THE ART

OF

LITERARY CRITICISM

Paul Robert Lieder

PROFESSOR OF ENGLISH LANGUAGE AND LITERATURE IN SMITH COLLEGE

and

Robert Withington

PROFESSOR OF ENGLISH LANGUAGE AND LITERATURE IN SMITH COLLEGE

D APPLETON-CENTURY COMPANY

INCORPORATED

NEW YORK   LONDON

441

TO

HERBERT DAVIS
CRITIC IN THE FAIR FIELD
OF THE ARTS

CONTENTS

Contents

PREFACE

IN this source-book the editors have brought together, within reasonable space, some of the significant critical writing from Plato to our own day—excluding the work of living authors. They have sought to let the critics speak for themselves, only occasionally offering suggestions to guide the reader. They have not included material dealing extensively with individual authors, such as Addison's discussion of Milton, but have aimed to emphasize principles which may be universal.

They have used, throughout, authoritative texts of the critics included, and have in general selected complete units, omitting passages which are clearly digressions or not germane to the subject. The older English texts have been modernized, although an attempt has been made to keep the earlier flavor, when this can be done without sacrificing clarity. Such notes have been furnished as will help the undergraduate; but the editors have not overburdened the text with explanations which the common books of reference can give. A selected bibliography and an index have been included.

The authors have been arranged mainly in the order of their birth, but in two or three instances—where a late work would come before one much earlier—a readjustment has been made. Thus Young, born before Pope, has been placed after Johnson; and Goethe, who survived Shelley, has been placed after Schiller, though he was ten years older. But the editors have left Tolstóy, whose life covered much of the nineteenth century, in his chronological place, although the work chosen follows Pater's by twenty-two years.

The dates affixed to the selections are, in general, those of publication, not of composition; but in the case of Shelley the former might confuse, as his essay was not printed until almost twenty years after the poet's death. The reader, accordingly, should bear in mind that the selections do not always fall into a chronological sequence.

Our thanks are due to the President and Fellows of Harvard College, for their permission to use the text of Quintilian in the Loeb Classics; to the Cambridge University Press and The Macmillan Company, for W. Rhys Roberts's translation of Longinus; to E. P. Dutton and Company for the translation of Dante's *De Vulgari Eloquentia* by A. G. Ferrers Howell, and of Lessing's *Laocoön*, by W. A. Steel; to The Macmillan Company for Arnold's essay introducing Ward's *The English Poets*; to Harcourt, Brace and Company for Randolph S. Bourne's translation of the *Supplement to Aristotle's "Poetics"* by Goethe; to The Clarendon Press, Oxford, for the extracts from Sidney's *Apology for Poetry*, edited by G. Gregory Smith, Jonson's *Timber*, edited by J. E. Spingarn, and Milton's Prefaces to *Paradise Lost* and *Samson Agonistes*, edited by R. C. Browne; to Doubleday, Doran and Company for the Preface to Conrad's *The Nigger of the "Narcissus,"* and to Professor John Masson Smith for his translation of Corneille's *Discourse on the Three Unities*, and his revision of van Laun's translation of Taine. We are also grateful to the Yale University Library for its kindness in sending us rare editions for proofreading.

It gives us especial pleasure to record our gratitude to our colleagues, Professors Sidney N. Deane, Michele F. Cantarella, Ruth E. Young, Vincent Guilloton, John M. Smith, for various fruitful suggestions, and to Miss Mary Dunham and Mrs. Margaret Storrs Grierson, of the Smith College Library, for bibliographical aid. To Mr. Dana H. Ferrin and Mr. F. S. Pease, of the D. Appleton-Century Company, we are grateful for their interest in the book and help in seeing it through the press.

P. R. L.
R. W.

Northampton, Massachusetts
April, 1941

INTRODUCTION

THIS volume is what is called in law-schools a case-book; that is, a collection of important analyses, from which a student evolves for himself a philosophy of criticism. Law-schools can teach the written law, or statutes, and enable a candidate to pass the bar examinations; but this candidate may not become a jurist, like the scholar who has studied the significant law cases of the last twenty-four centuries and formulated for himself a legal philosophy; he will remain a lawyer who follows the letter of the law. He will be like the rigid neo-classicist who applies accurately the standards that have been laid down. The jurist, said Justice Cardozo, interprets the law according to changing conditions. So likewise does the critic of literature.

II

To master the contents of this book the student should read slowly and carefully, especially in the beginning, scrutinizing every word or phrase, to establish what he thinks is the exact meaning. This advice applies to all reading, to be sure, but especially to material that is technical. An economist wrote recently: "In general, there are two important difficulties encountered by the layman when he attempts to understand the experts in almost any subject. The first is the repeated stumbling over unfamiliar words and phrases; but this difficulty can ordinarily be overcome by a little attention to definitions, unless the experts themselves are careless in using their special words. The second, and a greater, difficulty is the frequent use of common words that, when placed in different phrases and sentences, often have entirely different meanings. This pitfall is one that all too frequently traps the expert as well as the layman, usually with most unfortunate results."

Two of the common words that a student may stumble over in the earlier essays are *poet* and *poetry*. They are not used with their present-day purport. As Professor Kittredge has pointed out, we borrowed the word *poet* "in a special sense, so that we cannot use the literal meaning to interpret the English word." Literally, in Greek, *poet* means "maker," or "creator," and *poetry* is what he fashions. The best translation of the ancient word *poetry* is the German *Dichtung*. The nearest we have in English is "literature"; and the "poet" is he who creates through the medium of words, whether or not they are in rhyme or in metre.

III

This book is not a history of criticism. Although practically all the problems—and they are many—that have confronted critics from classical antiquity on have been presented here in one form or another, many critics have of necessity been omitted. Because of lack of space, the following, among others, were regretfully denied representation: Petronius, Petrarch, Boccaccio, Vida, Minturno, Scaliger, Castelvetro, Cinthio, du Bellay, Ronsard, Descartes, Rapin, Shaftesbury, Gottsched, the Schlegels, Dostoevski, Nietzsche, Baudelaire, Flaubert, Rimbaud, Bergson. Their ideas, however, are represented. For instance, the critical philosophy of Vida, and of Boileau's *L'Art Poétique*, echoed from Horace, appears in Pope; the three unities in the drama, first enunciated by Castelvetro in 1570, are discussed later by Corneille and Dryden; and du Bellay's spirited defense of the French language, or vernacular, is an application to French conditions of the method and ideas with which Dante established the Italian tongue; Baudelaire derives from Poe; and so on.

This book, again, is not a collection of readings in the field of pure æsthetics. The writers included are, for the most part, men who were themselves creative artists. Their treatment of literary problems is not theoretical or metaphysical, but, in the best sense of the word, practical.

IV

The careful reader of these selections may for a brief time be confused when he finds that great critics do not always agree—as, for instance, Plato and his pupil Aristotle. He may be disturbed when he finds, as he builds his critical philosophy, that he is altering or even discarding principles that he once thought good; but he will develop an independence and a self-confidence that will enable him to analyze a new poem, novel, or play, and find in the piece itself why it is so and not otherwise, and then to give a value to what he has found.

Appreciation and enjoyment depend upon taste. Taste is not innate, but can be developed through the application of tests which, in turn, increase one's sensitiveness. Analysis alone is not enough, even though critics in all ages have tried to make criticism scientifically accurate.

"Could a rule," said Coleridge, "be given from without, poetry would cease to be poetry, and sink into a mechanical art." Laws come from within, are not imposed; as Doctor Johnson observed: "It ought to be the first endeavor of a writer to distinguish nature from custom; or that which is established because it is right, from that which is right only because it is established; that he may neither violate essential principles by a desire of novelty, nor debar himself from the attainment of beauties within his view, by a needless fear of breaking rules which no literary dictator had authority to enact."

V

What this book purposes is suggested by two remarks of a great critic. "The judgment of literature," wrote Longinus to his friend Terentianus, seventeen hundred years ago, "is the final aftergrowth of much endeavor." Later, in his long epistle, he stated modestly and tolerantly, "Such are the decisions to which I have felt bound to come with regard to the questions proposed; but let every man cherish the view which pleases him best."

Plato

PLATO (*c* 427–347 B. C.) or, as he was really named, ARISTOCLES, was born at Ægina, of an aristocratic and wealthy family—Solon, the famous law-giver, was a collateral ancestor. His surname, Plátōn, was given him because of his broad shoulders. He received the best instruction possible in grammar, music, and gymnastics, which prepared him not only for the career of a poet but for that of a soldier. Early introduced to the philosophy of Heraclitus, he became later a pupil of Socrates; and upon the death of his master, in 399 B. C., he travelled widely, visiting the philosopher Euclid at Megara, studying mathematics at Cyrene and astronomy in Egypt. After a possible sojourn in Asia Minor, he went to the Greek cities of lower Italy and Sicily to acquaint himself with the Pythagorean doctrines, and here Dionysius the Elder, offended at his opinions, sold him (according to one report) to the Spartan ambassador, Pollis. Later ransomed, he returned to Athens, about 387 B. C. He founded his famous school, which took its name—the Academy—from the gardens said to have belonged, at the time of the Trojan War, to the hero Academus. Here he taught for more than forty years—a period interrupted only by two visits to Syracuse. He died at Athens in 347 B. C.

His works—supplementary to his oral teaching—were preserved by his disciples. His *Dialogues* have been variously arranged, but the order of their composition is unknown. Some debate whether they are links in a chain or independent works, written without a central plan.

Plato is the poet, the artist, among ancient Greek philoso-

phers and critics; as Sir Philip Sidney said, "Of all philosophers, I have ever esteemed [him] most worthy of reverence,
and with great reason, since of all philosophers he is the most
poetical." He creates characters, sometimes from actual men,
like Socrates, often entirely fictitious. These characters converse, and from their dialogues we obtain some of the greatest ideas in antiquity. This method of Plato's naturally confuses some students, who, expecting a tight philosophical
system, find, as they go from dialogue to dialogue, apparent
inconsistencies.

Being at heart and in practice a poet, Plato has amazed
many readers by his attacks upon poets. The reason for this
attitude may be explained as follows: The ancient Greeks,
although they produced incomparable beauty in all the arts,
felt that the main purpose in life was the search for truth
and the attainment of goodness. Plato, as a realist—that is, a
philosopher who believes that what we perceive is merely a
rendering of reality, of the idea behind the thing—reasoned
that the artist who copied nature was giving us something
thrice removed from the real truth. In other words, a work
of art took us still further away from what Longinus called
"the mighty thought of God." As for goodness, art produced
only pleasure, and since pleasure in itself, Plato felt, had no
purpose, art was morally hurtful. Because in his unified State,
everything and everybody should serve and contribute to the
idea of the State, he banished art. Grudgingly he admitted
music, only because it could stimulate men to work and to
fight.

In the dialogue given below, the speakers are Socrates and
Glaucon. The reader will quickly be able to determine which
is which, for Socrates is the master, Glaucon the disciple.

From THE REPUBLIC

(*c* 373 B. C.)

BOOK X [1]

Of the many excellences which I perceive in the order of our State, there is none which upon reflection pleases me better than the rule about poetry.

To what do you refer?

To the rejection of imitative poetry, which certainly ought not to be received; as I see far more clearly now that the parts of the soul have been distinguished.

What do you mean?

Speaking in confidence, for I should not like to have my words repeated to the tragedians and the rest of the imitative tribe—but I do not mind saying to you, that all poetical imitations are ruinous to the understanding of the hearers, and that the knowledge of their true nature is the only antidote to them.

Explain the purport of your remark.

Well, I will tell you, although I have always from my earliest youth had an awe and love of Homer, which even now makes the words falter on my lips, for he is the great captain and teacher of the whole of that charming tragic company; but a man is not to be reverenced more than the truth, and therefore I will speak out.

Very good, he said.

Listen to me then, or rather, answer me.

Put your question.

Can you tell me what imitation is? for I really do not know.

A likely thing, then, that I should know.

Why not? for the duller eye may often see a thing sooner than the keener.

Very true, he said; but in your presence, even if I had any faint notion, I could not muster courage to utter it. Will you enquire yourself?

Well then, shall we begin the enquiry in our usual manner: Whenever a number of individuals have a common name, we assume them to have also a corresponding idea or form:—do you understand me?

---

[1] Translated by Benjamin Jowett. The text is taken from the third edition, Oxford, 1888.

I do.

Let us take any common instance; there are beds and tables in the world—plenty of them, are there not?

Yes.

But there are only two ideas or forms of them—one the idea of a bed, the other of a table.

True.

And the maker of either of them makes a bed or he makes a table for our use, in accordance with the idea—that is our way of speaking in this and similar instances—but no artificer makes the ideas themselves: how could he?

Impossible.

And there is another artist,—I should like to know what you would say of him.

Who is he?

One who is the maker of all the works of all other workmen.

What an extraordinary man!

Wait a little, and there will be more reason for your saying so. For this is he who is able to make not only vessels of every kind, but plants and animals, himself and all other things—the earth and heaven, and the things which are in heaven or under the earth; he makes the gods also.

He must be a wizard and no mistake.

Oh! you are incredulous, are you? Do you mean that there is no such maker or creator, or that in one sense there might be a maker of all these things but in another not? Do you see that there is a way in which you could make them all yourself?

What way?

An easy way enough; or rather, there are many ways in which the feat might be quickly and easily accomplished, none quicker than that of turning a mirror round and round—you would soon enough make the sun and the heavens, and the earth and yourself, and other animals and plants, and all the other things of which we were just now speaking, in the mirror.

Yes, he said; but they would be appearances only.

Very good, I said, you are coming to the point now. And the painter too is, as I conceive, just such another—a creator of appearances, is he not?

Of course.

But then I suppose you will say that what he creates is untrue. And yet there is a sense in which the painter also creates a bed?

Yes, he said, but not a real bed.

And what of the maker of the bed? were you not saying that he too makes, not the idea which, according to our view, is the essence of the bed, but only a particular bed?

Yes, I did.

Then if he does not make that which exists he cannot make true existence, but only some semblance of existence; and if any one were to say that the work of the maker of the bed, or of any other workman, has real existence, he could hardly be supposed to be speaking the truth.

At any rate, he replied, philosophers would say that he was not speaking the truth.

No wonder, then, that his work too is an indistinct expression of truth.

No wonder.

Suppose now that by the light of the examples just offered we enquire who this imitator is?

If you please.

Well, then, here are three beds: one existing in nature, which is made by God, as I think that we may say—for no one else can be the maker?

No.

There is another which is the work of the carpenter?

Yes.

And the work of the painter is a third?

Yes.

Beds, then, are of three kinds, and there are three artists who superintend them: God, the maker of the bed, and the painter?

Yes, there are three of them.

God, whether from choice or from necessity, made one bed in nature and one only; two or more such ideal beds neither ever have been nor ever will be made by God.

Why is that?

Because even if He had made but two, a third would still appear behind them which both of them would have for their idea, and that would be the ideal bed and not the two others.

Very true, he said.

God knew this, and He desired to be the real maker of a real bed, not a particular maker of a particular bed, and therefore He created a bed which is essentially and by nature one only.

So we believe.

Shall we, then, speak of Him as the natural author or maker of the bed?

Yes, he replied; inasmuch as by the natural process of creation He is the author of this and of all other things.

And what shall we say of the carpenter—is not he also the maker of the bed?

Yes.

But would you call the painter a creator and maker?

Certainly not.

Yet if he is not the maker, what is he in relation to the bed?

I think, he said, that we may fairly designate him as the imitator of that which the others make.

Good, I said; then you call him who is third in the descent from nature an imitator?

Certainly, he said.

And the tragic poet is an imitator, and therefore, like all other imitators, he is thrice removed from the king and from the truth?

That appears to be so.

Then about the imitator we are agreed. And what about the painter?—I would like to know whether he may be thought to imitate that which originally exists in nature, or only the creations of artists?

The latter.

As they are or as they appear? you have still to determine this.

What do you mean?

I mean, that you may look at a bed from different points of view, obliquely or directly or from any other point of view, and the bed will appear different, but there is no difference in reality. And the same of all things.

Yes, he said, the difference is only apparent.

Now let me ask you another question: Which is the art of painting designed to be—an imitation of things as they are, or as they appear —of appearance or of reality?

Of appearance.

Then the imitator, I said, is a long way off the truth, and can do all things because he lightly touches on a small part of them, and that part an image. For example: A painter will paint a cobbler, carpenter, or any other artist, though he knows nothing of their arts; and, if he is a good artist, he may deceive children or simple persons, when he shows them his picture of a carpenter from a distance, and they will fancy that they are looking at a real carpenter.

Certainly.

And whenever any one informs us that he has found a man who knows all the arts, and all things else that anybody knows, and every single thing with a higher degree of accuracy than any other man—whoever tells us this, I think that we can only imagine him to be a simple creature who is likely to have been deceived by some wizard or actor whom he met, and whom he thought all-knowing, because he himself was unable to analyze the nature of knowledge and ignorance and imitation.

Most true.

And so, when we hear persons saying that the tragedians, and Homer, who is at their head, know all the arts and all things human, virtue as well as vice, and divine things too, for that the good poet cannot compose well unless he knows his subject, and that he who has not this knowledge can never be a poet, we ought to consider whether here also there may not be a similar illusion. Perhaps they may have come across imitators and been deceived by them; they may not have remembered when they saw their works that these were but imitations thrice removed from the truth, and could easily be made without any knowledge of the truth, because they are appearances only and not realities? Or, after all, they may be in the right, and poets do really know the things about which they seem to the many to speak so well?

The question, he said, should by all means be considered.

Now do you suppose that if a person were able to make the original as well as the image, he would seriously devote himself to the image-making branch? Would he allow imitation to be the ruling principle of his life, as if he had nothing higher in him?

I should say not.

The real artist, who knew what he was imitating, would be interested in realities and not in imitations; and would desire to leave as memorials of himself works many and fair; and, instead of being the author of encomiums, he would prefer to be the theme of them.

Yes, he said, that would be to him a source of much greater honor and profit.

Then, I said, we must put a question to Homer; not about medicine, or any of the arts to which his poems only incidentally refer: we are not going to ask him, or any other poet, whether he has cured patients like Asclepius, or left behind him a school of medicine such as the Asclepiads were, or whether he only talks about medicine and other arts at second-hand; but we have a right to know respecting military tactics, politics, education, which are the chiefest and noblest subjects of his poems, and we may fairly ask him about them. "Friend Homer," then we say to him, "if you are only in the second remove from truth in what you say of virtue, and not in the third —not an image maker or imitator—and if you are able to discern what pursuits make men better or worse in private or public life, tell us what State was ever better governed by your help? The good order of Lacedæmon is due to Lycurgus, and many other cities great and small have been similarly benefited by others; but who says that you have been a good legislator to them and have done them any good? Italy and Sicily boast of Charondas, and there is Solon who is renowned among us; but what city has anything to say about you?" Is there any city which he might name?

I think not, said Glaucon; not even the Homerids themselves pretend that he was a legislator.

Well, but is there any war on record which was carried on successfully by him, or aided by his counsels, when he was alive?

There is not.

Or is there any invention of his, applicable to the arts or to human life, such as Thales the Milesian or Anacharsis the Scythian, and other ingenious men have conceived, which is attributed to him?

There is absolutely nothing of the kind.

But, if Homer never did any public service, was he privately a guide, or teacher of any? Had he in his life-time friends who loved to associate with him, and who handed down to posterity an Homeric way of life, such as was established by Pythagoras who was so greatly beloved for his wisdom, and whose followers are to this day quite celebrated for the order which was named after him?

Nothing of the kind is recorded of him. For surely, Socrates, Creophylus, the companion of Homer, that child of flesh, whose name always makes us laugh, might be more justly ridiculed for his stupidity, if, as is said, Homer was greatly neglected by him and others in his own day when he was alive?

Yes, I replied, that is the tradition. But can you imagine, Glaucon, that if Homer had really been able to educate and improve mankind —if he had possessed knowledge and not been a mere imitator—can you imagine, I say, that he would not have had many followers, and been honored and loved by them? Protagoras of Abdera, and Prodicus of Ceos, and a host of others, have only to whisper to their contemporaries: "You will never be able to manage either your own house or your own State until you appoint us to be your ministers of education"—and this ingenious device of theirs has such an effect in making men love them that their companions all but carry them about on their shoulders. And is it conceivable that the contemporaries of Homer, or again of Hesiod, would have allowed either of them to go about as rhapsodists, if they had really been able to make mankind virtuous? Would they not have been as unwilling to part with them as with gold, and have compelled them to stay at home with them? Or, if the master would not stay, then the disciples would have followed him about everywhere, until they had got education enough?

Yet, Socrates, that, I think, is quite true.

Then must we not infer that all these poetical individuals, beginning with Homer, are only imitators; they copy images of virtue and the like, but the truth they never reach? The poet is like a painter who, as we have already observed, will make a likeness of a cobbler though he understands nothing of cobbling; and his picture is good enough for those who know no more than he does, and judge only by colors and figures.

Quite so.

In like manner the poet with his words and phrases [1] may be said to lay on the colors of the several arts, himself understanding their nature only enough to imitate them; and other people, who are as ignorant as he is, and judge only from his words, imagine that if he speaks of cobbling, or of military tactics, or of anything else, in metre and harmony and rhythm, he speaks very well—such is the sweet influence which melody and rhythm by nature have. And I think that you must have observed again and again what a poor appearance the tales of poets make when stripped of the colors which music puts upon them, and recited in simple prose.

Yes, he said.

They are like faces which were never really beautiful, but only blooming; and now the bloom of youth has passed away from them?

Exactly.

Here is another point: The imitator or maker of the image knows nothing of true existence; he knows appearances only. Am I not right?

Yes.

[1] Or, "with his nouns and verbs." (Jowett.)

Then let us have a clear understanding, and not be satisfied with half an explanation.

Proceed.

Of the painter we say that he will paint reins, and he will paint a bit?

Yes.

And the worker in leather and brass will make them?

Certainly.

But does the painter know the right form of the bit and reins? Nay, hardly even the workers in brass and leather who make them; only the horseman who knows how to use them—he knows their right form.

Most true.

And may we not say the same of all things?

What?

That there are three arts which are concerned with all things: one which uses, another which makes, a third which imitates them?

Yes.

And the excellence or beauty or truth of every structure, animate or inanimate, and of every action of man, is relative to the use for which nature or the artist has intended them.

True.

Then the user of them must have the greatest experience of them, and he must indicate to the maker the good or bad qualities which develop themselves in use; for example, the flute-player will tell the flute-maker which of his flutes is satisfactory to the performer; he will tell him how he ought to make them, and the other will attend to his instructions?

Of course.

The one knows and therefore speaks with authority about the goodness and badness of flutes, while the other, confiding in him, will do what he is told by him?

True.

The instrument is the same, but about the excellence or badness of it the maker will only attain to a correct belief; and this he will gain from him who knows, by talking to him and being compelled to hear what he has to say, whereas the user will have knowledge?

True.

But will the imitator have either? Will he know from use whether or no his drawing is correct or beautiful? or will he have right opinion from being compelled to associate with another who knows and gives him instructions about what he should draw?

Neither.

Then he will no more have true opinion than he will have knowledge about the goodness or badness of his imitations?

I suppose not.

The imitative artist will be in a brilliant state of intelligence about his own creations?

Nay, very much the reverse.

And still he will go on imitating without knowing what makes a thing good or bad, and may be expected therefore to imitate only that which appears to be good to the ignorant multitude?

Just so.

Thus far we are pretty well agreed that the imitator has no knowledge worth mentioning of what he imitates. Imitation is only a kind of play or sport, and the tragic poets, whether they write in Iambic or in Heroic verse, are imitators in the highest degree?

Very true.

And now tell me, I conjure you, has not imitation been shown by us to be concerned with that which is thrice removed from the truth?

Certainly.

And what is the faculty in man to which imitation is addressed?

What do you mean?

I will explain: The body which is large when seen near, appears small when seen at a distance?

True.

And the same objects appear straight when looked at out of the water, and crooked when in the water; and the concave becomes convex, owing to the illusion about colors to which the sight is liable. Thus every sort of confusion is revealed within us; and this is that weakness of the human mind on which the art of conjuring and of deceiving by light and shadow and other ingenious devices imposes, having an effect upon us like magic.

True.

And the arts of measuring and numbering and weighing come to the rescue of the human understanding—there is the beauty of them—and the apparent greater or less, or more or heavier, no longer have the mastery over us, but give way before calculation and measure and weight?

Most true.

And this, surely, must be the work of the calculating and rational principle in the soul?

To be sure.

And when this principle measures and certifies that some things are equal, or that some are greater or less than others, there occurs an apparent contradiction?

True.

But were we not saying that such a contradiction is impossible— the same faculty cannot have contrary opinions at the same time about the same thing?

Very true.

Then that part of the soul which has an opinion contrary to measure is not the same with that which has an opinion in accordance with measure?

True.

And the better part of the soul is likely to be that which trusts to measure and calculation?

Certainly.

And that which is opposed to them is one of the inferior principles of the soul?

No doubt.

This was the conclusion at which I was seeking to arrive when I said that painting or drawing, and imitation in general, when doing their own proper work, are far removed from truth, and the companions and friends and associates of a principle within us which is equally removed from reason, and that they have no true or healthy aim.

Exactly.

The imitative art is an inferior who marries an inferior, and has inferior offspring.

Very true.

And is this confined to the sight only, or does it extend to the hearing also, relating in fact to what we term poetry?

Probably the same would be true of poetry.

Do not rely, I said, on a probability derived from the analogy of painting; but let us examine further and see whether the faculty with which poetical imitation is concerned is good or bad.

By all means.

We may state the question thus:—Imitation imitates the actions of men, whether voluntary or involuntary, on which, as they imagine, a good or bad result has ensued, and they rejoice or sorrow accordingly. Is there anything more?

No, there is nothing else.

But in all this variety of circumstances is the man at unity with himself—or rather, as in the instance of sight there was confusion and opposition in his opinions about the same things, so here also is there not strife and inconsistency in his life? Though I need hardly raise the question again, for I remember that all this has been already admitted; and the soul has been acknowledged by us to be full of these and ten thousand similar oppositions occurring at the same moment?

And we were right, he said.

Yes, I said, thus far we were right; but there was an omission which must now be supplied.

What was the omission?

Were we not saying that a good man, who has the misfortune to lose his son or anything else which is most dear to him, will bear the loss with more equanimity than another?

Yes.

But will he have no sorrow, or shall we say that although he cannot help sorrowing, he will moderate his sorrow?

The latter, he said, is the truer statement.

Tell me: will he be more likely to struggle and hold out against his sorrow when he is seen by his equals, or when he is alone?

It will make a great difference whether he is seen or not.

When he is by himself he will not mind saying or doing many things which he would be ashamed of any one hearing or seeing him do?

True.

There is a principle of law and reason in him which bids him resist, as well as a feeling of his misfortune which is forcing him to indulge his sorrow?

True.

But when a man is drawn in two opposite directions, to and from the same object, this, as we affirm, necessarily implies two distinct principles in him?

Certainly.

One of them is ready to follow the guidance of the law?

How do you mean?

The law would say that to be patient under suffering is best, and that we should not give way to impatience, as there is no knowing whether such things are good or evil; and nothing is gained by impatience; also, because no human thing is of serious importance, and grief stands in the way of that which at the moment is most required.

What is most required? he asked.

That we should take counsel about what has happened, and when the dice have been thrown, order our affairs in the way which reason deems best; not, like children who have had a fall, keeping hold of the part struck and wasting time in setting up a howl, but always accustoming the soul forthwith to apply a remedy, raising up that which is sickly and fallen, banishing the cry of sorrow by the healing art.

Yes, he said, that is the true way of meeting the attacks of fortune.

Yes, I said; and the higher principle is ready to follow this suggestion of reason?

Clearly.

And the other principle, which inclines us to recollection of our troubles and to lamentation, and can never have enough of them, we may call irrational, useless, and cowardly?

Indeed, we may.

And does not the latter—I mean the rebellious principle—furnish a great variety of materials for imitation? Whereas the wise and calm temperament, being always nearly equable, is not easy to imitate or to appreciate when imitated, especially at a public festival when a promiscuous crowd is assembled in a theatre. For the feeling represented is one to which they are strangers. *The rabble*

Certainly.

Then the imitative poet who aims at being popular is not by nature made, nor is his art intended, to please or to affect the rational principle in the soul; but he will prefer the passionate and fitful temper, which is easily imitated?

Clearly.

And now we may fairly take him and place him by the side of the painter, for he is like him in two ways: first, inasmuch as his creations have an inferior degree of truth—in this, I say, he is like him; and he is also like him in being concerned with an inferior part of the soul; and therefore we shall be right in refusing to admit him into a well-ordered State, because he awakens and nourishes and strengthens the feelings and impairs the reason. As in a city when the evil are permitted to have authority and the good are put out of the way, so in the soul of man, as we maintain, the imitative poet implants an evil constitution, for he indulges the irrational nature which has no discernment of greater and less, but thinks the same thing at one time great and at another small—he is a manufacturer of images and is very far removed from the truth.

Exactly.

But we have not yet brought forward the heaviest count in our accusation:—the power which poetry has of harming even the good (and there are very few who are not harmed), is surely an awful thing?

Yes, certainly, if the effect is what you say.

Hear and judge: The best of us, as I conceive, when we listen to a passage of Homer, or one of the tragedians, in which he represents some pitiful hero who is drawling out his sorrows in a long oration, or weeping, and smiting his breast—the best of us, you know, delight in giving way to sympathy, and are in raptures at the excellence of the poet who stirs our feelings most.

Yes, of course I know.

But when any sorrow of our own happens to us, then you may observe that we pride ourselves on the opposite quality—we would fain be quiet and patient; this is the manly part, and the other which delighted us in the recitation is now deemed to be the part of a woman.

Very true, he said.

Now can we be right in praising and admiring another who is doing that which any one of us would abominate and be ashamed of in his own person?

No, he said, that is certainly not reasonable.

Nay, I said, quite reasonable from one point of view.

What point of view?

If you consider, I said, that when in misfortune we feel a natural hunger and desire to relieve our sorrow by weeping and lamentation, and that this feeling which is kept under control in our own calamities is satisfied and delighted by the poets;—the better nature in each of us, not having been sufficiently trained by reason or habit, allows the sympathetic element to break loose because the sorrow is another's; and the spectator fancies that there can be no disgrace to himself in praising and pitying any one who comes telling him what a good man he is, and making a fuss about his troubles; he thinks that the pleasure is a gain, and why should he be supercilious and lose this and the poem too? Few persons ever reflect, as I should imagine, that from the evil of other men something of evil is communicated to themselves. And so the feeling of sorrow which has gathered strength at the sight of the misfortunes of others is with difficulty repressed in our own.

How very true!

And does not the same hold also of the ridiculous? There are jests which you would be ashamed to make yourself, and yet on the comic stage, or indeed in private, when you hear them, you are greatly amused by them, and are not at all disgusted at their unseemliness; —the case of pity is repeated;—there is a principle in human nature which is disposed to raise a laugh, and this which you once restrained by reason, because you were afraid of being thought a buffoon, is now let out again; and having stimulated the risible faculty at the theatre, you are betrayed unconsciously to yourself into playing the comic poet at home.

Quite true, he said.

And the same may be said of lust and anger and all the other affections, of desire and pain and pleasure, which are held to be inseparable from every action—in all of them poetry feeds and waters the passions instead of drying them up; she lets them rule, although they ought to be controlled, if mankind are ever to increase in happiness and virtue.

I cannot deny it.

Therefore, Glaucon, I said, whenever you meet with any of the eulogists of Homer declaring that he has been the educator of Hellas, and that he is profitable for education and for the ordering of human things, and that you should take him up again and again and get to know him and regulate your whole life according to him, we may love and honor those who say these things—they are excellent people, as far as their lights extend; and we are ready to acknowledge that Homer is the greatest of poets and first of tragedy writers; but we must remain firm in our conviction that hymns to the gods and praises of famous men are the only poetry which ought to be admitted into our State. For if you go beyond this and allow the honeyed muse to enter, either in epic or lyric verse, not law and the reason of mankind, which by common consent have ever been deemed best, but pleasure and pain will be the rulers in our State.

That is most true, he said.

And now since we have reverted to the subject of poetry, let this our defence serve to show the reasonableness of our former judgment in sending away out of our State an art having the tendencies which we have described; for reason constrained us. But that she may not impute to us any harshness or want of politeness, let us tell her that there is an ancient quarrel between philosophy and poetry; of which there are many proofs, such as the saying of "the yelping hound howling at her lord," or of one "mighty in the vain talk of fools," and "the mob of sages circumventing Zeus," and the "subtle thinkers who are beggars after all"; and there are innumerable other signs of ancient enmity between them. Notwithstanding this, let us assure our sweet friend and the sister arts of imitation, that if she will only prove her title to exist in a well-ordered State we shall be delighted to receive her—we are very conscious of her charms; but we may not on that account betray the truth. I dare say, Glaucon, that you are as much charmed by her as I am, especially when she appears in Homer?

Yes, indeed, I am greatly charmed.

Shall I propose, then, that she be allowed to return from exile, but upon this condition only—that she make a defence of herself in lyrical or some other metre?

Certainly.

And we may further grant to those of her defenders who are lovers of poetry and yet not poets the permission to speak in prose on her behalf: let them show not only that she is pleasant but also useful to States and to human life, and we will listen in a kindly spirit; for if this can be proved we shall surely be the gainers—I mean, if there is a use in poetry as well as a delight?

Certainly, he said, we shall be the gainers.

If her defence fails, then, my dear friend, like other persons who are enamored of something, but put a restraint upon themselves when they think their desires are opposed to their interests, so too must we after the manner of lovers give her up, though not without a struggle. We too are inspired by that love of poetry which the education of noble States has implanted in us, and therefore we would have her appear at her best and truest; but so long as she is unable to make good her defence, this argument of ours shall be a charm to us, which we will repeat to ourselves while we listen to her strains; that we may not fall away into the childish love of her which captivates the many. At all events we are well aware that poetry being such as we have described is not to be regarded seriously as attaining to the truth; and he who listens to her, fearing for the safety of the city which is within him, should be on his guard against her seductions and make our words his law.

Yes, he said, I quite agree with you.

Yes, I said, my dear Glaucon, for great is the issue at stake, greater than appears, whether a man is to be good or bad. And what will any one be profited if under the influence of honor or money or power, aye, or under the excitement of poetry, he neglect justice and virtue?

Yes, he said; I have been convinced by the argument, as I believe that any one else would have been.

*   *   *   *

Aristotle

ARISTOTLE (384–322 B. C.) was born at Stagira, Macedonia, of a good family, Greek in origin, claiming descent from Æsculapius. His father, Nicomachus, was the physician and friend of Amyntas II, King of Macedonia, the father of Philip. At the age of seventeen, Aristotle went to Athens and became the pupil of Plato at the Academy, where he remained twenty years. His talents were soon recognized and he rapidly became a rival of his master. On Plato's death, he travelled, spending three years at Atarneus as a guest of Hermias, whose niece he afterward married. He later visited Mytilene, and in 343 B. C. was summoned to the Court of Macedon, to undertake the education of Philip's son, Alexander, then a boy of thirteen. The future conqueror formed an enthusiastic and lasting attachment for his teacher. When Alexander ascended the throne of Macedonia, Aristotle returned to Athens, and in 335 founded his school—called the Peripatetic, because the discussions were carried on while the philosophers walked about. The school was located, through a grant from the State, in the Lyceum, a gymnasium and exercise-ground, noted for its fine groves of plane-trees, near the temple of Apollo Lyceius. Here pupils gathered from all parts of Greece, and his school became the most popular in Athens. It is supposed that he composed the great bulk of his works during the time of his teaching at the Lyceum. In 323 B. C., on the death of Alexander, who had given Aristotle generous grants for his scientific investigations, anti-Macedonian revolutions broke out in Athens causing Aristotle's retirement to Chalcis in Eubœa, where he died a year later.

Aristotle is the scientific observer among the ancient critics. In all fields—natural science, art, ethics, law—he accepted what existed, and tried to find the underlying causes, good or bad. Like his admirer, Coleridge, he believed that "nothing can permanently please, which does not contain in itself the reason why it is so, and not otherwise." In the field of literature, accordingly, he analyzed the works of Homer, Æschylus, Sophocles, and Euripides, to find what general principles there might be within them to produce the beauty that he felt was there.

Since beauty did exist, he did not dismiss it, as Plato did, as something inimical to an individual's morals, and thereby to the State. He found its justification—in literature, at least—in the theory that he derived from his analysis of tragedy, his theory of *katharsis*. Art was a pleasing, but beneficent, medicine.

As an answer to the charge that art was not truth, Aristotle deduced from the writings that he knew, the theory of universality—holding that the true poet, while imitating nature, went beyond appearances and came nearer to the real truth that Plato desired than the latter would allow.

Thus Aristotle, who, as a philosopher, believed that his chief task was the search for truth, justified the contention —and he was the first so far as we know—that the fine arts exist primarily to give pleasure. More than two thousand years later, Matthew Arnold, thorough student of Aristotle's *Poetics,* wrote in the preface to his *Poems* (1854): "It is not enough that the Poet should add to the knowledge of men; it is required of him also that he should add to their happiness. 'All art,' says Schiller, 'is dedicated to joy, and there is no higher and no more serious problem than how to make men happy. The right art is that alone which creates the highest enjoyment.' "

Among other notable contributions that Aristotle made to the consideration of literature is his theory of *architectoniké.*

Again to quote Matthew Arnold, who in turn quotes a still
greater man: "What distinguishes the artist from the mere
amateur," says Goethe, "is *Architectoniké* in the highest
sense; that power of execution which creates, forms, and
constitutes: not the profoundness of single thoughts, not the
richness of imagery, not the abundance of illustration."

Aristotle, the "master of them that know," in Dante's
phrase, has had tremendous influence. He was not known
during the Middle Ages in the original Greek; but, through
the Latin commentaries of men like Albertus Magnus and
Thomas Aquinas, his ideas became almost gospel. To say *"ipse
dixit"* (the master has said it) was enough to clinch an argument.

From POETICS [1]

(*c* 335–320 B. C.)

I

I propose to treat of Poetry in itself and of its various kinds,
noting the essential quality of each; to inquire into the structure of
the plot as requisite to a good poem; into the number and nature
of the parts of which a poem is composed; and similarly into whatever else falls within the same inquiry. Following, then, the order of
nature, let us begin with the principles which come first.

2. Epic poetry and Tragedy, Comedy also and Dithyrambic
poetry, and the music of the flute and of the lyre in most of their
forms, are all in their general conception modes of imitation. 3. They
differ, however, from one another in three respects,—the medium,
the objects, the manner or mode of imitation, being in each case
distinct.

4. For as there are persons who, by conscious art or mere habit,
imitate and represent various objects through the medium of color
and form, or again by the voice; so in the arts above mentioned,
taken as a whole, the imitation is produced by rhythm, language, or
"harmony," either singly or combined.

Thus in the music of the flute and of the lyre, "harmony" and
rhythm alone are employed; also in other arts, such as that of the

[1] The text is S. H. Butcher's revised translation, London, 1898.

shepherd's pipe, which are essentially similar to these. 5. In dancing, rhythm alone is used without "harmony"; for even dancing imitates character, emotion, and action, by rhythmical movement.

6. There is another art which imitates by means of language alone, and that either in prose or verse—which verse, again, may either combine different metres or consist of but one kind—but this has hitherto been without a name. 7. For there is no common term we could apply to the mimes of Sophron and Xenarchus and the Socratic dialogues on the one hand; and, on the other, to poetic imitations in iambic, elegiac, or any similar metre. People do, indeed, add the word "maker" or "poet" to the name of the metre, and speak of elegiac poets, or epic (that is, hexameter) poets, as if it were not the imitation that makes the poet, but the verse that entitles them all indiscriminately to the name. 8. Even when a treatise on medicine or natural science is brought out in verse, the name of poet is by custom given to the author; and yet Homer and Empedocles have nothing in common but the metre, so that it would be right to call the one poet, the other physicist rather than poet. 9. On the same principle, even if a writer in his poetic imitation were to combine all metres, as Chæremon did in his *Centaur*, which is a medley composed of metres of all kinds, we should bring him too under the general term poet. So much then for these distinctions.

10. There are, again some arts which employ all the means above mentioned,—namely, rhythm, tune and metre. Such are Dithyrambic [1] and Nomic poetry, and also Tragedy and Comedy; but between them the difference is, that in the first two cases these means are all employed in combination, in the latter, now one means is employed, now another.

Such, then, are the differences of the arts with respect to the medium of imitation.

II

Since the objects of imitation are men in action, and these men must be either of a higher or a lower type (for moral character mainly answers to these divisions, goodness and badness being the distinguishing marks of moral differences), it follows that we must represent men either as better than in real life, or as worse, or as they are. It is the same in painting. Polygnotus depicted men as

---

1 The Dithyramb was sung to a flute accompaniment by a chorus in honor of Dionysus; the Nome was a solo sung to a harp accompaniment in honor of Apollo. (Fyfe).

nobler than they are, Pauson as less noble, Dionysius drew them true to life.

2. Now it is evident that each of the modes of imitation above mentioned will exhibit these differences, and become a distinct kind in imitating objects that are thus distinct. 3. Such diversities may be found even in dancing, flute-playing, and lyre-playing. So again in language, whether prose or verse unaccompanied by music. Homer, for example, makes men better than they are; Cleophon as they are; Hegemon the Thasian, the inventor of parodies, and Nicochares, the author of the *Deliad*, worse than they are. 4. The same thing holds good of Dithyrambs and Nomes; here too one may portray different types, as Timotheus and Philoxenus differed in representing the Cyclops. The same distinction marks off Tragedy from Comedy; for Comedy aims at representing men as worse, Tragedy as better than in actual life.

III

There is still a third difference—the manner in which each of these objects may be imitated. For the medium being the same, and the objects the same, the poet may imitate by narration—in which case he can either take another personality as Homer does, or speak in his own person, unchanged—or he may present all his characters as living and moving before us.

2. These, then, as we said at the beginning, are the three differences which distinguish artistic imitation—the medium, the objects and the manner. So that from one point of view, Sophocles is an imitator of the same kind as Homer—for both imitate higher types of character; from another point of view, of the same kind as Aristophanes—for both imitate persons acting and doing. 3. Hence, some say, the name of "drama" is given to such poems, as representing action. For the same reason the Dorians claim the invention both of Tragedy and Comedy. The claim to Comedy is put forward by the Megarians,—not only by those of Greece proper, who allege that it originated under their democracy, but also by the Megarians of Sicily, for the poet Epicharmus, who is much earlier than Chionides and Magnes, belonged to that country. Tragedy too is claimed by certain Dorians of the Peloponnese. In each case they appeal to the evidence of language. Villages, they say, are by them called κῶμαι, by the Athenians δῆμοι: and they assume that Comedians were so named not from κωμάζειν, "to revel," but because they wandered from vil-

lage to village (κατὰ κώμας), being excluded contemptuously from the city. They add also that the Dorian word for "doing" is δρᾶν, and the Athenian, πράττειν.

4. This may suffice as to the number and nature of the various modes of imitation.

IV

Poetry in general seems to have sprung from two causes, each of them lying deep in our nature. 2. First, the instinct of imitation is implanted in man from childhood, one difference between him and other animals being that he is the most imitative of living creatures; and through imitation he learns his earliest lessons; and no less universal is the pleasure felt in things imitated. 3. We have evidence of this in the facts of experience. Objects which in themselves we view with pain, we delight to contemplate when reproduced with minute fidelity: such as the forms of the most ignoble animals and of dead bodies. 4. The cause of this again is, that to learn gives the liveliest pleasure, not only to philosophers but to men in general; whose capacity, however, of learning is more limited. 5. Thus the reason why men enjoy seeing a likeness is, that in contemplating it they find themselves learning or inferring, and saying perhaps, "Ah, that is he." For if you happen not to have seen the original, the pleasure will be due not to the imitation as such, but to the execution, the coloring, or some such other cause.

6. Imitation, then, is one instinct of our nature. Next, there is the instinct for "harmony" and rhythm, metres being manifestly sections of rhythm. Persons, therefore, starting with this natural gift developed by degrees their special aptitudes, till their rude improvisations gave birth to Poetry.

7. Poetry now diverged in two directions, according to the individual character of the writers. The graver spirits imitated noble actions, and the actions of good men. The more trivial sort imitated the actions of meaner persons, at first composing satires, as the former did hymns to the gods and the praises of famous men. 8. A poem of the satirical kind cannot indeed be put down to any author earlier than Homer; though many such writers probably there were. But from Homer onward, instances can be cited,—his own *Margites,* for example, and other similar compositions. The appropriate metre was also here introduced; hence the measure is still called the iambic or lampooning measure, being that in which people lampooned one an-

other. 9. Thus the older poets were distinguished as writers of heroic
or of lampooning verse.

As, in the serious style, Homer is pre-eminent among poets, standing alone not only in the excellence, but also in the dramatic form
of his imitations, so he too first laid down the main lines of Comedy,
by dramatizing the ludicrous instead of writing personal satire. His
Margites bears the same relation to Comedy that the *Iliad* and
Odyssey do to Tragedy. 10. But when Tragedy and Comedy came
to light, the two classes of poets still followed their natural bent:
the lampooners became writers of Comedy, and the Epic poets were
succeeded by Tragedians, since the drama was a larger and higher
form of art.

11. Whether Tragedy has as yet perfected its proper types or not;
and whether it is to be judged in itself, or in relation also to the
audience,—this raises another question. 12. Be that as it may, Tragedy—as also Comedy—was at first mere improvisation. The one
originated with the leaders of the Dithyramb, the other with those
of the phallic songs, which are still in use in many of our cities.
Tragedy advanced by slow degrees; each new element that showed
itself was in turn developed. Having passed through many changes,
it found its natural form, and there it stopped.

13. Æschylus first introduced a second actor; he diminished the
importance of the Chorus, and assigned the leading part to the dialogue. Sophocles raised the number of actors to three, and added
scene-painting. 14. It was not till late that the short plot was discarded for one of greater compass, and the grotesque diction of
the earlier satyric form for the stately manner of Tragedy. The
iambic measure then replaced the trochaic tetrameter, which was
originally employed when the poetry was of the satyric order, and
had greater affinities with dancing. Once dialogue had come in, Nature herself discovered the appropriate measure. For the iambic is, of
all measures, the most colloquial: we see it in the fact that conversational speech runs into iambic form more frequently than into any
other kind of verse; rarely into hexameters, and only when we drop
the colloquial intonation. 15. The number of "episodes" or acts was
also increased, and the other embellishments added, of which tradition tells. These we need not here discuss; to enter into them in detail
would, doubtless, be a large undertaking.

V

Comedy is, as we have said, an imitation of characters of a lower type—not, however, in the full sense of the word bad, the Ludicrous being merely a subdivision of the ugly. It consists in some defect or ugliness which is not painful or destructive. To take an obvious example, the comic mask is ugly and distorted, but does not imply pain.
2. The successive changes through which Tragedy passed, and the authors of these changes, are well known, whereas Comedy has had no history, because it was not at first treated seriously. It was late before the Archon granted a comic chorus to a poet; the performers were till then voluntary. Comedy had already taken definite shape when comic poets, distinctively so called, are heard of. 3. Who introduced masks, or prologues, or increased the number of actors—these and other similar details remain unknown. As for the plot, it came originally from Sicily; but of Athenian writers Crates was the first who, abandoning the "iambic" or lampooning form, generalized his themes and plots.
4. Epic poetry agrees with Tragedy in so far as it is an imitation in verse of characters of a higher type. They differ, in that Epic poetry admits but one kind of metre, and is narrative in form. They differ, again, in the length of the action: for Tragedy endeavors, as far as possible, to confine itself to a single revolution of the sun, or but slightly to exceed this limit; whereas the Epic action has no limits of time. This, then, is a second point of difference; though at first the same freedom was admitted in Tragedy as in Epic poetry.
5. Of their constituent parts some are common to both, some peculiar to Tragedy. Whoever, therefore, knows what is good or bad Tragedy, knows also about Epic poetry: for all the elements of an Epic poem are found in Tragedy, but the elements of a Tragedy are not all found in the Epic poem.

VI

Of the poetry which imitates in hexameter verse, and of Comedy, we will speak hereafter. Let us now discuss Tragedy, resuming its formal definition, as resulting from what has been already said.
2. Tragedy then, is an imitation of an action that is serious, complete, and of a certain magnitude; in language embellished with each kind of artistic ornament, the several kinds being found in separate

parts of the play; in the form of action, not of narrative; through pity and fear effecting the proper purgation of these emotions. 3. By "language embellished," I mean language into which rhythm, "harmony," and song enter. By "the several kinds in separate parts," I mean, that some parts are rendered through the medium of verse alone, others again with the aid of song.

4. Now as tragic imitation implies persons acting, it necessarily follows, in the first place, that Scenic equipment will be a part of Tragedy. Next, Song and Diction, for these are the medium of imitation. By "Diction" I mean the mere metrical arrangement of the words: as for "Song," it is a term whose sense every one understands.

5. Again, Tragedy is the imitation of an action; and an action implies personal agents, who necessarily possess certain distinctive qualities both of character and thought. It is these that determine the qualities of actions themselves; these—thought and character— are the two natural causes from which actions spring: on these causes, again, all success or failure depends. 6. Hence, the Plot is the imitation of the action:—for by Plot I here mean the arrangement of the incidents. By Character I mean that in virtue of which we ascribe certain qualities to the agents. Thought is required wherever a statement is proved, or, it may be, a general truth enunciated. 7. Every Tragedy, therefore, must have six parts, which parts determine its quality—namely, Plot, Character, Diction, Thought, Scenery, Song. Two of the parts constitute the medium of imitation, one the manner, and three the objects of imitation. And these complete the list. 8. These elements have been employed, we may say, by the poets to a man; in fact, every play contains Scenic accessories as well as Character, Plot, Diction, Song, and Thought.

9. But most important of all is the structure of the incidents. For Tragedy is an imitation, not of men, but of an action and of life, and life consists in action, and its end is a mode of action, not a quality. 10. Now character determines men's qualities, but it is by their actions that they are happy or the reverse. Dramatic action, therefore, is not with a view to the representation of character: character comes in as subsidiary to the action. Hence the incidents and the plot are the end of a tragedy; and the end is the chief thing of all. 11. Again, without action there cannot be a tragedy; there may be without character. The tragedies of most of our modern poets fail in the rendering of character; and of poets in general this is often true. It is the

same in painting; and here lies the difference between Zeuxis and Polygnotus. Polygnotus delineates character well: the style of Zeuxis is devoid of ethical quality. 12. Again, if you string together a set of speeches expressive of character, and well finished in point of diction and thought, you will not produce the essential tragic effect nearly so well as with a play which, however deficient in these respects, yet has a plot and artistically constructed incidents. 13. Besides which, the most powerful elements of emotional interest in Tragedy—Reversal or Recoil of the Action, and Recognition scenes —are parts of the plot. 14. A further proof is, that novices in the art attain to finish of diction and precision of portraiture before they can construct the plot. It is the same with almost all the early poets.

The Plot, then, is the first principle, and, as it were, the soul of a tragedy: Character holds the second place. 15. A similar fact is seen in painting. The most beautiful colors, laid on confusedly, will not give as much pleasure as the chalk outline of a portrait. Thus Tragedy is the imitation of an action, and of the agents, mainly with a view to the action.

16. Third in order is Thought,—that is, the faculty of saying what is possible and pertinent in given circumstances. In the case of oratory, this is the function of the political art and of the art of rhetoric: and so indeed the older poets make their characters speak the language of civic life; the poets of our time, the language of the rhetoricians.

17. Character is that which reveals moral purpose, showing what kind of things a man chooses or avoids. Speeches, therefore, which do not make this manifest, or in which the speaker does not choose or avoid anything whatever, are not expressive of character. Thought, on the other hand, is found where something is proved to be or not to be, or a general maxim is enunciated.

18. Fourth among the elements enumerated comes Diction; by which I mean, as has been already said, the expression of our meaning in words; and its essence is the same both in verse and prose.

19. Of the remaining elements Song holds the chief place among the embellishments.

Scenery has, indeed, an emotional attraction of its own, but, of all the parts, it is the least artistic, and connected least with the art of poetry. For the power of Tragedy, we may be sure, is felt even apart from representation and actors. Besides, the production of spectacular effects depends more on the art of the stage machinist than on that of the poet.

VII

These principles being established, let us now discuss the proper structure of the Plot, since this is the first and most important part of Tragedy.

2. Now, according to our definition, Tragedy is an imitation of an action that is complete, and whole, and of a certain magnitude; for there may be a whole that is wanting in magnitude. 3. A whole is that which has a beginning, a middle, and an end. A beginning is that which does not itself follow anything by causal necessity, but after which something naturally is or comes to be. An end, on the contrary, is that which itself naturally follows some other thing, either by necessity, or as a rule, but has nothing following it. A middle is that which follows something as some other thing follows it. A well constructed plot, therefore, must neither begin nor end at haphazard, but conform to these principles.

4. Again, a beautiful object, whether it be a picture of a living organism or any whole composed of parts, must not only have an orderly arrangement of parts, but must also be of a certain magnitude; for beauty depends on magnitude and order. Hence an exceedingly small picture cannot be beautiful; for the view of it is confused, the object being seen in an almost imperceptible moment of time. Nor, again, can one of vast size be beautiful; for as the eye cannot take it all in at once, the unity and sense of the whole is lost for the spectator; as for instance if there were a picture a thousand miles long. 5. As, therefore, in the case of animate bodies and pictures a certain magnitude is necessary, and a magnitude which may be easily embraced in one view; so in the plot, a certain length is necessary, and a length which can be easily embraced by the memory. 6. The limit of length in relation to dramatic competition and sensuous presentment, is no part of artistic theory. For had it been the rule for a hundred tragedies to compete together, the performance would have been regulated by the water-clock—as indeed is the practice in certain other contests. 7. But the limit as fixed by the nature of the drama itself is this:—the greater the length, the more beautiful will the piece be, so far as beauty depends on size, provided that the whole be perspicuous. And to define the matter roughly, we may say that the proper magnitude is comprised within such limits, that the sequence of events, according to the law of probability or necessity, will admit of a change from bad fortune to good, or from good fortune to bad.

VIII

Unity of plot does not, as some persons think, consist in the unity of the hero. For infinitely various are the incidents in one man's life, which cannot be reduced to unity; and so, too, there are many actions of one man out of which we cannot make one action. 2. Hence the error, as it appears, of all poets who have composed a *Heracleid*, a *Theseid*, or other poems of the kind. They imagine that as Heracles was one man, the story of Heracles must also be a unity. 3. But Homer, as in all else he is of surpassing merit, here too—whether from art or natural genius—seems to have happily discerned the truth. In composing the *Odyssey* he did not include all the adventures of Odysseus—such as his wound on Parnassus, or his feigned madness at the mustering of the host—incidents between which there was no necessary or probable connection: but he made the *Odyssey*, and likewise the *Iliad*, to centre round an action that in our sense of the word is one. 4. As therefore, in the other imitative arts, the imitation is one when the object imitated is one, so the plot, being an imitation of an action, must imitate one action and that a whole, the structural union of the parts being such that, if any one of them is displaced or removed, the whole will be disjointed and disturbed. For a thing whose presence or absence makes no visible difference, is not an organic part of the whole.

IX

It is, moreover, evident from what has been said, that it is not the function of the poet to relate what has happened, but what may happen,—what is possible according to the law of probability or necessity. 2. The poet and the historian differ not by writing in verse or in prose. The work of Herodotus might be put into verse, and it would still be a species of history, with metre no less than without it. The true difference is that one relates what has happened, the other what may happen. 3. Poetry, therefore, is a more philosophical and a higher thing than history: for poetry tends to express the universal, history the particular. 4. By the universal I mean how a person of given character will on occasion speak or act, according to the law of probability or necessity; and it is this universality at which poetry aims in the names she attaches to the personages. The particular is—for example—what Alcibiades did or suffered. 5. In Comedy this is already apparent: for here the poet first constructs the plot on the lines of probability, and then inserts characteristic names;—unlike the lampooners who write about particular individuals. 6. But tragedians still keep to real names, the reason being that what is possible is credible: what has not happened we do not at once feel sure to be possible: but what has happened is manifestly possible: otherwise it would not have happened. 7. Still there are some tragedies in which there are only one or two well known names, the rest being fictitious. In others, none are well known,—as in Agathon's *Flower,* where incidents and names alike are fictitious, and yet they give none the less pleasure. 8. We must not, therefore, at all costs keep to the received legends, which are the usual subjects of Tragedy. Indeed, it would be absurd to attempt it; for even familiar subjects are familiar only to a few, and yet give pleasure to all. 9. It clearly follows that the poet or "maker" should be the maker of plots rather than of verses; since he is a poet because he imitates, and what he imitates are actions. And even if he chances to take an historical subject, he is none the less a poet; for there is no reason why some events that have actually happened should not conform to the law of the probable and possible, and in virtue of that quality in them he is their poet or maker.

10. Of all plots and actions the episodic are the worst. I call a plot "episodic" in which the episodes or acts succeed one another without probable or necessary sequence. Bad poets compose such pieces by their own fault; good poets, to please the players; for, as they write show pieces for competition, they stretch the plot beyond its capacity, and are often forced to break the natural continuity.

11. But again, Tragedy is an imitation not only of a complete action, but of events terrible and pitiful. Such an effect is best produced when the events come on us by surprise; and the effect is heightened when, at the same time, they follow from one another. 12. The tragic wonder will then be greater than if they happened of themselves or by accident; for even coincidences are most striking when they have an air of design. We may instance the statue of Mitys at Argos, which fell upon his murderer while he was a spectator at a festival, and killed him. Such events seem not to be due to mere chance. Plots, therefore, constructed on these principles are necessarily the best.

X

Plots are either Simple or Complex, for the actions in real life, of which the plots are an imitation, obviously show a similar distinction. 2. An action which is one and continuous in the sense above defined, I call Simple, when the change of fortune takes place without Reversal (or Recoil) of the Action and without Recognition.

A Complex action is one in which the change is accompanied by such Reversal, or by Recognition, or by both. 3. These last should arise from the internal structure of the plot, so that what follows should be the necessary or probable result of the preceding action. It makes all the difference whether any given event is a case of *propter hoc* or *post hoc*.

XI

Reversal (or Recoil) is a change by which a train of action produces the opposite of the effect intended, subject always to our rule of probability or necessity. Thus in the *Œdipus*, the messenger comes to cheer Œdipus and free him from his alarms about his mother, but by revealing who he is, he produces the opposite effect. Again in the *Lynceus,* Lynceus is being led away to his death, and Danaus goes with him, meaning to slay him; but the outcome of the action is, that Danaus is killed and Lynceus saved.

2. Recognition, as the name indicates, is a change from ignorance to knowledge, producing love or hate between the persons destined by the poet for good or bad fortune. The best form of recognition is coincident with a Reversal (or Recoil), as in the *Œdipus*. 3. There are indeed other forms. Even inanimate things of the most trivial kind may sometimes be objects of recognition. Again, we may recognize or discover whether a person has done a thing or not. But the recognition which is most intimately connected with the plot and action is, as we have said, the recognition of persons. 4. This recognition, combined with Reversal, will produce either pity or fear; and actions producing these effects are those which, by our definition, Tragedy represents. Moreover, it is upon such issues that fortune or misfortune will turn. 5. Recognition, then, being between persons, it may happen that one person only is recognized by the other—when the latter is already known—or it may be necessary that the recognition should be on both sides. Thus Iphigenia is revealed to Orestes by the sending of the letter; but another act of recognition is required to make Orestes known to Iphigenia.

6. Two parts, then, of the Plot—Reversal and Recognition—turn upon surprises. A third part is the Tragic Incident. The Tragic

Incident is a destructive or painful action, such as death on the stage, bodily agony, wounds, and the like.

XII

[Here Aristotle enumerates the technical names for the various parts of a Greek tragedy.]

XIII

As the sequel to what has already been said, we must proceed to consider what the poet should aim at, and what he should avoid, in constructing his plots; and by what means the specific effect of Tragedy will be produced.

2. A perfect tragedy should, as we have seen, be arranged not on the simple but on the complex plan. It should, moreover, imitate actions which excite pity and fear, this being the distinctive mark of tragic imitation. It follows plainly, in the first place, that the change of fortune presented must not be the spectacle of a virtuous man brought from prosperity to adversity: for this moves neither pity nor fear; it merely shocks us. Nor, again, that of a bad man passing from adversity to prosperity: for nothing can be more alien to the spirit of Tragedy; it possesses no single tragic quality; it neither satisfies the moral sense, nor calls forth pity or fear. Nor, again, should the downfall of the utter villain be exhibited. A plot of this kind would, doubtless, satisfy the moral sense, but it would inspire neither pity nor fear; for pity is aroused by unmerited misfortune, fear by the misfortune of a man like ourselves. Such an event, therefore, will be neither pitiful nor terrible. 3. There remains, then, the character between these two extremes,—that of a man who is not eminently good and just, yet whose misfortune is brought about not by vice or depravity, but by some error or frailty. He must be one who is highly renowned and prosperous,—a personage like Œdipus, Thyestes, or other illustrious men of such families.

4. A well constructed plot should, therefore, be single in its issue, rather than double as some maintain. The change of fortune should be not from bad to good, but, reversely, from good to bad. It should come about as the result not of vice, but of some great error or frailty, in a character either such as we have described, or better rather than worse. 5. The practice of the stage bears out our view. At first the poets recounted any legend that came in their way. Now,

tragedies are founded on the story of a few houses,—on the fortunes of Alcmæon, Œdipus, Orestes, Meleager, Thyestes, Telephus, and those others who have done or suffered something terrible. A tragedy, then, to be perfect according to the rules of art should be of this construction. 6. Hence they are in error who censure Euripides just because he follows this principle in his plays, many of which end unhappily. It is, as we have said, the right ending. The best proof is that on the stage and in dramatic competition, such plays, if they are well represented, are the most tragic in effect; and Euripides, faulty as he is in the general management of his subject, yet is felt to be the most tragic of the poets.

7. In the second rank comes the kind of tragedy which some place first. Like the *Odyssey*, it has a double thread of plot, and also an opposite catastrophe for the good and for the bad. It is accounted the best because of the weakness of the spectators; for the poet is guided in what he writes by the wishes of his audience. 8. The pleasure, however, thence derived is not the true tragic pleasure. It is proper rather to Comedy, where those who, in the piece, are the deadliest enemies—like Orestes and Ægisthus—quit the stage as friends at the close, and no one slays or is slain.

XIV

Fear and pity may be aroused by spectacular means; but they may also result from the inner structure of the piece, which is the better way, and indicates a superior poet. For the plot ought to be so constructed that, even without the aid of the eye, he who hears the tale told will thrill with horror and melt to pity at what takes place. This is the impression we should receive from hearing the story of the *Œdipus*. 2. But to produce this effect by the mere spectacle is a less artistic method, and dependent on extraneous aids. Those who employ spectacular means to create a sense not of the terrible but of the monstrous, are strangers to the purpose of Tragedy; for we must not demand of Tragedy any and every kind of pleasure, but only that which is proper to it. 3. And since the pleasure which the poet should afford is that which comes from pity and fear through imitation, it is evident that this quality must be impressed upon the incidents.

Let us then determine what are the circumstances which strike us as terrible or pitiful.

4. Actions capable of this effect must happen between persons

who are either friends or enemies or indifferent to one another. If an enemy kills an enemy, there is nothing to excite pity either in the act or the intention,—except so far as the suffering in itself is pitiful. So again with indifferent persons. But when the tragic incident occurs between those who are near or dear to one another— if, for example, a brother kills, or intends to kill, a brother, a son his father, a mother her son, a son his mother, or any other deed of the kind is done—these are the situations to be looked for by the poet. 5. He may not indeed destroy the framework of the received legends —the fact, for instance, that Clytemnestra was slain by Orestes and Eriphyle by Alcmæon—but he ought to show invention of his own, and skilfully handle the traditional material. Let us explain more clearly what is meant by skilful handling.

6. The action may be done consciously and with knowledge of the persons, in the manner of the older poets. It is thus indeed that Euripides makes Medea slay her children. Or, again, the deed of horror may be done, but done in ignorance, and the tie of kinship or friendship be discovered afterwards. The *Œdipus* of Sophocles is an example. Here, indeed, the incident is outside the drama proper; but cases occur where it falls within the action of the play: one may cite the *Alcmæon* of Astydamas, or Telegonus in the *Wounded Odysseus*. 7. Again, there is a third case where some one is just about to do some irreparable deed through ignorance, and makes the discovery before it is done. These are the only possible ways. For the deed must either be done or not done,—and that wittingly or unwittingly. But of all these ways, to be about to act knowing the persons, and then not to act, is the worst. It is shocking without being tragic, for no disaster follows. It is, therefore, never, or very rarely, found in poetry. One instance, however, is in the *Antigone*, where Hæmon threatens to kill Creon. 8. The next and better way is that the deed should be perpetrated. Still better, that it should be perpetrated in ignorance, and the discovery made afterwards. There is then nothing to shock us, while the discovery produces a startling effect. 9. The last case is the best, as when in the *Cresphontes* Merope is about to slay her son, but, recognizing who he is, spares his life. So in the *Iphigenia*, the sister recognizes the brother just in time. Again in the *Helle*, the son recognizes the mother when on the point of giving her up. This, then, is why a few families only, as has been already observed, furnish the subjects of tragedy. It was not art, but happy chance, that led poets to look for such situations and so impress the tragic quality upon their

plots. They are compelled, therefore, to have recourse to those houses whose history contains moving incidents like these.

Enough has now been said concerning the structure of the incidents, and the proper constitution of the plot.

XV

In respect of Character there are four things to be aimed at. First, and most important, it must be good. Now any speech or action that manifests moral purpose of any kind will be expressive of character: the character will be good if the purpose is good. This rule is relative to each class. Even a woman may be good, and also a slave; though the woman may be said to be an inferior being, and the slave quite worthless. 2. The second thing to aim at is propriety. There is a type of manly valor; but for a woman to be valiant, or terrible, would be inappropriate. 3. Thirdly, character must be true to life: for this is a distinct thing from goodness and propriety, as here described. 4. The fourth point is consistency: for though the subject of the imitation, who suggested the type, be inconsistent, still he must be consistently inconsistent. 5. As an example of character gratuitously bad, we have Menelaus in the *Orestes*: of character indecorous and inappropriate, the lament of Odysseus in the *Scylla*, and the speech of Melanippe: of inconsistency, the *Iphigenia at Aulis*,—for Iphigenia the suppliant in no way resembles her later self.

6. As in the structure of the plot, so too in the portraiture of character, the poet should always aim either at the necessary or the probable. Thus a person of a given character should speak or act in a given way, by the rule either of necessity or of probability; just as this event should follow that by necessary or probable sequence. 7. It is therefore evident that the unravelling of the plot, no less than the complication, must arise out of the plot itself; it must not be brought about by the *Deus ex Machina*—as in the *Medea,* or in the Return of the Greeks in the *Iliad.* The *Deus ex Machina* should be employed only for events external to the drama,—for antecedent or subsequent events, which lie beyond the range of human knowledge, and which require to be reported or foretold; for to the gods we ascribe the power of seeing all things. Within the action there must be nothing irrational. If the irrational cannot be excluded, it should be outside the scope of the tragedy. Such is the irrational element in the *Œdipus* of Sophocles.

8. Again, since Tragedy is an imitation of persons who are above the common level, the example of good portrait-painters should be followed. They, while reproducing the distinctive form of the original, make a likeness which is true to life and yet more beautiful. So too the poet, in representing men who are irascible or indolent, or have other defects of character, should preserve the type and yet ennoble it. In this way Achilles is portrayed by Agathon and Homer.

9. These then are rules the poet should observe. Nor should he neglect those appeals to the senses, which, though not among the essentials, are the concomitants of poetry; for here too there is much room for error. But of this enough has been said in the published treatises.

XVI

[This section, perhaps not Aristotle's, discusses "recognition" or "discovery" in Greek tragedy.]

XVII

In constructing the plot and working it out with the proper diction, the poet should place the scene, as far as possible, before his eyes. In this way, seeing everything with the utmost vividness, as if he were a spectator of the action, he will discover what is in keeping with it, and be most unlikely to overlook inconsistencies. The need of such a rule is shown by the fault found in Carcinus. Amphiaraus was on his way from the temple. This fact escaped the observation of one who did not see the situation. On the stage, however, the piece failed, the audience being offended at the oversight.

2. Again, the poet should work out his play, to the best of his power, with appropriate gestures; for those who feel emotion are most convincing by force of sympathy. One who is agitated storms, one who is angry rages, with the most life-like reality. Hence poetry implies either a happy gift of nature or a strain of madness. In the one case a man can take the mould of any character; in the other, he is lifted out of his proper self.

3. As for the story, whether the poet takes it ready made or constructs it for himself, he should first sketch its general outline, and then fill in the episodes and amplify in detail. The general plan may be illustrated by the *Iphigenia*. A young girl is sacrificed; she disappears mysteriously from the eyes of those who sacrificed her; she is transported to another country, where the custom is to offer up all

strangers to the goddess. To this ministry she is appointed. Some time later her brother chances to arrive. The fact that the oracle for some reason ordered him to go there, is outside the general plan of the play. The purpose, again, of his coming is outside the action proper. However, he comes, he is seized, and, when on the point of being sacrificed, reveals who he is. The mode of recognition may be either that of Euripides or of Polyeidus, in whose play he exclaims very naturally:—"So it was not my sister only, but I too, who was doomed to be sacrificed"; and by that remark he is saved.

4. After this, the names being once given, it remains to fill in the episodes. We must see that they are relevant to the action. In the case of Orestes, for example, there is the madness which led to his capture, and his deliverance by means of the purificatory rite. 5. In the drama, the episodes are short, but it is these that give extension to Epic poetry. Thus the story of the *Odyssey* can be stated briefly. A certain man is absent from home for many years; he is jealously watched by Poseidon, and left desolate. Meanwhile his home is in a wretched plight—suitors are wasting his substance and plotting against his son. At length, tempest-tossed, he himself arrives and reveals his true self; he attacks his enemies, destroys them and is himself preserved. This is the essence of the plot; the rest is episode.

XVIII

Every tragedy falls into two parts,—Complication and Unravelling (or *Dénouement*). Incidents extraneous to the action are frequently combined with a portion of the action proper, to form the Complication; the rest is the Unravelling. By the Complication I mean all that comes between the beginning of the action and the part which marks the turning-point to good or bad fortune. The Unravelling is that which comes between the beginning of the change and the end. Thus, in the *Lynceus* of Theodectes, the Complication consists of the incidents presupposed in the drama, the seizure of the child, and then again . . . [The Unravelling] extends from the accusation of murder to the end.

2. There are four kinds of Tragedy,—first the [Simple, then] the Complex, depending entirely on Reversal and Recognition; next the Pathetic (where the motive is passion),—such as the tragedies on Ajax and Ixion; next the Ethical (where the motives are ethical), —such as the *Phthiotides* and the *Peleus*. [We here exclude the supernatural kind], such as the *Phorcides*, the *Prometheus*, and trage-

dies whose scene is in the lower world. 3. The poet should endeavor, if possible, to combine all poetic merits; or failing that, the greatest number and those the most important; the more so, in face of the cavilling criticism of the day. For whereas there have hitherto been good poets, each in his own branch, the critics now expect one man to surpass all others in their several lines of excellence.

In speaking of a tragedy as the same or different, the best test to take is the plot. Identity exists where the Complication and Unravelling are the same. Many poets tie the knot well, but unravel it ill. Both arts, however, should always be mastered.

4. Again, the poet should remember what has been often said, and not make a Tragedy into an Epic structure. By an Epic structure I mean one with a multiplicity of plots: as if, for instance, you were to make a tragedy out of the entire story of the *Iliad*. In the Epic poem, owing to its length, each part assumes its proper magnitude. In the drama the result is far from answering to the poet's expectation. 5. The proof is that the poets who have dramatized the whole story of the Fall of Troy, instead of selecting portions, like Euripides; or who have taken the whole tale of Niobe, and not a part of her story, like Æschylus, either fail utterly or meet with poor success on the stage. Even Agathon has been known to fail from this one defect. In his Reversals of the Action, however, he shows a marvellous skill in the effort to hit the popular taste,—to produce a tragic effect that satisfies the moral sense. 6. This effect is produced when the clever rogue, like Sisyphus, is outwitted, or the brave villain defeated. Such an event is, moreover, probable in Agathon's sense of the word: "it is probable," he says, "that many things should happen contrary to probability."

7. The Chorus too should be regarded as one of the actors; it should be an integral part of the whole, and share in the action, in the manner not of Euripides but of Sophocles. As for the later poets, their choral songs pertain as little to the subject of the piece as to that of any other tragedy. They are, therefore, sung as mere interludes,—a practice first begun by Agathon. Yet what difference is there between introducing such choral interludes, and transferring a speech, or even a whole act, from one play to another?

XIX

It remains to speak of Diction and Thought, the other parts of Tragedy having been already discussed. Concerning Thought, we may assume what is said in the *Rhetoric*,[1] to which inquiry the subject more strictly belongs. 2. Under Thought is included every effect which has to be produced by speech; in particular,—proof and refutation; the excitation of the feelings, such as pity, fear, anger, and the like; the suggestion of importance or its opposite. 3. Further, it is evident that the dramatic incidents must be treated from the same points of view as the dramatic speeches, when the object is to evoke the sense of pity, fear, importance, or probability. The only difference is, that the incidents should speak for themselves without verbal exposition; while the effects aimed at in a speech should be produced by the speaker, and as a result of the speech. For what were the need of a speaker, if the proper impression were at once conveyed, quite apart from what he says?

4. Next, as regards Diction. One branch of the inquiry treats of the Modes of Expression. But this province of knowledge belongs to the art of Declamation, and to the masters of that science. It includes, for instance,—what is a command, a prayer, a narrative, a threat, a question, an answer, and so forth. 5. To know or not to know these things involves no serious censure upon the poet's art. For who can admit the fault imputed to Homer by Protagoras,— that in the words, "Sing, goddess, of the wrath," he gives a command under the idea that he utters a prayer? For to tell some one to do a thing or not to do it is, he says, a command. We may, therefore, pass this over as an inquiry that belongs to another art, not to poetry.

[XX, XXI, XXII deal mainly with the mechanics of rhetoric.]

XXIII

As to that poetic imitation which is narrative in form and employs a single metre, the plot manifestly ought, as in a tragedy, to be constructed on dramatic principles. It should have for its subject a single action, whole and complete, with a beginning, a middle, and an end. It will thus resemble a single and coherent picture of a living being, and produce the pleasure proper to it. It will differ in structure from historical compositions, which of necessity present not a single action, but a single period, and all that hap-

---

[1] Aristotle's great contribution to the study of literary criticism was, of course, his *Poetics*. He also wrote a *Rhetoric*. His opinion of this branch of study is expressed in a sentence from Book III: "Style was brought forward at ᴀ late period, and, if rightly conceived of, it appears a vulgar sort of thing." (Saintsbury's translation.)

pened within that period to one person or to many, little connected together as the events may be. 2. For as the sea-fight at Salamis and the battle with the Carthaginians in Sicily took place at the same time, but did not tend to one result, so in the sequence of events, one thing sometimes follows another, and yet the two may not work up to any common end. Such is the practice, we may say, of most poets. 3. Here again, then, as has been already observed, the transcendent excellence of Homer is manifest. He never attempts to make the whole war of Troy the subject of his poem, though that war had a beginning and an end. It would have been too vast a theme, and not easily embraced in a single view. If, again, he had kept it within moderate limits, it must have been over-complicated by the variety of the incidents. As it is, he detaches a single portion, and admits as episodes many events from the general story of the war—such as the Catalogue of the ships and others—thus diversifying the poem. All other poets take a single hero, a single period, or an action single indeed, but with a multiplicity of parts. Thus did the author of the *Cypria* and of the *Little Iliad*. 4. For this reason the *Iliad* and the *Odyssey* each furnish the subject of one tragedy, or, at most, of two; while the *Cypria* supplies materials for many, and the *Little Iliad* for eight—the *Award of the Arms*, the *Philoctetes*, the *Neoptolemus*, *Eurypylus*, the *Mendicant Odysseus*, the *Laconian Women*, the *Fall of Ilium*, the *Departure of the Fleet*.[1]

XXIV

Again, Epic poetry must have as many kinds as Tragedy: it must be simple, or complex, or "ethical," or "pathetic." The parts also, with the exception of song and scenery, are the same; for it requires Reversals, Recognitions, and Tragic Incidents. Moreover, the thoughts and the diction must be artistic. 2. In all these respects Homer is our earliest and sufficient model. Indeed each of his poems has a twofold character. The *Iliad* is at once simple and "pathetic," and the *Odyssey* complex (for Recognition scenes run through it), and at the same time "ethical." Moreover, in diction and thought he is supreme.

3. Epic poetry differs from Tragedy in the scale on which it is constructed, and in its metre. As regards scale or length, we have already laid down an adequate limit:—the beginning and the end must be capable of being brought within a single view. This con-

[1] The Greek text adds *Sinon* and *The Trojan Women*.

dition will be satisfied by poems on a smaller scale than the old epics, and answering in length to the group of tragedies presented at a single sitting.

4. Epic poetry has, however, a great—a special—capacity for enlarging its dimensions, and we can see the reason. In Tragedy we cannot imitate several actions carried on at one and the same time; we must confine ourselves to the action on the stage and the part taken by the players. But in Epic poetry, owing to the narrative form, many events simultaneously transacted can be presented; and these, if relevant to the subject, add mass and dignity to the poem. The Epic has here an advantage, and one that conduces to grandeur of effect, also diverting the mind of the hearer and relieving the story with varying episodes. For sameness of incident soon produces satiety, and makes tragedies fail on the stage.

5. As for the metre, the heroic measure has proved its fitness by the test of experience. If a narrative poem in any other metre or in many metres were now composed, it would be found incongruous. For of all measures the heroic is the stateliest and the most massive; and hence it most readily admits rare words and metaphors, which is another point in which the narrative form of imitation stands alone. On the other hand, the iambic and the trochaic tetrameter are stirring measures, the latter being akin to dancing, the former expressive of action. 6. Still more absurd would it be to mix together different metres, as was done by Chæremon. Hence no one has ever composed a poem on a great scale in any other than heroic verse. Nature herself, as we have said, teaches the choice of the proper measure.

7. Homer, admirable in all respects, has the special merit of being the only poet who rightly appreciates the part he should take himself. The poet should speak as little as possible in his own person, for it is not this that makes him an imitator. Other poets appear themselves upon the scene throughout, and imitate but little and rarely. Homer, after a few prefatory words, at once brings in a man, or woman, or other personage; none of them wanting in characteristic qualities, but each with a character of his own.

8. The element of the wonderful is admitted in Tragedy. The irrational, on which the wonderful depends for its chief effects, has wider scope in Epic poetry, because there the person acting is not seen. Thus, the pursuit of Hector would be ludicrous if placed upon the stage—the Greeks standing still and not joining in the pursuit, and Achilles waving them back. But in the Epic poem the absurdity

passes unnoticed. Now the wonderful is pleasing: as may be inferred from the fact that, in telling a story, every one adds something startling of his own, knowing that his hearers like it. 9. It is Homer who has chiefly taught other poets the art of telling lies skilfully. The secret of it lies in a fallacy. For, assuming that if one thing is or becomes, a second is or becomes, men imagine that, if the second is, the first likewise is or becomes. But this is a false inference. Hence, where the first thing is untrue, it is quite unnecessary, provided the second be true, to add that the first is or has become. For the mind, knowing the second to be true, falsely infers the truth of the first. There is an example of this in the Bath Scene of the *Odyssey*.

10. Accordingly, the poet should prefer probable impossibilities to improbable possibilities. The tragic plot must not be composed of irrational parts. Everything irrational should, if possible, be excluded; or, at all events, it should lie outside the action of the play (as, in the *Œdipus*, the hero's ignorance as to the manner of Laius' death); not within the drama,—as in the *Electra*, the messenger's account of the Pythian games; or, as in the *Mysians*, the man who comes from Tegea to Mysia without speaking. The plea that otherwise the plot would have been ruined, is ridiculous. Such a plot should not in the first instance be constructed. But once it has been framed and an air of likelihood imparted to it, the absurdity itself should be tolerated. Take the irrational incidents in the *Odyssey*, where Odysseus is left upon the shore of Ithaca. How intolerable even these might have been would be apparent if an inferior poet were to treat the subject. As it is, the absurdity is veiled by the poetic charm with which the poet invests it.

11. The diction should be elaborated in the pauses of the action, where there is no expression of character or thought. For, conversely, character and thought are merely obscured by a diction that is over brilliant.

XXV

With respect to critical difficulties and their solutions, the number and nature of the sources from which they may be drawn may be thus exhibited.

The poet being an imitator, like a painter or any other artist, must of necessity imitate one of three objects,—things as they were or are, things as they are said or thought to be, or things as they ought to be. 2. The vehicle of expression is language,—either current terms or, it may be, rare words or metaphors. There are also many modifications of language, which we concede to the poets. 3. Add to this, that the standard of correctness is not the same in poetry and politics, any more than in poetry and any other art. Within the art of poetry itself there are two kinds of faults,— those which touch its essence, and those which are accidental. 4. If a poet has proposed to himself to imitate something [but has imitated it incorrectly], through want of capacity, the error is inherent in the poetry. But if the failure is due to the thing he has proposed to do—if he has represented a horse as throwing out both his off legs at once, or introduced technical inaccuracies in medicine, for example, or in any other art—the error is not essential to the poetry. These are the points of view from which we should consider and answer the objections raised by the critics.

5. First we will suppose the poet has represented things impossible according to the laws of his own art. It is an error; but the error may be justified, if the end of the art be thereby attained (the end being that already mentioned),—if, that is, the effect of this or any other part of the poem is thus rendered more striking. A case in point is the pursuit of Hector. If, however, the end might have been as well, or better, attained without violating the special rules of the poetic art, the error is not justified: for every kind of error should, if possible, be avoided.

Again, does the error touch the essentials of the poetic art, or some accident of it? For example,—not to know that a hind has no horns is a less serious matter than to paint it inartistically.

6. Further, if it be objected that the description is not true to fact, the poet may perhaps reply,—"But the objects are as they ought to be": just as Sophocles said that he drew men as they ought to be; Euripides, as they are. 7. In this way the objection may be met. If, however, the representation be of neither kind, the poet may answer,—"This is how men say the thing is." This applies to tales about the gods. It may well be that these stories are not higher than fact nor yet true to fact: they are, very possibly, what Xenophanes says of them. But anyhow, "this is what is said." Again, a description may be no better than the fact: "still, it was the fact"; as in the passage about the arms: "Upright upon their butt-ends stood the spears." This was the custom then, as it now is among the Illyrians.

8. Again, in examining whether what has been said or done by some one is poetically right or not, we must not look merely to the particular act or saying, and ask whether it is poetically good or bad. We must also consider by whom it is said or done, to whom, when, in whose interest, or for what end; whether, for instance, it be to secure a greater good, or avert a greater evil.

[Sections 9–14 give illustrations of usage in Greek.]

15. Again, when a word seems to involve some inconsistency of meaning, we should consider how many senses it may bear in the particular passage. 16. For example: "there was stayed the spear of bronze"—we should ask in how many ways we may take "being checked there." The true mode of interpretation is the precise opposite of what Glaucus mentions. Critics, he says, jump at certain groundless conclusions; they pass adverse judgment and then proceed to reason on it; and, assuming that the poet has said whatever they happen to think, find fault if a thing is inconsistent with their own fancy. The question about Icarius has been treated in this fashion. The critics imagine he was a Lacedæmonian. They think it strange, therefore, that Telemachus should not have met him when he went to Lacedæmon. But the Cephallenian story may perhaps be the true one. They allege that Odysseus took a wife from among themselves, and that her father was Icadius not Icarius. It is merely a mistake, then, that gives plausibility to the objection.

17. In general, the impossible must be justified by reference to artistic requirements, or to the higher reality, or to received opinion. With respect to the requirements of art, a probable impossibility is to be preferred to a thing improbable and yet possible. Again, it may be impossible that there should be men such as Zeuxis painted. "Yes," we say, "but the impossible is the higher thing; for the ideal type must surpass the reality." To justify the irrational, we appeal to what is commonly said to be. In addition to which, we urge that the irrational sometimes does not violate reason; just as "it is probable that a thing may happen contrary to probability."

18. Things that sound contradictory should be examined by the same rules as in dialectical refutation—whether the same thing is meant, in the same relation, and in the same sense. We should therefore solve the question by reference to what the poet says himself, or to what is tacitly assumed by a person of intelligence.

19. The element of the irrational, and, similarly, depravity of

character, are justly censured when there is no inner necessity for introducing them. Such is the irrational element in the *Ægeus* of Euripides, and the badness of Menelaus in the *Orestes*.

20. Thus, there are five sources from which critical objections are drawn. Things are censured either as impossible, or irrational, or morally hurtful, or contradictory, or contrary to artistic correctness. The answers should be sought under the twelve heads above mentioned.

XXVI

The question may be raised whether the Epic or Tragic mode of imitation is the higher. If the more refined art is the higher, and the more refined in every case is that which appeals to the better sort of audience, the art which imitates anything and everything is manifestly most unrefined. The audience is supposed to be too dull to comprehend unless something of their own is thrown in by the performers, who therefore indulge in restless movements. Bad flute-players twist and twirl, if they have to represent "the quoit-throw," or hustle the coryphæus when they perform the "Scylla." [1] 2. Tragedy, it is said, has this same defect. We may compare the opinion that the older actors entertained of their successors. Mynniscus used to call Callippides "ape" on account of the extravagance of his action, and the same view was held of Pindarus. Tragic art, then, as a whole, stands to Epic in the same relation as the younger to the elder actors. So we are told that Epic poetry is addressed to a cultivated audience, who do not need gesture; Tragedy, to an inferior public. 3. Being then unrefined, it is evidently the lower of the two.

Now, in the first place, this censure attaches not to the poetic but to the histrionic art; for gesticulation may be equally overdone in epic recitation, as by Sosistratus, or in lyrical competition, as by Mnasitheus, the Opuntian. Next, all action is not to be condemned —any more than all dancing—but only that of bad performers. Such was the fault found in Callippides, as also in others of our own day, who are censured for representing degraded women. Again, Tragedy like Epic poetry produces its effect even without action; it reveals its power by mere reading. If, then, in all other respects it is superior, this fault, we say, is not inherent in it.

4. And superior it is, because it has all the epic elements—it may even use the epic metre—with the music and scenic effects as im-

[1] Either flute music descriptive of Scylla, or a dance accompanied by such music.

portant accessories; and these produce the most vivid of pleasures. Further, it has vividness of impression in reading as well as in representation. 5. Moreover, the art attains its end within narrower limits; for the concentrated effect is more pleasurable than one which is spread over a long time and so diluted. What, for example, would be the effect of the *Œdipus* of Sophocles, if it were cast into a form as long as the *Iliad*? 6. Once more, the Epic imitation has less unity; as is shown by this, that any Epic poem will furnish subjects for several tragedies. Now if the story be worked into a unity, it will, if concisely told, appear truncated; or, if it conform to the Epic canon of length, it must seem weak and watery. . . *.* What I mean by a story composed of several actions may be illustrated from the *Iliad* and *Odyssey*, which have many parts, each with a certain magnitude of its own. Yet these poems are as perfect as possible in structure; each is, in the highest degree attainable, an imitation of a single action.

7. If, then, Tragedy is superior to Epic poetry in all these respects, and, moreover, fulfils its specific function better as an art —for each art ought to produce, not any chance pleasure, but the pleasure proper to it, as already stated—it plainly follows that Tragedy is the higher art, as attaining its end more perfectly.

8. Thus much may suffice concerning Tragic and Epic poetry in general; their several kinds and parts, with the number of each and their differences; the causes that make a poem good or bad; the objections of the critics and the answers to these objections.[1] . . .

---

[1] Here the manuscript breaks off.

Horace

Quintus Horatius Flaccus, or HORACE (65–8 B. C.) was born in Venusia, Apulia, the son of a freedman. He was educated at Rome and Athens, where he studied philosophy; he later served in the Republican army under Brutus at Philippi (42 B. C.). Back from Greece, he was employed as secretary to one of the quæstors, and began to write poetry, notably satire. He became the friend of Vergil and Varius; and the rich Mæcenas, patron of literary men, became attached to him, showing appreciation of his talents by giving him a villa, or farm, in the Sabine Hills, near Tibur (Tivoli). Here he wrote, free from distractions and financial worries (he declined an offer to become secretary to the Emperor Augustus), the lyrics, satires, and poetic epistles on which his chief fame rests. He died in Rome.

The *Ars Poetica* (among his last works) represents the beginning of what is often called "neo-classicism." The feeling had grown, even in Horace's time, that the ancient Greeks had achieved perfection in everything. Just as Horace himself copied the metres of Sappho and Alcæus; and Plautus and Terence, in their comedies, followed meticulously Menander; so it was argued that it was futile to imitate nature in ways other than those the Greeks had discovered. As Alexander Pope later put it:

> Learn hence for ancient rules a just esteem;
> To copy nature is to copy them.

The Italian Vida, in his *Art of Poetry* (1527), the Frenchman Boileau, in his *Art of Poetry* (1680), and the English-

man Pope, in his *Essay on Criticism* (1711), all reflect the
ideas of Horace.

From ART OF POETRY [1]

(B. C. 8)

If in a picture (Piso) [2] you should see
A handsome woman with a fish's tail,
Or a man's head upon a horse's neck,
Or limbs of beasts of the most different kinds,
Covered with feathers of all sorts of birds,
Would you not laugh, and think the painter mad?
Trust me, that book is as ridiculous,
Whose incoherent style (like sick men's dreams)
Varies all shapes, and mixes all extremes.
Painters and poets have been still allowed
Their pencils, and their fancies unconfined.
This privilege we freely give and take;
But nature, and the common laws of sense
Forbid to reconcile antipathies,
Or make a snake engender with a dove,
And hungry tigers court the tender lambs.

Some that at first have promised mighty things,
Applaud themselves, when a few florid lines
Shine through the insipid dullness of the rest;
Here they describe a temple, or a wood,
Or streams that through delightful meadows run,
And there the rainbow, or the rapid Rhine,
But they misplace them all, and crowd them in,
And are as much to seek in other things,
As he that only can design a tree,
Would be to draw a shipwreck or a storm.
When you begin with so much pomp and show,
Why is the end so little and so low?
Be what you will, so you be still the same.

[1] Translated by the Earl of Roscommon (1633–1685), printed in *Works of English Poets from Chaucer to Cowper* (London, 1810), vol. viii, pp. 272, from Dr Rawlinson's copy, corrected by the Earl's own hand.
[2] This, the last of Horace's *Epistles*, was addressed to the Piso family.

Most poets fall into the grossest faults,
Deluded by a seeming excellence:
By striving to be short, they grow obscure;
And when they would write smoothly, they want strength,
Their spirits sink; while others that affect
A lofty style, swell to a tympany.
Some timorous wretches start at every blast,
And fearing tempests, dare not leave the shore;
Others, in love with wild variety,
Draw boars in waves, and dolphins in a wood;
Thus fear of erring, joined with want of skill,
Is a most certain way of erring still.

* * * *

Let poets match their subject to their strength,
And often try what weight they can support,
And what their shoulders are too weak to bear,
After a serious and judicious choice,
Method and eloquence will never fail.

As well the force as ornament of verse,
Consists in choosing a fit time for things,
And knowing when a muse should be indulged
In her full flight, and when she should be curbed.

Words must be chosen, and be placed with skill:
You gain your point, when by the noble art
Of good connection, an unusual word
Is made at first familiar to our ear.
But if you write of things abstruse or new,
Some of your own inventing may be used,
So it be seldom and discreetly done:
But he, that hopes to have new words allowed,
Must so derive them from the Grecian spring,
As they may seem to flow without constraint.
Can an impartial reader discommend
In Varius, or in Virgil, what he likes
In Plautus or Cæcilius? Why should I
Be envied for the little I invent,
When Ennius and Cato's copious style
Have so enriched, and so adorned, our tongue?

Men ever had, and ever will have, leave
To coin new words well suited to the age.
Words are like leaves, some wither every year,
And every year a younger race succeeds.
Death is a tribute all things owe to fate;
The Lucrine mole (Cæsar's stupendous work)
Protects our navies from the raging north;
And (since Cethegus drained the Pontine Lake)
We plough and reap where former ages rowed.
See how the Tiber (whose licentious waves
So often overflowed the neighboring fields)
Now runs a smooth and inoffensive course,
Confined by our great Emperor's command:
Yet this, and they, and all, will be forgot.
Why then should words challenge Eternity,
When greatest men and greatest actions die?
Use may revive the obsoletest words,
And banish those that now are most in vogue;
Use is the judge, the law, and rule of speech.

[Here Horace discusses metres, and states that they have
    been settled for all time.]

He that would have spectators share his grief,
Must write not only well, but movingly,
And raise men's passions to what height he will.
We weep and laugh, as we see others do:
He only makes me sad who shows the way,
And first is sad himself; then, Telephus,
I feel the weight of your calamities,
And fancy all your miseries my own.
But, if you act them ill, I sleep or laugh:
Your looks must alter, as your subject does,
From kind to fierce, from wanton to severe:
For Nature forms, and softens us within,
And writes our fortune's changes in our face.
Pleasure enchants, impetuous rage transports,
And grief dejects, and wrings the tortured soul,
And these are all interpreted by speech;
But he whose words and fortunes disagree,
Absurd, unpitied, grows a public jest.

Observe the characters of those that speak,
Whether an honest servant, or a cheat,
Or one whose blood boils in his youthful veins,
Or a grave matron, or a busy nurse,
Extorting merchants, careful husbandmen,
Argives, or Thebans, Asians, or Greeks.

Follow report, or feign coherent things;
Describe Achilles, as Achilles was,
Impatient, rash, inexorable, proud,
Scorning all judges, and all law but arms;
Medea must be all revenge and blood,
Ino all tears, Ixion all deceit,
Io must wander, and Orestes mourn.

If your bold muse dare tread unbeaten paths,
And bring new characters upon the stage,
Be sure you keep them up to their first height.
New subjects are not easily explained,
And you had better choose a well-known theme,
Than trust to an invention of your own:
For what originally others writ,
May be so well disguised, and so improved,
That with some justice it may pass for yours;
But then you must not copy trivial things,
Nor word for word too faithfully translate,
Nor (as some servile imitators do)
Prescribe at first such strict uneasy rules,
As you must ever slavishly observe,
Or all the laws of decency renounce.

Begin not as the old poetaster did,
"Troy's famous war, and Priam's fate, I sing."
In what will all this ostentation end?
The laboring mountain scarce brings forth a mouse:
How far is this from the Mæonian [1] style?
"Muse, speak the man, who, since the siege of Troy,
So many towns, such change of manners saw."
One with a flash begins, and ends in smoke,
The other out of smoke brings glorious light,

[1] Homeric.

And (without raising expectation high)
Surprises us with daring miracles,
The bloody Lestrygons,[1] Charybdis' gulf,
And frighted Greeks, who near the Ætna shore
Hear Scylla bark, and Polyphemus roar.
He doth not trouble us with Leda's eggs,
When he begins to write the Trojan war;
Nor, writing the return of Diomed,
Go back as far as Meleager's death:
Nothing is idle, each judicious line
Insensibly acquaints us with the plot;
He chooses only what he can improve,
And truth and fiction are so aptly mixed
That all seems uniform, and of a piece.

Now hear what every auditor expects;
If you intend that he should stay to hear
The epilogue, and see the curtain fall,
Mind how our tempers alter with our years,
And by those rules form all your characters.
One that hath newly learned to speak and go,
Loves childish plays, is soon provoked and pleased,
And changes every hour his wavering mind.
A youth, that first casts off his tutor's yoke,
Loves horses, hounds, and sports, and exercise,
Prone to all vice, impatient of reproof,
Proud, careless, fond, inconstant, and profuse.
Gain and ambition rule our riper years,
And make us slaves to interest and power.
Old men are only walking hospitals,
Where all defects, and all diseases, crowd
With restless pain, and more tormenting fear,
Lazy, morose, full of delays and hopes,
Oppressed with riches, which they dare not use;
Ill-natured censors of the present age,
And fond of all the follies of the past.
Thus all the treasure of our flowing years,
Our ebb of life for ever takes away.
Boys must not have the ambitious care of men,
Nor men the weak anxieties of age.

[1] cannibals.

Some things are acted, others only told;
But what we hear moves less than what we see;
Spectators only have their eyes to trust,
But auditors must trust their ears and you;
Yet there are things improper for a scene,
Which men of judgment only will relate.
Medea must not draw her murdering knife,
And spill her children's blood upon the stage,
Nor Atreus there his horrid feast prepare.
Cadmus and Progné's metamorphosis,
(She to a swallow turned, he to a snake)
And whatsoever contradicts my sense,
I hate to see, and never can believe.

Five acts are the just measure of a play.
Never presume to make a god appear,
But for a business worthy of a god;
And in one scene no more than three should speak.

A chorus should supply what action wants,
And hath a generous and manly part;
Bridles wild rage, loves rigid honesty,
And strict observance of impartial laws,
Sobriety, security, and peace,
And begs the gods to turn blind Fortune's wheel,
To raise the wretched, and pull down the proud.
But nothing must be sung between the acts
But what some way conduces to the plot.

First the shrill sound of a small rural pipe
(Not loud like trumpets, nor adorned as now)
Was entertainment for the infant stage,
And pleased the thin and bashful audience
Of our well-meaning, frugal ancestors.
But when our walls and limits were enlarged,
And men (grown wanton by prosperity)
Studied new arts of luxury and ease,
The verse, the music, and the scenes improved;
For how should ignorance be judge of wit,
Or men of sense applaud the jests of fools?
Then came rich clothes and graceful action in,

Then instruments were taught more moving notes,
And Eloquence with all her pomp and charms
Foretold as useful and sententious truths,
As those delivered by the Delphic god.

    The first tragedians found that serious style
Too grave for their uncultivated age,
And so brought wild and naked satyrs in,
Whose motion, words, and shape, were all a farce,
(As oft as decency would give them leave)
Because the mad ungovernable rout,
Full of confusion, and the fumes of wine,
Loved such variety and antic tricks.
But then they did not wrong themselves so much
To make a god, a hero, or a king,
(Stripped of his golden crown and purple robe)
Descend to a mechanic dialect,
Nor (to avoid such meanness) soaring high
With empty sound, and airy notions fly;
For Tragedy should blush as much to stoop
To the low mimic follies of a farce,
As a grave matron would, to dance with girls:
You must not think that a satiric style
Allows of scandalous and brutish words,
Or the confounding of your characters.
Begin with Truth, then give Invention scope,
And if your style be natural and smooth,
All men will try, and hope to write as well;
And (not without much pains) be undeceived.
So much good method and connection may
Improve the common and the plainest things.
A satyr, that comes staring from the woods,
Must not at first speak like an orator:
But, though his language should not be refined,
It must not be obscene and impudent;
The better sort abhors scurrility,
And often censures what the rabble likes.

    [Some fourteen lines, in which Horace again discusses metre,
    are omitted here.]

Unpolished verses pass with many men,
And Rome is too indulgent in that point;
But then, to write at a loose rambling rate,
In hope the world will wink at all our faults,
Is such a rash, ill-grounded confidence,
As men may pardon, but will never praise.
Be perfect in the Greek originals,
Read them by day, and think of them by night.
But Plautus was admired in former time
With too much patience (not to call it worse),
His harsh, unequal verse was music then,
And rudeness had the privilege of wit.

When Thespis first exposed the tragic Muse,
Rude were the actors, and a cart the scene,
Where ghastly faces stained with lees of wine
Frighted the children, and amused the crowd;
This Æschylus (with indignation) saw,
And built a stage, found out a decent dress,
Brought vizards in (a civiler disguise)
And taught men how to speak, and how to act.
Next Comedy appeared with great applause,
Till her licentious and abusive tongue
Wakened the magistrate's coercive power,
And forced it to suppress her insolence.

Our writers have attempted every way,
And they deserve our praise, whose daring Muse
Disdained to be beholden to the Greeks,
And found fit subjects for her verse at home.
Nor should we be less famous for our wit,
Than for the force of our victorious arms;
But that the time and care, that are required
To overlook, and file, and polish well,
Fright poets from that necessary toil.

Democritus was so in love with wit,
And some men's natural impulse to write,
That he despised the help of art and rules,
And thought none poets till their brains were cracked;
And this hath so intoxicated some,

That (to appear incorrigibly mad)
They cleanliness and company renounce
For lunacy beyond the cure of art,
With a long beard, and ten long dirty nails,
Pass current for Apollo's livery.
O my unhappy stars! if in the Spring
Some physic had not cured me of the spleen,
None would have writ with more success than I;
But I must rest contented as I am,
And only serve to whet that wit in you,
To which I willingly resign my claim.
Yet without writing I may teach to write,
Tell what the duty of a poet is;
Wherein his wealth and ornaments consist,
And how he may be formed, and how improved,
What fit, what not, what excellent or ill.

Sound judgment is the ground of writing well:
And when Philosophy directs your choice
To proper subjects rightly understood,
Words from your pen will naturally flow;
He only gives the proper characters,
Who knows the duty of all ranks of men,
And what we owe our country, parents, friends,
How judges, and how senators should act,
And what becomes a general to do;
Those are the likest copies, which are drawn
By the original of human life.
Sometimes in rough and undigested plays
We meet with such a lucky character,
As being humored right, and well pursued,
Succeeds much better than the shallow verse
And chiming trifles of more studious pens.

Greece had a genius, Greece had eloquence,
For her ambition and her end was fame.
Our Roman youth is diligently taught
The deep mysterious art of growing rich,
And the first words that children learn to speak,
Are of the value of the names of coin:
Can a penurious wretch, that with his milk

Hath sucked the basest dregs of usury,
Pretend to generous and heroic thoughts?
Can rust and avarice write lasting lines?
But you (brave youth), wise Numa's worthy heir,
Remember of what weight your judgment is,
And never venture to commend a book,
That has not passed all judges and all tests.

A poet should instruct, or please, or both;
Let all your precepts be succinct and clear,
That ready wits may comprehend them soon,
And faithful memories retain them long;
All superfluities are soon forgot.
Never be so conceited of your parts,
To think you may persuade us what you please,
Or venture to bring in a child alive,
That cannibals have murdered and devoured.
Old age explodes all but morality;
Austerity offends aspiring youths;
But he that joins instructions with delight,
Profit with pleasure, carries all the votes:
These are the volumes that enrich the shops,
These pass with admiration through the world,
And bring their author to eternal fame.

Be not too rigidly censorious,
A string may jar in the best master's hand,
And the most skilful archer miss his aim;
But in a poem elegantly writ,
I would not quarrel with a slight mistake,
Such as our nature's frailty may excuse;
But he that hath been often told his fault,
And still persists, is as impertinent,
As a musician that will always play,
And yet is always out at the same note;
When such a positive abandoned fop
(Among his numerous absurdities)
Stumbles upon some tolerable line,
I fret to see them in such company,
And wonder by what magic they came there.

But in long works sleep will sometimes surprise;
Homer himself hath been observed to nod.

Poems, like pictures, are of different sorts,
Some better at a distance, others near,
Some love the dark, some choose the clearest light,
And boldly challenge the most piercing eye;
Some please for once, some will for ever please.

But, Piso (though your knowledge of the world,
Joined with your father's precepts, make you wise),
Remember this as an important truth:
Some things admit of mediocrity.
A counsellor, or pleader at the bar,
May want Messala's powerful eloquence,
Or be less read than deep Cascellius;
Yet this indifferent lawyer is esteemed;
But no authority of gods nor men
Allow of any mean in poesy.
As an ill concert, and a coarse perfume,
Disgrace the delicacy of a feast,
And might with more discretion have been spared;
So poesy, whose end is to delight,
Admits of no degrees, but must be still
Sublimely good, or despicably ill.

In other things men have some reason left,
And one that cannot dance, or fence, or run,
Despairing of success, forbears to try;
But all (without consideration) write;
Some thinking that the omnipotence of wealth
Can turn them into poets when they please.
But, Piso, you are of too quick a sight
Not to discern which way your talent lies,
Or vainly with your genius to contend;
Yet if it ever be your fate to write,
Let your productions pass the strictest hands,
Mine and your father's, and not see the light,
Till time and care have ripened every line.
What you keep by you, you may change and mend
But words once spoke can never be recalled.

Orpheus, inspired by more than human power,
Did not (as poets feign) tame savage beasts,
But men as lawless, and as wild as they,
And first dissuaded them from rage and blood.
Thus, when Amphion built the Theban wall,
They feigned the stones obeyed his magic lute;
Poets, the first instructors of mankind,
Brought all things to their proper native use;
Some they appropriated to the gods,
And some to public, some to private, ends:
Promiscuous love by marriage was restrained,
Cities were built, and useful laws were made;
So great was the divinity of verse,
And such observance to a poet paid.
Then Homer's and Tyrtæus' martial Muse
Wakened the world, and sounded loud alarms.
To verse we owe the sacred oracles,
And our best precepts of morality;
Some have by verse obtained the love of kings,
(Who, with the Muses, ease their wearied minds)
Then blush not, noble Piso, to protect
What gods inspire, and kings delight to hear.

Some think that poets may be formed by Art,
Others maintain, that Nature makes them so;
I neither see what Art without a vein,
Nor Wit without the help of Art can do,
But mutually they crave each other's aid.
He that intends to gain the Olympic prize
Must use himself to hunger, heat, and cold,
Take leave of wine, and the soft joys of love;
And no musician dares pretend to skill,
Without a great expense of time and pains;
But every little busy scribbler now
Swells with the praises which he gives himself;
And, taking sanctuary in the crowd,
Brags of his impudence, and scorns to mend.

[The rest of the poem deals with critics who are flatterers and poets who are obstinate.]

Quintilian

Marcus Fabius Quintilianus, or QUINTILIAN (*c* 40–*c* 118), Roman rhetorician, was born in Calagurris (Calahorra), Spain, and educated at Rome. He began to practise law about the year 69 and subsequently became a teacher of rhetoric. Domitian bestowed consular rank upon him. His greatest work, *Institutio Oratoria,* was written in the early nineties of the first century; it combines a discussion of education with a consideration of the principles, scope, and matter of oratory, as well as its manner (style).

Quintilian is in many ways the ablest and the most helpful of Roman critics. His field is rhetoric, to be sure, rather than poetics, but his treatment of the mechanics of writing is so wise and clear, beginning with simple directions for a schoolboy, and proceeding to solid advice to the mature writer, that he rises above the mere rhetorician, and wins a deserved place among literary critics.

Aristotle had written a *Rhetoric.* His attitude toward style has already been quoted (see above, page 44, footnote 1). He thinks it vulgar, but it must be remembered that after the ancient Greeks, critics—Roman, Italian, French, German, even English—had first to consider the nature and capabilities of their native languages and then to discover how their countrymen as artists could emulate the sublimity of the Greeks.

Quintilian's distinction is that he not only offers solid advice to Romans in the craft of writing, but gives, in the end, insight into what literary art is.

From INSTITUTIO ORATORIA [1]

(c 93)

BOOK VIII, iii, 6–11

But such ornament must, as I have already said [in the introduction to this book, 19], be bold, manly, and chaste, free from all effeminate smoothness and the false hues derived from artificial dyes, and must glow with health and vigor. So true is this, that although, where ornament is concerned, vice and virtue are never far apart, those who employ a vicious style of embellishment disguise their vices with the name of virtue. Therefore let none of our decadents accuse me of being an enemy to those who speak with grace and finish. I do not deny the existence of such a virtue, I merely deny that they possess it. Shall I regard a farm as a model of good cultivation because its owner shows me lilies and violets and anemones and fountains of living water in place of rich crops and vines bowed beneath their clusters? Shall I prefer the barren plane and myrtles trimly clipped, to the fruitful olive and the elm that weds the vine? No, let such luxuries delight the rich: but where would their wealth be if they had nought save these? Again, is beauty an object of no consideration in the planting of fruit trees? Certainly not! For my trees must be planted in due order and at fixed intervals. What fairer sight is there than rows of trees planted in échelon which present straight lines to the eye from whatever angle they be viewed? But it has an additional advantage, since this form of plantation enables every tree to derive an equal share of moisture from the soil. When the tops of my olive trees rise too high, I lop them away, with the result that their growth expands laterally in a manner that is at once more pleasing to the eye and enables them to bear more fruit owing to the increase in the number of branches. A horse whose flanks are compact is not only better to look upon, but swifter in speed. The athlete whose muscles have been formed by exercise is a joy to the eye, but he is also better fitted for the contests in which he must engage. In fact true beauty and usefulness always go hand in hand.

BOOK IX, iv, 3–14

I am well aware that there are certain writers who would abso-

[1] Translated by H. E. Butler, M.A., printed in the Loeb Classical Library, vol. cxxvi (1922), and used by kind permission of the President and Fellows of Harvard College.

lutely bar all study of artistic structure and contend that language as it chances to present itself in the rough is more natural and even more manly. If by this they mean that only that is natural which originated with nature and has never received any subsequent cultivation, there is an end to the whole art of oratory. For the first men did not speak with the care demanded by that art nor in accordance with the rules that it lays down. They knew nothing of introducing their case by means of an exordium, of instructing the jury by a statement of facts, of proving by argument or of arousing the emotions. They lacked all these qualifications as completely as they lacked all knowledge of the theory of artistic structure. But if they were to be forbidden all progress in this respect, they ought equally to have been forbidden to exchange their huts for houses, their cloaks of skin for civilized raiment and their mountains and forests for cities. What art was ever born full-grown? What does not ripen with cultivation? Why do we train the vine? Why dig it? We clear the fields of brambles, and they too are natural products of the soil. We tame animals, and yet they are born wild. No, that which is most natural is that which nature permits to be done to the greatest perfection. How can a style which lacks orderly structure be stronger than one that is welded together and artistically arranged? It must not be regarded as the fault of the study of structure that the employment of feet consisting of short syllables such as characterize the Sotadean [1] and Galliambic [2] metres and certain prose rhythms closely resembling them in wildness, weakens the force of our matter. Just as river-currents are more violent when they run along a sloping bed that presents no obstacles to check their course, than when their waters are broken and baffled by rocks that obstruct the channel, so a style which flows in a continuous stream with all the full development of its force is better than one which is rough and broken. Why then should it be thought that polish is inevitably prejudicial to vigor, when the truth is that nothing can attain its full strength without the assistance of art; and that art is always productive of beauty? Is it not the fact that grace always goes with the highest skill in throwing the spear, and that the truer the archer's aim, the more comely is his attitude? Again in fencing and all the contests of the wrestling school, what one of all the tricks of attack and defence is there, that does not require movements and firmness of foot such as can only be acquired by art? Consequently in my

[1] The Greek poet Sotades (276 B.C.) wrote licentious verse in acatalectic tetrameter.
[2] A kind of Ionic verse (two iambic dimeters catalectic) used by the priests of Cybele.

opinion artistic structure gives force and direction to our thoughts just as the throwing-thong and the bowstring do to the spear and the arrow. And for this reason all the best scholars are convinced that the study of structure is of the utmost value, not merely for charming the ear, but for stirring the soul. For in the first place nothing can penetrate to the emotions that stumbles at the portals of the ear, and secondly man is naturally attracted by harmonious sounds. Otherwise it would not be the case that musical instruments, in spite of the fact that their sounds are inarticulate, still succeed in exciting a variety of different emotions in the hearer. In the sacred games different methods are employed to excite and calm the soul, different melodies are required for the war-song and the entreaty sung by the suppliant on bended knee, while the war-note of the trumpet that leads the army forth to battle has no resemblance to the call that sounds the retreat. It was the undoubted custom of the Pythagoreans, when they woke from slumber, to rouse their souls with the music of the lyre, that they might be more alert for action, and before they retired to rest, to soothe their minds by melodies from the same instrument, in order that all restlessness of thought might be lulled to orderly repose. But if there is such secret power in rhythm and melody alone, this power is found at its strongest in eloquence, and, however important the selection of words for the expression of our thoughts, the structural art which welds them together in the body of a period or rounds them off at the close, has at least an equal claim to importance. For there are some things which, despite triviality of thought and mediocrity of language, may achieve distinction in virtue of this excellence alone. In fact, if we break up and disarrange any sentence that may have struck us as vigorous, charming or elegant, we shall find that all its force, attraction and grace have disappeared. . . .

BOOK IX, iv, 60–63

. . . On the other hand the management of feet is far more difficult in prose than in verse, first because there are but few feet in a single line of verse which is far shorter than the lengthy periods of prose; secondly because each line of verse is always uniform and its movement is determined by a single definite scheme, whereas the structure of prose must be varied if it is to avoid giving offence by its monotony and standing convicted of affectation. Rhythm pervades the whole body of prose through all its extent. For we cannot speak without employing the long and short syllables of which feet are composed. Its presence is, however, most necessary and most apparent at the conclusion of the period, firstly because every group of connected thoughts has its natural limit and demands a reasonable interval to divide it from the commencement of what is to follow: secondly because the ear, after following the unbroken flow of the voice and being carried along down the stream of oratory, finds its best opportunity of forming a sound judgment on what it has heard, when the rush of words comes to a halt and gives it time for consideration. Consequently all harshness and abruptness must be avoided at this point, where the mind takes breath and recovers its energy. It is there that style has its citadel, it is this point that excites the eager expectation of the audience, it is from this that the declaimer wins all his glory. Next to the conclusion of the period, it is the beginning which claims the most care: for the audience have their attention fixed on this as well. But the opening of the sentence presents less difficulty, since it is independent and is not the slave of what has preceded. It merely takes what has preceded as a starting point, whereas the conclusion coheres with what has preceded, and however carefully constructed, its elegance will be wasted, if the path which leads up to it be interrupted. . . .

BOOK IX, iv, 116–119

The best judge as to rhythm is the ear, which appreciates fullness of rhythm or feels the lack of it, is offended by harshness, soothed by smooth and excited by impetuous movement, and approves stability, while it detects limping measures and rejects those that are excessive and extravagant. It is for this reason that those who have received a thorough training understand the theory of artistic structure, while even the untrained derive pleasure from it. There are some points, it is true, which are beyond the power of art to inculcate. For example, if the case, tense, or mood with which we have begun, produces a harsh rhythm, it must be changed. But is it possible to lay down any definite rule as to what the change of case, tense, or mood should be? It is often possible to help out the rhythm when it is in difficulties by introducing variety through the agency of a *figure*. But what is this *figure* to be? A *figure of speech* or a *figure of thought*? Can we give any general ruling on the subject? In such cases opportunism is our only salvation, and we must be guided by consideration of the special circumstances. Further with regard to the time-lengths, which are of such importance where rhythm is concerned, what standard is there by which they can be regulated, save that of the ear? Why do some sentences produce a full rhythmical effect, although the words which they contain are few, whereas others containing a greater number are abrupt and short in rhythm? Why again in periods do we get an impression of incompleteness, despite the fact that the sense is complete?

BOOK IX, iv, 142–147

As a general rule, however, if the choice were forced upon me, I should prefer my rhythm to be harsh and violent rather than nerveless and effeminate, as it is in so many writers, more especially in our own day, when it trips along in wanton measures that suggest the accompaniment of castanets. Nor will any rhythm ever be so admirable that it ought to be continued with the same recurrence of feet. For we shall really be indulging in a species of versification if we seek to lay down one law for all varieties of speech: further, to do so would lay us open to the charge of the most obvious affectation, a fault of which we should avoid even the smallest suspicion, while we should also weary and cloy our audience by the resulting monotony; the sweeter the rhythm, the sooner the orator who is detected in a studied adherence to its employment, will cease to carry conviction or to stir the passions and emotions. The judge will refuse to believe him or to allow him to excite his compassion or his anger, if he thinks that he has leisure for this species of refinement. It will therefore be desirable from time to time that in certain passages the rhythm should be deliberately dissolved: this is a task of no small difficulty, if the appearance of effort is to be avoided. In so doing we must not come to the assistance of the rhythm by introducing *hyperbata* [1] of extravagant length, for fear that we should betray the purpose of our action: and we should certainly never in our search for smoothness abandon for another any word that is apt and appropriate to our theme. As a matter of fact no word will be so intractable as to baffle all our attempts to find it a suitable position; but it must be remembered that when we avoid such words, we do so not to enhance the charm of our rhythm, but to evade a difficulty. I am not, however, surprised that Latin writers have paid more at-

[1] Transpositions. See VIII, vi, 62: *"Hyperbation,* that is, the transposition of a word, is often demanded by the structure of the sentence and the claims of elegance, and is consequently counted among the ornaments of style." (Butler.)

tention to rhythmical structure than the Athenians, since Latin words possess less correctness and charm. Nor again do I count it a fault in Cicero that, in this respect, he diverged to some extent from the practice of Demosthenes. However, my final book will explain the nature of the difference between our language and that of Greece. . . .

To sum up then, artistic structure must be decorous, pleasing, and varied. It consists of three parts, order, connection, and rhythm. The method of its achievement lies in addition, subtraction, and alteration of words. Its practice will depend upon the nature of our theme. The care which it demands is great, but, still, less than that demanded by expression and thought. Above all it is necessary to conceal the care expended upon it so that our rhythms may seem to possess a spontaneous flow, not to have been the result of elaborate search or compulsion.

Longinus

Dionysius Cassius LONGINUS (*c* 210–273) was an Athenian philosopher and student of literature. In philosophy, he was an ardent Platonist; in the field of literary criticism, he was the reputed author of the splendid treatise *On the Sublime*. Of his life we know little except that he was called by Queen Zenobia of Palmyra to be the instructor of her children and to be her Counsellor of State. When, in 272, the Roman Emperor Aurelian, waging war against Palmyra, captured Zenobia, she saved her life by sacrificing her ministers, among whom was Longinus. He was beheaded as a traitor by order of the emperor.

On the Sublime, one of the greatest critical essays of all time, has had a strange history. There are no references to it in ancient writings and no manuscript of it earlier than the tenth century. It was first printed, in the original Greek, by Robortello, in 1554; but the treatise remained little known until Boileau—the great neo-classic critic, curiously enough—translated it, in 1674, into French. (See his Introduction to the translation, p. 223, below.)

Longinus—if it was he that wrote the essay—is the first critic to state definitely that literature exists, not to teach, or to give us learning, but to arouse our emotions, to transport us into ecstasy, to give us pleasure. He admits the necessity of great and weighty thought, but believes that noble ideas give rise to deep emotions, lift us to sublimity, just as, conversely, a deep emotion may give rise to profound thought.

Longinus's attitude toward literature is an extraordinary one for his day. It is more like that of men such as Young, in

72

the so-called Romantic Period in England. And in his essay, he exemplifies the very qualities that he asserts should be inherent in all art. As Boileau, his translator, said: "In speaking of the sublime, he is himself sublime." So likewise Pope, who echoed Boileau more than once:

> Thee, bold Longinus! all the Nine inspire,
> And bless their critic with a poet's fire:
> An ardent judge, who, zealous in his trust,
> With warmth gives sentence, yet is always just;
> Whose own example strengthens all his laws,
> And is himself that great Sublime he draws.
> *Essay on Criticism*, 675–680.

From ON THE SUBLIME [1]

(*c* 250)

I

You will remember, my dear Postumius Terentianus, that when we examined together the treatise of Cæcilius on the Sublime, we found that it fell below the dignity of the whole subject, while it failed signally to grasp the essential points, and conveyed to its readers but little of that practical help which it should be a writer's principal aim to give. In every systematic treatise two things are required. The first is a statement of the subject; the other, which although second in order ranks higher in importance, is an indication of the methods by which we may attain our end. Now Cæcilius seeks to show the nature of the sublime by countless instances as though our ignorance demanded it, but the consideration of the means whereby we may succeed in raising our own capacities to a certain pitch of elevation he has, strangely enough, omitted as unnecessary. 2. However, it may be that the man ought not so much to be blamed for his shortcomings as praised for his happy thought and his enthusiasm. But since you have urged me, in my turn, to write a brief essay on the sublime for your special gratification, let us consider whether the views I have formed contain anything which will be of use to public men. You will yourself, my friend, in accordance with your nature and with what is fitting, join me in appraising each detail

[1] Translated by W. Rhys Roberts, Cambridge, 1907. Used by permission of the Cambridge University Press and the Macmillan Company.

with the utmost regard for truth; for he answered well who, when asked in what qualities we resemble the gods, declared that we do so in benevolence and truth. 3. As I am writing to you, my good friend, who are well versed in literary studies, I feel almost absolved from the necessity of premising at any length that sublimity is a certain distinction and excellence in expression, and that it is from no other source than this that the greatest poets and writers have derived their eminence and gained an immortality of renown. 4. The effect of elevated language upon an audience is not persuasion but transport. At every time and in every way imposing speech, with the spell it throws over us, prevails over that which aims at persuasion and gratification. Our persuasions we can usually control, but the influences of the sublime bring power and irresistible might to bear, and reign supreme over every hearer. Similarly, we see skill in invention, and due order and arrangement of matter, emerging as the hard-won result not of one thing nor of two, but of the whole texture of the composition, whereas Sublimity flashing forth at the right moment scatters everything before it like a thunderbolt, and at once displays the power of the orator in all its plentitude. But enough; for these reflections, and others like them, you can, I know well, my dear Terentianus, yourself suggest from your own experience.

II

First of all, we must raise the question whether there is such a thing as an art of the sublime or lofty. Some hold that those are entirely in error who would bring such matters under the precepts of art. A lofty tone, says one, is innate, and does not come by teaching; nature is the only art that can compass it. Works of nature are, they think, made worse and altogether feebler when wizened by the rules of art. 2. But I maintain that this will be found to be otherwise if it be observed that, while nature as a rule is free and independent in matters of passion and elevation, yet is she wont not to act at random and utterly without system. Further, nature is the original and vital underlying principle in all cases, but system can define limits and fitting seasons, and can also contribute the safest rules for use and practice. Moreover, the expression of the sublime is more exposed to danger when it goes its own way without the guidance of knowledge,—when it is suffered to be unstable and unballasted,— when it is left at the mercy of mere momentum and ignorant audacity. It is true that it often needs the spur, but it is also true that it often needs the curb. 3. Demosthenes expresses the view, with regard to human life in general, that good fortune is the greatest of blessings, while good counsel, which occupies the second place, is hardly inferior in importance, since its absence contributes inevitably to the ruin of the former. This we may apply to diction, nature occupying the position of good fortune, art that of good counsel. Most important of all, we must remember that the very fact that there are some elements of expression which are in the hands of nature alone, can be learnt from no other source than art. If, I say, the critic of those who desire to learn were to turn these matters over in his mind, he would no longer, it seems to me, regard the discussion of the subject as superfluous or useless.

* * * *

[III and IV discuss faults in rhetoric.]

V

All these ugly and parasitical growths arise in literature from a single cause, that pursuit of novelty in the expression of ideas which may be regarded as the fashionable craze of the day. Our defects usually spring, for the most part, from the same sources as our good points. Hence, while beauties of expression and touches of sublimity, and charming elegances withal, are favorable to effective composition, yet these very things are the elements and foundation, not only of success, but also of the contrary. Something of the kind is true also of variations and hyperboles and the use of the plural number, and we shall show subsequently the dangers to which these seem severally to be exposed. It is necessary now to seek and to suggest means by which we may avoid the defects which attend the steps of the sublime.

VI

The best means would be, my friend, to gain, first of all, clear knowledge and appreciation of the true sublime. The enterprise is, however, an arduous one. For the judgment of [literature] [1] is the last and crowning fruit of long experience. None the less, if I must speak in the way of precept, it is not impossible perhaps to acquire

[1] The editors take the liberty of substituting this word for the translator's *style*, believing it expresses the meaning of Longinus more clearly.

discrimination in these matters by attention to some such hints as those which follow.

VII

You must know, my dear friend, that it is with the sublime as in the common life of man. In life nothing can be considered great which it is held great to despise. For instance, riches, honors, distinctions, sovereignties, and all other things which possess in abundance the external trappings of the stage, will not seem, to a man of sense, to be supreme blessings, since the very contempt of them is reckoned good in no small degree, and in any case those who could have them, but are high-souled enough to disdain them, are more admired than those who have them. So also in the case of sublimity in poems and prose writings, we must consider whether some supposed examples have not simply the appearance of elevation with many idle accretions, so that when analyzed they are found to be mere vanity—objects which a noble nature will rather despise than admire. 2. For, as if instinctively, our soul is uplifted by the true sublime; it takes a proud flight, and is filled with joy and vaunting, as though it had itself produced what it has heard. 3. When, therefore, a thing is heard repeatedly by a man of intelligence, who is well versed in literature, and its effect is not to dispose the soul to high thoughts, and it does not leave in the mind more food for reflection than the words seem to convey, but falls, if examined carefully through and through, into disesteem, it cannot rank as true sublimity because it does not survive a first hearing. For that is really great which bears a repeated examination, and which it is difficult or rather impossible to withstand, and the memory of which is strong and hard to efface. 4. In general, consider those examples of sublimity to be fine and genuine which please all and always. For when men of different pursuits, lives, ambitions, ages, languages, hold identical views on one and the same subject, then that verdict which results, so to speak, from a concert of discordant elements makes our faith in the object of admiration strong and unassailable.

VIII

There are, it may be said, five principal sources of elevated language. Beneath these five varieties there lies, as though it were a common foundation, the gift of discourse, which is indispensable. First and most important is the power of forming great conceptions, as we have elsewhere explained in our remarks on Xenophon. Secondly, there is vehement and inspired passion. These two components of the sublime are for the most part innate. Those which remain are partly the product of art. The due formation of figures deals with two sorts of figures, first those of thought and secondly those of expression. Next there is noble diction, which in turn comprises choice of words, and use of metaphors, and elaboration of language. The fifth cause of elevation—one which is the fitting conclusion of all that have preceded it—is dignified and elevated composition. Come now, let us consider what is involved in each of these varieties, with this one remark by way of preface, that Cæcilius has omitted some of the five divisions, for example, that of passion. 2. Surely he is quite mistaken if he does so on the ground that these two, sublimity and passion, are a unity, and if it seems to him that they are by nature one and inseparable. For some passions are found which are far removed from sublimity and are of a low order, such as pity, grief, and fear; and on the other hand there are many examples of the sublime which are independent of passion, such as the daring words of Homer with regard to the Aloadæ, to take one out of numberless instances,

Yea, Ossa in fury they strove to upheave on Olympus on high,
With forest-clad Pelion above, that thence they might step to the sky.

And so of the words which follow with still greater force:—

Ay, and the deed had they done.

3. Among the orators, too, eulogies and ceremonial and occasional addresses contain on every side examples of dignity and elevation, but are for the most part void of passion. This is the reason why passionate speakers are the worst eulogists, and why, on the other hand, those who are apt in encomium are the least passionate. 4. If, on the other hand, Cæcilius thought that passion never contributes at all to sublimity, and if it was for this reason that he did not deem it worthy of mention, he is altogether deluded. I would affirm with confidence that there is no tone so lofty as that of genuine passion, in its right place, when it bursts out in a wild gust of mad enthusiasm and as it were fills the speaker's words with frenzy.

IX

Now the first of the conditions mentioned, namely elevation of mind, holds the foremost rank among them all. We must, therefore, in this case also, although we have to do rather with an endowment than with an acquirement, nurture our souls (as far as that is possible) to thoughts sublime, and make them always pregnant, so to say, with noble inspiration. 2. In what way, you may ask, is this to be done? Elsewhere I have written as follows: "Sublimity is the echo of a great soul." Hence also a bare idea, by itself and without a spoken word, sometimes excites admiration just because of the greatness of soul implied. Thus the silence of Ajax in the Underworld is great and more sublime than words. 3. First, then, it is absolutely necessary to indicate the source of this elevation, namely, that the truly eloquent must be free from low and ignoble thoughts. For it is not possible that men with mean and servile ideas and aims prevailing throughout their lives should produce anything that is admirable and worthy of immortality. Great accents we expect to fall from the lips of those whose thoughts are deep and grave.

* * * *

13. It is for the same reason, I suppose, that he has made the whole structure of the *Iliad*, which was written at the height of his inspiration, full of action and conflict, while the *Odyssey* for the most part consists of narrative, as is characteristic of old age. Accordingly, in the *Odyssey* Homer may be likened to a sinking sun, whose grandeur remains without its intensity. He does not in the *Odyssey* maintain so high a pitch as in those poems of Ilium. His sublimities are not evenly sustained and free from the liability to sink; there is not the same profusion of accumulated passions, nor the supple and oratorical style, packed with images drawn from real life. You seem to see henceforth the ebb and flow of greatness, and a fancy roving in the fabulous and incredible, as though the ocean were withdrawing into itself and were being laid bare within its own confines. 14. In saying this I have not forgotten the tempests in the *Odyssey* and the story of the Cyclops and the like. If I speak of old age, it is nevertheless the old age of Homer. The fabulous element, however, prevails throughout this poem over the real. The object of this digression has been, as I said, to show how easily great natures in their decline are sometimes diverted into absurdity, as in the incident of the wine-skin

and of the men who were fed like swine by Circe (*whining porkers,* as Zoilus called them), and of Zeus like a nestling nurtured by the doves, and of the hero who was without food for ten days upon the wreck, and of the incredible tale of the slaying of the suitors. For what else can we term these things than veritable dreams of Zeus? 15. These observations with regard to the *Odyssey* should be made for another reason—in order that you may know that the genius of great poets and prose-writers, as their passion declines, finds its final expression in the delineation of character. For such are the details which Homer gives, with an eye to characterization, of life in the home of Odysseus; they form as it were a comedy of manners.

X

Let us next consider whether we can point to anything further that contributes to sublimity of style. Now, there inhere in all things by nature certain constituents which are part and parcel of their substance. It must needs be, therefore, that we shall find one source of the sublime in the systematic selection of the most important elements, and the power of forming, by their mutual combination, what may be called one body. The former process attracts the hearer by the choice of the ideas, the latter by the aggregation of those chosen. For instance, Sappho everywhere chooses the emotions that attend delirious passion from its accompaniments in actual life. Wherein does she demonstrate her supreme excellence? In the skill with which she selects and binds together the most striking and vehement circumstances of passion.

[The rest of X, XI, and XII digress into the field of rhetoric.]

XIII

To return from my digression. Although Plato thus flows on with noiseless stream, he is none the less elevated. You know this because you have read the *Republic* and are familiar with his manner. "Those," says he, "who are destitute of wisdom and goodness and are ever present at carousals and the like are carried on the downward path, it seems, and wander thus throughout their life. They never look upwards to the truth, nor do they lift their heads, nor enjoy any pure and lasting pleasure, but like cattle they have their eyes ever cast downwards and bent upon the ground and upon their feeding-places, and they gaze and grow fat and breed, and through their insatiate desire of these delights they kick and butt with horns and hoofs of iron and kill one another in their greed."

2. This writer shows us, if only we were willing to pay him heed, that another way (beyond anything we have mentioned) leads to the sublime. And what, and what manner of way, may that be? It is the imitation and emulation of previous great poets and writers. And let this, my dear friend, be an aim to which we steadfastly apply ourselves. For many men are carried away by the spirit of others as if inspired, just as it is related of the Pythian priestess when she approaches the tripod, where there is a rift in the ground which (they say) exhales divine vapor. By heavenly power thus communicated she is impregnated and straightway delivers oracles in virtue of the afflatus. Similarly from the great natures of the men of old there are borne in upon the souls of those who emulate them (as from sacred caves) what we may describe as *effluences,* so that even those who seem little likely to be possesed are thereby inspired and succumb to the spell of the others' greatness. 3. Was Herodotus alone a devoted imitator of Homer? No, Stesichorus even before his time, and Archilochus, and above all Plato, who from the great Homeric source drew to himself innumerable tributary streams. And perhaps we should have found it necessary to prove this, point by point, had not Ammonius and his followers selected and recorded the particulars. 4. This proceeding is not plagiarism; it is like taking an impression from beautiful forms or figures or other works of art. And it seems to me that there would not have been so fine a bloom of perfection on Plato's philosophical doctrines, and that he would not in many cases have found his way to poetical subject-matter and modes of expression, unless he had with all his heart and mind struggled with Homer for the primacy, entering the lists like a young champion matched against the man whom all admire, and showing perhaps too much love of contention and breaking a lance with him as it were, but deriving some profit from the contest none the less. For, as Hesiod says, "This strife is good for mortals." And in truth that struggle for the crown of glory is noble and best deserves the victory in which even to be worsted by one's predecessors brings no discredit.

XIV

[This brief section states that it is good for a writer to consider how the great masters of the past would handle a certain passage.]

XV

Images, moreover, contribute greatly, my young friend, to dignity, elevation, and power as a pleader. In this sense some call them mental representations. In a general way the name of *image* or *imagination* is applied to every idea of the mind, in whatever form it presents itself, which gives birth to speech. But at the present day the word is predominantly used in cases where, carried away by enthusiasm and passion, you think you see what you describe, and you place it before the eyes of your hearers. 2. Further, you will be aware of the fact that an image has one purpose with the orators and another with the poets, and that the design of the poetical image is enthrallment, of the rhetorical—vivid description. Both, however, seek to stir the passions and the emotions.

[Here follow a few illustrations.]

XVI–XXIX

[These sections, dealing with figures of speech, are more in the field of rhetoric than of literary criticism.]

XXX

Since, however, it is the case that, in discourse, thought and diction are for the most part developed one through the other, come let us proceed to consider any branches of the subject of diction which have so far been neglected. Now it is, no doubt, superfluous to dilate to those who know it well upon the fact that the choice of proper and striking words wonderfully attracts and enthralls the hearer, and that such a choice is the leading ambition of all orators and writers, since it is the direct agency which ensures the presence in writings, as upon the fairest statues, of the perfection of grandeur, beauty, mellowness, dignity, force, power, and any other high qualities there may be, and breathes into dead things a kind of living voice. All this it is, I say, needless to mention, for beautiful words are in very truth the peculiar light of thought. 2. It may, however, be pointed out that stately language is not to be used everywhere, since to invest petty affairs with great and high-sounding names would seem just like putting a full-sized tragic mask upon an infant boy. But in poetry and . . .[1]

[1] Four pages of the manuscript are here lost.

XXXI

. . . full of vigor and racy; and so is Anacreon's line, "That Thracian mare no longer do I heed." In this way, too, that original expression of Theopompus merits praise. Owing to the correspondence between word and thing it seems to me to be highly expressive; and yet Cæcilius for some unexplained reason finds fault with it. "Philip," says Theopompus, "had a genius for *stomaching* things." Now a homely expression of this kind is sometimes much more telling than elegant language, for it is understood at once since it is drawn from common life, and the fact that it is familiar makes it only the more convincing. So the words "stomaching things" are used most strikingly of a man who, for the sake of attaining his own ends, patiently and with cheerfulness endures things shameful and vile. 2. So with the words of Herodotus. "Cleomenes," he says, "went mad, and with a small sword cut the flesh of his own body into strips, until he slew himself by making mincemeat of his entire person." And, "Pythes fought on shipboard, until he was utterly hacked to pieces." These phrases graze the very edge of vulgarity, but they are saved from vulgarity by their expressiveness.

XXXII

Further, with regard to the number of metaphors to be employed, Cæcilius seems to assent to the view of those who lay it down that not more than two, or at the most three, should be ranged together in the same passage. Demosthenes is, in fact, the standard in this as in other matters. The proper time for using metaphors is when the passions roll like a torrent and sweep a multitude of them down their resistless flood. 2. "Men," says he, "who are vile flatterers, who have maimed their own fatherlands each one of them, who have toasted away their liberty first to Philip and now to Alexander, who measure happiness by their belly and their lowest desires, and who have overthrown that liberty and that freedom from despotic mastery which to the Greeks of an earlier time were the rules and standards of good." Here the orator's wrath against the traitors throws a veil over the number of the tropes. 3. In the same spirit, Aristotle and Theophrastus point out that the following phrases serve to soften bold metaphors—"as if," and "as it were," and "if one may so say," and "if one may venture such an expression"; for the qualifying words mitigate, they say, the audacity of expression. 4. I accept that view, but still

for number and boldness of metaphors I maintain, as I said in dealing
with figures, that strong and timely passion and noble sublimity are
the appropriate palliatives. For it is the nature of the passions, in
their vehement rush, to sweep and thrust everything before them, or
rather to demand hazardous turns as altogether indispensable. They
do not allow the hearer leisure to criticize the number of the metaphors because he is carried away by the fervor of the speaker. 5.
Moreover, in the treatment of commonplaces and in descriptions
there is nothing so impressive as a number of tropes following close
one upon the other. It is by this means that in Xenophon the anatomy
of the human tabernacle is magnificently depicted, and still more
divinely in Plato. Plato says that its head is a citadel; in the midst,
between the head and the breast, is built the neck like some isthmus.
The vertebræ, he says, are fixed beneath like pivots. Pleasure is a bait
which tempts men to ill, the tongue the test of taste; the heart is the
knot of the veins and the wellspring of the blood that courses round
impetuously, and it is stationed in the guard-house of the body. The
passages by which the blood races this way and that he names alleys.
He says that the gods, contriving succor for the beating of the heart
(which takes place when dangers are expected, and when wrath
excites it, since it then reaches a fiery heat), have implanted the
lungs, which are soft and bloodless and have pores within, to serve
as a buffer, in order that the heart may, when its inward wrath boils
over, beat against a yielding substance and so escape injury. The seat
of the desires he compared to the women's apartments in a house, that
of anger to the men's. The spleen he called the napkin of the inward
parts, whence it is filled with secretions and grows to a great and fes-
tering bulk. After this, the gods canopied the whole with flesh, putting forward the flesh as a defence against injuries from without,
as though it were a hair-cushion. The blood he called the fodder of
the flesh. "In order to promote nutrition," he continues, "they irri-
gated the body, cutting conduits as in gardens, in order that, with
the body forming a set of tiny channels, the streams of the veins
might flow as from a never-failing source." When the end comes, he
says that the cables of the soul are loosed like those of a ship, and she
is allowed to go free. 6. Examples of a similar nature are to be found
in a never-ending series. But those indicated are enough to show that
figurative language possesses great natural power, and that metaphors contribute to the sublime; and at the same time that it is impassioned and descriptive passages which rejoice in them to the greatest extent. 7. It is obvious, however, even though I do not dwell upon

it, that the use of tropes, like all other beauties of expression, is apt to lead to excess. On this score Plato himself is much criticized, since he is often carried away by a sort of frenzy of words into strong and harsh metaphors and into inflated allegory. "For it is not readily observed," he says, "that a city ought to be mixed like a bowl, in which the mad wine seethes when it has been poured in, though when chastened by another god who is sober, falling thus into noble company, it makes a good and temperate drink." For to call water "a sober god," and mixing "chastening," is—the critics say—the language of a poet, and one who is in truth far from sober. 8. Fastening upon such defects, however, Cæcilius ventured, in his writings in praise of Lysias, to make the assertion that Lysias was altogether superior to Plato. In so doing he gave way to two blind impulses of passion. Loving Lysias better even than himself, he nevertheless hates Plato more perfectly than he loves Lysias. In fact, he is carried away by the spirit of contention, and even his premises are not, as he thought, admitted. For he prefers the orator as faultless and immaculate to Plato as one who has often made mistakes. But the truth is not of this nature, nor anything like it.

XXXIII

Come, now, let us take some writer who is really immaculate and beyond reproach. Is it not worth while, on this very point, to raise the general question whether we ought to give the preference, in poems and prose writings, to grandeur with some attendant faults, or to success which is moderate but altogether sound and free from error? Aye, and further, whether a greater number of excellences, or excellences higher in quality, would in literature rightly bear away the palm? For these are inquiries appropriate to a treatise on the sublime, and they imperatively demand a settlement. 2. For my part, I am well aware that lofty genius is far removed from flawlessness; for invariable accuracy incurs the risk of pettiness, and in the sublime, as in great fortunes, there must be something which is overlooked. It may be necessarily the case that low and average natures remain as a rule free from failing and in greater safety because they never run a risk or seek to scale the heights, while great endowments prove insecure because of their very greatness. 3. In the second place, I am not ignorant that it naturally happens that the worse side of human character is always the more easily recognized, and that the memory of errors remains indelible, while that of excellences quickly dies away.

4. I have myself noted not a few errors on the part of Homer and other writers of the greatest distinction, and the slips they have made afford me anything but pleasure. Still I do not term them wilful errors, but rather oversights of a random and casual kind, due to neglect and introduced with all the heedlessness of genius. Consequently I do not waver in my view that excellences higher in quality, even if not sustained throughout, should always on a comparison be voted the first place, because of their sheer elevation of spirit if for no other reason. Granted that Apollonius in his *Argonautica* shows himself a poet who does not trip, and that in his pastorals Theocritus is, except in a few externals, most happy, would you not, for all that, choose to be Homer rather than Apollonius? 5. Again: does Eratosthenes in the *Erigone* (a little poem which is altogether free from flaw) show himself a greater poet than Archilochus with the rich and disorderly abundance which follows in his train and with that outburst of the divine spirit within him which it is difficult to bring under the rules of law? Once more: in lyric poetry would you prefer to be Bacchylides rather than Pindar? And in tragedy to be Ion of Chios rather than—Sophocles? It is true that Bacchylides and Ion are faultless and entirely elegant writers of the polished school, while Pindar and Sophocles, although at times they burn everything before them as it were in their swift career, are often extinguished unaccountably and fail most lamentably. But would anyone in his senses regard all the compositions of Ion put together as an equivalent for the single play of the *Œdipus?*

XXXIV

If successful writing were to be estimated by number of merits and not by the true criterion, thus judged Hyperides would be altogether superior to Demosthenes. For he has a greater variety of accents than Demosthenes and a greater number of excellences, and like the pent-athlete [1] he falls just below the top in every branch. In all the contests he has to resign the first place to his rivals, while he maintains that place as against all ordinary persons. 2. Now Hyperides not only imitates all the strong points of Demosthenes with the exception of his composition, but he has embraced in a singular degree the excellences and graces of Lysias as well. For he talks with simplicity, where it is required, and does not adopt like Demosthenes one unvarying tone in all his utterances. He possesses the gift of

[1] i. e., the athlete who competes in the pentathlon.

characterization in a sweet and pleasant form and with a touch of piquancy. There are innumerable signs of wit in him—the most polished raillery, high-bred ease, supple skill in the contests of irony, jests not tasteless or rude after the well-known Attic manner but naturally suggested by the subject, clever ridicule, much comic power, biting satire with well-directed fun, and what may be termed an inimitable charm investing the whole. He is excellently fitted by nature to excite pity; in narrating a fable he is facile, and with his pliant spirit he is also most easily turned towards a digression (as for instance in his rather poetical presentation of the story of Leto), while he has treated his Funeral Oration in the epideictic [1] vein with probably unequalled success. 3. Demosthenes, on the other hand, is not an apt delineator of character, he is not facile, he is anything but pliant or epideictic, he is comparatively lacking in the entire list of excellences just given. Where he forces himself to be jocular and pleasant, he does not excite laughter but rather becomes the subject of it, and when he wishes to approach the region of charm, he is all the farther removed from it. If he had attempted to write the short speech about Phryne or about Athenogenes, he would have all the more commended Hyperides to our regard. 4. The good points of the latter, however, many though they be, are wanting in elevation; they are the staid utterances of a sober-hearted man and leave the hearer unmoved, no one feeling terror when he reads Hyperides. But Demosthenes draws—as from a store—excellences allied to the highest sublimity and perfected to the utmost, the tone of lofty speech, living passions, copiousness, readiness, speed (where it is legitimate), and that power and vehemence of his which forbid approach. Having, I say, absorbed bodily within himself these mighty gifts which we may deem heaven-sent (for it would not be right to term them *human*), he thus with the noble qualities which are his own routs all comers even where the qualities he does not possess are concerned, and overpowers with thunder and with lightning the orators of every age. One could sooner face with unflinching eyes a descending thunderbolt than meet with steady gaze his bursts of passion in their swift succession.

XXXV

But in the case of Plato and Lysias there is, as I said, a further point of difference. For not only in the degree of his excellences, but also in

---

[1] Full of display; showy.

their number, Lysias is much inferior to Plato; and at the same time he surpasses him in his faults still more than he falls below him in his excellences. 2. What fact, then, was before the eyes of those super-human writers who, aiming at everything that was highest in composition, contemned an all-pervading accuracy? This besides many other things, that Nature has appointed us men to be no base or ignoble animals; but when she ushers us into life and into the vast universe as into some great assembly, to be as it were spectators of the mighty whole and the keenest aspirants for honor, forthwith she implants in our souls the unconquerable love of whatever is elevated and more divine than we. 3. Wherefore not even the entire universe suffices for the thought and contemplation within the reach of the human mind, but our imaginations often pass beyond the bounds of space, and if we survey our life on every side and see how much more it everywhere abounds in what is striking, and great, and beautiful, we shall soon discern the purpose of our birth. 4. This is why, by a sort of natural impulse, we admire not the small streams, useful and pellucid though they be, but the Nile, the Danube or the Rhine, and still more the Ocean. Nor do we view the tiny flame of our own kindling (guarded in lasting purity as its light ever is) with greater awe than the celestial fires though they are often shrouded in darkness; nor do we deem it a greater marvel than the craters of Ætna, whose eruptions throw up stones from its depths and great masses of rock, and at times pour forth rivers of that pure and unmixed subterranean fire. 5. In all such matters we may say that what is useful or necessary men regard as common-place, while they reserve their admiration for that which is astounding.

XXXVI

Now as regards the manifestations of the sublime in literature, in which grandeur is never, as it sometimes is in nature, found apart from utility and advantage, it is fitting to observe at once that, though writers of this magnitude are far removed from faultlessness, they none the less all rise above what is mortal; that all other qualities prove their possessors to be men, but sublimity raises them near the majesty of God; and that, while immunity from errors relieves from censure, it is grandeur that excites admiration. 2. What need to add thereto that each of these supreme authors often redeems all his failures by a single sublime and happy touch, and (most important of all) that if one were to pick out and mass together the blunders of

Homer, Demosthenes, Plato, and all the rest of the greatest writers, they would be found to be a very small part, nay an infinitesimal fraction, of the triumphs which those heroes achieve on every hand? This is the reason why the judgment of all posterity—a verdict which envy itself cannot convict of perversity—has brought and offered those meeds of victory which up to this day it guards intact and seems likely still to preserve,

Long as earth's waters shall flow, and her tall trees burgeon and bloom.

3. In reply, however, to the writer who maintains that the faulty Colossus is not superior to the Spearman of Polycleitus, it is obvious to remark among many other things that in art the utmost exactitude is admired, grandeur in the works of nature; and that it is by nature that man is a being gifted with speech. In statues likeness to man is the quality required; in discourse we demand, as I said, that which transcends the human. 4. Nevertheless—and the counsel about to be given reverts to the beginning of our memoir—since freedom from failings is for the most part the successful result of art, and excellence (though it may be unevenly sustained) the result of sublimity, the employment of art is in every way a fitting aid to nature; for it is the conjunction of the two which tends to ensure perfection.

Such are the decisions to which we have felt bound to come with regard to the questions proposed; but let every man cherish the view which pleases him best.

XXXVII

Closely related to Metaphors (for we must return to our point) are comparisons and similes, differing only in this respect. . . .[1]

XXXVIII

. . . such Hyperboles as: "unless you carry your brains trodden down in your heels." It is necessary, therefore, to know where to fix the limit in each case; for an occasional overshooting of the mark ruins the hyperbole, and such expressions, when strained too much, lose their tension, and sometimes swing round and produce the contrary effect. 2. Isocrates, for example, fell into unaccountable pueril-

---

[1] Here two pages of the manuscript are lost.

ity owing to the ambition which made him desire to describe everything with a touch of amplification. The theme of his *Panegyric* is that Athens surpasses Lacedæmon in benefits conferred upon Greece, and yet at the very outset of his speech he uses these words: "Further, language has such capacity that it is possible thereby to debase things lofty and invest things small with grandeur, and to express old things in a new way, and to discourse in ancient fashion about what has newly happened." "Do you then, Isocrates," it may be asked, "mean in that way to interchange the facts of Lacedæmonian and Athenian history?" For in his eulogy of language he has, we may say, published to his hearers a preamble warning them to distrust himself. 3. Perhaps, then, as we said in dealing with figures generally, those hyperboles are best in which the very fact that they are hyperboles escapes attention. This happens when, through stress of strong emotion, they are uttered in connection with some great crisis, as is done by Thucydides in the case of those who perished in Sicily. "The Syracusans," he says, "came down to the water's edge and began the slaughter of those chiefly who were in the river, and the water at once became polluted, but none the less it was swallowed although muddy and mixed with blood, and to most it was still worth fighting for." That a draught of blood and mud should still be worth fighting for, is rendered credible by the intensity of the emotion at a great crisis. 4. So with the passage in which Herodotus tells of those who fell at Thermopylæ. "On this spot," he says, "the barbarians buried them as they defended themselves with daggers—those of them who had daggers still left—and with hands and mouths." Here you may be inclined to protest against the expressions "fight with their very mouths" against men in armor, and "being buried" with darts. At the same time the narrative carries conviction; for the event does not seem to be introduced for the sake of the hyperbole, but the hyperbole to spring naturally from the event. 5. For (as I never cease to say) the deeds and passions which verge on transport are a sufficient lenitive and remedy for every audacity of speech. This is the reason why the quips of comedy, although they may be carried to the extreme of absurdity, are plausible because they are so amusing. For instance,

> Smaller his field was than a Spartan letter.

For mirth, too, is an emotion, an emotion which has its root in pleasure. 6. Hyperboles are employed in describing things small as well as great, since exaggeration is the common element in both cases. And, in a sense, ridicule is an amplification of the paltriness of things.

XXXIX

The fifth of those elements contributing to the sublime which we mentioned, my excellent friend, at the beginning, still remains to be dealt with, namely the arrangement of the words in a certain order. In regard to this, having already in two treatises sufficiently stated such results as our inquiry could compass, we will add, for the purpose of our present undertaking, only what is absolutely essential, namely the fact that harmonious arrangement is not only a natural source of persuasion and pleasure among men but also a wonderful instrument of lofty utterance and of passion. 2. For does not the flute instill certain emotions into its hearers and as it were make them beside themselves and full of frenzy, and supplying a rhythmical movement constrain the listener to move rhythmically in accordance therewith and to conform himself to the melody, although he may be utterly ignorant of music? Yes, and the tones of the harp, although in themselves they signify nothing at all, often cast a wonderful spell, as you know, over an audience by means of the variations of sounds, by their pulsation against one another, and by their mingling in concert. 3. And yet these are mere semblances and spurious copies of persuasion, not (as I have said) genuine activities of human nature. Are we not, then, to hold that composition (being a harmony of that language which is implanted by nature in man and which appeals not to the hearing only but to the soul itself), since it calls forth manifold shapes of words, thoughts, deeds, beauty, melody, all of them born at our birth and growing with our growth, and since by means of the blending and variation of its own tones it seeks to introduce into the minds of those who are present the emotion which affects the speaker and since it always brings the audience to share in it and by the building of phrase upon phrase raises a sublime and harmonious structure: are we not, I say, to hold that harmony by these selfsame means allures us and invariably disposes us to stateliness and dignity and elevation and every emotion which it contains within itself, gaining absolute mastery over our minds? But it is folly to dispute concerning matters which are generally admitted, since experience is proof sufficient. 4. An example of a conception which is usually thought sublime and is really admirable is that which Demosthenes associates with the decree: "This decree caused the danger which then beset the city to pass by just-as a cloud." But it owes its happy sound no less to the harmony than to the thought itself. For the thought is expressed throughout in dactylic rhythms, and these are most noble and productive of sublimity; and therefore it is that they constitute the heroic, the finest metre that we know. For if you derange the words of the sentence and transpose them in whatever way you will, as for example "This decree just-as a cloud caused the danger of the time to pass by"; nay, if you cut off a single syllable only and say "caused to pass by as a cloud," you will perceive to what an extent harmony is in unison with sublimity. For the very words "just-as a cloud" begin with a long rhythm, which consists of four metrical beats; but if one syllable is cut off and we read "as a cloud," we immediately maim the sublimity by the abbreviation. Conversely, if you elongate the word and write "caused to pass by just-as-if a cloud," it means the same thing, but no longer falls with the same effect upon the ear, inasmuch as the abrupt grandeur of the passage loses its energy and tension through the lengthening of the concluding syllables.

XL

Among the chief causes of the sublime in speech, as in the structure of the human body, is the collocation of members, a single one of which if severed from another possesses in itself nothing remarkable, but all united together make a full and perfect organism. So the constituents of grandeur, when separated from one another, carry with them sublimity in distraction this way and that, but when formed into a body by association and when further encircled in a chain of harmony they become sonorous by their very rotundity; and in periods sublimity is, as it were, a contribution made by a multitude. 2. We have, however, sufficiently shown that many writers and poets who possess no natural sublimity and are perhaps even wanting in elevation have nevertheless, although employing for the most part common and popular words with no striking associations of their own, by merely joining and fitting these together, secured dignity and distinction and the appearance of freedom from meanness. Instances will be furnished by Philistus among many others, by Aristophanes in certain passages, by Euripides in most. 3. In the last-mentioned author, Heracles, after the scene in which he slays his children, uses the words:—

Full-fraught am I with woes—no space for more.

The expression is a most ordinary one, but it has gained elevation through the aptness of the structure of the line. If you shape the sentence in a different way, you will see this plainly, the fact being that Euripides is a poet in virtue of his power of composition rather than of his invention. 4. In the passage which describes Dirce torn away by the bull:—

> Whitherso'er he turned
> Swift wheeling round, he haled and hurled withal
> Dame, rock, oak, intershifted ceaselessly,

the conception itself is a fine one, but it has been rendered more forcible by the fact that the harmony is not hurried or carried as it were on rollers, but the words act as buttresses for one another and find support in the pauses, and issue finally in a well-grounded sublimity.

XLI

There is nothing in the sphere of the sublime that is so lowering as broken and agitated movement of language, such as is characteristic of pyrrhics and trochees and dichorees, which fall altogether to the level of dance-music. For all over-rhythmical writing is at once felt to be affected and finical and wholly lacking in passion owing to the monotony of its superficial polish. 2. And the worst of it all is that, just as petty lays draw their hearer away from the point and compel his attention to themselves, so also over-rhythmical style does not communicate the feeling of the words but simply the feeling of the rhythm. Sometimes, indeed, the listeners knowing beforehand the due terminations stamp their feet in time with the speaker, and as in a dance give the right step in anticipation. 3. In like manner those words are destitute of sublimity which lie too close together, and are cut up into short and tiny syllables, and are held together as if with wooden bolts by sheer inequality and ruggedness.

XLII

Further, excessive concision of expression tends to lower the sublime, since grandeur is marred when the thought is brought into too narrow a compass. Let this be understood not of proper compression, but of what is absolutely petty and cut into segments. For concision curtails the sense, but brevity goes straight to the mark. It is plain that, *vice versa*, prolixities are frigid, for so is everything that resorts to unseasonable length.

XLIII

Triviality of expression is also apt to disfigure sublimity. In Herodotus, for example, the tempest is described with marvellous effect in all its details, but the passage surely contains some words below the dignity of the subject. The following may serve as an instance—"when the sea seethed." The word "seethed" detracts greatly from the sublimity because it is an ill-sounding one. Further, "the wind," he says, "grew fagged," and those who clung to the spars met "an unpleasant end." The expression "grew fagged" is lacking in dignity, being vulgar; and the word "unpleasant" is inappropriate to so great a disaster. 2. Similarly, when Theopompus had dressed out in marvellous fashion the descent of the Persian king upon Egypt, he spoiled the whole by some petty words. "For which of the cities (he says) or which of the tribes in Asia did not send envoys to the Great King? Which of the products of the earth or of the achievements of art was not, in all its beauty of preciousness, brought as an offering to his presence? Consider the multitude of costly coverlets and mantles, in purple or white or embroidery; the multitude of pavilions of gold furnished with all things useful; the multitude, too, of tapestries and costly couches. Further, gold and silver plate richly wrought, and goblets and mixing-bowls, some of which you might have seen set with precious stones, and others finished with care and at great price. In addition to all this, countless myriads of Greek and barbaric weapons, and beasts of burden beyond all reckoning and victims fattened for slaughter, and many bushels of condiments, and many bags and sacks and sheets of papyrus and all other useful things, and an equal number of pieces of salted flesh from all manner of victims, so that the piles of them were so great that those who were approaching from a distance took them to be hills and eminences confronting them." 3. He runs off from the more elevated to the more lowly, whereas he should, on the contrary, have risen higher and higher. With his wonderful description of the whole outfit he mixes bags and condiments and sacks, and conveys the impression of a confectioner's shop! For just as if, in the case of those very adornments, between the golden vessels and the jewelled mixing-bowls and the silver plate and the pavilions of pure gold and the goblets, a man were to bring and set in the midst paltry bags and sacks, the proceeding would have been offensive to the eye, so do such words when introduced out of season constitute deformities and as it were blots on the diction. 4. He might have described the scene in broad outline just as he says that hills blocked their way, and with regard to the preparations generally have spoken of "waggons and camels and the multitude of beasts of burden carrying everything that ministers to the luxury and enjoyment of the table," or have used some such expression as "piles of all manner of grain and things which conduce pre-eminently to good cookery and comfort of body," or if he must necessarily put it in so uncompromising a way, he might have said that "all the dainties of cooks and caterers were there." 5. In lofty passages we ought not to descend to sordid and contemptible language unless constrained by some overpowering necessity, but it is fitting that we should use words worthy of the subject and imitate nature, the artificer of man, for she has not placed in full view our grosser parts or the means of purging our frame, but has hidden them away as far as was possible, and as Xenophon says has put their channels in the remotest background, so as not to sully the beauty of the entire creature. 6. But enough; there is no need to enumerate, one by one, the things which produce triviality. For since we have previously indicated those qualities which render style noble and lofty, it is evident that their opposites will for the most part make it low and base.

XLIV

It remains however (as I will not hesitate to add, in recognition of your love of knowledge) to clear up, my dear Terentianus, a question which a certain philosopher has recently mooted. "I wonder," he says, "as no doubt do many others, how it happens that in our time there are men who have the gift of persuasion to the utmost extent, and are well fitted for public life, and are keen and ready, and particularly rich in all the charms of language, yet there no longer arise really lofty and transcendent natures unless quite exceptionally. So great and world-wide a dearth of high utterance attends our age." 2. "Can it be," he continued, "that we are to accept the trite explanation that democracy is the kind nursing-mother of genius, and that literary power may be said to share its rise and fall with democracy and democracy alone? For freedom, it is said, has power to feed the imaginations of the lofty-minded and to inspire hope, and where it prevails there spreads abroad the eagerness of mutual rivalry and the emulous pursuit of the foremost place. 3. Moreover, owing to the prizes which are open to all under popular government, the mental excellences of the orator are continually exercised and sharpened, and as it were rubbed bright, and shine forth (as it is natural they should) with all the freedom which inspires the doings of the state. To-day," he went on, "we seem in our boyhood to learn the lessons of a righteous servitude, being all but enswathed in its customs and observances, when our thoughts are yet young and tender, and never tasting the fairest and most productive source of eloquence (by which," he added, "I mean freedom), so that we emerge in no other guise than that of sublime flatterers." 4. This is the reason, he maintained, why no slave ever becomes an orator, although all other faculties may belong to menials. In the slave there immediately burst out signs of fettered liberty of speech, of the dungeon as it were, of a man habituated to buffetings. 5. "For the day of slavery," as Homer has it, "takes away half our manhood." "Just as," he proceeded, "the cages (if what I hear is true) in which are kept the Pygmies, commonly called *nani,* not only hinder the growth of the creatures confined within them, but actually attenuate them through the bonds which beset their bodies, so one has aptly termed all servitude (though it be most righteous) the cage of the soul and a public prison-house." 6. I answered him thus: "It is easy, my good sir, and characteristic of human nature, to find fault with the age in which one lives. But consider whether it may not be true that it is not the world's peace that ruins great natures, but far rather this war illimitable which holds our desires in its grasp, aye, and further still those passions which occupy as with troops our present age and utterly harry and plunder it. For the love of money, (a disease from which we all now suffer sorely) and the love of pleasure make us their thralls, or rather, as one may say, drown us body and soul in the depths, the love of riches being a malady which makes men petty, and the love of pleasure one which makes them most ignoble. 7. On reflection I cannot discover how it is possible for us, if we value boundless wealth so highly, or (to speak more truly) deify it, to avoid allowing the entrance into our souls of the evils which are inseparable from it. For vast and unchecked wealth is accompanied, in close conjunction and step for step as they say, by extravagance, and as soon as the former opens the gates of cities and houses, the latter immediately enters and abides. And when time has passed the pair build nests in the lives of men, as the wise say, and quickly give themselves to the rearing of offspring, and breed ostentation, and vanity, and luxury, no spurious progeny of theirs, but only too legitimate. If these children of wealth are permitted to come to maturity, straightway they beget in the soul inexorable masters—insolence, and lawlessness, and shamelessness. 8. This must necessarily happen, and men will no longer lift up their eyes or have any further regard for fame, but the ruin of such lives will gradually reach its complete consummation and sublimities of soul fade and wither away and become contemptible, when men are lost in admiration of their own mortal parts and omit to exalt that which is immortal. 9. For a man who has once accepted a bribe for a judicial decision cannot be an unbiassed and upright judge of what is just and honorable (since to the man who is venal his own interests must seem honorable and just), and the same is true where the entire life of each of us is ordered by bribes, and huntings after the death of others, and the laying of ambushes for legacies, while gain from any and every source we purchase—each one of us—at the price of life itself, being the slaves of pleasure. In an age which is ravaged by plagues so sore, is it possible for us to imagine that there is still left an unbiassed and incorruptible judge of works that are great and likely to reach posterity, or is it not rather the case that all are influenced in their decisions by the passion for gain? 10. Nay, it is perhaps better for men like ourselves to be ruled than to be free, since our appetites, if let loose without restraint upon our neighbors like beasts from a cage, would set the world on fire with deeds of evil. 11. Summing up, I maintained that among the banes of the natures which our age produces must be reckoned that half-heartedness in which the life of all of us with few exceptions is passed, for we do not labor or exert ourselves except for the sake of praise and pleasure, never for those solid benefits which are a worthy object of our own efforts and the respect of others. 12. But " 'tis best to leave these riddles unresolved," and to proceed to what next presents itself, namely the subject of the Passions, about which I previously undertook to write in a separate treatise. These form, as it seems to me, a material part of discourse generally and of the Sublime itself. . . .[1]

---

[1] Here the manuscript breaks off.

Boethius

Anicius Manlius Severinus Boethius (c 480–524) was born in Italy and educated at Rome. He gained positions of power and influence under Theodoric, King of the Ostrogoths, then master of Italy. His influence on the administration of this monarch was of the best; he was trusted by the sovereign and loved by the people. But as the king grew old and suspicious, Boethius lost his power; the enemies that his integrity had made succeeded in prejudicing the king against him, and he faced an accusation of treason. Arrested and imprisoned, he was executed about 524.

In prison, Boethius wrote his famous book on philosophy, *De Consolatione Philosophiæ*. The brief quotation below, taken from Chaucer's translation, shows how Plato's attitude toward literature persisted in maintaining the belief that the fine arts, because they aroused one's emotions, killed one's power of reasoning. For Boethius, as for Plato, the search for truth was man's first task. This was the attitude, too, of the Church Fathers and the Puritan moralists.

From DE CONSOLATIONE PHILOSOPHIÆ [1]
(c 520)

BOOK I, PROSE i

And when Philosophy saw these poetical Muses approach about my bed, and relate words which caused me to weep, she was a little moved, and glowed with cruel eyes. "Who," quoth she, "hath suffered to approach to this sick man these common strumpets of such a place that men call the theatre? They will not only not assuage his

[1] Translated by Geoffrey Chaucer, modernized.

97

sorrows with any remedies, but they will feed and nourish him with sweet poison. Forsooth, these be the ones that with thorns and prickings of talents or affections, which, because they be in no way fructifying nor profitable, destroy the plenteous corn of the fruits of reason; for they hold the hearts of men in habit, but they do not deliver any folk from sickness. But if you Muses had withdrawn from me, with your flattery, any uncunning and unprofitable man, as men are wont to be found commonly among the people, I would surely suffer the less grievously: because in such an unprofitable man, my designs were in no wise damaged. But ye withdraw from me this man that hath been nourished in the studies or schools of Elea and of the Academy in Greece. But go now rather away, ye mermaidens, which are sweet until it be at the last, and suffer this man to be cured and healed by my Muses—that is to say by useful sciences." And thus this company of Muses, blamed, cast angrily their faces downward to the earth; and showing by redness their shame, they passed sorrowfully across the threshold. And I, whose sight plunged in tears was darkened, so that I might not know what that woman was, of such imperial authority, I waxed all abashed and astonished, and cast my sight down to the earth, and began still to abide what she would do afterward. Then came she near, and sat her down upon the outermost corner of my bed; and she, beholding my face, that was cast upon the earth, heavy and grievous of weeping, complained, with these words that I shall say, the perturbation of my thought.

BOOK II, PROSE i

*   *   *   *

And with Rhetoric came forth Music, a damsel of our house, that sings now lighter modes, now heavier. "What aileth thee, man? What is it that hath cast thee into mourning and into weeping? I trow that thou hast seen some new thing, and uncouth. Thou weenest that Fortune be changed against thee; but thou weenest wrong, if thou weenest that. Always these are her manners; she hath rather kept, as to thee, her proper stableness in the changing of herself. Right such was she when she flattered thee, and deceived thee with unpermissible attractions of false well-being. Thou hast now known and apprehended the doubtful or double visage of this same blind goddess Fortune. She, that yet covereth herself and conceals herself to other folk, hath shown herself completely to thee. If you approve her, and think that she is good, use her courteously, and do not complain. And if you dread her false treachery, despise and cast away her that playeth so harmfully; for she, that is now cause of so much sorrow to thee, should be cause to thee of peace and joy. She hath forsaken thee, forsooth; nor is there man surely that she hath not forsaken.

*   *   *   *

Dante

DANTE (contracted from Durante) Alighieri (1265–1321), was born in Florence, of a family belonging to the lower nobility. His education was confided to the eminent philosopher and statesman, Brunetto Latini, supplemented (it is thought) by studies at various Italian universities, as well as at Paris and Oxford. He was a musician and painter, theologian and linguist. In his youth he saw, and ever afterward loved, Beatrice Portinari, who, in 1287, married a noble Florentine, Simone Bardi. Dante's love for her awakened in him a new life, and he devoted his powers to immortalizing her. The record of these early years is set down in the *Vita Nuova.*

The political turbulence of Italy did not leave Dante untouched. He took part in the wars between Guelphs and Ghibellines, on the side of the former; and, in 1291, married into one of the most powerful families of this faction. In a Florentine revolution, he cast his lot with the citizens' party, and in 1300 was nominated a prior of the trades. Taking part in various civic struggles, he was fined and banished, becoming a wanderer—well-nigh a beggar. His sympathies later changed to the Ghibelline party. After the death of the emperor, Henry VII (1313), he seems to have lived chiefly at Verona and Ravenna, where he died.

Dante is often called "the father of Italian literature." His *Divina Commedia,* written "in the middle of my life," that is, when he was thirty-five, has won him an undisputed place with the great writers of the world. Among literary critics he ranks high, because, at a time when most writers used Latin or Greek, he boldly proclaimed that every author should use his own native language, the vernacular. How revolutionary his ideas were is suggested by the fact that it was two and a half centuries later that du Bellay, in his *Defence and Illustration of the French Language,* 1549, accomplished for what may be called modern French literature what Dante had already done for the Italian.

To realize the import of Dante's pronouncement, one need only recall that Sir Thomas More, in 1516, wrote his *Utopia* first in Latin; that in the Elizabethan period Bacon felt that works in the vernacular would not last; that Milton composed many of his poems in Latin; and that in our own day Maeterlinck, a Belgian, instead of using one of the Belgian dialects (a term not opprobrious), chose to write in French. For that matter, it was a long time before Americans dared to write American.

Dante is the greatest critic of the Middle Ages. In his criticism and in his creative writing he is the last of the old, and the first of the moderns.

From DE VULGARI ELOQUENTIA [1]

(c 1305)

BOOK I, CHAPTER I

Since we do not find that any one before us has treated of the science of the vernacular language, while in fact we see that this language is highly necessary for all, inasmuch as not only men, but even women and children, strive, in so far as nature allows them, to acquire it; and since it is our wish to enlighten to some little extent the discernment of those who walk through the streets like blind men, generally fancying that those things which are [really] in front of them are behind them, we will endeavor, the Word aiding us from heaven, to be of service to the vernacular speech; not only drawing the water of our own wit for such a drink, but mixing with it the best of what we have taken or compiled from others, so that we may thence be able to give draughts of the sweetest hydromel. But be-

---

[1] Translated by A. G. Ferrers Howell. Used by the kind permission of E. P. Dutton and Company Inc.

cause the business of every science is not to prove but to explain its subject, in order that men may know what that is with which the science is concerned, we say (to come quickly to the point) that what we call the vernacular speech is that to which children are accustomed by those who are about them when they first begin to distinguish words; or to put it more shortly, we say that the vernacular speech is that which we acquire without any rule, by imitating our nurses. There further springs from this another secondary speech, which the Romans called grammar. And this secondary speech the Greeks also have, as well as others, but not all. Few, however, acquire the use of this speech, because we can only be guided and instructed in it by the expenditure of much time, and by assiduous study. Of these two kinds of speech also, the vernacular is the nobler, as well because it was the first employed by the human race, as because the whole world makes use of it, though it has been divided into forms differing in pronunciation and vocabulary. It is also the nobler as being natural to us, whereas the other is rather of an artificial kind; and it is of this our nobler speech that we intend to treat.

Having therefore found what we were searching for, we declare the illustrious, cardinal, courtly, and curial vernacular language in Italy to be that which belongs to all the towns in Italy but does not appear to belong to any one of them, and by which all the municipal dialects of the Italians are measured, weighed, and compared.

CHAPTER XVII

We must now set forth why it is that we call this language we have found by the epithets illustrious, cardinal, courtly, and curial; and by doing this we disclose the nature of the language itself more clearly. First, then, let us lay bare what we mean by the epithet illustrious, and why we call the language illustrious. Now we understand by this term "illustrious" something which shines forth illuminating and illuminated. And in this way we call men illustrious either because, being illuminated by power, they illuminate others by justice and charity; or else because, having been excellently trained, they in turn give excellent training, like Seneca and Numa Pompilius. And the vernacular of which we are speaking has both been exalted by training and power, and also exalts its followers by honor and glory.

Now it appears to have been exalted by training, inasmuch as from amid so many rude Italian words, involved constructions, faulty expressions, and rustic accents we see that it has been chosen out in such degree of excellence, clearness, completeness, and polish as is displayed by Cino of Pistoja and his friend in their canzoni.

And that it has been exalted by power is plain; for what is of greater power than that which can sway the hearts of men, so as to make an unwilling man willing, and a willing man unwilling, just as this language has done and is doing?

Now that it exalts by honor is evident. Do not they of its household surpass in renown kings, marquises, counts, and all other magnates? This has no need at all of proof.

But how glorious it makes its familiar friends we ourselves know, who for the sweetness of this glory cast our exile behind our back. Wherefore we ought deservedly to proclaim this language illustrious.

BOOK II, CHAPTER II

After having proved that not all those who write verse, but only those of the highest excellence, ought to use the illustrious vernacular, we must in the next place establish whether every subject ought to be handled in it, or not; and if not, we must set out by themselves those subjects that are worthy of it. And in reference to this we must first find out what we understand by that which we call *worthy*. We say that a thing which has worthiness is worthy, just as we say that a thing which has nobility is noble; and if when that which confers the habit is known, that on which the habit is conferred is [also] known, as such, then if we know what worthiness is, we shall know also what *worthy* is. Now worthiness is an effect or end of deserts; so that when any one has deserved well we say that he has arrived at worthiness of good; but when he has deserved ill, at worthiness of evil. Thus we say that a soldier who has fought well has arrived at worthiness of victory; one who has ruled well, at worthiness of a kingdom; also that a liar has arrived at worthiness of shame, and a robber at worthiness of death.

But inasmuch as [further] comparisons are made among those who deserve well, and also among those who deserve ill, so that some deserve well, some better, and some best; some badly, some worse, and some worst; while such comparisons are only made with respect to the end of deserts, which (as has been mentioned before) we call *worthiness*, it is plain that worthinesses are compared together according as they are greater or less, so that some are great, some greater, and some greatest; and, consequently, it is obvious that one thing is worthy, another worthier, and another worthiest. And whereas there can be no such comparison of worthinesses with regard to the same object [of desert] but [only] with regard to different objects, so that we call *worthier* that which is worthy of greater objects, and *worthiest* that which is worthy of the greatest, because no thing can be more worthy [than another] in virtue of the same qualification, it is evident that the best things are worthy of the best [objects of desert], according to the requirement of the things. Whence it follows that, since the language we call illustrious is the best of all the other forms of the vernacular, the best subjects alone are worthy of being handled in it, and these we call the *worthiest* of those subjects which can be handled; and now let us hunt out what they are. And, in order to make this clear, it must be observed that, as man has been endowed with a threefold life, namely, vegetable, animal, and rational, he journeys along a threefold road; for in so far as he is vegetable he seeks for what is useful, wherein he is of like nature with plants; in so far as he is animal he seeks for that which is pleasurable, wherein he is of like nature with the brutes; in so far as he is rational he seeks for what is right—and in this he stands alone, or is a partaker of the nature of the angels. It is by these three kinds of life that we appear to carry out whatever we do; and because in each one of them some things are greater, some greatest, within the range of their kind, it follows that those which are greatest appear the ones which ought to be treated of supremely, and consequently, in the greatest vernacular.

But we must discuss what things are greatest; and first in respect of what is useful. Now in this matter, if we carefully consider the object of all those who are in search of what is useful, we shall find that it is nothing else but safety. Secondly, in respect of what is pleasurable; and here we say that that is most pleasurable which gives pleasure by the most exquisite object of appetite, and this is love. Thirdly, in respect of what is right; and here no one doubts that virtue has the first place. Wherefore these three things, namely, safety, love, and virtue, appear to be those capital matters which ought to be treated of supremely, I mean the things which are most important in respect of them, as prowess in arms, the fire of love, and the direction of the will.

[The remainder of this chapter gives illustrations from Italian poetry.]

CHAPTER IV

Having then labored by a process of disentangling [to show] what persons and things are worthy of the courtly vernacular, as well as the form of verse which we deem worthy of such honor that it alone is fitted for the highest vernacular, before going off to other topics, let us explain the form of the canzone, which many appear to adopt rather at haphazard than with art; and let us unlock the workshop of the art of that form which has hitherto been adopted in a casual way, omitting the form of ballate and sonnets, because we intend to explain this in the fourth book of this work, when we shall treat of the middle vernacular language.

Reviewing, therefore, what has been said, we remember that we have frequently called those who write verse in the vernacular poets; and this we have doubtless ventured to say with good reason, because they are in fact poets, if we take a right view of poetry, which is nothing else but a rhetorical composition set to music. But these poets differ from the great poets, that is, the regular ones, for the language of the great poets was regulated by art, whereas these, as has been said, write at haphazard. It therefore happens that the more closely we copy the great poets, the more correct is the poetry we write; whence it behooves us, by devoting some trouble to the work of teaching, to emulate their poetic teaching.

Before all things therefore we say that each one ought to adjust the weight of the subject to his own shoulders, so that their strength may not be too heavily taxed, and he be forced to tumble into the mud. This is the advice our master Horace gives us when he says in the beginning of his *Art of Poetry* ["Ye who write] take up a subject [suited to your strength"].

[The rest of the chapter deals with style.]

Sidney

Sir Philip SIDNEY (1554–1586) was born at Penshurst, Kent, the son of Sir Henry Sidney, and nephew of Robert Dudley, Earl of Leicester, the favorite of Elizabeth. He was educated at Shrewsbury School, and at Oxford University. At the Court of Queen Elizabeth he met many who were interested in literature, and became a friend of Spenser, who dedicated his *Shepherd's Calendar* to him. He travelled abroad on various diplomatic missions for Queen Elizabeth, and was in Paris at the time of the Massacre of St. Bartholomew. In 1580, while in retirement, he wrote for his sister's amusement the celebrated pastoral romance *Arcadia,* which, when published ten years later, became exceedingly popular and exerted an influence, almost as great as Lyly's *Euphues,* upon English style. In 1583 he married a daughter of Sir Francis Walsingham, and in 1586 was killed at Zutphen, in Holland, while fighting with the Dutch against the Spaniards.

Sidney wrote sonnets (including the sequence *Astrophel and Stella*), and made a translation of the Psalms; in reply to Gosson's *School of Abuse* (1579), dedicated to him, he wrote his *Defence of Poesie* (first called *Apologie for Poetrie*), which was not published until 1595.

Sir Philip, the complete gentleman of the Renaissance, whose heroic death on the field of battle caused both the Court and the City to go into mourning "for many months," and called forth Spenser's *Astrophel,* one of the great elegies in the language, is England's first important literary critic. He may be regarded in English literature as foremost in the development of the novel, the sonnet, and the pure lyric. In literary criticism, however, he achieved greatness.

For a background, Sidney had a wide knowledge of ancient as well as of modern literature; and he had read with understanding his predecessors in criticism—Plato, Aristotle, Horace, and others—weighing their ideas and then formulating his own.

In his answer to the Puritans' charge that literature, since it gave only pleasure, was therefore something useless, if not bad, and that it killed reason—an attitude of mind familiar to readers of Plato and Boethius—Sidney came out boldly, as did Longinus before him, stating without reservations, "that moving is of a higher degree than teaching." Like many another critic, he felt that criticism of literature was intertwined with criticism of life. He felt that one could be moved by poetry "more than with a trumpet" to good, noble living. Sidney, the aristocrat, was a Cavalier, but also, in the best sense, a Puritan.

The extract that follows is a model of urbanity and keen insight.

From AN APOLOGY FOR POETRY [1]

(c 1583)

. . . I will give you a nearer example of myself, who (I know not by what mischance) in these my not old years and idlest times, having slipped into the title of a Poet, am provoked to say something unto you in the defence of that my unelected vocation, which if I handle with more good will than good reasons, bear with me, since the scholar is to be pardoned that followeth the steps of his master. And yet I must say that as I have just cause to make a pitiful defence of poor Poetry, which from almost the highest estimation of learning is fallen to be the laughing-stock of children; so have I need to bring some more available proofs; since the former is by no means barred of his deserved credit, the silly latter hath had even the names of philosophers used to the defacing of it, with great

[1] The text is from G. Gregory Smith, *Elizabethan Critical Essays*, vol. 1, Oxford, 1904, modernized by the editors. It is used with the kind permission of The Clarendon Press, Oxford.

danger of civil war among the Muses. And first, truly to all them that professing learning inveigh against poetry, may justly be objected, that they go very near to ungratefulness, to seek to deface that which, in the noblest nations and languages that are known, hath been the first light-giver to ignorance, and first nurse, whose milk by little and little enabled them to feed afterwards on tougher knowledges; and will they now play the hedgehog that, being received into the den, drove out his host? or rather the vipers, that with their birth kill their parents? Let learned Greece in any of her manifold sciences be able to show me one book before Musæus, Homer, and Hesiod, all three nothing else but poets. Nay, let any history be brought that can say any writers were there before them, if they were not men of the same skill, as Orpheus, Linos, and some others are named; who, having been the first of that country that made pens deliverers of their knowledge to their posterity, may justly challenge to be called their fathers in learning; for not only in time they had this priority (although in itself antiquity be venerable) but went before them, as causes to draw with their charming sweetness the wild untamed wits to an admiration of knowledge. So as Amphion was said to move stones with his poetry to build Thebes, and Orpheus to be listened to by beasts, indeed stony and beastly people, so among the Romans were Livy, Andronicus, and Ennius; so in the Italian language, the first that made it aspire to be a treasure-house of science were the poets Dante, Boccaccio, and Petrarch; so in our English were Gower and Chaucer.

After whom, encouraged and delighted with their excellent foregoing, others have followed, to beautify our mother tongue, as well in the same kind as in other arts. This did so notably show itself, that the philosophers of Greece durst not a long time appear to the world but under the masks of poets; so Thales, Empedocles, and Parmenides sang their natural philosophy in verses; so did Pythagoras and Phocylides their moral counsels; so did Tyrtæus in war matters, and Solon in matters of policy; or rather, they being poets, did exercise their delightful vein in those points of highest knowledge, which, before them, lay hid to the world. For that wise Solon was directly a poet it is manifest, having written in verse the notable fable of the Atlantic island, which was continued by Plato.

And truly, even Plato, whosoever well considereth, shall find that in the body of his work, though the inside and strength were philosophy, the skin as it were and beauty depended most of poetry; for all standeth upon Dialogues, wherein he feigneth many honest burgesses of Athens to speak of such matters, that, if they had been set on the rack, they would never have confessed them. Besides, his poetical describing the circumstances of their meetings, as the well-ordering of a banquet, the delicacy of a walk, with interlacing mere tales, as Gyges's ring and others, which who knoweth not to be flowers of poetry did never walk into Apollo's garden.

*   *   *   *

Among the Romans, a poet was called *vates*, which is as much as a "diviner," "foreseer," or "prophet," as by its conjoined words, *vaticinium* and *vaticinari* is manifest; so heavenly a title did that excellent people bestow upon this heart-ravishing knowledge. And so far were they carried into the admiration thereof, that they thought in the chanceable hitting upon any such verses great foretokens of their following fortunes were placed. Whereupon grew the word of *sortes Virgilianæ*, when, by sudden opening Virgil's book, they lighted upon any verse of his making; whereof the histories of the emperors' lives are full: as of Albinus, the governor of our island, who in his childhood met with this verse:

Arma amens capio; nec sat rationis in armis,[1]

and in his age performed it; which, although it were a very vain and godless superstition, as also it was to think that spirits were commanded by such verses—whereupon this word "charms," derived from *carmina*, cometh—so yet serveth it to show the great reverence those wits were held in. And altogether not without ground, since both the oracles of Delphi and the Sibyl's prophecies were wholly delivered in verses. For that same exquisite observing of number and measure in words, and that high-flying liberty of conceit [2] proper to the poet, did seem to have some divine force in it.

And may I not presume a little further, to show the reasonableness of this word *vates*? and say that the holy David's Psalms are a divine poem? If I do, I shall not do it without the testimony of great learned men, both ancient and modern; but even the name *Psalms* will speak for me, which, being interpreted, is nothing but songs; then that it is fully written in metre, as all learned Hebricians agree, although the rules be not yet fully found. Lastly and principally, his handling his prophecy, which is merely poetical. For what

[1] "Mad I take arms, nor in arms have I reason enough." Vergil, *Æneid*, ii, 314.
[2] conception.

else is the awaking his musical instruments; the often and free changing of persons; his notable *prosopopeias*,[1] when he maketh you, as it were, see God coming in his majesty; his telling of the beasts' joyfulness, and hills leaping, but a heavenly poesy, wherein almost he showeth himself a passionate lover of that unspeakable and everlasting beauty to be seen by the eyes of the mind only cleared by faith? But truly now having named him, I fear me I seem to profane that holy name, applying it to poetry, which is among us thrown down to so ridiculous an estimation; but they that with quiet judgments will look a little deeper into it, shall find the end and working of it such, as being rightly applied, deserveth not to be scourged out of the Church of God.

But now, let us see how the Greeks named it, and how they deemed of it. The Greeks called him a Poet, which name hath, as the most excellent, gone through other languages. It cometh from this word *poiein*, which is "to make"; wherein I know not whether by luck or wisdom, we Englishmen have met with the Greeks in calling him a "maker"; which name, how high and incomparable a title it is, I had rather were known by marking the scope of other sciences than by my partial allegation.

There is no art delivered to mankind that hath not the works of Nature for its principal object, without which they could not consist, and on which they so depend, that they become actors and players, as it were, of what Nature will have set forth. So doth the astronomer look upon the stars, and by that he seeth, setteth down what order Nature hath taken therein; so do the geometrician and arithmetician, in their diverse sorts of quantities; so doth the musician in times tell you which by nature agree, which not. The natural philosopher thereon hath his name, and the moral philosopher standeth upon the natural virtues, vices, and passions of man; and "follow Nature" (saith he) "therein, and thou shalt not err." The lawyer saith what men have determined. The historian, what men have done. The grammarian speaketh only of the rules of speech; and the rhetorician and logician, considering what in nature will soonest prove and persuade, thereon give artificial rules, which still are compassed within the circle of a question, according to the proposed matter. The physician weigheth the nature of a man's body, and the nature of things helpful or hurtful unto it. And the metaphysic[ian], though it be in the second[ary] and abstract notions, and therefore be counted supernatural, yet doth he indeed build

[1] personification.

upon the depth of Nature. Only the poet, disdaining to be tied to any such subjection, lifted up with the vigor of his own invention, doth grow in effect another nature, in making things either better than nature bringeth forth, or, quite anew, forms such as never were in nature, as the heroes, demigods, cyclops, chimæras, furies, and suchlike; so as he goeth hand in hand with Nature, not enclosed within the narrow warrant of her gifts, but freely ranging only within the zodiac of his own wit.

Nature never set forth the earth in so rich tapestry as divers poets have done, neither with pleasant rivers, fruitful trees, sweet-smelling flowers, nor whatsoever else may make the too-much-loved earth more lovely. Her world is brazen, the poets only deliver a golden.

*   *   *   *

Poesy, therefore, is an art of imitation, for so Aristotle termeth it in his word *mimesis,* that is to say, "a representing," "counterfeiting," or "figuring forth"; to speak metaphorically, a "speaking picture"; with this end, to teach and delight. Of this [there] have been three several kinds.

*   *   *   *

Now therefore it shall not be amiss first to weigh this latter sort of poetry by [the poet's] works, and then by his parts; and if in neither of these anatomies he be condemnable, I hope we shall obtain a more favorable sentence. This purifying of wit, this enriching of memory, enabling of judgment, and enlarging of conceit, which commonly we call learning, under what name soever it come forth, or to what immediate end soever it be directed, the final end is to lead and draw us to as high a perfection as our degenerate souls, made worse by their clayey lodgings, can be capable of. This, according to the inclination of the man, bred many formed impressions. For some that thought this felicity principally to be gotten by knowledge, and no knowledge to be so high and heavenly as acquaintance with the stars, gave themselves to astronomy; others, persuading themselves to be demigods if they knew the causes of things, became natural and supernatural philosophers; some, an admirable delight drew to music; and some, the certainty of demonstration to the mathematics; but all, one and other, having this scope: to know, and by knowledge to lift up the mind from the dungeon of the body to the enjoying his own divine essence. But when by the balance of experience it was found that the astronomer looking to the stars might fall into a ditch, that the enquiring philosopher might be blind in himself, and the mathematician might draw forth a straight line with a crooked heart, then, lo, did proof, the overruler of opinions, make manifest that all these are but serving sciences, which as they have each a private end in themselves, so yet are they all directed to the highest end of the mistress, Knowledge, by the Greeks called *architechtoniké*, which stands (as I think) in the knowledge of a man's self, in the ethic[al] and politic[al] consideration, with the end of well-doing, and not of well-knowing only; even as the saddler's next end is to make a good saddle, but his farther end to serve a nobler faculty, which is horsemanship; so the horseman's to soldiery, and the soldier not only to have the skill, but to perform the practice of a soldier; so that, the ending end of all earthly learning being virtuous action, those skills that most serve to bring forth that, have a most just title to be princes over all the rest.

*   *   *   *

Now doth the peerless poet perform both: [1] for whatsoever the philosopher saith should be done, he giveth a perfect picture of it in some one, by whom he presupposeth it was done; so that he coupleth the general notion with the particular example. A perfect picture I say, for he yieldeth to the powers of the mind an image of that whereof the philosopher bestoweth but a wordish description; which doth neither strike, pierce, nor possess the sight of the soul so much as that other doth.

For as in outward things, to a man that had never seen an elephant or a rhinoceros, who should tell him most exquisitely all their shapes, color, bigness, and particular marks; or of a gorgeous palace, the architecture, with declaring the full beauties, might well make the hearer able to repeat, as it were by rote, all he had heard, yet should never satisfy his inward conceits with being witness to itself of a true lively knowledge: but the same man, as soon as he might see those beasts well painted, or the house well in model, should straightways grow, without need of any description, to a judicial comprehending of them; so no doubt the philosopher with his learned definition, be it of virtue, vices, matters of public policy or private government, replenisheth the memory with many infallible grounds of wisdom, which, notwithstanding, lie dark before the

---

[1] I. e., the task of the philosopher and of the historian.

imaginative and judging power, if they be not illuminated or figured forth by the speaking picture of poesy.

* * * *

But now may it be alleged that if this imagining of matters be so fit for the imagination, then must the historian needs surpass, who bringeth you images of true matters, such as indeed were done, and not such as fantastically or falsely may be suggested to have been done. Truly, Aristotle himself, in his discourse of Poesy, plainly determineth this question, saying that poetry is *philosophoteron* and *spoudaioteron*, that is to say, it is more philosophical and more studiously serious than history. His reason is, because poesy dealeth with *katholou*, that is to say, with the universal consideration; and the history with *kathekaston*, the particular. "Now," saith he, "the universal weighs what is fit to be said or done, either in likelihood or necessity (which the poesy considereth in his imposed names), and the particular only marks whether Alcibiades did, or suffered, this or that." Thus far, Aristotle; which reason of his (as all his) is most full of reason. For indeed, if the question were whether it were better to have a particular act truly or falsely set down, there is no doubt which is to be chosen, no more than whether you had rather have Vespasian's picture right as he was, or at the painter's pleasure nothing resembling. But if the question be for your own use and learning, whether it be better to have it set down as it should be, or as it was, then certainly is more doctrinable [1] the feigned Cyrus in Xenophon than the true Cyrus in Justinus, and the feigned Æneas in Virgil than the right Æneas in Dares Phrygius.

* * * *

For suppose it may be granted (that which I suppose with great reason may be denied) that the philosopher, in respect of his methodical proceeding, doth teach more perfectly than the poet, yet do I think that no man is so much *philophilosophos* [2] as to compare the philosopher, in moving, with the poet.

And that moving is of a higher degree than teaching, it may by this appear, that it is wellnigh the cause and the effect of teaching. For who will be taught, if he be not moved with desire to be taught? and what so much good doth that teaching bring forth (I speak

---

[1] instructive.

[2] A lover of philosophers. (G. Gregory Smith suggests that the word may be Sidney's own coinage.)

still of moral doctrine) as that it moveth one to do that which it doth teach? for, as Aristotle saith, it is not *gnosis* but *praxis* [1] must be the fruit. And how *praxis* cannot be, without being moved to practice, it is no hard matter to consider.

The philosopher showeth you the way, he informeth you of the particularities, as well of the tediousness of the way, as of the pleasant lodging you shall have when your journey is ended, as of the many bye-turnings that may divert you from your way. But this is to no man but to him that will read him, and read him with attentive studious painfulness. Which constant desire, whosoever hath in him, hath already passed half the hardness of the way, and therefore is beholden to the philosopher but for the other half. Nay, truly, learned men have learnedly thought that, where once reason hath so much over-mastered passion as that the mind hath a free desire to do well, the inward light each mind hath in itself is as good as a philosopher's book; seeing in nature we know it is well to do well, and what is well and what is evil, although not in the words of art which philosophers bestow upon us. For out of natural conceit the philosophers drew it; but to be moved to do that which we know, or to be moved with desire to know, *hoc opus, hic labor est*. [2]

Now therein of all sciences (I speak still of human, and according to the human conceits) is our poet the monarch. For he doth not only show the way, but giveth so sweet a prospect into the way, as will entice any man to enter into it. Nay, he doth, as if your journey should lie through a fair vineyard, at the first give you a cluster of grapes, that, full of that taste, you may long to pass further. He beginneth not with obscure definitions, which must blur the margin with interpretations, and load the memory with doubtfulness; but he cometh to you with words sent in delightful proportion, either accompanied with, or prepared for, the well-enchanting skill of music; and with a tale forsooth he cometh unto you, with a tale which holdeth children from play, and old men from the chimney corner. And, pretending no more, [he] doth intend the winning of the mind from wickedness to virtue; even as the child is often brought to take most wholesome things by hiding them in such others as have a pleasant taste; which, if one should begin to tell them the nature of [the] aloes or rhubarb they should receive, would sooner take their physic at their ears than at their mouth.

*   *   *   *

[1] Not knowledge but deeds.
[2] "This is the work, this is the labor." Vergil, *Æneid*, vi, 129.

That imitation, whereof poetry is, hath the most conveniency [1] to nature of all other, insomuch that, as Aristotle saith, those things which in themselves are horrible, as cruel battles, unnatural monsters, are made in poetical imitation delightful. Truly, I have known men, that even with reading *Amadis de Gaul* (which, God knoweth, wanteth much of a perfect poesy) have found their hearts moved to the exercise of courtesy, liberality, and especially courage. Who readeth [of] Æneas carrying old Anchises on his back, that wisheth not it were his fortune to perform so excellent an act?

*   *   *   *

But it is not the tragedy they do mislike; for it were too absurd to cast out so excellent a representation of whatsoever is most worthy to be learned. Is it the lyric that most displeaseth, who with his tuned lyre and well-accorded voice, giveth praise, the reward of virtue, to virtuous acts? who gives moral precepts, and natural problems, who sometimes raiseth up his voice to the height of the heavens, in singing the lauds of the immortal God? Certainly I must confess my own barbarousness: I never heard the old song of *Percy and Douglas* that I found not my heart moved more than with a trumpet; and yet is it sung but by some blind crowder,[2] with no rougher voice than rude style; which being so evil apparelled in the dust and cobwebs of that uncivil age, what would it work trimmed in the gorgeous eloquence of Pindar? In Hungary I have seen it the manner at all feasts, and other such meetings, to have songs of their ancestors' valor, which that right soldier-like nation think the chiefest kindlers of brave courage. The incomparable Lacedæmonians did not only carry that kind of music ever with them to the field, but even at home, as such songs were made, so were they all content to be the singers of them, when the lusty men were to tell what they did, the old men what they had done, and the young men what they would do. And where a man may say that Pindar many times praiseth highly victories of small moment, matters rather of sport than virtue, it may be answered, it was the fault of the poet, and not of the poetry; so indeed the chief fault was in the time and custom of the Greeks, who set these toys at so high a price that Philip of Macedon reckoned a horse-race won at Olympus among his three fearful felicities. But as the unimitable Pindar often did, so is that kind most capable and

---

[1] fittingness.
[2] fiddler.

most fit to awake the thoughts from the sleep of idleness, to embrace honorable enterprises.

*   *   *   *

Our tragedies and comedies (not without cause cried out against), observing rules neither of honest civility nor of skilful poetry, excepting *Gorboduc* (again, I say, of those that I have seen), which notwithstanding, as it is full of stately speeches and well-sounding phrases, climbing to the height of Seneca his style, and as full of notable morality, which it doth most delightfully teach, and so obtain the very end of poesy, yet in truth it is very defectious in the circumstances, which grieveth me, because it might not remain as an exact model of all tragedies. For it is faulty both in place and time, the two necessary companions of all corporal actions. For where the stage should always represent but one place, and the uttermost time presupposed in it should be, both by Aristotle's precept and common reason, but one day, there is both many days, and many places, inartificially imagined. But if it be so in *Gorboduc*, how much more in all the rest? where you shall have Asia on the one side, and Africa on the other, and so many under-kingdoms, that the player, when he cometh in, must ever begin with telling where he is, or else the tale will not be conceived. Now ye shall have three ladies walk to gather flowers, and then we must believe the stage to be a garden. By and by, we hear news of shipwreck in the same place, and then we are to blame if we accept it not for a rock. Upon the back of that, comes out a hideous monster, with fire and smoke, and then the miserable beholders are bound to take it for a cave. While in the meantime two armies fly in, represented with four swords and bucklers, and then what hard heart will not receive it for a pitched field? Now, of time they are much more liberal, for ordinary it is that two young princes fall in love. After many traverses,[1] she is got with child, delivered of a fair boy; he is lost, groweth a man, falls in love, and is ready to get another child; and all this in two hours' space; which how absurd it is in sense even sense may imagine, and art hath taught, and all ancient examples justified, and, at this day, the ordinary players in Italy will not err in. Yet will some bring in an example of *Eunuchus* in Terence, that containeth matter of two days, yet far short of twenty years. True it is, and so was it to be played in two days, and so fitted to the time it set forth. And though

[1] adventures.

Plautus hath in one place done amiss, let us hit with him, and not miss with him. But they will say, how then shall we set forth a story, which containeth both many places and many times? And do they not know that a tragedy is tied to the laws of poesy, and not of history? not bound to follow the story, but, having liberty, either to feign a quite new matter, or to frame the history to the most tragical conveniency? Again, many things may be told which cannot be showed, if they know the difference betwixt reporting and representing. As, for example, I may speak (though I am here) of Peru, and in speech digress from that to the description of Calcutta; but in action I cannot represent it without Pacolet's horse; [1] and so was the manner the ancients took, by some Nuntius, to recount things done in former time or other place. Lastly, if they will represent an history, they must not (as Horace saith) begin *ab ovo*,[2] but they must come to the principal point of that one action which they will represent. By example this will be best expressed. I have a story of young Polydorus, delivered for safety's sake, with great riches, by his father Priam to Polymnestor, king of Thrace, in the Trojan war time. He after some years, hearing the overthrow of Priam, for to make the treasure his own, murdereth the child; the body of the child is taken up by Hecuba; she the same day findeth a slight to be revenged most cruelly of the tyrant. Where now would one of our tragedy writers begin, but with the delivery of the child? Then should he sail over into Thrace, and so spend I know not how many years, and travel numbers of places. But where doth Euripides [begin]? Even with the finding of the body, leaving the rest to be told by the spirit of Polydorus. This needs no further to be enlarged; the dullest wit may conceive it.

But besides these gross absurdities, how all their plays be neither right tragedies, nor right comedies; mingling kings and clowns, not because the matter so carrieth it, but thrust in clowns by head and shoulders, to play a part in majestical matters, with neither decency nor discretion; so as neither the admiration and commiseration, nor the right sportfulness, is by their mongrel tragi-comedy obtained. I know Apuleius did some-what so, but that is a thing recounted with space of time, not represented in one moment; and I know the ancients have one or two examples of tragi-comedies, as Plautus hath *Amphitryon*. But, if we mark them well, we shall find that they

---

[1] A swift horse; a reference to the horse of Pacolet, a dwarf in an old romance.

[2] From the egg.

never, or very daintily, match hornpipes and funerals. So falleth it out that, having indeed no right comedy, in that comical part of our tragedy we have nothing but scurrility, unworthy of any chaste ears, or some extreme show of doltishness, indeed fit to lift up a loud laughter, and nothing else; where the whole tract [1] of a comedy should be full of delight, as the tragedy should be still maintained in a well-raised admiration. But our comedians think there is no delight without laughter; which is very wrong, for though laughter may come with delight, yet cometh it not of delight, as though delight should be the cause of laughter; but well may one thing breed both together: nay, rather in themselves they have, as it were, a kind of contrariety; for delight we scarcely do but in things that have a conveniency to ourselves or to the general nature: laughter almost ever cometh of things most disproportioned to ourselves and nature. Delight hath a joy in it, either permanent or present. Laughter hath only a scornful tickling. For example, we are ravished with delight to see a fair woman, and yet are far from being moved to laughter. We laugh at deformed creatures, wherein certainly we cannot delight. We delight in good chances, we laugh at mischances; we delight to hear the happiness of our friends, or country, at which he were worthy to be laughed at that would laugh; we shall, contrarily, laugh sometimes to find a matter quite mistaken and go down the hill against the bias, in the mouth of some such men, as for the respect of them one shall be heartily sorry, yet he cannot choose but laugh, and so is rather pained than delighted with laughter. Yet deny I not but that they may go well together; for as in Alexander's picture well set out we delight without laughter, and in twenty mad antics we laugh without delight, so in Hercules, painted with his great beard and furious countenance, in woman's attire, spinning at Omphale's commandment, it breedeth both delight and laughter. For the representing of so strange a power in love procureth delight; and the scornfulness of the action stirreth laughter. But I speak to this purpose, that all the end of the comical part be not upon such scornful matters as stirreth laughter only, but, mixed with it, that delightful teaching which is the end of poesy. And the great fault even in that point of laughter, and forbidden plainly by Aristotle, is that they stir laughter in sinful things, which are rather execrable than ridiculous; or in miserable, which are rather to be pitied than scorned. For what is it to make folks gape at a wretched beggar, or a beggarly clown? or,

[1] treatment.

against law of hospitality, to jest at strangers, because they speak not English so well as we do? what do we learn? since it is certain

> *Nil habet infelix paupertas durius in se,*
> *Quam quod ridiculos homines facit.*[1]

But rather a busy loving courtier, a heartless threatening Thraso,[2] a self-wise-seeming schoolmaster, an awry-transformed traveller: these if we saw walk in stage names, which we play naturally, therein were delightful laughter, and teaching delightfulness; as in the other, the tragedies of Buchanan do justly bring forth a divine admiration. But I have lavished out too many words of this play matter. I do it because as they are excellent parts of poesy, so there is none so much used in England, and none can be more pitifully abused. Which, like an unmannerly daughter, showing a bad education, causeth her mother Poesy's honesty to be called in question.

*　　*　　*　　*

So that since the ever-praiseworthy Poesy is full of virtue-breeding delightfulness, and void of no gift that ought to be in the noble name of learning; since the blames laid against it are either false or feeble; since the cause why it is not esteemed in England is the fault of poet-apes, not poets; since, lastly, our tongue is most fit to honor poesy, and to be honored by poesy, I conjure you all that have had the evil luck to read this ink-wasting toy of mine, even in the name of the nine Muses, no more to scorn the sacred mysteries of poesy, no more to laugh at the name of poets, as though they were next inheritors to fools; no more to jest at the reverend title of a rimer; but to believe, with Aristotle, that they were the ancient treasurers of the Grecians' divinity; to believe, with Bembus, that they were first bringers-in of all civility; to believe, with Scaliger, that no philosopher's precepts can sooner make you an honest man than the reading of Virgil; to believe, with Clauserus, the translator of Cornutus, that it pleased the heavenly deity, by Hesiod and Homer, under the veil of fables, to give us all knowledge, logic, rhetoric, philosophy, natural and moral; and *quid non?*[3] to believe with me, that there are many mysteries contained in poetry, which of purpose were written darkly, lest by profane wits it should be abused;

---

[1] "Unhappy poverty has in it nothing harder than the fact that it makes men ridiculous." Juvenal, *Sat.*, iii, 152–3.

[2] A braggart soldier in Terence's *Eunuchus*.

[3] Why not?

to believe, with Landin, that they are so beloved of the gods that whatsoever they write proceeds from a divine fury. Lastly, to believe themselves, when they tell you they will make you immortal by their verses.

*   *   *   *

Jonson

Ben JONSON (1573–1637) was born in poverty in West-minster, of a North of England family. His youth is clouded in obscurity; he may have been put to the trade of his step-father, a bricklayer. We know that he was educated at West-minster School, through the kindness of Camden, the master. Tradition has it that he later matriculated at Cambridge, but there is no record of his taking a degree. He seems to have joined the army, and may have fought against the Spaniards in the Netherlands. When he returned to England, he became an actor. In 1598, having killed a fellow-actor, he was tried for murder, but escaped severe punishment, pleading "benefit of clergy." The same year his first successful play, *Every Man in His Humor,* was produced, with Shakespeare in the cast. Other plays followed rapidly, including satires on fellow-dramatists in the so-called "War of the Theatres." His satiri-cal comedies, based on Latin models, pointed the way to the comedies of the Restoration. Most of his important plays were written before 1616, when a folio collection of his "works" appeared. He went to Scotland in 1618, paying his famous visit to Drummond at Hawthornden; his *obiter dicta,* pre-served by his host, have a certain critical interest. On his re-turn to London, he wrote many Court masques, some plays, verse, and criticism, most of which is contained in *Timber, or Discoveries,* which was not published until after his death. He was the leader of a school of poets (the "sons of Ben") and did much to establish the classical standards of taste which dominated English literature for a century and a half after his death.

Jonson's *Timber, or Discoveries* is to a great extent a "commonplace book," that is, a journal in which a writer puts not only his own ideas, but reactions to, and often quotations or translations from, his reading. Such was the practice of many authors, including Emerson and Thoreau. When Jonson made an extract from a book, the selection fitted in so well with his temperament and attitude that it seemed his own. We know now that some of the passages that the poet Swinburne greatly admired are Jonson's translations from commentaries on Aristotle, written in Latin by the Dutchmen, Heinsius and Lipsius.

Jonson is a far greater critic than is generally admitted. He was a classicist in the best sense of the word, knowing and appreciating what the ancients had accomplished in literature and in criticism, but realizing that in an age of exuberance, such as the Elizabethan, a Shakespeare could break the accepted rules and by his genius alone be great. Like Quintilian, he displays uncommon sense. His critical comments invite and merit careful reading.

From TIMBER, or DISCOVERIES [1]
(1620–35?)

*   *   *   *

Censura de Poetis. Nothing in our age, I have observed, is more preposterous than the running judgments upon poetry and poets; when we shall hear those things commended and cried up for the best writings, which a man would scarce vouchsafe to wrap any wholesome drug in; he would never light his tobacco with them; and those men almost named for miracles, who yet are so vile that if a man should go about to examine and correct them, he must make all they have done but one blot. Their good is so entangled with their bad, as forcibly one must draw on the other's death with it. A sponge dipped in ink will do all:

[1] The text is that of J. E. Spingarn in his *Critical Essays of the Seventeenth Century,* Oxford, 1908, modernized by the editors. It is used with the kind permission of The Clarendon Press, Oxford.

Comitetur punica librum

Spongia.[1]

Et paulò post,[2]

Non possunt . . . multæ una litura potest.[3]

Yet their vices have not hurt them; nay, a great many they have profited, for they have been loved for nothing else. And this false opinion grows strong against the best men, if once it take root with the ignorant. Cestius, in his time, was preferred to Cicero, so far as the ignorant durst. They learned him without book, and had him often in their mouths; but a man cannot imagine that thing so foolish or rude but will find and enjoy an admirer; at least, a reader or spectator. The puppets are seen now in despite of the players; Heath's *Epigrams* and the Sculler's [4] poems have their applause. There are never wanting [those] that dare prefer the worst preachers, the worst pleaders, the worst poets; not that the better have left to write or speak better, but that they that hear them judge worse: *Non illi pejus dicunt, sed hi corruptius judicant.* Nay, if it were put to the question of the Water-rimer's works against Spenser's, I doubt not but they would find more suffrages; because the most favor common vices, out of a prerogative the vulgar have to lose their judgments, and like that which is naught.

Poetry, in this latter age, hath proved but a mean mistress to such as have wholly addicted themselves to her, or given their names up to her family. They who have but saluted her on the by, and now and then tendered their visits, she hath done much for, and advanced in the way of their own professions (both the law and the gospel) beyond all they could have hoped or done for themselves without her favor. Wherein she doth emulate the judicious but preposterous bounty of the time's grandees, who accumulate all they can upon the parasite or freshman in their friendship, but think an old client or honest servant bound by his place to write and starve.

Indeed, the multitude commend writers as they do fencers or wrestlers, who, if they come in robustiously and put for it with a deal of violence, are received for the braver fellows; when many times their own rudeness is a cause of their disgrace, and a slight

---

[1] Let a Punic sponge go with the book.
[2] A little later.
[3] Many erasures are not enough; a single sponging will suffice.
[4] John Taylor, the "water poet" (1580–1653), a Thames waterman and versifier.

touch of their adversary gives all that boisterous force the foil. But in these things the unskilful are naturally deceived, and judging wholly by the bulk, think rude things greater than polished, and scattered more numerous than composed. Nor think this only to be true in the sordid multitude, but the neater sort of our gallants; for all are the multitude, only they differ in clothes, not in judgment or understanding.

De Shakespeare nostrat. I remember the players have often mentioned it as an honor to Shakespeare that in his writing, whatsoever he penned, he never blotted out line. My answer hath been, Would he had blotted a thousand, which they thought a malevolent speech. I had not told posterity this, but for their ignorance who choose that circumstance to commend their friend by wherein he most faulted, and to justify mine own candor, for I loved the man, and do honor his memory, on this side idolatry, as much as any. He was indeed honest, and of an open and free nature, had an excellent fancy, brave notions, and gentle expressions, wherein he flowed with that facility that sometimes it was necessary he should be stopped: *sufflaminandus erat,*[1] as Augustus said of Haterius. His wit was in his own power; would the rule of it had been so, too. Many times he fell into those things, could not escape laughter—as when he said in the person of Cæsar, one speaking to him: *Cæsar, thou dost me wrong.* He replied: *Cæsar did never wrong but with just cause;* and such like, which were ridiculous. But he redeemed his vices with his virtues. There was ever more in him to be praised than to be pardoned.

Ingeniorum discrimina. In the difference of wits, I have observed there are many notes: And it is a little mastery to know them, to discern what every nature, every disposition will bear. For before we sow our land, we should plough it. There are no fewer forms of minds than of bodies amongst us. The variety is incredible, and therefore we must search. Some are fit to make divines, some poets, some lawyers, some physicians, some to be sent to the plough and trades.

There is no doctrine will do good where nature is wanting. Some wits are swelling and high, others low and still; some hot and fiery, others cold and dull; one must have a bridle, the other a spur.

There be some that are forward and bold, and these will do every little thing easily: I mean that [which] is hard by, and next them, which they will utter unretarded without any shamefacedness.

[1] He had to be suppressed.

These never perform much, but quickly. They are what they are on the sudden; they show presently like grain that, scattered on the top of the ground, shoots up, but takes no root, has a yellow blade, but the ear empty. They are wits of good promise at first, but there is an *Ingeni-stitium*: [1] They stand still at sixteen, they get no higher.

You have others that labor only to ostentation, and are ever more busy about the colors and surface of a work than in the matter and foundation; for that is hid, the other is seen.

Others that in composition are nothing but what is rough and broken: *Quæ per salebras altaque saxa cadunt.*[2] And if it would come gently, they trouble it of purpose. They would not have it run without rubs, as if that style were more strong and manly, that stroke the ear with a kind of uneven-ness. These men err not by chance, but knowingly and willingly; they are like men that affect a fashion by themselves, have some singularity in a ruff, cloak, or hat-band, or their beards specially cut to provoke beholders, and set a mark upon themselves. They would be reprehended while they are looked on. And this vice, one that is in authority with the rest, loving, delivers over to them to be imitated, so that oft-times the faults which he fell into, the others seek for. This is the danger, when vice becomes a precedent.

Others there are that have no composition at all; but a kind of tuning and riming fall in what they write. It runs and slides, and only makes a sound. Women's poets, they are called, as you have women's tailors.

> *They write a verse as smooth, as soft as cream,*
> *In which there is no torrent, nor scarce stream.*

You may sound these wits and find the depth of them with your middle finger. They are cream-bowl, or but puddle, deep.

Some that turn over all books, and are equally searching in all papers; that write out of what they presently find or meet, without choice; by which means it happens that what they have discredited and impugned in one work, they have before or after extolled the same in another. Such are all the essayists, even their master, Montaigne. These in all they write confess still what books they have read last, and therein their own folly so much that they bring it to the stake raw and undigested; not that the place did need it neither, but that they thought themselves furnished, and would vent it.

[1] A standing-still of wit.
[2] That fall over the rough ways, and high rocks. (Martial.)

Some again, who, after they have got authority, or, which is less, opinion, by their writings, to have read much, dare presently to feign whole books and authors, and lie safely. For what never was will not easily be found, not by the most curious.

And some, by a cunning protestation against all reading, and false venditation of their own naturals,[1] think to divert the sagacity of their readers from themselves, and cool the scent of their own fox-like thefts, when yet they are so rank as a man may find whole pages together usurped from one author, their necessities compelling them to read for present use, which could not be in many books, and so come forth more ridiculously and palpably guilty than those who, because they cannot trace, they yet would slander their industry.

But the wretcheder are the obstinate condemners of all helps and arts, such as presuming on their own naturals, which perhaps are excellent, dare deride all diligence, and seem to mock at the terms when they understand not the things, thinking that way to get off wittily with their ignorance. These are imitated often by such as are their peers in negligence, though they cannot be in nature. And they utter all they can think with a kind of violence and indisposition, unexamined, without relation either to person, place, or any fitness else; and the more wilful and stubborn they are in it, the more learned they are esteemed of the multitude, through their excellent vice of judgment: who think those things the stronger that have no art, as if to break were better than to open, or to rend asunder gentler than to loose.

It cannot but come to pass that these men who commonly seek to do more than enough may sometimes happen on some thing that is good and great; but very seldom. And when it comes, it doth not recompense the rest of their ill. For their jests and their sentences, which they only and ambitiously seek for, stick out and are more eminent, because all is sordid and vile about them; as lights are more discerned in a thick darkness than a faint shadow. Now because they speak all they can, however unfitly, they are thought to have the greater copy. Where the learned use ever election, and a mean, they look back to what they intended at first, and make all an even and proportioned body. The true artificer will not run away from nature, as he were afraid of her, or depart from life and the likeness of truth, but speak to the capacity of his hearers. And though his language differ from the vulgar somewhat, it shall not fly from

[1] Constantly displaying, as if for sale, their natural abilities.

all humanity, with the Tamerlanes and Tamer-Chams of the late age, which had nothing in them but the scenical strutting and furious vociferation to warrant them to the ignorant gapers. He knows it is his only art so to carry it, as none but artificers perceive it. In the meantime perhaps he is called barren, dull, lean, a poor writer, or by what contumelious word can come in their cheeks, by these men who, without labor, judgment, knowledge, or almost sense, are received or preferred before him. He gratulates them and their fortune. Another age, or juster men, will acknowledge the virtues of his studies, his wisdom in dividing, his subtlety in arguing, with what strength he doth inspire his readers, with what sweetness he strokes them; in inveighing, what sharpness; in jest, what urbanity he uses; how he doth reign in men's affections; how invade and break in upon them, and makes their minds like the thing he writes. Then in his elocution to behold what word is proper, which hath ornament, which height, what is beautifully translated, where figures are fit, which gentle, which strong, to show the composition manly: and how he hath avoided faint, obscure, obscene, sordid, humble, improper, or effeminate phrase, which is not only praised of the most, but commended, which is worse, especially for that it is naught.

Ignorantia animæ. I know no disease of the soul but ignorance, not of the arts and sciences, but of itself. Yet relating to those it is a pernicious evil, the darkener of man's life, the disturber of his reason, and common confounder of truth, with which a man goes groping in the dark, no otherwise than if he were blind. Great understandings are most wrecked and troubled with it. Nay, sometimes they will rather choose to die than not to know the things they study for. Think then what an evil it is, and what good the contrary.

Scientia. Knowledge is the action of the soul, and is perfect without the senses, as having the seeds of all science and virtue in itself, but not without the service of the senses; by those organs the soul works. She is a perpetual agent, prompt and subtle, but often flexible and erring, entangling herself like a silk-worm: but her reason is a weapon with two edges, and cuts through. In her indagations [1] oft-times new scents put her by, and she takes in errors into her by the same conduits she does truths.

Otium studiorum. Ease and relaxation are profitable to all studies. The mind is like a bow, the stronger by being unbent. But the temper

---

[1] investigations.

in spirits is all, when to command a man's wit, when to favor it. I have known a man vehement on both sides, that knew no mean, either to intermit his studies or call upon them again. When he hath set himself to writing, he would join night to day, press upon himself without release, not minding it till he fainted; and when he left off, resolve himself into all sports and looseness again, that it was almost a despair to draw him to his book; but once got to it, he grew stronger and more earnest by the ease. His whole powers were renewed; he would work out of himself what he desired, but with such excess as his study could not be ruled; he knew not how to dispose his own abilities, or husband them; he was of that immoderate power against himself. Nor was he only a strong, but an absolute speaker and writer; but his subtlety did not show itself; his judgment thought that a vice: for the ambush hurts more than is hid. He never forced his language, nor went out of the high way of speaking, but for some great necessity or apparent profit. For he denied figures to be invented for ornament, but for aid; and still thought it an extreme madness to bend or wrest that which ought to be right.

Et stili eminentia. It is no wonder men's eminence appears but in their own way. Virgil's felicity left him in prose, as Tully's forsook him in verse. Sallust's orations are read in the honor of story; yet the most eloquent Plato's speech, which he made for Socrates, is neither worthy of the patron or the person defended. Nay, in the same kind of oratory, and where the matter is one, you shall have him that reasons strongly, open negligently; another that prepares well, not fit so well; and this happens, not only to brains, but to bodies. One can wrestle well, another run well, a third leap or throw the bar, a fourth lift or stop a cart going: each hath his way of strength. So in other creatures, some dogs are for the deer, some for the wild boar, some are fox-hounds, some otter-hounds. Nor are all horses for the coach or saddle; some are for the cart and panniers.

De claris oratoribus. I have known many excellent men that would speak suddenly, to the admiration of their hearers, who upon study and premeditation have been forsaken by their own wits, and no way answered their fame. Their eloquence was greater than their reading; and the things they uttered, better than those they knew. Their fortune deserved better of them than their care. For men of present spirits, and of greater wits than study, do please more in the things they invent than in those they bring. And I have heard some of them compelled to speak, out of necessity, that have so infinitely exceeded themselves, as it was better both for them and their auditory that they were so surprised, not prepared. Nor was it safe then to cross them, for their adversary, their anger made them more eloquent. Yet these men I could not but love and admire, that they returned to their studies. They left not diligence, as many do, when their rashness prospered. For diligence is a great aid, even to an indifferent wit, when we are not contented with the examples of our own age, but would know the face of the former. Indeed, the more we confer with, the more we profit by, if the persons be chosen.

Dominus Verulanus.[1] One, though he be excellent and the chief, is not to be imitated alone. For never no imitator ever grew up to his author; likeness is always on this side truth. Yet there happened in my time one noble speaker who was full of gravity in his speaking. His language, where he could spare or pass by a jest, was nobly censorious. No man ever spoke more neatly, more pressly, more weightily, or suffered less emptiness, less idleness, in what he uttered. No member of his speech but consisted of [his] own graces. His hearers could not cough or look aside from him without loss. He commanded where he spoke, and had his judges angry and pleased at his devotion. No man had their affections more in his power. The fear of every man that heard him was lest he should make an end.

Scriptorum catalogus.[2] Cicero is said to be the only wit that the people of Rome had equalled to their empire. *Ingenium par imperio.* We have had many, and in their several ages (to take in but the former *seculum*) Sir Thomas More, the elder Wyatt, Henry, Earl of Surrey, Chaloner, Smith, Eliot, B[ishop] Gardiner, were for their times admirable; and the more because they began eloquence with us. Sir Nico[las] Bacon was singular and almost alone in the beginning of Queen Elizabeth's times. Sir Philip Sidney and Mr. Hooker, in different matter, grew great masters of wit and language, and in whom all vigor of invention and strength of judgment met. The Earl of Essex, noble and high, and Sir Walter Raleigh, not to be condemned either for judgment or style; Sir Henry Savile, grave and truly lettered; Sir Edwin Sandys, excellent in both; Lo[rd] Egerton, the Chancellor, a grave and great orator,

---

[1] Sir Francis Bacon, Lord Verulam, Viscount St. Albans.
[2] A catalogue of writers—here all Tudor authors.

and best when he was provoked. But his learned and able, though unfortunate, successor [1] is he who hath filled up all numbers, and performed that in our tongue which may be compared or preferred either to insolent Greece or haughty Rome. In short, within his view and about his times were all the wits born that could honor a language or help study. Now things daily fall; wits grow downward and eloquence grows backward: so that he may be named and stand as the mark and ἀκμή [2] of our language.

De augmentis scientiarum. I have ever observed it to have been the office of a wise patriot, among the greatest affairs of the state, to take care of the commonwealth of learning. For schools, they are the seminaries of state; and nothing is worthier the study of a statesman than that part of the republic which we call the advancement of letters. Witness the care of Julius Cæsar, who in the heat of the civil war wrote his books of *Analogie,* and dedicated them to Tully. This made the late Lord St. Albans entitle his work *Novum Organum:* which, though by the most of superficial men, who cannot get beyond the title of *Nominals,*[3] it is not penetrated nor understood, it really openeth all defects of learning whatsoever, and is a book

Qui longum noto scriptori porriget ævum.[4]

My conceit of his person was never increased toward him by his place or honors. But I have and do reverence him for the greatness that was only proper to himself, in that he seemed to me ever, by his work, one of the greatest men, and most worthy of admiration, that had been in many ages. In his adversity I ever prayed that God would give him strength; for greatness he could not want. Neither could I condole in a word or syllable for him, as knowing no accident could do harm to virtue, but rather help to make it manifest.

De corruptela morum. There cannot be one color of the mind, another of the wit. If the mind be staid, grave, and composed, the wit is so; that vitiated, the other is blown and deflowered. Do we not see, if the mind languish, the members are dull? Look upon an effeminate person; his very gait confesseth him. If a man be fiery, his motion is so; if angry, 'tis troubled and violent. So that we may

[1] Bacon.
[2] acme.
[3] Mere names.
[4] That ready wits may comprehend them soon,
   And faithful memories retain them long. (Horace, *Ars Poetica.* Roscommon's translation.)

conclude: wheresoever manners and fashions are corrupted, language is. It imitates the public riot. The excess of feasts and apparel are the notes of a sick state, and the wantonness of language, of a sick mind.

＊　　＊　　＊　　＊

Poesis et pictura. Poetry and picture are arts of a like nature, and both are busy about imitation. It was excellently said of Plutarch, Poetry was a speaking Picture, and Picture a mute Poesie. For they both invent, feign, and devise many things, and accommodate all they invent to the use and service of nature. Yet of the two the pen is more noble than the pencil: for that can speak to the understanding, the other but to the sense. They both behold pleasure and profit as their common object; but should abstain from all base pleasures, lest they should err from their end, and, while they seek to better men's minds, destroy their manners. They both are born artificers, not made. Nature is more powerful in them than study.

＊　　＊　　＊　　＊

De stilo, et optimo scribendi genere. For a man to write well, there are required three necessaries: to read the best authors, observe the best speakers, and much exercise of his own style. In style, to consider what ought to be written and after what manner: he must first think and excogitate his matter, then choose his words, and examine the weight of either. Then take care, in placing and ranking both matter and words, that the composition be comely; and to do this with diligence and often. No matter how slow the style be at first, so it be labored and accurate; seek the best, and be not glad of the forward conceits,[1] or first words that offer themselves to us; but judge of what we invent, and order what we approve. Repeat often what we have formerly written; which beside that it helps the consequence, and makes the juncture better, it quickens the heat of imagination, that often cools in the time of setting down, and gives it new strength, as if it grew lustier by the going back. As we see in the contention of leaping, they jump farthest that fetch their race largest; or, as in throwing a dart or javelin, we force back our arms to make our loose the stronger. Yet, if we have a fair gale of wind, I forbid not the steering out of our sail, so the favor of the gale deceive us not. For all that we invent doth please us in the conception or birth, else we would never set it down. But the safest

---

[1] Ideas; cleverness in expressing conceptions.

is to return to our judgment, and handle over again those things the easiness of which might make them justly suspected. So did the best writers in their beginnings; they imposed upon themselves care and industry. They did nothing rashly. They obtained first to write well, and then custom made it easy and a habit. By little and little their matter showed itself to them more plentifully, their words answered, their compositions followed; and all, as in a well-ordered family, presented itself in the place. So that the sum of all is: Ready writing makes not good writing, but good writing brings on ready writing. Yet when we think we have got the faculty, it is even then good to resist it, as to give a horse a check sometimes with bit, which doth not so much stop his course as stir his mettle. Again, whither a man's genius is best able to reach, thither it should more and more contend, lift, and dilate itself; as men of low stature raise themselves on their toes, and so oft times get even, if not eminent. Besides, as it is fit for grown and able writers to stand of themselves, and work with their own strength, to trust and endeavor by their own faculties, so it is fit for the beginner and learner to study others and the best. For the mind and memory are more sharply exercised in comprehending another man's things than our own; and such as accustom themselves and are familiar with the best authors shall ever and anon find somewhat of them in themselves, and in the expression of their minds, even when they feel it not, be able to utter something like theirs, which hath an authority above their own. Nay, sometimes it is the reward of a man's study, the praise of quoting another man fitly: and though a man be more prone and able for one kind of writing than another, yet he must exercise all. For as in an instrument, so in style, there must be a harmony and consent of parts.

Precipiendi modi. I take this labor in teaching others, that they should not be always to be taught, and I would bring my precepts into practice. For rules are ever of less force and value than experiments. Yet with this purpose, rather to show the right way to those that come after, than to detect any that have slipped before by error; and I hope it will be more profitable; for men do more willingly listen, and with more favor, to precept than reprehension. Among diverse opinions of an art, and most of them contrary in themselves, it is hard to make election; and therefore, though a man cannot invent new things after so many, he may do a welcome work yet to help posterity to judge rightly of the old. But arts and precepts avail nothing, except nature be beneficial and aiding. And therefore these things are no more written to a dull disposition than rules of husbandry to a barren soil. No precepts will profit a fool, no more than beauty will the blind, or music the deaf. As we should take care that our style in writing be neither dry nor empty, we should look again it be not winding, or wanton with far-fetched descriptions. Either is a vice. But that is worse which proceeds out of want than that which riots out of plenty. The remedy of fruitfulness is easy, but no labor will help the contrary. I will like and praise some things in a young writer which yet, if he continue in, I cannot but justly hate him for the same. There is a time to be given all things for maturity, and that even your country-husbandman can teach, who to a young plant will not put the pruning knife, because it seems to fear the iron, as not able to admit the scar. No more would I tell a green writer all his faults, lest I should make him grieve and faint, and at last despair. For nothing doth more hurt than to make him so afraid of all things as he can endeavor nothing. Therefore youth ought to be instructed betimes, and in the best things; for we hold those longest we take soonest, as the first scent of a vessel lasts, and that tinct the wool first receives. Therefore a master should temper his own powers, and descend to the other's infirmity. If you pour a glut of water upon a bottle, it receives little of it; but with a funnel, and by degrees, you shall fill many of them, and spill little of your own; to their capacity they will all receive and be full. And as it is fit to read the best authors to youth first, so let them be of the openest and clearest: as Livy before Sallust, Sidney before Donne; and beware of letting them taste Gower or Chaucer at first, lest falling too much in love with antiquity, and not apprehending the weight, they grow rough and barren in language only. When their judgments are firm and out of danger,[1] let them read both the old and the new; but no less take heed that their new flowers and sweetness do not as much corrupt as the others' dryness and squalor, if they choose not carefully. Spenser, in affecting the ancients, writ no language; yet I would have him read for his matter, but as Virgil read Ennius. The reading of Homer and Virgil is counselled by Quintilian as the best way of informing youth and confirming man. For, besides that the mind is raised with the height and sublimity of such a verse, it takes spirit from the greatness of the matter, and is tincted with the best things. Tragic and lyric poetry is good too; and comic with the best, if the manners of the reader be once in safety. In the Greek poets, as also

[1] domination.

in Plautus, we shall see the economy and disposition of poems better observed than in Terence and the later, who thought the sole grace and virtue of their fable [1] the sticking in of sentences [2] as ours do the forcing in of jests.

* * * *

Præcept. element. It is not the passing through these learnings that hurts us, but the dwelling and sticking about them. To descend to those extreme anxieties and foolish cavils of grammarians is able to break a wit in pieces; being a work of manifold misery and vainness to be *Elementarii senes.*[3] Yet even letters are, as it were, the bank of words, and restore themselves to an author as the pawns of language. But talking and eloquence are not the same: to speak, and to speak well, are two things. A fool may talk, but a wise man speaks, and out of the observation, knowledge, and use of things. Many writers perplex their readers and hearers with mere nonsense. Their writings need sunshine. Pure and neat language I love, yet plain and customary. A barbarous phrase hath often made me out of love with a good sense, and doubtful [4] writing hath wracked me beyond my patience. The reason why a poet is said that he ought to have all knowledges, is that he should not be ignorant of the most, especially of those he will handle. And indeed, when the attaining of them is possible, it were a sluggish and base thing to despair. For frequent imitation of anything becomes a habit quickly. If a man should prosecute as much as could be said of every thing, his work would find no end.

De orationis dignitate.[5] Speech is the only benefit man hath to express his excellence of mind above other creatures. It is the instrument of society. Therefore Mercury who is the President of Language, is called *Deorum hominumque interpres.*[6] In all speech, words and sense are as the body and the soul. The sense is as the life and soul of language, without which all words are dead. Sense is wrought out of experience, the knowledge of human life and actions, or of the liberal arts, which the Greeks called Ἐγκυκλοπαιδείαν. Words are the people's, yet there is a choice of them to be made. For *Verborum*

[1] plot.
[2] philosophical maxims.
[3] Old men beginning to learn.
[4] ambiguous.
[5] Concerning the dignity of speech.
[6] Interpreter between gods and men.

delectus origo est eloquentiæ.[1] They are to be chosen according to the persons we make speak, or the things we speak of. Some are of the camp, some of the council-board, some of the shop, some of the sheep-cote, some of the pulpit, some of the bar, &c.

Metaphora. And herein is seen their elegance and propriety, when we use them fitly, and draw them forth to their just strength and nature by way of translation or Metaphor. But in this translation we must only serve necessity (*Nam temerè nihil transfertur à prudenti* [2]), or commodity, which is a kind of necessity; that is, when we either absolutely want a word to express by, and that is necessity; or when we have not so fit a word, and that is commodity. As when we avoid loss by it, and escape obsceneness, and gain in the grace and property which helps significance. Metaphors far-fet[ched] hinder to be understood; and affected, lose their grace. Or when the person fetcheth his translations from a wrong place: as if a privy-councillor should at the table take his metaphor from a dicing-house, or ordinary,[3] or a vintner's vault; or a justice of the peace draw his similitudes from the mathematics; or a divine from a bawdy-house, or taverns; or a gentleman of Northampton-shire, Warwickshire, or the Midland, should fetch all his illustrations to his country neighbors from shipping, and tell them of the main sheet and the bowline. Metaphors are thus many times deformed, as in him that said, *Castratam morte Africani rempublicam.*[4] And another, *stercus curiæ Glauciam.*[5] And *Canâ nive conspuit Alpes.*[6] All attempts that are new in this kind are dangerous, and somewhat hard, before they be softened with use. A man coins not a new word without some peril and less fruit; for if it happens to be received, the praise is but moderate; if refused, the scorn is assured. Yet we must adventure; for things at first hard and rough are by use made tender and gentle. It is an honest error that is committed, following great chiefs.

Consuetudo. Custom is the most certain mistress of language, as the public stamp makes the current money. But we must not be too frequent with the mint, every day coining; nor fetch words

---

[1] The choice of words is the source of eloquence.

[2] A wise writer never coins a metaphor carelessly.

[3] inn.

[4] The State was gelded by the death of Africanus.

[5] Glaucia, the excrement of the Senate-house.

[6] [Jove] with white snow the Alps bespewed. These three metaphors are from Quintilian, *Inst. Orat.* viii.

from the extreme and utmost ages; since the chief virtue of a style is perspicuity [1] and nothing so vicious in it as to need an interpreter. Words borrowed of antiquity do lend a kind of majesty to style, and are not without their delight sometimes.

Authoritas. For they have the authority of years, and out of their intermission do win to themselves a kind of grace-like newness. But the eldest of the present, and newest of the past language, is the best. For what was the ancient language, which some men so dote upon, but the ancient custom? Yet when I name custom, I understand not the vulgar custom: for that were a precept no less dangerous to language than life, if we should speak or live after the manners of the vulgar. But that I call custom of speech, which is the consent of the learned; as custom of life, which is the consent of the good. Virgil was most loving of antiquity; yet how rarely doth he insert *aquai* and *pictai*!

Chaucerisms. Lucretius is scabrous and rough in these; he seeks them, as some do Chaucerisms with us, which were better expunged and banished. Some words are to be culled out for ornament and color, as we gather flowers to strew houses or make garlands; but they are better when they grow to our style, as in a meadow, where, though the mere grass and greenness delights, yet the variety of flowers doth heighten and beautify.

Paronomasia. Marry, we must not play or riot too much with them, as in paronomasias, nor use too swelling or ill-sounding words: *Quæ per salebras altaque saxa cadunt.*[2] It is true, there is no sound but shall find some lovers, as the bitterest confections are grateful to some palates. Our composition must be more accurate in the beginning and end than in the midst, and in the end more than in the beginning; for through the midst the stream bears us. And this is attained by custom more than care or diligence. We must express readily and fully, not profusely. There is [a] difference between a liberal and a prodigal hand. As it is a great point of art, when our matter requires it, to enlarge and veer out all sail, so to take it in and contract it is of no less praise when the argument doth ask it. Either of them hath their fitness in the place. A good man always profits by his endeavor, by his help; yea, when he is absent; nay, when he is dead, by his example and memory.

De stilo. So good authors in their style. A strict and succinct style is that where you can take away nothing without loss, and

[1] clarity.
[2] Cf. above, p. 125.

that loss to be manifest. The brief style is that which expresseth much in little. The concise style, which expresseth not enough, but leaves somewhat to be understood. The abrupt style, which hath many breaches, and doth not seem to end but fall. The congruent and harmonious fitting of parts in a sentence hath almost the fastening and force of knitting and connection, as in stones well squared, which will rise strong a great way without mortar.

Periodi. Periods are beautiful when they are not too long; for so they have their strength too, as in a pike or javelin. As we must take the care that our words and sense be clear, so if the obscurity happen through the hearers' or readers' want of understanding, I am not to answer for them, no more than for their not listening or marking; I must neither find them ears nor mind. But a man cannot put a word so in sense but some thing about it will illustrate it, if the writer understand himself. For order helps much to perspicuity, as confusion hurts: *Rectitudo lucem adfert; obliquitas et circumductio offuscat.* We should therefore speak what we can the nearest way, so as we keep our gait, not leap; for too short may as well be not let into the memory, as too long not kept in. Whatsoever loseth the grace and clearness converts into a riddle; the obscurity is marked, but not the value. That perisheth, and is passed by, like the pearl in the fable.

Obscuritas offundit tenebras.[1] Our style should be like a skein of silk, to be carried and found by the right thread, not ravelled and perplexed; then all is a knot, a heap. There are words that do as much raise a style as others can depress it.

Superlatio. Superlation and overmuchness amplifies. It may be above faith, but never above a mean. It was ridiculous in Cestius, when he said of Alexander:

Fremit Oceanus, quasi indignetur, quod terras relinquas;[2]

But propitiously from Virgil:

Credas innare revulsas
Cycladas.[3]

He doth not say it was so, but seemed to be so. Although it be somewhat incredible, that is excused before it be spoken. But there are hyperboles which will become one language, that will by no

[1] Obscurity [of phrase] spreads darkness [of meaning].
[2] Oceanus shuddered as if he were indignant that lands should be left.
[3] You would have thought that the Cyclades, uprooted, were swimming.

means admit another. As *Eos esse* P[opuli] R[omani] *exercitus, qui cœlum possint perrumpere:* [1] who would say this with us, but a mad man? Therefore we must consider in every tongue what is used, what received. Quintilian warns us that in no kind of translation, or metaphor, or allegory, we make a turn from what we began: as, if we fetch the original of our metaphor from sea and billows, we end not in flames and ashes: it is a most foul inconsequence. Neither must we draw out our allegory too long, lest either we make ourselves obscure, or fall into affectation, which is childish. But why do men depart at all from the right and natural ways of speaking? Sometimes for necessity, when we are driven, or think it fitter, to speak that in obscure words, or by circumstance, which uttered plainly would offend the hearers; or to avoid obsceneness, or sometimes for pleasure and variety, as travellers turn out of the highway, drawn either by the commodity of a footpath, or the delicacy or freshness of the fields. And all this is called ἐσχηματισμένη, or figured language.

Oratio imago animi. Language most shows a man; speak, that I may see thee. It springs out of the most retired and inmost parts of us, and is the image of the parent of it, the mind. No glass renders a man's form or likeness so true as his speech.

Structura et statura. Nay, it is likened to a man; and as we consider feature and composition in a man, so words in language, in the greatness, aptness, sound, structure, and harmony of it. Some men are tall and big, so some language is high and great. Then the words are chosen, their sound ample, the composition full, the absolution plenteous, and powered out, all grave, sinewy, and strong. Some are little and dwarfs; so of speech, it is humble and low, the words poor and flat, the members and periods thin and weak, without knitting or number.

Mediocris plana et placida. The middle are of a just stature. There the language is plain and pleasing: even without stopping; round without swelling; all well-turned, composed, elegant, and accurate.

Tumens. Enormis. Affectata. Abjecta. The vicious language is vast and gaping, swelling and irregular; when it contends to be high, full of rock, mountain, and pointedness; as it affects to be low, it is abject, and creeps, full of bogs and holes. And according to their subject these styles vary, and lose their names; for that which is

---

[1] They are the kind of Roman army that can smash the heavens.

high and lofty, declaring excellent matter, becomes vast and tumorous, speaking of petty and inferior things; so that which was even and apt in a mean and plain subject, will appear most poor and humble in a high argument. Would you not laugh to meet a great counsellor of state in a flat cap, with his trunk hose, and a hobby-horse cloak, his gloves under his girdle, and yond haberdasher in a velvet gown, furred with sables? There is a certain latitude in these things, by which we find the degrees.

* * * *

Notæ Domini St. Albani de doctrin: intemper. It was well noted by the late L[ord] St. Albans, that the study of words is the first distemper of learning; vain matter, the second; and a third distemper is deceit, or the likeness of truth; imposture held up by credulity. All these are the cobwebs of learning, and to let them grow in us is either sluttish or foolish.

Dictator. Nothing is more ridiculous than to make an author a dictator, as the schools have done Aristotle. The damage is infinite [which] knowledge receives by it. For to many things a man should owe but a temporary belief, and a suspension of his own judgment, not an absolute resignation of himself, or a perpetual captivity. Let Aristotle and others have their dues; but if we can make farther discoveries of truth and fitness than they, why are we envied? Let us beware, while we strive to add, we do not diminish or deface; we may improve, but not augment. By discrediting falsehood, truth grows in request. We must not go about like men anguished and perplexed for vicious affectation of praise, but calmly study the separation of opinions, find the errors [which] have intervened, awake antiquity, call former times into question; but make no parties with the present, nor follow any fierce undertakers, mingle no matter of doubtful credit with the simplicity of truth, but gently stir the mould about the root of the question, and avoid all digladiations,[1] facility of credit, or superstitious simplicity; seek the consonancy and concatenation of truth; stoop only to point of necessity, and what leads to convenience. Then make exact animadversion where style hath degenerated, where flourished and thrived in choiceness of phrase, round and clean composition of sentence, sweet falling of the clause, varying an illustration by tropes and figures, weight of matter, worth of subject, soundness of argument,

[1] wrangling, disputing.

life of invention, and depth of judgment. This is *monte potiri,* to get the hill; for no perfect discovery can be made upon a flat or a level.

De optimo scriptore. Now that I have informed you in the knowing these things, let me lead you by the hand a little farther, in the direction of the use, and make you an able writer by practice. The conceits of the mind are pictures of things, and the tongue is the interpreter of those pictures. The order of God's creatures in themselves is not only admirable and glorious, but eloquent; then he who could apprehend the consequence of things in their truth, and utter his apprehensions as truly, were the best writer or speaker. Therefore Cicero said much, when he said, *Dicere rectè nemo potest, nisi qui prudenter intelligit.*[1] The shame of speaking unskilfully were small if the tongue only thereby were disgraced; but as the image of a king in his seal ill-represented is not so much a blemish to the wax, or the signet that sealed it, as to the prince it representeth, so disordered speech is not so much injury to the lips that give it forth, as to the disproportion and incoherence of things in themselves, so negligently expressed. Neither can his mind be thought to be in tune, whose words do jar; nor his reason in frame, whose sentence is preposterous; nor his elocution clear and perfect, whose utterance breaks itself into fragments and uncertainties. Were it not a dishonor to a mighty prince, to have the majesty of his embassage spoiled by a careless ambassador? and is it not as great an indignity that an excellent conceit and capacity, by the indiligence of an idle tongue,.should be disgraced? Negligent speech doth not only discredit the person of the speaker, but it discrediteth the opinion of his reason and judgment; it discrediteth the force and uniformity of the matter and substance. If it be so then in words, which fly and escape censure, and where one good phrase begs pardon for many incongruities and faults, how shall he then be thought wise whose penning is thin and shallow? How shall you look for wit from him whose leisure and head, assisted with the examination of his eyes, yield you no life or sharpness in his writing?

De stilo epistolari. Inventio. In writing there is to be regarded the invention and the fashion. For the invention, that ariseth upon your business; whereof there can be no rules of more certainty, or precepts of better direction given, than conjecture can lay down from the several occasions of men's particular lives and vocations. But sometimes men make baseness of kindness: as, *I could not satisfy*

[1] No one can speak correctly, unless he understands intelligently.

myself till I had discharged my remembrance, and charged my let-
ters with commendations to you; or, *My business is no other than to*
testify my love to you, and to put you in mind of my willingness to
do you all kind offices; or, *Sir, have you leisure to descend to the*
remembering of that assurance you have long possessed in your
servant, and upon your next opportunity make him happy with some
commands from you? Or the like; that go a-begging for some meaning, and labor to be delivered of the great burden of nothing. When
you have invented, and that your business be matter, and not bare
form or mere ceremony, but some earnest, then are you to proceed
to the ordering of it, and digesting the parts, which is had out of
two circumstances. One is the understanding of the persons to whom
you are to write; the other is the coherence of your sentence; for
men's capacity to weigh what will be apprehended with greatest
attention or leisure, what next regarded and longed for especially,
and what last will leave satisfaction, and, as it were, the sweetest
memorial and belief of all that is past in his understanding whom
you write to. For the consequence of sentences, you must be sure
that every clause do give the cue one to the other, and be bespoken
ere it come. So much for invention and order.

Modus. 1. Brevitas. Now for fashion: it consists in four things,
which are qualities of your style. The first is *brevity:* for they must
not be treatises or discourses (your letters) except it be to learned
men. And even among them there is a kind of thrift and saving
of words. Therefore you are to examine the clearest passages of your
understanding, and through them to convey the sweetest and most
significant words you can devise, that you may the easier teach them
the readiest way to another man's apprehension, and open their
meaning fully, roundly, and distinctly, so as the reader may not
think a second view cast away upon your letter. And though respect be a part following this, yet now here, and still I must remember it, if you write to a man, whose estate and cense,[1] as senses,
you are familiar with, you may the bolder (to set a task to his
brain) venture on a knot. But if to your superior, you are bound
to measure him in three farther points: first, your interest in him;
secondly, his capacity in your letters; thirdly, his leisure to peruse
them. For your interest or favor with him, you are to be the shorter
or longer, more familiar or submiss[iv]e, as he will afford you time.
For his capacity you are to be quicker and fuller of those reaches
and glances of wit or learning, as he is able to entertain them. For

[1] position, rank.

his leisure, you are commanded to the greater briefness, as his place is of greater discharges and cares. But with your betters, you are not to put riddles of wit, by being too scarce of words; not to cause the trouble of making *breviates* by writing too riotous and wastingly. Brevity is attained in matter by avoiding idle compliments, prefaces, protestations, parentheses, superfluous circuit of figures and digressions; also in the composition, by omitting conjunctions—*not only, but also; both the one and the other; whereby it cometh to pass*—and suchlike idle particles, that have no great business in a serious letter but breaking of sentences, as often times a short journey is made long by unnecessary baits.

But as Quintilian saith, there is a briefness of the parts sometimes that makes the whole long; as, "I came to the stairs, I took a pair of oars, they launched out, rowed a pace, I landed at the Courtgate, I paid my fare, went up to the Presence, asked for my Lord, I was admitted." All this is but, "I went to the Court, and spake with my Lord." This is the fault of some Latin writers, within these last hundred years, of my reading, and perhaps Seneca may be appeached of it; I accuse him not.

2. *Perspicuitas.* The next property of espistolary style is perspicuity, and is often times [lost] by affectation of some wit ill angled for, or ostentation of some hidden terms of art. Few words they darken speech, and so do too many; as well too much light hurteth the eyes as too little; and a long Bill of Chancery confounds the understanding as much as the shortest note. Therefore, let not your letters be penned like English statutes, and this is obtained. These vices are eschewed by pondering your business well and distinctly concerning yourself, which is much furthered by uttering your thoughts, and letting them as well come forth to the light and judgment of your own outward senses as to the censure of other men's ears; for that is the reason why many good scholars speak but fumblingly; like a rich man, that for want of particular note and difference can bring you no certain ware readily out of his shop. Hence it is that talkative, shallow men do often content the hearers more than the wise. But this may find a speedier redress in writing, where all comes under the last examination of the eyes. First mind it well, then pen it, then examine it, then amend it, and you may be in the better hope of doing reasonably well. Under this virtue may come plainness, which is not to be curious in the order, as to answer a letter as if you were to answer to interrogatories: as to the first, first; and to the second, secondly, &c. But both in method

to use (as ladies do in their attire) a diligent kind of negligence, and their sportive freedom; though with some men you are not to jest, or practice tricks; yet the delivery of the most important things may be carried with such a grace, as that it may yield a pleasure to the conceit of the reader. There must be store, though no excess of terms; as, if you are to name *store*, sometimes you may call it choice, sometimes plenty, sometimes copiousness, or variety; but ever so, that the word which comes in lieu have not such difference of meaning as that it may put the sense of the first in hazard to be mistaken. You are not to cast a ring for the perfumed terms of the time, as *accommodation, compliment, spirit, &c.* But use them properly in their place, as others.

3. *Vigor.* There followeth life and quickness, which is the strength and sinews, as it were, of your penning by pretty sayings, similitudes, and conceits, allusions, some known history, or other commonplace, such as are in the *Courtier* and the second book of Cicero's *De Oratore*.

4. *Discretio.* The last is, respect to discern what fits yourself, him to whom you write, and that which you handle, which is a quality fit to conclude the rest, because it doth include all. And that must proceed from ripeness of judgment, which, as one truly saith, is gotten by four means: God, Nature, Diligence, and Conversation. Serve the first well, and the rest will serve you.

*   *   *   *

WHAT IS A POET?

Poeta. A poet is that which by the Greeks is called κατ᾽ ἐξοχήν, ὁ Ποιητής,[1] a maker, or a feigner; his art, an art of imitation or feigning, expressing the life of man in fit measure, numbers, and harmony, according to Aristotle; from the word ποιεῖν, which signifies to make or feign. Hence he is called a *poet*, not he which writeth in measure only, but that feigneth and formeth a fable, and writes things like the truth. For the fable and fiction is, as it were, the form and soul of any poetical work, or poem.

WHAT MEAN YOU BY A POEM?

Poema. A poem is not alone any work or composition of the poet's in many or few verses; but even one alone verse sometimes

---

[1] Par excellence, the poet.

makes a perfect poem. As when Æneas hangs up and consecrates the arms of Abas with this inscription:

> *Æneas hæc de Danais victoribus arma,*[1]

and calls it a poem, or *carmen.* Such are those in Martial:

> *Omnia, Castor, emis: sic fiet, ut omnia vendas,*[2]

and:

> *Pauper videri Cinna vult, & est pauper.*[3]

So were Horace's *Odes* called *Carmina,* his lyric songs. And Lucretius designs a whole book in his sixth:

> *Quod in primo quoque carmine claret.*[4]

Epicum, Dramaticum, Liricum, Elegiacum, Epigramat. Poesis. And anciently all the oracles were called *carmina;* or whatever sentence was expressed, were it much or little, it was called an epic, dramatic, lyric, elegiac, or epigrammatic poem.

But How Differs a Poem from What We Call Poesy?

A poem, as I have told you, is the work of the poet, the end and fruit of his labor and study. Poesy is his skill or craft of making; the very fiction itself, the reason or form of the work. And these three voices differ, as the thing done, the doing, and the doer; the thing feigned, the feigning, and the feigner: so the poem, the poesy, and the poet.

Artium regina. Now the poesy is the habit or the art; nay, rather the queen of arts, which had her original from heaven, received thence from the Hebrews, and had in prime estimation with the Greeks, transmitted to the Latins and all nations that professed civility. The study of it, if we will trust Aristotle, offers to mankind a certain rule and pattern of living well and happily, disposing us to all civil offices of society. If we will believe Tully, it nourisheth and instructeth our youth, delights our age, adorns our prosperity, comforts our adversity, entertains us at home, keeps us company abroad, travels with us, watches, divides the times of our

---

[1] These arms Æneas [won] from the victorious Greeks.
[2] You buy all things, Castor; so it will come to pass that you will have to sell all things.
[3] Cinna wishes to seem poor, and he is poor.
[4] Let what was clear in the beginning be so also in my song.

earnest [1] and sports, shares in our country recesses and recreations; insomuch as the wisest and best learned have thought her the absolute mistress of manners and nearest of kin to virtue. And whereas they entitle philosophy to be a rigid and austere poesy, they have, on the contrary, styled poesy a dulcet and gentle philosophy, which leads on and guides us by the hand to action with a ravishing delight and incredible sweetness.

Poet: differentiæ. But before we handle the kinds of poems, with their special differences, or make court to the art itself as a mistress, I would lead you to the knowledge of our poet by a perfect information, what he is or should be by nature, by exercise, by imitation, by study, and so bring him down through the disciplines of grammar, logic, rhetoric, and the ethics, adding somewhat out of all, peculiar to himself, and worthy of your admittance or reception.

1. Ingenium. First, we require in our poet or maker (for that title our language affords him elegantly with the Greek) a goodness of natural wit. For whereas all other arts consist of doctrine and precepts, the poet must be able by nature and instinct to pour out the treasure of his mind, and as Seneca saith, *Aliquando secundum Anacreontem insanire jucundum esse;* [2] by which he understands the poetical rapture. And according to that of Plato, *Frustrà poeticas fores sui compos pulsavit:* [3] and of Aristotle, *Nullum magnum ingenium sine mixturâ dementiæ fuit. Nec potest grande aliquid & supra cæteros loqui, nisi mota mens.* [4] Then it riseth higher, as by a divine instinct, when it contemns common and known conceptions. It utters somewhat above a mortal mouth. Then it gets aloft and flies away with his rider, whither before it was doubtful to ascend. This the poets understood by their Helicon, Pegasus, or Parnassus; and this made Ovid to boast:

> *Est Deus in nobis, agitante calescimus illo:*
> *Sedibus æthereis spiritus ille venit.* [5]

And Lipsius to affirm, *Scio poetam neminem præstantem fuisse, sine parte quadam uberiore divinæ auræ.* [6] And hence it is that the com-

---

[1] labors.

[2] Sometimes it is delightful to rave, like a second Anacreon.

[3] One who is master of himself beats in vain against the doors of poetry.

[4] There was never any great genius without an admixture of madness. Nor can there be anything sublime, to be mentioned above other things, unless the mind be excited.

[5] There is a god within us, and we glow when he stirs us; from the seats of the upper air this spirit comes.

[6] I know that no poet has been illustrious who has not in him an abundant portion of the divine breath.

ing up of good poets (for I mind not *mediocres* or *imos* [1]) is so thin
and rare among us. Every beggarly corporation affords the state a
mayor or two bailiffs yearly; but *solus rex aut poeta non quotannis
nascitur.* [2]

2. *Exercitatio.* To this perfection of nature in our poet we require exercise of those parts, and frequent. If his wit will not arrive
suddenly at the dignity of the ancients, let him not yet fall out with
it, quarrel, or be over hastily angry, offer to turn it away from study
in a humor; but come to it again upon better cogitation, try another
time with labor. If then it succeed not, cast not away the quills yet,
nor scratch the wainscot, beat not the poor desk, but bring all to the
forge and file again; turn it anew. There is no statute law of the
kingdom bids you be a poet against your will or the first quarter. If
it comes in a year or two, it is well. The common rimers pour forth
verses, such as they are, extempore; but there never comes from them
one sense worth the life of a day. A rimer and a poet are two things. It
is said of the incomparable Virgil that he brought forth his verses
like a bear, and after formed them with licking. Scaliger the father
writes it of him, that he made a quantity of verses in the morning,
which afore night he reduced to a less number. But that which
Valerius Maximus hath left recorded of Euripides, the tragic poet,
his answer to Alcestis, another poet, is as memorable as modest:
who when it was told to Alcestis that Euripides had in three days
brought forth but three verses, and those with some difficulty and
throes, Alcestis glorying [3] he could with ease have sent forth a hundred in the space, Euripides roundly replied: Like enough, but here
is the difference: thy verses will not last those three days, mine will
to all time. Which was as to tell him he could not write a verse. I
have met many of these rattles that made a noise and buzzed. They
had their hum, and no more. Indeed, things wrote with labor deserve to be so read, and will last their age.

3. *Imitatio.* The third requisite in our poet or maker is imitation, to be able to convert the substance or riches of another poet
to his own use. To make choice of one excellent man above the rest,
and so to follow him till he grow very *he,* or so like him as the copy
may be mistaken for the principal. Not as a creature that swallows
what it takes in, crude, raw, or indigested, but that feeds with an
appetite, and hath a stomach to concoct, divide, and turn all into

---

[1] ordinary or inferior.
[2] It is only the king or poet who is not born every year.
[3] boasting.

nourishment. Not to imitate servilely, as Horace saith, and catch at vices for virtue, but to draw forth out of the best and choicest flowers, with the bee, and turn all into honey, work it into one relish and savor; make our imitation sweet; observe how the best writers have imitated, and follow them: how Virgil and Statius have imitated Homer; how Horace, Archilochus, how Alcæus and the other lyric[ist]s; and so of the rest.

4. Lectio. But that which we especially require in him is an exactness of study and multiplicity of reading, which maketh a full man, not alone enabling him to know the history or argument of a poem, and to report it, but so to master the matter and style, as to show he knows how to handle, place, or dispose of either with elegance when need shall be; and not think he can leap forth suddenly a poet by dreaming he hath been in Parnassus, or having washed his lips, as they say, in Helicon. There goes more to his making than so; for to nature, exercise, imitation, and study, art must be added to make all these perfect.

Ars coron. And though these challenge to themselves much in the making up of our maker, it is art only [which] can lead him to perfection, and leave him there in possession, as planted by her hand. It is the assertion of Tully, if to an excellent nature there happen an accession or confirmation of learning and discipline, there will then remain somewhat noble and singular. For, as Simylus saith in *Stobæus,* Οὔτε φύσις ἱκανὴ γίνεται τέχνης ἄτερ, οὔτε πᾶν τέχνη μὴ φύσιν κεκτημένη,[1] without art, nature can never be perfect, & without nature art can claim no being. But our poet must beware that his study be not only to learn of himself; for he that shall affect to do that confesseth his ever having a fool to his master. He must read many, but ever the best and choicest; those that can teach him anything he must ever account his masters, and reverence; among whom Horace and he that taught him, Aristotle, deserved to be the first in estimation. Aristotle was the first accurate critic and truest judge, nay, the greatest philosopher, the world ever had; for he noted the vices of all knowledges in all creatures, and out of many men's perfections in a science he formed still one art. So he taught us two offices together: how we ought to judge rightly of others, and what we ought to imitate specially in ourselves; but all this in vain without a natural wit and a poetical nature in chief. For

---

[1] Neither nature without art, nor again art unassociated with nature is sufficient to anyone for any accomplishment. The reader will note that Jonson usually paraphrases the Latin or Greek that he quotes.

no man, so soon as he knows this or reads it, shall be able to write the better; but as he is adapted to it by nature, he shall grow the perfecter writer. He must have civil prudence and eloquence, & that whole, not taken up by snatches or pieces, in sentences or remnants, when he will handle business or carry counsels, as if he came then out of the declaimers' gallery, or shadow, but furnished out of the body of the state, which commonly is the school of men.

Virorum schola Respub. The poet is the nearest borderer upon the orator, and expresseth all his virtues, though he be tied more to numbers, is his equal in ornament, and above him in his strengths. And of the kind the comic comes nearest; because in moving the minds of men, and stirring of affections, in which oratory shows, and especially approves her eminence, he chiefly excels. What figure of a body was Lysippus ever able to form with his graver, or Apelles to paint with his pencil, as the comedy to life expresseth so many and various affections of the mind? There shall the spectator see some insulting [1] with joy, others fretting with melancholy, raging with anger, mad with love, boiling with avarice, undone with riot, tortured with expectation, consumed with fear; no perturbation in common life but the orator finds an example of it in the scene.

*   *   *   *

I am not of that opinion to conclude a poet's liberty within the narrow limits of laws which either the grammarians or philosophers prescribe. For before they found out those laws there were many excellent poets that fulfilled them, amongst whom none more perfect than Sophocles, who lived a little before Aristotle.

Which of the Greeklings durst ever give precepts to Demosthenes? or to Pericles, whom the age surnamed *heavenly,* because he seemed to thunder and lighten with his language? or to Alcibiades, who had rather nature for his guide than art for his master?

But whatsoever nature at any time dictated to the most happy, or long exercise to the most laborious, that the wisdom and learning of Aristotle hath brought into an art, because he understood the causes of things; and what other men did by chance or custom he doth by reason; and not only found out the way not to err, but the short way we should take not to err.

Many things in Euripides hath Aristophanes wittily reprehended, not out of art, but out of truth. For Euripides is sometimes peccant,

[1] jumping.

as he is most times perfect. But judgment when it is greatest, if reason doth not accompany it, is not ever absolute.

To judge of poets is only the faculty of poets; and not of all poets, but the best. *Nemo infæliciùs de poetis judicavit, quàm qui de poetis scripsit.*[1] But some will say, Critics are a kind of tinkers, that make more faults than they mend ordinarily. See their diseases and those of grammarians. It is true, many bodies are the worse for the meddling with; and the multitude of physicians hath destroyed many sound patients with their wrong practice. But the office of a true critic or censor is not to throw by a letter anywhere, or damn an innocent syllable, but lay the words together, and amend them; judge sincerely of the author and his matter, which is the sign of solid and perfect learning in a man. Such was Horace, an author of much civility, and, if any one among the heathen can be, the best master both of virtue and wisdom; an excellent and true judge upon cause and reason, not because he thought so, but because he knew so, out of use and experience.

*   *   *   *

The parts of a Comedy and Tragedy. The parts of a comedy are the same with a tragedy, and the end [2] is partly the same: for they both delight and teach; and the comics are called διδάσκαλοι [3] of the Greeks no less than the tragics.

Nor is the moving of laughter always the end of comedy; that is rather a fowling for the people's delight, or their fooling. For, as Aristotle says rightly, the moving of laughter is a fault in comedy, a kind of turpitude that depraves some part of man's nature without a disease; as a wry face without pain moves laughter, or a deformed vizard, or a rude clown dressed in a lady's habit and using her actions; we dislike and scorn such representations, which made the ancient philosophers ever think laughter unfitting in a wise man. And this induced Plato to esteem of Homer as a sacrilegious person, because he presented the gods sometimes laughing. As also it is divinely said of Aristotle, that to seem ridiculous is a part of dishonesty, and foolish.

So that what either in the words or sense of an author, or in the language or actions of men, is awry or depraved doth strangely

---

[1] Nobody judged of poets more unhappily than he who wrote about poets.
[2] aim.
[3] teachers.

stir mean affections, and provoke for the most part to laughter.

The wit of the old Comedy. And therefore it was clear that all insolent and obscene speeches, jest[s] upon the best men, injuries to particular persons, perverse and sinister sayings, and the rather unexpected, in the old comedy did move laughter, especially where it did imitate any dishonesty; and scurrility came forth in the place of wit; which, who[ever] understands the nature and genius of laughter cannot but perfectly know.

Of which Aristophanes affords an ample harvest, having not only outgone Plautus or any other in that kind, but expressed all the moods and figures of what is ridiculous oddly. In short, as vinegar is not accounted good until the wine be corrupted, so jests that are true and natural seldom raise laughter with the beast, the multitude. They love nothing that is right and proper. The farther it runs from reason or possibility with them the better it is.

What could have made them laugh, like to see Socrates presented, that example of all good life, honesty, and virtue, to have him hoisted up with a pulley, and there play the philosopher in a basket: measure how many feet a flea could skip geometrically, by a just scale, and edify the people from the engine!

Theatrical wit. This was theatrical wit, right stage-jesting, and relishing a playhouse, invented for scorn and laughter; whereas, if it had savored of equity, truth, perspicuity, and candor, to have tasten a wise or a learned palate, spit it out presently! this is bitter and profitable, this instructs, and would inform us; what need we know anything, that are nobly born, more than a horse-race or a hunting-match, our day to break with citizens, and such innate mysteries?

The Cart. This is truly leaping from the stage to the tumbrel again, reducing all wit to the original dung-cart.

Of the Magnitude and Compass of any Fable, Epic or Dramatic

What the measure of a Fable is. The Fable or Plot of a Poem defined. To the resolving of this question we must first agree in the definition of the fable. The fable is called the imitation of one entire and perfect action, whose parts are so joined and knit together, as nothing in the structure can be changed or taken away without impairing or troubling the whole, of which there is a proportionable magnitude in the members. As, for example, if a man would build a house, he would first appoint a place to build it in, which he would define within certain bounds; so in the constitution of a poem, the action is aimed at by the poet, which answers place in a building, and that action hath his [1] largeness, compass, and proportion.

The epic fable differing from the dramatic. But as a court, or king's palace, requires other dimensions than a private house, so the epic asks a magnitude from other poems, since what is place in the one is action in the other; the difference is in space. So that by this definition we conclude the fable to be the *imitation* of one perfect and entire action, as one perfect and entire place is required to a building. By perfect, we understand that to which nothing is wanting, as place to the building that is raised, and action to the fable that is formed. It is perfect, perhaps not for a court or king's palace, which requires a greater ground, but for the structure we would raise; so the space of the action may not prove large enough for the epic fable, yet be perfect for the dramatic, and whole.

What we understand by Whole. Whole we call that, and perfect, which hath a *beginning*, a *midst*, and an *end*. So the place of any building may be whole and entire for that work, though too little for a palace. As to a tragedy or a comedy, the action may be convenient and perfect that would not fit an epic poem in magnitude; so a lion is a perfect creature in himself, though it be less than that of a buffalo or a rhinoceros. They differ but in specie; either in the kind is absolute. Both have their parts, and either the whole. Therefore, as in every body, so in every action, which is the subject of a just work, there is required a certain proportionable greatness, neither too vast nor too minute. For that which happens to the eyes when we behold a body, the same happens to the memory when we contemplate an action. I look upon a monstrous giant, as Tityus, whose body covered nine acres of land, and mine eye sticks upon every part; the whole that consists of those parts will never be taken in at one entire view. So in a fable, if the action be too great, we can never comprehend the whole together in our imagination. Again, if it be too little, there ariseth no pleasure out of the object; it affords the view no stay; it is beheld, and vanisheth at once. As if we should look upon an ant or pismire, the parts fly the sight, and the whole considered is almost nothing. The same happens in action, which is the object of memory, as the body is of sight. Too vast oppresseth the eyes, and exceeds the memory; too little scarce admits either.

What the utmost bound of a fable [is]. Now, in every action it behooves the poet to know which is his utmost bound, how far with

[1] its.

fitness and a necessary proportion he may produce and determine it; that is, till either good fortune change into the worse, or the worse into the better. For as a body without proportion cannot be goodly, no more can the action, either in comedy or tragedy, without his fit bounds. And every bound, for the nature of the subject, is esteemed the best that is the largest, till it can increase no more; so it behooves the action in tragedy or comedy to be let grow till the necessity ask a conclusion; wherein two things are to be considered: first, that it exceed not the compass of one day; next, that there be place left for digression and art. For the episodes and digressions in a fable are the same that household stuff and other furniture are in a house. And so far for the measure and extent of a fable dramatic.

What [is meant] by one, and entire. Now, that it should be one and entire. One is considerable two ways: either as it is only separate, and by itself, or as being composed of many parts, it begins to be one as those parts grow or are wrought together. That it should be one the first way alone, and by itself, no man that hath tasted letters ever would say, especially having required before a just magnitude and equal proportion of the parts in themselves. Neither of which can possibly be, if the action be single and separate, not composed of parts, which laid together in themselves, with an equal and fitting proportion, tend to the same end; which thing out of antiquity itself hath deceived many, and more this day it doth deceive.

So many there be of old that have thought the action of one man to be one: as of Hercules, Theseus, Achilles, Ulysses, and other heroes; which is both foolish and false, since by one and the same person many things may be severally done which cannot fitly be referred or joined to the same end: which not only the excellent tragic poets, but the best masters of the epic, Homer and Virgil, saw. For though the argument of an epic poem be far more diffused & poured out than that of tragedy, yet Virgil, writing of Æneas, hath pretermitted many things. He neither tells how he was born, how brought up, how he fought with Achilles, how he was snatched out of the battle by Venus; but that one thing, how he came into Italy, he prosecutes in twelve books. The rest of his journey, his error by sea, the sack of Troy, are put not as the argument of the work, but episodes of the argument. So Homer laid by many things of Ulysses, and handled no more than he saw tended to one and the same end.

Contrary to which, and foolishly, those poets did, whom the philosopher taxeth: of whom one gathered all the actions of Theseus, another put all the labors of Hercules in one work. So did he whom

Juvenal mentions in the beginning, "hoarse Codrus," that recited a volume compiled, which he called his *Theseide*, not yet finished, to the great trouble both of his hearers and himself; amongst which there were many parts [which] had no coherence nor kindred one with [an]other, so far were they from being one action, one fable. For as a house, consisting of diverse materials, becomes one structure and one dwelling, so an action, composed of diverse parts, may become one fable, epic or dramatic. For example, in a tragedy, look upon Sophocles's *Ajax*: Ajax, deprived of Achilles's armor, which he hoped from the suffrage of the Greeks, disdains, and growing impatient of the injury, rageth and turns mad. In that humor he doth many senseless things, and at last falls upon the Grecian flock, and kills a great ram for Ulysses; returning to his sense, he grows ashamed of the scorn, and kills himself; and is by the chiefs of the Greeks forbidden burial. These things agree and hang together, not as they were done, but as seeming to be done, which made the action whole, entire, and absolute.

The conclusion concerning the Whole and the Parts. For the whole, as it consisteth of parts, so without all the parts it is not the whole; and to make it absolute is required not only the parts, but such parts as are true. For a part of the whole was true, which, if you take away, you either change the whole or it is not the whole.

Which are Episodes. For if it be such a part, as, being present or absent, nothing concerns the whole, it cannot be called a part of the whole; and such are the *episodes*, of which hereafter. For the present, here is one example: the single combat of Ajax with Hector, as it is at large described in Homer, nothing belongs to this Ajax of Sophocles.

*   *   *   *

Corneille

Pierre CORNEILLE (1606–1684) was born at Rouen and graduated from the Jesuit College of his native town with high honors; after studying law, he was admitted to the Bar in 1624, and in 1629 began his career as a dramatist. Comedies, melodramas, and tragedies succeeded each other; *Le Cid* appeared in 1636, *Horace* in 1640, *Cinna*, the same year, and *Le Mort de Pompée* in 1643, in the same year as *Polyeucte*, sometimes regarded as his greatest work, and *Le Menteur*, his finest comedy. Many other plays followed, including *Rodogune* (1644), *Theodora* (1645), and *Heraclius* (1647). Besides his plays he wrote poetry, and made a translation of the *Imitation of Christ* (1653–1656). His criticism is found chiefly in three Discourses: "Sur le Poème Dramatique," "Sur la Tragédie," and "Sur les Trois Unités," as well as in his analyses of his plays. In 1647 he was made a member of the Académie Française, of which he was the dean when he died.

Corneille is generally regarded as a neo-classic critic—that is, one who follows the rules laid down by Horace and his successors. This appraisement is not quite true, because often, like his contemporary Boileau, Corneille displays independent judgment, based upon his scrutiny of original sources.

In the extract below, from an essay that Dryden knew well (as the reader will see shortly), Corneille does not accept blindly the law of the three unities, first expounded by the Italian Castelvetro (1570) in his commentary on Aristotle. Corneille knew that Aristotle insisted only upon unity of action; that Aristotle saw that in some plays there was unity of time; but that nowhere did he mention unity of place.

From DISCOURSE ON THE THREE UNITIES [1]
(1660)

The two preceding Discourses [on *The Dramatic Poem* and on *Tragedy*] and the discussion of the plays contained in my first two volumes have furnished me so many opportunities to explain my thoughts about these matters that there would remain little for me to say, if I refused to repeat myself.

I hold, and I have already said so, that the unity of action in comedy consists of the unity of plot or of obstacle to the plans of the protagonists, and in tragedy of the unity of peril, whether the hero succumbs to it or escapes from it. Not that I maintain one cannot admit several perils in the one, and several obstacles in the other, provided that one falls necessarily from the one into the other; for then the escape from the first peril leaves the action incomplete, since it brings on a second; and the surmounting of one obstacle does not leave the actors at rest since it faces them with a new one. My memory does not furnish me with any ancient examples of this multiplicity of perils so bound to each other as not to destroy the unity of action; but I have noted the independent duplicity as a fault in *Horace* and in *Theodora*, where it is not at all necessary that the first kill his sister after his victory, nor that the second offer herself as a martyr after having escaped prostitution; and I am much mistaken if the death of Polyxena and that of Astyanax in Seneca's *Trojan Women* are not examples of the same irregularity.

In the second place, this phrase, "unity of action," does not mean that tragedy should show only one action on the stage. Whatever the poet chooses for his subject should have a beginning, a middle, and an end; and these three parts not only are so many actions which bear on the principal one, but in addition each may contain several with the same subordination. There ought to be only one complete action, one which will leave the mind of the auditor calm; but this action can only become complete through the aid of several other imperfect ones, which serve as steps toward its completion, and hold the auditor in an agreeable suspense. This must be achieved at the end of each act to make the action continuous. It is not necessary that one know precisely what the actors are doing during the intervals between acts, nor even that they be active when they do not appear

---

[1] Translated for this volume by John Masson Smith. The French text on which this is based is that of Charles Joseph Marty-Laveaux.

upon the stage; but it is necessary that each act arouse an expectation concerning something which is to be developed in the following act.

* * * *

The linking of scenes which unites all the separate actions of each act . . . is an important ornament in a poem and helps greatly in forming a continuity of action by means of continuity of performance; but after all, it is an ornament and not a rule. The ancients did not always subject themselves to this, although most of their acts contained no more than two or three scenes; this made it much easier for them than for us who sometimes give them nine or ten scenes. I shall cite only two examples of the disregard they have shown for this practice; one is in Sophocles's *Ajax,* in which the monologue, before he kills himself, has no connection with the scene which goes before, nor with that which follows; the other is from the third act of the *Eunuchus* of Terence, where the scene in which Antiphon is alone has no connection with Chremes and Pythias, who leave the stage as he comes on. Scholars of our time, who have taken these writers as models in the tragedies which they have left us, have neglected this linking even more than they, and to prove it we have only to glance at the plays of Buchanan, of Grotius, and of Heinsius,[1] of which I spoke in the analysis of *Polyeucte.* We have so accustomed our public to this that they cannot now see a detached scene without noting it as an artistic fault; the eye and the ear are shocked by it before the mind can have taken it in. The fourth act of *Cinna* is weaker than all the others, because of this shortcoming, and that which was formerly not a rule has become so now by dint of usage.

* * * *

Although the action of a dramatic poem should have its unity, we have to consider it as having two parts—the knot (*nœud*) and its untying (*dénouement*). According to Aristotle, the knot is composed, in part, of that which has happened off-stage before the beginning of the action and in part, of that which takes place on the

---

[1] George Buchanan (1506–1582), a Scotsman, wrote two Latin tragedies—one on Jephthah (1554), translated by Brinon, who divided it into seven acts, and one on St. John the Baptist; Grotius (Hugh de Groot) (1583–1645), a Dutchman, scholar and publicist, wrote three Latin tragedies on Biblical subjects: *Adam's Fall (Adamus Exsul),* on the Passion of Christ (*Christus Patiens*), and the third on the elevation of Joseph (*Sophompaneas*), the Savior of the world. Daniel Heinsius, philologist, was born at Ghent in 1580, and died at Leyden in 1665; he wrote *Herodes Infanticida,* criticized by Balzac, but much admired. (Marty-Laveaux).

stage; the rest belongs to the dénouement. The change from one fortune to another marks the separation of these two parts. All that precedes it belongs to the first: and this change, with what follows, to the second.[1] The "knot" depends entirely on the choice and the industrious imagination of the poet, and no rule can be given for it, save that he should arrange everything according to the probable or the necessary—of which matters I spoke in my second Discourse [concerning *Tragedy*]; to which I add a bit of advice: to be concerned as little as possible with things which happen before the action begins. The narration of these events usually annoys the auditors, because they do not expect it, and are bothered because they have to burden their memory with things which happened ten or twelve years before, in order to understand what they are looking at; but the telling of what happens off-stage after the action has begun, always produces a better effect, because it is awaited with some curiosity, and plays a part in the action which is presented. One of the reasons *Cinna* received so many distinguished votes of approval, giving it first place among my works, is that it has no narration of past events, so that Cinna's conspiracy with Émilie becomes rather an ornament which tickles the mind of the spectators than necessary exposition of details which they ought to know, and to impress on their memory in order to understand what follows. Émilie lets them know clearly enough, in the two first scenes, that he has been conspiring against Augustus in her favor; and even if Cinna should say no more to her than that the conspirators were ready for action the next day, he would be advancing the action just as much as he does by the hundred lines which he uses to tell her what he said to them, and how they took it. There are plots which begin with the birth of the hero—like that of *Heraclius;* but these great efforts of imagination demand an extraordinary amount of attention from the spectator, and often prevent his taking an unmixed pleasure in the early scenes, so much do they tire him.

In the dénouement I find two things to avoid: the simple change of will, and the machine. It is no great trick to end a poem, if he who has thwarted the plans of the protagonists for four acts ceases to do so in the fifth without being forced to do so by some notable event. I spoke of this in my first Discourse, and shall make no further comment here. The machine is no cleverer, when it serves only to make a god come down to arrange everything when the actors do not know how to end the play. This is what Apollo does in *Orestes:*

---

[1] Aristotle, *Poetics*, xviii, i. (Marty-Laveaux.)

this prince and his friend Pylades, accused by Tyndareus and Menelaus of the death of Clytemnestra, and condemned at their trial, seize Helen and Hermione; they kill, or think they have killed, the first, and threaten to kill the other, if the sentence pronounced against them is not revoked. To iron out these difficulties, Euripides does not look for cleverer means than to make Apollo descend from heaven; the god orders, with arbitrary authority, Orestes to marry Hermione, and Pylades, Electra; and fearing that the death of Helen might serve as a hindrance to this, it being unlikely that Hermione would marry Orestes, who had just killed her mother, he tells them that she is not dead, that he circumvented their blows and carried her off to the skies at the moment they thought they had killed her. This sort of machine is entirely inappropriate, having no basis in the rest of the play, and making a vicious solution. But I find a certain severity in the judgment of Aristotle, who puts into this class the chariot which Medea uses to escape from Corinth after the vengeance which she has taken on Creon. It seems to me that this has been amply prepared for, by making her a magician, and referring in the poem to many actions quite as supernatural as the one condemned. After what she did for Jason at Colchis, after she made Æson young again, after she fastened invisible fires to the gift which she made Creusa, this flying chariot is not beyond the bounds of probability; and the poem does not need to prepare us further for this extraordinary performance. Seneca warns us in this line, where Medea says to her nurse

Tuum quoque ipsa corpus hinc mecum aveham; [1]

and I, by that which she speaks to Ægeus:

Je vous suivrai demain par un chemin nouveau. [2]

And so the condemnation of Euripides, who made use of no precautions, may be fair, and should fall neither on Seneca nor on me; and I have no need to contradict Aristotle in order to defend myself on this head.

From the action I pass to the acts, each of which should contain a part of it, but not so equally divided that more is not saved for the last than for the others, and less given to the first than to the others. One may even do nothing more in this first act than portray

---

[1] I myself shall also take you away with me.
[2] I shall follow you tomorrow by a new road.

the manners of the characters, and show just where they are in the story which is to be told. Aristotle does not prescribe the number; Horace limits it to five; and though he forbids using fewer, the Spanish persist in stopping at three, and the Italians often do the same. The Greeks separated them by the singing of the chorus, and as I have reason to believe that in some of their poems they made the chorus sing more than four times, I should not undertake to say that they never raised the number beyond five. This method of separating them was more unsatisfactory than ours; for either one paid attention to what the chorus was singing, or one didn't; if attention was paid to it, the mind of the auditor was too tense and had no time for relaxation; if none was paid, his attention was so scattered by the length of the song that when another act began, he had to prod his memory to recall what he had already seen and at what point the action had stopped. Our use of violins has neither of these inconveniences. The spectator's mind relaxes while they play, and he even thinks about what he has seen, criticizing favorably or unfavorably, according as it has pleased or displeased him; and the short duration of the music leaves his memory so clear that when the actors return, he does not need to make an effort to bring back or renew his attention.

The number of scenes in each act is governed by no rule; but as each act should have a certain number of verses to make its length proportionate to the others, one may put in it more or fewer scenes, according as they are shorter or longer, in order to fill out the time allotted to it. One must if possible justify the entrance and the exit of each actor. Especially for the exit, I consider this rule indispensable; and there is nothing so unseemly as an actor who leaves the stage merely because he has no more verses to recite.

I should not be so exacting in regard to entrances. The audience is expecting the actor; and although the stage represents the chamber or room of the speaker, he cannot appear there unless he comes from behind the scenery; and it is not always easy to explain what he has been doing in town before returning home, since at times it is probable that he has not been out. I have never seen anyone shocked at seeing Émilie begin *Cinna* without saying why she has just entered her room: she is presumed to be there before the play begins, and it is only the necessity of staging that makes her come from the wings to get there.[1] And so, I should gladly free from this requirement all first scenes of each act, but not the others, because when an actor is

---

[1] No curtain was used in Corneille's time. (Translator's note.)

once on the stage, no one should enter who does not have a reason
to speak to him, or at least who has not a reason to seize the opportunity when it presents itself. Especially when an actor enters twice
in one act, whether in comedy or tragedy, he should without exception either give us reason to think he will soon be back, when he
goes out the first time, as Horace does in the second act, and Julie in
the third act of the same play,[1] or else explain on entering why he is
back so soon.

Aristotle states that the well-constructed tragedy should be beautiful and capable of pleasing without the help of actors and stage.
To make this pleasure easier for the reader, his mind must not be
hampered any more than the spectator's, because the effort he is
obliged to make, in order to understand and to picture the action
in his own mind, diminishes the satisfaction he should derive from
it. Therefore, I am of the opinion that the poet should take great
care to indicate in marginal notes the minute details which are not
important enough to be expressed in his verses, and which would
even take away some of their dignity, were he to stoop to include
them. Acting easily takes their place in the theatre, but in the book
one would fairly often be reduced to guesswork, and sometimes one
might even guess badly, unless furnished with these details in this
way. I confess that such is not the practice of the ancients, but I must
confess also that for lack of it, they leave us many obscure passages
in their poems which only masters of the art can clarify; and I am
not sure whether even they succeed in doing so every time they think
they have. If we should bind ourselves to follow their method to the
letter, we should have to omit all divisions into acts and scenes as did
the Greeks. This omission is frequently the cause of my not knowing
into how many acts their plays are divided, or whether at the end of
an act a player withdraws to let the chorus sing, because neither the
poets nor their annotators have deigned to give us a word of explanation in marginal notes.

We have still another special reason not to neglect, as they have
done, these small aids to understanding. The printing of our plays
puts them into the hands of provincial actors to whom we cannot
otherwise explain what they have to do. They would be guilty of
strange mistakes if we did not help them with these notes. They
would find themselves in great difficulty in the fifth acts of plays
which end happily, in which we bring all the actors on to the stage
at once; a thing which the ancients did not do. They would often say

[1] *Horace.*

to one what was meant for another, especially when the same actor has to speak to three or four persons, one after the other. When there is some order to be whispered to someone, as when Cleopatra whispers to Laonice to get her some poison,[1] an *aside* would be necessary to express it in verse, if one wished to do without marginal directions, and the former seems to me much more unsatisfactory than the latter, which gives us the true and only means of making the tragedy as beautiful when read as it is when acted (as Aristotle thinks it should be), by putting within easy reach of the reader's imagination all that the stage makes visible to the spectator.

The rule of the unity of time is based upon a statement of Aristotle: *The tragedy must confine the duration of its action within a revolution of the sun, or try not to exceed that limit very much.*[2] These words are the cause of the famous discussion as to whether they mean a natural day of twenty-four hours, or an artificial day of twelve: two opinions, each of which has eminent supporters. As for me, I find there are subjects so hard to confine within so short a time, that I should not only grant them the full twenty-four hours, but I should avail myself of the privilege, accorded by this critic, of exceeding them somewhat, and should even increase the number without scruple, to thirty. We have a maxim in law which says, *we must be lenient rather than severe* [in pronouncing sentence]: *odia restringenda, favores ampliandi;* and yet I find that an author is much hampered by this restriction which has forced some of our ancient writers to be guilty of absurdity. Euripides in *The Suppliants* has Theseus set out from Athens with an army, give battle before the walls of Thebes twelve or fifteen leagues distant, and come back victorious in the following act; and from the time of his departure to the arrival of the messenger who comes to tell of the victory, Æthra and the chorus have only thirty-six verses to recite. That is using such a short time to rather good advantage. Æschylus brings Agamemnon back from Troy with even greater speed. He had promised his wife Clytemnestra that as soon as the city was taken, he would signal the word to her from mountain to mountain by torches, the second of which should be lighted as soon as the first was seen, the third at sight of the second, and so on; and by this means she should have the great news the first night. However she had barely received the message of the lighted torches when Agamemnon arrived. His ship, though lashed by a tempest, if I remem-

---

[1] See *Rodogune*, act V, sc. iii. (Marty-Laveaux.)
[2] Aristotle, *Poetics*, v, 4. (Marty-Laveaux.)

ber correctly, must have been as swift in its crossing as the eye in discerning the lights. *The Cid* and *Pompey*, in which the action is somewhat rushed, are far from using such licence; and if they stretch normal probability a bit, at least they are not guilty of such impossibilities.

Many object to this rule, which they say is tyrannical, and they would be right if it were founded only upon Aristotle; but the natural reason upon which it is based should make it acceptable. The dramatic poem is an imitation, or better still, a portrait of men's actions, and there is no doubt that the best portraits are those which resemble most the original. The play takes two hours acting time, and would be a perfect resemblance, if the action which it presents required no more time in reality. So, let us not decide upon twelve or twenty-four hours; rather let us limit the action of the poem to the shortest length of time possible so that the picture will better resemble reality, and consequently be more perfect. Let us allow, if we can, to the one only the two hours the other takes. I do not think that *Rodogune* requires more than that, and perhaps that would suffice for *Cinna*. If we cannot limit it to two hours, then let us take four, six, ten, but let us not go far beyond the twenty-four, lest we become immoderate, and so reduce the scale of the portrait that its just proportions and perfection would vanish. Above all, I should leave the length of time to the imagination of the audience; and never state it if the subject does not so require, especially when probability is somewhat forced, as in the *Cid*, because that would serve only to call attention to the crowding of events. Even when nothing in the poem is forced as a result of the necessity of obeying this rule, what need is there of indicating at the beginning of a play that the sun is rising, that it is noon in the third act, and that the sun is setting at the end of the last? This is an affectation which serves only to annoy. It is sufficient that the possibility of the thing within the time allotted be established and that we be able to calculate the time, if we wish to do so, without being forced, in spite of ourselves, to turn our attention to it. Even in actions which require no more than the acting time, it would be poor taste to indicate that a half-hour had elapsed between acts.

I repeat what I have said elsewhere,[1] that when we take a longer time, ten hours for example, I should prefer that the eight hours we must drop from the acting time be consumed by the intervals between the acts, and that each one of these acts have at its disposal the

---

[1] In the analysis of *Mélite*, which in early editions immediately preceded this Discourse.

time the acting requires, especially when there is continuous linking of scenes, for this linking permits of no pause between two scenes. I consider, however, that the fifth act, by special privilege, has some right to compress the real time somewhat so that its share of the action should represent more time than is required for the acting. The reason for this is that the spectator is impatient to see the end, and that when the end depends upon the actors who have left the stage, all the lines given those who remain on the stage languish and seem lifeless. . . . When the end depends on actors who have not left the stage, and who therefore do not keep us waiting for news from them, as in *Cinna* and in *Rodogune,* the fifth act has no need of this privilege, because then all the action is visible to the eye, which is not true when part of it takes place off-stage after the act has begun. The other acts do not deserve the same indulgence. If enough time is not available to bring back an actor who has left, or to make known what he has done after he left, one can wait and give an account of it in the following act; and the violin which separates one act from the next, can take up as much time as is necessary; but in the fifth, no delay is possible. Attention is exhausted; one must get on to the end.

I cannot forget that, although we must reduce every tragic action to a day, that does not prevent the tragedy from telling, by narration or some other more clever means, what its hero has done for several years, since the plots of some are based upon the obscurity of the hero's birth, which must be clarified, as in *Œdipus.* I shall not repeat that the less we burden ourselves with past events, the more hold we have upon our audience, for by putting everything before their eyes, we do not place them under the strain of remembering any thing they have not seen; but I cannot forget that the choice of an illustrious day long looked forward to, is a great ornament for a poem. Opportunities for this do not always present themselves, and in all I have written so far, you will find only four.

*   *   *   *

As for unity of place, I find no precept for it either in Aristotle or in Horace. This leads some to believe that the rule has been established only as a consequence of the unity of time, and to maintain that it may be extended to include the distance a man can go and return in twenty-four hours. This is a rather bold interpretation of it, for if an actor were dispatched by mail-coach the two sides of the stage might represent Paris and Rouen. I should like nothing better than that, in order not to annoy the spectator, what we present before him in two hours, might in fact take place in two hours, and that what we show him on the stage which does not change, might be confined to a room or a hall, according to the choice we have made; but often that is so difficult, not to say impossible, that we must of necessity find some expansion of place and time.

*   *   *   *

The ancients who brought their kings into public squares to speak found it easy to observe the strict unity of place in their tragedies. Sophocles, however, did not do so in his *Ajax*, where the hero leaves the stage to find a secluded spot to kill himself, and kills himself there before the eyes of the audience. This easily leads us to suppose that the place where he killed himself was not the one he was seen to leave, since he left it to choose another.

We do not take this same liberty of bringing kings and princesses out of their private apartments, and since often the difference and opposition of interests of those who live in the same palace do not permit them to utter their confidences and reveal their secrets in the same room, we must seek some other adjustment to satisfy the unity of place, if we wish to keep it in all our poems. Otherwise we should have to condemn many whom we see succeed brilliantly.

I hold, therefore, that we must observe the strict unity in so far as it is possible; but since it does not suit all kinds of subjects, I should willingly concede that what one presents as having happened in a single city has unity of place. Not that I should like to have the whole city represented on the stage—that would be too vast—but only two or three particular places within the city walls.

*   *   *   *

These are my opinions, or, if you prefer, my heresies, about the chief points of dramatic art; and I know no better way of reconciling ancient rules with modern taste. I have no doubt that it would be easy to find better means of doing so, and I shall be quite ready to adopt them when they have been put into practice with as fortunate results as mine have been seen to achieve.

Milton

John MILTON (1608–1674) was born in London, the son of a Puritan scrivener. Trained by his father in music, and by a Scottish clergyman in the classics, Milton went to St. Paul's School and Cambridge University. He had thought of entering the Anglican Church, and for a time considered the law, but finally decided to devote himself to literature. He spent six years on his father's estate at Horton, continuing his studies and the poetic composition he had begun at college. In 1638 he travelled abroad, chiefly in Italy, where he met many famous scholars and writers. News of impending political troubles in England brought him home, and the second period of his life —that of controversy and political pamphleteering—began: his unhappy marriage led him to support divorce; he defended the freedom of the press; he became Latin Secretary to Cromwell's Council of State and carried on diplomatic correspondence. His polemical writings tried his eyesight and resulted in ultimate blindness, the subject of his most famous sonnet. He wrote other sonnets on political and personal themes, changing the emphasis from the love-sonnets of the Elizabethans. Four years after his wife's death, he married again; his second wife died the next year (1657); and in 1663 he married a third time. With the fall of the Commonwealth, his liberty was threatened, but he was included in the amnesty. He then turned his attention to the epic poems he had long planned. The final period of his life saw the publication of *Paradise Lost*, *Paradise Regained*, and *Samson Agonistes*.

Milton, in his criticism, is a true classicist. Like Ascham, Webbe, and other Elizabethans, he was (except in his youth) against rhyme, striving in *Paradise Lost* and *Samson Agonistes* for the sonorousness and dignity of the Greek hexameters. In *Samson* his aim was to produce, not a neo-classic play, but a tragedy in the mood and the form of Æschylus and Sophocles. In the chorus he was particularly successful.

A modern poet, a counterpart—though on a much smaller scale—of Milton in his religious and poetic intensity, Gerard Manley Hopkins, admired greatly and was deeply affected in his technique by the choral parts of *Samson*.

THE PREFACE TO *PARADISE LOST* [1]

THE VERSE

(1668)

The measure is English heroic verse without rime, as that of Homer in Greek, and of Virgil in Latin; rime being no necessary adjunct or true ornament of poem or good verse, in longer works especially, but the invention of a barbarous age to set off wretched matter and lame metre; graced indeed since by the use of some famous modern poets, carried away by custom, but much to their own vexation, hindrance, and constraint to express many things otherwise, and for the most part worse, than else they would have expressed them. Not without cause therefore, some both Italian and Spanish poets of prime note have rejected rime both in longer and shorter works, as have long since our best English tragedies; as a thing of itself, to all judicious ears, trivial and of no true musical delight; which consists only in apt numbers, fit quantity of syllables, and the sense variously drawn out from one verse into another; not in the jingling sound of like endings, a fault avoided by the learned ancients both in poetry and all good oratory. This neglect then of rime so little is to be taken for a defect, though it may seem so perhaps to vulgar readers, that it is rather to be esteemed an example set, the first in English, of ancient liberty recovered to heroic poem, from the troublesome and modern bondage of riming.

---

[1] The Milton texts are from R. C. Browne, *English Poems by John Milton*, 2 vols., Oxford, 1902. Prefixed to the 1668 edition of *Paradise Lost,* appeared the following "address" of the printer to the reader: "Courteous Reader, there was no *Argument* at first intended to the book; but for the satisfaction of many that have desired it, I have procured it, and withal a reason of that which stumbled many others, why the poem rimes not." The texts are used with the kind permission of The Clarendon Press, Oxford.

THE PREFACE TO *SAMSON AGONISTES*

OF THAT SORT OF DRAMATIC POEM WHICH IS CALLED "TRAGEDY" [1]

(1671)

Tragedy, as it was anciently composed, hath been ever held the gravest, moralest, and most profitable of all other poems; therefore said by Aristotle to be of power by raising pity and fear, or terror, to purge the mind of those and suchlike passions; that is, to temper and reduce them to just measure with a kind of delight, stirred up by reading or seeing those passions well imitated. Nor is Nature wanting in her own effects to make good his assertion; for so in physic things of melancholic hue and quality are used against melancholy, sour against sour, salt to remove salt humors. Hence philosophers and other gravest writers, as Cicero, Plutarch, and others, frequently cite out of tragic poets, both to adorn and illustrate their discourse. The Apostle Paul himself thought it not unworthy to insert a verse of Euripides into the text of Holy Scripture, 1 *Corinthians* xv:33; and Paræus, commenting on the *Revelation,* divides the whole book as a tragedy, into acts, distinguished each by a chorus of heavenly harpings and song between. Heretofore men in highest dignity have labored not a little to be thought able to compose a tragedy. Of that honor Dionysius the Elder was no less ambitious than before of his attaining to the tyranny. Augustus Cæsar also had begun his *Ajax,* but unable to please his own judgment with what he had begun, left it unfinished. Seneca, the philosopher, is by some thought the author of those tragedies (at least the best of them) that go under that name. Gregory Nazianzen, a Father of the Church, thought it not unbeseeming the sanctity of his person to write a tragedy, which he entitled *Christ Suffering.* This is mentioned to vindicate tragedy from the small esteem, or rather infamy, which in the account of many it undergoes at this day with other common interludes; happening through the poet's error of intermixing comic stuff with tragic sadness and gravity; or introducing trivial and vulgar persons, which by all judicious hath been counted absurd and brought in without discretion, corruptly to gratify the people. And though ancient tragedy use no prologue, yet using sometimes in case of self-defence, or explanation, that which Martial calls

---

[1] In Browne's edition, this preface is introduced by a few phrases from the sixth book of Aristotle's *Poetics,* with a Latin translation recalling for the reader Aristotle's famous definition of tragedy.

an epistle, in behalf of this tragedy coming forth after the ancient manner, much different from what among us passes for best, thus much beforehand may be epistled; that Chorus is here introduced after the Greek manner, not ancient only but modern, and still in use among the Italians. In the modelling therefore of this poem, with good reason, the ancients and Italians are rather followed, as of much more authority and fame. The measure of verse used in the Chorus is of all sorts, called by the Greeks Monostrophic or rather Apolelymenon,[1] without regard had to Strophe, Antistrophe, or Epode, which were a kind of stanzas framed only for the music then used with the Chorus that sung; not essential to the poem and therefore not material; or being divided into stanzas or pauses they may be called Allœostropha.[2] Division into act and scene, referring chiefly to the stage (to which this work never was intended), is here omitted.

It suffices if the whole drama be found not produced beyond the fifth act. Of the style and uniformity, and that commonly called the plot, whether intricate or explicit—which is nothing indeed but such economy or disposition of the fable as may stand best with verisimilitude and decorum—they only will best judge who are not unacquainted with Æschylus, Sophocles, and Euripides, the three tragic poets unequalled yet by any, and the best rule to all who endeavor to write tragedy. The circumscription of time wherein the whole drama begins and ends is, according to ancient rule and best example, within the space of twenty-four hours.

[1] resolved.
[2] irregular stanzas.

Dryden

John DRYDEN (1631–1700) was born in Northampton-shire, of a good Puritan family. Educated at Westminster School and Cambridge University, he went to London in 1657, seeking a career. Various political poems—in honor of Cromwell and Charles II—were followed by plays for the newly-reopened theatres; but his first attempts were not successful. His later comedies and "heroic" dramas captured the public taste, and his poems and criticisms commanded public attention. In 1663 he married Lady Elizabeth Howard, daughter of the Earl of Berkshire; in 1668 his *Essay on Dramatic Poetry*, and the *Defence of the Essay*, appeared; in 1670 he was appointed poet-laureate and royal historiographer, and given a pension. He continued his dramatic composition and produced satirical poems, including *Absalom and Achitophel* (1681), *The Medal*, and *MacFlecknoe* (1682). In 1686, after the accession of James II, he joined the Roman Church, which he defends in *The Hind and the Panther*. The Revolution of 1688 deprived him of his appointments and pension. He wrote a few more plays and translated classical authors, including Vergil (1697). In the year before his death, he published *Fables, Ancient and Modern,* paraphrases and translations from Ovid, Chaucer, and Boccaccio. He was buried in Westminster Abbey, between Chaucer and Cowley.

Dryden, "the father of English prose," may also be called, to use Dr. Johnson's phrase, "the father of English criticism." Learned and widely read, Dryden accepted from previous writers only what he thought was good, and then proceeded boldly to build his own critical philosophy. At a time when most commentators accepted whole-heartedly the precepts of Horace, either directly, or through Vida or Boileau, Dryden spoke out with good sense, refusing to be cowed by the weight of authority, bravely proclaiming, with keen reasoning, the greatness of Englishmen like Chaucer, Shakespeare, and Fletcher. He realized their shortcomings, but his judicial analysis of their qualities proved to him their rank in the literature of the world.

In his "Remarks on Rymer"—who was called by Macaulay "the worst critic who ever lived"—he framed, in brief compass, what might be regarded as the Magna Charta of English literary criticism: "It is not enough that Aristotle has said so, for Aristotle drew his models of tragedy from Sophocles and Euripides; *and, if he had seen ours, might have changed his mind.*"

From AN ESSAY OF DRAMATIC POESY [1]
(1668)

It was that memorable day, in the first summer of the late war, when our navy engaged the Dutch; a day wherein the two most mighty and best appointed fleets which any age had ever seen disputed the command of the greater half of the globe, the commerce of nations, and the riches of the universe. While these vast floating bodies, on either side, moved against each other in parallel lines, and our countrymen, under the happy conduct of his Royal Highness, went breaking, by little and little, into the line of the enemies, the noise of the cannon from both navies reached our ears about the City, so that all men being alarmed with it, and in a dreadful suspense of the event which we knew was then deciding, every one went following the sound as his fancy led him; and leaving the town almost empty, some took towards the park, some cross the river, others down it; all seeking the noise in the depth of silence.

Among the rest, it was the fortune of Eugenius, Crites, Lisideius,

---

[1] The text of Dryden has been compared with that of W. P. Ker, Oxford, 1926, based on the edition of 1668, collated with those of 1684 and 1693—with a few changes by the editors.

and Neander,[1] to be in company together; three of them persons whom their wit and quality have made known to all the town; and whom I have chose to hide under these borrowed names, that they may not suffer by so ill a relation as I am going to make of their discourse.

Taking then a barge, which a servant of Lisideius had provided for them, they made haste to shoot the bridge, and left behind them that great fall of waters which hindered them from hearing what they desired: after which, having disengaged themselves from many vessels which rode at anchor in the Thames, and almost blocked up the passage towards Greenwich, they ordered the watermen to let fall their oars more gently; and then, every one favoring his own curiosity with a strict silence, it was not long ere they perceived the air break about them like the noise of distant thunder, or of swallows in a chimney: those little undulations of sound, though almost vanishing before they reached them, yet still seeming to retain somewhat of their first horror, which they had betwixt the fleets. After they had attentively listened till such time as the sound by little and little went from them, Eugenius, lifting up his head, and taking notice of it, was the first who congratulated to the rest that happy omen of our Nation's victory: adding, we had but this to desire in confirmation of it, that we might hear no more of that noise, which was now leaving the English coast. When the rest had concurred in the same opinion, Crites, a person of a sharp judgment, and somewhat too delicate a taste in wit, which the world have mistaken in him for ill-nature, said, smiling to us, that if the concernment of this battle had not been so exceeding great, he could scarce have wished the victory at the price he knew he must pay for it, in being subject to the reading and hearing of so many ill verses as he was sure would be made upon it. Adding, that no argument could scape some of those eternal rhymers, who watch a battle with more diligence than the ravens and birds of prey; and the worst of them surest to be first in upon the quarry: while the better able, either out of modesty writ not at all, or set that due value upon their poems, as to let them be often called for and long expected! "There are some of those impertinent people you speak of," answered Lisideius, "who to my knowledge are already so provided, either way, that they can produce not only a panegyric upon the victory, but, if need be, a fu-

[1] With these names, Dryden masks Charles Sackville, Lord Buckhurst (created Earl of Middlesex, 1675; succeeded as sixth Earl of Dorset, 1677; F.R.S., 1699); Sir Robert Howard, Dryden's brother-in-law; Sir Charles Sedley; and Dryden himself.

neral elegy on the Duke; and, after they had crowned his valor with many laurels, at last deplore the odds under which he fell, concluding that his courage deserved a better destiny." All the company smiled at the conceit of Lisideius; but Crites, more eager than before, began to make particular exceptions against some writers, and said, the public magistrate ought to send betimes to forbid them; and that it concerned the peace and quiet of all honest people, that ill poets should be as well silenced as seditious preachers. "In my opinion," replied Eugenius, "you pursue your point too far; for as to my own particular, I am so great a lover of poesy, that I could wish them all rewarded who attempt but to do well; at least, I would not have them worse used than Sylla the Dictator did one of their brethren heretofore:—*Quem in concione vidimus* (says Tully), *cum ei libellum malus poeta de populo subjecisset, quod epigramma in eum fecisset tantummodo alternis versibus longiusculis, statim ex iis rebus quas tunc vendebat jubere ei praemium tribui, sub ea conditione ne quid postea scriberet.*" [1] "I could wish with all my heart," replied Crites, "that many whom we know were as bountifully thanked upon the same condition,—that they would never trouble us again. For amongst others, I have a mortal apprehension of two poets, whom this victory, with the help of both her wings, will never be able to escape." " 'Tis easy to guess whom you intend," said Lisideius; "and without naming them, I ask you, if one of them does not perpetually pay us with clenches [2] upon words, and a certain clownish kind of raillery? if now and then he does not offer at a catachresis or Clevelandism,[3] wresting and torturing a word into another meaning: in fine, if he be not one of those whom the French would call *un mauvais buffon;* [4] one that is so much a well-willer to the satire, that he spares no man; and though he cannot strike a blow to hurt any, yet ought to be punished for the malice of the action, as our witches are justly hanged, because they think themselves so; and suffer deservedly for believing they did mischief, because they meant it." "You have described him," said Crites, "so exactly, that I am afraid to come after you with my

---

[1] "In an assembly once, we recall, when a bad poet in the crowd handed him a book of which he had composed long-winded epigrams, he ordered that the poet be given a reward from the things he was selling on condition that he write nothing thereafter." Cicero, *Pro Arch.,* x, 25.

[2] Paronomasia, or plays upon words, puns.

[3] John Cleveland (1613–1658), a satirical poet, given to extreme "conceits." κατάχρησις, (catachresis)—a mixed metaphor, or misuse of words.

[4] A bad clown.

other extremity of poetry. He is one of those who, having had some advantage of education and converse, knows better than the other what a poet should be, but puts it into practice more unluckily than any man; his style and matter are everywhere alike: he is the most calm, peaceable writer you ever read: he never disquiets your passions with the least concernment, but still leaves you in as even a temper as he found you; he is a very leveller in poetry: he creeps along with ten little words in every line,[1] and helps out his numbers with *for to,* and *unto,* and all the pretty expletives he can find, till he drags them to the end of another line; while the sense is left tired half way behind it: he doubly starves all his verses, first for want of thought, and then of expression; his poetry neither has wit in it, nor seems to have it; like him in Martial:

Pauper videri *Cinna* vult, et est pauper.[2]

"He affects plainness, to cover his want of imagination: when he writes the serious way, the highest flight of his fancy is some miserable antithesis, or seeming contradiction; and in the comic he is still reaching at some thin conceit, the ghost of a jest, and that too flies before him, never to be caught; these swallows which we see before us on the Thames are the just resemblance of his wit: you may observe how near the water they stoop, how many proffers they make to dip, and yet how seldom they touch it; and when they do, 'tis but the surface: they skim over it but to catch a gnat, and then mount into the air and leave it."

"Well, gentlemen," said Eugenius, "you may speak your pleasure of these authors; but though I and some few more about the town may give you a peaceable hearing, yet assure yourselves, there are multitudes who would think you malicious and them injured: especially him whom you first described; he is the very Withers[3] of the City: they have bought more editions of his works than would serve to lay under all their pies at the Lord Mayor's Christmas. When his famous poem first came out in the year 1660, I have seen them reading it in the midst of 'Change time; nay so vehement they were at it, that they lost their bargain by the candles' ends;[4] but what will you say if he has been received amongst the great ones? I can assure you he is, this day, the envy of a great Person who is lord in the art of

---

[1] Cf. Pope, *Essay on Criticism,* 347.

[2] Cf. p. 144.

[3] With perhaps a punning reference to George Wither, the poet (1588–1667).

[4] Bids were accepted as long as the candle-end burned. (Ker.)

quibbling, and who does not take it well that any man should intrude so far into his province." "All I would wish," replied Crites, "is that they who love his writings, may still admire him, and his fellow poet: *Qui Bavium non odit, etc.*,[1] is curse sufficient." "And farther," added Lisideius, "I believe there is no man who writes well, but would think himself very hardly dealt with, if their admirers should praise anything of his: *Nam quos contemnimus, eorum quoque laudes contemnimus.*"[2] "There are so few who write well in this age," says Crites, "that methinks any praises should be welcome; they neither rise to the dignity of the last age, nor to any of the Ancients: and we may cry out of the writers of this time, with more reason than Petronius of his, *Pace vestrâ liceat dixisse, primi omnium eloquentiam perdidistis:*[3] you have debauched the true old poetry so far, that Nature, which is the soul of it, is not in any of your writings."

"If your quarrel," said Eugenius, "to those who now write, be grounded only on your reverence to antiquity, there is no man more ready to adore those great Greeks and Romans than I am: but on the other side, I cannot think so contemptibly of the age I live in, or so dishonorably of my own country, as not to judge we equal the Ancients in most kinds of poesy, and in some surpass them; neither know I any reason why I may not be as zealous for the reputation of our age as we find the Ancients themselves in reference to those who lived before them. For you hear your Horace saying,

> Indignor quidquam reprehendi, non quia crasse
> Compositum, illepidève putetur, sed quia nuper.[4]

And after:

> Si meliora dies, ut vina, poemata reddit,
> Scire velim, pretim chartis quotus arroget annus?[5]

"But I see I am engaging in a wide dispute, where the arguments are not like to reach close on either side; for poesy is of so large an

---

[1] "Who does not hate Bavius [a third-rate poet] loves your poems, Mævius."—Vergil, *Eclogues*, III. 90.

[2] For we despise also the praise of people whom we despise.

[3] "With your leave, let me say that you have lost the eloquence of all your predecessors."—Petronius, *Satyr.*, 2.

[4] I am indignant when I hear anything abused, not because it is thought rudely or ungracefully put together, but because it is modern.

[5] If time improves books, as it does wines, let me ask what year of their age bestows value upon them?

extent, and so many both of the Ancients and Moderns have done well in all kinds of it, that in citing one against the other, we shall take up more time this evening than each man's occasions will allow him: therefore I would ask Crites to what part of Poesy he would confine his arguments, and whether he would defend the general cause of the Ancients against the Moderns, or oppose any age of the Moderns against this of ours?"

Crites, a little while considering upon this demand, told Eugenius, he approved his propositions, and if he pleased, he would limit their dispute to Dramatic Poesy; in which he thought it not difficult to prove, either that the Ancients were superior to the Moderns, or the last age of this of ours.

Eugenius was somewhat surprised, when he heard Crites make choice of that subject. "For aught I see," said he, "I have undertaken a harder province than I imagined; for though I never judged the plays of the Greek or Roman poets comparable to ours, yet, on the other side, those we now see acted come short of many which were written in the last age: but my comfort is, if we are o'ercome, it will be only by our own countrymen: and if we yield to them in this one part of poesy, we more surpass them in all the other: for in the epic or lyric way, it will be hard for them to show us one such amongst them, as we have many now living, or who lately were so: they can produce nothing so courtly writ, or which expresses so much the conversation of a gentleman, as Sir John Suckling; [1] nothing so even, sweet, and flowing as Mr. Waller; nothing so majestic, so correct, as Sir John Denham; nothing so elevated, so copious, and full of spirit as Mr. Cowley; as for the Italian, French, and Spanish plays, I can make it evident, that those who now write surpass them; and that the Drama is wholly ours."

All of them were thus far of Eugenius his [2] opinion, that the sweetness of English verse was never understood or practiced by our fathers; even Crites himself did not much oppose it; and every one was willing to acknowledge how much our poesy is improved by the happiness of some writers yet living; who first taught us to mould our thoughts into easy and significant words; to retrench the superfluities of expression, and to make our rhyme so properly a part of the verse,

---

[1] Sir John Suckling (1609–1642), Edmund Waller (1606–1687), Sir John Denham (1615–1669), Abraham Cowley (1618–1667), all poets of Dryden's time. Cf. Pope's "easy vigor of a line where Denham's strength and Waller's sweetness join," (*Essay on Criticism*).

[2] A common use of the pronoun to give the inflection of the noun. (Ker.)

that it should never mislead the sense, but itself be led and governed by it.

Eugenius was going to continue this discourse, when Lisideius told him it was necessary, before they proceeded further, to take a standing measure of their controversy; for how was it possible to be decided who writ the best plays, before we know what a play should be? But, this once agreed on by both parties, each might have recourse to it, either to prove his own advantages, or to discover the failings of his adversary.

He had no sooner said this, but all desired the favor of him to give the definition of a play; and they were the more importunate, because neither Aristotle, nor Horace, nor any other, who writ of that subject, had ever done it.

Lisideius, after some modest denials, at last confessed he had a rude notion of it; indeed, rather a description than a definition; but which served to guide him in his private thoughts, when he was to make a judgment of what others writ: that he conceived a play ought to be, *A just and lively image of human nature, representing its passions and humors, and the changes of fortune to which it is subject, for the delight and instruction of mankind.*

This definition, though Crites raised a logical objection against it; that it was only *a genere et fine,*[1] and so not altogether perfect; was yet well received by the rest: and after they had given order to the watermen to turn their barge, and row softly, that they might take the cool of the evening in their return, Crites, being desired by the company to begin, spoke on behalf of the Ancients, in this manner:

"If confidence presage a victory, Eugenius, in his own opinion, has already triumphed over the Ancients: nothing seems more easy to him, than to overcome those whom it is our greatest praise to have imitated well; for we do not only build upon their foundation, but by their models. Dramatic Poesy had time enough, reckoning from Thespis (who first invented it) to Aristophanes, to be born, to grow up, and to flourish in maturity. It has been observed of arts and sciences, that in one and the same century they have arrived to a great perfection; and no wonder, since every age has a kind of universal genius, which inclines those that live in it to some particular studies: the work then being pushed on by many hands, must of necessity go forward.

---

[1] "By general classification and by purpose." The description might be used of a narrative poem, or of a novel, as well as of a play. Dryden thought that the specific difference between drama and narrative was not likely to be mistaken, and was therefore of less importance than the points here described. (Ker).

"Is it not evident, in these last hundred years (when the study of philosophy has been the business of all the virtuosi in Christendom), that almost a new Nature has been revealed to us?—that more errors of the school have been detected, more useful experiments in philosophy have been made, more noble secrets in optics, medicine, anatomy, astronomy, discovered, than in all those credulous and doting ages from Aristotle to us?—so true is it, that nothing spreads more fast than science, when rightly and generally cultivated.

"Add to this, the more than common emulation that was in those times of writing well; which though it be found in all ages and all persons that pretend to the same reputation, yet Poesy, being then in more esteem than now it is, had greater honors decreed to the professors of it, and consequently the rivalship was more high between them; they had judges ordained to decide their merit, and prizes to reward it; and historians have been diligent to record of Æschylus, Euripides, Sophocles, Lycophron, and the rest of them, both who they were that vanquished in these wars of the theatre, and how often they were crowned: while the Asian kings and Grecian commonwealths scarce afforded them a nobler subject than the unmanly luxuries of a debauched court, or giddy intrigues of a factious city:— *Alit æmulatio ingenia* (says Paterculus), *et nunc invidia, nunc admiratio incitatio nem accendit*: Emulation is the spur of wit; and sometimes envy, sometimes admiration, quickens our endeavors.

"But now, since the rewards of honor are taken away, that virtuous emulation is turned into direct malice; yet so slothful, that it contents itself to condemn and cry down others, without attempting to do better: 'tis a reputation too unprofitable, to take the necessary pains for it; yet, wishing they had it is incitement enough to hinder others from it. And this, in short, Eugenius, is the reason why you have now so few good poets, and so many severe judges. Certainly, to imitate the Ancients well, much labor and long study is required; which pains, I have already shown, our poets would want encouragement to take, if yet they had ability to go through with it. Those Ancients have been faithful imitators and wise observers of that Nature which is so torn and ill represented in our plays; they have handed down to us a perfect resemblance of her; which we, like ill copiers, neglecting to look on, have rendered monstrous, and disfigured. But, that you may know how much you are indebted to those your masters, and be ashamed to have so ill requited them, I must remember you, that all the rules by which we practice the Drama at this day, (either such as relate to the justness and symmetry of the plot, or the episodical ornaments, such as descriptions, narrations, and other beauties, which are not essential to the play,) were delivered to us from the observations which Aristotle made, of those poets, who either lived before him, or were his contemporaries: we have added nothing of our own, except we have the confidence to say our wit is better; of which none boast in this our age, but such as understand not theirs. Of that book which Aristotle has left us, περὶ τῆς Ποιητικῆς, Horace his *Art of Poetry* is an excellent comment, and, I believe, restores to us that Second Book of his concerning *Comedy*, which is wanting in him.

"Out of these two have been extracted the famous Rules, which the French call *Des Trois Unités*, or, the Three Unities, which ought to be observed in every regular play; namely, of Time, Place, and Action.

"The Unity of Time they comprehend in twenty-four hours, the compass of a natural day, or as near as it can be contrived; and the reason of it is obvious to every one,—that the time of the feigned action, or fable of the play, should be proportioned as near as can be to the duration of that time in which it is represented: since, therefore, all plays are acted on the theatre in a space of time much within the compass of twenty-four hours, that play is to be thought the nearest imitation of nature, whose plot or action is confined within that time; and, by the same rule which concludes this general proportion of time, it follows, that all the parts of it are to be equally subdivided; as namely, that one act take not up the supposed time of half a day, which is out of proportion to the rest; since the other four are then to be straitened within the compass of the remaining half: for it is unnatural that one act, which being spoke or written is not longer than the rest, should be supposed longer by the audience; 'tis therefore the poet's duty, to take care that no act should be imagined to exceed the time in which it is represented on the stage; and that the intervals and inequalities of time be supposed to fall out between the acts.

"This rule of time, how well it has been observed by the Ancients, most of their plays will witness; you see them in their tragedies (wherein to follow this rule is certainly most difficult), from the very beginning of their plays, falling close into that part of the story which they intend for the action or principal object of it, leaving the former part to be delivered by narration: so that they set the audience, as it were, at the post where the race is to be concluded; and, saving them the tedious expectation of seeing the poet set out and ride the beginning of the course, you behold him not till he is in sight of the goal, and just upon you.

"For the second Unity, which is that of Place, the Ancients meant by it, that the scene ought to be continued through the play, in the same place where it was laid in the beginning: for the stage on which it is represented being but one and the same place, it is unnatural to conceive it many; and those far distant from one another. I will not deny but, by the variation of painted scenes,[1] the fancy, which in these cases will contribute to its own deceit, may sometimes imagine it several places, with some appearance of probability; yet it still carries the greater likelihood of truth, if those places be supposed so near each other, as in the same town or city; which may all be comprehended under the larger denomination of one place; for a greater distance will bear no proportion to the shortness of time which is allotted, in the acting, to pass from one of them to another; for the observation of this, next to the Ancients, the French are to be most commended. They tie themselves so strictly to the Unity of Place that you never see in any of their plays a scene changed in the middle of an act: if the act begins in a garden, a street, or chamber, 'tis ended in the same place; and that you may know it to be the same, the stage is so supplied with persons, that it is never empty all the time: he that enters the second, has business with him who was on before; and before the second quits the stage, a third appears who has business with him. This Corneille calls *la liaison des scènes,* the continuity or joining of the scenes; and 'tis a good mark of a well-contrived play, when all the persons are known to each other, and every one of them has some affairs with all the rest.

"As for the third Unity, which is that of Action, the Ancients meant no other by it than what the logicians do by their *finis,* the end or scope of any action; that which is the first in intention, and last in execution: now the poet is to aim at one great and complete action, to the carrying on of which all things in his play, even the very obstacles, are to be subservient; and the reason of this is as evident as any of the former.

"For two actions, equally labored and driven on by the writer, would destroy the unity of the poem; it would be no longer one play, but two: not but that there may be many actions in a play, as Ben Jonson has observed in his *Discoveries;* but they must be all

---

[1] While the Court Masques of the Stuart Court were given against an elaborate background, there was little scenery in the regular theatre until the Restoration. Davenant's *Siege of Rhodes* was one of the first plays to use "sets" in England.

subservient to the great one, which our language happily expresses in the name of *under-plots:* such as in Terence's *Eunuch* is the difference and reconcilement of Thais and Phædria, which is not the chief business of the play, but promotes the marriage of Chærea and Chremes's sister, principally intended by the poet. There ought to be but one action, says Corneille, that is, one complete action, which leaves the mind of the audience in a full repose; but this cannot be brought to pass but by many other imperfect actions, which conduce to it, and hold the audience in a delightful suspense of what will be.

"If by these rules (to omit many other drawn from the precepts and practice of the Ancients) we should judge our modern plays, 'tis probable that few of them would endure the trial: that which should be the business of a day, takes up in some of them an age; instead of one action, they are the epitomes of a man's life; and for one spot of ground (which the stage should represent) we are sometimes in more countries than the map can show us.

"But if we allow the Ancients to have contrived well, we must acknowledge them to have writ better; questionless we are deprived of a great stock of wit in the loss of Menander among the Greek poets, and of Cæcilius, Afranius, and Varius, among the Romans; we may guess at Menander's excellency by the plays of Terence, who translated some of his; and yet wanted so much of him, that he was called by C. Cæsar the half-Menander; and may judge of Varius, by the testimonies of Horace, Martial, and Velleius Paterculus.[1] 'Tis probable that these, could they be recovered, would decide the controversy; but so long as Aristophanes in the old Comedy, and Plautus in the new are extant, while the tragedies of Euripides, Sophocles, and Seneca are to be had, I can never see one of those plays which are now written, but it increases my admiration of the Ancients. And yet I must acknowledge farther, that to admire them as we ought, we should understand them better than we do. Doubtless many things appear flat to us, the wit of which depended on some custom or story, which never came to our knowledge; or perhaps on some criticism in their language, which being so long dead, and only remaining in their books, 'tis not possible they should make us understand perfectly. To read Macrobius,[2] explaining the propriety and elegancy of many words in Virgil, which I had before passed over

---

[1] Ker notes that Velleius Paterculus does not mention Varius.

[2] Amerosius Theodosius Macrobius, Roman grammarian and philosopher, fl. fourth century, A. D. Ker refers to his *Saturnalia, passim.*

without consideration as common things, is enough to assure me that I ought to think the same of Terence; and that in the purity of his style (which Tully so much valued that he ever carried his works about him) there is yet left in him great room for admiration, if I knew but where to place it. In the mean time I must desire you to take notice that the greatest man of the last age (Ben Jonson) was willing to give place to them in all things: he was not only a professed imitator of Horace, but a learned plagiary of all the others; you track him everywhere in their snow: if Horace, Lucan, Petronius Arbiter, Seneca, and Juvenal had their own from him, there are few serious thoughts which are new in him: you will pardon me, therefore, if I presume he loved their fashion, when he wore their clothes. But since I have otherwise a great veneration for him, and you, Eugenius, prefer him above all other poets, I will use no farther argument to you than his example: I will produce Father Ben to you, dressed in all the ornaments and colors of the Ancients; you will need no other guide to our party, if you follow him; and whether you consider the bad plays of our age, or regard the good ones of the last, both the best and worst of the modern poets will equally instruct you to esteem the Ancients."

Crites had no sooner left speaking, but Eugenius, who had waited with some impatience for it, thus began:

"I have observed in your speech, that the former part of it is convincing as to what the Moderns have profited by the rules of the Ancients; but in the latter you are careful to conceal how much they have excelled them; we own all the helps we have from them, and want neither veneration nor gratitude, while we acknowledge that to overcome them we must make use of the advantages we have received from them: but to these assistances we have joined our own industry; for, had we sat down with a dull imitation of them, we might then have lost somewhat of the old perfection, but never acquired any that was new. We draw not therefore after their lines, but those of Nature; and having the life before us, besides the experience of all they knew, it is no wonder if we hit some airs and features which they have missed. I deny not what you urge of arts and sciences, that they have flourished in some ages more than others; but your instance in philosophy makes for me: for if natural causes be more known now than in the time of Aristotle, because more studied, it follows that poesy and other arts may, with the same pains, arrive still nearer to perfection; and, that granted, it will rest for you to prove that they wrought more perfect images of human life than we; which seeing in your discourse you have avoided to make good, it shall now be my task to show you some part of their defects, and some few excellencies of the Moderns. And I think there is none among us can imagine I do it enviously, or with purpose to detract from them; for what interest of fame or profit can the living lose by the reputation of the dead? On the other side, it is a great truth which Velleius Paterculus affirms: *Audita visis libentius laudamus; et præsentia invidia, præterita admiratione prosequimur; et his nos obrui, illis instrui credimus:* [1] that praise or censure is certainly the most sincere, which unbribed posterity shall give us.

"Be pleased then in the first place to take notice that the Greek poesy, which Crites has affirmed to have arrived to perfection in the reign of the Old Comedy, was so far from it that the distinction of it into acts was not known to them; or if it were, it is yet so darkly delivered to us that we cannot make it out.

"All we know of it is, from the singing of their Chorus; and that too is so uncertain, that in some of their plays we have reason to conjecture they sung more than five times. Aristotle [2] indeed divides the integral parts of a play into four. First, the *Protasis*, or entrance, which gives light only to the characters of the persons, and proceeds very little into any part of the action. Secondly, the *Epitasis*, or working up of the plot; where the play grows warmer, the design or action of it is drawing on, and you see something promising that it will come to pass. Thirdly, the *Catastasis,* or counterturn, which destroys that expectation, imbroils the action in new difficulties, and leaves you far distant from that hope in which it found you; as you may have observed in a violent stream resisted by a narrow passage,—it runs round to an eddy, and carries back the waters with more swiftness than it brought them on. Lastly, the *Catastrophe,* which the Grecians called λύσις, the French *le dénouement,* [3] and we the discovery, or unravelling of the plot: there you see all things settling again upon their first foundations; and, the obstacles which hindered the design or action of the play once removed, it ends with that resemblance of truth and nature, that the audience are satisfied with the conduct of it. Thus this great man delivered to us the image of a play; and I must confess it is so lively, that from

[1] "We praise things heard more freely than things seen; and we join envy for the present with admiration [veneration] for the past; we believe ourselves buried by the former and set up by the latter,"—*Hist. Rom.,* ii, 92; Ker notes, for *admiratione* read *veneratione.*

[2] Ker refers to Scaliger, *Poet.,* i, 9.

[3] Lit. unknotting, untying a knot.

thence much light has been derived to the forming it more perfectly into acts and scenes: but what poet first limited to five the number of the acts, I know not; only we see it so firmly established in the time of Horace, that he gives it for a rule in comedy,—*Neu brevior quinto, neu sit productior actu.*[1] So that you see the Grecians cannot be said to have consummated this art; writing rather by entrances than by acts, and having rather a general indigested notion of a play, than knowing how and where to bestow the particular graces of it.

"But since the Spaniards at this day allow but three acts, which they call *Jornadas*,[2] to a play, and the Italians in many of theirs follow them, when I condemn the Ancients, I declare it is not altogether because they have not five acts to every play, but because they have not confined themselves to one certain number: it is building an house without a model; and when they succeeded in such undertakings, they ought to have sacrificed to Fortune, not to the Muses.

"Next, for the plot, which Aristotle called τὸ μύθος, and often τῶν πραγμάτων σύνθεσις,[3] and from him the Romans *Fabula*, it has already been judiciously observed by a late writer,[4] that in their tragedies it was only some tale derived from Thebes or Troy, or at least something that happened in those two ages; which was worn so threadbare by the pens of all the epic poets, and even by tradition itself of the talkative Greeklings (as Ben Jonson calls them), that before it came upon the stage it was already known to all the audience: and the people, so soon as ever they heard the name of Œdipus, knew as well as the poet, that he had killed his father by a mistake, and committed incest with his mother, before the play; that they were now to hear of a great plague, an oracle, and the ghost of Laius: so that they sat with a yawning kind of expectation, till he was to come with his eyes pulled out, and speak a hundred or two of verses in a tragic tone, in complaint of his misfortunes. But one Œdipus, Hercules, or Medea, had been tolerable: poor people, they scaped not so good cheap; they had still the *chapon bouillé*[5] set before them, till their appetites were cloyed with the same dish,

---

[1] "Let it be neither shorter nor longer than five acts." Horace, *Ars Poetica,* 189.

[2] Ker notes that the Spanish poets borrowed the term (*journée*) from the old French mysteries, and that the term was still in use in seventeenth-century France, not for an act, but for the several parts of a play.

[3] Lit., the placing together, or synthesis, of the actions, or things done.

[4] Ker suggests Ménage.

[5] (*Fr.*) boiled capon; *i. e.*, hash, or the same dish served over.

and, the novelty being gone, the pleasure vanished; so that one main end of Dramatic Poesy in its definition, which was to cause delight, was of consequence destroyed.

[Here Dryden enters upon a digression of five pages on Roman comedy.]

"But, to return from whence I have digressed, to the consideration of the Ancients' writing, and their wit; of which by this time you will grant us in some measure to be fit judges. Though I see many excellent thoughts in Seneca, yet he of them who had a genius most proper for the stage, was Ovid; he had a way of writing so fit to stir up a pleasing admiration and concernment, which are the objects of a tragedy, and to show the various movements of a soul combating betwixt two different passions, that, had he lived in our age, or in his own could have writ with our advantages, no man but must have yielded to him; and therefore I am confident the *Medea* is none of his: for, though I esteem it for the gravity and sententiousness of it, which he himself concludes to be suitable to a tragedy, —*Omne genus scripti gravitate tragœdia vincit,*[1]—yet it moves not my soul enough to judge that he, who in the epic way wrote things so near the drama as the story of Myrrha, of Caunus and Biblis, and the rest, should stir up no more concernment where he most endeavored it. The masterpiece of Seneca I hold to be that scene in the *Troades*, where Ulysses is seeking for Astyanax to kill him; there you see the tenderness of a mother so represented in Andromache, that it raises compassion to a high degree in the reader, and bears the nearest resemblance of any thing in their tragedies to the excellent scenes of passion in Shakespeare, or in Fletcher: for love-scenes, you will find few among them; their tragic poets dealt not with that soft passion, but with lust, cruelty, revenge, ambition, and those bloody actions they produced; which were more capable of raising horror than compassion in an audience: leaving love untouched, whose gentleness would have tempered them, which is the most frequent of all the passions, and which, being the private concernment of every person, is soothed by viewing its own image in a public entertainment.

"Among their comedies, we find a scene or two of tenderness, and that where you would least expect it, in Plautus; but to speak generally, their lovers say little, when they see each other, but *anima*

---

[1] "Tragedy surpasses every kind of writing in gravity." Ovid, *Tristia*, ii, 381.

mea, vita mea; ζωὴ καὶ ψυχή,[1] as the women in Juvenal's time used to cry out in the fury of their kindness: then indeed to speak sense were an offence. Any sudden gust of passion (as an ecstasy of love in an unexpected meeting) cannot better be expressed than in a word and a sigh, breaking one another. Nature is dumb on such occasions; and to make her speak would be to represent her unlike herself. But there are a thousand other concernments of lovers, as jealousies, complaints, contrivances, and the like, where not to open their minds at large to each other, were to be wanting to their own love, and to the expectation of the audience; who watch the movements of their minds, as much as the changes of their fortunes. For the imaging of the first is properly the work of a poet; the latter he borrows of the historian."

Eugenius was proceeding in that part of his discourse, when Crites interrupted him. "I see," said he, "Eugenius and I are never like to have this question decided betwixt us; for he maintains the Moderns have acquired a new perfection in writing; I can only grant they have altered the mode of it. Homer described his heroes men of great appetites, lovers of beef broiled upon the coals, and good fellows; contrary to the practice of the French Romances, whose heroes neither eat, nor drink, nor sleep, for love. Virgil makes Æneas a bold avower of his own virtues:

> Sum pius Æneas, fama super æthera notus; [2]

which, in the civility of our poets is the character of a fanfaron or Hector [3]: for with us the knight takes occasion to walk out, or sleep, to avoid the vanity of telling his own story, which the trusty squire is ever to perform for him. So in their love-scenes, of which Eugenius spoke last, the Ancients were more hearty, we more talkative; they writ love as it was then the mode to make it; and I will grant thus much to Eugenius, that perhaps one of their poets, had he lived in our age, *si foret hoc nostrum fato delapsus in ævum* [4] (as Horace says of Lucilius), he had altered many things; not that they were not as natural before, but that he might accommodate himself to the age he lived in. Yet in the mean time, we are not to conclude any thing rashly against those great men, but preserve to

---

[1] My soul, my life.

[2] "I am that pious Æneas, famed above the heavens." *Æneid*, i, 378–79.

[3] A hector, or bully, was portrayed by Samuel Butler, among his *Characters*; *fanfaron* means braggart, or empty boaster.

[4] "If he had been dropped by fate into our age." *Sat.*, i, 10, 68.

them the dignity of masters, and give that honor to their memories, *quos Libitina sacravit*,[1] part of which we expect may be paid to us in future times."

This moderation of Crites, as it was pleasing to all the company, so it put an end to that dispute; which Eugenius, who seemed to have the better of the argument, would urge no farther: but Lisideius, after he had acknowledged himself of Eugenius his opinion concerning the Ancients, yet told him, he had forborne, till his discourse were ended, to ask him why he preferred the English plays above those of other nations? and whether we ought not to submit our stage to the exactness of our next neighbors?

"Though," said Eugenius, "I am at all times ready to defend the honor of my country against the French, and to maintain, we are as well able to vanquish them with our pens, as our ancestors have been with their swords; yet, if you please," added he, looking upon Neander, "I will commit this cause to my friend's management; his opinion of our plays is the same with mine, and besides, there is no reason, that Crites and I, who have now left the stage, should re-enter so suddenly upon it; which is against the laws of comedy."

"If the question had been stated," replied Lisideius, "who had writ best, the French or English, forty years ago, I should have been of your opinion, and adjudged the honor to our own nation; but since that time" (said he, turning towards Neander), "we have been so long together bad Englishmen, that we had not leisure to be good poets. Beaumont, Fletcher, and Jonson (who were only capable of bringing us to that degree of perfection which we have) were just then leaving the world; as if (in an age of so much horror) wit, and those milder studies of humanity, had no farther business among us. But the Muses, who ever follow peace, went to plant in another country: it was then that the great Cardinal of Richelieu began to take them into his protection; and that, by his encouragement, Corneille, and some other Frenchmen, reformed their theatre, which before was as much below ours, as it now surpasses it and the rest of Europe. But because Crites in his discourse for the Ancients has prevented [2] me, by touching upon many rules of the stage which the Moderns have borrowed from them, I shall only, in short, demand of you, whether you are not convinced that of all nations the French have best observed them? In the Unity of Time you find them so scrupulous, that it yet remains a dispute among their poets,

---

1 "Which Libitina has made sacred." Horace, *Epist.*, ii, 1, 49.
2 anticipated.

whether the artificial day of twelve hours, more or less, be not meant by Aristotle, rather than the natural one of twenty-four; and consequently, whether all plays ought not to be reduced into that compass. This I can testify, that in all their dramas writ within these last twenty years and upwards, I have not observed any that have extended the time to thirty hours: in the Unity of Place they are full as scrupulous; for many of their critics limit it to that very spot of ground where the play is supposed to begin; none of them exceed the compass of the same town or city. The Unity of Action in all plays is yet more conspicuous; for they do not burden them with underplots, as the English do: which is the reason why many scenes of our tragi-comedies carry on a design that is nothing of kin to the main plot; and that we see two distinct webs in a play, like those in ill-wrought stuffs; and two actions, that is, two plays, carried on together, to the confounding of the audience; who, before they are warm in their concernments for one part, are diverted to another; and by that means espouse the interest of neither. From hence likewise it arises, that the one half of our actors are not known to the other. They keep their distances, as if they were Montagues and Capulets, and seldom begin an acquaintance till the last scene of the fifth act, when they are all to meet upon the stage. There is no theatre in the world has anything so absurd as the English tragicomedy; 'tis a drama of our own invention, and the fashion of it is enough to proclaim it so; here a course of mirth, there another of sadness and passion, a third of honor and fourth a duel: thus, in two hours and a half, we run through all the fits of Bedlam. The French affords you as much variety on the same day, but they do it not so unseasonably, or *mal à propos*, as we: our poets present you the play and the farce together; and our stages still retain somewhat of the original civility of the *Red Bull*: [1]

Atque ursum et pugiles media inter carmina poscunt.[2]

The end of tragedies or serious plays, says Aristotle, is to beget admiration, compassion, or concernment; but are not mirth and compassion things incompatible? and is it not evident that the poet must of necessity destroy the former by intermingling of the latter? that is, he must ruin the sole end and object of his tragedy, to introduce somewhat that is forced in, and is not of the body of it.

[1] Before the Restoration, the favorite theatre for "drolls." In 1664, Pepys went to the Red Bull to see a prize-fight.
[2] "In the middle of plays they demand a bear or boxers." Horace, *Epist.*, ii, 1, 185.

Would you not think that physician mad, who, having prescribed a purge, should immediately order you to take restringents upon it?

"But to leave our plays, and return to theirs. I have noted one great advantage they have had in the plotting of their tragedies; that is, they are always grounded upon some known history: according to that of Horace, *Ex noto fictum carmen sequar;* [1] and in that they have so imitated the Ancients that they have surpassed them. For the Ancients, as was observed before, took for the foundation of their plays some poetical fiction, such as under that consideration could move but little concernment in the audience, because they already knew the event of it. But the French goes farther:

> Atque ita mentitur, sic veris falsa remiscet
> Primo ne medium, medio ne discrepet imum. [2]

He so interweaves truth with probable fiction that he puts a pleasing fallacy upon us; mends the intrigues of fate, and dispenses with the severity of history, to reward that virtue which has been rendered to us there unfortunate. Sometimes the story has left the success so doubtful, that the writer is free, by the privilege of a poet, to take that which of two or more relations will best suit with his design: as for example, the death of Cyrus, whom Justin and some others report to have perished in the Scythian war, but Xenophon affirms to have died in his bed of extreme old age. Nay more, when the event is past dispute, even then we are willing to be deceived, and the poet, if he contrives it with appearance of truth, has all the audience of his party; at least during the time his play is acting: so naturally we are kind to virtue, when our own interest is not in question, that we take it up as the general concernment of mankind. On the other side, if you consider the historical plays of Shakespeare, they are rather so many chronicles of kings, or the business many times of thirty or forty years, cramped into a representation of two hours and an half; which is not to imitate or paint Nature, but rather to draw her in miniature, to take her in little; to look upon her through the wrong end of a perspective,[3] and receive her images not only much less, but infinitely more imperfect than the life: this, instead of making a play delightful, renders it ridiculous:—

---

[1] "I should fashion a poem based upon a well-known plot." Horace, *Ars Poet.*, 240.

[2] "He so lies and mixes the true and false that the middle is out of harmony with the beginning, and the end with the middle." *Ibid.*, 151.

[3] telescope.

Quodcunque ostendis mihi sic, incredulus odi.[1]

For the spirit of man cannot be satisfied but with truth, or at least verisimility; and a poem is to contain, if not τὰ ἔτυμα,[2] yet ἐτύμοισιν ὁμοῖα,[3] as one [4] of the Greek poets has expressed it.

"Another thing in which the French differ from us and from the Spaniards, is, that they do not embarrass, or cumber themselves with too much plot; they only represent so much of a story as will constitute one whole and great action sufficient for a play; we, who undertake more, do but multiply adventures; which, not being produced from one another, as effects from causes, but barely following, constitute many actions in the drama, and consequently make it many plays.

"But by pursuing close one argument, which is not cloyed with many turns, the French have gained more liberty for verse, in which they write; they have leisure to dwell on a subject which deserves it; and to represent the passions (which we have acknowledged to be the poet's work), without being hurried from one thing to another, as we are in the plays of Calderón, which we have seen lately upon our theatres, under the name of Spanish plots. I have taken notice but of one tragedy of ours, whose plot has that uniformity and unity of design in it, which I have commended in the French; and that is *Rollo*, or rather, under the name of Rollo,[5] the story of Bassianus and Geta in Herodian: there indeed the plot is neither large nor intricate, but just enough to fill the minds of the audience, not to cloy them. Besides, you see it founded upon the truth of history, only the time of the action is not reduceable to the strictness of the rules; and you see in some places a little farce mingled, which is below the dignity of the other parts; and in this all our poets are extremely peccant: even Ben Jonson himself, in *Sejanus* and *Catiline*, has given us this oleo [6] of a play, this unnatural mixture of comedy and tragedy; which to me sounds just as ridiculously as the history of David and the merry humors of Golias.[7]

---

[1] "Whatever you show me thus, I dislike, not believing it." Horace, *Ars Poet.*, 188.
[2] the truth.
[3] Like the truth.
[4] Homer, *Od.*, xix, 203.
[5] *The Bloody Brother*, or *The Tragedy of Rollo, Duke of Normandy*, by John Fletcher. Herodian (170–240) was a Greek writer on Roman history.
[6] medley.
[7] A jolly bishop (probably invented by Walter Map in the twelfth century), a symbol of gluttony and lechery.

In *Sejanus* you may take notice of the scene betwixt Livia and the physician, which is a pleasant satire upon the artificial helps of beauty: in *Catiline* you may see the parliament of women; the little envies of them to one another; and all that passes betwixt Curio and Fulvia: scenes admirable in their kind, but of an ill mingle with the rest.

"But I return again to the French writers, who, as I have said, do not burden themselves too much with plot, which has been reproached to them by an *ingenious person* of our nation as a fault; for, he says, they commonly make but one person considerable in a play; they dwell on him, and his concernments, while the rest of the persons are only subservient to set him off. If he intends this by it, that there is one person in the play who is of greater dignity than the rest, he must tax, not only theirs, but those of the Ancients, and which he would be loth to do, the best of ours; for it is impossible but that one person must be more conspicuous in it than any other, and consequently the greatest share in the action must devolve on him. We see it so in the management of all affairs; even in the most equal aristocracy, the balance cannot be so justly poised, but some one will be superior to the rest, either in parts, fortune, interest, or the consideration of some glorious exploit; which will reduce the greatest part of business into his hands.

"But, if he would have us to imagine, that in exalting one character the rest of them are neglected, and that all of them have not some share or other in the action of the play, I desire him to produce any of Corneille's tragedies, wherein every person, like so many servants in a well-governed family, has not some employment, and who is not necessary to the carrying on of the plot, or at least to your understanding it.

"There are indeed some protatic [1] persons in the Ancients, whom they make use of in their plays, either to hear or give the relation: but the French avoid this with great address, making their narrations only to, or by such, who are some way interested in the main design. And now I am speaking of relations, I cannot take a fitter opportunity to add this in favor of the French, that they often use them with better judgment and more *à propos* than the English do. Not that I commend narrations in general,—but there are two sorts of them. One, of those things which are antecedent to the play, and are related to make the conduct of it more clear to us. But 'tis a fault to choose such subjects for the stage as will force us on that rock, be-

---

[1] Protatic persons are those appearing only in the introductory part of the play.

cause we see they are seldom listened to by the audience, and that is many times the ruin of the play; for, being once let pass without attention, the audience can never recover themselves to understand the plot: and indeed it is somewhat unreasonable that they should be put to so much trouble, as that, to comprehend what passes in their sight, they must have recourse to what was done, perhaps, ten or twenty years ago.

"But there is another sort of relations, that is, of things happening in the action of the play, and supposed to be done behind the scenes; and this is many times both convenient and beautiful; for by it the French avoid the tumult which we are subject to in England, by representing duels, battles, and the like; which renders our stage too like the theatres where they fight prizes. For what is more ridiculous than to represent an army with a drum and five men behind it; all which the hero of the other side is to drive in before him; or to see a duel fought, and one slain with two or three thrusts of the foils, which we know are so blunted, that we might give a man an hour to kill another in good earnest with them.

"I have observed that in all our tragedies, the audience cannot forbear laughing when the actors are to die; it is the most comic part of the whole play. All *passions* may be lively represented on the stage, if to the well-writing of them the actor supplies a good commanded voice, and limbs that move easily, and without stiffness; but there are many *actions* which can never be imitated to a just height: dying especially is a thing which none but a Roman gladiator could naturally perform on the stage, when he did not imitate or represent, but naturally do it; and therefore it is better to omit the representation of it.

"The words of a good writer, which describe it lively, will make a deeper impression of belief in us than all the actor can persuade us to, when he seems to fall dead before us; as a poet in the description of a beautiful garden, or a meadow, will please our imagination more than the place itself can please our sight. When we see death represented, we are convinced it is but fiction; but when we hear it related, our eyes, the strongest witnesses, are wanting, which might have undeceived us; and we are all willing to favor the sleight, when the poet does not too grossly impose on us. They therefore who imagine these relations would make no concernment in the audience, are deceived, by confounding them with the other, which are of things antecedent to the play: those are made often in cold blood, as I may say, to the audience; but these are warmed with our concernments, which were before awakened in the play. What the philosophers say of motion, that, when it is once begun, it continues of itself, and will do so to eternity, without some stop put to it, is clearly true on this occasion: the soul, being already moved with the characters and fortunes of those imaginary persons, continues going of its own accord; and we are no more weary to hear what becomes of them when they are not on the stage, than we are to listen to the news of an absent mistress. But it is objected, that if one part of the play may be related, then why not all? I answer, some parts of the action are more fit to be represented, some to be related. Corneille says judiciously, that the poet is not obliged to expose to view all particular actions which conduce to the principal: he ought to select such of them to be seen, which will appear with the greatest beauty, either by the magnificence of the show, or the vehemence of passions which they produce, or some other charm which they have in them; and let the rest arrive to the audience by narration. 'Tis a great mistake in us to believe the French present no part of the action on the stage; every alteration or crossing of a design, every new-sprung passion, and turn of it, is a part of the action, and much the noblest, except we conceive nothing to be action till they come to blows; as if the painting of the hero's mind were not more properly the poet's work than the strength of his body. Nor does this anything contradict the opinion of Horace, where he tells us,

> Segnius irritant animos demissa per aurem,
> Quam quæ sunt oculis subjecta fidelibus.[1]

For he says immediately after,

> Non tamen intus
> Digna geri promes in scenam; multaq; tolles
> Ex oculis, quæ mox narret facundia præsens.[2]

Among which many he recounts some:

> Nec pueros coram populo Medea trucidet,
> Aut in avem Progné mutetur, Cadmus in anguem; etc.[3]

[1] "Things communicated by the ear impress the mind less than things which have been witnessed by the unmistaking eyes." Horace, *Ars Poet.*, 180.

[2] Yet there are things improper for a scene,
   Which men of judgment only will relate. (Roscommon.)

[3] Medea should not slaughter her children in the face of the audience, or Progné be changed into a bird, or Cadmus into a snake.

That is, those actions which by reason of their cruelty will cause aversion in us, or by reason of their impossibility, unbelief, ought either wholly to be avoided by a poet, or only delivered by narration. To which we may have leave to add such as to avoid tumult (as was before hinted), or to reduce the plot into a more reasonable compass of time, or for defect of beauty in them, are rather to be related than presented to the eye. Examples of all these kinds are frequent, not only among all the Ancients, but in the best received of our English poets. We find Ben Jonson using them in his *Magnetic Lady*, where one comes out from dinner, and relates the quarrels and disorders of it, to save the undecent appearance of them on the stage, and to abbreviate the story; and this in express imitation of Terence, who had done the same before him in his *Eunuch*, where Pythias makes the like relation of what had happened within at the Soldier's entertainment. The relations likewise of Sejanus's death, and the prodigies before it, are remarkable; the one of which was hid from sight, to avoid the horror and tumult of the representation; the other, to shun the introducing of things impossible to be believed. In that excellent play, *The King and no King*, Fletcher goes yet farther; for the whole unravelling of the plot is done by narration in the fifth act, after the manner of the Ancients; and it moves great concernment in the audience, though it be only a relation of what was done many years before the play. I could multiply other instances, but these are sufficient to prove that there is no error in choosing a subject which requires this sort of narrations; in the ill managing of them, there may.

"But I find I have been too long in this discourse, since the French have many other excellencies not common to us; as that you never see any of their plays end with a conversion, or simple change of will, which is the ordinary way which our poets use to end theirs. It shows little art in the conclusion of a dramatic poem, when they who have hindered the felicity during the four acts, desist from it in the fifth, without some powerful cause to take them off their design; and though I deny not but such reasons may be found, yet it is a path that is cautiously to be trod, and the poet is to be sure he convinces the audience that the motive is strong enough. As for example, the conversion of the Usurer in *The Scornful Lady* seems to me a little forced; for, being an Usurer, which implies a lover of money to the highest degree of covetousness (and such the poet has represented him), the account he gives for the sudden change is, that he has been duped by the wild young fellow; which in reason might render him more wary another time, and make him punish himself with harder fare and coarser clothes, to get it up again: but that he should look on it as a judgment, and so repent, we may expect to hear of in a sermon, but I should never endure it in a play.

"I pass by this; neither will I insist on the care they take, that no person after his first entrance shall ever appear, but the business which brings him upon the stage shall be evident; which rule, if observed, must needs render all the events in the play more natural; for there you see the probability of every accident, in the cause that produced it; and that which appears chance in the play, will seem so reasonable to you, that you will there find it almost necessary: so that in the exits of the actors you have a clear account of their purpose and design in the next entrance (though, if the scene be well wrought, the event will commonly deceive you), for there is nothing so absurd, says Corneille, as for an actor to leave the stage, only because he has no more to say.

"I should now speak of the beauty of their rhyme, and the just reason I have to prefer that way of writing in tragedies before ours in blank verse; but because it is partly received by us, and therefore not altogether peculiar to them, I will say no more of it in relation to their plays. For our own, I doubt not but it will exceedingly beautify them; and I can see but one reason why it should not generally obtain, that is, because our poets write so ill in it. This indeed may prove a more prevailing argument than all others which are used to destroy it, and therefore I am only troubled when great and judicious poets, and those who are acknowledged such, have writ or spoke against it: as for others, they are to be answered by that one sentence of an ancient author:—*Sed ut primo ad consequendos eos quos priores ducimus, accendimur, ita ubi aut præteriri, aut æquari eos posse desperavimus, studium cum spe senescit: quod, scilicet, assequi non potest, sequi desinit; . . . præteritoque eo in quo eminere non possumus, aliquid in quo nitamur, conquirimus.*" [1]

Lisideius concluded in this manner; and Neander, after a little pause, thus answered him:

"I shall grant Lisideius, without much dispute, a great part of what

[1] "But as we are inspired to follow those whom we consider leaders, so when we have given up hope of passing or equalling them, our eagerness flags with our hope; naturally, since it cannot attain, it gives up following . . . After what we were unable to be prominent in has passed by, we look around for something in which we may shine." Velleius, i, 17.

he has urged against us; for I acknowledge that the French contrive their plots more regularly, and observe the laws of comedy, and decorum of the stage (to speak generally), with more exactness than the English. Farther, I deny not but he has taxed us justly in some irregularities of ours, which he has mentioned; yet, after all, I am of opinion that neither our faults nor their virtues are considerable enough to place them above us.

"For the lively imitation of Nature being in the definition of a play, those which best fulfil that law ought to be esteemed superior to the others. 'Tis true, those beauties of the French poesy are such as will raise perfection higher where it is, but are not sufficient to give it where it is not: they are indeed the beauties of a statue, but not of a man, because not animated with the soul of Poesy, which is imitation of humor and passions: and this Lisideius himself, or any other, however biassed to their party, cannot but acknowledge, if he will either compare the humors of our comedies, or the characters of our serious plays, with theirs. He that will look upon theirs which have been written till these last ten years, or thereabouts, will find it an hard matter to pick out two or three passable humors amongst them. Corneille himself, their arch-poet, what has he produced except *The Liar*,[1] and you know how it was cried up in France; but when it came upon the English stage, though well translated, and that part of Dorant acted to so much advantage by Mr. Hart [2] as I am confident it never received in its own country, the most favorable to it would not put it in competition with many of Fletcher's or Ben Jonson's. In the rest of Corneille's comedies you have little humor; he tells you himself, his way is, first to show two lovers in good intelligence with each other; in the working up of the play to embroil them by some mistake, and in the latter end to clear it up, and reconcile them.

"But of late years de Molière, the younger Corneille, Quinault,[3] and some others, have been imitating afar off the quick turns and graces of the English stage. They have mixed their serious plays with mirth, like our tragi-comedies, since the death of Cardinal Richelieu; which Lisideius and many others not observing, have commended that in them for a virtue which they themselves no longer practice. Most of their new plays are, like some of ours, derived from the

---

[1] *Le Menteur* (1644), founded on a Spanish play; translated into English as *The Mistaken Beauty, or the Lyar*.

[2] Charles Hart, grand-nephew of Shakespeare; see *D.N.B.*

[3] Molière (1621–1673), Thomas Corneille (1625–1709) and Philippe Quinault (1635–1688) had written many plays; the latter also wrote the books of Lulli's operas.

Spanish novels. There is scarce one of them without a veil, and a trusty Diego, who drolls much after the rate of the *Adventures*.[1] But their humors, if I may grace them with that name, are so thin-sown, that never above one of them comes up in any play. I dare take upon me to find more variety of them in some one play of Ben Jonson's, than in all theirs together; as he who has seen *The Alchemist, The Silent Woman*, or *Bartholomew Fair*, cannot but acknowledge with me.

"I grant the French have performed what was possible on the ground-work of the Spanish plays; what was pleasant before, they have made regular: but there is not above one good play to be writ on all those plots; they are too much alike to please often; which we need not the experience of our own stage to justify. As for their new way of mingling mirth with serious plot, I do not, with Lisideius, condemn the thing, though I cannot approve their manner of doing it. He tells us, we cannot so speedily recollect ourselves after a scene of great passion and concernment, as to pass to another of mirth and humor, and to enjoy it with any relish: but why should he imagine the soul of man more heavy than his senses? Does not the eye pass from an unpleasant object to a pleasant in a much shorter time than is required to this? and does not the unpleasantness of the first commend the beauty of the latter? The old rule of logic might have convinced him, that contraries, when placed near, set off each other. A continued gravity keeps the spirit too much bent; we must refresh it sometimes, as we bait in a journey, that we may go on with greater ease. A scene of mirth, mixed with tragedy, has the same effect upon us which our music has betwixt the acts; and that we find a relief to us from the best plots and language of the stage, if the discourses have been long. I must therefore have stronger arguments, ere I am convinced that compassion and mirth in the same subject destroy each other; and in the mean time cannot but conclude, to the honor of our nation, that we have invented, increased, and perfected a more pleasant way of writing for the stage, than was ever known to the ancients or moderns of any nation, which is tragi-comedy.

"And this leads me to wonder why Lisideius and many others should cry up the barrenness of the French plots above the variety and copiousness of the English. Their plots are single; they carry on one design, which is pushed forward by all the actors, every

[1] Ker notes that Diego is the comic servant in the *Adventures of Five Hours* (1663), adapted, by Sir Samuel Tuke, from *Los Empeños de seis Horas*, attributed to Calderón.

scene in the play contributing and moving towards it. Our plays, besides the main design, have under-plots or by-concernments, of less considerable persons and intrigues, which are carried on with the motion of the main plot: just as they say the orb of the fixed stars, and those of the planets, though they have motions of their own, are whirled about by the motion of the *Primum Mobile*,[1] in which they are contained. That similitude expresses much of the English stage; for if contrary motions may be found in nature to agree; if a planet can go east and west at the same time, one way by virtue of his own motion, the other by the force of the First Mover, it will not be difficult to imagine how the under-plot, which is only different, not contrary to the great design, may naturally be conducted along with it.

"Eugenius has already shown us, from the confession of the French poets, that the Unity of Action is sufficiently preserved, if all the imperfect actions of the play are conducing to the main design; but when those petty intrigues of a play are so ill ordered, that they have no coherence with the other, I must grant that Lisideius has reason to tax that want of due connection; for co-ordination in a play is as dangerous and unnatural as in a state. In the mean time he must acknowledge, our variety, if well ordered, will afford a greater pleasure to the audience.

"As for his other argument, that by pursuing one single theme they gain an advantage to express and work up the passions, I wish any example he could bring from them would make it good; for I confess their verses are to me the coldest I have ever read. Neither, indeed, is it possible for them, in the way they take, so to express passion, as that the effects of it should appear in the concernment of an audience, their speeches being so many declamations, which tire us with the length; so that instead of persuading us to grieve for their imaginary heroes, we are concerned for our own trouble, as we are in the tedious visits of bad company; we are in pain till they are gone. When the French stage came to be reformed by Cardinal Richelieu, those long harangues were introduced, to comply with the gravity of a churchman. Look upon the *Cinna* and the *Pompey*; they are not so properly to be called plays, as long discourses of reason of state; and *Polyeucte* in matters of religion is as solemn as the long stops upon our organs. Since that time it is grown into a custom, and their actors speak by the hour-glass, like our parsons;

[1] In the old astronomy, the sphere beyond the sphere of the fixed stars, which gives to the lower spheres their daily motion from east to west, round the centre of the earth.

nay, they account it the grace of their parts, and think themselves disparaged by the poet, if they may not twice or thrice in a play entertain the audience with a speech of an hundred or two hundred lines. I deny not but this may suit well enough with the French; for as we, who are a more sullen people, come to be diverted at our plays, so they, who are of an airy and gay temper, come thither to make themselves more serious: and this I conceive to be one reason why comedy is more pleasing to us, and tragedies to them. But to speak generally: it cannot be denied that short speeches and replies are more apt to move the passions and beget concernment in us, than the other; for it is unnatural for any one in a gust of passion to speak long together, or for another in the same condition to suffer him, without interruption. Grief and passion are like floods raised in little brooks by a sudden rain; they are quickly up; and if the concernment be poured unexpectedly in upon us, it overflows us: but a long sober shower gives them leisure to run out as they came in, without troubling the ordinary current. As for Comedy, repartee is one of its chiefest graces; the greatest pleasure of the audience is a chase of wit, kept up on both sides, and swiftly managed. And this our forefathers, if not we, have had in Fletcher's plays, to a much higher degree of perfection than the French poets can arrive at.

"There is another part of Lisideius his discourse, in which he rather excused our neighbors, than commended them; that is, for aiming only to make one person considerable in their plays. 'Tis very true what he has urged, that one character in all plays, even without the poet's care, will have advantage of all the others; and that the design of the whole drama will chiefly depend on it. But this hinders not that there may be more shining characters in the play: many persons of a second magnitude, nay, some so very near, so almost equal to the first, that greatness may be opposed to greatness, and all the persons be made considerable, not only by their quality, but their action. 'Tis evident that the more the persons are, the greater will be the variety of the plot. If then the parts are managed so regularly, that the beauty of the whole be kept entire, and that the variety become not a perplexed and confused mass of accidents, you will find it infinitely pleasing to be led in a labyrinth of design, where you see some of your way before you, yet discern not the end till you arrive at it. And that all this is practicable, I can produce for examples many of our English plays: as *The Maid's Tragedy*, *The Alchemist*, *The Silent Woman*: I was

going to have named *The Fox*, but that the unity of design seems
not exactly observed in it; for there appear two actions in the play;
the first naturally ending with the fourth act; the second forced
from it in the fifth: which yet is the less to be condemned in him,
because the disguise of Volpone, though it suited not with his character as a crafty or covetous person, agreed well enough with that of
a voluptuary; and by it the poet gained the end he aimed at, the
punishment of vice, and the reward of virtue, which that disguise
produced. So that to judge equally of it, it was an excellent fifth
act, but not so naturally proceeding from the former.

"But to leave this, and pass to the latter part of Lisideius his discourse, which concerns relations: I must acknowledge with him,
that the French have reason when they hide that part of the action
which would occasion too much tumult on the stage, and choose
rather to have it made known by narration to the audience. Farther,
I think it very convenient, for the reasons he has given, that all
incredible actions were removed; but, whether custom has so in-
sinuated itself into our countrymen, or nature has so formed them
to fierceness, I know not; but they will scarcely suffer combats and
other objects of horror to be taken from them. And indeed, the in-
decency of tumults is all which can be objected against fighting:
for why may not our imagination as well suffer itself to be deluded
with the probability of it, as with any other thing in the play? For
my part, I can with as great ease persuade myself that the blows
which are struck, are given in good earnest, as I can that they who
strike them are kings or princes, or those persons which they represent. For objects of incredibility, I would be satisfied from Lisideius, whether we have any so removed from all appearance of
truth, as are those of Corneille's *Andromède;* a play which has been
frequented the most of any he has writ. If the Perseus, or the son
of an heathen god, the Pegasus, and the Monster, were not capable to
choke a strong belief, let him blame any representation of ours
hereafter. Those indeed were objects of delight; yet the reason is
the same as to the probability: for he makes it not a Ballette or
masque, but a play, which is to resemble truth. But for death, that
it ought not to be represented, I have, besides the arguments alleged
by Lisideius, the authority of Ben Jonson, who has forborne it in
his tragedies; for both the death of Sejanus and Catiline are related:
though in the latter I cannot but observe one irregularity of that
great poet; he has removed the scene in the same act from Rome to
Catiline's army, and from thence again to Rome; and besides, has

allowed a very inconsiderable time, after Catiline's speech, for the striking of the battle, and the return of Petreius, who is to relate the event of it to the senate: which I should not animadvert on him, who was otherwise a painful observer of τὸ πρέπον, or the *decorum* of the stage, if he had not used extreme severity in his judgment on the incomparable Shakespeare for the same fault.—To conclude on this subject of relations; if we are to be blamed for showing too much of the action, the French are as faulty for discovering too little of it: a mean betwixt both should be observed by every judicious writer, so as the audience may neither be left unsatisfied by not seeing what is beautiful, or shocked by beholding what is either incredible or undecent.

"I hope I have already proved in this discourse, that though we are not altogether so punctual as the French in observing the laws of Comedy, yet our errors are so few, and little, and those things wherein we excel them so considerable, that we ought of right to be preferred before them. But what will Lisideius say, if they themselves acknowledge they are too strictly tied up by those laws, for breaking which he has blamed the English? I will allege Corneille's words, as I find them in the end of his Discourse of the Three Unities: *Il est facile aux spéculatifs d'être sévères*, etc. ' 'Tis easy for speculative persons to judge severely; but if they would produce to public view ten or twelve pieces of this nature, they would perhaps give more latitude to the rules than I have done, when, by experience, they had known how much we are bound up and constrained by them, and how many beauties of the stage they banished from it.' To illustrate a little what he has said: by their servile observations of the Unities of Time and Place, and integrity of scenes, they have brought on themselves that dearth of plot, and narrowness of imagination, which may be observed in all their plays. How many beautiful accidents might naturally happen in two or three days, which cannot arrive with any probability in the compass of twenty-four hours? There is time to be allowed also for maturity of design, which, amongst great and prudent persons, such as are often represented in Tragedy, cannot, with any likelihood of truth, be brought to pass at so short a warning. Farther; by tying themselves strictly to the Unity of Place, and unbroken scenes, they are forced many times to omit some beauties which cannot be shown where the act began; but might, if the scene were interrupted, and the stage cleared for the persons to enter in another place; and therefore the French poets are often forced upon absurdities; for if the act begins in a chamber, all the persons in the play must have some business or other to come thither, or else they are not to be shown that act; and sometimes their characters are very unfitting to appear there. As, suppose it were the king's bed-chamber; yet the meanest man in the tragedy must come and dispatch his business there, rather than in the lobby or courtyard (which is fitter for him), for fear the stage should be cleared, and the scenes broken. Many times they fall by it in a greater inconvenience; for they keep their scenes unbroken, and yet change the place; as in one of their newest plays, where the act begins in the street.[1] There a gentleman is to meet his friend; he sees him with his man, coming out from his father's house; they talk together, and the first goes out: the second, who is a lover, has made an appointment with his mistress; she appears at the window, and then we are to imagine the scene lies under it. This gentleman is called away, and leaves his servant with his mistress; presently her father is heard from within; the young lady is afraid the serving-man should be discovered, and thrusts him in through a door, which is supposed to be her closet. After this, the father enters to the daughter, and now the scene is in a house; for he is seeking from one room to another for this poor Philipin, or French Diego, who is heard from within, drolling and breaking many a miserable conceit upon his sad condition. In this ridiculous manner the play goes on, the stage being never empty all the while: so that the street, the window, the houses, and the closet, are made to walk about, and the persons to stand still. Now what, I beseech you, is more easy than to write a regular French play, or more difficult than to write an irregular English one, like those of Fletcher, or of Shakespeare?

"If they content themselves, as Corneille did, with some flat design, which, like an ill riddle, is found out ere it be half proposed, such plots we can make every way regular, as easily as they; but whene'er they endeavor to rise to any quick turns and counterturns of plot, as some of them have attempted, since Corneille's plays have been less in vogue, you see they write as irregularly as we, though they cover it more speciously. Hence the reason is perspicuous, why no French plays, when translated, have, or ever can, succeed on the English stage. For, if you consider the plots, our own are fuller of variety; if the writing, ours are more quick and

---

[1] Ker thinks Dryden inaccurately remembers a scene from Thomas Corneille's *L'Amour à la Mode*, confusing it with a similar scene in Quinault's *L'Amant Indiscret*, where the servant is Philipin.

fuller of spirit; and therefore 'tis a strange mistake in those who decry the way of writing plays in verse, as if the English therein imitated the French. We have borrowed nothing from them; our plots are weaved in English looms: we endeavor therein to follow the variety and greatness of characters which are derived to us from Shakespeare and Fletcher; the copiousness and well-knitting of the intrigues we have from Jonson; and for the verse itself we have English precedents of elder date than any of Corneille's plays. Not to name our old comedies before Shakespeare, which were all writ in verse of six feet, or Alexandrines,[1] such as the French now use, I can show in Shakespeare many scenes of rhyme together, and the like in Ben Jonson's tragedies: in *Catiline* and *Sejanus* sometimes thirty or forty lines, I mean besides the Chorus, or the monologues; which, by the way, showed Ben no enemy to this way of writing, especially if you look upon his *Sad Shepherd*, which goes sometimes on rhyme, sometimes on blank verse, like an horse who eases himself on trot and amble. You find him likewise commending Fletcher's pastoral of *The Faithful Shepherdess*, which is for the most part rhyme, though not refined to that purity to which it hath since been brought. And these examples are enough to clear us from a servile imitation of the French.

"But to return from whence I have digressed: I dare boldly affirm these two things of the English drama;—First, that we have many plays of ours as regular as any of theirs, and which, besides, have more variety of plot and characters; and secondly, that in most of the irregular plays of Shakespeare or Fletcher (for Ben Jonson's are for the most part regular), there is a more masculine fancy and greater spirit in the writing, than there is in any of the French. I could produce, even in Shakespeare's and Fletcher's works, some plays which are almost exactly formed; as *The Merry Wives of Windsor*, and *The Scornful Lady*: but because (generally speaking) Shakespeare, who writ first, did not perfectly observe the laws of Comedy, and Fletcher, who came nearer to perfection, yet through carelessness made many faults; I will take the pattern of a perfect play from Ben Jonson, who was a careful and learned observer of the dramatic laws, and from all his comedies I shall select *The Silent Woman*; of which I will make a short examen, according to those rules which the French observe."

As Neander was beginning to examine *The Silent Woman*, Eugenius, looking earnestly upon him; "I beseech you, Neander,"

---

[1] Not a strictly true statement.

said he, "gratify the company, and me in particular, so far, as before you speak of the play, to give us a character of the author; and tell us frankly your opinion, whether you do not think all writers, both French and English, ought to give place to him."

"I fear," replied Neander, "that in obeying your commands I shall draw a little envy on myself. Besides, in performing them, it will be first necessary to speak somewhat of Shakespeare and Fletcher, his rivals in poesy; and one of them, in my opinion, at least his equal, perhaps his superior.

"To begin, then, with Shakespeare. He was the man who of all modern, and perhaps ancient poets, had the largest and most comprehensive soul. All the images of Nature were still present to him, and he drew them, not laboriously, but luckily; when he describes anything, you more than see it, you feel it too. Those who accuse him to have wanted learning, give him the greater commendation: he was naturally learned; he needed not the spectacles of books to read Nature; he looked inwards, and found her there. I cannot say he is everywhere alike; were he so, I should do him injury to compare him with the greatest of mankind. He is many times flat, insipid; his comic wit degenerating into clenches, his serious swelling into bombast. But he is always great, when some great occasion is presented to him; no man can say he ever had a fit subject for his wit, and did not then raise himself as high above the rest of poets,

Quantum lenta solent inter viburna cupressi.[1]

The consideration of this made Mr. Hales of Eton [2] say, that there was no subject of which any poet ever writ, but he would produce it much better treated of in Shakespeare; and however others are now generally preferred before him, yet the age wherein he lived, which had contemporaries with him Fletcher and Jonson, never equalled them to him in their esteem: and in the last King's Court, when Ben's reputation was at highest, Sir John Suckling, and with him the greater part of the courtiers, set our Shakespeare far above him.[3]

[1] "As cypresses usually do among bending shrubs." Vergil, *Eclogues*, i, 25.

[2] John Hales (1584–1656), Fellow of Eton, 1612. Ker, referring to Rowe's *Life of Shakespeare*, notes a story of his being present when Jonson was speaking of Shakespeare's want of learning.

[3] Until the end of the century, Beaumont and Fletcher were twice as popular on the stage as Shakespeare. See A. C. Sprague, *Beaumont and Fletcher on the Restoration Stage* (1926) p. 25, citing Dryden. But on p. 121 he notes that by 1710, Shakespeare was as popular as the others; he "had not been crowded out by the new drama; Beaumont and Fletcher were beginning to be."

"Beaumont and Fletcher, of whom I am next to speak, had, with the advantage of Shakespeare's wit, which was their precedent, great natural gifts, improved by study: Beaumont especially being so accurate a judge of plays, that Ben Jonson, while he lived, submitted all his writings to his censure, and, 'tis thought, used his judgment in correcting, if not contriving, all his plots. What value he had for him, appears by the verses he writ to him; and therefore I need speak no farther of it. The first play that brought Fletcher and him in esteem was their *Philaster*: for before that, they had written two or three very unsuccessfully, as the like is reported of Ben Jonson, before he writ *Every Man in His Humor*. Their plots were generally more regular than Shakespeare's, especially those which were made before Beaumont's death; and they understood and imitated the conversation of gentlemen much better; whose wild debaucheries, and quickness of wit in repartees, no poet can ever paint as they have done. Humor, which Ben Jonson derived from particular persons, they made it not their business to describe: they represented all the passions very lively, but above all, love. I am apt to believe the English language in them arrived to its highest perfection: what words have since been taken in, are rather superfluous than ornamental. Their plays are now the most pleasant and frequent entertainments of the stage; two of theirs being acted through the year for one of Shakespeare's or Jonson's: the reason is, because there is a certain gaiety in their comedies, and pathos in their more serious plays, which suits generally with all men's humors. Shakespeare's language is likewise a little obsolete, and Ben Jonson's wit comes short of theirs.

"As for Jonson, to whose character I am now arrived, if we look upon him while he was himself (for his last plays were but his dotages), I think him the most learned and judicious writer which any theatre ever had. He was a most severe judge of himself, as well as others. One cannot say he wanted wit, but rather that he was frugal of it. In his works you find little to retrench or alter. Wit, and language, and humor also in some measure, we had before him; but something of art was wanting to the drama till he came. He managed his strength to more advantage than any who preceded him. You seldom find him making love in any of his scenes, or endeavoring to move the passions; his genius was too sullen and saturnine to do it gracefully, especially when he knew he came after those who had performed both to such an height. Humor was his proper sphere; and in that he delighted most to represent mechanic people.[1] He was deeply conversant in the Ancients, both Greek and Latin, and he borrowed boldly from them: there is scarce a poet or historian among the Roman authors of those times whom he has not translated in *Sejanus* and *Catiline*. But he has done his robberies so openly, that one may see he fears not to be taxed by any law. He invades authors like a monarch; and what would be theft in other poets is only victory in him. With the spoils of these writers he so represents old Rome to us, in its rites, ceremonies, and customs, that if one of their poets had written either of his tragedies, we had seen less of it than in him. If there was any fault in his language, 'twas that he weaved it too closely and laboriously, in his serious plays: perhaps, too, he did a little too much Romanize our tongue, leaving the words which he translated almost as much Latin as he found them: wherein, though he learnedly followed the idiom of their language, he did not enough comply with the idiom of ours. If I would compare him with Shakespeare, I must acknowledge him the more correct poet, but Shakespeare the greater wit. Shakespeare was the Homer, or father of our dramatic poets; Jonson was the Virgil, the pattern of elaborate writing; I admire him, but I love Shakespeare. To conclude of him; as he has given us the most correct plays, so in the precepts which he has laid down in his *Discoveries,* we have as many and profitable rules for perfecting the stage, as any wherewith the French can furnish us."

[Here follows an analysis of Jonson's *Silent Woman.*]

This was the substance of what was then spoken on that occasion; and Lisideius, I think, was going to reply, when he was prevented thus by Crites: "I am confident," said he, "that the most material things that can be said have been already urged on either side; if they have not, I must beg of Lisideius that he will defer his answer till another time: for I confess I have a joint quarrel to you both, because you have concluded, without any reason given for it, that rhyme is proper for the stage. I will not dispute how ancient it hath been among us to write this way; perhaps our ancestors knew no better till Shakespeare's time. I will grant it was not altogether left by him, and that Fletcher and Ben Jonson used it frequently in their Pastorals, and sometimes in other plays. Farther, I will not argue whether we received it originally from our own countrymen, or

[1] Tradesmen, or laboring men.—Cf. *Antony and Cleopatra,* V, ii, 209; and *A Midsummer Night's Dream,* III, ii, 9; also "mechanic dialect," above, p. 59.

from the French; for that is an inquiry of as little benefit, as theirs who, in the midst of the great Plague, were not so solicitous to provide against it, as to know whether we had it from the malignity of our own air, or by transportation from Holland. I have therefore only to affirm, that it is not allowable in serious plays; for comedies, I find you already concluding with me. To prove this, I might satisfy myself to tell you, how much in vain it is for you to strive against the stream of the people's inclination; the greatest part of which are prepossessed so much with those excellent plays of Shakespeare, Fletcher, and Ben Jonson, which have been written out of rhyme, that except you could bring them such as were written better in it, and those too by persons of equal reputation with them, it will be impossible for you to gain your cause with them, who will still be judges. This it is to which, in fine, all your reasons must submit. The unanimous consent of an audience is so powerful, that even Julius Cæsar (as Macrobius reports of him), when he was perpetual dictator, was not able to balance it on the other side. But when Laberius, a Roman Knight, at his request contended in the Mime with another poet, he was forced to cry out, *Etiam favente me victus es, Laberi.*[1] But I will not on this occasion take the advantage of the greater number, but only urge such reasons against rhyme, as I find in the writings of those who have argued for the other way. First, then, I am of opinion that rhyme is unnatural in a play, because dialogue there is presented as the effect of sudden thought: for a play is the imitation of Nature; and since no man, without premeditation, speaks in rhyme, neither ought he to do it on the stage. This hinders not but the fancy may be there elevated to an higher pitch of thought than it is in ordinary discourse; for there is a probability that men of excellent and quick parts may speak noble things *ex tempore*: but those thoughts are never fettered with the numbers or sound of verse without study, and therefore it cannot be but unnatural to present the most free way of speaking in that which is the most constrained. For this reason, says Aristotle, 'tis best to write tragedy in that kind of verse which is the least such, or which is nearest prose: and this amongst the Ancients was the iambic, and with us is blank verse, or the measure of verse kept exactly without rhyme. These numbers therefore are fittest for a play; the others for a paper of verses, or a poem; blank verse being as much below them as rhyme is improper for the drama. And if it be objected that neither are blank verses made *ex tempore*, yet, as

[1] Even with me favoring you, Laberius, you are defeated.

nearest nature, they are still to be preferred.—But there are two particular exceptions, which many besides myself have had to verse; by which it will appear yet more plainly how improper it is in plays. And the first of them is grounded on that very reason for which some have commended rhyme; they say, the quickness of repartees in argumentative scenes receives an ornament from verse. Now what is more unreasonable than to imagine that a man should not only light upon the wit, but the rhyme too, upon the sudden? This nicking of him who spoke before both in sound and measure, is so great an happiness, that you must at least suppose the persons of your play to be born poets: *Arcades omnes, et cantare pares, et respondere parati*: [1] they must have arrived to the degree of *quicquid conabar dicere*; [2]—to make verses almost whether they will or no. If they are anything below this, it will look rather like the design of two, than the answer of one: it will appear that your actors hold intelligence together; that they perform their tricks like fortune-tellers, by confederacy. The hand of art will be too visible in it, against that maxim of all professions, *Ars est celare artem;* that it is the greatest perfection of art to keep itself undiscovered. Nor will it serve you to object, that however you manage it, 'tis still known to be a play; and, consequently, the dialogue of two persons understood to be the labor of one poet. For a play is still an imitation of Nature; we know we are to be deceived, and we desire to be so; but no man ever was deceived but with a probability of truth; for who will suffer a gross lie to be fastened on him? Thus we sufficiently understand, that the scenes which represent cities and countries to us are not really such, but only painted on boards and canvas; but shall that excuse the ill painture or designment of them? Nay, rather ought they not be labored with so much the more diligence and exactness, to help the imagination? since the mind of man does naturally tend to, and seek after truth; and therefore the nearer any thing comes to the imitation of it, the more it pleases.

"Thus, you see, your rhyme is incapable of expressing the greatest thoughts naturally, and the lowest it cannot with any grace: for what is more unbefitting the majesty of verse, than to call a servant, or bid a door be shut in rhyme? and yet this miserable necessity you are often forced upon. But verse, you say, circumscribes a quick and luxuriant fancy, which would extend itself too far on every subject, did not the labor which is required to well-turned and

[1] All Arcadians, ready either to sing or to answer.
[2] What I was trying to say.

polished rhyme, set bounds to it. Yet this argument, if granted, would only prove that we may write better in verse, but not more naturally. Neither is it able to evince that; for he who wants judgment to confine his fancy in blank verse, may want it as much in rhyme: and he who has it will avoid errors in both kinds. Latin verse was as great a confinement to the imagination of those poets, as rhyme to ours; and yet you find Ovid saying too much on every subject. *Nescivit* (says Seneca) *quod bene cessit relinquere*: [1] of which he gives you one famous instance in his description of the deluge:

> Omnia pontus erat, deerant quoque litora ponto.
>
> Now all was sea, nor had that sea a shore.

Thus Ovid's fancy was not limited by verse, and Virgil needed not verse to have bounded his.

"In our own language we see Ben Jonson confining himself to what ought to be said, even in the liberty of blank verse; and yet Corneille, the most judicious of the French poets, is still varying the same sense an hundred ways, and dwelling eternally on the same subject, though confined by rhyme. Some other exceptions I have to verse; but since these I have named are for the most part already public, I conceive it reasonable they should first be answered."

"It concerns me less than any," said Neander (seeing he had ended), "to reply to this discourse; because when I should have proved that verse may be natural in plays, yet I should always be ready to confess, that those which I have written in this kind come short of that perfection which is required. Yet since you are pleased I should undertake this province, I will do it, though with all imaginable respect and deference, both to that person from whom you have borrowed your strongest arguments, and to whose judgment, when I have said all, I finally submit. But before I proceed to answer your objections, I must first remember you, that I exclude all Comedy from my defence; and next that I deny not but blank verse may be also used; and content myself only to assert, that in serious plays where the subject and characters are great, and the plot unmixed with mirth, which might allay or divert these concernments which are produced, rhyme is there as natural and more effectual than blank verse.

"And now having laid down this as a foundation,—to begin with

---

[1] "He did not know how to leave off when it was well." M. Seneca, *Controv.*, ix, 5,— quoting Ovid.

Crites, I must crave leave to tell him, that some of his arguments against rhyme reach no farther than, from the faults or defects of ill rhyme, to conclude against the use of it in general. May not I conclude against blank verse by the same reason? If the words of some poets who write in it are either ill chosen, or ill placed, which makes not only rhyme, but all kind of verse in any language unnatural,[1] shall I, for their vicious affectation, condemn those excellent lines of Fletcher, which are written in that kind? Is there anything in rhyme more constrained than this line in blank verse?—*I heaven invoke, and strong resistance make?* where you see both the clauses are placed unnaturally, that is, contrary to the common way of speaking, and that without the excuse of a rhyme to cause it: yet you would think me very ridiculous, if I should accuse the stubbornness of blank verse for this, and not rather the stiffness of the poet. Therefore, Crites, you must either prove that words, though well chosen, and duly placed, yet render not rhyme natural in itself; or that, however natural and easy the rhyme may be, yet it is not proper for a play. If you insist on the former part, I would ask you, what other conditions are required to make rhyme natural in itself, besides an election of apt words, and a right disposing of them? For the due choice of your words expresses your sense naturally, and the due placing them adapts the rhyme to it.[2] If you object that one verse may be made for the sake of another, though both the words and rhyme be apt, I answer, it cannot possibly so fall out; for either there is a dependence of sense betwixt the first line and the second, or there is none: if there be that connection, then in the natural position of the words the latter line must of necessity flow from the former; if there be no dependence, yet still the due ordering of words makes the last line as natural in itself as the other: so that the necessity of a rhyme never forces any but bad or lazy writers to say what they would not otherwise. 'Tis true, there is both care and art required to write in verse. A good poet never concludes upon the first line, till he has sought out such a rhyme as may fit the sense, already prepared to heighten the second: many times the close of the sense falls into the middle of the next verse, or farther off, and he may often prevail himself of the same advantages in English which Virgil had in Latin; he may break off

[1] The mother who says to her child, "Come, lay your knife and fork across your plate," may not be inspired, but she speaks a metrically perfect blank verse line. It is certainly not "unnatural," and one may suggest that iambic pentameter is natural in English.

[2] Cf. *David Copperfield*, ch. lxiii: ". . . and friends is dear, and I am here.—Which is verse," said Mr. Peggotty, surprised to find it out, "though I hadn't such intentions."

in the hemistich, and begin another line. Indeed, the not observing these two last things makes plays which are writ in verse so tedious: for though, most commonly, the sense is to be confined to the couplet, yet nothing that does *perpetuo tenore fluere*, run in the same channel, can please always. 'Tis like the murmuring of a stream, which not varying in the fall, causes at first attention, at last drowsiness. Variety of cadences is the best rule; the greatest help to the actors, and refreshment to the audience.

"If, then, verse may be made natural in itself, how becomes it improper to a play? You say the stage is the representation of Nature, and no man in ordinary conversation speaks in rhyme. But you foresaw when you said this, that it might be answered—neither does any man speak in blank verse, or in measure without rhyme. Therefore you concluded, that which is nearest Nature is still to be preferred. But you took no notice that rhyme might be made as natural as blank verse, by the well placing of the words, &c. All the difference between them, when they are both correct, is, the sound in one, which the other wants; and if so, the sweetness of it, and all the advantage resulting from it, which are handled in the Preface to *The Rival Ladies*, will yet stand good. As for that place of Aristotle, where he says, plays should be writ in that kind of verse which is nearest prose, it makes little for you; blank verse being properly but measured prose. Now measure alone, in any modern language, does not constitute verse; those of the Ancients in Greek and Latin consisted in quantity of words, and a determinate number of feet. But when, by the inundation of the Goths and Vandals into Italy, new languages were brought in, and barbarously mingled with the Latin, of which the Italian, Spanish, French, and ours (made out of them and the Teutonic) are dialects, a new way of poesy was practiced; new, I say, in those countries, for in all probability it was that of the conquerors in their own nations. This new way consisted in measure or number of feet, and rhyme; the sweetness of rhyme, and observation of accent, supplying the place of quantity in words, which could neither exactly be observed by those Barbarians, who knew not the rules of it, neither was it suitable to their tongues, as it had been to the Greek and Latin. No man is tied in modern poesy to observe any farther rule in the feet of his verse, but that they be dissyllables; whether spondee, trochee, or iambic, it matters not; only he is obliged to rhyme. Neither do the Spanish, French, Italian, or Germans acknowledge at all, or very rarely, any such kind of poesy as blank verse amongst them. Therefore, at most 'tis but a poetic prose, a *sermo pedestris;* and as such, most fit for comedies, where I acknowledge rhyme to be improper. Farther; as to that quotation of Aristotle, our couplet verses may be rendered as near prose as blank verse itself, by using those advantages I lately named, —as breaks in a hemistich, or running the sense into another line, —thereby making art and order appear as loose and free as nature: or not tying ourselves to couplets strictly, we may use the benefit of the Pindaric way practiced in *The Siege of Rhodes;* where the numbers vary, and the rhyme is disposed carelessly, and far from often chiming. Neither is that other advantage of the Ancients to be despised, of changing the kind of verse when they please, with the change of the scene, or some new entrance; for they confine not themselves always to iambics, but extend their liberty to all lyric numbers, and sometimes even to hexameter. But I need not go so far to prove that rhyme, as it succeeds to all other offices of Greek and Latin verse, so especially to this of plays, since the custom of all nations at this day confirms it; all the French, Italian, and Spanish tragedies are generally writ in it; and sure the universal consent of the most civilized parts of the world ought in this, as it doth in other customs, to include the rest.

"But perhaps you may tell me, I have proposed such a way to make rhyme natural, and consequently proper to plays, as is unpracticable; and that I shall scarce find six or eight lines together in any play, where the words are so placed and chosen as is required to make it natural. I answer, no poet need constrain himself at all times to it. It is enough he makes it his general rule; for I deny not but sometimes there may be a greatness in placing the words otherwise; and sometimes they may sound better; sometimes also the variety itself is excuse enough. But if, for the most part, the words be placed as they are in the negligence of prose, it is sufficient to denominate the way practicable; for we esteem that to be such, which in the trial oftener succeeds than misses. And thus far you may find the practice made good in many plays: where you do not, remember still, that if you cannot find six natural rhymes together, it will be as hard for you to produce as many lines in blank verse, even among the greatest of our poets, against which I cannot make some reasonable exception.

"And this, Sir, calls to my remembrance the beginning of your discourse, where you told us we should never find the audience favorable to this kind of writing, till we could produce as good plays in rhyme as Ben Jonson, Fletcher, and Shakespeare had writ out of it. But it is to raise envy to the living, to compare them with the dead. They are honored, and almost adored by us, as they deserve; neither do I know any so presumptuous of themselves as to contend with them. Yet give me leave to say thus much, without injury to their ashes; that not only we shall never equal them, but they could never equal themselves, were they to rise and write again. We acknowledge them our fathers in wit; but they have ruined their estates themselves, before they came to their children's hands. There is scarce an humor, a character, or any kind of plot, which they have not blown upon. All comes sullied or wasted to us: and were they to entertain this age, they could not make so plenteous treatments out of such decayed fortunes. This therefore will be a good argument to us, either not to write at all, or to attempt some other way. There is no bays to be expected in their walks: *tentanda via est, quà me quoque possum tollere humo.*[1]

"This way of writing in verse they have only left free to us; our age is arrived to a perfection in it, which they never knew; and which (if we may guess by what of theirs we have seen in verse, as *The Faithful Shepherdess*, and *Sad Shepherd*) 'tis probable they never could have reached. For the genius of every age is different; and though ours excel in this, I deny not but that to imitate Nature in that perfection which they did in prose, is a greater commendation than to write in verse exactly. As for what you have added, that the people are not generally inclined to like this way; if it were true, it would be no wonder, that betwixt the shaking off an old habit, and the introducing of a new, there should be difficulty. Do we not see them stick to Hopkins' and Sternhold's Psalms,[2] and forsake those of David,—I mean Sandys his translation of them? If by the people you understand the multitude, the οἱ πολλοί, 'tis no matter what they think; they are sometimes in the right, sometimes in the wrong: their judgment is a mere lottery. *Est ubi plebs rectè putat, est ubi peccat.*[3] Horace says it of the vulgar, judging poesy. But if you mean the mixed audience of the populace and the noblesse, I dare confidently affirm that a great part of the latter sort are already favorable to verse; and that no serious plays written since the King's return have been more kindly received by them

---

1 "A method must be tried by which I may also raise myself from the ground."— Vergil, *Georgics*, iii, 8. (Vergil wrote *temptanda* and *possim*.)

2 John Hopkins and Thomas Sternhold, sixteenth-century authors, together made a metrical version of the Psalms.—George Sandys (1578–1644) wrote a metrical *Paraphrase on the Psalms* (1636), with music by Henry Lawes.

3 There are times when the rabble thinks rightly, times when it is mistaken.

than *The Siege of Rhodes*, the *Mustapha*, *The Indian Queen*, and *Indian Emperor*.

"But I come now to the inference of your first argument. You said the dialogue of plays is presented as the effect of sudden thought, but no man speaks suddenly, or *ex tempore*, in rhyme; and you inferred from thence, that rhyme, which you acknowledge to be proper to epic poesy, cannot equally be proper to dramatic, unless we could suppose all men born so much more than poets, that verses should be made in them, not by them.

"It has been formerly urged by you, and confessed by me, that since no man spoke any kind of verse *ex tempore*, that which was nearest Nature was to be preferred. I answer you, therefore, by distinguishing betwixt what is nearest to the nature of Comedy, which is the imitation of common persons and ordinary speaking, and what is nearest the nature of a serious play: this last is indeed the representation of Nature, but 'tis Nature wrought up to an higher pitch. The plot, the characters, the wit, the passions, the descriptions, are all exalted above the level of common converse, as high as the imagination of the poet can carry them, with proportion to verisimility. Tragedy, we know, is wont to image to us the minds and fortunes of noble persons, and to portray these exactly; heroic rhyme is nearest Nature, as being the noblest kind of modern verse.

> Indignatur enim privatis et prope socco
> Dignis carminibus narrari cœna Thyestæ [1]

says Horace: and in another place,

> Effutire leves indigna tragœdia versus.[2]

Blank verse is acknowledged to be too low for a poem, nay more, for a paper of verses; but if too low for an ordinary sonnet,[3] how much more for Tragedy, which is by Aristotle, in the dispute betwixt the epic poesy and the dramatic, for many reasons he there alleges, ranked above it?

"But setting this defence aside, your argument is almost as strong against the use of rhyme in poems as in plays; for the epic way is everywhere interlaced with dialogue, or discoursive scenes; and

---

[1] "It is unbecoming that the banquet of Thyestes be described in familiar verses fit for comedy." Horace, *Ars Poet.*, 90.

[2] "Tragedy unfit to chatter light verses." *Ibid.*, 231.

[3] Any short poem—not the fourteen-line iambic pentameter composition to which we apply the word now.

therefore you must either grant rhyme to be improper there, which is contrary to your assertion, or admit it into plays by the same title which you have given it to poems. For though Tragedy be justly preferred above the other, yet there is a great affinity between them, as may easily be discovered in that definition of a play which Lisideius gave us. The *genus* of them is the same, a just and lively image of human nature, in its actions, passions, and traverses of fortune: so is the end, namely, for the delight and benefit of mankind. The characters and persons are still the same, viz. the greatest of both sorts; only the manner of acquainting us with those actions, passions, and fortunes, is different. Tragedy performs it *viva voce*, or by action, in dialogue; wherein it excels the Epic Poem, which does it chiefly by narration, and therefore is not so lively an image of human nature. However, the agreement betwixt them is such, that if rhyme be proper for one, it must be for the other. Verse, 'tis true, is not the effect of sudden thought; but this hinders not that sudden thought may be represented in verse, since those thoughts are such as must be higher than Nature can raise them without premeditation, especially to a continuance of them, even out of verse; and consequently you cannot imagine them to have been sudden either in the poet or in the actors. A play, as I have said, to be like Nature, is to be set above it; as statues which are placed on high are made greater than the life, that they may descend to the sight in their just proportion.

"Perhaps I have insisted too long on this objection; but the clearing of it will make my stay shorter on the rest. You tell us, Crites, that rhyme appears most unnatural in repartees, or short replies: when he who answers, it being presumed he knew not what the other would say, yet makes up that part of the verse which was left incomplete, and supplies both the sound and measure of it. This, you say, looks rather like the confederacy of two, than the answer of one.

"This, I confess, is an objection which is in every one's mouth, who loves not rhyme: but suppose, I beseech you, the repartee were made only in blank verse, might not part of the same argument be turned against you? for the measure is as often supplied there, as it is in rhyme; the latter half of the hemistich as commonly made up, or a second line subjoined as a reply to the former; which any one leaf in Jonson's plays will sufficiently clear to you. You will often find in the Greek tragedians, and in Seneca, that when a scene grows up into the warmth of repartees, which is the close fighting of it, the latter part of the trimeter is supplied by him who answers;

and yet it was never observed as a fault in them by any of the ancient or modern critics. The case is the same in our verse, as it was in theirs; rhyme to us being in lieu of quantity to them. But if no latitude is to be allowed a poet, you take from him not only his licence of *quidlibet audendi*,[1] but you tie him up in a straiter compass than you would a philosopher. This is indeed *Musas colere severiores*.[2] You would have him follow Nature, but he must follow her on foot: you have dismounted him from his Pegasus. But you tell us, this supplying the last half of a verse, or adjoining a whole second to the former, looks more like the design of two, than the answer of one. Suppose we acknowledge it: how comes this confederacy to be more displeasing to you, than in a dance which is well contrived? You see there the united design of many persons to make up one figure: after they have separated themselves in many petty divisions, they rejoin one by one into a gross: the confederacy is plain amongst them, for chance could never produce anything so beautiful; and yet there is nothing in it that shocks your sight. I acknowledge the hand of art appears in repartee, as of necessity it must in all kinds of verse. But there is also the quick and poignant brevity of it (which is an high imitation of Nature in those sudden gusts of passion) to mingle with it; and this, joined with the cadency and sweetness of the rhyme, leaves nothing in the soul of the hearer to desire. 'Tis an art which appears; but it appears only like the shadowings of painture, which being to cause the rounding of it, cannot be absent; but while that is considered, they are lost: so while we attend to the other beauties of the matter, the care and labor of the rhyme is carried from us, or at least drowned in its own sweetness, as bees are sometimes buried in their honey. When a poet has found the repartee, the last perfection he can add to it, is to put it into verse. However good the thought may be, however apt the words in which 'tis couched, yet he finds himself at a little unrest, while rhyme is wanting: he cannot leave it till that comes naturally, and then is at ease, and sits down contented.

"From replies, which are the most elevated thoughts of verse, you pass to the most mean ones, those which are common with the lowest of household conversation. In these, you say, the majesty of verse suffers. You instance in the calling of a servant, or commanding a door to be shut, in rhyme. This, Crites, is a good observation of yours, but no argument: for it proves no more but that such thoughts

---

[1] "Of daring whatever he wishes." Horace, *Ars Poet.*, 10.
[2] "To cultivate the stricter Muses." Martial, *Epig.*, ix, 12.

should be waived, as often as may be, by the address of the poet. But suppose they are necessary in the places where he uses them, yet there is no need to put them into rhyme. He may place them in the beginning of a verse, and break it off, as unfit, when so debased, for any other use: or granting the worst,—that they require more room than the hemistich will allow,—yet still there is a choice to be made of the best words, and least vulgar (provided they be apt) to express such thoughts. Many have blamed rhyme in general, for this fault, when the poet with a little care might have redressed it. But they do it with no more justice than if English Poesy should be made ridiculous for the sake of the Water Poet's rhymes.[1] Our language is noble, full, and significant; and I know not why he who is master of it may not clothe ordinary things in it as decently as the Latin, if he use the same diligence in his choice of words: *delectus verborum origo est eloquentiæ.*[2] It was the saying of Julius Cæsar, one so curious[3] in his, that none of them can be changed but for a worse. One would think, *unlock the door,* was a thing as vulgar as could be spoken; and yet Seneca could make it sound high and lofty in his Latin:

> Reserate clusos regii postes laris.[4]
>
> Set wide the palace gates.

"But I turn from this exception, both because it happens not above twice or thrice in any play that those vulgar thoughts are used; and then too, were there no other apology to be made, yet the necessity of them, which is alike in all kind of writing, may excuse them. Besides that the great eagerness and precipitation with which they are spoken makes us rather mind the substance than the dress; that for which they are spoken, rather than what is spoke. For they are always the effect of some hasty concernment, and something of consequence depends on them.

"Thus, Crites, I have endeavored to answer your objections; it remains only that I should vindicate an argument for verse, which you have gone about to overthrow. It had formerly been said, that the easiness of blank verse renders the poet too luxuriant, but that the labor of rhyme bounds and circumscribes an over-fruitful fancy; the sense there being commonly confined to the couplet, and

---

1 See above, p. 123, note 4.
2 "The origin of eloquence lies in the choice of words." Cicero, quoting Cæsar in his *Brutus.*
3 careful.
4 Seneca, *Phædra,* 871. Dryden prints *clusos* for *clausos* in all editions, as Ker notes.

the words so ordered that the rhyme naturally follows them, not they the rhyme. To this you answered, that it was no argument to the question in hand; for the dispute was not which way a man may write best, but which is most proper for the subject on which he writes.

"First, give me leave, Sir, to remember you, that the argument against which you raised this objection was only secondary: it was built on this hypothesis, that to write in verse was proper for serious plays. Which supposition being granted (as it was briefly made out in that discourse, by showing how verse might be made natural), it asserted, that this way of writing was an help to the poet's judgment, by putting bounds to a wild overflowing fancy. I think, therefore, it will not be hard for me to make good what it was to prove. But you add, that were this let pass, yet he who wants judgment in the liberty of his fancy, may as well show the defect of it when he is confined to verse; for he who has judgment will avoid errors, and he who has it not, will commit them in all kinds of writing.

"This argument, as you have taken it from a most acute person, so I confess it carries much weight in it: but by using the word judgment here indefinitely, you seem to have put a fallacy upon us. I grant, he who has judgment, that is, so profound, so strong, so infallible a judgment, that he needs no helps to keep it always poised and upright, will commit no faults either in rhyme or out of it. And on the other extreme, he who has a judgment so weak and crazed that no helps can correct or amend it, shall write scurvily out of rhyme, and worse in it. But the first of these judgments is nowhere to be found, and the latter is not fit to write at all. To speak therefore of judgment as it is in the best poets; they who have the greatest proportion of it, want other helps than from it, within. As for example, you would be loth to say, that he who was endued with a sound judgment had no need of History, Geography, or Moral Philosophy, to write correctly. Judgment is indeed the master-workman in a play; but he requires many subordinate hands, many tools to his assistance. And verse I affirm to be one of these; 'tis a rule and line by which he keeps his building compact and even, which otherwise lawless imagination would raise either irregularly or loosely. At least, if the poet commits errors with this help, he would make greater and more without it: 'tis, in short, a slow and painful, but the surest kind of working. Ovid, whom you accuse for luxuriancy in verse, had perhaps been farther guilty of it, had he writ in prose.

And for your instance of Ben Jonson, who, you say, writ exactly without the help of rhyme; you are to remember, 'tis only an aid to a luxuriant fancy, which his was not: as he did not want imagination, so none ever said he had much to spare. Neither was verse then refined so much, to be an help to that age, as it is to ours. Thus then the second thoughts being usually the best, as receiving the maturest digestion from judgment, and the last and most mature product of those thoughts being artful and labored verse, it may well be inferred, that verse is a great help to a luxuriant fancy; and this is what that argument which you opposed was to evince."

Neander was pursuing this discourse so eagerly that Eugenius had called him twice or thrice, ere he took notice that the barge stood still, and that they were at the foot of Somerset Stairs,[1] where they had appointed it to land. The company were all sorry to separate so soon, though a great part of the evening was already spent; and stood awhile looking back on the water, which the moonbeams played upon, and made it appear like floating quick-silver: at last they went up through a crowd of French people, who were merrily dancing in the open air, and nothing concerned for the noise of guns which had alarmed the town that afternoon. Walking thence together to the Piazze,[2] they parted there; Eugenius and Lisideius to some pleasant appointment they had made, and Crites and Neander to their several lodgings.

From A DEFENCE OF *AN ESSAY*
OF DRAMATIC POESY [3]

(1668)

* * * *

. . . But to return to verse; whether it be natural or not in plays, is a problem which is not demonstrable of either side: 'tis enough for me that he [4] acknowledges he had rather read good verse than prose: for if all the enemies of verse will confess as much, I shall not need to prove that it is natural. I am satisfied, if it cause delight;

---

[1] Somerset Stairs lay to the west of old Somerset House, on the Strand. They were designed by Inigo Jones.

[2] The Piazzas were on the north and east sides of Covent Garden.

[3] Prefixed to the second edition of *The Indian Emperor*.

[4] The author of *The Great Favorite, or The Duke of Lerma*, whom Dryden in this essay has called "a noble and most ingenious person." The preface to his play called forth this *Defence*.

for delight is the chief, if not the only, end of poesy: instruction can be admitted but in the second place; for poesy only instructs as it delights. 'Tis true, that to imitate well is a poet's work; but to affect the soul, and excite the passions, and above all to move admiration, which is the delight of serious plays, a bare imitation will not serve. The converse, therefore, which a poet is to imitate, must be heightened with all the arts and ornaments of poesy; and must be such as, strictly considered, could never be supposed spoken by any without premeditation.

As for what he urges, that *a play will still be supposed to be a composition of several persons speaking* ex tempore; *and that good verses are the hardest things which can be imagined to be so spoken;* I must crave leave to dissent from his opinion, as to the former part of it: for, if I am not deceived, a play is supposed to be the work of the poet, imitating or representing the conversation of several persons; and this I think to be as clear as he thinks the contrary.

But I will be bolder, and do not doubt to make it good, though a paradox, that one great reason why prose is not to be used in serious plays, is, because it is too near the nature of converse: there may be too great a likeness; as the most skilful painters affirm, that there may be too near a resemblance in a picture: to take every lineament and feature is not to make an excellent piece; but to take so much only as will make a beautiful resemblance of the whole; and, with an ingenious flattery of nature, to heighten the beauties of some parts, and hide the deformities of the rest. For so says Horace:

> Ut pictura poesis erit. . . .
> Hæc amat obscurum, vult hæc sub luce videri,
> Judicis argutum quæ non formidat acumen.
>   . . . et quæ
> Desperat tractata nitescere posse, relinquit.[1]

In *Bartholomew Fair,* or the lowest kind of comedy, that degree of heightening is used, which is proper to set off that subject. It is true the author was not there to go out of prose, as he does in his

---

[1] Poems, like pictures, are of diff'rent sorts, . . .
  Some love the dark, some choose the clearest light,
  And boldly challenge the most piercing eye . . .
  In other things men have some reason left,
  And one . . .
  Despairing of success, forbears to try. (Roscommon.)

higher arguments of comedy, *The Fox*, and *Alchemist*; yet he does so raise his matter in that prose as to render it delightful; which he could never have performed had he only said or done those very things that are daily spoken or practiced in the Fair; for then the Fair itself would be as full of pleasure to an ingenious person as the play; which we manifestly see it is not. But he hath made an excellent lazar [1] of it: the copy is of price, though the original be vile. You see in *Catiline* and *Sejanus*, where the argument is great, he sometimes ascends to verse, which shows he thought it not unnatural in serious plays; and had his genius been as proper for rhyme as it was for humor, or had the age in which he lived attained to as much knowledge in verse as ours, it is probable he would have adorned those subjects with that kind of writing.

Thus prose, though the rightful prince, yet is by common consent deposed, as too weak for the government of serious plays; and he failing, there now start up two competitors; one, the nearer in blood, which is blank verse; the other, more fit for the ends of government, which is rhyme. Blank verse is, indeed, the nearer prose, but he is blemished with the weakness of his predecessor. Rhyme (for I will deal clearly) has somewhat of the usurper in him; but he is brave and generous, and his dominion pleasing. For this reason of delight, the Ancients (whom I will still believe as wise as those who so confidently correct them) wrote all their tragedies in verse, though they knew it most remote from conversation.

But I perceive I am falling into the danger of another rebuke from my opponent; for when I plead that the Ancients used verse, I prove not that they would have admitted rhyme, had it then been written. All I can say is only this, that it seems to have succeeded verse by the general consent of poets in all modern languages; for almost all their serious plays are written in it; which, though it be no demonstration that therefore they ought to be so, yet at least the practice first, and then the continuation of it, shows that it attained the end,—which was to please; and if that cannot be compassed here, I will be the first who shall lay it down. For I confess my chief endeavors are to delight the age in which I live. If the humor of this be for low comedy, small accidents, and raillery, I will force my genius to obey it, though with more reputation I could write in verse. I know I am not so fitted by nature to write comedy: I want that gaiety of humor which is required to it. My conversation is slow and dull, my humor saturnine and reserved: in short, I am

[1] leper.

none of those who endeavor to break jests in company, or make repartees. So that those who decry my comedies do me no injury, except it be in point of profit: reputation in them is the last thing to which I shall pretend.

*   *   *   *

Boileau

Nicholas Boileau-Despréaux, known as BOILEAU (1636–1711), was born at Paris and educated first for the law; later he applied himself to theology, but eventually devoted himself to literature. His prolific writing included satires, translations of the classics, the famous epistles, and miscellaneous comments on art and music. He was a friend of Racine, and historiographer of Louis XIV. In 1684 he was made a member of the Académie Française. The end of his life was marked by neglect and trouble, and he died in Paris at the age of seventy-five.

Boileau is the foremost of the neo-classicists of his day. His influence, not only in France but in England, was extraordinary. This influence derived mainly from his *L'Art Poétique*, an essay in verse after the manner, and with most of the ideas, of Horace and Vida.

Since the reader has already become acquainted with Horace's *Ars Poetica*, and will presently encounter Pope's *Essay on Criticism*—which is for England what Boileau's poem is for France—*L'Art Poétique* is here omitted. Instead, the editors have chosen a less-known critical essay of Boileau's, which, in its generous appreciation of Longinus, displays a far different side of Boileau's temperament, suggesting that underneath his neo-classicism there was a genuine feeling for literature that did not obey the rules.

PREFACE BY THE TRANSLATOR OF THE TREATISE *ON THE SUBLIME* BY LONGINUS [1]

(1674)

This little treatise, the translation of which I give to the public, is a piece which has escaped from the shipwreck of several other works which Longinus composed. Even so, it did not come to us intact; for, although the volume is not very thick, there are several *lacunæ*; and we have lost the treatise on the passions, of which subject the author made a separate work, which was a natural sequel to this. Nevertheless, disfigured as it is, enough of it is left to give us an excellent idea of its author, and to make us keenly regret the loss of his other works. Nor is the number of them negligible. Suidas [2] counts nine, of which nothing remains except rather confused titles. They were all works on criticism. And surely no one can sufficiently mourn the loss of these outstanding works which, judging by the one we have, should be masterpieces of good sense, erudition, and eloquence. I say of eloquence, because Longinus has never been contented—as are Aristotle and Hermogenus—to give us dry precepts, stripped of ornaments. He did not want to fall into the error for which he reproaches Cæcilius,[3] who, he says, wrote of the sublime in a low style. In treating of the beauties of elocution, he employed all the fine distinctions of elocution. Often he uses the figure he is talking about, and, in speaking of the sublime, he is himself sublime. Nevertheless he does so appropriately, and with so much art, that no one can accuse him in any one place of getting out of the didactic style. This has given to his book the high reputation which it has acquired among scholars, who have all considered it a very precious gift of antiquity to our age in matters of rhetoric. Casaubon [4] calls it a book of gold, wishing to indicate by this phrase the weight of this little work which, despite its small size, can balance very heavy volumes.

And never was a man, even in his own time, estimated more highly than was Longinus. The philosopher Porphyry,[5] who had been his

---

[1] Translated by the editors. This preface is the expanded version, made some twenty years after the first edition, as Boileau notes in the text.

[2] A Greek author of the twelfth century.

[3] Boileau notes that he was a Sicilian rhetorician of the time of Augustus—a contemporary of Dionysius of Halicarnassus, with whom he lived on close friendly terms.

[4] Isaac Casaubon (1559–1614) was an industrious and learned critic.

[5] A Syrian Neoplatonist philosopher in Alexandria (233–304).

disciple, speaks of him as of a prodigy. If we can believe him, Longinus's judgment was the rule of sense; his decisions concerning books were considered as a royal decree, and nothing was good or bad save as Longinus approved or condemned. Eunapius [1] in his *Lives of the Sophists* goes even further. To express his esteem for Longinus, he lets himself be carried away by extravagant hyperboles, and cannot bring himself to speak in a reasonable manner of a merit as extraordinary as that of this author. But Longinus was not merely a clever critic—he was a statesman of considerable authority; and it is a sufficient sign of his importance, to say that he was highly thought of by Zenobia, the famous Queen of Palmyra, who dared to call herself Queen of the Orient after the death of her husband Odenathus. She had called Longinus to her court originally to teach her Greek—but from her Greek teacher she promoted him to be one of her chief ministers. He was the one who encouraged the queen to assume the rank of Queen of the Orient, who comforted her heart in adversity, and who furnished her with the haughty words which she sent to Aurelian when that emperor called for her surrender. This cost our author his life; but his death was as glorious for him as it was shameful for Aurelian, whose memory, one may say, has been forever disgraced by it. As this death is one of the most famous historical events of those days, the reader will perhaps not be sorry to have me quote here what Flavius Vopiscus [2] has written about it. This author relates how the army of Zenobia and her allies, having been put to flight near the city of Emessa, Aurelian went to lay siege to Palmyra, whither the princess had retired. He encountered a greater resistance than he expected, which he did not suppose could be reasonably laid to the resolution of a woman. Annoyed by the length of the siege, he tried to get the city by offering terms, and wrote a letter to Zenobia, giving her her life and a place to which she could retire, provided she would surrender within a certain time. Zenobia, adds Vopiscus, replied to this letter with a greater pride than her situation warranted. She thought she would inspire terror in Aurelian by her answer, which I give:

Zenobia, Queen of the Orient, to Emperor Aurelian.

Nobody has ever made a demand comparable to yours. It is justice, Aurelian, which ought to win completely in a war. You command me to put myself into your hands, as if you did not know that Cleopatra would rather die with her title of queen than live with any other honor. We await

[1] A Greek author of the fourth century.
[2] An historian, born at Syracuse in the third century.

the help of the Persians; the Saracens are arming on our behalf; the Armenians have declared themselves in our favor. A robber band in Syria has defeated your army; you can judge what you ought to expect when these forces have come together. You will humble the pride with which, as if you were master of everything, you order me to surrender myself.

This letter, adds Vopiscus, gave Aurelian more anger than shame. The city of Palmyra was taken a few days later, and Zenobia was captured as she was fleeing to the Persians. The whole army asked for her death, but Aurelian would not dishonor his victory by the death of a woman. So he saved Zenobia for his triumph, and contented himself with killing those who had helped her with their advice. Among them (this historian continues) the philosopher Longinus was much mourned. He had been called to teach her Greek. Aurelian killed him for having written the foregoing letter; for, although it was written in the Syriac language, he was suspected of being the author of it. The historian Zosima [1] bears witness that Zenobia herself accused him of it. "Zenobia," he said, "finding herself arrested, threw all blame on her ministers, who had, she said, taken advantage of her weakness." Among others, she named Longinus, of whom we have still some very valuable writings. Aurelian ordered him to be put to the torture. This great person, says Zosima, suffered death with admirable courage, even consoling, as he died, those who were touched with pity and indignation by his misfortune.

So one can see that Longinus was not only a clever rhetorician, like Quintilian and Hermogenus, but a philosopher worthy of being compared with Socrates and the Catos. His book does not deny the claims I have just made. His character as an honest man is visible throughout it, and his sentiments have an indefinable something which indicates not only a sublime spirit, but a soul raised high above common life. I have, therefore, no regrets in having employed some of my watchful nights in explaining such an excellent work, which I can say has not been understood until now, except by a very small number of scholars. Muret was the first who undertook to translate it into Latin, at the request of Manutius; but he did not finish his work, either because the difficulties of it dismayed him, or because death overtook him; [2] Gabriel de Pétra some time later, was more

[1] A writer of the fifth century.

[2] In the 1894 edition of the French text it is noted that Paul Manuce died in 1574, while Muret lived until 1585. Gabriel de Pétra, who died in 1616, was professor of Greek at Lausanne.

courageous; and we owe to him the Latin translation which we now have. There are two others; but they are so shapeless and so clumsy that it would be doing too much honor to their authors to name them. Even that of de Pétra, which is infinitely better, is not completely finished; for, besides the fact that he often speaks Greek in Latin, there are several places where one can say that he has not understood his author very well. I do not want to accuse so scholarly a man of ignorance, nor establish my reputation on the ruins of his. I know what it is to be the first to puzzle out an author; and I admit, besides, that his work has been of great help to me, as well as the notes of Langbaine and M. Le Febvre; [1] but I am glad to find excuses, in the faults of the Latin translation, for those which may have escaped me in the French. I have, however, made every effort to translate the book as accurately as possible; and to say the truth, I have found no small difficulties. It is easy for one translating into Latin to get along, even in the places which he does not understand. He has only to translate the Greek word for word, and to express things which one can at least suspect to be intelligible. As a matter of fact, the reader, who very often comprehends nothing, criticizes himself rather than suspects the ignorance of the translator. It is not the same with translations into the vernacular. All that the reader does not understand is called nonsense, for which the translator alone is responsible. Even the faults of his author are laid at the translator's door; and in many places he has to correct them, unless he dares to ignore them.

And so, however small this volume of Longinus may be, I do not believe I have made a negligible gift of it to the public, if I have made a good translation into our tongue. I have spared neither care nor effort. But one must not expect to find here a timid or over-nice version of Longinus's words. While I have tried not to get a step away from the rules of true translation, I have nevertheless taken an honest liberty, above all in the passages which count. I have supposed that my task is not only to translate Longinus, but to give the public a *Treatise on the Sublime* which can be useful. With all that, there may be people who not only will not approve my translation, but will criticize the original. I expect that there will be several who will decline to accept the authority of Longinus, who will condemn that of which he approves, who will praise the things he blames.

---

[1] Gérard Langbaine, who died in 1657 or 1658, was the author, with Le Febvre, of an edition of Longinus in English. Le Febvre was the father of Mme Dacier, whose husband furnished some of the notes to Boileau's translation—which was made from the Greek.

This is the treatment we ought to expect of the majority of critics in our century. These men, accustomed to the excesses of modern poets, who admire only what they do not understand, will not believe that an author has taken flight, unless they have lost sight of him entirely; these narrow minds, I say, will doubtless not be much struck by the judicious boldness of Homer, Plato, and Demosthenes. They will often seek the sublime in the sublime; and perhaps they will laugh at the exclamations which Longinus sometimes makes about passages which, though quite sublime, remain simple and natural, and which rather seize the soul than blaze out before the eyes. Whatever assurance these gentlemen may have of the clearness of their light, I beg them to consider that I do not offer them here the work of an apprentice, but the masterpiece of one of the most scholarly critics of antiquity; that if they do not see the beauty of these passages, this failure may just as well come from the feebleness of their vision as from the dimness of the lustre of these passages. If worse comes to worst, I advise them to accuse the translation; because it is too true that I have not attained, nor can I attain, the perfection of the excellent original; and I declare to them in advance that if there are any faults in it, they can only come from me.

The only thing that remains in concluding this preface, is to explain what Longinus means by *sublime;* for, as he writes on this subject after Cæcilius, who had used almost his whole book to show what the sublime was, he did not feel it necessary to rehash a subject which had been only too much discussed by another. We must, therefore, realize that by *sublime* Longinus does not understand what orators call the sublime style, but the extraordinary and wonderful quality which strikes us in speech, which causes a work to lift, enchant, and delight us. The sublime style always needs lofty words, but the sublime can be found in a single thought, a simple figure, in a single phrase. A thing can be in the sublime style, and nevertheless not be sublime—that is to say, have nothing extraordinary or astonishing in it. For example: "The sovereign arbiter of nature with a single word created light": that is in the sublime style, but it is not sublime, because there is nothing there very marvellous, which one could not easily find. But: "God said, Let there be light; and there was light"; this extraordinary expression, which indicates so well the obedience of the creature to the orders of the Creator, is truly sublime, and has something of the divine in it. We must therefore understand by *sublime* in Longinus the extraordinary, the astonishing, and, as I have translated it, the marvellous.

I have reminded you of these words of *Genesis* because they were the most appropriate ones to make my meaning clear, and I used the passage the more willingly because this expression is quoted with approbation by Longinus himself, who, in the midst of the shadows of paganism, was not prevented from recognizing the divine quality of these Scriptural words. But what can we say of one of the most scholarly men of our century,[1] who, enlightened by the rays from the Gospel, cannot find the beauty in this passage—who has dared, I say, to put forth in a book which he has written to demonstrate the Christian religion, that Longinus made a mistake when he thought these words were sublime? I have at least the satisfaction of knowing that people[2] no less notable for their piety than for their profound erudition, who gave us a short while ago a translation of the Book of *Genesis,* have not shared the opinion of this scholar; and in their preface, among other excellent proofs which they have adduced to show that the Holy Spirit dictated this book, they have cited the passage from Longinus to show how much Christians should be persuaded of a clear truth which even a heathen has felt by the light of reason alone.

Finally, while I was working on the last edition of my book,[3] M. Dacier, who gave us a short time ago the odes of Horace in French, passed on to me some very scholarly notes which he had made on Longinus, in which he sought new meanings hitherto unknown to his interpreters. I have adopted some of them, but as I may be wrong in those with which I do not agree, it is well to let the readers judge; and to make this possible, I have put them after my own comments. M. Dacier is not only a man of great erudition, and very sensitive appreciation, but of a courtesy all the more to be esteemed because we do not often find it joined with so much learning. He was a disciple of the celebrated M. Le Febvre, the father of that scholarly daughter to whom we owe the first translation which has yet appeared in French of Anacreon, and who is now working to give us Aristophanes, Sophocles, and Euripides in our tongue.

I have left in all my other editions my preface, such as it was when I printed it for the first time more than twenty years ago, and I have added nothing to it; but to-day, when I saw the proofs, and was about to send them back to the printer, it struck me that it

---

[1] In the 1894 edition is noted: Huet, Archbishop of Avranches.

[2] In the 1894 edition is noted: The writers of the Port-Royal, particularly the Master of Sacy.

[3] That of 1683.

would not be a bad idea, in order to make it more clearly understood what Longinus means by this word *sublime,* to add to the passage which I quoted from the Bible another example taken from another source. Here is one which comes happily enough to my memory. It is taken from M. Corneille's *Horace.* In this tragedy, the first three acts of which are, in my opinion, the best work of this illustrious writer, a woman who had been present at the fight of the three Horaces, but who withdrew a little too soon, without seeing the end of it, came in an ill-advised moment to announce to the old Horace, their father, that two of his sons had been killed, and that the third, not being able to resist longer, had fled. Then the old Roman, full of the love of his country, without taking time to lament the loss of his two sons, who had died so gloriously, mourns only the shameless flight of the last, who has (he says) by such a cowardly act stamped an eternal shame on the name of Horace. And their sister, who was there present, having asked him

> What would you wish that he did against three?

he replied shortly,

> That he died.

Here are some very short words, but there is no one who cannot feel the heroic greatness wrapped up in this phrase, "That he died," which is the more sublime because it is simple and natural, and because one can see in it that it is from the depths of his heart that the old hero speaks in the transports of an anger truly Roman. As a matter of fact, the situation would have lost much of its strength if, instead of saying, "That he died," he had said, "That he followed the example of his two brothers," or, "That he should sacrifice his life to the success and glory of his fatherland." It is the simplicity of the phrase which makes its greatness. These are the things which Longinus calls sublime, and which he would have admired much more in Corneille, had he lived in the time of Corneille, than those grandiloquent speeches with which Ptolemy fills his mouth at the beginning of *The Death of Pompey,* to exaggerate the futile circumstances of a defeat which he had not seen.

Addison

Joseph ADDISON (1672–1719), son of the Reverend Lance-
lot Addison, who became Dean of Lichfield, was born in
Milston, near Amesbury, Wiltshire. He was educated at the
Charterhouse, where he made the acquaintance of his future
collaborator, Richard Steele, and at Oxford, where he had a
distinguished career, taking his M.A. in 1693, and was later
elected a Fellow of Magdalen College. This Fellowship, which
he held from 1699 to 1711, did not keep Addison from
other pursuits. After abandoning the idea of taking orders,
he turned to literature. He soon came under the notice of
Dryden for some translations that he had made from the
Latin; Congreve introduced him to various influential politicians, including Lord Halifax; Lord Somers also became his
patron, and through him Addison's work was recognized by
a pension. He went abroad and was about to begin a diplomatic career when, at the death of William III, his friends lost
power and he his pension. During his travels he had written a
great deal, and when the first ministry of Queen Anne wished
to celebrate the victory of Blenheim, the promising young
literary man was commissioned to undertake the task. The resulting poem, *The Campaign,* brought him political prefer-
ment: he was made Under-Secretary of State in 1705, and in
1708 was elected to Parliament.

In 1709 Steele started the *Tatler,* and Addison soon became
associated with his old friend in this venture, which was followed, in 1711, by the *Spectator.* In this periodical, much of
Addison's critical work appeared. In 1716 he married (unhappily) the Dowager Countess of Warwick, to whose son he had

been tutor; and in 1718 he retired from the Secretaryship of State, with a large pension. He died the next year at Holland House.

Addison is noteworthy in literary criticism for his explanation of what imagination is, and his division of imagination into primary and secondary. The papers in which he presents his views were written, it is believed, while he was an undergraduate. Years later, revised, they appeared in the *Spectator*.

The ideas that Addison expresses on imagination, wit, judgment, and other literary problems, are not wholly his own. They grew out of observations made by a philosopher whom he cites with admiration—John Locke. The latter's revolutionary *Essay Concerning Human Understanding* (1690), which may be called in all justice the foundation of modern analytic philosophy, was in particular Addison's source of inspiration.

From *THE SPECTATOR* [1]

(1712)

No. 411.   Saturday, June 21, [1712]

> *Avia Pieridum peragro loca, nullius ante*
> *Trita solo; juvat integros accedere fonteis,*
> *Atque haurire————.—*LUCRETIUS.[2]

Our sight is the most perfect and most delightful of all our senses. It fills the mind with the largest variety of ideas, converses with its objects at the greatest distance, and continues the longest in action without being tired or satiated with its proper enjoyments. The sense of feeling can indeed give us a notion of extension, shape, and all other ideas that enter at the eye, except colors; but at the same time, it is very much straitened and confined in its operations, to the number, bulk, and distance of its particular objects. Our sight seems

[1] The text is based on the eight-volume edition of *The Spectator*, "carefully corrected," London, 1754, compared with G. Gregory Smith's text, reprinted in the *Everyman's Library*. The spelling and punctuation have, in general, been modernized.

[2]   —Inspired I trace the Muses' seats,
    Untrodden yet: 'tis sweet to visit first
    Untouch'd and virgin streams, and quench my thirst.
                                        CREECH.

designed to supply all these defects, and may be considered as a more delicate and diffusive kind of touch, that spreads itself over an infinite multitude of bodies, comprehends the largest figures, and brings into our reach some of the most remote parts of the universe.

It is this sense which furnishes the imagination with its ideas; so that by the pleasures of the imagination or fancy (which I shall use promiscuously) I here mean such as arise from visible objects, either when we have them actually in our view, or when we call up their ideas into our minds by paintings, statues, descriptions, or any the like occasion. We cannot indeed have a single image in the fancy that did not make its first entrance through the sight; but we have the power of retaining, altering, and compounding those images, which we have once received, into all the varieties of picture and vision that are most agreeable to the imagination; for by this faculty a man in a dungeon is capable of entertaining himself with scenes and landscapes more beautiful than any that can be found in the whole compass of nature.

There are few words in the English language which are employed in a more loose and uncircumscribed sense than those of the *fancy* and the *imagination*. I therefore thought it necessary to fix and determine the notion of these two words, as I intend to make use of them in the thread of my following speculations, that the reader may conceive rightly what is the subject which I proceed upon. I must therefore desire him to remember, that by the pleasures of the imagination, I mean only such pleasures as arise originally from sight, and that I divide these pleasures into two kinds: my design being first of all to discourse of those primary pleasures of the imagination, which entirely proceed from such objects as are before our eyes; and in the next place to speak of those secondary pleasures of the imagination which flow from the ideas of visible objects, when the objects are not actually before the eye, but are called up into our memories, or formed into agreeable visions of things that are either absent or fictitious.

The pleasures of the imagination, taken in the full extent, are not so gross as those of sense, nor so refined as those of the understanding. The last are, indeed, more preferable, because they are founded on some new knowledge or improvement in the mind of man; yet it must be confessed, that those of the imagination are as great and as transporting as the other. A beautiful prospect delights the soul, as much as a demonstration; and a description in Homer has charmed more readers than a chapter in Aristotle. Besides, the pleasures of the imagination have this advantage, above those of the understanding, that they are more obvious, and more easy to be acquired. It is but opening the eye, and the scene enters. The colors paint themselves on the fancy, with very little attention of thought or application of mind in the beholder. We are struck, we know not how, with the symmetry of any thing we see, and immediately assent to the beauty of an object, without enquiring into the particular causes and occasions of it.

A man of a polite imagination is let into a great many pleasures, that the vulgar are not capable of receiving. He can converse with a picture, and find an agreeable companion in a statue. He meets with a secret refreshment in a description, and often feels a greater satisfaction in the prospect of fields and meadows, than another does in the possession. It gives him, indeed, a kind of property in every thing he sees, and makes the most rude uncultivated parts of nature administer to his pleasures: so that he looks upon the world, as it were, in another light, and discovers in it a multitude of charms, that conceal themselves from the generality of mankind.

There are, indeed, but very few who know how to be idle and innocent, or have a relish of any pleasures that are not criminal; every diversion they take is at the expense of some one virtue or another, and their very first step out of business is into vice or folly. A man should endeavor, therefore, to make the sphere of his innocent pleasures as wide as possible, that he may retire into them with safety, and find in them such a satisfaction as a wise man would not blush to take. Of this nature are those of the imagination, which do not require such a bent of thought as is necessary to our more serious employments, nor, at the same time, suffer the mind to sink into that negligence and remissness, which are apt to accompany our more sensual delights, but, like a gentle exercise to the faculties, awaken them from sloth and idleness, without putting them upon any labor or difficulty.

We might here add, that the pleasures of the fancy are more conducive to health, than those of the understanding, which are worked out by dint of thinking, and attended with too violent a labor of the brain. Delightful scenes, whether in nature, painting, or poetry, have a kindly influence on the body, as well as the mind; and not only serve to clear and brighten the imagination, but are able to disperse grief and melancholy, and to set the animal spirits in pleasing and agreeable motions. For this reason Sir Francis Bacon, in his essay upon health, has not thought it improper to prescribe to his reader a poem or a prospect, where he particularly dissuades him from knotty and subtle disquisitions, and advises him to pursue studies that fill the mind with splendid and illustrious objects, as histories, fables, and contemplations of nature.

I have in this paper, by way of introduction, settled the notion of those pleasures of the imagination which are the subject of my present undertaking, and endeavored, by several considerations, to recommend to my reader the pursuit of those pleasures. I shall, in my next paper, examine the several sources from whence these pleasures are derived.

No. 412.   Monday, June 23.

——*Divisum sic breve fiet opus.*—MARTIAL [1]

I shall first consider those pleasures of the imagination, which arise from the actual view and survey of outward objects: And these, I think, all proceed from the sight of what is *Great, Uncommon,* or *Beautiful.* There may, indeed, be something so terrible or offensive, that the horror or loathsomeness of an object may overbear the pleasure which results from its greatness, novelty or beauty; but still there will be such a mixture of delight in the very disgust it gives us, as any of these three qualifications are most conspicuous and prevailing.

By *Greatness,* I do not only mean the bulk of any single object, but the largeness of a whole view, considered as one entire piece. Such are the prospects of an open champain [2] country, a vast uncultivated desert, of huge heaps of mountains, high rocks and precipices, or a wide expanse of waters, where we are not struck with the novelty or beauty of the sight, but with that rude kind of magnificence which appears in many of these stupendous works of nature. Our imagination loves to be filled with an object, or to grasp at any thing that is too big for its capacity. We are flung into a pleasing astonishment at such unbounded views, and feel a delightful stillness and amazement in the soul at the apprehension of them. The mind of man naturally hates every thing that looks like a restraint upon it, and is apt to fancy itself under a sort of confinement, when the sight is pent up in a narrow compass, and shortened on every side by the neighborhood of walls or mountains. On the contrary, a spacious horizon is an image of liberty, where the eye has room to

---

[1] The work, divided aptly, shorter grows.
[2] Cf. the French *champagne,* "a field."

range abroad, to expatiate at large on the immensity of its views, and to lose itself amidst the variety of objects that offer themselves to its observation. Such wide and undetermined prospects are as pleasing to the fancy, as the speculations of eternity or infinitude are to the understanding. But if there be a beauty or uncommonness joined with this grandeur, as in a troubled ocean, a heaven adorned with stars and meteors, or a spacious landscape cut out into rivers, woods, rocks, and meadows, the pleasure still grows upon us, as it arises from more than a single principle.

Every thing that is *new* or *uncommon* raises a pleasure in the imagination, because it fills the soul with an agreeable surprise, gratifies its curiosity, and gives it an idea of which it was not before possessed. We are indeed so often conversant with one set of objects, and tired out with so many repeated shows of the same things, that whatever is *new* or *uncommon* contributes a little to vary human life, and to divert our minds, for a while, with the strangeness of its appearance: it serves us for a kind of refreshment, and takes off from that satiety we are apt to complain of in our usual and ordinary entertainments. It is this that bestows charms on a monster, and makes even the imperfections of nature please us. It is this that recommends variety, where the mind is every instant called off to something new, and the attention not suffered to dwell too long, and waste itself on any particular object. It is this, likewise, that improves what is great or beautiful, and makes it afford the mind a double entertainment. Groves, fields, and meadows are at any season of the year pleasant to look upon, but never so much as in the opening of the spring, when they are all new and fresh, with their first gloss upon them, and not yet too much accustomed and familiar to the eye. For this reason there is nothing that more enlivens a prospect than rivers, jets-d'eau, or falls of water, where the scene is perpetually shifting, and entertaining the sight every moment with something that is new. We are quickly tired with looking upon hills and valleys, where every thing continues fixed and settled in the same place and posture, but find our thoughts a little agitated and relieved at the sight of such objects as are ever in motion, and sliding away from beneath the eye of the beholder.

But there is nothing that makes its way more directly to the soul than *beauty*, which immediately diffuses a secret satisfaction and complacency through the imagination, and gives a finishing to any thing that is great or uncommon. The very first discovery of it strikes the mind with an inward joy, and spreads a cheerfulness and delight through all its faculties. There is not perhaps any real beauty or deformity more in one piece of matter than another, because we might have been so made, that whatsoever now appears loathsome to us, might have shown itself agreeable; but we find by experience that there are several modifications of matter which the mind, without any previous consideration, pronounces at first sight beautiful or deformed. Thus we see that every different species of sensible creatures has its different notions of beauty, and that each of them is most affected with the beauties of its own kind. This is nowhere more remarkable than in birds of the same shape and proportion, where we often see the male determined in his courtship by the single grain or tincture of a feather, and never discovering any charms but in the color of its species. . . . [Here Addison inserts a Latin poem of his own composition, the following translation of which was added in later editions.]

> The feathered husband, to his partner true,
> Preserves connubial rites inviolate.
> With cold indifference every charm he sees,
> The milky whiteness of the stately neck,
> The shining down, proud crest, and purple wings:
> But cautious with a searching eye explores
> The female tribes, his proper mate to find,
> With kindred colors marked: did he not so,
> The grove with painted monsters would abound,
> Th' ambiguous product of unnatural love.
> The black-bird hence selects her sooty spouse;
> The nightingale her musical compeer,
> Lured by the well-known voice: the bird of night,
> Smit with his dusky wings, and greenish eyes,
> Woos his dun paramour. The beauteous race
> Speak the chaste loves of their progenitors;
> When, by the spring invited, they exult
> In woods and fields, and to the sun unfold
> Their plumes, that with paternal colors glow.

There is a second kind of *Beauty* that we find in the several products of art and nature, which does not work in the imagination with that warmth and violence as the beauty that appears in our proper species, but is apt however to raise in us a secret delight, and a kind of fondness for the places or objects in which we discover it. This consists either in the gaiety or variety of colors, in the symmetry and proportion of parts, in the arrangement and disposition of bodies, or in a just mixture and concurrence of all together. Among these several kinds of beauty the eye takes most delight in colors. We nowhere meet with a more glorious or pleasing show in nature than what appears in the heavens at the rising and setting of the sun, which is wholly made up of those different stains of light that show themselves in clouds of a different situation. For this reason we find the poets, who are always addressing themselves to the imagination, borrowing more of their epithets from colors than from any other topic.

As the fancy delights in every thing that is great, strange, or beautiful, and is still more pleased the more it finds of these perfections in the same object, so it is capable of receiving a new satisfaction by the assistance of another sense. Thus any continued sound, as the music of birds, or a fall of water, awakens every moment the mind of the beholder, and makes him more attentive to the several beauties of the place that lie before him. Thus if there arises a fragrancy of smells or perfumes, they heighten the pleasures of the imagination, and make even the colors and verdure of the landscape appear more agreeable; for the ideas of both senses recommend each other, and are pleasanter together, than when they enter the mind separately: as the different colors of a picture, when they are well disposed, set off one another, and receive an additional beauty from the advantage of their situation.

No. 413.   Tuesday, June 24.

————*Causa latet: vis est notissima*————.—Ovid.[1]

Though in yesterday's paper we considered how everything that is great, new, or beautiful is apt to affect the imagination with pleasure, we must own that it is impossible for us to assign the necessary cause of this pleasure, because we know neither the nature of an idea, nor the substance of a human soul, which might help us to discover the conformity or disagreeableness of the one to the other; and therefore, for want of such a light, all that we can do in speculations of this kind, is to reflect on those operations of the soul that are most agreeable, and to range, under their proper heads, what is pleasing or displeasing to the mind, without being able to trace out the several necessary and efficient causes from whence the pleasure or displeasure arises.

[1] The cause is secret, but th' effect is known.
ADDISON

Final causes lie more bare and open to our observation, as there are often a greater variety that belong to the same effect; and these, though they are not altogether so satisfactory, are generally more useful than the other, as they give us greater occasion of admiring the goodness and wisdom of the first contriver.

One of the final causes of our delight, in any thing that is *great*, may be this. The supreme author of our being has so formed the soul of man, that nothing but himself can be its last, adequate, and proper happiness. Because, therefore, a great part of our happiness must arise from the contemplation of his being, that he might give our souls a just relish of such a contemplation, he has made them naturally delight in the apprehension of what is great or unlimited. Our admiration, which is a very pleasing motion of the mind, immediately rises at the consideration of any object that takes up a great deal of room in the fancy, and, by consequence, will improve into the highest pitch of astonishment and devotion when we contemplate his nature, that is neither circumscribed by time nor place, nor to be comprehended by the largest capacity of a created being.

He has annexed a secret pleasure to the idea of any thing that is *new* or *uncommon*, that he might encourage us in the pursuit after knowledge, and engage us to search into the wonders of his creation; for every new idea brings such a pleasure along with it, as rewards any pains we have taken in its acquisition, and consequently serves as a motive to put us upon fresh discoveries.

He has made every thing that is beautiful in our own species pleasant, that all creatures might be tempted to multiply their kind, and fill the world with inhabitants; for 'tis very remarkable that, wherever nature is crossed in the production of a monster (the result of any unnatural mixture), the breed is incapable of propagating its likeness, and of founding a new order of creatures; so that, unless all animals were allured by the beauty of their own species, generation would be at an end, and the earth unpeopled.

In the last place, he has made every thing that is beautiful in all other objects pleasant, or rather has made so many objects appear beautiful, that he might render the whole creation more gay and delightful. He has given almost every thing about us the power of raising an agreeable idea in the imagination: so that it is impossible for us to behold his works with coldness or indifference, and to survey so many beauties without a secret satisfaction and complacency. Things would make but a poor appearance to the eye, if we saw them only in their proper figures and motions: And what reason can we assign for their exciting in us many of those ideas which are different from any thing that exists in the objects themselves (for such are light and colors), were it not to add supernumerary ornaments to the universe, and make it more agreeable to the imagination? We are everywhere entertained with pleasing shows and apparitions; we discover imaginary glories in the heavens, and in the earth, and see some of this visionary beauty poured out upon the whole creation; but what a rough unsightly sketch of nature should we be entertained with, did all her coloring disappear, and the several distinctions of light and shade vanish? In short, our souls are at present delightfully lost and bewildered in a pleasing delusion, and we walk about like the enchanted hero in a romance, who sees beautiful castles, woods and meadows; and at the same time hears the warbling of birds, and the purling of streams; but, upon the finishing of some secret spell, the fantastic scene breaks up, and the disconsolate knight finds himself on a barren heath, or in a solitary desert. It is not improbable that something like this may be the state of the soul after its first separation, in respect of the images it will receive from matter; though indeed the ideas of colors are so pleasing and beautiful in the imagination, that it is possible the soul will not be deprived of them, but perhaps find them excited by some other occasional cause, as they are at present by the different impressions of the subtle matter on the organ of sight.

I have here supposed that my reader is acquainted with that great modern discovery, which is at present universally acknowledged by all the enquirers into natural philosophy: namely, that light and colors, as apprehended by the imagination, are only ideas in the mind, and not qualities that have any existence in matter. As this is a truth which has been proved incontestably by many modern philosophers, and is indeed one of the finest speculations in that science, if the English reader would see the notion explained at large, he may find it in the eighth chapter of the second book of Mr. Locke's *Essay on Human Understanding*.

No. 414.   Wednesday, June 25.

————*Alterius sic*
Altera poscit opem res & conjurat amice.—HORACE [1]

[1] But naturally they need each other's help.
ROSCOMMON

If we consider the works of nature and art, as they are qualified to entertain the imagination, we shall find the last very defective, in comparison of the former; for though they may sometimes appear as beautiful or strange, they can have nothing in them of that vastness and immensity, which afford so great an entertainment to the mind of the beholder. The one may be as polite and delicate as the other, but can never show herself so august and magnificent in the design. There is something more bold and masterly in the rough careless strokes of nature, than in the nice touches and embellishments of art. The beauties of the most stately garden or palace lie in a narrow compass, the imagination immediately runs them over, and requires something else to gratify her; but, in the wide fields of nature, the sight wanders up and down without confinement, and is fed with an infinite variety of images, without any certain stint or number. For this reason we always find the poet in love with a country-life, where nature appears in the greatest perfection, and furnishes out all those scenes that are most apt to delight the imagination.

> *Scriptorum chorus omnis amat nemus et fugit urbes.*—HORACE [1]

> *Hic secura quies, et nescia fallere vita,*
> *Dives opum variarum, hic latis otia fundis,*
> *Speluncæ, vivique lacus, hic frigida tempe,*
> *Mugitusque boum, mollesque sub arbore somni.*—VIRGIL [2]

But though there are several of these wild scenes, that are more delightful than any artificial shows; yet we find the works of nature still more pleasant, the more they resemble those of art: for in this case our pleasure rises from a double principle; from the agreeableness of the objects to the eye, and from their similitude to other ob-

---

[1] —To grottoes and to groves we run,
To ease and silence every Muse's son.
                                        POPE

[2] Here easy quiet, a secure retreat,
A harmless life that knows not how to cheat,
With homebred plenty the rich owner bless,
And rural pleasures crown his happiness.
Unvexed with quarrels, undisturbed with noise,
The country king his peaceful realm enjoys:
Cool grots, and living lakes, the flow'ry pride
Of meads and streams that through the valley glide;
And shady groves that easy sleep invite,
And, after toilsome days, a short repose at night.
                                        DRYDEN.

jects: We are pleased as well with comparing their beauties, as with surveying them, and can represent them to our minds, either as copies or originals. Hence it is that we take delight in a prospect which is well laid out, and diversified with fields and meadows, woods and rivers; in those accidental landscapes of trees, clouds and cities, that are sometimes found in the veins of marble; in the curious fret-work of rocks and grottos; and, in a word, in any thing that hath such a variety or regularity as may seem the effect of design in what we call the works of chance.

If the products of nature rise in value, according as they more or less resemble those of art, we may be sure that artificial works receive a greater advantage from their resemblance of such as are natural; because here the similitude is not only pleasant, but the pattern more perfect. The prettiest landscape I ever saw, was one drawn on the walls of a dark room, which stood opposite on one side to a navigable river, and on the other to a park. The experiment is very common in optics. Here you might discover the waves and fluctuations of the water in strong and proper colors, with the picture of a ship entering at one end, and sailing by degrees through the whole piece. On another there appeared the green shadows of trees, waving to and fro with the wind, and herds of deer among them in miniature, leaping about upon the wall. I must confess, the novelty of such a sight may be one occasion of its pleasantness to the imagination, but certainly the chief reason is its near resemblance to nature, as it does not only, like other pictures, give the color and figure, but the motion of the things it represents.

We have before observed, that there is generally in nature something more grand and august, than what we meet with in the curiosities of art. When, therefore, we see this imitated in any measure, it gives us a nobler and more exalted kind of pleasure than what we receive from the nicer and more accurate productions of art. On this account our English gardens are not so entertaining to the fancy as those in France and Italy, where we see a large extent of ground covered over with an agreeable mixture of garden and forest, which represent everywhere an artificial rudeness, much more charming than that neatness and elegancy which we meet with in those of our own country. It might, indeed, be of ill consequence to the public, as well as unprofitable to private persons, to alienate so much ground from pasturage, and the plough, in many parts of a country that is so well peopled, and cultivated to a far greater advantage. But why may not a whole estate be thrown into a kind of garden by frequent plantations, that may turn as much to the profit, as the pleasure of the owner? A marsh overgrown with willows, or a mountain shaded with oaks, are not only more beautiful, but more beneficial, than when they lie bare and unadorned. Fields of corn make a pleasant prospect, and if the walks were a little taken care of that lie between them, if the natural embroidery of the meadows were helped and improved by some small additions of art, and the several rows of hedges set off by trees and flowers, that the soil was capable of receiving, a man might make a pretty landscape of his own possessions.

Writers, who have given us an account of China, tell us the inhabitants of that country laugh at the plantations of our Europeans, which are laid out by the rule and line; because, they say, any one may place trees in equal rows and uniform figures. They choose rather to show a genius in works of this nature, and therefore always conceal the art by which they direct themselves. They have a word, it seems, in their language, by which they express the particular beauty of a plantation that thus strikes the imagination at first sight, without discovering what it is that has so agreeable an effect. Our British gardeners, on the contrary, instead of humoring nature, love to deviate from it as much as possible. Our trees rise in cones, globes, and pyramids. We see the marks of the scissors upon every plant and bush. I do not know whether I am singular in my opinion, but, for my own part, I would rather look upon a tree in all its luxuriancy and diffusion of boughs and branches, than when it is thus cut and trimmed into a mathematical figure; and cannot but fancy that an orchard in flower looks infinitely more delightful than all the little labyrinths of the most finished parterre. But as our great modellers of gardens have their magazines of plants to dispose of, it is very natural for them to tear up all the beautiful plantations of fruit trees, and contrive a plan that may most turn to their own profit, in taking off their evergreens, and the like moveable plants, with which their shops are plentifully stocked.

Pope

Alexander POPE (1688–1744) was born in London, the son of a Roman Catholic linen merchant, who was comfortably off. After a desultory education, interrupted, when he was twelve years old, by a severe illness brought on by overapplication, he carried on his own schooling, studying the classics, which he read with ease if not with accuracy. He wrote much verse in his youth, some of which attracted the attention of Congreve and Wycherley, who introduced him to the men of letters in London. In 1709 his *Pastorals* were published, and two years later his *Essay on Criticism*, which Addison praised. Other poems followed, including the *Rape of the Lock* (1714), and in 1715 he began his translation of Homer, which brought him a fortune. The *Iliad* (1720) was followed by the *Odyssey* (1725–26). On the death of his father, he moved with his mother to Twickenham, near London, where he received the visits of famous authors, wits, statesmen, and beauties of the day. His edition of Shakespeare appeared in 1725, and the *Miscellanies* (with Swift) in 1727–28. In the *Dunciad* (first published in 1728; with later additions, in 1729 and 1742), he attacked all sorts of critics. His *Epistles* (1731–35) were followed by his *Essay on Man* (1733) and the *Imitations of Horace* (1733–39). His naturally delicate constitution, his deformity, his sensitiveness, combined with overexcitement and overwork, brought about his death at a relatively early age.

Pope, who succeeded Dryden as arbiter of British letters, is, in the opinion of some authorities, the greatest English poet of the eighteenth century. His reputation as a literary critic is based on *An Essay on Criticism,* a beautiful mosaic of ideas taken mainly from Horace, Vida, and Boileau, but also from Dionysius, Vergil, Cicero, Pliny, Petronius, Quintilian, Rapin, Le Bossu, Dryden, Temple, Roscommon, Buckingham, Sheffield, Rochester, Cowley, and Addison.

He holds the well-known neo-classic tenets, expressing them so tersely and so neatly that they, along with Pope's accompanying remarks, have become almost proverbs in the English language. Pope, however, like many neo-classic critics, realized that in great literature there are qualities which no rules can teach. A master will "snatch a grace beyond the reach of art"—a line that he takes, it may be remarked, from Rapin.

AN ESSAY ON CRITICISM [1]

(1711)

PART I

'Tis hard to say, if greater want of skill
Appear in writing or in judging ill;
But, of the two, less dang'rous is th' offence
To tire our patience, than mislead our sense [2]:
Some few in that, but numbers err in this;
Ten censure wrong for one who writes amiss;
A fool might once himself alone expose;
Now one in verse makes many more in prose.
 'Tis with our judgments as our watches, none
Go just alike, yet each believes his own.   10
In poets as true genius is but rare,
True taste as seldom is the critic's share;
Both must alike from Heav'n derive their light,
These born to judge, as well as those to write.
Let such teach others who themselves excel,
And censure freely, who have written well.
Authors are partial to their wit, 'tis true,

---

[1] The text is based on that of the Cambridge Edition of Pope, edited by Henry W. Boynton, Houghton Mifflin Company.
[2] judgment.

But are not critics to their judgment too?
   Yet, if we look more closely, we shall find
Most have the seeds of judgment in their mind.   20
Nature affords at least a glimm'ring light;
The lines, tho' touch'd but faintly, are drawn right:
But as the slightest sketch, if justly trac'd,
Is by ill coloring but the more disgrac'd,
So by false learning is good sense defac'd:
Some are bewilder'd in the maze of schools,
And some made coxcombs Nature meant but fools:
In search of wit, these lose their common sense,
And then turn critics in their own defence:
Each burns alike, who can or cannot write,   30
Or with a rival's, or an eunuch's spite.
All fools have still an itching to deride,
And fain would be upon the laughing side.
If Mævius [1] scribble in Apollo's spite,
There are who judge still worse than he can write.
   Some have at first for wits,[2] then poets past,
Turn'd critics next, and prov'd plain fools at last.
Some neither can for wits nor critics pass,
As heavy mules are neither horse nor ass.
Those half-learn'd witlings, num'rous in our isle,   40
As half-form'd insects on the banks of Nile;
Unfinish'd things, one knows not what to call,
Their generation's so equivocal;
To tell them would a hundred tongues require,
Or one vain wit's, that might a hundred tire.
   But you who seek to give and merit fame,
And justly bear a critic's noble name,
Be sure yourself and your own reach to know,
How far your genius, taste, and learning go;
Launch not beyond your depth, but be discreet,   50
And mark that point where sense and dulness meet.
   Nature to all things fix'd the limits fit,
And wisely curb'd proud man's pretending wit.
As on the land while here the ocean gains,
In other parts it leaves wide sandy plains;

[1] A minor poet of the Augustan age, ridiculed by Vergil and Horace, whom he had attacked.
[2] Men of learning.

Thus in the soul while memory prevails,
The solid pow'r of understanding fails;
Where beams of warm imagination play,
The memory's soft figures melt away.
One science only will one genius fit;   60
So vast is art, so narrow human wit:
Not only bounded to peculiar arts,
But oft in those confin'd to single parts.
Like kings we lose the conquests gain'd before,
By vain ambition still to make them more:
Each might his sev'ral [1] province well command,
Would all but stoop to what they understand.
     First follow Nature, and your judgment frame
By her just standard, which is still the same:
Unerring Nature, still divinely bright,   70
One clear, unchang'd, and universal light,
Life, force, and beauty, must to all impart,
At once the source, and end, and test of art.
Art from that fund each just supply provides
Works without show, and without pomp presides.
In some fair body thus th' informing soul
With spirits feeds, with vigor fills the whole;
Each motion guides, and ev'ry nerve sustains,
Itself unseen, but in th' effects remains.
Some, to whom Heav'n in wit has been profuse,   80
Want as much more to turn it to its use;
For wit and judgment often are at strife,
Tho' meant each other's aid, like man and wife.
'Tis more to guide, than spur the Muse's steed;
Restrain his fury, than provoke his speed:
The winged courser, like a gen'rous horse,
Shows most true mettle when you check his course.
     Those rules of old, discover'd, not devis'd,
Are Nature still, but Nature methodiz'd:
Nature, like liberty, is but restrain'd   90
By the same laws which first herself ordain'd.
     Hear how learn'd Greece her useful rules indites,
When to repress, and when indulge our flights:
High on Parnassus' top her sons she show'd,
And pointed out those arduous paths they trod;

1 peculiar, separate.

Held from afar, aloft, th' immortal prize,
And urg'd the rest by equal steps to rise.
Just precepts thus from great examples giv'n,
She drew from them what they deriv'd from Heav'n.
The gen'rous critic fann'd the poet's fire,   100
And taught the world with reason to admire.
Then criticism the Muse's handmaid prov'd,
To dress her charms, and make her more belov'd:
But following wits from that intention stray'd;
Who could not win the mistress woo'd the maid;
Against the poets their own arms they turn'd,
Sure to hate most the men from whom they learn'd.
So modern 'pothecaries, taught the art
By doctors' bills [1] to play the doctor's part,
Bold in the practice of mistaken rules,   110
Prescribe, apply, and call their masters fools.
Some on the leaves of ancient authors prey;
Nor time nor moths e'er spoil'd so much as they:
Some dryly plain, without invention's aid,
Write dull receipts how poems may be made;
These leave the sense their learning to display,
And those explain the meaning quite away.
    You then whose judgment the right course would steer,
Know well each ancient's proper character:
His fable, subject, scope in ev'ry page;   120
Religion, country, genius of his age:
Without all these at once before your eyes,
Cavil you may, but never criticize.
Be Homer's works your study and delight,
Read them by day, and meditate by night;
Thence form your judgment, thence your maxims bring,
And trace the Muses upward to their spring.
Still with itself compar'd, his text peruse;
And let your comment be the Mantuan Muse.
    When first young Maro [2] in his boundless mind   130
A work t' outlast immortal Rome design'd,
Perhaps he seem'd above the critic's law,
And but from Nature's fountain scorn'd to draw:
But when t' examine ev'ry part he came,

---

[1] prescriptions.
[2] Publius Vergilius Maro (Vergil) was born at Mantua.

Nature and Homer were, he found, the same.
Convinc'd, amaz'd, he checks the bold design,
And rules as strict his labor'd work confine
As if the Stagyrite [1] o'erlook'd each line.
Learn hence for ancient rules a just esteem;
To copy Nature is to copy them.   140
    Some beauties yet no precepts can declare,
For there's a happiness as well as care.
Music resembles poetry; in each
Are nameless graces which no methods teach,
And which a master-hand alone can reach.
If, where the rules not far enough extend,
(Since rules were made but to promote their end)
Some lucky licence answer to the full
Th' intent propos'd, that licence is a rule.
Thus Pegasus, a nearer way to take,   150
May boldly deviate from the common track.
Great wits sometimes may gloriously offend,
And rise to faults true critics dare not mend;
From vulgar bounds with brave disorder part,
And snatch a grace beyond the reach of art,
Which, without passing thro' the judgment, gains
The heart, and all its ends at once attains.
In prospects [2] thus some objects please our eyes,
Which out of Nature's common order rise,
The shapeless rock, or hanging precipice.   160
But tho' the ancients thus their rules invade
(As kings dispense with laws themselves have made),
Moderns, beware! or if you must offend
Against the precept, ne'er transgress its end;
Let it be seldom, and compell'd by need;
And have, at least, their precedent to plead;
The critic else proceeds without remorse,
Seizes your fame, and puts his laws in force.
    I know there are, to whose presumptuous thoughts
Those freer beauties, ev'n in them, seem faults.   170
Some figures monstrous and mis-shap'd appear,
Consider'd singly, or beheld too near,
Which, but proportion'd to their light, or place,

---

[1] Aristotle was born at Stagira in Macedonia.
[2] Views or landscapes.

Due distance reconciles to form and grace.
A prudent chief not always must display
His pow'rs in equal ranks, and fair array,
But with th' occasion and the place comply,
Conceal his force, nay, seem sometimes to fly.
Those oft are stratagems which errors seem,
Nor is it Homer nods, but we that dream.   180
    Still green with bays each ancient altar stands,
Above the reach of sacrilegious hands;
Secure from flames, from envy's fiercer rage,
Destructive war, and all-involving age.
See, from each clime, the learn'd their incense bring;
Hear, in all tongues consenting pæans ring!
In praise so just let ev'ry voice be join'd,
And fill the gen'ral chorus of mankind.
Hail, bards triumphant! born in happier days;
Immortal heirs of universal praise!   190
Whose honors with increase of ages grow,
As streams roll down, enlarging as they flow;
Nations unborn your mighty names shall sound,
And worlds applaud that must not yet be found!
O may some spark of your celestial fire
The last, the meanest of your sons inspire,
(That on weak wings, from far, pursues your flights,
Glows while he reads, but trembles as he writes)
To teach vain wits a science little known,
T' admire superior sense, and doubt their own!   200

PART II

    Of all the causes which conspire to blind
Man's erring judgment, and misguide the mind,
What the weak head with strongest bias rules,
Is pride, the never-failing vice of fools.
Whatever Nature has in worth denied,
She gives in large recruits of needful pride;
For as in bodies, thus in souls, we find
What wants in blood and spirits, swell'd with wind:
Pride, where wit fails, steps in to our defence,
And fills up all the mighty void of sense: 210
If once right reason drives that cloud away,

Truth breaks upon us with resistless day.
Trust not yourself; but, your defects to know,
Make use of ev'ry friend—and ev'ry foe.
    A little learning is a dang'rous thing;
Drink deep, or taste not the Pierian [1] spring:
There shallow draughts intoxicate the brain,
And drinking largely sobers us again.
Fir'd at first sight with what the Muse imparts,
In fearless youth we tempt the heights of arts,   220
While from the bounded level of our mind,
Short views we take, nor see the lengths behind;
But more advanc'd, behold with strange surprise,
New distant scenes of endless science rise!
So pleas'd at first the tow'ring Alps we try,
Mount o'er the vales, and seem to tread the sky;
Th' eternal snows appear already past,
And the first clouds and mountains seem the last:
But those attain'd, we tremble to survey
The growing labors of the lengthen'd way;   230
Th' increasing prospect tires our wand'ring eyes,
Hills peep o'er hills, and Alps on Alps arise!
    A perfect judge will read each work of wit
With the same spirit that its author writ;
Survey the whole, nor seek slight faults to find
Where Nature moves, and rapture warms the mind;
Nor lose, for that malignant dull delight,
The gen'rous pleasure to be charm'd with wit.
But in such lays as neither ebb nor flow,
Correctly cold, and regularly low,   240
That, shunning faults, one quiet tenor keep,
We cannot blame indeed—but we may sleep.
In wit, as Nature, what affects our hearts
Is not th' exactness of peculiar parts;
'Tis not a lip, or eye, we beauty call,
But the joint force and full result of all.
Thus when we view some well-proportion'd dome,
(The world's just wonder, and ev'n thine, O Rome!)
No single parts unequally surprise,
All comes united to th' admiring eyes;   250

[1] Mount Pierus, in Thessaly, sacred to the Muses.

No monstrous height, or breadth, or length, appear;
The whole at once is bold, and regular.
   Whoever thinks a faultless piece to see,
Thinks what ne'er was, nor is, nor e'er shall be.
In ev'ry work regard the writer's end,
Since none can compass more than they intend;
And if the means be just, the conduct true,
Applause, in spite of trivial faults, is due.
As men of breeding, sometimes men of wit,
T' avoid great errors, must the less commit;   260
Neglect the rules each verbal critic lays,
For not to know some trifles is a praise.
Most critics, fond of some subservient art,
Still make the whole depend upon a part:
They talk of principles, but notions prize,
And all to one lov'd folly sacrifice.
   Once on a time, La Mancha's Knight, they say,
A certain bard encount'ring on the way,
Discours'd in terms as just, with looks as sage,
As e'er could Dennis,[1] of the Grecian stage;   270
Concluding all were desp'rate sots and fools,
Who durst depart from Aristotle's rules.
Our author, happy in a judge so nice,
Produc'd his play, and begg'd the knight's advice;
Made him observe the subject, and the plot,
The manners, passions, unities; what not?
All which, exact to rule, were brought about,
Were but a combat in the lists left out.
"What! leave the combat out?" exclaims the knight.
"Yes, or we must renounce the Stagyrite."   280
"Not so, by Heav'n!" (he answers in a rage)
"Knights, squires, and steeds, must enter on the stage."
"So vast a throng, the stage can ne'er contain."
"Then build a new, or act it in a plain."
   Thus critics of less judgment than caprice,
Curious, not knowing, not exact but nice,
Form short ideas, and offend in arts

---

[1] John Dennis (1657–1734), a mediocre critic of Pope's time, is ridiculed in the *Dunciad*. He is referred to as Appius in line 585 below; his unsuccessful play, *Appius and Virginia*, appeared in 1709,—the year in which this essay was written.

(As most in manners) by a love to parts.
　　Some to conceit [1] alone their taste confine,
And glitt'ring thoughts struck out at ev'ry line;　　　290
Pleas'd with a work where nothing's just or fit;
One glaring chaos and wild heap of wit.
Poets, like painters, thus unskill'd to trace
The naked nature, and the living grace,
With golds and jewels cover ev'ry part,
And hide with ornaments their want of art.
True wit is Nature to advantage dress'd;
What oft was thought, but ne'er so well express'd;
Something, whose truth convinc'd at sight we find,
That gives us back the image of our mind.　　　300
As shades more sweetly recommend the light,
So modest plainness sets off sprightly wit:
For works may have more wit than does them good,
As bodies perish thro' excess of blood.
　　Others for language all their care express,
And value books, as women men, for dress:
Their praise is still,—the style is excellent;
The sense, they humbly take upon content.
Words are like leaves, and where they most abound,
Much fruit of sense beneath is rarely found.　　　310
False eloquence, like the prismatic glass,
Its gaudy colors spreads on ev'ry place;
The face of Nature we no more survey,
All glares alike, without distinction gay;
But true expression, like th' unchanging sun,
Clears and improves whate'er it shines upon;
It gilds all objects, but it alters none.
Expression is the dress of thought, and still
Appears more decent, as more suitable.
A vile conceit in pompous words express'd　　　320
Is like a clown in regal purple dress'd:
For diff'rent styles with diff'rent subjects sort,
As sev'ral garbs with country, town, and court.
Some by old words to fame have made pretence,
Ancients in phrase, mere Moderns in their sense;
Such labor'd nothings, in so strange a style,
Amaze th' unlearn'd, and make the learned smile.

[1] Affected or fanciful notions.

Unlucky, as Fungoso in the play,[1]
These sparks [2] with awkward vanity display
What the fine gentleman wore yesterday;   330
And but so mimic ancient wits at best,
As apes our grandsires, in their doublets drest.
In words, as fashions, the same rule will hold,
Alike fantastic, if too new or old:
Be not the first by whom the new are try'd,
Nor yet the last to lay the old aside.
    But most by numbers judge a poet's song,
And smooth or rough, with them, is right or wrong:
In the bright Muse, tho' thousand charms conspire,
Her voice is all these tuneful fools admire;   340
Who haunt Parnassus but to please their ear,
Not mend their minds; as some to church repair
Not for the doctrine, but the music there.
These equal syllables alone require,
Tho' oft the ear the open vowels tire,
While expletives their feeble aid do join,
And ten low words oft creep in one dull line:
While they ring round the same unvary'd chimes,
With sure returns of still expected rhymes;
Where'er you find "the cooling western breeze,"   350
In the next line, it "whispers thro' the trees:"
If crystal streams "with pleasing murmurs creep,"
The reader's threaten'd (not in vain) with "sleep:"
Then, at the last and only couplet, fraught
With some unmeaning thing they call a thought,
A needless Alexandrine ends the song,
That, like a wounded snake, drags its slow length along.
Leave such to tune their own dull rhymes, and know
What's roundly smooth, or languishingly slow;
And praise the easy vigor of a line   360
Where Denham's strength, and Waller's sweetness join.
True ease in writing comes from art, not chance,
As those move easiest who have learn'd to dance.
'Tis not enough no harshness gives offence;
The sound must seem an echo to the sense.
Soft is the strain when zephyr gently blows,

[1] A character in Jonson's *Every Man Out of His Humor.*
[2] beaux.

And the smooth stream in smoother numbers flows;
But when loud surges lash the sounding shore,
The hoarse, rough verse should like the torrent roar.
When Ajax strives some rock's vast weight to throw,   370
The line too labors, and the words move slow:
Not so when swift Camilla scours the plain,[1]
Flies o'er th' unbending corn, and skims along the main.
Hear how Timotheus'[2] vary'd lays surprise,
And bid alternate passions fall and rise,
While at each change, the son of Libyan Jove[3]
Now burns with glory, and then melts with love;
Now his fierce eyes with sparkling fury glow,
Now sighs steal out, and tears begin to flow:
Persians and Greeks like turns of nature found,   380
And the world's victor stood subdu'd by sound!
The pow'r of music all our hearts allow,
And what Timotheus was, is Dryden now.[4]
   Avoid extremes, and shun the fault of such
Who still are pleas'd too little or too much.
At ev'ry trifle scorn to take offence,
That always shows great pride, or little sense:
Those heads, as stomachs, are not sure the best,
Which nauseate all, and nothing can digest.
Yet let not each gay turn thy rapture move;   390
For fools admire, but men of sense approve:
As things seem large which we thro' mists descry,
Dulness is ever apt to magnify.
   Some foreign writers, some our own despise;
The Ancients only, or the Moderns prize.
Thus wit, like faith, by each man is apply'd
To one small sect, and all are damn'd beside.
Meanly they seek the blessing to confine,
And force that sun but on a part to shine,
Which not alone the southern wit sublimes,   400

[1] A madrigal by Thomas Bateson (*c* 1600) begins:
    "Camilla fair tripped o'er the plain,
       I followed quickly after . . ."
[2] The dithyrambic poet of Miletus (*c* 400 B. C.); cf. Dryden's *Alexander's Feast*.
[3] Alexander was declared by the priests of Libya to be the son of Jupiter.
[4] Johnson said that both Dryden and Pope drove coaches and six, but while Dryden's horses are either galloping or stumbling, Pope's go at a steady, even trot. Pope was a constant reader and ardent admirer of Dryden from early youth.

But ripens spirits in cold northern climes;
Which from the first has shone on ages past,
Enlights the present, and shall warm the last;
Tho' each may feel increases and decays,
And see now clearer and now darker days;
Regard not then if wit be old or new,
But blame the false, and value still the true.
    Some ne'er advance a judgment of their own,
But catch the spreading notion of the town;
They reason and conclude by precedent,   410
And own stale nonsense which they ne'er invent.
Some judge of authors' names, not works, and then
Nor praise nor blame the writings, but the men.
Of all this servile herd, the worst is he
That in proud dulness joins with quality;
A constant critic at the great man's board,
To fetch and carry nonsense for my lord.
What woeful stuff this madrigal would be,
In some starv'd hackney sonneteer, or me!
But let a lord once own the happy lines,   420
How the wit brightens! how the style refines!
Before his sacred name flies ev'ry fault,
And each exalted stanza teems with thought!
    The vulgar thus thro' imitation err,
As oft the learn'd by being singular;
So much they scorn the crowd, that if the throng
By chance go right, they purposely go wrong:
So schismatics the plain believers quit,
And are but damn'd for having too much wit.
Some praise at morning what they blame at night,   430
But always think the last opinion right.
A muse by these is like a mistress us'd,
This hour she's idoliz'd, the next abus'd;
While their weak heads, like towns unfortify'd,
'Twixt sense and nonsense daily change their side.
Ask them the cause; they're wiser still they say;
And still to-morrow's wiser than to-day.
We think our fathers fools, so wise we grow;
Our wiser sons, no doubt, will think us so.
Once school-divines this zealous isle o'erspread;   440
Who knew most sentences was deepest read:

Faith, gospel, all, seem'd made to be disputed,
And none had sense enough to be confuted.
Scotists and Thomists [1] now in peace remain,
Amidst their kindred cobwebs in Duck Lane.[2]
If faith itself has diff'rent dresses worn,
What wonder modes in wit should take their turn?
Oft, leaving what is natural and fit,
The current folly proves the ready wit;
And authors think their reputation safe,   450
Which lives as long as fools are pleas'd to laugh.
   Some, valuing those of their own side or mind,
Still make themselves the measure of mankind:
Fondly we think we honor merit then,
When we but praise ourselves in other men.
Parties in wit attend on those of state,
And public faction doubles private hate.
Pride, malice, folly, against Dryden rose,
In various shapes of parsons, critics, beaus;
But sense surviv'd when merry jests were past;   460
For rising merit will buoy up at last.
Might he return, and bless once more our eyes,
New Blackmores and new Milbournes [3] must arise:
Nay, should great Homer lift his awful head,
Zoilus [4] again would start up from the dead.
Envy will merit, as its shade, pursue;
But like a shadow, proves the substance true:
For envy'd wit, like Sol eclips'd, makes known
Th' opposing body's grossness, not its own.
When first that sun too pow'rful beams displays,   470
It draws up vapors which obscure its rays;
But ev'n those clouds at last adorn its way,
Reflect new glories, and augment the day.
   Be thou the first true merit to befriend;
His praise is lost who stays till all commend.

[1] Followers of Duns Scotus and Thomas Aquinas, Schoolmen of the fourteenth century, who argued on theological matters.

[2] A centre of the book trade, which was located in St. Paul's Churchyard. See line 623, below.

[3] Sir Richard Blackmore (1650–1729), court physician and minor poet; the Rev. Luke Milbourne was a just critic of Dryden.

[4] Zoilus (fl. 4th cent. B.C.) so severely criticized Homer that he was called "Homeromastix" ("Scourge of Homer").

Short is the date, alas! of modern rhymes,
And 'tis but just to let them live betimes.
No longer now that golden age appears,
When patriarch wits surviv'd a thousand years;
Now length of fame (our second life) is lost,   480
And bare threescore is all ev'n that can boast;
Our sons their fathers' failing language see,
And such as Chaucer is, shall Dryden be.
So when the faithful pencil has design'd
Some bright idea of the master's mind,
Where a new world leaps out at his command,
And ready Nature waits upon his hand;
When the ripe colors soften and unite,
And sweetly melt into just shade and light;
When mellowing years their full perfection give,   490
And each bold figure just begins to live,
The treach'rous colors the fair art betray,
And all the bright creation fades away!
   Unhappy wit, like most mistaken things,
Atones not for that envy which it brings;
In youth alone its empty praise we boast,
But soon the short-liv'd vanity is lost;
Like some fair flow'r the early spring supplies,
That gaily blooms, but ev'n in blooming dies.
What is this wit, which must our cares employ?   500
The owner's wife, that other men enjoy;
Then most our trouble still when most admir'd,
And still the more we give, the more requir'd;
Whose fame with pains we guard, but lose with ease,
Sure some to vex, but never all to please;
'Tis what the vicious fear, the virtuous shun,
By fools 'tis hated, and by knaves undone!
   If wit so much from ignorance undergo,
Ah, let not learning too commence its foe!
Of old, those met rewards who could excel,   510
And such were prais'd who but endeavor'd well:
Tho' triumphs were to gen'rals only due,
Crowns were reserv'd to grace the soldiers too.
Now they who reach Parnassus' lofty crown
Employ their pains to spurn some others down;
And while self-love each jealous writer rules,

Contending wits become the sport of fools;
But still the worst with most regret commend,
For each ill author is as bad a friend.
To what base ends, and by what abject ways,   520
Are mortals urg'd thro' sacred lust of praise!
Ah, ne'er so dire a thirst of glory boast,
Nor in the critic let the man be lost.
Good nature and good sense must ever join;
To err is human, to forgive, divine.
   But if in noble minds some dregs remain,
Not yet purg'd off, of spleen and sour disdain,
Discharge that rage on more provoking crimes,
Nor fear a dearth in these flagitious times.
No pardon vile obscenity should find,   530
Tho' wit and art conspire to move your mind;
But dulness with obscenity must prove
As shameful sure as impotence in love.
In the fat age of pleasure, wealth, and ease
Sprung the rank weed, and thriv'd with large increase:
When love was all an easy monarch's care;
Seldom at council, never in a war,
Jilts rul'd the state, and statesmen farces writ;
Nay, wits had pensions, and young lords had wit;
The fair sat panting at a courtier's play,   540
And not a mask went unimprov'd away;
The modest fan was lifted up no more,
And virgins smil'd at what they blush'd before.
The following licence of a foreign reign
Did all the dregs of bold Socinus ¹ drain;
Then unbelieving priests reform'd the nation,
And taught more pleasant methods of salvation;
Where Heav'n's free subjects might their rights dispute,
Lest God himself should seem too absolute:
Pulpits their sacred satire learn'd to spare,   550
And vice admir'd to find a flatt'rer there!
Encourag'd thus, wit's Titans braved the skies,
And the press groan'd with licenc'd blasphemies.
These monsters, Critics! with your darts engage,
Here point your thunder, and exhaust your rage!

---

¹ Lelio Sozzini, an Italian theologian (1525–1562), with his nephew Fausto Sozzini (1539–1604), advanced the Unitarian doctrines held by the Socinians.

Yet shun their fault, who, scandalously nice,
Will needs mistake an author into vice:
All seems infected that th' infected spy,
As all looks yellow to the jaundic'd eye.

PART III

Learn then what morals critics ought to show,   560
For 'tis but half a judge's task, to know.
'Tis not enough, taste, judgment, learning, join;
In all you speak, let truth and candor shine,
That not alone what to your sense is due
All may allow, but seek your friendship too.
Be silent always when you doubt your sense,
And speak, tho' sure, with seeming diffidence:
Some positive, persisting fops we know,
Who, if once wrong, will needs be always so;
But you with pleasure own your errors past,   570
And make each day a critique on the last.
'Tis not enough your counsel still be true;
Blunt truths more mischief than nice falsehoods do.
Men must be taught as if you taught them not,
And things unknown propos'd as things forgot.
Without good-breeding truth is disapprov'd;
That only makes superior sense belov'd.
Be niggards of advice on no pretence,
For the worst avarice is that of sense.
With mean complacence ne'er betray your trust,   580
Nor be so civil as to prove unjust.
Fear not the anger of the wise to raise;
Those best can bear reproof, who merit praise.
'Twere well might critics still this freedom take,
But Appius reddens at each word you speak,
And stares, tremendous, with a threat'ning eye,
Like some fierce tyrant in old tapestry.
Fear most to tax an honorable fool,
Whose right it is, uncensur'd, to be dull:
Such, without wit, are poets when they please,   590
As without learning they can take degrees.
Leave dang'rous truths to unsuccessful satires,
And flattery to fulsome dedicators,

Whom, when they praise, the world believes no more,
Than when they promise to give scribbling o'er.
'Tis best sometimes your censure to restrain,
And charitably let the dull be vain;
Your silence there is better than your spite,
For who can rail so long as they can write?
Still humming on, their drowsy course they keep,   600
And lash'd so long, like tops, are lash'd asleep.
False steps but help them to renew the race,
As, after stumbling, jades will mend their pace.
What crowds of these, impenitently bold,
In sounds and jingling syllables grown old,
Still run on poets in a raging vein,
Ev'n to the dregs and squeezing of the brain,
Strain out the last dull droppings of their sense,
And rhyme with all the rage of impotence.
　　Such shameless bards we have; and yet, 'tis true,   610
There are as mad, abandon'd critics too.
The bookful blockhead, ignorantly read,
With loads of learned lumber in his head,
With his own tongue still edifies his ears,
And always list'ning to himself appears:
All books he reads, and all he reads assails,
From Dryden's *Fables* down to Durfey's [1] *Tales*.
With him most authors steal their works, or buy;
Garth [2] did not write his own *Dispensary*.
Name a new play, and he's the poet's friend,   620
Nay, show'd his faults—but when would poets mend?
No place so sacred from such fops is barr'd,
Nor is Paul's church more safe than Paul's churchyard:
Nay, fly to altars, there they'll talk you dead;
For fools rush in where angels fear to tread.
Distrustful sense with modest caution speaks,
It still looks home, and short excursions makes;
But rattling nonsense in full volleys breaks,
And never shock'd, and never turn'd aside,
Bursts out, resistless, with a thund'ring tide.   630
　　But where's the man who counsel can bestow,

---

[1] Thomas D'Urfey (1653–1723), dramatist and humorous poet.
[2] Sir Samuel Garth (1661–1719), physician and poet, whose *Dispensary* was a poetical satire on apothecaries and physicians.

Still pleas'd to teach, and yet not proud to know?
Unbias'd, or by favor, or by spite,
Not dully prepossess'd, nor blindly right;
Tho' learn'd, well-bred; and tho' well-bred, sincere;
Modestly bold, and humanly severe;
Who to a friend his faults can freely show,
And gladly praise the merit of a foe?
Bless'd with a taste exact, yet unconfin'd,
A knowledge both of books and human-kind;   640
Gen'rous converse; a soul exempt from pride;
And love to praise, with reason on his side?

    Such once were critics; such the happy few
Athens and Rome in better ages knew.
The mighty Stagyrite first left the shore,
Spread all his sails, and durst the deeps explore;
He steer'd securely, and discover'd far,
Led by the light of the Mæonian star.[1]
Poets, a race long unconfin'd and free,
Still fond and proud of savage liberty,   650
Receiv'd his laws, and stood convinc'd 'twas fit,
Who conquer'd Nature should preside o'er wit.

    Horace still charms with graceful negligence,
And without method talks us into sense;
Will, like a friend, familiarly convey
The truest notions in the easiest way.
He, who supreme in judgment, as in wit,
Might boldly censure, as he boldly writ,
Yet judg'd with coolness, tho' he sung with fire;
His precepts teach but what his works inspire.   660
Our critics take a contrary extreme,
They judge with fury, but they write with phlegm:
Nor suffers Horace more in wrong translations
By wits, than critics in as wrong quotations.

    See Dionysius [2] Homer's thoughts refine,
And call new beauties forth from ev'ry line!

    Fancy and art in gay Petronius please,
The scholar's learning, with the courtier's ease.

---

[1] Homer, who was believed by some to have been born in Mæonia (Asia Minor).

[2] A Greek critic and historian (d. 7 B. C.)—not to be confused with the tyrants of Syracuse—is known by the name of his birthplace, Halicarnassus, though he spent most of his life at Rome.

In grave Quintilian's copious work we find
The justest rules, and clearest method join'd. 670
Thus useful arms in magazines we place,
All rang'd in order, and dispos'd with grace;
But less to please the eye, than arm the hand,
Still fit for use, and ready at command.
  Thee, bold Longinus! all the Nine inspire,
And bless their critic with a poet's fire:
An ardent judge, who, zealous in his trust,
With warmth gives sentence, yet is always just;
Whose own example strengthens all his laws,
And is himself that great Sublime he draws. 680
  Thus long succeeding critics justly reign'd,
Licence repress'd, and useful laws ordain'd.
Learning and Rome alike in empire grew,
And arts still follow'd where her eagles flew;
From the same foes, at last, both felt their doom,
And the same age saw learning fall, and Rome.
With tyranny, then superstition join'd,
As that the body, this enslav'd the mind;
Much was believ'd, but little understood,
And to be dull was constru'd to be good; 690
A second deluge learning thus o'er-run,
And the monks finish'd what the Goths begun.
  At length Erasmus, that great injur'd name,
(The glory of the priesthood, and the shame!)
Stemm'd the wild torrent of a barb'rous age,
And drove those holy Vandals off the stage.
  But see! each Muse, in Leo's [1] golden days,
Starts from her trance, and trims her wither'd bays·
Rome's ancient Genius, o'er its ruins spread,
Shakes off the dust, and rears his rev'rend head. 700
Then Sculpture and her sister arts revive;
Stones leap'd to form, and rocks began to live;
With sweeter notes each rising temple rung;
A Raphael painted, and a Vida sung.
Immortal Vida! on whose honor'd brow
The poet's bays and critic's ivy grow:

---

[1] Giovanni de' Medici (1475–1521), second son of Lorenzo, became Pope as Leo X (from 1513 to 1521); he was a patron of art and learning; his court was the meeting-place for scholars.

Cremona now shall ever boast thy name,
As next in place to Mantua, next in fame!
   But soon by impious arms from Latium chas'd,
Their ancient bounds the banish'd Muses pass'd: 710
Thence arts o'er all the northern world advance,
But critic learning flourish'd most in France;
The rules a nation, born to serve, obeys;
And Boileau still in right of Horace sways.
But we, brave Britons, foreign laws despis'd,
And kept unconquer'd, and unciviliz'd;
Fierce for the liberties of wit, and bold,
We still defy'd the Romans, as of old.
Yet some there were, among the sounder few
Of those who less presum'd, and better knew,   720
Who durst assert the juster ancient cause,
And here restor'd wit's fundamental laws.
Such was the Muse, whose rules and practice tell
"Nature's chief masterpiece is writing well."
Such was Roscommon, not more learn'd than good,
With manners gen'rous as his noble blood;
To him the wit of Greece and Rome was known,
And ev'ry author's merit, but his own.
Such late was Walsh [1]—the Muse's judge and friend,
Who justly knew to blame or to commend;   730
To failings mild, but zealous for desert;
The clearest head, and the sincerest heart.
Thus humble praise, lamented shade! receive;
This praise at least a grateful Muse may give:
The Muse, whose early voice you taught to sing,
Prescrib'd her heights, and prun'd her tender wing,
(Her guide now lost) no more attempts to rise,
But in low numbers short excursions tries;
Content, if hence th' unlearn'd their wants may view,
The learn'd reflect on what before they knew: 740
Careless of censure, nor too fond of fame;
Still pleas'd to praise, yet not afraid to blame;
Averse alike to flatter, or offend;
Not free from faults, nor yet too vain to mend.

---

[1] William Walsh (1663–1709), poet, friend of Dryden and Pope.

Johnson

Samuel JOHNSON (1709–1784) was the son of a Lichfield bookseller. After attending the grammar-school of his town and reading widely in his father's shop, he entered Oxford University, which he left shortly because of poverty, without taking a degree. For a while he taught school at Market Bosworth, but the routine was irksome and he resigned his position, finding employment with a publisher in Birmingham, where he gained a meagre livelihood. In 1735 he married a widow, older than himself, and opened, near Lichfield, an academy which was not a success. Two years later, with a pupil, David Garrick, he went to London, where he had a hard struggle, doing literary hack-work and writing satirical poetry. In 1747 he began his great *Dictionary*, which was published in 1755. *The Vanity of Human Wishes* appeared in 1749, in the same year that Garrick produced his tragedy, *Irene*. He started, in 1750, the *Rambler*, a bi-weekly somewhat on the lines of the *Spectator*, which he edited for two years. In 1752 his wife died, and in 1755, when the *Dictionary* appeared, Oxford conferred on him an M.A. degree; later both Oxford and Dublin honored him with an LL.D.

Johnson was now the friend of men like Reynolds, Burke, and Goldsmith, and was the dominant member of the Literary Club. The *Idler*, another periodical of his, ran from 1758 to 1760. In 1759, he wrote *Rasselas*. A pension was conferred upon him in 1762, and in the next year he made the acquaintance of Boswell, who later became his biographer. During the rest of his life, he published his edition of Shakespeare (1765), the *Journey to the Western Isles* (1775), and his last great work, the *Lives of the Poets* (1779–81). He was the literary dictator of London, following Ben Jonson, Dryden, and Pope; and when he died he was buried in Westminster Abbey.

Dr. Johnson may be called the last of the neo-classic critics in English. His criticism of Milton's verse is rigid and dogmatic, leaning heavily on the "rules." He made some foolish statements about Shakespeare, but he perceived, as had Dryden, the greatness of the man and his works. Dr. Johnson's essential good sense is best shown by the last paragraph of the first essay below.

From *THE RAMBLER* [1]

(1751)

No. 156. *Saturday, September 14, 1751.*

Nunquam aliud natura, aliud sapienta dicit.
                                             JUVENAL
For wisdom ever echoes nature's voice.

Every government, say the politicians, is perpetually degenerating towards corruption, from which it must be rescued at certain periods by the resuscitation of its first principles, and the re-establishment of its original constitution. Every animal body, according to the methodic physicians, is, by the predominance of some exuberant quality, continually declining towards disease and death, which must be obviated by a seasonable reduction of the peccant humor to the just equipoise which health requires.

In the same manner the studies of mankind, all at least which, not being subject to rigorous demonstration, admit the influence of fancy and caprice, are perpetually tending to error and confusion. Of the great principles of truth which the first speculatists discovered, the simplicity is embarrassed by ambitious additions, or the evidence obscured by inaccurate argumentation; and as they descend from one succession of writers to another, like light transmitted from room to room, they lose their strength and splendor, and fade at last in total evanescence.

The systems of learning therefore must be sometimes reviewed,

[1] The text is taken from *The British Essayists,* edited by Lionel Thomas Berguer, London, 1823, vols. 21 and 22.

complication analyzed into principles, and knowledge disentangled from opinion. It is not always possible, without a close inspection, to separate the genuine shoots of consequential reasoning, which grow out of some radical postulate, from the branches which art has engrafted on it. The accidental prescriptions of authority, when time has procured them veneration, are often confounded with the laws of nature, and those rules are supposed co-eval with reason, of which the first rise cannot be discovered.

Criticism has sometimes permitted fancy to dictate the laws by which fancy ought to be restrained, and fallacy to perplex the principles by which fallacy is to be detected; her superintendence of others has betrayed her to negligence of herself; and, like the ancient Scythians, by extending her conquests over distant regions, she has left her throne vacant to her slaves.

Among the laws of which the desire of extending authority, or ardor of promoting knowledge, has prompted the prescription, all which writers have received had not the same original right to our regard. Some are to be considered as fundamental and indispensable, others only as useful and convenient; some as dictated by reason and necessity, others as enacted by despotic antiquity; some as invincibly supported by their conformity to the order of nature and operations of the intellect; others as formed by accident, or instituted by example, and therefore always liable to dispute and alteration.

That many rules have been advanced without consulting nature or reason, we cannot but suspect, when we find it peremptorily decreed by the ancient masters, that *only three speaking personages should appear at once upon the stage*; a law which, as the variety and intricacy of modern plays has made it impossible to be observed, we now violate without scruple, and, as experience proves, without inconvenience.

The original of this precept was merely accidental. Tragedy was a monody, or solitary song in honor of Bacchus, improved afterwards into a dialogue by the addition of another speaker; but the ancients, remembering that the tragedy was at first pronounced only by one, durst not for some time venture beyond two; at last, when custom and impunity had made them daring, they extended their liberty to the admission of three, but restrained themselves by a critical edict from further exorbitance.

By what accident the number of acts was limited to five, I know not that any author has informed us; but certainly it is not determined by any necessity arising either from the nature of action or propriety of exhibition. An act is only the representation of such a part of the business of the play as proceeds in an unbroken tenor, or without any intermediate pause. Nothing is more evident than that of every real, and by consequence of every dramatic, action the intervals may be more or fewer than five; and indeed the rule is upon the English stage every day broken in effect, without any other mischief than that which arises from an absurd endeavor to observe it in appearance. Whenever the scene is shifted the act ceases, since some time is necessarily supposed to elapse while the personages of the drama change their place.

With no greater right to our obedience have the critics confined the dramatic action to a certain number of hours. Probability requires that the time of action should approach somewhat nearly to that of exhibition, and those plays will always be thought most happily conducted which crowd the greatest variety into the least space. But since it will frequently happen that some delusion must be admitted, I know not where the limits of imagination can be fixed. It is rarely observed that minds, not prepossessed by mechanical criticism, feel any offence from the extension of the intervals between the acts; nor can I conceive it absurd or impossible, that he who can multiply three hours into twelve or twenty-four, might imagine with equal ease a greater number.

I know not whether he who professeth to regard no other laws than those of nature, will not be inclined to receive tragi-comedy to his protection, whom, however generally condemned, her own laurels have hitherto shaded from the fulminations of criticism. For what is there in the mingled drama which impartial reason can condemn? The connection of important with trivial incidents, since it is not only common but perpetual in the world, may surely be allowed upon the stage, which pretends only to be the mirror of life. The impropriety of suppressing passions before we have raised them to the intended agitation, and of diverting the expectation from an event which we keep suspended only to raise it, may be speciously urged. But will not experience show this objection to be rather subtle than just? Is it not certain that the tragic and comic affections have been moved alternately with equal force; and that no plays have oftener filled the eye with tears, and the breast with palpitation, than those which are variegated with interludes of mirth?

I do not, however, think it safe to judge of works of genius merely by the event. The resistless vicissitudes of the heart, this alternate prevalence of merriment and solemnity, may sometimes be more properly ascribed to the vigor of the writer than the justness of the design: and, instead of vindicating tragi-comedy by the success of Shakespeare, we ought, perhaps, to pay new honors to that transcendent and unbounded genius that could preside over the passions in sport; who, to actuate the affections, needed not the slow gradation of common means, but could fill the heart with instantaneous jollity or sorrow, and vary our disposition as he changed his scenes. Perhaps the effect even of Shakespeare's poetry might have been yet greater, had he not counteracted himself; and we might have been more interested in the distresses of his heroes, had we not been so frequently diverted by the jokes of his buffoons.

There are other rules more fixed and obligatory. It is necessary that of every play the chief action should be single; for, since a play represents some transaction through its regular maturation to its final event, two actions equally important must evidently constitute two plays.

As the design of tragedy is to instruct by moving the passions, it must always have a hero, a personage apparently and incontestably superior to the rest, upon whom the attention may be fixed, and the anxiety suspended. For though, of two persons opposing each other with equal abilities and equal virtue, the auditor will inevitably, in time, choose his favorite; yet, as that choice must be without any cogency of conviction, the hopes or fears which it raises will be faint and languid. Of two heroes acting in confederacy against a common enemy, the virtues or dangers will give little emotion, because each claims our concern with the same right, and the heart lies at rest between equal motives.

It ought to be the first endeavor of a writer to distinguish nature from custom; or that which is established because it is right, from that which is right only because it is established; that he may neither violate essential principles by a desire of novelty, nor debar himself from the attainment of beauties within his view, by a needless fear of breaking rules which no literary dictator had authority to enact.

No. 158. *Saturday, September 21, 1751.*

Grammatici certant, et adhuc sub judice lis est.
HORACE

. . . Critics yet contend,
And of their vain disputings find no end.
FRANCIS

Criticism, though dignified from the earliest ages by the labors of men eminent for knowledge and sagacity, and, since the revival of polite literature, the favorite study of European scholars, has not yet attained the certainty and stability of science. The rules hitherto received are seldom drawn from any settled principle or self-evident postulate, or adapted to the natural and invariable constitution of things; but will be found, upon examination, the arbitrary edicts of legislators, authorized only by themselves, who out of various means by which the same end may be attained, selected such as happened to occur to their own reflection, and then, by a law which idleness and timidity were too willing to obey, prohibited new experiments of wit, restrained fancy from the indulgence of her innate inclination to hazard and adventure, and condemned all future flights of genius to pursue the path of the Mæonian [1] eagle.

This authority may be more justly opposed, as it is apparently derived from them whom they endeavor to control; for we owe few of the rules of writing to the acuteness of critics, who have generally no other merit than that, having read the works of great authors with attention, they have observed the arrangement of their matter, or the graces of their expression, and then expected honor and reverence for precepts which they never could have invented; so that practice has introduced rules, rather than rules have directed practice.

For this reason the laws of every species of writing have been settled by the ideas of him who first raised it to reputation, without inquiry whether his performances were not yet susceptible of improvement. The excellencies and faults of celebrated writers have been equally recommended to posterity; and so far has blind reverence prevailed that even the number of their books has been thought worthy of imitation.

The imagination of the first authors of lyric poetry was vehement and rapid, and their knowledge various and extensive. Living in an age when science had been little cultivated, and when the minds of their auditors, not being accustomed to accurate inspection, were easily dazzled by glaring ideas, they applied themselves to instruct, rather by short sentences and striking thoughts, than by regular argumentation; and, finding attention more successfully excited by sudden sallies and unexpected exclamations, than by the more artful and placid beauties of methodical deduction, they loosed

[1] Cf. p. 56, n. 1, and p. 261, n. 1.

their genius to its own course, passed from one sentiment to another without expressing the intermediate ideas, and roved at large over the ideal world with such lightness and agility, that their footsteps are scarcely to be traced.

From this accidental peculiarity of the ancient writers the critics deduce the rules of lyric poetry, which they have set free from all the laws by which other compositions are confined, and allow to neglect the niceties of transition, to start into remote digressions, and to wander without restraint from one scene of imagery to another.

A writer of later times has, by the vivacity of his essays, reconciled mankind to the same licentiousness in short dissertations; and he, therefore, who wants skill to form a plan, or diligence to pursue it, needs only entitle his performance an essay, to acquire the right of heaping together the collections of half his life, without order, coherence, or propriety.

In writing, as in life, faults are endured without disgust when they are associated with transcendent merit, and may be sometimes recommended to weak judgments by the lustre which they obtain from their union with excellence; but it is the business of those who presume to superintend the taste or morals of mankind to separate delusive combinations, and distinguish that which may be praised from that which can only be excused. As vices never promote happiness, though, when overpowered by more active and more numerous virtues, they cannot totally destroy it; so confusion and irregularity produce no beauty, though they cannot always obstruct the brightness of genius and learning. To proceed from one truth to another, and connect distant propositions by regular consequences, is the great prerogative of man. Independent and unconnected sentiments flashing upon the mind in quick succession, may, for a time, delight by their novelty; but they differ from systematical reasoning, as single notes from harmony, as glances of lightning from the radiance of the sun.

When rules are thus drawn, rather from precedents than reason, there is danger not only from the faults of an author, but from the errors of those who criticize his works; since they may often mislead their pupils by false representations, as the Ciceronians of the sixteenth century were betrayed into barbarisms by corrupt copies of their darling writer.

It is established, at present, that the pro-emial lines of a poem, in which the general subject is proposed, must be void of glitter and embellishment. "The first lines of *Paradise Lost*," says Addison, "are perhaps as plain, simple, and unadorned, as any of the whole poem; in which particular the author has conformed himself to the example of Homer, and the precept of Horace."

This observation seems to have been made by an implicit adoption of the common opinion, without consideration either of the precept or example. Had Horace been consulted, he would have been found to direct only what should be comprised in the proposition, not how it should be expressed; and to have commended Homer in opposition to a meaner poet, not for the gradual elevation of his diction, but the judicious expansion of his plan; for displaying unpromised events, not for producing unexpected elegancies:

> . . . *Speciosa dehinc miracula promit,*
> *Antiphaten Scyllamque, & cum Cyclope Charybdim.*

> But from a cloud of smoke he breaks to light,
> And pours his specious miracles to sight;
> Antiphates his hideous feast devours,
> Charybdis barks, and Polyphemus roars.

FRANCIS

If the exordial verses of Homer be compared with the rest of the poem, they will not appear remarkable for plainness or simplicity, but rather eminently adorned and illuminated:

[Here Johnson quotes the passage in Greek, followed by Pope's translation.]

> The man for wisdom's various arts renown'd,
> Long exercis'd in woes, O muse! resound;
> Who, when his arms had wrought the destin'd fall
> Of sacred Troy, and raz'd her heav'n-built wall,
> Wand'ring from clime to clime observant stray'd,
> Their manners noted, and their states survey'd:
> On stormy seas unnumber'd toils he bore,
> Safe with his friends to gain his natal shore:
> Vain toils! their impious folly dar'd to prey
> On herds devoted to the god of day:
> The god vindictive doom'd them never more
> (Ah! men unblest) to touch that natal shore.
> O snatch some portion of these acts from fate,
> Celestial muse! and to our world relate.

POPE

The first verses of the *Iliad* are in like manner particularly splendid, and the proposition of the *Æneid* closes with dignity and magnificence not often to be found even in the poetry of Virgil.

The intent of the introduction is to raise expectation, and suspend it: something therefore must be discovered, and something concealed; and the poet, while the fertility of his invention is yet unknown, may properly recommend himself by the grace of his language.

He that reveals too much, or promises too little; he that never irritates the intellectual appetite, or that immediately satiates it, equally defeats his own purpose. It is necessary to the pleasure of the reader that the events should not be anticipated; and how then can his attention be invited, but by grandeur of expression?

No. 168. *Saturday, October 26, 1751.*

> . . . *Decipit*
> *Frons prima multos, rara mens intelligit*
> *Quod interiore condidit cura angulo.*
>   PHÆDRUS.
> The tinsel glitter, and the specious mien,
> Delude the most; few pry behind the scene.

It has been observed by Boileau, that "a mean or common thought expressed in pompous diction, generally pleases more than a new or noble sentiment delivered in low and vulgar language; because the number is greater of those whom custom has enabled to judge of words than whom study has qualified to examine things."

This solution might satisfy, if such only were offended with meanness of expression as are unable to distinguish propriety of thought, and to separate propositions or images from the vehicles by which they are conveyed to the understanding. But this kind of disgust is by no means confined to the ignorant or superficial; it operates uniformly and universally upon readers of all classes; every man, however profound or abstracted, perceives himself irresistibly alienated by low terms; they who profess the most zealous adherence to truth are forced to admit that she owes part of her charms to her ornaments; and loses much of her power over the soul, when she appears disgraced by a dress uncouth or ill-adjusted.

We are all offended by low terms, but are not disgusted alike by the same compositions, because we do not all agree to censure the same terms as low. No word is naturally or intrinsically meaner than another; our opinion therefore of words, as of other things arbitrarily and capriciously established, depends wholly upon accident and custom. The cottager thinks those apartments splendid and spacious, which an inhabitant of palaces will despise for their inelegance; and to him who has passed most of his hours with the delicate and polite, many expressions will seem sordid, which another, equally acute, may hear without offence; but a mean term never fails to displease him to whom it appears mean, as poverty is certainly and invariably despised, though he who is poor in the eyes of some, may by others be envied for his wealth.

Words become low by the occasions to which they are applied, or the general character of them who use them; and the disgust which they produce arises from the revival of those images with which they are commonly united. Thus if, in the most solemn discourse, a phrase happens to occur which has been successfully employed in some ludicrous narrative, the gravest auditor finds it difficult to refrain from laughter, when they who are not prepossessed by the same accidental association are utterly unable to guess the reason of his merriment. Words which convey ideas of dignity in one age, are banished from elegant writing or conversation in another, because they are in time debased by vulgar mouths, and can be no longer heard without the involuntary recollection of unpleasing images.

When Macbeth is confirming himself in the horrid purpose of stabbing his king, he breaks out amidst his emotions into a wish natural to a murderer:

> . . . Come, thick night!
> And pall thee in the dunnest smoke of hell,
> That my keen knife see not the wound it makes;
> Nor heav'n peep through the blanket of the dark,
> To cry, Hold, hold!

In this passage is exerted all the force of poetry; that force which calls new powers into being, which embodies sentiment, and animates matter; yet, perhaps, scarce any man now peruses it without some disturbance of his attention from the counteraction of the words to the ideas. What can be more dreadful than to implore the presence of night, invested, not in common obscurity, but in the smoke of hell? Yet the efficacy of this invocation is destroyed by the insertion of an epithet now seldom heard but in the stable, and *dun* night may come or go without any other notice than contempt.

If we start into raptures when some hero of the *Iliad* tells us that δόρυ μαίνεται, his lance rages with eagerness to destroy; if we are alarmed at the terror of the soldiers commanded by Cæsar to hew down the sacred grove, who dreaded, says Lucan, lest the axe aimed at the oak should fly back upon the striker:

> . . . *Si robora sacra ferirent,*
> *In sua credebant redituras membra secures,*
>
> None dares with impious steel the grove to rend,
> Lest on himself the destin'd stroke descend;

we cannot surely but sympathize with the horrors of a wretch about to murder his master, his friend, his benefactor, who suspects that the weapon will refuse its office, and start back from the breast which he is preparing to violate. Yet this sentiment is weakened by the name of an instrument used by butchers and cooks in the meanest employments; we do not immediately conceive that any crime of importance is to be committed with a *knife;* or who does not, at last, from the long habit of connecting a knife with sordid offices, feel aversion rather than terror?

Macbeth proceeds to wish, in the madness of guilt, that the inspection of heaven may be intercepted, and that he may, in the involutions of infernal darkness, escape the eye of Providence. This is the utmost extravagance of determined wickedness; yet this is so debased by two unfortunate words, that while I endeavor to impress on my reader the energy of the sentiment, I can scarce check my risibility, when the expression forces itself upon my mind; for who, without some relaxation of his gravity, can hear of the avengers of guilt *peeping through a blanket?* [1]

These imperfections of diction are less obvious to the reader, as he is less acquainted with common usages; they are therefore wholly imperceptible to a foreigner, who learns our language from books, and will strike a solitary academic less forcibly than a modish lady.

Among the numerous requisites that most concur to complete an author, few are of more importance than an early entrance into the living world. The seeds of knowledge may be planted in solitude, but must be cultivated in public. Argumentation may be taught in colleges, and theories formed in retirement; but the artifice of embellishment, and the powers of attraction, can be gained only by a general converse.

---

[1] Dr. Johnson forgets that to the Elizabethan the word might well suggest the curtain of a theatre.

An acquaintance with prevailing customs and fashionable elegance is necessary likewise for other purposes. The injury that grand imagery suffers from unsuitable language, personal merit may fear from rudeness and indelicacy. When the success of Æneas depended on the favor of the queen upon whose coasts he was driven, his celestial protectress thought him not sufficiently secured against rejection by his piety or bravery, but decorated him for the interview with preternatural beauty. Whoever desires, for his writings or himself, what none can reasonably contemn, the favor of mankind, must add grace to strength, and make his thoughts agreeable as well as useful. Many complain of neglect who never tried to attract regard. It cannot be expected that the patrons of science or virtue should be solicitous to discover excellencies, which they who possess them shade and disguise. Few have abilities so much needed by the rest of the world as to be caressed on their own terms; and he that will not condescend to recommend himself by external embellishments must submit to the fate of just sentiment meanly expressed, and be ridiculed and forgotten before he is understood.

Young

Edward YOUNG (1683-1765), son of the rector of Upham, Hampshire, was educated at Winchester and Oxford. He began to write in 1713, and had two plays produced in London—*Busiris* in 1719 and *Revenge* in 1721, both of which were satirized genially by Henry Fielding in his *Tom Thumb* (1730). He took orders, and in 1729 was appointed one of the Royal Chaplains, being given the living of Welwyn (Herts) in 1730. The next year he married the widowed daughter of the Earl of Lichfield, to whom, as to her daughter by her first marriage, he was warmly attached. After their deaths, he wrote a series of poems called *The Complaint, or Night Thoughts on Life, Death, and Immortality* (1742-45), which won a quick and long-enduring popularity; it is pious, gloomy, and lofty, if strained and artificial in places. In 1759, after an extended correspondence upon the subject with Richardson, the novelist, Young published anonymously, in the *Gentleman's Magazine*, his *Conjectures on Original Composition*. In 1761 he was made Clerk of the Closet to the Dowager Princess of Wales. Four years later he died at Welwyn.

In his *Conjectures*, Young, like the poet Gray and the brothers Warton, is far in advance of his time, pointing, decades before the change took place, to the Romantic Movement in English poetry. For him, the rigid rules of the neo-classicists must give way to original genius. He is like Longinus in preferring a noble work with imperfections to a correct work that has no flair. Imitation of the classics, restraint, hard work, constant revision, and the other precepts of the neo-classicists have for him no validity. He takes the view, romantic yet sensible, that progress in literature can be achieved only by breaking away from superimposed laws and by trying for originality, in the best sense of the word.

Just as many neo-classic critics show romantic tendencies, so Young is classic, like Milton, standing against rhyme—in his *Conjectures,* but not in practice.

From CONJECTURES ON ORIGINAL COMPOSITION

IN A LETTER TO THE AUTHOR OF *Sir Charles Grandison* [1]

(1759)

DEAR SIR—We confess the follies of youth without a blush; not so, those of age. However, keep me a little in countenance, by considering that age wants amusements more, though it can justify them less, than the preceding periods of life. How you may relish the pastime here sent you, I know not. It is miscellaneous in its nature, somewhat licentious in its conduct; and, perhaps, not over important in its end. However, I have endeavored to make some amends, by digressing into subjects more important, and more suitable to my season of life. A serious thought standing single among many of a lighter nature will sometimes strike the careless wanderer after amusement only with useful awe: as monumental marbles scattered in a wide pleasure-garden (and such there are) will call to recollection those who would never have sought it in a churchyard-walk of mournful yews.

To one such monument I may conduct you, in which is a hidden lustre, like the sepulchral lamps of old; but not like them will this be extinguished, but shine the brighter for being produced, after so long concealment, into open day.

You remember that your worthy patron, and our common friend, put some questions on the serious drama, at the same time when he desired our sentiments on original, and on moral, composition. Though I despair of breaking through the frozen obstructions of age, and care's incumbent cloud, into that flow of thought, and brightness of expression, which subjects so polite require; yet will I hazard some conjectures on them.

[1] The text, modernized by the editors, is based on the Dublin edition of 1759, kindly lent by the Yale University Library.

I begin with original composition; but, first, a few thoughts on composition in general. Some are of opinion, that its growth, at present, is too luxuriant; and that the press is overcharged. Overcharged, I think, it could never be, if none were admitted, but such as brought their Imprimatur from sound understanding, and the public good. Wit, indeed, however brilliant, should not be permitted to gaze self-enamored on its useless charms, in that fountain of fame (if so I may call the press), if beauty is all that it has to boast; but, like the first Brutus, it should sacrifice its most darling offspring to the sacred interests of virtue, and real service of mankind.

This restriction allowed, the more composition the better. To men of letters, and leisure, it is not only a noble amusement, but a sweet refuge; it improves their parts, and promotes their peace: It opens a back-door out of the bustle of this busy, and idle world, into a delicious garden of moral and intellectual fruits and flowers; the key of which is denied to the rest of mankind. When stung with idle anxieties, or teased with fruitless impertinence, or yawning over insipid diversions, then we perceive the blessing of a lettered recess. With what a gust do we retire to our disinterested and immortal friends in our closet, and find our minds, when applied to some favorite theme, as naturally, and as easily quieted, and refreshed, as a peevish child (and peevish children are we all till we fall asleep) when laid to the breast? Our happiness no longer lives on charity; nor bids fair for a fall, by leaning on that most precarious, and thorny pillow, another's pleasure, for our repose. How independent of the world is he, who can daily find new acquaintance, that at once entertain, and improve him, in the little world, the minute but fruitful creation, of his own mind?

These advantages composition affords us, whether we write ourselves, or in more humble amusement peruse the works of others. While we bustle through the thronged walks of public life, it gives us a respite, at least, from care; a pleasing pause of refreshing recollection. If the country is our choice, or fate, there it rescues us from sloth and sensuality, which, like obscene vermin, are apt gradually to creep unperceived into the delightful bowers of our retirement, and to poison all its sweets. Conscious guilt robs the rose of its scent, and lily of its lustre; and makes an Eden a deflowered, and dismal scene.

Moreover, if we consider life's endless evils, what can be more prudent, than to provide for consolation under them? A consolation under them the wisest of men have found in the pleasures of the pen. Witness, among many more, Thucydides, Xenophon, Tully, Ovid, Seneca, Pliny the younger, who says *In uxoris infirmitate, & amicorum periculo, aut morte turbatus, ad studia, unicum doloris levamentum, confugio.*[1] And why not add to these their modern equals, Raleigh, Milton, Clarendon, under the same shield, unwounded by misfortune, and nobly smiling in distress?

Composition was a cordial to these under the frowns of fortune; but evils there are, which her smiles cannot prevent, or cure. Among these are the languors of old age. If those are held honorable, who in a hand benumbed by time have grasped the just sword in defence of their country; shall they be less esteemed, whose unsteady pen vibrates to the last in the cause of religion, of virtue, of learning? Both these are happy in this, that by fixing their attention on objects most important, they escape numberless little anxieties, and that *tædium vitæ* [2] which hangs often so heavy on its evening hours. May not this insinuate some apology for my spilling ink, and spoiling paper, so late in life?

But there are, who write with vigor, and success, to the world's delight, and their own renown. These are the glorious fruits where genius prevails. The mind of a man of genius is a fertile and pleasant field, pleasant as Elysium, and fertile as Tempe; it enjoys a perpetual spring. Of that spring, originals are the fairest flowers: imitations are of quicker growth, but fainter bloom. Imitations are of two kinds; one of nature, one of authors: The first we call originals, and confine the term "Imitation" to the second. I shall not enter into the curious enquiry of what is, or is not, strictly speaking, original, content with what all must allow, that some compositions are more so than others; and the more they are so, I say, the better. Originals are, and ought to be, great favorites, for they are great benefactors; they extend the republic of letters, and add a new province to its dominion: imitators only give us a sort of duplicates of what we had, possibly much better, before; increasing the mere drug of books, while all that makes them valuable, *knowledge* and *genius,* are at a stand. The pen of an original writer, like Armida's [3] wand, out of a barren waste calls a blooming spring: Out of that blooming spring an imitator is a transplanter of laurels, which sometimes die on removal, always languish in a foreign soil.

[1] If my wife is ill, my friends in danger, or I am troubled with the thought of death, I fly to my studies, the sole lightener of grief.

[2] Weariness of life.

[3] A beautiful sorceress in Tasso's *Jerusalem Delivered.*

But suppose an imitator to be most excellent (and such there are), yet still he but nobly builds on another's foundation; his debt is, at least, equal to his glory; which therefore, on the balance, cannot be very great. On the contrary, an original, though but indifferent (its originality being set aside), yet has something to boast; it is something to say with him in Horace,

Meo sum pauper in ære; [1]

and to share ambition with no less than Cæsar, who declared he had rather be the first in a village, than the second at Rome.

Still farther: An imitator shares his crown, if he has one, with the chosen object of his imitation; an original enjoys an undivided applause. An original may be said to be of a vegetable nature; it rises spontaneously from the vital root of genius; it *grows*, it is not *made*: imitations are often a sort of manufacture wrought up by those mechanics, art, and labor, out of pre-existent materials not their own.

Again: We read imitation with somewhat of his languor, who listens to a twice-told tale: Our spirits rouse at an original; that is a perfect stranger, and all throng to learn what news from a foreign land: And though it comes, like an Indian prince, adorned with feathers only, having little of weight; yet of our attention it will rob the more solid, if not equally new: thus every telescope is lifted at a new-discovered star; it makes a hundred astronomers in a moment, and denies equal notice to the sun. But if an original, by being as excellent, as new, adds admiration to surprise, then are we at the writer's mercy; on the strong wing of his imagination, we are snatched from Britain to Italy, from climate to climate, from pleasure to pleasure; we have no home, no thought, of our own; till the magician drops his pen: And then falling down into ourselves, we awake to flat realities, lamenting the change, like the beggar who dreamed himself a prince.

It is with thoughts, as it is with words; and with both, as with men; they may grow old, and die. Words tarnished, by passing through the mouths of the vulgar, are laid aside as inelegant, and obsolete. So thoughts, when become too common, should lose their currency; and we should send new metal to the mint, that is, new meaning to the press. The division of tongues at Babel did not more effectually debar men from "making themselves a name" (as the Scripture [2] speaks,) than the too great concurrence, or union of

---

[1] I am poor in my own money, (with the implication that I owe no one).
[2] Cf. Gen. xi: 4.

tongues will do for ever. We may as well grow good by another's virtue, or fat by another's food, as famous by another's thought. The world will pay its debt of praise but once; and instead of applauding, explode a second demand, as a cheat.

If it is said, that most of the Latin classics, and all the Greek, except, perhaps, Homer, Pindar, and Anacreon, are in the number of imitators, yet receive our highest applause; our answer is, That they, though not real, are accidental originals; the works they imitated, few excepted, are lost: They, on their father's decease, enter, as lawful heirs, on their estates in fame: The fathers of our copyists are still in possession; and secured in it, in spite of Goths, and flames, by the perpetuating power of the press. Very late must a modern imitator's fame arrive, if it waits for their decease.

An original enters early upon reputation: Fame, fond of new glories, sounds her trumpet in triumph at its birth; and yet how few are awakened by it into the noble ambition of like attempts? Ambition is sometimes no vice in life; it is always a virtue in composition. High in the towering Alps is the fountain of the Po; high in fame, and in antiquity, is the fountain of an imitator's undertaking; but the river, and the imitation, humbly creep along the vale. So few are our originals, that, if all other books were to be burned, the lettered world would resemble some metropolis in flames, where a few incombustible buildings, a fortress, temple, or tower, lift their heads, in melancholy grandeur, amid the mighty ruin. Compared with this conflagration, old Omar lighted up but a small bonfire, when he heated the baths of the barbarians, for eight months together, with the famed Alexandrian library's inestimable spoils, that no profane book might obstruct the triumphant progress of his holy Alcoran round the globe.

But why are originals so few? not because the writer's harvest is over, the great reapers of antiquity having left nothing to be gleaned after them; nor because the human mind's teeming time is past, or because it is incapable of putting forth unprecedented births; but because illustrious examples engross, prejudice, and intimidate. They engross our attention, and so prevent a due inspection of ourselves; they prejudice our judgment in favor of their abilities, and so lessen the sense of our own; and they intimidate us with the splendor of their renown, and thus under diffidence bury our strength. Nature's impossibilities, and those of diffidence, lie wide asunder.

Let it not be suspected, that I would weakly insinuate anything in favor of the moderns, as compared with ancient authors; no, I am lamenting their great inferiority. But I think it is no necessary inferiority; that it is not from divine destination, but from some cause far beneath the moon: I think that human souls, through all periods, are equal; that due care, and exertion, would set us nearer our immortal predecessors than we are at present; and he who questions and confutes this, will show abilities not a little tending toward a proof of that equality, which he denies.

After all, the first ancients had no merit in being originals: They could not be imitators. Modern writers have a choice to make; and therefore have a merit in their power. They may soar in the regions of liberty, or move in the soft fetters of easy imitation; and imitation has as many plausible reasons to urge, as pleasure had to offer to Hercules. Hercules made the choice of an hero, and so became immortal.

Yet let not assertors of classic excellence imagine that I deny the tribute it so well deserves. He that admires not ancient authors betrays a secret he could conceal, and tells the world that he does not understand them. Let us be as far from neglecting, as from copying, their admirable compositions: Sacred be their rights, and inviolable their fame. Let our understanding feed on theirs; they afford the noblest nourishment: But let them nourish, not annihilate, our own. When we read, let our imagination kindle at their charms; when we write, let our judgment shut them out of our thoughts; treat even Homer himself as his royal admirer was treated by the cynic; bid him stand aside, nor shade our composition from the beams of our own genius; for nothing original can rise, nothing immortal, can ripen, in any other sun.

Must we then, you say, not imitate ancient authors? Imitate them, by all means; but imitate aright. He that imitates the divine *Iliad* does not imitate Homer; but he who takes the same method, which Homer took, for arriving at a capacity of accomplishing a work so great. Tread in his steps to the sole fountain of immortality; drink where he drank, at the true Helicon, that is, at the breast of nature: Imitate; but imitate not the composition, but the man. For may not this paradox pass into a maxim? *viz.* "The less we copy the renowned ancients, we shall resemble them the more."

But possibly you may reply, that you must either imitate Homer, or depart from nature. Not so: for suppose you was to change place, in time, with Homer; then, if you write naturally, you might as well charge Homer with an imitation of you. Can you be said to imitate Homer for writing so, as you would have written, if Homer had never been? As far as a regard to nature, and sound sense, will permit a departure from your great predecessors; so far, ambitiously, depart from them; the farther from them in similitude, the nearer are you to them in excellence; you rise by it into an original; become a noble collateral, not an humble descendant from them. Let us build our compositions with the spirit, and in the taste, of the ancients; but not with their materials: Thus will they resemble the structures of Pericles at Athens, which Plutarch commends for having had an air of antiquity as soon as they were built. All eminence, and distinction, lies out of the beaten road; excursion, and deviation, are necessary to find it; and the more remote your path from the highway, the more reputable; if, like poor Gulliver (of whom anon), you fall not into a ditch, in your way to glory.

What glory to come near, what glory to reach, what glory (presumptuous thought!) to surpass, our predecessors? And is that then in nature absolutely impossible? Or is it not, rather, contrary to nature to fail in it? Nature herself sets the ladder, all wanting is our ambition to climb. For by the bounty of nature we are as strong as our predecessors; and by the favor of time (which is but another round in nature's scale) we stand on higher ground. As to the first, were they more than men? Or are we less? Are not our minds cast in the same mould with those before the flood? The flood affected matter; mind escaped. As to the second; though we are moderns, the world is an ancient; more ancient far, than when they filled it with their fame whom we most admire. Have we not their beauties, as stars, to guide; their defects, as rocks, to be shunned; the judgment of ages on both, as a chart to conduct, and a sure helm to steer us in our passage to greater perfection than theirs? And shall we be stopped in our rival pretensions to fame by this just reproof?

Stat contra, dicitque tibi tua pagina, fur es.[1]

MARTIAL

It is by a sort of noble contagion, from a general familiarity with their writings, and not by any particular sordid theft, that we can be the better for those who went before us. Hope we, from plagiarism, any dominion in literature; as that of Rome arose from a nest of thieves?

Rome was a powerful ally to many states; ancient authors are our powerful allies; but we must take heed, that they do not succor, till they enslave, after the manner of Rome. Too formidable an idea of their superiority, like a spectre, would fright us out of a proper

---

[1] Your written page is against you and declares you are a thief.

use of our wits; and dwarf our understanding, by making a giant of theirs. Too great awe for them lays genius under restraint, and denies it that free scope, that full elbow-room, which is requisite for striking its most masterly strokes. Genius is a master-workman, learning is but an instrument; and an instrument, though most valuable, yet not always indispensable. Heaven will not admit of a partner in the accomplishment of some favorite spirits; but rejecting all human means, assumes the whole glory to itself. Have not some, though not famed for erudition, so written, as almost to persuade us that they shone brighter, and soared higher, for escaping the boasted aid of that proud ally?

Nor is it strange; for what, for the most part, mean we by genius, but the power of accomplishing great things without the means generally reputed necessary to that end? A genius differs from a good understanding, as a magician from a good architect; that raises his structure by means invisible; this by the skilful use of common tools. Hence genius has ever been supposed to partake of something divine. *Nemo unquam vir magnus fuit, sine aliquo afflatu divino.*[1]

Learning, destitute of this superior aid, is fond, and proud, of what has cost it much pains; is a great lover of rules, and boaster of famed examples: As beauties less perfect, who owe half their charms to cautious art, [learning] inveighs against natural unstudied graces, and small harmless indecorums, and sets rigid bounds to that liberty, to which genius often owes its supreme glory; but the no-genius its frequent ruin. For unprescribed beauties, and unexampled excellence, which are characteristics of genius, lie without the pale of learning's authorities, and laws; which pale, genius must leap to come at them: But by that leap, if genius is wanting, we break our necks; we lose that little credit, which possibly we might have enjoyed before. For rules, like crutches, are a needful aid to the lame, though an impediment to the strong. A Homer casts them away; and, like his Achilles,

Jura negat sibi nata, nihil non arrogat,[2]

by native force of mind. There is something in poetry beyond prose-reason; there are mysteries in it not to be explained, but admired; which render mere prose-men infidels to their divinity. And here pardon a second paradox; *viz.* "Genius often then deserves most to be

---

[1] No man was ever great without some divine inspiration.

[2] He denies that the laws were formed for him; there is nothing he does not claim for himself.

praised, when it is most sure to be condemned; that is, when its excellence, from mounting high, to weak eyes is quite out of sight."

If I might speak farther of learning, and genius, I would compare genius to virtue, and learning to riches. As riches are most wanted where there is least virtue; so learning where there is least genius. As virtue without much riches can give happiness, so genius without much learning can give renown. As it is said in Terence, *Pecuniam [in loco] negligere interdum maximum est lucrum;* [1] so to neglect of learning, genius sometimes owes its greater glory. Genius, therefore, leaves but the second place, among men of letters, to the learned. It is their merit, and ambition, to fling light on the works of genius, and point out its charms. We most justly reverence their informing radius for that favor; but we must much more admire the radiant stars pointed out by them.

A star of the first magnitude among the moderns was Shakespeare; among the ancients, Pindar; who (as Vossius tells us) boasted of his no-learning, calling himself the eagle, for his flight above it. And such genii as these may, indeed, have much reliance on their own native powers. For genius may be compared to the body's natural strength; learning to the super-induced accoutrements of arms: if the first is equal to the proposed exploit, the latter rather encumbers, than assists; rather retards, than promotes, the victory. *Sacer nobis inest Deus,* [2] says Seneca. With regard to the moral world, conscience, with regard to the intellectual, genius, is that god within. Genius can set us right in composition, without the rules of the learned; as conscience sets us right in life, without the laws of the land: This, singly, can make us good, as men: that, singly, as writers, can, sometimes, make us great.

I say, sometimes, because there is a genius, which stands in need of learning to make it shine. Of genius there are two species, an earlier, and a later; or call them infantine and adult. An adult genius comes out of nature's hand, as Pallas out of Jove's head, at full growth, and mature: Shakespeare's genius was of this kind: On the contrary, Swift stumbled at the threshold, and set out for distinction on feeble knees: His was an infantine genius; a genius, which, like other infants, must be nursed, and educated, or it will come to nought: Learning is its nurse, and tutor; but this nurse may overlay with an indigested load, which smothers common sense;

[1] "To despise money on occasion is now and then a very great gain." *Adelphi,* II, ii, 8.
[2] Sacred within us is God.

and this tutor may mislead, with pedantic prejudice, which vitiates the best understanding: As too great admirers of the Fathers of the Church have sometimes set up their authority against the true sense of Scripture; so too great admirers of the classical fathers have sometimes set up their authority, or example, against reason.

Neve minor, neu sit quinto productior actu fabula.[1]

So says Horace, so says ancient example. But reason has not subscribed. I know but one book that can justify our implicit acquiescence in it.

But superstition set aside, the classics are for ever our rightful and revered masters in composition; and our understandings bow before them: But when? When a master is wanted; which, sometimes, as I have shown, is not the case. Some are pupils of nature only, nor go farther to school: From such we reap often a double advantage; they not only rival the reputation of the great ancient authors, but also reduce the number of mean ones among the moderns. For when they enter on subjects which have been in former hands, such is their superiority, that, like a tenth wave, they overwhelm, and bury in oblivion all that went before: And thus not only enrich and adorn, but remove a load, and lessen the labor, of the lettered world.

But, you say, since originals can arise from genius only, and since genius is so very rare, it is scarce worth while to labor a point so much, from which we can reasonably expect so little. To show that genius is not so very rare as you imagine, I shall point out strong instances of it, in a far distant quarter from that mentioned above. The minds of the schoolmen were almost as much cloistered as their bodies; they had but little learning, and few books; yet may the most learned be struck with some astonishment at their so singular natural sagacity, and most exquisite edge of thought. Who would expect to find Pindar and Scotus, Shakespeare and Aquinas, of the same party? Both equally show an original, unindebted, energy; the *vigor igneus,* and *cœlestis origo,*[2] burns in both; and leaves us in doubt if genius is more evident in the sublime flights and beauteous flowers of poetry, or in the profound penetrations, and marvellously keen and minute distinctions, called the thorns of the schools. There might have been more able consuls called from the plough, than ever arrived at that honor: Many a genius, probably,

---

[1] "Five acts are the just measure of a play." (Roscommon's translation.)
[2] Fiery vigor and celestial origin.

there has been, which could neither write, nor read. So that genius, that supreme lustre of literature, is less rare than you conceive.

By the praise of genius we detract not from learning; we detract not from the value of gold, by saying that diamond has greater still. He who disregards learning, shows that he wants its aid; and he that overvalues it, shows that its aid has done him harm. Overvalued indeed it cannot be, if genius, as to composition, is valued more. Learning we thank, genius we revere; that gives us pleasure, this gives us rapture; that informs, this inspires; and is itself inspired; for genius is from Heaven, learning from man: this sets us above the low, and illiterate; that, above the learned, and polite. Learning is borrowed knowledge; genius is knowledge innate, and quite our own. Therefore, as Bacon observes, it may take a nobler name, and be called Wisdom; in which sense of wisdom, some are born wise.

But here a caution is necessary against the most fatal of errors in those automaths, those self-taught philosophers of our age, who set up genius, and often, mere fancied genius, not only above human learning, but divine truth. I have called genius wisdom; but let it be remembered, that in the most renowned ages of the most refined heathen wisdom (and theirs is not Christian) "the world by wisdom knew not God, and it pleased God by the foolishness of preaching to save those that believed." [1] In the fairyland of fancy, genius may wander wild; there it has a creative power, and may reign arbitrarily over its own empire of chimæras. The wide field of nature also lies open before it, where it may range unconfined, make what discoveries it can, and sport with its infinite objects uncontrolled, as far as visible nature extends, painting them as wantonly as it will: But what painter of the most unbounded and exalted genius can give us the true portrait of a seraph? He can give us only what by his own or others' eyes, has been seen; though that indeed infinitely compounded, raised, burlesqued, dishonored, or adorned: In like manner, who can give us divine truth unrevealed? Much less should any presume to set aside divine truth when revealed, as incongruous to their own sagacities.—Is this too serious for my subject? I shall be more so before I close.

Having put in a caveat against the most fatal of errors, from the too great indulgence of genius, return we now to that too great suppression of it, which is detrimental to composition; and endeavor to rescue the writer, as well as the man. I have said, that some are

[1] 1 Corinthians, i: 21.

born wise; but they, like those that are born rich, by neglecting the cultivation and produce of their own possessions, and by running in debt, may be beggared at last; and lose their reputations, as younger brothers estates, not by being born with less abilities than the rich heir, but at too late an hour.

Many a great man has been lost to himself, and the public, purely because great ones were born before him. Hermias, in his collections on Homer's blindness, says, that Homer requesting the gods to grant him a sight of Achilles, that hero rose, but in armor so bright, that it struck Homer blind with the blaze. Let not the blaze of even Homer's muse darken us to the discernment of our own powers; which may possibly set us above the rank of imitators; who, though most excellent, and even immortal (as some of them are) yet are still but *Dii minorum gentium*,[1] nor can expect the largest share of incense, the greatest profusion of praise, on their secondary altars.

But farther still: a spirit of imitation hath many ill effects; I shall confine myself to three. First, it deprives the liberal and politer arts of an advantage which the mechanic enjoy: In these, men are ever endeavoring to go beyond their predecessors; in the former, to follow them. And since copies surpass not their originals, as streams rise not higher than their spring, rarely so high; hence, while arts mechanic are in perpetual progress, and increase, the liberal are in retrogradation, and decay. These resemble pyramids, are broad at bottom, but lessen exceedingly as they rise; those resemble rivers which, from a small fountain-head, are spreading ever wider and wider, as they run. Hence it is evident, that different portions of understanding are not (as some imagine) allotted to different periods of time; for we see, in the same period, understanding rising in one set of artists, and declining in another. Therefore nature stands absolved, and our inferiority in composition must be charged on ourselves.

Nay, so far are we from complying with a necessity, which nature lays us under, that, secondly, by a spirit of imitation we counteract nature, and thwart her design. She brings us into the world all originals: no two faces, no two minds, are just alike; but all bear nature's evident mark of separation on them. Born originals, how comes it to pass that we die copies? That meddling ape imitation, as soon as we come to years of indiscretion (so let me speak), snatches the pen, and blots out nature's mark of separation, cancels her kind intention, destroys all mental individuality; the lettered world no longer consists of singulars, it is a medley, a mass; and a hundred books, at

[1] Gods of inferior peoples.

bottom, are but one. Why are monkeys such masters of mimicry? Why receive they such a talent at imitation? Is it not as the Spartan slaves received a licence for ebriety; that their betters might be ashamed of it?

The third fault to be found with a spirit of imitation is, that with great incongruity it makes us poor, and proud: makes us think little, and write much; gives us huge folios, which are little better than more reputable cushions to promote our repose. Have not some sevenfold volumes put us in mind of Ovid's sevenfold channels of the Nile at the conflagration?

> Ostia septem
> Pulverulenta vacant septem sine flumine valles.[1]

Such leaden labors are like Lycurgus's iron money, which was so much less in value than in bulk, that it required barns for strong-boxes, and a yoke of oxen to draw five hundred pounds.

But notwithstanding these disadvantages of imitation, imitation must be the lot (and often an honorable lot it is) of most writers. If there is a famine of invention in the land, like Joseph's brethren, we must travel far for food; we must visit the remote, and rich, ancients; but an inventive genius may safely stay at home; that, like the widow's cruse,[2] is divinely replenished from within; and affords us a miraculous delight. Whether our own genius be such, or not, we diligently should inquire; that we may not go a-begging with gold in our purse. For there is a mine in man, which must be deeply dug ere we can conjecture its contents. Another often sees that in us, which we see not ourselves; and may there not be that in us which is unseen by both? That there may, chance often discovers, either by a luckily chosen theme, or a mighty premium, or an absolute necessity of exertion, or a noble stroke of emulation from another's glory; as that on Thucydides from hearing Herodotus repeat part of his history at the Olympic games: Had there been no Herodotus, there might have been no Thucydides, and the world's admiration might have begun at Livy for excellence in that province of the pen. Demosthenes had the same stimulation on hearing Callistratus; or Tully might have been the first of consummate renown at the bar.

Quite clear of the dispute concerning ancient and modern learning, we speak not of performance, but powers. The modern powers

---

[1] Its seven outlets are empty and dusty, seven valleys without water.
[2] See 1 Kings, xvii: 16.

are equal to those before them; modern performance in general is deplorably short. How great are the names just mentioned? Yet who will dare affirm, that as great may not rise up in some future, or even in the present age? Reasons there are why talents may not appear, none why they may not exist, as much in one period as another. An evocation of vegetable fruits depends on rain, air, and sun; an evocation of the fruits of genius no less depends on externals. What a marvellous crop bore it in Greece, and Rome? And what a marvellous sunshine did it there enjoy? What encouragement from the nature of their governments, and the spirit of their people? Virgil and Horace owed their divine talents to Heaven; their immortal works, to men; thank Mæcenas and Augustus for them. Had it not been for these, the genius of those poets had lain buried in their ashes. Athens expended on her theatre, painting, sculpture, and architecture a tax levied for the support of a war. Cæsar dropped his papers when Tully spoke; and Philip trembled at the voice of Demosthenes: And has there shone but one Tully, one Demosthenes, in so long a course of years? The powerful eloquence of them both in one stream, should never bear me down into the melancholy persuasion that several have not been born, though they have not emerged. The sun as much exists in a cloudy day, as in a clear; it is outward, accidental circumstance that with regard to genius either in nation, or age,

Collectas fugat nubes, solemque reducit.[1]

VIRGIL

As great, perhaps, greater than those mentioned (presumptuous as it may sound) may, possibly, arise; for who hath fathomed the mind of man? Its bounds are as unknown, as those of the creation; since the birth of which, perhaps, not one has so far exerted, as not to leave his possibilities beyond his attainments, his powers beyond his exploits. Forming our judgments altogether by what has been done, without knowing, or at all inquiring, what possibly might have been done, we naturally enough fall into too mean an opinion of the human mind. If a sketch of the divine *Iliad* before Homer wrote, had been given to mankind, by some superior being, or otherwise, its execution would, probably, have appeared beyond the power of man. Now, to surpass it, we think impossible. As the first of these opinions would evidently have been a mistake, why may

---

[1] Disperses the gathered clouds, and leads back the sun.

not the second be so too? Both are founded on the same bottom; on our ignorance of the possible dimensions of the mind of man.

Nor are we only ignorant of the dimensions of the human mind in general, but even of our own. That a man may be scarce less ignorant of his own powers than an oyster of its pearl, or a rock of its diamond; that he may possess dormant, unsuspected abilities, till awakened by loud calls, or stung up by striking emergencies, is evident from the sudden eruption of some men, out of perfect obscurity, into public admiration, on the strong impulse of some animating occasion; not more to the world's great surprise, than their own. Few authors of distinction but have experienced something of this nature, at the first beamings of their yet unsuspected genius on their hitherto dark composition: The writer starts at it, as at a lucid meteor in the night; is much surprised; can scarce believe it true. During his happy confusion, it may be said to him, as to Eve at the lake,

> What there thou seest, fair creature, is thyself.
>
> MILTON

Genius, in this view, is like a dear friend in our company under disguise; who, while we are lamenting his absence, drops his mask, striking us, at once, with equal surprise and joy. This sensation, which I speak of in a writer, might favor, and so promote, the fable of poetic inspiration: A poet of a strong imagination, and stronger vanity, on feeling it, might naturally enough realize the world's mere compliment, and think himself truly inspired. Which is not improbable; for enthusiasts of all kinds do no less.

Since it is plain that men may be strangers to their own abilities; and by thinking meanly of them without just cause, may possibly lose a name, perhaps a name immortal; I would find some means to prevent these evils. Whatever promotes virtue, promotes something more, and carries its good influence beyond the moral man: To prevent these evils, I borrow two golden rules from ethics, which are no less golden in composition, than in life. 1. *Know thyself;* 2dly, *Reverence thyself.* I design to repay ethics in a future letter, by two rules from rhetoric for its service.

1st. *Know thyself.* Of ourselves it may be said, as Martial says of a bad neighbor,

> Nil tam prope, proculque nobis.[1]

---

[1] Nothing so near us and yet so far.

Therefore dive deep into thy bosom; learn the depth, extent, bias, and full fort of thy mind; contract full intimacy with the stranger within thee; excite and cherish every spark of intellectual light and heat, however smothered under former negligence, or scattered through the dull, dark mass of common thoughts; and collecting them into a body, let thy genius rise (if a genius thou hast) as the sun from chaos; and if I should then say, like an Indian, Worship it, (though too bold) yet should I say little more than my second rule enjoins, (*viz.*) *Reverence thyself.*

That is, let not great examples, or authorities, browbeat thy reason into too great a diffidence of thyself: Thyself so reverence, as to prefer the native growth of thy own mind to the richest import from abroad; such borrowed riches make us poor. The man who thus reverences himself, will soon find the world's reverence to follow his own. His works will stand distinguished; his the sole property of them; which property alone can confer the noble title of an author; that is, of one who (to speak accurately) thinks, and composes; while other invaders of the press, how voluminous, and learned soever (with due respect be it spoken), only read, and write.

This is the difference between those two luminaries in literature, the well-accomplished scholar, and the divinely-inspired enthusiast; the first is, as the bright morning star; the second, as the rising sun. The writer who neglects those two rules above will never stand alone; he makes one of a group, and thinks in wretched unanimity with the throng: Incumbered with the notions of others, and impoverished by their abundance, he conceives not the least embryo of new thought; opens not the least vista through the gloom of ordinary writers, into the bright walks of rare imagination, and singular design; while the true genius is crossing all public roads into fresh untrodden ground; he, up to the knees in antiquity, is treading the sacred footsteps of great examples, with the blind veneration of a bigot saluting the papal toe; comfortably hoping full absolution for the sins of his own understanding, from the powerful charm of touching his idol's infallibility.

Such meanness of mind, such prostration of our own powers, proceeds from too great admiration of others. Admiration has, generally, a degree of two very bad ingredients in it; of ignorance, and of fear; and does mischief in composition, and in life. Proud as the world is, there is more superiority in it given, than assumed: And its grandees of all kinds owe more of their elevation to the littleness of others' minds, than to the greatness of their own. Were not prostrate spirits their voluntary pedestals, the figure they make among mankind would not stand so high. Imitators and translators are somewhat of the pedestal-kind, and sometimes rather raise their original's reputation, by showing him to be by them inimitable, than their own. Homer has been translated into most languages; Ælian tells us, that the Indians (hopeful tutors!) have taught him to speak their tongue. What expect we from them? Not Homer's Achilles, but something, which, like Patroclus, assumes his name, and, at its peril, appears in his stead; nor expect we Homer's Ulysses, gloriously bursting out of his cloud into royal grandeur, but an Ulysses under disguise, and a beggar to the last. Such is that inimitable father of poetry, and oracle of all the wise, whom Lycurgus transcribed; and for an annual public recital of whose works Solon enacted a law; that it is much to be feared, that his so numerous translations are but as the published testimonials of so many nations, and ages, that this author so divine is untranslated still.

But here,

> Cynthius aurem
> Vellit,—[1]
>
> VIRGIL

and demands justice for his favorite, and ours. Great things he has done; but he might have done greater. What a fall is it from Homer's numbers, free as air, lofty and harmonious as the spheres, into childish shackles, and tinkling sounds! But, in his fall, he is still great—

> Nor appears
> Less than archangel ruined, and the excess
> Of glory obscured.—
>
> MILTON

Had Milton never wrote, Pope had been less to blame: But when in Milton's genius, Homer, as it were, personally rose to forbid Britons doing him that ignoble wrong, it is less pardonable, by that effeminate decoration, to put Achilles in petticoats a second time: How much nobler had it been, if his numbers had rolled on in full flow, through the various modulations of masculine melody, into those grandeurs of solemn sound, which are indispensably demanded by

---

[1] Apollo twitches my ear.

the native dignity of heroic song? How much nobler, if he had resisted the temptation of that Gothic dæmon, which modern poesy tasting, became mortal? O how unlike the deathless, divine harmony of three great names (how justly joined), of Milton, Greece, and Rome? His verse, but for this little speck of mortality, in its extreme parts, as his hero had in his heel; like him, had been invulnerable, and immortal. But, unfortunately, that was undipped in Helicon; as this, in Styx. Harmony as well as eloquence is essential to poesy; and a murder of his music is putting half Homer to death. Blank is a term of diminution; what we mean by blank verse, is, verse unfallen, uncursed; verse reclaimed, reinthroned in the true language of the gods; who never thundered nor suffered their Homer to thunder, in rhyme; and therefore, I beg you, my friend, to crown it with some nobler term; nor let the greatness of the thing lie under the defamation of such a name.

But supposing Pope's *Iliad* to have been perfect in its kind; yet it is a translation still; which differs as much from an original, as the moon from the sun.

> —Phœben alieno jusserat igne
> Impleri, solemque suo.[1]
> CLAUDIAN

But as nothing is more easy than to write originally wrong; originals are not here recommended, but under the strong guard of my first rule—*Know thyself*. Lucian, who was an original, neglected not this rule, if we may judge by his reply to one who took some freedom with him. He was, at first, an apprentice to a statuary; and when he was reflected on as such, by being called Prometheus, he replied, "I am indeed the inventor of new work, the model of which I owe to none; and, if I do not execute it well, I deserve to be torn by twelve vultures, instead of one."

If so, O Gulliver! dost thou not shudder at thy brother Lucian's vultures hovering o'er thee? Shudder on! they cannot shock thee more than decency has been shocked by thee. How have thy Houyhnhnms thrown thy judgment from its seat, and laid thy imagination in the mire? In what ordure hast thou dipped thy pencil? What a monster hast thou made of the

> Human face divine?
> MILTON

[1] He had ordered Phoebe to shine with another's light, the sun with its own.

This writer has so satirized human nature, as to give a demonstration in himself, that it deserves to be satirized. But, say his wholesale admirers, few could so have written; true, and fewer would. If it required great abilities to commit the fault, greater still would have saved him from it. But whence arise such warm advocates for such a performance? From hence, *viz.* before a character is established, merit makes fame; afterwards fame makes merit. Swift is not commended for this piece, but this piece for Swift. He has given us some beauties which deserve all our praise; and our comfort is that his faults will not become common; for none can be guilty of them, but who have wit as well as reputation to spare. His wit had been less wild, if his temper had not jostled his judgment. If his favorite Houyhnhnms could write, and Swift had been one of them, every horse with him would have been an ass, and he would have written a panegyric on mankind, saddling with much reproach the present heroes of his pen: On the contrary, being born amongst men, and, of consequence, piqued by many, and peevish at more, he has blasphemed a nature little lower than that of angels, and assumed by far higher than they: But surely the contempt of the world is not a greater virtue, that the contempt of mankind is a vice. Therefore I wonder that, though forborne by others, the laughter-loving Swift was not reproved by the venerable Dean, who could sometimes be very grave.

For I remember, as I and others were taking with him an evening's walk, about a mile out of Dublin, he stopped short; we passed on; but perceiving that he did not follow us, I went back; and found him fixed as a statue, and earnestly gazing upward at a noble elm, which in its uppermost branches was much withered, and decayed. Pointing at it, he said, "I shall be like that tree, I shall die at the top." As in this he seemed to prophesy like the Sybils; if, like one of them, he had burned part of his works, especially this blasted branch of a noble genius, like her too, he might have risen in his demand for the rest.

Would not his friend Pope have succeeded better in an original attempt? Talents untried are talents unknown. All that I know, is that, contrary to these sentiments, he was not only an avowed professor of imitation, but a zealous recommender of it also. Nor could he recommend any thing better, except emulation, to those who write. One of these all writers must call to their aid; but aids they are of unequal repute. Imitation is inferiority confessed; emulation is superiority contested, or denied; imitation is servile, emulation generous; that fetters, this fires; that may give a name; this, a name immortal: This made Athens to succeeding ages the rule of taste, and the standard of perfection. Her men of genius struck fire against each other; and kindled, by conflict, into glories, which no time shall extinguish. We thank Æschylus for Sophocles; and Parrhasius for Zeuxis; emulation, for both. That bids us fly the general fault of imitators; bids us not be struck with the loud report of former fame, as with a knell, which damps the spirits; but, as with a trumpet, which inspires ardor to rival the renowned. Emulation exhorts us, instead of learning our discipline for ever, like raw troops, under ancient leaders in composition, to put those laurelled veterans in some hazard of losing their superior posts in glory.

Such is emulation's high-spirited advice, such her immortalizing call. Pope would not hear, pre-engaged with imitation, which blessed him with all her charms. He chose rather, with his namesake of Greece, to triumph in the old world, than to look out for a new. His taste partook the error of his religion; it denied not worship to saints and angels; that is, to writers, who, canonized for ages, have received their apotheosis from established and universal fame. True poesy, like true religion, abhors idolatry; and though it honors the memory of the exemplary, and takes them willingly (yet cautiously) as guides in the way to glory; real, though unexampled, excellence is its only aim; nor looks it for any inspiration less than divine.

Though Pope's noble muse may boast her illustrious descent from Homer, Virgil, Horace, yet is an original author more nobly born. As Tacitus says of Curtius Rufus, an original author is born of himself, is his own progenitor, and will probably propagate a numerous offspring of imitators, to eternize his glory; while mule-like imitators die without issue. Therefore, though we stand much obliged for his giving us an Homer, yet had he doubled our obligation, by giving us—a Pope. Had he a strong imagination, and the true sublime? That granted, we might have had two Homers, instead of one, if longer had been his life; for I heard the dying swan talk over an epic plan a few weeks before his decease.

Bacon, under the shadow of whose great name I would shelter my present attempt in favor of originals, says, "Men seek not to know their own stock, and abilities; but fancy their possessions to be greater, and their abilities less, than they really are." Which is, in effect, saying, "That we ought to exert more than we do; and that, on exertion, our probability of success is greater than we conceive."

Nor have I Bacon's opinion only, but his assistance too, on my side. His mighty mind travelled round the intellectual world; and, with a more than eagle's eye, saw, and has pointed out, blank spaces, or dark spots in it, on which the human mind never shone. Some of these have been enlightened since; some are benighted still.

Moreover, so boundless are the bold excursions of the human mind, that, in the vast void beyond real existence, it can call forth shadowy beings, and unknown worlds, as numerous, as bright, and, perhaps, as lasting, as the stars; such quite-original beauties we may call paradisaical.

Natos sine semine flores.[1]

OVID

When such an ample area for renowned adventure in original attempts lies before us, shall we be as mere leaden pipes, conveying to the present age small streams of excellence from its grand reservoir in antiquity; and those too, perhaps, muddied in the pass? Originals shine, like comets; have no peer in their path; are rivalled by none, and the gaze of all: All other compositions (if they shine at all) shine in clusters; like the stars in the galaxy; where, like bad neighbors, all suffer from all; each particular being diminished, and almost lost in the throng.

If thoughts of this nature prevailed; if ancients and moderns were no longer considered as masters and pupils, but as hard-matched rivals for renown; then moderns, by the longevity of their labors, might, one day, become ancients themselves: And old time, that best weigher of merits, to keep his balance even, might have the golden weight of an Augustan age in both his scales: Or rather our scale might descend; and antiquity (as a modern match for it strongly speaks), might *kick the beam.*

And why not? For, consider, since an impartial Providence scatters talents indifferently, as through all orders of persons, so through all periods of time; since, a marvellous light, unenjoyed of old, is poured on us by revelation, with larger prospects extending our understanding, with brighter objects enriching our imagination, with an inestimable prize setting our passions on fire, thus strengthening every power that enables composition to shine; since, there has been no fall in man on this side Adam, who left no works, and the works of all other ancients are our auxiliaries against themselves, as being perpetual spurs to our ambition, and shining lamps in our

---

[1] Flowers born without seed.

path to fame; since this world is a school, as well for intellectual, as moral, advance; and the longer human nature is at school, the better scholar it should be; since, as the moral world expects its glorious millennium, the world intellectual may hope, by the rules of analogy, for some superior degrees of excellence to crown her later scenes; nor may it only hope, but must enjoy them too; for Tully, Quintilian, and all true critics, allow that virtue assists genius, and that the writer will be more able, when better is the man— All these particulars, I say, considered, why should it seem altogether impossible that heaven's latest editions of the human mind may be the most correct, and fair; that the day may come, when the moderns may proudly look back on the comparative darkness of former ages, on the children of antiquity; reputing Homer and Demosthenes as the dawn of divine genius; and on Athens as the cradle of infant fame; what a glorious revolution would this make in the rolls of renown!

What a rant, say you, is here?— I partly grant it: Yet, consider, my friend! knowledge physical, mathematical, moral, and divine, increases; all arts and sciences are making considerable advance; with them, all the accommodations, ornaments, delights, and glories of human life; and these are new food to the genius of a polite writer; these are as the root, and composition, as the flower; and as the root spreads, and thrives, shall the flower fail? As well may a flower flourish, when the root is dead. It is prudence to read, genius to relish, glory to surpass, ancient authors; and wisdom to try our strength in an attempt in which it would be no great dishonor to fail.

Why condemned Maro his admirable epic to the flames? Was it not because his discerning eye saw some length of perfection beyond it? And what he saw, may not others reach? And who bid fairer than our countrymen for that glory? Something new may be expected from Britons particularly; who seem not to be more severed from the rest of mankind by the surrounding sea, than by the current in their veins; and of whom little more appears to be required, in order to give us originals, than a consistency of character, and making their compositions of a piece with their lives.

In polite composition, in natural, and mathematical, knowledge, we have great originals already—Bacon, Boyle, Newton, Shakespeare, Milton, have showed us that all the winds cannot blow the British flag farther, than an original spirit can convey the British fame; their names go round the world; and what for-

eign genius strikes not as they pass? Why should not their posterity embark in the same bold bottom of new enterprise, and hope
the same success? Hope it they may; or you must assert that either
those originals, which we already enjoy, were written by angels, or
deny that we are men. As Simonides said to Pausanias, reason should
say to the writer, "Remember thou art a man." And for man not to
grasp at all which is laudable within his reach, is a dishonor to
human nature, and a disobedience to the divine; for as heaven does
nothing in vain, its gift of talents implies an injunction of their use.

A friend of mine [1] has obeyed that injunction; he has relied on
himself, and with a genius, as well moral, as original (to speak in
bold terms), has cast out evil spirits; has made a convert to virtue
of a species of composition, once most its foe. As the first Christian
emperors expelled dæmons, and dedicated their temples to the living
God.

But you, I know, are sparing your praise of this author; therefore
I will speak of one, which is sure of your applause. Shakespeare
mingled no water with his wine, lowered his genius by no vapid
imitation. Shakespeare gave us a Shakespeare, nor could the first in
ancient fame have given us more! Shakespeare is not their son, but
brother; their equal; and that, in spite of all his faults. Think you
this too bold? Consider, in those ancients what is it the world admires? Not the fewness of their faults, but the number and brightness of their beauties; and if Shakespeare is their equal (as he doubtless is) in that, which in them is admired, then is Shakespeare as
great as they; and not impotence, but some other cause, must be
charged with his defects. When we are setting these great men in
competition, what but the comparative size of their genius is the
subject of our inquiry? And a giant loses nothing of his size, though
he should chance to trip in his race. But it is a compliment to those
heroes of antiquity to suppose Shakespeare their equal only in dramatic powers; therefore, though his faults had been greater, the scale
would still turn in his favor. There is at least as much genius on the
British as on the Grecian stage, though the former is not swept so
clean; so clean from violations not only of the dramatic, but moral
rule; for an honest heathen, on reading some of our celebrated
scenes, might be seriously concerned to see, that our obligations to
the religion of nature were cancelled by Christianity.

Jonson, in the serious drama, is as much an imitator, as Shake-

---

[1] W. Thomas, *Le Poète Edward Young,* Paris, 1901, p. 474, identifies this friend as
Richardson himself.

speare is an original. He was very learned, as Samson was very strong, to his own hurt: Blind to the nature of tragedy, he pulled down all antiquity on his head, and buried himself under it; we see nothing of Jonson, nor indeed, of his admired (but also murdered) ancients; for what shone in the historian is a cloud on the poet; and *Catiline* might have been a good play, if Sallust had never writ.

Who knows if Shakespeare might not have thought less, if he had read more? Who knows if he might not have labored under the load of Jonson's learning, as Enceladus under Ætna? His mighty genius, indeed, through the most mountainous oppression would have breathed out some of his inextinguishable fire; yet, possibly, he might not have risen up into that giant, that much more than common man, at which we now gaze with amazement, and delight. Perhaps he was as learned as his dramatic province required; for whatever other learning he wanted, he was master of two books, unknown to many of the profoundly read, though books, which the last conflagration alone can destroy; the book of nature, and that of man. These he had by heart, and has transcribed many admirable pages of them, into his immortal works. These are the fountainhead, whence the Castalian streams of original composition flow; and these are often muddied by other waters, though waters in their distinct channel, most wholesome and pure: As two chemical liquors, separately clear as crystal, grow foul by mixture, and offend the sight. So that he had not only as much learning as his dramatic province required, but, perhaps, as it could safely bear.

Dryden, destitute of Shakespeare's genius, had almost as much learning as Jonson, and, for the buskin, quite as little taste. He was a stranger to the pathos, and by numbers, expression, sentiment, and every other dramatic cheat, strove to make amends for it; as if a saint could make amends for the want of conscience; a soldier, for the want of valor; or a vestal, of modesty. The noble nature of tragedy disclaims an equivalent; like virtue, it demands the heart; and Dryden had none to give. Let epic poets think, the tragedian's point is rather to feel; such distant things are a tragedian and a poet, that the latter indulged, destroys the former. Look on Barnwell, and Essex, and see how as to these distant characters Dryden excels, and is excelled. But the strongest demonstration of his no-taste for the buskin are his tragedies fringed with rhyme; which, in epic poetry, is a sore disease, in the tragic, absolute death. To Dryden's enormity, Pope's was a light offence. As lacemen are foes to mourning, these two authors, rich in rhyme, were no great friends to those solemn ornaments which the noble nature of their works required.

Must rhyme then, say you, be banished? I wish the nature of our language could bear its entire expulsion; but our lesser poetry stands in need of a toleration for it; it raises that, but it sinks the great; as spangles adorn children, but expose men. Prince Henry bespangled all over in his oylet-hole [1] suit, with glittering pins; and an Achilles, or an Almanzor, in his Gothic array; are very much on a level, as to the majesty of the poet, and the prince. Dryden had a great, but a general capacity; and as for a general genius, there is no such thing in nature: A genius implies the rays of the mind concentered, and determined to some particular point; when they are scattered widely, they act feebly, and strike not with sufficient force, to fire, or dissolve, the heart. As what comes from the writer's heart, reaches ours; so what comes from his head, sets our brains at work, and our hearts at ease. It makes a circle of thoughtful critics, not of distressed patients; and a passive audience is what tragedy requires. Applause is not to be given, but extorted; and the silent lapse of a single tear does the writer more honor, than the rattling thunder of a thousand hands. Applauding hands, and dry eyes (which during Dryden's theatrical reign often met) are a satire on the writer's talent, and the spectator's taste. When by such judges the laurel is blindly given, and by such a poet proudly received, they resemble an intoxicated host, and his tasteless guests, over some sparkling adulteration, commending their champagne.

But Dryden has his glory, though not on the stage: What an inimitable original is his ode? A small one, indeed, but of the first lustre, and without a flaw; and, amid the brightest boasts of antiquity, it may find a foil.

Among the brightest of the moderns, Mr. Addison must take his place. Who does not approach his character with great respect? They who refuse to close with the public in his praise, refuse at their peril. But, if men will be fond of their own opinions, some hazard must be run. He had, what Dryden and Jonson wanted, a warm, and feeling heart; but, being of a grave and bashful nature, through a philosophic reserve, and a sort of moral prudery, he concealed it, where he should have let loose all his fire, and have showed the most tender sensibilities of heart. At his celebrated *Cato,* few tears are shed, but Cato's own; which, indeed, are truly great, but unaffecting, except to the noble few who love their country better than themselves. The bulk of mankind want virtue enough to be touched by them.

[1] Decorated with small perforations, or eye-lets.

His strength of genius has reared up one glorious image, more lofty, and truly golden, than that in the plains of Dura,[1] for cool admiration to gaze at, and warm patriotism (how rare!) to worship; while those two throbbing pulses of the drama, by which alone it is shown to live, terror and pity, neglected through the whole, leave our unmolested hearts at perfect peace. Thus the poet, like his hero, through mistaken excellence, and virtue overstrained, becomes a sort of suicide; and that which is most dramatic in the drama, dies. All his charms of poetry are but as funeral flowers, which adorn; all his noble sentiments but as rich spices, which embalm the tragedy deceased.

Of tragedy, pathos is not only the life and soul, but the soul inextinguishable; it charms us through a thousand faults. Decorations, which in this author abound, though they might immortalize other poesy, are the *splendida peccata*[2] which damn the drama; while, on the contrary, the murder of all other beauties is a venial sin, nor plucks the laurel from the tragedian's brow.

Socrates frequented the plays of Euripides; and, what living Socrates would decline the theatre, at the representation of *Cato*? Tully's assassins found him in his litter, reading the *Medea* of the Grecian poet, to prepare himself for death. Part of *Cato* might be read to the same end. In the weight and dignity of moral reflection, Addison resembles that poet, who was called the dramatic philosopher; and is himself, as he says of *Cato*, "ambitiously sententious." But as to the singular talent so remarkable in Euripides, at melting down hearts into the tender streams of grief and pity, there the resemblance fails. His beauties sparkle, but do not warm; they sparkle as stars in a frosty night. There is, indeed, a constellation in his play; there is the philosopher, patriot, orator, and poet; but where is the tragedian? And, if that is wanting,

Cur in theatrum Cato severe venisti?[3]

MARTIAL

And, when I recollect what passed between him and Dryden in relation to this drama, I must add the next line,

An ideo tantum veneras, ut exires?[4]

[1] See Daniel, iii: 1.
[2] magnificent sins.
[3] Why, severe Cato, did you come to the theatre?
[4] Did you come only that you might go away?

For, when Addison was a student at Oxford, he sent up this play to his friend Dryden, as a proper person to recommend it to the theatre, if it deserved it; who returned it, with very great commendation; but with his opinion, that, on the stage, it could not meet with its deserved success. But though the performance was denied the theatre,[1] it brought its author on the public stage of life. For persons in power inquiring soon after of the head of his college for a youth of parts, Addison was recommended, and readily received, by means of the great reputation which Dryden had just then spread of him above.

There is this similitude between the poet and the play; as this is more fit for the closet than the stage; so, that shone brighter in private conversation than on the public scene. They both had a sort of local excellency, as the heathen gods a local divinity; beyond such a bound they, unadmired; and these, unadored. This puts me in mind of Plato, who denied Homer to the public; that Homer, which, when in his closet, was rarely out of his hand. Thus, though Cato is not calculated to signalize himself in the warm emotions of the theatre, yet we find him a most amiable companion, in our calmer delights of recess.

Notwithstanding what has been offered, this, in many views, is an exquisite piece. But there is so much more of art than nature in it that I can scarce forbear calling it an exquisite piece of statuary,

> Where the smooth chisel all its skill has shown,
> To soften into flesh the rugged stone.
>
> ADDISON

That is, where art has taken great pains to labor undramatic matter into dramatic life; which is impossible. However, as it is, like Pygmalion, we cannot but fall in love with it, and wish it was alive. How would a Shakespeare, or an Otway, have answered our wishes? They would have outdone Prometheus, and, with their heavenly fire, have given him not only life, but immortality. At their dramas (such is the force of nature) the poet is out of sight, quite hid behind his Venus, never thought of, till the curtain falls. Art brings our author forward, he stands before his piece; splendidly indeed, but unfortunately; for the writer must be forgotten by his audience, during the representation, if for ages he would be remembered by posterity. In the theatre, as in life, delusion is the charm; and we

---

[1] Young is in error here. *Cato* had, for its day, a successful run at Drury Lane.

are undelighted, the first moment we are undeceived. Such demonstration have we, that the theatre is not yet opened, in which solid
happiness can be found by man; because none are more than comparatively good; and folly has a corner in the heart of the wise.

A genius fond of ornament should not be wedded to the tragic
muse, which is in mourning: We want not to be diverted at an entertainment, where our greatest pleasure arises from the depth of our
concern. But whence (by the way) this odd generation of pleasure
from pain? The movement of our melancholy passions is pleasant,
when we ourselves are safe: We love to be, at once, miserable, and
unhurt: So are we made; and so made, perhaps, to show us the divine
goodness; to show that none of our passions were designed to give us
pain, except when being pained is for our advantage on the whole;
which is evident from this instance, in which we see, that passions
the most painful administer greatly, sometimes, to our delight.

*   *   *   *

[We omit the concluding pages of Young's essay, where he discusses Pope, Swift, and again Addison.]

Lessing

Gotthold Ephraim LESSING (1729–1781) was born at Kamenz, Saxony, the son of a strict clergyman of scanty means. He went to school at Meissen, and from there to the University of Leipzig, where his interest turned from theology to literature; he was particularly drawn to the theatre (much to his father's disapproval), and when in 1748 the local company broke up, he went to Berlin to begin a career as critic and journalist, meeting many literary figures. In 1755 he produced *Miss Sara Sampson,* a prose tragedy modelled on the English domestic drama. Shortly afterward, he went to the University of Wittenberg to continue his studies, and later lived in Leipzig for a time, returning in 1758 to Berlin. Two years later he became secretary to the Governor of Breslau. His independence led him to refuse several offers, including a chair at Königsberg, the tenure of which required an annual eulogy of the king. In 1765 he became director of the theatre at Hamburg, and in 1770, librarian to the Duke of Brunswick at Wolfenbüttel—an office which he held until his death. The most celebrated of his writings are his plays, *Minna von Barnhelm* (1765), *Emilia Galotti* (1772), and *Nathan der Weise* (1779); his great critical work, *Laocoön* (1766), and the theatrical criticism entitled *Hamburgische Dramaturgie* (1767–68).

Lessing is one of the greatest analytical critics since Aristotle. Like the latter, his practice is to examine a work of art objectively, in order to discover what its inherent qualities are, and then to deduce from these qualities principles that may be universal concerning the nature of beauty. This method he used with brilliant success in his *Laocoön,* settling with finality the problem underlying the statement *"ut pictura poesis"* ("poetry is like painting"). This theory first received wide currency in Horace's *Ars Poetica,* and was cited by critics down through Jonson and Dryden.

At a time when German writers were uncertain whether to follow the French or the English, Lessing turned the balance in favor of the English, having read in particular the authors of Queen Anne's time, and having been deeply influenced by Swift, Steele, Addison, and Pope. With the Frenchman Diderot, he realized the import of the middle-class, prose, domestic tragedies of Lillo and Moore, which, poor as they are as literature, point towards the "rights of man," and the revolutions that were to come in France and the American colonies. In his *Hamburgische Dramaturgie,* a series of articles on the drama and the theatre, Lessing made clear the genius of Shakespeare. His vivid observations led to the Schlegel-Tieck translations of the plays, the most adequate version in any foreign language. Lessing, accordingly, is the prime reason for Shakespeare's being known better in Germany than in any foreign country, and for his plays being performed more often, since that time, than they have been even in the country which gave him birth.

Lessing was a great analytical critic. But he was modest about what he had done in criticism. "I here remind my readers," he says at the end of essay 95 of the *Hamburgische Dramaturgie* (29 March 1768), "that these articles are not supposed to contain a whole dramatic system. So I am not obliged to give a solution for all the difficulties that I raise. My thoughts may seem to hang loosely together—nay, even seem to be inconsistent: I wish only that they be thoughts providing material for original thinking. I seek here merely to scatter *fermenta cognitionis* [the seeds of knowledge]."

From LAOCOÖN [1]

(1766)

II

Whether it be fable or history that Love prompted the first attempt in the plastic arts, it is at least certain that she was never weary of lending her guiding hand to the ancient masters. For if painting, as the art which imitates bodies on plane surfaces, is now generally practiced with an unlimited range of subject, certainly the wise Greek set her much straiter bounds, and confined her solely to the imitation of beautiful bodies. His artist portrayed nothing but the beautiful; even the ordinary beautiful, beauty of inferior kinds, was for him only an occasional theme, an exercise, a recreation. In his work the perfection of the subject itself must give delight; he was too great to demand of those who beheld it that they should content themselves with the bare, cold pleasure arising from a well-caught likeness or from the daring of a clever effort; in his art nothing was dearer to him, and to his thinking nothing nobler, than the ultimate purpose of art.

"Who will wish to paint you, when no one wishes to see you?" says an old epigrammatist concerning an extremely misshapen man. Many a more modern artist would say, "Be you as misshapen as is possible, I will paint you nevertheless. Though, indeed, no one may wish to see you, people will still wish to see my picture; not in so far as it represents you, but in so far as it is a demonstration of my art, which knows how to make so good a likeness of such a monster."

To be sure, with pitiful dexterities that are not ennobled by the worth of their subjects, the propensity to such rank boasting is too natural for the Greeks to have escaped without their Pauson, their Pyreicus. They had them; but they did strict justice upon them. Pauson, who confined himself entirely to the beauty of vulgar things and whose lower taste delighted most in the faulty and ugly in human shape, lived in the most sordid poverty. And Pyreicus, who painted, with all the diligence of a Dutch artist, nothing but barbers' shops, filthy factories, donkeys and cabbages, as if that kind of thing had so much charm in Nature and were so rarely to be seen, got the nickname of the rhyparograph, the dirt-painter, although the

---

[1] Translated by W. A. Steel, and published in the Everyman's Library. Reprinted here by the kind permission of E. P. Dutton and Company, Inc., New York.

luxurious rich weighed his works against gold, to help out their merit by this imaginary value.

The magistrates themselves considered it not unworthy of their attention to keep the artist by force in his proper sphere. The law of the Thebans, which commanded him in his imitation to add to beauty, and forbade under penalties the exaggeration of the ugly, is well known. It was no law against the bungler, as it is usually, and even by Junius, considered. It condemned the Greek "Ghezzi"; the unworthy artifice of achieving likeness by exaggeration of the uglier parts of the original: in a word, caricature.

*　　*　　*　　*

III

But, as we have already seen, Art in these later days has been assigned far wider boundaries. Let her imitative hand, folks say, stretch out to the whole of visible Nature, of which the Beautiful is only a small part. Let fidelity and truth of expression be her first law, and as Nature herself at all times sacrifices beauty to higher purposes, so also must the artist subordinate it to his general aim and yield to it no further than fidelity of expression permits. Enough, if by truth and faithful expression an ugliness of Nature be transformed into a beauty of Art.

Granted that one would willingly, to begin with, leave these conceptions uncontested in their worth or worthlessness, ought not other considerations quite independent of them to be examined—namely, why the artist is obliged to set bounds to expression and never to choose for it the supreme moment of an action?

The fact that the material limits of Art confine her imitative effort to one single moment will, I believe, lead us to similar conclusions.

If the artist can never, in the presence of ever-changing Nature, choose and use more than one single moment, and the painter in particular can use this single moment only from one point of vision; if, again, their works are made not merely to be seen, but to be considered, to be long and repeatedly contemplated, then it is certain that that single moment, and the single viewpoint of that moment, can never be chosen too significantly. Now that alone is significant and fruitful which gives free play to the imagination. The more we see, the more must we be able to add by thinking. The more we add thereto by thinking, so much the more can we believe ourselves to see. In the whole gamut of an emotion, however, there is no moment less advantageous than its topmost note. Beyond it there is nothing further, and to show us the uttermost is to tie the wings of fancy and oblige her, as she cannot rise above the sensuous impression, to busy herself with weaker pictures below it, the visible fullness of expression acting as a frontier which she dare not transgress. When, therefore, Laocoön sighs, the imagination can hear him shriek; but if he shrieks, then she cannot mount a step higher from this representation, nor, again, descend a step lower without seeing him in a more tolerable and consequently more uninteresting condition. She hears him only groan, or she sees him already dead.

*   *   *   *

IV

Glancing at the reasons adduced why the artist of the Laocoön was obliged to observe restraint in the expression of physical pain, I find that they are entirely drawn from the peculiar nature of Art and its necessary limits and requirements. Hardly, therefore, could any one of them be made applicable to poetry.

Without inquiring here how far the poet can succeed in depicting physical beauty, so much at least is undeniable, that, as the whole immeasurable realm of perfection lies open to his imitative skill, this visible veil, under which perfection becomes beauty, can be only one of the smallest means by which he undertakes to interest us in his subject. Often he neglects this means entirely, being assured that if his hero has won our goodwill, then his nobler qualities either so engage us that we do not think at all of the bodily form, or, if we think of it, so prepossess us that we do, on their very account, attribute to him, if not a beautiful one, yet at any rate one that is not uncomely. At least, with every single line which is not expressly intended for the eye, he will still take this sense into consideration. When Virgil's Laocoön cries aloud, to whom does it occur then that a wide mouth is needful for a cry, and that this must be ugly? Enough, that *clamores horrendos ad sidera tollit* [1] is an excellent feature for the hearing, whatever it might be for the vision. Whosoever demands here a beautiful picture, for him the poet has entirely failed of his intention.

[1] He lifts his terrifying cries to the stars.

In the next place, nothing requires the poet to concentrate his picture on one single moment. He takes up each of his actions, as he likes, from its very origin and conducts it through all possible modifications to its final close. Every one of these modifications, which would cost the artist an entire separate canvas or marble-block, costs the poet a single line; and if this line, taken in itself, would have misled the hearer's imagination, it was either so prepared for by what preceded, or so modified and supplemented by what followed, that it loses its separate impression, and in its proper connection produces the most admirable effect in the world. Were it therefore actually unbecoming to a man to cry out in the extremity of pain, what damage can this trifling and transient impropriety do in our eyes to one whose other virtues have already taken us captive? Virgil's Laocoön shrieks aloud, but this shrieking Laocoön we already know and love as the wisest of patriots and the most affectionate of fathers. We refer his cries not to his character but purely to his unendurable suffering. It is this alone we hear in his cries, and the poet could make it sensible to us only through them. Who shall blame him then, and not much rather confess that, if the artist does well not to permit Laocoön to cry aloud, the poet does equally well in permitting him?

* * * *

VI

My hypothesis—that the artists [1] imitated the poet—does not redound to their disparagement. On the contrary, this imitation sets their wisdom in the fairest light. They followed the poet without allowing themselves to be misled by him in the slightest. They had a pattern, but as they had to transpose this pattern from one art into another, they found opportunity enough to think for themselves. And these thoughts of theirs, which are manifest in their deviation from their model, prove that they were just as great in their art as he in his own.

And now I will reverse the hypothesis and suppose the poet to have imitated the artists. There are scholars who maintain this supposition to be the truth. Whether they had historical grounds for that, I do not know. But when they found the work of art so superlatively beautiful, they could not persuade themselves that it might

---

[1] It is generally believed now that a father and his two sons were the sculptors, probably in the first century, A. D.

belong to a late period. It must be of the age [1] when Art was in its perfect flower, because it deserved to be of that age.

It has been shown that, admirable as Virgil's picture is, there are yet various features of it which the artists could not use. The statement thus admits of being reduced to this, that a good poetic description must also yield a good actual painting, and that the poet has only so far described well when the artist can follow him in every feature. One is inclined to presume this restricted sense, even before seeing it confirmed by examples; merely from consideration of the wider sphere of poetry, from the boundless field of our imagination, and from the spiritual nature of the pictures, which can stand side by side in the greatest multitude and variety without one obscuring or damaging another, just as the things themselves would do or the natural signs of the same within the narrow bounds of space and time.

* * * *

VII

When one says that the artist imitates the poet, or that the poet imitates the artist, this is capable of two interpretations. Either the one makes the work of the other the actual subject of his imitation, or they have both the same subject and the one borrows from the other the style and fashion of the imitation. When Virgil describes the shield of Æneas, it is in the first of these senses that he imitates the artist who made it. The work of art itself, not that which is represented upon it, is the subject of his imitation, and although certainly he describes at the same time what one sees represented thereon, yet he describes it only as a part of the shield, and not the thing itself. If Virgil, on the other hand, had imitated the Laocoön group, this would be an imitation of the second kind. For he would not have imitated the group, but what the group represents, and only the characteristics of his imitation would have been borrowed from it. In the first imitation the poet is original, in the second he is a copyist. The former is a part of the general imitation which constitutes the essence of his art, and he works as genius, whether his subject be a work of other arts or of Nature. The latter, on the contrary, degrades him wholly from his dignity; instead of the things themselves, he

---

[1] I. e., the age of Pericles, fifth century, B. C., when the Parthenon was built, and Phidias was the great sculptor.

imitates the imitations of them, and gives us cold recollections of features from another's genius in place of original features of his own.

* * * *

XVI

But I will turn to the foundations and try to argue the matter from first principles.

My conclusion is this. If it is true that painting employs in its imitations quite other means or signs than poetry employs, the former—that is to say, figures and colors in space—but the latter articulate sounds in time; as, unquestionably, the signs used must have a definite relation to the thing signified, it follows that signs arranged together side by side can express only subjects which, or the various parts of which, exist thus side by side, whilst signs which succeed each other can express only subjects which, or the various parts of which, succeed each other.

Subjects which, or the various parts of which, exist side by side, may be called *bodies*. Consequently, bodies with their visible properties form the proper subjects of painting.

Subjects which, or the various parts of which, succeed each other may in general be called *actions*. Consequently, actions form the proper subjects of poetry.

Yet all bodies exist not in space alone, but also in time. They continue, and may appear differently at every moment and stand in different relations. Every one of these momentary appearances and combinations is the effect of one preceding and can be the cause of one following, and accordingly be likewise the central point of an action. Consequently, painting can also imitate actions, but only by way of suggestion through bodies.

On the other hand, actions cannot subsist for themselves, but must attach to certain things or persons. Now in so far as these things are bodies or are regarded as bodies, poetry too depicts bodies, but only by way of suggestion through actions.

Painting, in her co-existing compositions, can use only one single moment of the action, and must therefore choose the most pregnant, from which what precedes and follows will be most easily apprehended.

Just in the same manner poetry also can use, in her continuous imitations, only one single property of the bodies, and must therefore choose that one which calls up the most living picture of the body on that side from which she is regarding it. Here, indeed, we find the origin of the rule which insists on the unity and consistency of descriptive epithets, and on economy in the delineations of bodily subjects.

This is a dry chain of reasoning, and I should put less trust in it if I did not find it completely confirmed by Homer's practice, or if, rather, it were not Homer's practice itself which had led me to it. Only by these principles can the great manner of the Greeks be settled and explained, and its rightness established against the opposite manner of so many modern poets, who would emulate the painter in a department where they must necessarily be outdone by him.

Homer, I find, paints nothing but continuous actions, and all bodies, all single things, he paints only by their share in those actions, and in general only by one feature. What wonder, then, that the painter, where Homer himself paints, finds little or nothing for him to do, his harvest arising only there where the story brings together a multitude of beautiful bodies, in beautiful attitudes, in a place favorable to art, the poet himself painting these bodies, attitudes, places, just as little as he chooses? Let the reader run through the whole succession of pictures piece by piece, as Caylus [1] suggests, and he will discover in every one of them evidence for our contention.

Here, then, I leave the Count, who wishes to make the painter's palette the touchstone of the poet, that I may expound in closer detail the manner of Homer.

For one thing, I say, Homer commonly names one feature only. A ship is to him now the black ship, now the hollow ship, now the swift ship, at most the well-rowed black ship. Beyond that he does not enter on a picture of the ship. But certainly of the navigating, the putting to sea, the disembarking of the ship, he makes a detailed picture, one from which the painter must make five or six separate pictures if he would get it in its entirety upon his canvas.

If indeed special circumstances compel Homer to fix our glance for a while on some single corporeal object, in spite of this no picture is made of it which the painter could follow with his brush; for Homer knows how, by innumerable artifices, to set this object in a succession of moments, at each of which it assumes a different appearance, and in the last of which the painter must await it in order to show us, fully arisen, what in the poet we see arising. For instance,

---

[1] Anne Claude Philippe de Tubières, Count de Caylus (1692–1765), a French antiquary and writer, who, in his discussion of Homer, states that poetry is best when it can be visualized as pictures.

if Homer wishes to let us see the chariot of Juno, then Hebe must put it together piece by piece before our eyes. We see the wheels, the axles, the seat, the pole and straps and traces, not so much as it is when complete, but as it comes together under the hands of Hebe. On the wheels alone does the poet expend more than one feature, showing us the brazen spokes, the golden rims, the tires of bronze, the silver hub, in fullest detail. We might suggest that as there were more wheels than one, so in the description just as much more time must be given to them as their separate putting-on would actually itself require.

* * * *

XVII

But, some will object, the signs or characters which poetry employs are not solely such as succeed each other; they may be also arbitrary; and, as arbitrary signs, they are certainly capable of representing bodies just as they exist in space. We find instances of this in Homer himself, for we have only to remember his shield of Achilles in order to have the most decisive example in how detailed and yet poetical a manner some single thing can be depicted, with its various parts side by side.[1]

I will reply to this twofold objection. I call it twofold, because a just conclusion must prevail even without examples, and, on the other hand, the example of Homer weighs with me even if I know not how to justify it by any argument. It is true, as the signs of speech are arbitrary, so it is perfectly possible that by it we can make the parts of a body follow each other just as truly as in actuality they are found existing side by side. Only this is a property of speech and its signs in general, but not in so far as it suits best the purposes of poetry. The poet is not concerned merely to be intelligible; his representations should not merely be clear and plain, though this may satisfy the prose writer. He desires rather to make the ideas awakened by him within us living things, so that for the moment we realize the true sensuous impressions of the objects he describes, and cease in this moment of illusion to be conscious of the means— namely, his words—which he employs for his purpose. This is the substance of what we have already said of the poetic picture. But the

[1] In describing the scene that Hephæstus had engraved deep in the gold of Achilles's shield, Homer said (in Bosanquet's excellent rendering): "And behind the plough the earth went black, and looked like ploughed ground, though it was made of gold; that was a very miracle of his craft."

poet should always paint; and now let us see how far bodies with their parts set side by side are suitable for this kind of painting.

How do we arrive at the distinct representation of a thing in space? First we regard its parts singly, then the combination of these parts, and finally the whole. Our senses perform these various operations with so astonishing a swiftness that they seem to us but one, and this swiftness is imperatively necessary if we are to arrive at a conception of the whole, which is nothing more than the result of the conceptions of the parts and their combination. Provided, then, the poet leads us in the most beautiful order from one part of the object to another; provided he knows also how to make the combination of those parts equally clear—how much time does he need for that? What the eye sees at a glance, he counts out to us gradually, with a perceptible slowness, and often it happens that when we come to the last feature we have already forgotten the first. Nevertheless, we have to frame a whole from those features; to the eye the parts beheld remain constantly present, and it can run over them again and again; for the ear, on the contrary, the parts heard are lost if they do not abide in the memory. And if they so abide, what trouble, what effort it costs to renew their impressions, all of them in their due order, so vividly, to think of them together with even a moderate swiftness, and thus to arrive at an eventual conception of the whole.

* * * *

XX

I rather turn gladly to my own road, if a rambler can be said to have a road.

What I have said of physical objects in general is even more pertinent to beautiful physical objects. Physical beauty arises from the harmonious effect of manifold parts that can be taken in at one view. It demands also that these parts shall subsist side by side; and as things whose parts subsist side by side are the proper subject of painting, so it, and it alone, can imitate physical beauty. The poet, who can only show the elements of beauty one after another, in succession, does on that very account forbear altogether the description of physical beauty, as beauty. He recognizes that those elements, arranged in succession, cannot possibly have the effect which they have when placed side by side; that the concentrating gaze which we would direct upon them immediately after their enumeration still affords us no harmonious picture; that it passes the human imagination to represent to itself what kind of effect this mouth, and this nose, and these eyes together have if one cannot recall from Nature or art a similar composition of such features.

*   *   * . *

XXI

But does not Poetry lose too much if we take from her all pictures of physical beauty? Who wishes to do so? If we seek to close to her one single road, on which she hopes to achieve such pictures by following in the footsteps of a sister art, where she stumbles painfully without ever attaining the same goal, do we, then, at the same time close to her every other road, where Art in her turn can but follow at a distance?

Even Homer, who with evident intention refrains from all piece-meal delineation of physical beauties, from whom we can scarcely once learn in passing that Helen had white arms and beautiful hair—even he knows how, nevertheless, to give us such a conception of her beauty as far outpasses all that Art in this respect can offer. Let us recall the passage where Helen steps into the assembly of the Elders of the Trojan people. The venerable old men looked on her, and one said to the other:—

> Οὐ νέμεσις Τρῶας καὶ ἐυκνήμιδας Ἀχαιοὺς
> Τοιῇδ' ἀμφὶ γυναικὶ πολὺν χρόνον ἄλγεα πάσχειν·
> Αἰνῶς ἀθανάτῃσι θεῇς εἰς ὦπα ἔοικεν.[1]

What can convey a more vivid idea of Beauty than to have frigid age confessing her well worth the war that has cost so much blood and so many tears? [2] What Homer could not describe in its component parts, he makes us feel in its working. Paint us, then, poet, the satisfaction, the affection, the love, the delight, which beauty produces,

---

[1] Small blame is theirs, if both the Trojan knights
And brazen-mailed Achaians have endured
So long so many evils for the sake
Of that one woman. She is wholly like
In feature to the deathless goddesses.
Iliad, III. (Translated by W. C. Bryant.)

[2] Cf., of course, Marlowe's famous lines in *Doctor Faustus* (xiii, 93 ff.), when Faustus, seeing Helen, exclaims:
"Was this the face that launched a thousand ships,
And burned the topless towers of Ilium?
Sweet Helen, make me immortal with a kiss."

and you have painted beauty itself. Who can imagine as ill-favored the beloved object of Sappho, the very sight of whom she confesses robbed her of her senses and her reason? Who does not fancy he beholds with his own eyes the fairest, most perfect form, as soon as he sympathizes with the feeling which nothing but such a form can awaken? Not because Ovid shows us the beautiful body of his Lesbia part by part:—

> *Quos humeros, quales vidi tetigique lacertos!*
> *Forma papillarum quam fuit apta premi!*
> *Quam castigato planus sub pectore venter!*
> *Quantum et quale latus! quam juvenile femur!*—[1]

but because he does so with the voluptuous intoxication in which it is so easy to awaken our longing, we imagine ourselves enjoying the same sight of exquisite beauty which he enjoyed.

Another way in which poetry in its turn overtakes art in delineation of physical beauty is by transmuting beauty into charm. Charm is beauty in motion, and just for that reason less suitable to the painter than to the poet. The painter can only help us to guess the motion, but in fact his figures are motionless. Consequently grace with him is turned into grimace. But in poetry it remains what it is —a transitory beauty which we want to see again and again. It comes and goes; and as we can generally recall a movement more easily and more vividly than mere forms and colors, charm can in such a case work more powerfully on us than beauty.

* * * *

XXIII

A single defective part can destroy the harmonious working of many parts towards beauty. Yet the object does not necessarily therefore become ugly. Even ugliness demands several defective parts which likewise must be seen at one view if we are to feel by it the contrary of that with which beauty inspires us.

Accordingly, ugliness also in its essential nature would not be a reproach to poetry; and yet Homer has depicted the extremest ugliness in Thersites, and depicted it, moreover, in its elements set side

---

[1] "What shoulders, what arms it was my privilege to behold and to touch. What bliss to press a bosom shaped so perfectly for such caresses. How soft and smooth her skin beneath her lovely breasts, how divine her figure, how firm and plump her thighs." *Amores*, i, 5, 19–22. (Translated by J. Lewis May.)

by side. Why was that permitted to him with ugliness which in the case of beauty he renounced with so fine a discernment? Is the effect of ugliness not just as much hindered by the successive enumeration of its elements as the effect of beauty is nullified by the like enumeration of its elements? To be sure it is, but herein lies also Homer's justification. Just because ugliness becomes in the poet's delineation a less repulsive vision of physical imperfection, and so far as effect is concerned ceases as it were to be ugliness, it becomes usable to the poet; and what he cannot use for its own sake, he uses as an ingredient in order to produce or intensify certain mixed states of feeling with which he must entertain us in default of feelings purely pleasurable.

* * * *

XXIV

It is thus the poet uses the ugliness of forms; what use of them is permitted to the painter? Painting, as imitative dexterity, can express ugliness; but painting, as beautiful art, will not express it. To her, as the former, all visible objects belong; but, as the latter, she confines herself solely to those visible objects which awaken agreeable sensations.

But do not even the disagreeable sensations please in the imitation of them? Not all. A sagacious critic has already made the remark concerning the sensation of disgust. "The representations of fear," he says, "of sadness, of terror, of pity and so on, can only excite discomfort in so far as we take the evil to be actual. These, therefore, can be resolved into pleasant sensations by the recollection that it is but an artistic deceit. The unpleasant sensation of disgust, however, in virtue of the laws of the imagination, ensues on the mere representation in the mind whether the subject be considered as actual or not. Of what use is it, therefore, to the offended soul if Art thus betrays herself by a surrender to imitation? Her discomfort arose not from the foreboding that the evil was actual, but from the mere presentation of the same, and this *is* actual. The sensations of disgust are therefore always nature, never imitation."

The same principle holds good of the ugliness of forms. This ugliness offends our sight, is repugnant to our taste for order and harmony, and awakens aversion without respect to the actual existence of the subject in which we perceive it. We do not want to see Thersites, either in Nature or in picture, and if in fact his picture displeases us less, this happens not for the reason that the ugliness of his form ceases in the imitation to be ugliness, but because we have the power of abstracting our attention from this ugliness and satisfying ourselves merely with the art of the painter. Yet even this satisfaction will every moment be interrupted by the reflection how ill the art has been bestowed, and this reflection will seldom fail to be accompanied by contempt for the artist.

Aristotle suggests another reason why things on which we look in Nature with repugnance do yet afford us pleasure even in the most faithful copy—namely, the universal curiosity of mankind. We are glad if we either can learn from the copy τὶ ἕχαστον, what anything is, or if we can conclude from it ὅτι οὖτος ἐχεῖνος, that it is this or that. But even from this there follows no advantage to ugliness in imitation. The pleasure that arises from the satisfaction of our curiosity is momentary, and merely accidental to the subject from which it arises; the dissatisfaction, on the contrary, that accompanies the sight of ugliness is permanent, and essential to the subject that excites it. How, then, can the former balance the latter? Still less can the momentary agreeable amusement which the showing of a likeness gives us overcome the disagreeable effect of ugliness. The more closely I compare the ugly copy with the ugly original, the more do I expose myself to this effect, so that the pleasure of comparison vanishes very quickly, and there remains to me nothing more than the untoward impression of the twofold ugliness. To judge by the examples given by Aristotle, it appears as if he himself had been unwilling to reckon the ugliness of forms as amongst the unpleasing subjects which might yet please in imitation. These subjects are corpses and ravening beasts. Ravening wild beasts excite terror even though they are not ugly; and this terror, and not their ugliness, it is that is resolved into pleasant sensations by imitation. So, too, with corpses: the keener feeling of pity, the terrible reminder of our own annihilation it is that makes a corpse in Nature a repulsive subject to us; in the imitation, however, that pity loses its sharper edge by the conviction of the illusion, and from the fatal reminder an alloy of flattering circumstances can either entirely divert us, or unite so inseparably with it that we seem to find in it more of the desirable than the terrible.

As, therefore, the ugliness of forms cannot by and for itself be a theme of painting as fine art, because the feeling which it excites, while unpleasing, is not of that sort of unpleasing sensations which may be transformed into pleasing ones by imitation; yet the question might still be asked whether it could not to painting as well as to poetry be useful as an ingredient, for the intensifying of other sensations. May painting, then, avail itself of ugly forms for the arriving at the laughable and the terrible?

I will not venture to give this question a point-blank negative. It is undeniable that harmless ugliness can even in painting be made laughable, especially when there is combined with it an affectation of charm and dignity. It is just as incontestable that mischievous ugliness does in painting, just as in Nature, excite horror, and that this laughable and this horrible element, which in themselves are mingled feelings, attain by imitation a new degree of offensiveness or of pleasure.

I must at the same time point out that, nevertheless, painting is not here completely in the same case with poetry. In poetry, as I have already remarked, the ugliness of forms does by the transmutation of their co-existing parts into successive parts lose its unpleasant effect almost entirely; from this point of view it ceases, as it were, to be ugliness, and can therefore ally itself more intimately with other appearances in order to produce a new and distinct effect. In painting, on the contrary, the ugliness has all its forces at hand, and works almost as strongly as in Nature itself. Consequently, harmless ugliness cannot well remain laughable for long; the unpleasant sensation gains the upper hand, and what was farcical to begin with becomes later merely disgusting. Nor is it otherwise with mischievous ugliness; the terrible is gradually lost and the monstrous remains alone and unchangeable.

*   *   *   *

Schiller

Johann Christoph Friedrich von SCHILLER (1759–1805) was born at Marbach, Württemberg, the son of an army surgeon. Educated originally for the law, and later for medicine, he began his career as a dramatist with *Die Räuber* (1781). When his professional work interfered with his literary labors, he gave up his position as regimental physician in Stuttgart, and was soon afterward made poet to the theatre at Mannheim. In 1785 he went to Leipzig, where he enjoyed the friendship of Huber and Körner; when the latter married and moved to Dresden, Schiller followed him. Here he began his studies for a history of the revolt of the Netherlands, which was not published until 1788, and wrote *Don Carlos*, which was produced in 1787; the same year he went to Weimar, where he was received cordially by the poets Wieland and Herder. In 1788, on Goethe's return from Italy, the two men met; and in 1789—partly through the influence of Goethe—Schiller was appointed to a chair of history at Jena, which he accepted after some hesitation. At Jena he wrote several philosophical and critical papers, among them, the essay *Of Naïve and Sentimental Poetry* (1795), and began his *History of the Thirty Years' War*, which was published in 1793. In 1799 the dramatic trilogy *Wallenstein* was completed (it was translated in part by Coleridge the next year), and Schiller moved to Weimar, to be near Goethe, the Duke having offered him a pension. His later works include the well-known plays *Maria Stuart* (1800); *Die Jungfrau von Orleans* (1801); *Die Braut von Messina* (1802); and *Wilhelm Tell* (1804). In 1805 he died.

In his youth, Schiller, through his play *Die Räuber,* became a leader, with Herder and Goethe, of a romantic movement called *Sturm und Drang*—"Storm and Stress," in Carlyle's translation. Later, however, he developed, like Goethe, a profound admiration for the Greek classics. This reverence is expressed most forcibly in his essay, *Of Naïve and Sentimental Poetry.* It will guide the reader to know that by *naïve,* or "simple," Schiller meant, in general, "classic," and by *sentimental,* "romantic."

From OF NAÏVE AND SENTIMENTAL POETRY [1]

(1795)

* * * *

. . . Simplicity in our mode of thinking brings with it of necessity simplicity in our mode of expression, simplicity in terms as well as movement; and it is in this that grace especially consists. Genius expresses its most sublime and its deepest thoughts with this simple grace; they are the divine oracles that issue from the lips of a child. While the scholastic spirit, always anxious to avoid error, tortures all its words, all its ideas, and makes them pass through the crucible of grammar and logic, hard and rigid, in order to keep from vagueness, and uses few words in order not to say too much, enervates and blunts thought in order not to wound the reader who is not on his guard, genius gives to its expression, with a single and happy stroke of the brush, a precise, firm, and yet perfectly free form. In the case of grammar and logic, the sign and the thing signified are always heterogeneous and strangers to each other: with genius, on the contrary, the expression gushes forth spontaneously from the idea, the language and the thought are one and the same, so that even though the expression thus gives it a body, the spirit appears as if disclosed in a nude state. This fashion of expression, when the sign disappears entirely in the thing signified, when the tongue, so to speak, leaves the thought it translates naked, whilst the other mode of expression cannot represent thought without veiling it at the same time is what is called originality and inspiration in style.

[1] The text, compared with the German by the editors, is that edited by Nathan Haskell Dole.

This freedom, this natural mode by which genius expresses itself in works of intellect, is also the expression of the innocence of heart in the intercourse of life. Every one knows that in the world men have departed from simplicity, from the rigorous veracity of language, in the same proportion as they have lost the simplicity of feelings. The guilty conscience easily wounded, the imagination easily seduced, make an anxious decency necessary. Without telling what is false, people often speak differently from what they think; we are obliged to make circumlocutions to say certain things, which, however, can never afflict any but a sickly self-love, and that have no danger except for a depraved imagination. The ignorance of these laws of propriety (conventional laws), coupled with a natural sincerity which despises all kinds of bias and all appearance of falsity (sincerity, I mean, not coarseness, for coarseness dispenses with forms because it is hampered), gives rise in the intercourse of life to a simplicity of expression that consists in naming things by their proper name without circumlocution. This is done because we do not venture to designate them as they are, or only to do so by artificial means. The ordinary expressions of children are of this kind. They make us smile because they are in opposition to received manners; but men would always agree in the bottom of their hearts that the child is right.

*   *   *   *

Whence can arise this difference between the spirit of the ancients and the modern spirit? How comes it that, being, for all that relates to nature, incomparably below the ancients, we are superior to them precisely on this point, that we render a more complete homage to nature; that we have a closer attachment to it; and that we are capable of embracing even the inanimate world with the most ardent sensibility? It is because nature, in our time, is no longer in man, and that we no longer encounter it in its primitive truth, except out of humanity, in the inanimate world. It is not because we are more *conformable to nature*—quite the contrary; it is because in our social relations, in our mode of existence, in our manners, we are in *opposition with nature*. This is what leads us, when the instinct of truth and of simplicity is awakened—this instinct which, like the moral aptitude from which it proceeds, lives incorruptible and indelible in every human heart—to procure for it in the physical world the satisfaction which there is no hope of finding in the moral order. This is the reason why the feeling that attaches us to nature is connected so closely with that which makes us regret our infancy, forever flown, and our primitive innocence. Our childhood is all that remains of nature in humanity, such as civilization has made it, of untouched, unmutilated nature. It is, therefore, not wonderful, when we meet outside of us an impress of nature, that we are always brought back to the idea of our childhood.

It was quite different with the Greeks in antiquity.[1] Civilization with them did not degenerate, nor was it carried to such an excess that it was necessary to break with nature. The entire structure of their social life reposed on feelings, and not on a factitious conception, on a work of art. Their very theology was the inspiration of a simple spirit, the fruit of a joyous imagination, and not, like the ecclesiastical dogmas of modern nations, subtle combinations of the understanding. Since, therefore, the Greeks had not lost sight of nature in humanity, they had no reason, when meeting it out of man, to be surprised at their discovery, and they would not feel very imperiously the need of objects in which nature could be retraced. In accord with themselves, happy in feeling themselves men, they would of necessity keep for humanity what was greatest in it, and they must needs try to make all the rest approach it; while we, who are not in accord with ourselves—we who are discontented with the experience we have made of our humanity—have no more pressing interest than to fly out of it and to remove from our sight such an ill-fashioned form. The feeling of which we are treating here is, therefore, not that which was known by the ancients; it approaches far more nearly that *which we ourselves experience for the ancients.* The ancients felt naturally; we, on our part, feel what is natural. It was certainly a very different inspiration that filled the soul of Homer, when he depicted his divine cowherd giving hospitality to Ulysses, from that which agitated the soul of the young Werther at the moment when he read the *Odyssey* on issuing from an assembly in which he had only found tedium. The feeling we experience for nature resembles that of a sick man for health.

As soon as nature gradually vanishes from human life—that is, in proportion as it ceases to be *experienced* as a *subject* (active and passive)—we see it dawn and increase in the poetical world in the guise of an *idea* and as an *object*. The people who have carried farthest the want of nature, and at the same time the reflections on that matter, must needs have been the people who at the same time

[1] Here Schiller appends a note in which he contrasts the spirit of Ossian with that of the Greeks.

were most struck with this phenomenon of the *simple*, and gave it a name. If I am not mistaken, this people was the French. But the feeling of the simple, and the interest we take in it, must naturally go much farther back, and it dates from the time when the moral sense and the æsthetical sense began to be corrupt. This modification in the manner of feeling is exceedingly striking in Euripides, for example, if compared with his predecessors, especially Æschylus; and yet Euripides was the favorite poet of his time. The same revolution is perceptible in the ancient historians. Horace, the poet of a cultivated and corrupt epoch, praises, under the shady groves of Tibur, the calm and happiness of the country, and he might be termed the true founder of this sentimental poetry, of which he has remained the unsurpassed model. In Propertius, Virgil, and others, we find also traces of this mode of feeling; less of it is found in Ovid, who would have required for that more abundance of heart, and who in his exile at Tomes sorrowfully regrets the happiness that Horace so readily dispensed with in his villa at Tibur.

It is in the fundamental idea of poetry that the poet is everywhere the *guardian* of nature. When he can no longer entirely fill this part, and has already in himself suffered the deleterious influence of arbitrary and factitious forms, or has had to struggle against this influence, he presents himself as the *witness* of nature and as its avenger. The poet will, therefore, be the *expression* of nature itself, or his part will be to *seek* it, if men have lost sight of it. Hence arise two kinds of poetry, which embrace and exhaust the entire field of poetry. All poets—I mean those who are really so—will belong, according to the time when they flourish, according to the accidental circumstances that have influenced their education generally, and the different dispositions of mind through which they pass, will belong, I say, to the order of the *sentimental* poetry or to *simple* poetry.

The poet of a young world, simple and inspired, as also the poet who at an epoch of artificial civilization approaches nearest to the primitive bards, is austere and prudish, like the virginal Diana in her forests. Wholly unconfiding, he hides himself from the heart that seeks him, from the desire that wishes to embrace him. It is not rare for the dry truth with which he treats his subject to resemble insensibility. The whole object possesses him, and to reach his heart it does not suffice, as with metals of little value, to stir up the surface; as with pure gold, you must go down to the lowest depths. Like the Deity behind this universe, the simple poet hides himself behind his work; he is *himself* his work, and his work is *himself*. A man must be no longer worthy of the work, nor understand it, or be tired of it, to be even anxious to learn who is its author.

Such appears to us, for instance, Homer in antiquity, and Shakespeare among moderns: two natures infinitely different and separated in time by an abyss, but perfectly identical as to this trait of character. When, at a very youthful age, I became first acquainted with Shakespeare, I was displeased with his coldness, with his insensibility, which allows him to jest even in the most pathetic moments, to disturb the impression of the most harrowing scenes in *Hamlet,* in *King Lear,* and in *Macbeth,* etc., by mixing with them the buffooneries of a madman. I was revolted by his insensibility, which allowed him to pause sometimes at places where my sensibility would bid me hasten and urge me along, and which sometimes carried him away with indifference when my heart would be so happy to pause. Though I was accustomed, by the practice of modern poets, to seek at once the poet in his works, to meet *his* heart, to reflect *with him* in his theme—in a word, to see the object in the subject— I could not bear that the poet could in Shakespeare never be seized, that he would never give me an account of himself. For some years Shakespeare had been the object of my study and of all my respect before I had learned to love his personality.

*   *   *   *

I have previously remarked that the poet *is* nature, or he *seeks* nature. In the former case, he is a simple poet; in the second case, a sentimental poet.

The poetic spirit is immortal, nor can it disappear from humanity; it can only disappear with humanity itself, or with the aptitude to be a man, a human being. And actually, though man by the freedom of his imagination and of his understanding departs from simplicity, from truth, from the necessity of nature, not only a road always remains open to him to return to it, but, moreover, a powerful and indestructible instinct, the moral instinct, brings him incessantly back to nature; and it is precisely the poetical faculty that is united to this instinct by the ties of the closest relationship. Thus man does not lose the poetic faculty directly he parts with the simplicity of nature; but this faculty merely works in another direction.

Even at present nature is the only flame that kindles and warms the poetic soul. From nature alone it obtains all its force; to nature alone it speaks in the artificial culture-seeking man. Any other form of displaying its activity is remote from the poetic spirit. Accordingly it may be remarked that it is incorrect to apply the expression poetic to any of the so-styled productions of wit, though the high credit given to French literature has led people for a long period to class them in that category. I repeat that at present, even in the existing phase of culture, it is still nature that powerfully stirs up the poetic spirit; only its present relation to nature is of a different order from formerly.

As long as man dwells in a state of pure nature (I mean pure and not coarse nature), all his being acts at once like a simple sensuous unity, like a harmonious whole. The senses and reason, the receptive faculty and the spontaneously active faculty, have not been as yet separated in their respective functions: much less are they yet in contradiction with each other. Then the feelings of man are not the formless play of chance; nor are his thoughts an empty play of the imagination, without any value. His feelings proceed from the law of necessity; his *thoughts* from *reality*. But when man enters the state of civilization, and art has fashioned him, this *sensuous* harmony which was in him disappears, and henceforth he can only manifest himself as a *moral unity*, that is, as aspiring to unity. The harmony that existed as a *fact* in the former state, the harmony of feeling and thought, only exists now in an *ideal* state. It is no longer in him, but out of him; it is a conception of thought which he must begin by realizing in himself; it is no longer a fact, a reality of his life. Well, now let us take the idea of poetry, which is nothing else than *expressing humanity as completely as possible,* and let us apply this idea to these two states. We shall be brought to infer that, on the one hand, in the state of natural simplicity, when all the faculties of man are exerted together, his being still manifests itself in a harmonious unity; and consequently (the *totality* of man's nature expressing itself in reality), the part of the *poet* is necessarily to imitate the real as completely as is possible. In the state of civilization, on the contrary, when this harmonious co-operation of the whole of human nature is no longer anything but an idea, the part of the poet is necessarily to raise reality to the ideal, or, what amounts to the same thing, *to represent the ideal.* And, actually, these are the only two ways in which, in general, the poetic genius can manifest itself. Their great difference is quite evident, but though there be great opposition between them, a higher idea exists that embraces both, and there is no cause to be astonished if this idea coincides with the very idea of humanity.

This is not the place to pursue this thought any further, as it would require a separate discussion to place it in its full light. But if we only compare the modern and ancient poets together,[1] not according to the accidental forms which they may have employed, but according to their spirit, we shall be easily convinced of the truth of this thought. The thing that touches us in the ancient poets is nature; it is the truth of sense, it is a present and a living reality: modern poets touch us through the medium of ideas. The path followed by modern poets is moreover that necessarily followed by man generally, individuals as well as the species. Nature reconciles man with himself; art divides and disunites him; the ideal brings him back to unity. Now, the ideal being an infinite that he never succeeds in reaching, it follows that civilized man can never become perfect in his kind, while the man of nature can become so in his. Accordingly in relation to perfection one would be infinitely below the other, if we only considered the relation in which they are both to their own kind and to their maximum. If, on the other hand, it is the kinds that are compared together, it becomes clear that the end to which man tends by civilization is infinitely superior to that which he reaches through nature. Thus one has his reward, because, having for an object a finite magnitude, he completely reaches this object; the merit of the other is to approach an object that is of infinite magnitude. Now, as there are only degrees, and as there is only progress in the second of these evolutions, it follows that the relative merit of the man engaged in the ways of civilization is never determinable in general, though this man, taking the individuals separately, is necessarily at a disadvantage, compared with the man in whom nature acts in all its perfection. But we know also that humanity cannot reach its final end except by *progress*, and that the man of nature cannot make progress save through culture, and consequently by passing himself through the way of civilization. Accordingly there is no occasion to ask with which of the two the advantage must remain, considering this final aim.

* * * *

1 Schiller here expands this idea in a note.

Goethe

Johann Wolfgang von GOETHE (1749–1832) was born at Frankfurt-am-Main, the son of a Councillor, a man of wealth, education, and good social position, who provided excellent instructors for the precocious boy. At the age of sixteen, Goethe went to the University of Leipzig, and in 1770 to Strassburg, where he met Herder and took his degree in law in 1771. His first play, *Götz von Berlichingen* (1773), was followed by *Die Leiden des jungen Werthers* (1774), a romance which made him world-famous. In 1775 he was invited by the Duke to Weimar, where he made his home for the rest of his life. For a decade he was occupied by administrative work in connection with the army, mines, roads, financial organization, and other public activities, which slackened his literary productivity, although it gave him material for his future work. In 1786 he went to Italy, where he stayed almost two years, painting, studying, and writing. Here he completed his *Iphigenie auf Tauris* and *Egmont,* and began *Tasso.* Soon after his return he met Schiller, and in 1794 their acquaintance ripened into a friendship which lasted, with increasing cordiality, until Schiller's death. In 1791 Goethe was appointed director of the ducal theatre at Weimar—a post which he held for twenty-two years, during which he also gave much time to painting, to scientific research, and metaphysical speculations. The first part of his *Faust* was published as a fragment in 1790; *Wilhelm Meisters Lehrjahre* in 1796; *Hermann und Dorothea* in 1797; *Dichtung und Wahrheit* in 1811; *Wilhelm Meisters*

Wanderjahre in 1821, and the second part of *Faust* in 1833, the year after his death.

Goethe's literary criticism is not systematic. It is scattered throughout his works or recorded in fragments by the faithful Eckermann. All of it is marked by admirable sense. Like Schiller, he was, with his *Götz von Berlichingen,* a leader in the movement called *Sturm und Drang,* but he soon rebelled against the excesses of romanticism, and, like Schiller, turned back to the Greek classics. His attitude is expressed briefly and clearly in the entry, below, for 2 April 1829.

SUPPLEMENT TO ARISTOTLE'S *POETICS* [1]

In connection with this *Supplement,* it is interesting to note Goethe's opinion of Aristotle, as expressed in a letter to Schiller, thirty years earlier.

"I have just re-read the *Poetics* of Aristotle with the greatest pleasure; intelligence in its highest manifestation is a fine thing. It is really remarkable how Aristotle limits himself entirely to experience, and so appears, if perhaps somewhat material, for the most part all the more solid. It was also stimulating to me to see with what liberality he always shields the poet against the fault-finders and the hypercritical, how he always insists on essentials, and in everything else is so lax that in more than one place I was simply amazed. It is this that makes his whole view of poetry, and especially of his favorite forms, so vivifying that I shall soon take up the book again, especially in regard to some important passages which are not quite clear and the meaning of which I wish to investigate further."—Goethe to Schiller, 28 April, 1797.

(1827)

Every one who has concerned himself at all about the theory of poetic art—and of tragedy in particular—will remember a passage in Aristotle which has caused the commentators much difficulty, without their ever having been able to convince themselves wholly of its meaning. In his definition of tragedy this great writer seems to demand of it that, through the representation of stirring deeds and events, which should arouse pity and fear, the soul of the spectator should be purified of these passions.

[1] Translated by Randolph S. Bourne. Reprinted from *Goethe's Literary Essays,* selected by J. E. Spingarn, New York, copyright 1921, by Harcourt, Brace and Company.

My thoughts and convictions in regard to this passage I can best impart by a translation of it:—

Tragedy is the imitation of a significant and complete action, which has a certain extension in time and is portrayed in beautiful language by separate individuals, each of whom plays a rôle, instead of having all represented by one person as in the narration of a story or epic. After a course of events arousing pity and fear, the action closes with the equilibration of these passions.

In the foregoing translation, I believe I have made this hitherto dubious passage clear; it will only be necessary to add the following remarks: Could Aristotle, notwithstanding his always objective manner—as, for instance, here, where he seems to be speaking exclusively of the technique of tragedy—be really thinking of the effect, indeed the distant effect, upon the *spectator*? By no means! He speaks clearly and definitely: When the course of action is one arousing pity and fear, the tragedy must close *on the stage* with an equilibration, a reconciliation, of these emotions.

By "catharsis," he understands this reconciling culmination, which is demanded of all drama, indeed of all poetical works.

This occurs in the tragedy through a kind of human sacrifice, whether it be rigidly worked out with the death of the victim, or, under the influence of a favoring divinity, be satisfied by a substitute, as in the case of Abraham and Agamemnon. But this reconciliation, this release, is necessary at the end if the tragedy is to be a perfect work of art. This release, on the other hand, when effected through a favorable or desirable outcome, rather makes the work resemble an intermediate species of art, as in the return of Alcestis. In comedy, on the contrary, for the clearing up of all complications, which in themselves are of little significance from the point of view of arousing fear and hope, a marriage is usually introduced; and this, even if it does not end life completely, does make in it an important and serious break. Nobody wants to die, everybody wants to marry; and in this lies the half-jocose, half-serious difference between tragedy and comedy in practical æsthetics.

We shall perceive further that the Greeks did make use of their "trilogy" for such a purpose; for there is no loftier "catharsis" than the *Œdipus at Colonus*, where a half-guilty delinquent—a man who, through a demonic strain in his nature, through the sombre vehemence as well as greatness of his character, and through a headstrong course of action, puts himself at the mercy of the ever-inscrutable, unalterable powers—plunges himself and his family into the deepest, irreparable misery, and yet finally, after having made atonement and reparation, is raised to the company of the gods, as the auspicious protecting spirit of a region, revered with special sacrifices and services.

Here we find the principle of the great master, that the hero of a tragedy must be regarded and represented neither as wholly guilty nor as wholly innocent. In the first case the catharsis would merely result from the nature of the story, and the murdered wretch would appear only to have escaped the common justice which would have fallen upon him anyway by law. In the second case, it is not feasible either; for then there would seem to fall on human power or fate the weight of an all-too-heavy burden of injustice.

But on this subject I do not wish to wax polemical, any more than on any other; I have only to point out here how up to the present time people have been inclined to put up with a dubious interpretation of this passage. Aristotle had said in the *Politics* that music could be made use of in education for ethical purposes, since by means of the sacred melodies the minds of those raised to frenzy by the orgies were quieted and soothed again; thus he thought other emotions and passions could be calmed and equilibrated. That the argument here is from analogous cases we cannot deny; yet we think they are not identical. The effect of music depends on its particular character, as Händel has worked out in his *Alexander's Feast,* and as we can see evidenced at every ball, where perhaps after a chaste and dignified polonaise, a waltz is played and whirls the whole company of young people away in a bacchic frenzy.

For music, like all the arts, has little power directly to influence morality, and it is always wrong to demand such results from them. Philosophy and Religion alone can accomplish this. If piety and duty must be stimulated, the arts can only casually effect this stimulation. What they can accomplish, however, is a softening of crude manners and morals; yet even this may, on the other hand, soon degenerate into effeminacy.

Whoever is on the path of a truly moral and spiritual self-cultivation, will feel and acknowledge that tragedy and tragic romance do not quiet and satisfy the mind, but rather tend to unsettle the emotions and what we call the heart, and induce a vague, unquiet mood. Youth is apt to love this mood and is for that reason passionately devoted to such productions.

We now return to our original point, and repeat: Aristotle speaks of the *technique* of tragedy, in the sense that the poet, making it the object of his attention, contrives to create something pleasing to eye and ear in the course of a completed action.

If the poet has fulfilled this purpose and his duty on his side, tying together his knots of meaning and unravelling them again, the same process will pass before the mind of the spectator; the complications will perplex him, the solution enlighten him, but he will not go home any the better for it all. He will be inclined perhaps, if he is given to reflection, to be amazed at the state of mind in which he finds himself at home again—just as frivolous, as obstinate, as zealous, as weak, as tender or as cynical as he was when he went out. On this point we believe we have said all we can until a further working out of the whole subject makes it possible to understand it more clearly.

From CONVERSATIONS WITH ECKERMANN [1]

(18 April, 1827)

*   *   *   *

When the rest had departed, and I also prepared to go, he begged of me to remain a little longer. He ordered a portfolio, with engravings and etchings by Dutch masters, to be brought in.

"I will treat you with something good, by way of dessert," said he. With these words, he placed before me a landscape by Rubens.

"You have already seen this picture," said he; "but nobody can look often enough at anything really excellent—besides, there is something very particular in this. Will you tell me what you see?"

"I begin from the distance," said I. "I see in the farthest background a very clear sky, as if after sunset. Then, still in the far distance, a village and a town, in the light of evening. In the middle of the picture there is a road, along which a flock of sheep is hastening to the village. At the right hand of the picture are several haystacks, and a wagon which appears well laden. Unharnessed horses are grazing near. On one side, among the bushes, are several mares with their foals, which appear as if they were going to remain out of doors all night. Then, nearer to the foreground, there is a group of large trees; and lastly, quite in the foreground to the left, there are various laborers returning homewards."

"Good," said Goethe, "that is apparently all. But the principal

---

[1] Translated by John Oxenford. The *Conversations* were published between 1836 and 1848.

point is still wanting. All these things, which we see represented, the flock of sheep, the wagon with hay, the horses, the returning laborers—on which side are they lighted?"

"They receive light," said I, "from the side turned to us, and the shadow is thrown into the picture. The returning laborers in the foreground are especially in the light, which produces an excellent effect."

"But how has Rubens produced this beautiful effect?"

"By making these light figures appear on a dark ground," said I.

"But this dark ground," said Goethe, "whence does it arise!"

"It is the powerful shadow thrown by the group of trees towards the figures," said I. "But how?" continued I, with surprise; "the figures cast their shadows into the picture; the group of trees, on the contrary, cast theirs towards the spectator. We have, thus, light from two different sides, which is quite contrary to Nature."

"That is the point," returned Goethe, with a smile. "It is by this that Rubens proves himself great, and shows to the world that he, with a free spirit, stands *above* Nature, and treats her conformably to his high purposes. The double light is certainly a violent expedient, and you certainly say that it is contrary to Nature. But if it is contrary to Nature, I still say it is higher than Nature; I say it is the bold stroke of the master, by which he, in a genial [1] manner, proclaims to the world, that art is not entirely subject to natural necessities, but has laws of its own.

"The artist," continued Goethe, "must, indeed, in his details faithfully and reverently copy Nature; he must not arbitrarily change the structure of the bones, or the position of the muscles and sinews of an animal, so that the peculiar character is destroyed. This would be annihilating Nature. But in the higher regions of artistical production, by which a picture really becomes a picture, he has freer play; and here he may have recourse to *fictions*, as Rubens has done with the double light in this landscape.

"The artist has a twofold relation to Nature; he is at once her master and her slave. He is her slave, inasmuch as he must work with earthly things, in order to be understood; but he is her master, inasmuch as he subjects these earthly means to his higher intentions, and renders them subservient.

"The artist would speak to the world through an entirety; he does not find this entirety in Nature—it is the fruit of his own mind; or, if you like it, of the aspiration of a fructifying divine breath.

[1] I. e., of a genius.

"If we observe this landscape by Rubens cursorily, everything appears as natural to us as if it had been copied exactly from Nature. But this is not so. So beautiful a picture has never been seen in Nature —any more than a landscape by Poussin or Claude Lorraine, which appears very natural to us, but which we vainly seek in the actual world."

"Are there not," said I, "bold strokes of artistic fiction, similar to this double light of Rubens, to be found in literature?"

"We need not go far," said Goethe, after some reflection; "I could show you a dozen of them in Shakespeare. Only take *Macbeth*. When the lady would animate her husband to the deed, she says:

> I have given suck, *etc.*

Whether this be true or not does not appear; but the lady says it, and she must say it, in order to give emphasis to her speech. But in the course of the piece, when Macduff hears of the account of the destruction of his family, he exclaims in wild rage:

> He has no children!

These words of Macduff contradict those of Lady Macbeth; but this does not trouble Shakespeare. The grand point with him is the force of each speech; and as the lady, in order to give the highest emphasis to her words, must say 'I have given suck,' so, for the same purpose, Macduff must say 'He has no children.'

"Generally," continued Goethe, "we must not judge too exactly and narrowly of the pencil touches of a painter, or the words of a poet; we should rather contemplate and enjoy a work of art that has been produced in a bold and free spirit, and if possible with the same spirit.

"Thus it would be foolish, if, from the words of Macbeth:

> Bring forth men children only! *etc.*

it were concluded that the lady was a young creature who had not yet borne any children. It would be equally foolish if we were to go still further, and say that the lady must be represented on the stage as a very youthful person.

"Shakespeare does not make Macbeth say these words to show the youth of the lady. Like those of Lady Macbeth and Macduff, which I quoted just now, they are introduced merely for rhetorical purposes, and prove nothing more than that the poet always makes his character say whatever is proper, effective, and good in each *particular place*, without troubling himself to calculate whether these words may perhaps fall into apparent contradition with some other passage.

"Shakespeare, in writing his pieces, could hardly have thought that they would appear in print, so as to be told over, and compared one with another; he had rather the stage in view when he wrote; he regarded his plays as a lively and moving scene, that would pass rapidly before the eyes and ears upon the stage, not as one that was to be held firmly, and carped at in detail. Hence, his only point was to be effective and significant for the moment."

*   *   *   *

(2 April, 1829)

*   *   *   *

We then came to the newest French poets, and the meaning of the terms "classic" and "romantic."

"A new expression occurs to me," said Goethe, "which does not ill define the state of the case. I call the classic *healthy*, the romantic *sickly*. In this sense, the *Nibelungenlied* is as classic as the *Iliad*, for both are vigorous and healthy. Most modern productions are romantic—not because they are new; but because they are weak, morbid, and sickly. And the antique is classic—not because it is old; but because it is strong, fresh, joyous, and healthy. If we distinguish 'classic' and 'romantic' by these qualities, it will be easy to see our way clearly."

*   *   *   *

(17 March, 1830)

*   *   *   *

"The distinction between classical and romantic poetry, which is now spread over the whole world and occasions so many quarrels and divisions, came originally from Schiller and myself. I laid down the maxim of objective treatment in poetry, and would allow no other; but Schiller, who worked quite in the subjective way, deemed his own fashion right, and to defend himself against me, wrote the treatise upon *Naïve and Sentimental Poetry*. He proved to me that I, against my will, was romantic, and that my *Iphigenia*, through the predominance of sentiment, was by no means so classical and so much in the antique spirit as some people supposed.

"The Schlegels took up this idea, and carried it further, so that it has now been diffused over the whole world; and everybody talks about classicism and romanticism—of which nobody thought fifty years ago."

* * * *

[The following is the last conversation with Goethe that Eckermann records.]

[March,[1] 1832], some days later.

We talked of the tragic idea of Destiny among the Greeks.

"It no longer suits our way of thinking," said Goethe; "it is obsolete, and is also in contradiction with our religious views. If a modern poet introduces such antique ideas into a drama, it always has an air of affectation. It is a costume long since out of fashion; which, like the Roman toga, no longer suits us.

"It is better for us moderns to say with Napoleon, 'Politics are Destiny.' But let us beware of saying, with our latest *literati*, that politics are poetry, or a suitable subject for the poet. The English poet Thomson wrote a very good poem on the Seasons, but a very bad one on Liberty; and that not from want of poetry in the poet, but from want of poetry in the subject.

"If a poet would work politically, he must give himself up to a party; and so soon as he does that, he is lost as a poet—he must bid farewell to his free spirit, his unbiased view, and draw over his ears the cap of bigotry and blind hatred.

"The poet, as a man and citizen, will love his native land; but the native land of his *poetic* powers and poetic action is the good, noble, and beautiful, which is confined to no particular province or country, and which he seizes upon and forms wherever he finds it. Therein is he like the eagle, who hovers with free gaze over whole countries, and to whom it is of no consequence whether the hare on which he pounces is running in Prussia or in Saxony.

"And, then, what is meant by love of one's country? what is meant by patriotic deeds? If the poet has employed a life in battling with pernicious prejudices, in setting aside narrow views, in enlightening the minds, purifying the tastes, ennobling the feelings and thoughts of his countrymen, what better could he have done? how could he have acted more patriotically?

"To make such ungrateful and unsuitable demands upon a poet is just as if we required the captain of a regiment to show himself

[1] Goethe died on the 22nd of the month.

a patriot by taking part in political innovations and thus neglecting his proper calling. The captain's country is his regiment; and he will show himself an excellent patriot by troubling himself about political matters only so far as they concern him, and bestowing all his mind and all his care on the battalions under him, trying so to train and discipline them that they may do their duty if ever their native land should be in peril.

"I hate all bungling like sin; but, most of all, bungling in state affairs, which produces nothing but mischief to thousands and millions.

"You know that, on the whole, I care little what is written about me; but yet it comes to my ears, and I know well enough that, hard as I have toiled all my life, all my labors are as nothing in the eyes of certain people, just because I have disdained to mingle in political parties. To please such people I must have become a member of a Jacobin club, and preached bloodshed and murder. However, not a word more upon this wretched subject, lest I become unwise in railing against folly."

In the same manner he blamed the political course, so much praised by others, of Uhland.

"Mind," said he, "the politician will devour the poet. To be a member of the States, and to live amid daily jostlings and excitements, is not for the delicate nature of a poet. His song will cease, and that is in some sort to be lamented. Swabia has plenty of men, sufficiently well educated, well meaning, able, and eloquent, to be members of the States; but only one poet of Uhland's class."

*　　*　　*　　*

Wordsworth

William WORDSWORTH (1770–1850) was born at Cocker-mouth, Cumberland, the son of an attorney. The wild beauties of his native county gave him early in life a love of nature. He was still a child when his parents died, and relatives helped with his education. After schooling in Hawkshead, Lancashire, Wordsworth went to Cambridge University, from which he was graduated in 1791. He then spent a year in France, where he became interested in revolutionary politics, and fell in love with Annette Vallon, who bore him a daughter. Fearing for his safety in disturbed France, his friends stopped his funds and forced his return to England in 1792. He hesitated to study for the Church, and turned his attention to literature, for which he had shown an early taste, but his poetry at first attracted little attention and sold slowly. It led, however, to his friendship with Coleridge, who recognized his genius. A legacy from a friend enabled him to make a home for himself and his sister—first in Dorset-shire, and then in Somersetshire, near Coleridge, with whom, in 1798, he published the *Lyrical Ballads*. After a winter in Germany with his sister and Coleridge, he settled in Grasmere, in the Lake District, where he remained, save for visits abroad and to Scotland, in domestic and poetic seclusion. In 1802 he married a childhood friend, Mary Hutchinson, and in 1813 he moved to Rydal Mount, which was his home for thirty-seven years, until his death. He held various official positions; in 1839 he was made a D. C. L. by Oxford University; and in 1843, on the death of Southey, became poet-laureate.

Wordsworth, one of the five or six outstanding poets in

the English language, wrote his most inspired verse before 1807, the year in which he printed *The Ode to Duty*. He produced much after this, but most of these later poems were far inferior to his previous accomplishment. His long, autobiographical poem, *The Prelude*, considered by many the greatest poem of its kind in English literature, was not published until after his death, though it was finished in 1805.

The publication of the *Lyrical Ballads* in 1798 was one of the momentous events in the history of English literature. To be sure, other poets, like Burns, had used a "selection of the real language of men." But Wordsworth was the first to impress readers with the possibilities of the new vocabulary, not only by the example of his poems, but also by the explanation that he wrote as the preface to the second edition of the volume in 1800.

Wordsworth in his prose is often prolix. When his intellect and his emotion merge, however, he can produce compact, cogent paragraphs like those on pages 342 and 344. He is not bookish; for instance, he does not know Aristotle at first hand; but he has a sensitivity that leads him to intuitions which illumine the subject.

Coleridge, Wordsworth's partner in the enterprise of the *Lyrical Ballads*, did not agree wholly with his friend's views. His objections will be found in the selections from *Biographia Literaria* below.

PREFACE[1] TO THE *LYRICAL BALLADS*
(1800)

The first volume of these poems has already been submitted to general perusal. It was published as an experiment, which I hoped might be of some use to ascertain how far, by fitting to metrical arrangement a selection of the real language of men in a state of vivid

[1] This appeared in the second edition of the *Lyrical Ballads*, two years after the poems had first been printed.

sensation, that sort of pleasure and that quantity of pleasure may be imparted, which a poet may rationally endeavor to impart.

I had formed no very inaccurate estimate of the probable effect of those poems: I flattered myself that they who should be pleased with them would read them with more than common pleasure: and, on the other hand, I was well aware that by those who should dislike them they would be read with more than common dislike. The result has differed from my expectation in this only, that a greater number have been pleased than I ventured to hope I should please.

．　　．　　．　　．　　．　　．

Several of my friends are anxious for the success of these poems, from a belief that, if the views with which they were composed were indeed realized, a class of poetry would be produced, well adapted to interest mankind permanently, and not unimportant in the quality and in the multiplicity of its moral relations: and on this account they have advised me to prefix a systematic defence of the theory upon which the poems were written. But I was unwilling to undertake the task, knowing that on this occasion the reader would look coldly upon my arguments, since I might be suspected of having been principally influenced by the selfish and foolish hope of *reasoning* him into an approbation of these particular poems; and I was still more unwilling to undertake the task, because adequately to display the opinions, and fully to enforce the arguments, would require a space wholly disproportionate to a preface. For to treat the subject with the clearness and coherence of which it is susceptible, it would be necessary to give a full account of the present state of the public taste in this country, and to determine how far this taste is healthy or depraved; which, again, could not be determined, without pointing out in what manner language and the human mind act and re-act on each other, and without retracing the revolutions, not of literature alone, but likewise of society itself. I have therefore altogether declined to enter regularly upon this defence; yet I am sensible that there would be something like impropriety in abruptly obtruding upon the public, without a few words of introduction, poems so materially different from those upon which general approbation is at present bestowed.

It is supposed that by the act of writing in verse an author makes a formal engagement that he will gratify certain known habits of association; that he not only thus apprises the reader that certain classes of ideas and expressions will be found in his book, but that others will be carefully excluded. This exponent or symbol held forth by metrical language must in different eras of literature have excited very different expectations: for example, in the age of Catullus, Terence, and Lucretius, and that of Statius or Claudian; and in our own country, in the age of Shakespeare and Beaumont and Fletcher, and that of Donne and Cowley, or Dryden, or Pope. I will not take upon me to determine the exact import of the promise which, by the act of writing in verse, an author in the present day makes to his reader; but it will undoubtedly appear to many persons that I have not fulfilled the terms of an engagement thus voluntarily contracted. They who have been accustomed to the gaudiness and inane phraseology of many modern writers, if they persist in reading this book to its conclusion, will, no doubt, frequently have to struggle with feelings of strangeness and awkwardness: they will look round for poetry, and will be induced to inquire by what species of courtesy these attempts can be permitted to assume that title. I hope, therefore, the reader will not censure me for attempting to state what I have proposed to myself to perform; and also (as far as the limits of a preface will permit) to explain some of the chief reasons which have determined me in the choice of my purpose: that at least he may be spared any unpleasant feeling of disappointment, and that I myself may be protected from one of the most dishonorable accusations which can be brought against an author; namely, that of an indolence which prevents him from endeavoring to ascertain what is his duty, or, when his duty is ascertained, prevents him from performing it.

The principle object, then, proposed in these poems was to choose incidents and situations from common life, and to relate or describe them, throughout, as far as was possible in a selection of language really used by men, and, at the same time, to throw over them a certain coloring of imagination, whereby ordinary things should be presented to the mind in an unusual aspect; and further, and above all, to make these incidents and situations interesting by tracing in them, truly though not ostentatiously, the primary laws of our nature: chiefly, as far as regards the manner in which we associate ideas in a state of excitement. Humble and rustic life was generally chosen, because in that condition the essential passions of the heart find a better soil in which they can attain their maturity, are less under restraint, and speak a plainer and more emphatic language; because in that condition of life our elementary feelings co-exist in a state of greater simplicity, and consequently may be more accurately contemplated and more forcibly communicated; because the manners of rural life germinate from those elementary feelings, and, from the necessary character of rural occupations, are more easily comprehended, and are more durable; and, lastly, because in that condition the passions of men are incorporated with the beautiful and permanent forms of nature. The language, too, of these men has been adopted (purified indeed from what appear to be its real defects, from all lasting and rational causes of dislike or disgust), because such men hourly communicate with the best objects from which the best part of language is originally derived; and because, from their rank in society and the sameness and narrow circle of their intercourse, being less under the influence of social vanity, they convey their feelings and notions in simple and unelaborated expressions. Accordingly, such a language, arising out of repeated experience and regular feelings, is a more permanent and a far more philosophical language than that which is frequently substituted for it by poets, who think that they are conferring honor upon themselves and their art, in proportion as they separate themselves from the sympathies of men, and indulge in arbitrary and capricious habits of expression, in order to furnish food for fickle tastes, and fickle appetites, of their own creation.[1]

I cannot, however, be insensible to the present outcry against the triviality and meanness, both of thought and language, which some of my contemporaries have occasionally introduced into their metrical compositions; and I acknowledge that this defect, where it exists, is more dishonorable to the writer's own character than false refinement or arbitrary innovation, though I should contend at the same time that it is far less pernicious in the sum of its consequences. From such verses the poems in these volumes will be found distinguished at least by one mark of difference, that each of them has a worthy *purpose*. Not that I always began to write with a distinct purpose formally conceived; but habits of meditation have, I trust, so prompted and regulated my feelings, that my descriptions of such objects as strongly excite those feelings will be found to carry along with them a *purpose*. If this opinion be erroneous, I can have little right to the name of a poet. For all good poetry is the spontaneous overflow of powerful feelings: and though this be true, poems to which any value can be attached were never produced on any variety

---

[1] It is worth while here to observe that the affecting parts of Chaucer are almost always expressed in language pure and universally intelligible even to this day. (Wordsworth.)

of subjects but by a man who, being possessed of more than usual organic sensibility, had also thought long and deeply. For our continued influxes of feeling are modified and directed by our thoughts, which are indeed the representatives of all our past feelings; and, as by contemplating the relation of these general representatives to each other, we discover what is really important to men, so, by the repetition and continuance of this act, our feelings will be connected with important subjects, till at length, if we be originally possessed of much sensibility, such habits of mind will be produced that, by obeying blindly and mechanically the impulses of those habits, we shall describe objects, and utter sentiments, of such a nature, and in such connection with each other, that the understanding of the reader must necessarily be in some degree enlightened, and his affections strengthened and purified.

It has been said that each of these poems has a purpose. Another circumstance must be mentioned which distinguishes these poems from the popular poetry of the day; it is this, that the feeling therein developed gives importance to the action and situation, and not the action and situation to the feeling.

A sense of false modesty shall not prevent me from asserting that the reader's attention is pointed to this mark of distinction, far less for the sake of these particular poems than from the general importance of the subject. The subject is indeed important! For the human mind is capable of being excited without the application of gross and violent stimulants; and he must have a very faint perception of its beauty and dignity who does not know this, and who does not further know that one being is elevated above another in proportion as he possesses this capability. It has therefore appeared to me that to endeavor to produce or enlarge this capability is one of the best services in which, at any period, a writer can be engaged; but this service, excellent at all times, is especially so at the present day. For a multitude of causes, unknown to former times, are now acting with a combined force to blunt the discriminating powers of the mind, and, unfitting it for all voluntary exertion, to reduce it to a state of almost savage torpor. The most effective of these causes are the great national events which are daily taking place, and the increasing accumulation of men in cities, where the uniformity of their occupations produces a craving for extraordinary incident, which the rapid communication of intelligence hourly gratifies. To this tendency of life and manners the literature and theatrical exhibitions of the country have conformed themselves. The invaluable works of our elder writers, I had almost said the works of Shakespeare and Milton, are driven into neglect by frantic novels, sickly and stupid German tragedies, and deluges of idle and extravagant stories in verse. When I think upon this degrading thirst after outrageous stimulation, I am almost ashamed to have spoken of the feeble endeavor made in these volumes to counteract it; and, reflecting upon the magnitude of the general evil, I should be oppressed with no dishonorable melancholy, had I not a deep impression of certain inherent and indestructible qualites of the human mind, and likewise of certain powers in the great and permanent objects that act upon it, which are equally inherent and indestructible; and were there not added to this impression a belief that the time is approaching when the evil will be systematically opposed by men of greater powers, and with far more distinguished success.

Having dwelt thus long on the subjects and aim of these poems, I shall request the reader's permission to apprise him of a few circumstances relating to their *style,* in order, among other reasons, that he may not censure me for not having performed what I never attempted. The reader will find that personifications of abstract ideas rarely occur in these volumes, and are utterly rejected, as an ordinary device to elevate the style, and raise it above prose. My purpose was to imitate, and, as far as possible, to adopt the very language of men; and assuredly such personifications do not make any natural or regular part of that language. They are, indeed, a figure of speech occasionally prompted by passion, and I have made use of them as such; but have endeavored utterly to reject them as a mechanical device of style, or as a family language which writers in metre seem to lay claim to by prescription. I have wished to keep the reader in the company of flesh and blood, persuaded that by so doing I shall interest him. Others who pursue a different track will interest him likewise; I do not interfere with their claim, but wish to prefer a claim of my own. There will also be found in these volumes little of what is usually called poetic diction; as much pains has been taken to avoid it as is ordinarily taken to produce it; this has been done for the reason already alleged, to bring my language near to the language of men; and further, because the pleasure which I have proposed to myself to impart is of a kind very different from that which is supposed by many persons to be the proper object of poetry. Without being culpably particular, I do not know how to give my reader a more exact notion of the style in which it was my wish and intention to write, than by informing him that I have at all times endeavored to look steadily at my subject; consequently there is, I hope, in these poems little falsehood of description, and my ideas are expressed in language fitted to their respective importance. Something must have been gained by this practice, as it is friendly to one property of all good poetry, namely, good sense: but it has necessarily cut me off from a large portion of phrases and figures of speech which from father to son have long been regarded as the common inheritance of poets. I have also thought it expedient to restrict myself still further, having abstained from the use of many expressions, in themselves proper and beautiful, but which have been foolishly repeated by bad poets, till such feelings of disgust are connected with them as it is scarcely possible by any art of association to overpower.

If in a poem there should be found a series of lines, or even a single line, in which the language, though naturally arranged, and according to the strict laws of metre, does not differ from that of prose, there is a numerous class of critics, who, when they stumble upon these prosaisms, as they call them, imagine that they have made a notable discovery, and exult over the poet as over a man ignorant of his own profession. Now these men would establish a canon of criticism which the reader will conclude he must utterly reject, if he wishes to be pleased with these volumes. And it would be a most easy task to prove to him that not only the language of a large portion of every good poem, even of the most elevated character, must necessarily, except with reference to the metre, in no respect differ from that of good prose, but likewise that some of the most interesting parts of the best poems will be found to be strictly the language of prose when prose is well written. The truth of this assertion might be demonstrated by innumerable passages from almost all the poetical writings, even of Milton himself. To illustrate the subject in a general manner, I will here adduce a short composition of Gray, who was at the head of those who, by their reasonings, have attempted to widen the space of separation betwixt prose and metrical composition, and was more than any other man curiously elaborate in the structure of his own poetic diction.

> In vain to me the smiling mornings shine,
> And reddening Phœbus lifts his golden fire:
> The birds in vain their amorous descant join,
> Or cheerful fields resume their green attire.
> These ears, alas! for other notes repine;
> *A different object do these eyes require;*
> *My lonely anguish melts no heart but mine;*

And in my breast the imperfect joys expire;
Yet morning smiles the busy race to cheer,
And new-born pleasure brings to happier men;
The fields to all their wonted tribute bear;
To warm their little loves the birds complain.
I fruitless mourn to him that cannot hear,
And weep the more because I weep in vain.[1]

It will easily be perceived, that the only part of this sonnet which is of any value is the lines printed in italics; it is equally obvious that, except in the rhyme, and in the use of the single word "fruitless" for "fruitlessly," which is so far a defect, the language of these lines does in no respect differ from that of prose.

By the foregoing quotation it has been shown that the language of prose may yet be well adapted to poetry; and it was previously asserted that a large portion of the language of every good poem can in no respect differ from that of good prose. We will go further. It may be safely affirmed that there neither is, nor can be, any *essential* difference between the language of prose and metrical composition. We are fond of tracing the resemblance between poetry and painting, and, accordingly, we call them sisters: but where shall we find bonds of connection sufficiently strict to typify the affinity betwixt metrical and prose composition? They both speak by and to the same organs; the bodies in which both of them are clothed may be said to be of the same substance, their affections are kindred, and almost identical, not necessarily differing even in degree; poetry [2] sheds no tears "such as angels weep," but natural and human tears; she can boast of no celestial ichor that distinguishes her vital juices from those of prose; the same human blood circulates through the veins of them both.

If it be affirmed that rhyme and metrical arrangement of themselves constitute a distinction which overturns what has just been said on the strict affinity of metrical language with that of prose, and paves the way for other artificial distinctions which the mind voluntarily admits, I answer that the language of such poetry as is

---

[1] *Sonnet on the Death of Mr. Richard West.*

[2] I here use the word Poetry (though against my own judgment) as opposed to the word Prose, and synonymous with metrical composition. But much confusion has been introduced into criticism by this contradistinction of Poetry and Prose, instead of the more philosophical one of Poetry and Matter of Fact, or Science. The only strict antithesis to Prose is Metre; nor is this, in truth, a *strict* antithesis, because lines and passages of metre so naturally occur in writing prose, that it would be scarcely possible to avoid them, even were it desirable. (Wordsworth.)

here recommended is, as far as is possible, a selection of the language really spoken by men; that this selection, wherever it is made with true taste and feeling, will of itself form a distinction far greater than would at first be imagined, and will entirely separate the composition from the vulgarity and meanness of ordinary life; and, if metre be superadded thereto, I believe that a dissimilitude will be produced altogether sufficient for the gratification of a rational mind. What other distinction would we have? Whence is it to come? And where is it to exist? Not, surely, where the poet speaks through the mouths of his characters: it cannot be necessary here, either for elevation of style, or any of its supposed ornaments: for, if the poet's subject be judiciously chosen, it will naturally, and upon fit occasion, lead him to passions the language of which, if selected truly and judiciously, must necessarily be dignified and variegated, and alive with metaphors and figures. I forbear to speak of an incongruity which would shock the intelligent reader, should the poet interweave any foreign splendor of his own with that which the passion naturally suggests: it is sufficient to say that such addition is unnecessary. And surely it is more probable that those passages which with propriety abound with metaphors and figures will have their due effect, if, upon other occasions where the passions are of a milder character, the style also be subdued and temperate.

But, as the pleasure which I hope to give by the poems now presented to the reader must depend entirely on just notions upon this subject, and as it is in itself of high importance to our taste and moral feelings, I cannot content myself with these detached remarks. And if, in what I am about to say, it shall appear to some that my labor is unnecessary, and that I am like a man fighting a battle without enemies, such persons may be reminded that, whatever be the language outwardly holden by men, a practical faith in the opinions which I am wishing to establish is almost unknown. If my conclusions are admitted, and carried as far as they must be carried if admitted at all, our judgments concerning the works of the greatest poets both ancient and modern will be far different from what they are at present, both when we praise, and when we censure; and our moral feelings influencing and influenced by these judgments will, I believe, be corrected and purified.

Taking up the subject, then, upon general grounds, let me ask, what is meant by the word *Poet?* What is a poet? To whom does he address himself? And what language is to be expected from him? —He is a man speaking to men: a man, it is true, endowed with more lively sensibility, more enthusiasm and tenderness, who has a greater knowledge of human nature, and a more comprehensive soul, than are supposed to be common among mankind; a man pleased with his own passions and volitions, and who rejoices more than other men in the spirit of life that is in him; delighting to contemplate similar volitions and passions as manifested in the goings-on of the universe, and habitually impelled to create them where he does not find them. To these qualities he has added a disposition to be affected more than other men by absent things as if they were present; an ability of conjuring up in himself passions which are indeed far from being the same as those produced by real events, yet (especially in those parts of the general sympathy which are pleasing and delightful) do more nearly resemble the passions produced by real events than anything which, from the motions of their own minds merely, other men are accustomed to feel in themselves:—whence, and from practice, he has acquired a greater readiness and power in expressing what he thinks and feels, and especially those thoughts and feelings which, by his own choice, or from the structure of his own mind, arise in him without immediate external excitement.

But whatever portion of this faculty we may suppose even the greatest poet to possess, there cannot be a doubt that the language which it will suggest to him must often, in liveliness and truth, fall short of that which is uttered by men in real life under the actual pressure of those passions, certain shadows of which the poet thus produces, or feels to be produced, in himself.

However exalted a notion we would wish to cherish of the character of a poet, it is obvious that while he describes and imitates passions, his employment is in some degree mechanical, compared with the freedom and power of real and substantial action and suffering. So that it will be the wish of the poet to bring his feelings near to those of the persons whose feelings he describes,—nay, for short spaces of time, perhaps, to let himself slip into an entire delusion, and even confound and identify his own feelings with theirs; modifying only the language which is thus suggested to him by a consideration that he describes for a particular purpose, that of giving pleasure. Here, then, he will apply the principle of selection which has been already insisted upon. He will depend upon this for removing what would otherwise be painful or disgusting in the passion; he will feel that there is no necessity to trick out or to elevate nature: and, the more industriously he applies this principle, the deeper will be his faith that no words which *his* fancy or imagination can suggest will be compared with those which are the emanations of reality and truth.

But it may be said by those who do not object to the general spirit of these remarks, that, as it is impossible for the poet to produce upon all occasions language as exquisitely fitted for the passion as that which the real passion itself suggests, it is proper that he should consider himself as in the situation of a translator, who does not scruple to substitute excellencies of another kind for those which are unattainable by him, and endeavors occasionally to surpass his original, in order to make some amends for the general inferiority to which he feels that he must submit. But this would be to encourage idleness and unmanly despair. Further, it is the language of men who speak of what they do not understand; who talk of poetry as of a matter of amusement and idle pleasure; who will converse with us as gravely about a *taste* for poetry, as they express it, as if it were a thing as indifferent as a taste for rope-dancing, or Frontiniac or Sherry.[1] Aristotle, I have been told, has said that poetry is the most philosophic of all writing: it is so: its object is truth, not individual and local, but general, and operative; not standing upon external testimony, but carried alive into the heart by passion; truth which is its own testimony, which gives competence and confidence to the tribunal to which it appeals, and receives them from the same tribunal. Poetry is the image of man and nature. The obstacles which stand in the way of the fidelity of the biographer and historian, and of their consequent utility, are incalculably greater than those which are to be encountered by the poet who comprehends the dignity of his art. The poet writes under one restriction only, namely, the necessity of giving immediate pleasure to a human being possessed of that information which may be expected from him, not as a lawyer, a physician, a mariner, an astronomer, or a natural philosopher, but as a man. Except this one restriction, there is no object standing between the poet and the image of things; between this, and the biographer and historian, there are a thousand.

Nor let this necessity of producing immediate pleasure be considered as a degradation of the poet's art. It is far otherwise. It is an acknowledgment of the beauty of the universe, an acknowledgment the more sincere, because not formal, but indirect; it is a task light and easy to him who looks at the world in the spirit of love: further, it is a homage paid to the native and naked dignity of man, to the grand elementary principle of pleasure, by which he knows,

[1] kinds of wine.

and feels, and lives, and moves. We have no sympathy but what is propagated by pleasure: I would not be misunderstood; but wherever we sympathize with pain, it will be found that the sympathy is produced and carried on by subtle combinations with pleasure. We have no knowledge, that is, no general principles drawn from the contemplation of particular facts, but what has been built up by pleasure, and exists in us by pleasure alone. The man of science, the chemist and mathematician, whatever difficulties and disgusts they may have had to struggle with, know and feel this. However painful may be the objects with which the anatomist's knowledge is connected, he feels that his knowledge is pleasure; and where he has no pleasure he has no knowledge. What then does the poet? He considers man and the objects that surround him as acting and reacting upon each other, so as to produce an infinite complexity of pain and pleasure; he considers man in his own nature and in his ordinary life as contemplating this with a certain quantity of immediate knowledge, with certain convictions, intuitions, and deductions, which from habit acquire the quality of intuitions; he considers him as looking upon this complex scene of ideas and sensations, and finding everywhere objects that immediately excite in him sympathies which, from the necessities of his nature, are accompanied by an over-balance of enjoyment.

To this knowledge which all men carry about with them, and to these sympathies in which, without any other discipline than that of our daily life, we are fitted to take delight, the poet principally directs his attention. He considers man and nature as essentially adapted to each other, and the mind of man as naturally the mirror of the fairest and most interesting properties of nature. And thus the poet, prompted by this feeling of pleasure, which accompanies him through the whole course of his studies, converses with general nature, with affections akin to those which, through labor and length of time, the man of science has raised up in himself, by conversing with those particular parts of nature which are the objects of his studies. The knowledge both of the poet and the man of science is pleasure; but the knowledge of the one cleaves to us as a necessary part of our existence, our natural and unalienable inheritance; the other is a personal and individual acquisition, slow to come to us, and by no habitual and direct sympathy connecting us with our fellow-beings. The man of science seeks truth as a remote and unknown benefactor; he cherishes and loves it in his solitude: the poet, singing a song in which all human beings join with him, rejoices in the presence of truth as our visible friend and hourly companion. Poetry is the breath and finer spirit of all knowledge; it is the impassioned expression which is in the countenance of all science. Emphatically may it be said of the poet, as Shakespeare hath said of man, that "he looks before and after." He is the rock of defence for human nature; an upholder and preserver, carrying everywhere with him relationship and love. In spite of difference of soil and climate, of language and manners, of laws and customs: in spite of things silently gone out of mind, and things violently destroyed; the poet binds together by passion and knowledge the vast empire of human society, as it is spread over the whole earth, and over all time. The objects of the poet's thoughts are everywhere; though the eyes and senses of man are, it is true, his favorite guides, yet he will follow wheresoever he can find an atmosphere of sensation in which to move his wings. Poetry is the first and last of all knowledge—it is as immortal as the heart of man. If the labors of men of science should ever create any material revolution, direct or indirect, in our condition, and in the impressions which we habitually receive, the poet will sleep then no more than at present; he will be ready to follow the steps of the man of science, not only in those general indirect effects, but he will be at his side, carrying sensation into the midst of the objects of the science itself. The remotest discoveries of the chemist, the botanist, or mineralogist, will be as proper objects of the poet's art as any upon which it can be employed, if the time should ever come when these things shall be familiar to us, and the relations under which they are contemplated by the followers of these respective sciences shall be manifestly and palpably material to us as enjoying and suffering beings. If the time should ever come when what is now called science, thus familiarized to men, shall be ready to put on, as it were, a form of flesh and blood, the poet will lend his divine spirit to aid the transfiguration, and will welcome the being thus produced, as a dear and genuine inmate of the household of man.—It is not, then, to be supposed that any one who holds that sublime notion of poetry which I have attempted to convey, will break in upon the sanctity and truth of his pictures by transitory and accidental ornaments, and endeavor to excite admiration of himself by arts, the necessity of which must manifestly depend upon the assumed meanness of his subject.

What has been thus far said applies to poetry in general, but especially to those parts of composition where the poet speaks through the mouths of his characters; and upon this point it appears to authorize the conclusion that there are few persons of good sense who would not allow that the dramatic parts of composition are defective, in proportion as they deviate from the real language of nature, and are colored by a diction of the poet's own, either peculiar to him as an individual poet or belonging simply to poets in general,—to a body of men who, from the circumstance of their compositions being in metre, it is expected will employ a particular language.

It is not, then, in the dramatic parts of composition that we look for this distinction of language; but still it may be proper and necessary where the poet speaks to us in his own person and character. To this I answer by referring the reader to the description before given of a poet. Among the qualities there enumerated as principally conducing to form a poet, is implied nothing differing in kind from other men, but only in degree. The sum of what was said is, that the poet is chiefly distinguished from other men by a greater promptness to think and feel without immediate external excitement, and a greater power in expressing such thoughts and feelings as are produced in him in that manner. But these passions and thoughts and feelings are the general passions and thoughts and feelings of men. And with what are they connected? Undoubtedly with our moral sentiments and animal sensations, and with the causes which excite these; with the operations of the elements, and the appearances of the visible universe; with storm and sunshine, with the revolutions of the seasons, with cold and heat, with loss of friends and kindred, with injuries and resentments, gratitude and hope, with fear and sorrow. These, and the like, are the sensations and objects which the poet describes, as they are the sensations of other men, and the objects which interest them. The poet thinks and feels in the spirit of human passions. How, then, can his language differ in any material degree from that of all other men who feel vividly and see clearly? It might be *proved* that it is impossible. But supposing that this were not the case, the poet might then be allowed to use a peculiar language when expressing his feelings for his own gratification, or that of men like himself. But poets do not write for poets alone, but for men. Unless, therefore, we are advocates for that admiration which subsists upon ignorance, and that pleasure which arises from hearing what we do not understand, the poet must descend from this supposed height; and, in order to excite rational sympathy, he must express himself as other men express themselves. To this it may be added that while he is only selecting from the real language of men, or, which amounts to the same thing, composing accurately in the spirit of such selection, he is treading upon safe ground, and we know what we are to expect from him. Our feelings are the same with respect to metre; for, as it may be proper to remind the reader, the distinction of metre is regular and uniform, and not, like that which is produced by what is usually called POETIC DICTION, arbitrary, and subject to infinite caprices upon which no calculation whatever can be made. In the one case, the reader is utterly at the mercy of the poet, respecting what imagery or diction he may choose to connect with the passion; whereas in the other, the metre obeys certain laws, to which the poet and reader both willingly submit because they are certain, and because no interference is made by them with the passion, but such as the concurring testimony of ages has shown to heighten and improve the pleasure which co-exists with it.

It will now be proper to answer an obvious question, namely, Why, professing these opinions, have I written in verse? To this, in addition to such answer as is included in what has been already said, I reply, in the first place, Because, however I may have restricted myself, there is still left open to me what confessedly constitutes the most valuable object of all writing, whether in prose or verse—the great and universal passions of men, the most general and interesting of their occupations, and the entire world of nature before me—to supply endless combinations of forms and imagery. Now, supposing for a moment that whatever is interesting in these objects may be as vividly described in prose, why should I be condemned for attempting to superadd to such description the charm which, by the consent of all nations, is acknowledged to exist in metrical language? To this, by such as are yet unconvinced, it may be answered that a very small part of the pleasure given by poetry depends upon the metre, and that it is injudicious to write in metre, unless it be accompanied with the other artificial distinctions of style with which metre is usually accompanied, and that, by such deviation, more will be lost from the shock which will thereby be given to the reader's associations than will be counterbalanced by any pleasure which he can derive from the general power of numbers. In answer to those who still contend for the necessity of accompanying metre with certain appropriate colors of style in order to the accomplishment of its appropriate end, and who also, in my opinion, greatly underrate the power of metre in itself, it might, perhaps, as far as relates to these volumes, have been almost sufficient to observe that poems are extant, written upon more humble subjects, and in a still more naked and simple style, which have continued to give pleasure from generation to generation. Now, if nakedness and simplicity be a defect, the fact here mentioned affords a strong presumption that poems somewhat less naked and simple are capable of affording pleasure at the present day; and, what I wished *chiefly* to attempt, at present, was to justify myself for having written under the impression of this belief.

But various causes might be pointed out why, when the style is manly, and the subject of some importance, words metrically arranged will long continue to impart such a pleasure to mankind as he who proves the extent of that pleasure will be desirous to impart. The end of poetry is to produce excitement in co-existence with an overbalance of pleasure; but, by the supposition, excitement is an unusual and irregular state of the mind; ideas and feelings do not, in that state, succeed each other in accustomed order. If the words, however, by which this excitement is produced be in themselves powerful, or the images and feelings have an undue proportion of pain connected with them, there is some danger that the excitement may be carried beyond its proper bounds. Now the co-presence of something regular, something to which the mind has been accustomed in various moods and in a less excited state, cannot but have great efficacy in tempering and restraining the passion by an intertexture of ordinary feeling, and of feeling not strictly and necessarily connected with the passion. This is unquestionably true; and hence, though the opinion will at first appear paradoxical, from the tendency of metre to divest language, in a certain degree, of its reality, and thus to throw a sort of half-consciousness of unsubstantial existence over the whole composition, there can be little doubt but that more pathetic situations and sentiments, that is, those which have a greater proportion of pain connected with them, may be endured in metrical composition, especially in rhyme, than in prose. The metre of the old ballads is very artless, yet they contain many passages which would illustrate this opinion; and, I hope, if the following poems be attentively perused, similar instances will be found in them. This opinion may be further illustrated by appealing to the reader's own experience of the reluctance with which he comes to the reperusal of the distressful parts of *Clarissa Harlowe,* or *The Gamester*; while Shakespeare's writings, in the most pathetic scenes, never act upon us as pathetic, beyond the bounds of pleasure—an effect which, in a much greater degree than might at first be imagined, is to be ascribed to small but continual and regular impulses of pleasurable surprise from the metrical arrangement.—On the other hand (what it must be allowed will much more frequently happen), if the poet's words should be incommensurate with the passion, and inadequate to raise the reader to a height of desirable excitement, then (unless the poet's choice of his metre has been grossly injudicious) in the feelings of pleasure which the reader has been accustomed to connect with metre in general, and in the feeling, whether cheerful or melancholy, which he has been accustomed to connect with that particular movement of metre, there will be found something which will greatly contribute to impart passion to the words, and to effect the complex end which the poet proposes to himself.

If I had undertaken a SYSTEMATIC defence of the theory here maintained, it would have been my duty to develop the various causes upon which the pleasure received from metrical language depends. Among the chief of these causes is to be reckoned a principle which must be well known to those who have made any of the arts the object of accurate reflection; namely, the pleasure which the mind derives from the perception of similitude in dissimilitude. This principle is the great spring of the activity of our minds, and their chief feeder. From this principle the direction of the sexual appetite, and all the passions connected with it, take their origin: it is the life of our ordinary conversation; and upon the accuracy with which similitude in dissimilitude, and dissimilitude in similitude are perceived, depend our taste and our moral feelings. It would not be a useless employment to apply this principle to the consideration of metre, and to show that metre is hence enabled to afford much pleasure, and to point out in what manner that pleasure is produced. But my limits will not permit me to enter upon this subject, and I must content myself with a general summary.

I have said that poetry is the spontaneous overflow of powerful feelings; it takes its origin from emotion recollected in tranquillity: the emotion is contemplated till, by a species of reaction, the tranquillity gradually disappears, and an emotion, kindred to that which was before the subject of contemplation, is gradually produced, and does itself actually exist in the mind. In this mood successful composition generally begins, and in a mood similar to this it is carried on; but the emotion, of whatever kind, and in whatever degree, from various causes, is qualified by various pleasures, so that in describing any passions whatsoever, which are voluntarily described, the mind will, upon the whole, be in a state of enjoyment. If Nature be thus cautious to preserve in a state of enjoyment a being so employed, the poet ought to profit by the lesson held forth to him, and ought especially to take care that, whatever passions he communicates to his reader, those passions, if his reader's mind be sound and vigorous, should always be accompanied with an overbalance of pleasure. Now the music of harmonious metrical language, the sense of difficulty overcome, and the blind association of pleasure which has been previously received from works of rhyme or metre of the same or similar construction, an indistinct perception perpetually renewed of language closely resembling that of real life, and yet, in the circumstance of metre, differing from it so widely—all these imperceptibly make up a complex feeling of delight, which is of the most important use in tempering the painful feeling always found intermingled with powerful descriptions of the deeper passions. This effect is always produced in pathetic and impassioned poetry; while in lighter compositions the ease and gracefulness with which the poet manages his numbers are themselves confessedly a principal source of the gratification of the reader. All that it is *necessary* to say, however, upon this subject, may be effected by affirming, what few persons will deny, that of two descriptions, either of passions, manners, or characters, each of them equally well executed, the one in prose and the other in verse, the verse will be read a hundred times where the prose is read once.

Having thus explained a few of my reasons for writing in verse, and why I have chosen subjects from common life, and endeavored to bring my language near to the real language of men, if I have been too minute in pleading my own cause, I have at the same time been treating a subject of general interest; and for this reason a few words shall be added with reference solely to these particular poems, and to some defects which will probably be found in them. I am sensible that my associations must have sometimes been particular instead of general, and that, consequently, giving to things a false importance, I may have sometimes written upon unworthy subjects; but I am less apprehensive on this account, than that my language may frequently have suffered from those arbitrary connections of feelings and ideas with particular words and phrases, from which no man can altogether protect himself. Hence I have no doubt that, in some instances, feelings, even of the ludicrous, may be given to my readers by expressions which appeared to me tender and pathetic. Such faulty expressions, were I convinced they were faulty at present, and that they must necessarily continue to be so, I would willingly take all reasonable pains to correct. But it is dangerous to make these alterations on the simple authority of a few individuals, or even of certain classes of men; for where the understanding of an author is not convinced, or his feelings altered, this cannot be done without great injury to himself: for his own feelings are his stay and support; and, if he set them aside in one instance, he may be induced to repeat this act till his mind shall lose all confidence in itself, and become utterly debilitated. To this it may be added that the critic ought never to forget that he is himself exposed to the same errors as the poet, and perhaps in a much greater degree: for there can be no presumption in saying of most readers that it is not probable they will be so well acquainted with the various stages of meaning through which words have passed, or with the fickleness or stability of the relations of particular ideas to each other; and, above all, since they are so much less interested in the subject, they may decide lightly and carelessly.

Long as the reader has been detained, I hope he will permit me to caution him against a mode of false criticism which has been applied to poetry, in which the language closely resembles that of life and nature. Such verses have been triumphed over in parodies, of which Dr. Johnson's stanza is a fair specimen:—

> I put my hat upon my head
> And walked into the Strand,
> And there I met another man
> Whose hat was in his hand.

Immediately under these lines let us place one of the most justly admired stanzas of the *Babes in the Wood*.

> These pretty babes with hand in hand
> Went wandering up and down;
> But never more they saw the man
> Approaching from the town.

In both these stanzas the words, and the order of the words, in no respect differ from the most unimpassioned conversation. There are words in both, for example, "the Strand," and "the town," connected with none but the most familiar ideas; yet the one stanza we admit as admirable, and the other as a fair example of the superlatively contemptible. Whence arises this difference? Not from the metre, not from the language, not from the order of the words; but the *matter* expressed in Dr. Johnson's stanza is contemptible. The proper method of treating trivial and simple verses, to which Dr. Johnson's stanza would be a fair parallelism, is not to say, This is a bad kind of poetry, or, This is not poetry; but, This wants sense; it is neither interesting in itself, nor can *lead* to anything interesting; the images neither originate in that sane state of feeling which arises out of thought, nor can excite thought or feeling in the reader. This is the only sensible manner of dealing with such verses. Why trouble yourself about the species till you have previously decided upon the genus? Why take pains to prove that an ape is not a Newton, when it is self-evident that he is not a man?

One request I must make of my reader, which is, that in judging these poems he would decide by his own feelings genuinely, and not by reflection upon what will probably be the judgment of others. How common is it to hear a person say, I myself do not object to this style of composition, or this or that expression, but to such and such classes of people it will appear mean or ludicrous! This mode of criticism, so destructive of all sound unadulterated judgment, is almost universal: let the reader then abide, independently, by his own feelings, and, if he finds himself affected, let him not suffer such conjectures to interfere with his pleasure.

If an author, by any single composition, has impressed us with respect for his talents, it is useful to consider this as affording a presumption that on other occasions, where we have been displeased, he nevertheless may not have written ill or absurdly; and further, to give him so much credit for this one composition as may induce us to review what has displeased us with more care than we should otherwise have bestowed upon it. This is not only an act of justice, but, in our decisions upon poetry especially, may conduce in a high degree to the improvement of our own taste; for an *accurate* taste in poetry, and in all the other arts, as Sir Joshua Reynolds has observed, is an *acquired* talent, which can only be produced by thought and a long-continued intercourse with the best models of composition. This is mentioned, not with so ridiculous a purpose as to prevent the most inexperienced reader from judging for himself (I have already said that I wish him to judge for himself), but merely to temper the rashness of decision, and to suggest that, if poetry be a subject on which much time has not been bestowed, the judgment may be erroneous; and that, in many cases, it necessarily will be so.

Nothing would, I know, have so effectually contributed to further the end which I have in view, as to have shown of what kind the pleasure is, and how that pleasure is produced, which is confessedly produced by metrical composition essentially different from that which I have here endeavored to recommend: for the reader will say that he has been pleased by such composition; and what more can be done for him? The power of any art is limited; and he will suspect that, if it be proposed to furnish him with new friends, that can be only upon condition of his abandoning his old friends. Besides, as I have said, the reader is himself conscious of the pleasure which he has received from such composition, composition to which he has peculiarly attached the endearing name of poetry; and all men feel an habitual gratitude, and something of an honorable bigotry, for the objects which have long continued to please them: we not only wish to be pleased, but to be pleased in that particular way in which we have been accustomed to be pleased. There is in these feelings enough to resist a host of arguments; and I should be the less able to combat them successfully, as I am willing to allow that, in order entirely to enjoy the poetry which I am recommending, it would be necessary to give up much of what is ordinarily enjoyed. But, would my limits have permitted me to point out how this pleasure is produced, many obstacles might have been removed, and the reader assisted in perceiving that the powers of language are not so limited as he may suppose; and that it is possible for poetry to give other enjoyments, of a purer, more lasting, and more exquisite nature. This part of the subject has not been altogether neglected, but it has not been so much my present aim to prove that the interest excited by some other kinds of poetry is less vivid, and less worthy of the nobler powers of the mind, as to offer reasons for presuming that, if my purpose were fulfilled, a species of poetry would be produced which is genuine poetry, in its nature well adapted to interest mankind permanently, and likewise important in the multiplicity and quality of its moral relations.

From what has been said, and from a perusal of the poems, the reader will be able clearly to perceive the object which I had in view: he will determine how far it has been attained; and, what is a much more important question, whether it be worth attaining: and upon the decision of these two questions will rest my claim to the approbation of the public.

Coleridge

Samuel Taylor COLERIDGE (1772–1834) was the son of the vicar-schoolmaster of Ottery St. Mary, Devonshire. Educated at Christ's Hospital, London, where he was a school-fellow of Lamb, he entered Cambridge University, which he left to enlist in the army. His service did not last long, and he returned to Cambridge for a short time, taking no degree. Making the acquaintance of Southey, he became interested in a project for founding a "pantisocracy" on the banks of the Susquehanna River, but the plan was never carried out. The two poets married sisters, and Coleridge settled at Clevedon, later moving to Nether Stowey, Somerset, where Wordsworth was his neighbor. About 1796 he formed the habit of taking laudanum, which he fought unsuccessfully for the rest of his life. He published some poetry and joined with Wordsworth in producing the *Lyrical Ballads* in 1798, to which his best-known contribution was *The Ancient Mariner*. He had become a Unitarian, and was much sought after as a preacher; for a few weeks in 1798 he served a parish at Shrewsbury, where young Hazlitt first met him. This same year the Wedgwoods gave him an annuity, on condition that he should devote himself to literature, and soon after, with the Wordsworths, he spent a year in Germany, where his interest was aroused in German philosophy and letters. Returning to England, he continued his literary labors, despite bad health, which a journey to Malta and Italy improved. At Malta he acted for a while as secretary to the Governor, and at Rome he met Tieck, Humboldt, and Bunsen. At the end of 1806 he went back to England, and in 1808 delivered in London his first course of lectures on Shakespeare. He left his family with Southey at Keswick while he lived with Wordsworth at Grasmere, where he started *The Friend,* a short-lived periodical. There followed a period of visits to various people, during which he continued his lecturing and writing. While he was with John Morgan at Calne, he published *Christabel* and *Kubla Khan* (1816), and *Biographia Literaria* and *Sybilline Leaves* (1817). He appeared as a lecturer for the last time in 1818. In 1819 he took up his residence in the household of James Gillman, a surgeon, at Highgate, where, though far from well, he became the centre of a group of disciples, who spread the influence of his philosophical and theological thought. Toward the end of his life he grew conservative in politics, and returned to Trinitarianism, defending the State religion. His fame as a conversationalist—or rather as a monologist—has become traditional.

As a critic, Coleridge is to England what Lessing is to Germany, and Aristotle to Greece. He is objective, scientific in his analysis, thorough, adopting with full faith what has been tested and found good in the past, but pushing forward with new investigations of his own. After his brief but remarkable career as a poet, he became the first writer in England to devote himself almost entirely to criticism. Where previous critics had written, at most, a few essays, he wrote the *Biographia Literaria*—the greatest single book on literary criticism in our language. Much of his criticism is scattered in various places, in his *Table Talk* and in the reminiscences of men who heard his penetrating, almost inspired, discussions around the Gillman fireplace in Highgate.

Coleridge, like his immediate predecessor, Lessing, whom he called "a model of acute, spirited, sometimes stinging, but always argumentative and honorable criticism," refrains from laying down rigid laws, as did the neo-classicists, seeking only to find in a work of art the principles that underlie it. His creed is suggested in a sentence from the chapter on the *Lyrical Bal-*

lads in the *Biographia:* "Nothing can permanently please,
which does not contain in itself the reason why it is so, and not
otherwise." Trying to find this reason, he evolved his ideas on
imagination and fancy, poetry and what a poem is, the theory
of opposites, and other trenchant conclusions which the student will find in the pages below. His analysis of his friend
Wordsworth's poem is a model of incisive yet kindly criticism.

From BIOGRAPHIA LITERARIA

(1817)

CHAPTER XIV

Occasion of the *Lyrical Ballads,* and the objects originally proposed—
Preface to the second edition— The ensuing controversy, its causes and
acrimony— Philosophic definitions of a Poem and Poetry with scholia.

During the first year that Mr. Wordsworth and I were neighbors,
our conversations turned frequently on the two cardinal points of
poetry, the power of exciting the sympathy of the reader by a faithful adherence to the truth of nature, and the power of giving the
interest of novelty by the modifying colors of imagination. The
sudden charm which accidents of light and shade, which moonlight
or sunset diffused over a known and familiar landscape, appeared
to represent the practicability of combining both. These are the
poetry of nature. The thought suggested itself (to which of us I do
not recollect) that a series of poems might be composed of two sorts.
In the one, the incidents and agents were to be, in part at least,
supernatural; and the excellence aimed at was to consist in the interesting of the affections by the dramatic truth of such emotions
as would naturally accompany such situations, supposing them real.
And real in this sense they have been to every human being who,
from whatever source of delusion, has at any time believed himself
under supernatural agency. For the second class, subjects were to
be chosen from ordinary life; the characters and incidents were to
be such as will be found in every village and its vicinity, where there
is a meditative and feeling mind to seek after them, or to notice
them when they present themselves.

In this idea originated the plan of the *Lyrical Ballads;* in which
it was agreed that my endeavors should be directed to persons and

characters supernatural, or at least romantic; yet so as to transfer from our inward nature a human interest and a semblance of truth sufficient to procure for these shadows of imagination that willing suspension of disbelief for the moment, which constitutes poetic faith. Mr. Wordsworth, on the other hand, was to propose to himself as his object, to give the charm of novelty to things of every day, and to excite a feeling analogous to the supernatural, by awakening the mind's attention from the lethargy of custom, and directing it to the loveliness and the wonders of the world before us; an inexhaustible treasure, but for which, in consequence of the film of familiarity and selfish solicitude, we have eyes yet see not, ears that hear not, and hearts that neither feel nor understand.

With this view I wrote *The Ancient Mariner,* and was preparing, among other poems, *The Dark Ladie* and the *Christabel,* in which I should have more nearly realized my ideal than I had done in my first attempt. But Mr. Wordsworth's industry had proved so much more successful, and the number of his poems so much greater, that my compositions, instead of forming a balance, appeared rather an interpolation of heterogeneous matter. Mr. Wordsworth added two or three poems written in his own character, in the impassioned, lofty, and sustained diction which is characteristic of his genius. In this form the *Lyrical Ballads* were published, and were presented by him as an *experiment* whether subjects which from their nature rejected the usual ornaments and extra-colloquial style of poems in general, might not be so managed in the language of ordinary life as to produce the pleasurable interest which it is the peculiar business of poetry to impart. To the second edition he added a preface of considerable length; in which, notwithstanding some passages of apparently a contrary import, he was understood to contend for the extension of this style to poetry of all kinds, and to reject as vicious and indefensible all phrases and forms of style that were not included in what he (unfortunately, I think, adopting an equivocal expression) called the language of *real* life. From this preface, prefixed to poems in which it was impossible to deny the presence of original genius, however mistaken its direction might be deemed, arose the whole long-continued controversy. For from the conjunction of perceived power with supposed heresy I explain the inveteracy and in some instances, I grieve to say, the acrimonious passions, with which the controversy has been conducted by the assailants.

Had Mr. Wordsworth's poems been the silly, the childish things, which they were for a long time described as being; had they been really distinguished from the compositions of other poets merely by meanness of language and inanity of thought; had they indeed contained nothing more than what is found in the parodies and pretended imitations of them; they must have sunk at once, a dead weight, into the slough of oblivion, and have dragged the preface along with them. But year after year increased the number of Mr. Wordsworth's admirers. They were found, too, not in the lower classes of the reading public, but chiefly among young men of strong sensibility and meditative minds; and their admiration (inflamed perhaps in some degree by opposition) was distinguished by its intensity, I might almost say by its religious fervor. These facts, and the intellectual energy of the author, which was more or less consciously felt, where it was outwardly and even boisterously denied, meeting with sentiments of aversion to his opinions and of alarm at their consequences, produced an eddy of criticism which would of itself have borne up the poems by the violence with which it whirled them round and round. With many parts of this preface, in the sense attributed to them and which the words undoubtedly seem to authorize, I never concurred; but on the contrary objected to them as erroneous in principle and as contradictory (in appearance at least) both to other parts of the same preface and to the author's own practice in the greater number of the poems themselves. Mr. Wordsworth in his recent collection has, I find, degraded this prefatory disquisition to the end of his second volume, to be read or not at the reader's choice. But he has not, as far as I can discover, announced any change in his poetic creed. At all events, considering it as the source of a controversy in which I have been honored more than I deserve by the frequent conjunction of my name with his, I think it expedient to declare once for all in what points I coincide with his opinions, and in what points I altogether differ. But in order to render myself intelligible I must previously, in as few words as possible, explain my ideas, first, of a Poem, and secondly, of Poetry itself, in kind and in essence.

The office of philosophical disquisition consists in just distinction; while it is the privilege of the philosopher to preserve himself constantly aware that distinction is not division. In order to obtain adequate notions of any truth, we must intellectually separate its distinguishable parts; and this is the technical process of philosophy. But having so done, we must then restore them in our conceptions to the unity in which they actually co-exist, and this is the result of philosophy. A poem contains the same elements as a prose composition; the difference, therefore, must consist in a different combination of them, in consequence of a different object proposed. According to the difference of the object will be the difference of the combination. It is possible that the object may be merely to facilitate the recollection of any given facts or observations by artificial arrangement; and the composition will be a poem merely because it is distinguished from prose by metre, or by rhyme, or by both conjointly. In this, the lowest sense, a man might attribute the name of a poem to the well-known enumeration of the days in the several months:—

> Thirty days hath September,
> April, June, and November, &c.

and others of the same class and purpose. And as a particular pleasure is found in anticipating the recurrence of sounds and quantities, all compositions that have this charm superadded, whatever be their contents, *may* be entitled poems.

So much for the superficial form. A difference of object and contents supplies an additional ground of distinction. The immediate purpose may be the communication of truths,—either of truth absolute and demonstrable, as in works of science, or of facts experienced and recorded, as in history. Pleasure, and that of the highest and most permanent kind, may result from the attainment of the end, but it is not itself the immediate end. In other works the communication of pleasure may be the immediate purpose; and though truth, either moral or intellectual, ought to be the ultimate end, yet this will distinguish the character of the author, not the class to which the work belongs. Blessed indeed is that state of society in which the immediate purpose would be baffled by the perversion of the proper ultimate end; in which no charm of diction or imagery could exempt the *Bathyllus* even of an Anacreon, or the *Alexis* of Virgil, from disgust and aversion!

But the communication of pleasure may be the immediate object of a work not metrically composed; and that object may have been in a high degree attained, as in novels and romances. Would, then, the mere superaddition of metre, with or without rhyme, entitle these to the name of poems? The answer is, that nothing can permanently please which does not contain in itself the reason why it is so and not otherwise. If metre be superadded, all other parts must be made consonant with it. They must be such as to justify the perpetual and distinct attention to each part, which an exact correspondent recurrence of accent and sound are calculated to excite. The final definition, then, so deduced, may be thus worded. A poem is that species of composition which is opposed to works of science, by proposing for its *immediate* object pleasure, not truth; and from all other species (having this object in common with it) it is discriminated by proposing to itself such delight from the *whole* as is compatible with a distinct gratification from each component *part*.

Controversy is not seldom excited in consequence of the disputants attaching each a different meaning to the same word; and in few instances has this been more striking than in disputes concerning the present subject. If a man chooses to call every composition a poem which is rhyme, or measure, or both, I must leave his opinion uncontroverted. The distinction is at least competent to characterize the writer's intention. If it were subjoined that the whole is likewise entertaining or affecting, as a tale or as a series of interesting reflections, I of course admit this as another fit ingredient of a poem, and an additional merit. But if the definition sought for be that of a *legitimate* poem, I answer, it must be one the parts of which mutually support and explain each other, all in their proportion harmonizing with and supporting the purpose and known influences of metrical arrangement. The philosophic critics of all ages coincide with the ultimate judgment of all countries, in equally denying the praises of a just poem, on the one hand, to a series of striking lines or distiches each of which, absorbing the whole attention of the reader to itself, disjoins it from its context, and makes it a separate whole instead of a harmonizing part, and on the other hand, to an unsustained composition from which the reader collects rapidly the general result, unattracted by the component parts. The reader should be carried forward, not merely or chiefly by the mechanical impulse of curiosity, or by a restless desire to arrive at the final solution, but by the pleasurable activity of mind excited by the attractions of the journey itself. Like the motion of a serpent, which the Egyptians made the emblem of intellectual power, or like the path of sound through the air, at every step he pauses and half recedes, and from the retrogressive movement collects the force which again carries him onward. "Præcipitandus est liber spiritus," [1] says Petronius Arbiter most happily. The epithet *liber* here balances the preceding verb; and it is not easy to conceive more meaning condensed in fewer words.

[1] From the *Satyricon*, 118. "The free spirit must be urged onward."

But if this should be admitted as a satisfactory character of a poem, we have still to seek for a definition of poetry. The writings of Plato, and Bishop Taylor, and the *Theoria Sacra* of Burnet,[1] furnish undeniable proofs that poetry of the highest kind may exist without metre, and even without the contradistinguishing objects of a poem. The first chapter of *Isaiah* (indeed a very large portion of the whole book) is poetry in the most emphatic sense; yet it would be not less irrational than strange to assert that pleasure, and not truth, was the immediate object of the prophet. In short, whatever specific import we attach to the word poetry, there will be found involved in it, as a necessary consequence, that a poem of any length neither can be, nor ought to be, all poetry. Yet if an harmonious whole is to be produced, the remaining parts must be preserved in keeping with the poetry; and this can be no otherwise effected than by such a studied selection and artificial arrangement as will partake of one, though not a peculiar, property of poetry. And this again can be no other than the property of exciting a more continuous and equal attention than the language of prose aims at, whether colloquial or written.

My own conclusions on the nature of poetry, in the strictest use of the word, have been in part anticipated in the preceding disquisition on the fancy and imagination. What is poetry? is so nearly the same question with, What is a poet? that the answer to the one is involved in the solution of the other. For it is a distinction resulting from the poetic genius itself, which sustains and modifies the images, thoughts, and emotions of the poet's own mind.

The poet, described in ideal perfection, brings the whole soul of man into activity, with the subordination of its faculties to each other, according to their relative worth and dignity. He diffuses a tone and spirit of unity, that blends and (as it were) *fuses* each into each, by that synthetic and magical power to which we have exclusively appropriated the name of imagination. This power, first put in action by the will and understanding, and retained under their irremissive, though gentle and unnoticed, control (*laxis effertur habenis*),[2] reveals itself in the balance or reconciliation of opposite or discordant qualities: of sameness, with difference; of the general, with the concrete; the idea, with the image; the individual, with the representative; the sense of novelty and freshness, with old and

---

[1] Published in Latin, 1681; in English, 1684. Thomas Burnet (1635–1715) was a Yorkshire divine and master of the Charterhouse. His *Sacred Theory of the Earth* was highly praised by Addison.

[2] Carried along with loosened reins.

familiar objects; a more than usual state of emotion, with more than usual order; judgment ever awake, and steady self-possession, with enthusiasm and feeling profound or vehement; and while it blends and harmonizes the natural and the artificial, still subordinates art to nature, the manner to the matter, and our admiration of the poet to our sympathy with the poetry. "Doubtless," as Sir John Davies [1] observes of the soul (and his words may with slight alteration be applied, and even more appropriately, to the poetic imagination),—

> Doubtless this could not be, but that she turns
> Bodies to spirit by sublimation strange,
> As fire converts to fire the things it burns,
> As we our food into our nature change.
>
> From their gross matter she abstracts their forms,
> And draws a kind of quintessence from things;
> Which to her proper nature she transforms,
> To bear them light on her celestial wings.
>
> Thus does she, when from individual states
> She doth abstract the universal kinds;
> Which then, recloth'd in divers names and fates,
> Steal access through our senses to our minds.

Finally, good sense is the body of poetic genius, fancy its drapery, motion its life, and imagination the soul that is everywhere, and in each, and forms all into one graceful and intelligent whole.

CHAPTER XVII

Examination of the tenets peculiar to Mr. Wordsworth—Rustic life (above all, low and rustic life) especially unfavorable to the formation of a human diction—The best parts of language the product of philosophers, not of clowns or shepherds—Poetry essentially ideal and generic—The language of Milton as much the language of real life, yea, incomparably more so than that of the cottager.

As far then as Mr. Wordsworth in his preface contended, and most ably contended, for a reformation in our poetic diction; as far as he has evinced the truth of passion, and the dramatic propriety of those figures and metaphors in the original poets, which, stripped of their justifying reasons, and converted into mere artifices of con-

[1] A too-little known Elizabethan poet (1569–1626), whose *Nosce Teipsum* has been praised by Coleridge and by John Masefield.

nection or ornament, constitute the characteristic falsity in the poetic style of the moderns; and as far as he has, with equal acuteness and clearness, pointed out the process by which this change was effected, and the resemblances between that state into which the reader's mind is thrown by the pleasurable confusion of thought from an unaccustomed train of words and images, and that state which is induced by the natural language of empassioned feeling,—he undertook a useful task, and deserves all praise both for the attempt and for the execution. The provocations to this remonstrance in behalf of truth and nature were still of perpetual recurrence before and after the publication of this preface. I cannot likewise but add that the comparison of such poems of merit as have been given to the public within the last ten or twelve years, with the majority of those produced previously to the appearance of that preface, leave no doubt on my mind that Mr. Wordsworth is fully justified in believing his efforts to have been by no means ineffectual. Not only in the verses of those who have professed their admiration of his genius, but even of those who have distinguished themselves by hostility to his theory, and depreciation of his writings, are the impressions of his principles plainly visible. It is possible that with these principles others may have been blended, which are not equally evident, and some which are unsteady and subvertible from the narrowness or imperfection of their basis. But it is more than possible that these errors of defect or exaggeration, by kindling and feeding the controversy, may have conduced not only to the wider propagation of the accompanying truths, but that, by their frequent presentation to the mind in an excited state, they may have won for them a more permanent and practical result. A man will borrow a part from his opponent the more easily, if he feels himself justified in continuing to reject a part. While there remain important points in which he can still feel himself in the right, in which he still finds firm footing for continued resistance, he will gradually adopt those opinions which were the least remote from his own convictions, as not less congruous with his own theory than with that which he reprobates. In like manner, with a kind of instinctive prudence, he will abandon by little and little his weakest posts, till at length he seems to forget that they had ever belonged to him, or affects to consider them at most as accidental and "petty annexments," the removal of which leaves the citadel unhurt and unendangered.

My own differences from certain supposed parts of Mr. Wordsworth's theory ground themselves on the assumption that his words had been rightly interpreted as purporting that the proper diction for poetry in general consists altogether in a language taken, with due exceptions, from the mouths of men in real life,—a language which actually constitutes the natural conversation of men under the influence of natural feelings. My objection is, first, that in any sense this rule is applicable only to certain classes of poetry; secondly, that even to these classes it is not applicable except in such a sense as hath never by any one (as far as I know or have read) been denied or doubted; and lastly, that as far as, and in that degree in which it is practicable, it is yet as a rule useless, if not injurious, and therefore either need not or ought not to be practiced. The poet informs his reader that he had generally chosen low and rustic life, but not as low and rustic, or in order to repeat that pleasure, of doubtful moral effect, which persons of elevated rank and of superior refinement oftentimes derive from a happy imitation of the rude unpolished manners and discourse of their inferiors. For the pleasure so derived may be traced to three exciting causes. The first is the naturalness, in fact, of the things represented. The second is the apparent naturalness of the representation, as raised and qualified by an imperceptible infusion of the author's own knowledge and talent, which infusion does indeed constitute it an *imitation* as distinguished from a mere *copy*. The third cause may be found in the reader's conscious feeling of his superiority awakened by the contrast presented to him, even as for the same purpose the kings and great barons of yore retained sometimes actual clowns and fools, but more frequently shrewd and witty fellows in that character. These, however, were not Mr. Wordsworth's objects. He chose low and rustic life, "because in that condition the essential passions of the heart find a better soil, in which they can attain their maturity, are less under restraint, and speak a plainer and more emphatic language; because in that condition of life our elementary feelings co-exist in a state of greater simplicity, and consequently may be more accurately contemplated, and more forcibly communicated; because the manners of rural life germinate from those elementary feelings; and from the necessary character of rural occupations are more easily comprehended, and are more durable; and lastly, because in that condition the passions of men are incorporated with the beautiful and permanent forms of nature."

Now it is clear to me that, in the most interesting of the poems, in which the author is more or less dramatic, as *The Brothers*, *Michael*, *Ruth*, *The Mad Mother*, and others, the persons introduced are by no means taken from low or rustic life in the common acceptation of those words; and it is not less clear that the sentiments and language, as far as they can be conceived to have been really transferred from the minds and conversation of such persons, are attributable to causes and circumstances not necessarily connected with "their occupations and abode." The thoughts, feelings, language, and manners of the shepherd-farmers in the vales of Cumberland and Westmoreland, as far as they are actually adopted in those poems, may be accounted for from causes which will and do produce the same results in every state of life, whether in town or country. As the two principal I rank that independence, which raises a man above servitude, or daily toil for the profit of others, yet not above the necessity of industry and a frugal simplicity of domestic life, and the accompanying unambitious but solid and religious education, which has rendered few books familiar but the Bible and the liturgy or hymn-book. To this latter cause, indeed, which is so far accidental that it is the blessing of particular countries and a particular age, not the product of particular places or employments, the poet owes the show of probability that his personages might really feel, think, and talk with any tolerable resemblance to his representation. It is an excellent remark of Dr. Henry More's, that "a man of confined education, but of good parts, by constant reading of the Bible will naturally form a more winning and commanding rhetoric than those that are learned, the intermixture of tongues and of artificial phrases debasing *their* style." (*Enthusiasmus Triumphatus*,[1] Sec. xxxv.)

It is, moreover, to be considered that to the formation of healthy feelings, and a reflecting mind, negations involve impediments not less formidable than sophistication and vicious intermixture. I am convinced that for the human soul to prosper in rustic life a certain vantage-ground is prerequisite. It is not every man that is likely to be improved by a country life or by country labors. Education, or original sensibility, or both, must pre-exist, if the changes, forms, and incidents of nature are to prove a sufficient stimulant. And where these are not sufficient, the mind contracts and hardens by want of stimulants, and the man becomes selfish, sensual, gross, and hardhearted. Let the management of the Poor Laws in Liverpool, Manchester, or Bristol be compared with the ordinary dispensation of the poor-rates in agricultural villages, where the farmers are the overseers and guardians of the poor. If my own experience has not been particularly unfortunate, as well as that of the many respectable

---

[1] Published 1656. Henry More (1614-1687) was a leader of the Cambridge Platonists.

country clergymen with whom I have conversed on the subject, the result would engender more than skepticism concerning the desirable influences of low and rustic life in and for itself. Whatever may be concluded on the other side, from the stronger local attachments and enterprising spirit of the Swiss and other mountaineers, applies to a particular mode of pastoral life, under forms of property that permit and beget manners truly republican, not to rustic life in general, or to the absence of artificial cultivation. On the contrary, the mountaineers, whose manners have been so often eulogized, are in general better educated and greater readers than men of equal rank elsewhere. But where this is not the case, as among the peasantry of North Wales, the ancient mountains, with all their terrors and all their glories, are pictures to the blind and music to the deaf.

I should not have entered so much into detail upon this passage, but here seems to be the point to which all the lines of difference converge as to their source and centre. (I mean, as far as, and in whatever respect, my poetic creed does differ from the doctrines promulgated in this preface.) I adopt with full faith the principle of Aristotle, that poetry as poetry is essentially ideal, that it avoids and excludes all accident; that its apparent individualities of rank, character, or occupation must be representative of a class; and that the persons of poetry must be clothed with generic attributes, with the common attributes of the class,—not with such as one gifted individual might possibly possess, but such as from his situation it is most probable beforehand that he would possess. If my premises are right and my deductions legitimate, it follows that there can be no poetic medium between the swains of Theocritus and those of an imaginary golden age.

The characters of the vicar and the shepherd-mariner in the poem of *The Brothers*, that of the shepherd of Greenhead Ghyll in the *Michael*, have all the verisimilitude and representative quality that the purposes of poetry can require. They are persons of a known and abiding class, and their manners and sentiments the natural product of circumstances common to the class.

* * * *

On the other hand, in the poems which are pitched at a lower note, as the *Harry Gill*, and *Idiot Boy*, the feelings are those of human nature in general, though the poet has judiciously laid the scene in the country, in order to place himself in the vicinity of interesting images, without the necessity of ascribing a sentimental perception of their beauty to the persons of his drama. In the *Idiot Boy*, indeed, the mother's character is not so much a real and native product of a "situation where the essential passions of the heart find a better soil, in which they can attain their maturity and speak a plainer and more emphatic language," as it is an impersonation of an instinct abandoned by judgment. Hence the two following charges seem to me not wholly groundless: at least, they are the only plausible objections which I have heard to that fine poem. The one is, that the author has not, in the poem itself, taken sufficient care to preclude from the reader's fancy the disgusting images of ordinary morbid idiocy, which yet it was by no means his intention to represent. He has even by the "burr, burr, burr," uncounteracted by any preceding description of the boy's beauty, assisted in recalling them. The other is, that the idiocy of the boy is so evenly balanced by the folly of the mother as to present to the general reader rather a laughable burlesque on the blindness of anile dotage, than an analytic display of maternal affection in its ordinary workings.

In *The Thorn* the poet himself acknowledges in a note the necessity of an introductory poem, in which he should have portrayed the character of the person from whom the words of the poem are supposed to proceed: a superstitious man, moderately imaginative, of slow faculties and deep feelings, "a captain of a small trading vessel, for example, who, being past the middle age of life, had retired upon an annuity, or small independent income, to some village or country town of which he was not a native, or in which he had not been accustomed to live. Such men, having nothing to do, become credulous and talkative from indolence." But in a poem, still more in a lyric poem (and the Nurse in Shakespeare's *Romeo and Juliet* alone prevents me from extending the remark even to dramatic poetry, if indeed the Nurse itself can be deemed altogether a case in point), it is not possible to imitate truly a dull and garrulous discourser, without repeating the effects of dullness and garrulity. However this may be, I dare assert that the parts (and these form the far larger portion of the whole) which might as well or still better have proceeded from the poet's own imagination, and have been spoken in his own character, are those which have given, and which will continue to give, universal delight; and that the passages exclusively appropriate to the supposed narrator, such as the last couplet of the third stanza,[1] the seven last lines of the tenth, and the five following stanzas, with the exception of the four admirable lines at the commencement of

---

[1] Here Coleridge quotes about sixty lines from an earlier version of *The Thorn*.

the fourteenth, are felt by many unprejudiced and unsophisticated hearts as sudden and unpleasant sinkings from the height to which the poet had previously lifted them, and to which he again re-elevates both himself and his reader.

If, then, I am compelled to doubt the theory by which the choice of characters was to be directed, not only *a priori*, from grounds of reason, but both from the few instances in which the poet himself need be supposed to have been governed by it, and from the comparative inferiority of those instances; still more must I hesitate in my assent to the sentence which immediately follows the former citation, and which I can neither admit as particular fact or as general rule. "The language too of these men is adopted (purified indeed from what appear to be its real defects, from all lasting and rational causes of dislike or disgust), because such men hourly communicate with the best objects from which the best part of language is originally derived; and because, from their rank in society and the sameness and narrow circle of their intercourse, being less under the action of social vanity, they convey their feelings and notions in simple and unelaborated expressions." To this I reply that a rustic's language, purified from all provincialism and grossness, and so far reconstructed as to be made consistent with the rules of grammar (which are in essence no other than the laws of universal logic, applied to psychological materials), will not differ from the language of any other man of common sense, however learned or refined he may be, except as far as the notions which the rustic has to convey are fewer and more indiscriminate. This will become still clearer, if we add the consideration (equally important though less obvious) that the rustic, from the more imperfect development of his faculties, and from the lower state of their cultivation, aims almost solely to convey insulated facts, either those of his scanty experience or his traditional belief; while the educated man chiefly seeks to discover and express those connections of things, or those relative bearings of fact to fact, from which some more or less general law is deducible. For facts are valuable to a wise man chiefly as they lead to the discovery of the indwelling law which is the true being of things, the sole solution of their modes of existence, and in the knowledge of which consists our dignity and our power.

As little can I agree with the assertion that from the objects with which the rustic hourly communicates the best part of language is formed. For first, if to communicate with an object implies such an acquaintance with it as renders it capable of being discriminately reflected on, the distinct knowledge of an uneducated rustic would furnish a very scanty vocabulary. The few things, and modes of action, requisite for his bodily conveniences, would alone be individualized, while all the rest of nature would be expressed by a small number of confused general terms. Secondly, I deny that the words and combinations of words derived from the objects with which the rustic is familiar, whether with distinct or confused knowledge, can be justly said to form the best part of language. It is more than probable that many classes of the brute creation possess discriminating sounds, by which they can convey to each other notices of such objects as concern their food, shelter, or safety. Yet we hesitate to call the aggregate of such sounds a language, otherwise than metaphorically. The best part of human language, properly so called, is derived from reflection on the acts of the mind itself. It is formed by a voluntary appropriation of fixed symbols to internal acts, to processes and results of imagination, the greater part of which have no place in the consciousness of uneducated man, though in civilized society, by imitation and passive remembrance of what they hear from their religious instructors and other superiors, the most uneducated share in the harvest which they neither sowed nor reaped. If the history of the phrases in hourly currency among our peasants were traced, a person not previously aware of the fact would be surprised at finding so large a number which three or four centuries ago were the exclusive property of the universities and the schools, and at the commencement of the Reformation had been transferred from the school to the pulpit, and thus gradually passed into common life. The extreme difficulty, and often the impossibility, of finding words for the simplest moral and intellectual processes of the languages of uncivilized tribes has proved perhaps the weightiest obstacle to the progress of our most zealous and adroit missionaries. Yet these tribes are surrounded by the same nature as our peasants are, but in still more impressive forms, and they are, moreover, obliged to particularize many more of them. When, therefore, Mr. Wordsworth adds, "accordingly, such a language" (meaning, as before, the language of rustic life purified from provincialism), "arising out of repeated experience and regular feelings, is a more permanent, and a far more philosophical language, than that which is frequently substituted for it by poets, who think they are conferring honor upon themselves and their art in proportion as they indulge in arbitrary and capricious habits of expression,"—it may be answered that the language which he has in view can be attributed to rustics with no greater right than the style of Hooker or Bacon to Tom Brown or Sir Roger L'Estrange.[1] Doubtless, if what is peculiar to each were omitted in each, the result must needs be the same. Further, that the poet who uses an illogical diction, or a style fitted to excite only the low and changeable pleasure of wonder by means of groundless novelty, substitutes a language of folly and vanity, not for that of the rustic, but for that of good sense and natural feeling.

Here let me be permitted to remind the reader that the positions which I controvert are contained in the sentences: "a selection of the real language of men"; "the language of these men" (i.e. men in low and rustic life) "I propose to myself to imitate, and, as far as is possible, to adopt the very language of men." "Between the language of prose and that of metrical composition, there neither is, nor can be, any essential difference." It is against these exclusively that my opposition is directed.

I object, in the very first instance, to an equivocation in the use of the word "real." Every man's language varies, according to the extent of his knowledge, the activity of his faculties, and the depth or quickness of his feelings. Every man's language has, first, its individualities; secondly, the common properties of the class to which he belongs; and thirdly, words and phrases of universal use. The language of Hooker, Bacon, Bishop Taylor, and Burke differs from the common language of the learned class only by the superior number and novelty of the thoughts and relations which they had to convey. The language of Algernon Sidney [2] differs not at all from that which every well-educated gentleman would wish to write, and (with due allowances for the undeliberateness, and less connected train of thinking natural and proper to conversation) such as he would wish to talk. Neither one nor the other differ half as much from the general language of cultivated society as the language of Mr. Wordsworth's homeliest composition differs from that of a common peasant. For "real," therefore, we must substitute ordinary, or *lingua communis*. And this, we have proved, is no more to be found in the phraseology of low and rustic life than in that of any other class. Omit the peculiarities of each, and the result of course must be common to all. And assuredly the omissions and changes to be made in the language

---

[1] Thomas Brown (1663–1704) and Roger L'Estrange (1616–1704), satirists and pamphleteers.

[2] Grand-nephew of Sir Philip (1622–1683), was active in politics until his implication in the Rye House Plot for which he was tried and executed. His *Discourses Concerning Government* was published in 1698, after his death.

of rustics, before it could be transferred to any species of poem (except the drama or other professed imitation), are at least as numerous and weighty as would be required in adapting to the same purpose the ordinary language of tradesmen and manufacturers. Not to mention that the language so highly extolled by Mr. Wordsworth varies in every county, nay in every village, according to the accidental character of the clergyman, the existence or non-existence of schools, or even, perhaps, as the exciseman, publican, or barber happen to be, or not to be, zealous politicians and readers of the weekly newspaper *pro bono publico*. Anterior to cultivation, the *lingua communis* of every country, as Dante has well observed, exists everywhere in parts, and nowhere as a whole.

Neither is the case rendered at all more tenable by the words "in a state of excitement." For the nature of a man's words, when he is strongly affected by joy, grief, or anger, must necessarily depend on the number and quality of the general truths, conceptions, and images, and of the words expressing them, with which his mind had been previously stored. For the property of passion is not to create, but to set in increased activity. At least, whatever new connections of thoughts or images, or (which is equally, if not more than equally, the appropriate effect of strong excitement) whatever generalizations of truth or experience the heat of passion may produce, yet the terms of their conveyance must have pre-existed in his former conversations, and are only collected and crowded together by the unusual stimulation. It is indeed very possible to adopt in a poem the unmeaning repetitions, habitual phrases, and other blank counters, which an unfurnished or confused understanding interposes at short intervals, in order to keep hold of his subject, which is still slipping from him, and to give him time for recollection, or, in mere aid of vacancy, as in the scanty companies of a country stage the same player pops backwards and forwards, in order to prevent the appearance of empty spaces, in the procession of *Macbeth* or *Henry VIII*. But what assistance to the poet, or ornament to the poem, these can supply, I am at a loss to conjecture. Nothing assuredly can differ in origin or in mode more widely from the apparent tautologies of intense and turbulent feeling, in which the passion is greater and of longer endurance than to be exhausted or satisfied by a single representation of the image or incident exciting it. Such repetitions I admit to be a beauty of the highest kind, as illustrated by Mr. Wordsworth himself from the song of Deborah:

"At her feet he bowed, he fell, he lay down; at her feet he bowed, he fell; where he bowed, there he fell down dead." [1]

Chapter XVIII

Language of metrical composition, why and wherein essentially different from that of prose—Origin and elements of metre—Its necessary consequences, and the conditions thereby imposed on the metrical writer in the choice of his diction.

I conclude, therefore, that the attempt is impracticable; and that, were it not impracticable, it would still be useless. For the very power of making the selection implies the previous possession of the language selected. Or where can the poet have lived? And by what rules could he direct his choice, which would not have enabled him to select and arrange his words by the light of his own judgment? We do not adopt the language of a class by the mere adoption of such words exclusively as that class would use, or at least understand; but likewise by following the order in which the words of such men are wont to succeed each other. Now this order, in the intercourse of uneducated men, is distinguished from the diction of their superiors in knowledge and power by the greater disjunction and separation in the component parts of that, whatever it be, which they wish to communicate. There is a want of that prospectiveness of mind, that surview, which enables a man to foresee the whole of what he is to convey, appertaining to any one point; and by this means so to subordinate and arrange the different parts according to their relative importance, as to convey it at once, and as an organized whole.

Now I will take the first stanza, on which I have chanced to open, in the *Lyrical Ballads*. It is one of the most simple and the least peculiar in its language:

> In distant countries I have been,
> And yet I have not often seen
> A healthy man, a man full grown,
> Weep in the public roads, alone.
> But such a one, on English ground,
> And in the broad highway, I met;
> Along the broad highway he came,

[1] Judges, v: 27.

His cheeks with tears were wet.
Sturdy he seemed, though he was sad,
And in his arms a lamb he had.

The words here are doubtless such as are current in all ranks of life: and of course not less so in the hamlet and cottage, than in the shop, manufactory, college, or palace. But is this the order in which the rustic would have placed the words? I am grievously deceived, if the following less compact mode of commencing the same tale be not a far more faithful copy. "I have been in a many parts far and near, and I don't know that I ever saw before a man crying by himself in the public road; a grown man I mean, that was neither sick nor hurt," etc., etc. But when I turn to the following stanza in *The Thorn:*

At all times of the day and night
This wretched woman thither goes,
And she is known to every star
And every wind that blows:
And there beside the thorn she sits,
When the blue daylight's in the skies:
And when the whirlwind's on the hill,
Or frosty air is keen and still;
And to herself she cries,
Oh misery! Oh misery!
Oh woe is me! Oh misery!

and compare this with the language of ordinary men, or with that which I can conceive at all likely to proceed, in real life, from such a narrator as is supposed in the note to the poem—compare it either in the succession of the images or of the sentences—I am reminded of the sublime prayer and hymn of praise which Milton, in opposition to an established liturgy, presents as a fair specimen of common extemporary devotion, and such as we might expect to hear from every self-inspired minister of a conventicle! And I reflect with delight, how little a mere theory, though of his own workmanship, interferes with the processes of genuine imagination in a man of true poetic genius, who possesses, as Mr. Wordsworth, if ever man did, most assuredly does possess,

The Vision and the Faculty divine.

One point then alone remains, but that the most important; its examination having been, indeed, my chief inducement for the preceding inquisition. "There neither is or can be any essential difference between the language of prose and metrical composition." Such is Mr. Wordsworth's assertion. Now prose itself, at least in all argumentative and consecutive works, differs, and ought to differ, from the language of conversation; even as reading ought to differ from talking. Unless, therefore, the difference denied be that of the mere words, as materials common to all styles of writing, and not of the style itself in the universally admitted sense of the term, it might be naturally presumed that there must exist a still greater between the ordonnance of poetic composition and that of prose, than is expected to distinguish prose from ordinary conversation.

There are not, indeed, examples wanting in the history of literature, of apparent paradoxes that have summoned the public wonder as new and startling truths, but which on examination have shrunk into tame and harmless truisms; as the eyes of a cat, seen in the dark, have been mistaken for flames of fire. But Mr. Wordsworth is among the last men to whom a delusion of this kind would be attributed by any one who had enjoyed the slightest opportunity of understanding his mind and character. Where an objection has been anticipated by such an author as natural, his answer to it must needs be interpreted in some sense which either is, or has been, or is capable of being controverted. My object, then, must be to discover some other meaning for the term "essential difference" in this place, exclusive of the indistinction and community of the words themselves. For whether there ought to exist a class of words in the English in any degree resembling the poetic dialect of the Greek and Italian, is a question of very subordinate importance. The number of such words would be small indeed in our language; and even in the Italian and Greek, they consist not so much of different words as of slight differences in the forms of declining and conjugating the same words; forms, doubtless, which having been, at some period more or less remote, the common grammatic flexions of some tribe or province, had been accidentally appropriated to poetry by the general admiration of certain master intellects, the first established lights of inspiration, to whom that dialect happened to be native.

Essence, in its primary signification, means the principle of individuation, the inmost principle of the possibility of any thing, as that particular thing. It is equivalent to the idea of a thing, whenever we use the word *idea* with philosophic precision. Existence, on the other hand, is distinguished from essence by the superinduction of reality. Thus we speak of the essence and essential properties of a circle; but we do not therefore assert, that any thing which really exists is mathematically circular. Thus too, without any tautology, we contend for the existence of the Supreme Being; that is, for a reality correspondent to the idea. There is, next, a secondary use of the word essence, in which it signifies the point or ground of contra-distinction between two modifications of the same substance or sub-ject. Thus we should be allowed to say, that the style of architecture of Westminster Abbey is essentially different from that of Saint Paul's, even though both had been built with blocks cut into the same form, and from the same quarry. Only in this latter sense of the term must it have been denied by Mr. Wordsworth (for in this sense alone is it affirmed by the general opinion) that the language of poetry (*i. e.*, the formal construction, or architecture, of the words and phrases) is essentially different from that of prose. Now the burthen of the proof lies with the oppugner, not with the sup-porters of the common belief. Mr. Wordsworth, in consequence, assigns as the proof of his position, "that not only the language of a large portion of every good poem, even of the most elevated charac-ter, must necessarily, except with reference to the metre, in no respect differ from that of good prose, but likewise that some of the most interesting parts of the best poems will be found to be strictly the language of prose, when prose is well written. The truth of this assertion might be demonstrated by innumerable passages from al-most all the poetical writings even of Milton himself." He then quotes Gray's sonnet:

> In vain to me the smiling mornings shine,
> And reddening Phœbus lifts his golden fire;
> The birds in vain their amorous descant join
> Or cheerful fields resume their green attire;
> These ears, alas! for other notes repine;
> *A different object do these eyes require;*
> *My lonely anguish melts no heart but mine,*
> *And in my breast the imperfect joys expire!*
> Yet morning smiles the busy race to cheer,
> And new-born pleasure brings to happier men;
> The fields to all their wonted tribute bear,
> To warm their little loves the birds complain.
> *I fruitless mourn to him who cannot hear,*
> *And weep the more because I weep in vain;*

and adds the following remark: "It will easily be perceived, that the only part of this sonnet which is of any value is the lines printed in italics. It is equally obvious that, except in the rhyme, and in the use of the single word 'fruitless' for 'fruitlessly,' which is so far a defect, the language of these lines does in no respect differ from that of prose."

An idealist defending his system by the fact, that when asleep we often believe ourselves awake, was well answered by his plain neighbor, "Ah! but when awake do we ever believe ourselves asleep?" Things identical must be convertible. The preceding passage seems to rest on a similar sophism. For the question is not, whether there may not occur in prose an order of words, which would be equally proper in a poem; nor whether there are not beautiful lines and sentences of frequent occurrence in good poems, which would be equally becoming as well as beautiful in good prose; for neither the one or the other has ever been either denied or doubted by any one. The true question must be, whether there are not modes of expression, a construction, and an order of sentences, which are in their fit and natural place in a serious prose composition, but would be disproportionate and heterogeneous in metrical poetry; and, *vice versâ*, whether in the language of a serious poem there may not be an arrangement both of words and sentences, and a use and selection of (what are called) figures of speech, both as to their kind, their frequency, and their occasions, which on a subject of equal weight would be vicious and alien in correct and manly prose. I contend, that in both cases this unfitness of each for the place of the other frequently will and ought to exist.

And, first, from the origin of metre. This I would trace to the balance in the mind effected by that spontaneous effort which strives to hold in check the workings of passion. It might be easily explained likewise in what manner this salutary antagonism is assisted by the very state which it counteracts; and how this balance of antagonists became organized into metre (in the usual acceptation of that term) by a supervening act of the will and judgment, consciously and for the foreseen purpose of pleasure. Assuming these principles as the data of our argument, we deduce from them two legitimate conditions, which the critic is entitled to expect in every metrical work. First, that as the elements of metre owe their existence to a state of increased excitement, so the metre itself should be accompanied by the natural language of excitement. Secondly, that as these elements are formed into metre artificially, by a voluntary act, with the design and for the purpose of blending delight with emotion, so the traces of present volition should throughout the metrical language be proportionally discernible. Now these two conditions must be reconciled and co-present. There must be not only a partnership, but a union; an interpenetration of passion and of will, of spontaneous impulse and of voluntary purpose. Again, this union can be manifested only in a frequency of forms and figures of speech (originally the off-spring of passion, but now the adopted children of power) greater than would be desired or endured, where the emotion is not voluntarily encouraged, and kept up for the sake of that pleasure, which such emotion so tempered and mastered by the will is found capable of communicating. It not only dictates, but of itself tends to produce, a more frequent employment of picturesque and vivifying language than would be natural in any other case in which there did not exist, as there does in the present, a previous and well understood, though tacit, compact between the poet and his reader, that the latter is entitled to expect, and the former bound to supply, this species and degree of pleasurable excitement. We may in some measure apply to this union the answer of Polixenes, in the *Winter's Tale,* to Perdita's neglect of the streaked gilly-flowers, because she had heard it said:

> There is an art which in their piedness shares
> With great creating nature.
>
> Pol.   Say there be.
> Yet nature is made better by no mean,
> But nature makes that mean. So over that art,
> Which you say adds to nature, is an art
> That nature makes! You see, sweet maid, we marry
> *A gentler scion to the wildest stock:*
> And make conceive a bark of baser kind
> By bud of nobler race. This is an art,
> Which does mend nature—change it rather; but
> The art itself is nature.

Secondly, I argue from the effects of metre. As far as metre acts in and for itself, it tends to increase the vivacity and susceptibility both of the general feelings and of the attention. This effect it produces by the continued excitement of surprise, and by the quick reciprocations of curiosity still gratified and still re-excited, which are too slight indeed to be at any one moment objects of distinct consciousness, yet become considerable in their aggregate influence. As a medicated atmosphere, or as wine during animated conversation, they act powerfully, though themselves unnoticed. Where, therefore, correspondent food and appropriate matter are not provided for the attention and feelings thus roused, there must needs be a disappointment felt; like that of leaping in the dark from the last step of a staircase, when we had prepared our muscles for a leap of three or four.

The discussion on the powers of metre in the preface is highly ingenious, and touches at all points on truth. But I cannot find any statement of its powers considered abstractly and separately. On the contrary, Mr. Wordsworth seems always to estimate metre by the powers which it exerts during (and, as I think, in consequence of) its combination with other elements of poetry. Thus the previous difficulty is left unanswered, what the elements are with which it must be combined in order to produce its own effects to any pleasurable purpose. Double and trisyllable rhymes, indeed, form a lower species of wit, and, attended to exclusively for their own sake, may become a source of momentary amusement; as in poor Smart's [1] distich to the Welch Squire who had promised him a hare:

> Tell me, thou son of great Cadwallader!
> Hast sent the hare? or hast thou swallow'd her?

But for any poetic purposes, metre resembles (if the aptness of the simile may excuse its meanness) yeast, worthless or disagreeable by itself, but giving vivacity and spirit to the liquor with which it is proportionally combined.

The reference to the *Children in the Wood* by no means satisfies my judgment. We all willingly throw ourselves back for awhile into the feelings of our childhood. This ballad, therefore, we read under such recollections of our own childish feelings, as would equally endear to us poems which Mr. Wordsworth himself would regard as faulty in the opposite extreme of gaudy and technical ornament. Before the invention of printing and, in a still greater degree, before the introduction of writing, metre, especially alliterative metre (whether alliterative at the beginning of the words, as in *Pierce Plowman*, or at the end as in rhymes), possessed an independent value as assisting the recollection, and consequently the preservation, of any series of truths or incidents. But I am not convinced by the collation of facts that the *Children in the Wood* owes either its preservation or its popularity to its metrical form. Mr. Marshal's repository affords a number of tales in prose inferior in pathos and general merit, some of as old a date, and many as widely popular. *Tom Hickathrift, Jack the Giant Killer, Goody Two Shoes*, and *Little Red*

---

[1] Christopher Smart (1722–1771), poet and satirist, died insane and in debt.

Riding Hood are formidable rivals. And that they have continued in prose cannot be fairly explained by the assumption that
the comparative meanness of their thoughts and images precluded
even the humblest forms of metre. The scene of *Goody Two Shoes*
in the church is perfectly susceptible of metrical narration; and
among the Θαύματα θαυμαστότατα [1] even of the present age, I do not
recollect a more astonishing image than that of the "whole rookery,
that flew out of the giant's beard," scared by the tremendous voice
with which this monster answered the challenge of the heroic Tom
Hickathrift!

If from these we turn to compositions universally, and independently of all early associations, beloved and admired, would the *Maria,
The Monk,* or the *Poor Man's Ass* of Sterne, be read with more delight, or have a better chance of immortality, had they, without any
change in the diction, been composed in rhyme, than in their present
state? If I am not grossly mistaken, the general reply would be in the
negative. Nay, I will confess, that in Mr. Wordsworth's own volumes, the *Anecdote for Fathers, Simon Lee, Alice Fell,* the *Beggars,*
and the *Sailor's Mother,* notwithstanding the beauties which are to
be found in each of them where the poet interposes the music of
his own thoughts, would have been more delightful to me in prose,
told and managed as by Mr. Wordsworth they would have been, in
a moral essay or pedestrian tour.

Metre in itself is simply a stimulant of the attention, and therefore excites the question, Why is the attention to be thus stimulated?
Now the question cannot be answered by the pleasure of the metre
itself: for this we have shown to be conditional, and dependent on
the appropriateness of the thoughts and expressions to which the
metrical form is superadded. Neither can I conceive any other answer
that can be rationally given, short of this: I write in metre, because
I am about to use a language different from that of prose. Besides,
where the language is not such, how interesting soever the reflections
are that are capable of being drawn by a philosophic mind from the
thoughts or incidents of the poem, the metre itself must often become feeble. Take the three last stanzas of the *Sailor's Mother,* for
instance. If I could for a moment abstract from the effect produced
on the author's feelings as a man, by the incident at the time of its
real occurrence, I would dare appeal to his own judgment, whether in
the metre itself he found sufficient reason for their being written
metrically?

[1] Wonder of wonders.

And thus continuing, she said
I had a Son, who many a day
Sailed on the seas; but he is dead;
In Denmark he was cast away:
And I have travelled far as Hull to see
What clothes he might have left, or other property.

The Bird and Cage, they both were his;
'T was my Son's Bird; and neat and trim
He kept it: many voyages
This Singing-bird hath gone with him;
When last he sailed he left the Bird behind;
As it might be, perhaps, from bodings of his mind.

He to a fellow-lodger's care
Had left it, to be watched and fed,
Till he came back again; and there
I found it when my Son was dead;
And now, God help me for my little wit!
I trail it with me, Sir! he took so much delight in it.

If disproportioning the emphasis we read these stanzas so as to make the rhymes perceptible, even trisyllable rhymes could scarcely produce an equal sense of oddity and strangeness, as we feel here in finding rhymes at all in sentences so exclusively colloquial. I would further ask whether, but for that visionary state into which the figure of the woman and the susceptibility of his own genius had placed the poet's imagination (a state which spreads its influence and coloring over all, that co-exists with the exciting cause, and in which

> The simplest, and the most familiar things
> Gain a strange power of spreading awe around them [1]) —

I would ask the poet whether he would not have felt an abrupt down-fall in these verses from the preceding stanza?

[1] Altered from the description of Night-Mair in the *Remorse*.
> Oh Heaven! 't was frightful! Now run down and stared at,
> By hideous shapes that cannot be remembered:
> Now seeing nothing and imagining nothing:
> But only being afraid—stifled with fear!
> While every goodly or familiar form
> Had a strange power of spreading terror round me.

N.B. Though Shakespeare has for his own all-justifying purposes introduced the *Night-Mare* with her own foals, yet Mair means a Sister, or perhaps a Hag. (Coleridge.)

The ancient spirit is not dead;
Old times, thought I, are breathing there!
Proud was I, that my country bred
Such strength, a dignity so fair!
She begged an alms, like one in poor estate;
I looked at her again, nor did my pride abate.

It must not be omitted, and is besides worthy of notice, that those stanzas furnish the only fair instance that I have been able to discover in all Mr. Wordsworth's writings of an actual adoption, or true imitation, of the real and very language of low and rustic life, freed from provincialisms.

Thirdly, I deduce the position from all the causes elsewhere assigned, which render metre the proper form of poetry, and poetry imperfect and defective without metre. Metre therefore having been connected with poetry most often and by a peculiar fitness, whatever else is combined with metre must, though it be not itself essentially poetic, have nevertheless some property in common with poetry, as an intermedium of affinity, a sort (if I may dare borrow a well-known phrase from technical chemistry) of *mordaunt* between it and the superadded metre. Now poetry, Mr. Wordsworth truly affirms, does always imply passion: which word must be here understood, in its most general sense, as an excited state of the feelings and faculties. And as every passion has its proper pulse, so will it likewise have its characteristic modes of expression. But where there exists that degree of genius and talent which entitles a writer to aim at the honors of a poet, the very act of poetic composition itself is, and is allowed to imply and to produce, an unusual state of excitement, which of course justifies and demands a correspondent difference of language, as truly, though not perhaps in as marked a degree, as the excitement of love, fear, rage, or jealousy. The vividness of the descriptions or declamations in Donne, or Dryden, is as much and as often derived from the force and fervor of the describer, as from the reflections, forms, or incidents which constitute their subject and materials. The wheels take fire from the mere rapidity of their motion. To what extent, and under what modifications, this may be admitted to act, I shall attempt to define in an after remark on Mr. Wordsworth's reply to this objection, or rather on his objection to this reply, as already anticipated in his preface.

Fourthly, and as intimately connected with this, if not the same argument in a more general form, I adduce the high spiritual instinct of the human being impelling us to seek unity by harmonious adjustment, and thus establishing the principle, that all the parts of an organized whole must be assimilated to the more important and essential parts. This and the preceding arguments may be strengthened by the reflection, that the composition of a poem is among the imitative arts; and that imitation, as opposed to copying, consists either in the interfusion of the same throughout the radically different, or of the different throughout a base radically the same.

Lastly, I appeal to the practice of the best poets, of all countries and in all ages, as authorizing the opinion (deduced from all the foregoing) that in every import of the word essential, which would not here involve a mere truism, there may be, is, and ought to be, an essential difference between the language of prose and of metrical composition.

In Mr. Wordsworth's criticism of Gray's *Sonnet*, the reader's sympathy with his praise or blame of the different parts is taken for granted rather perhaps too easily. He has not, at least, attempted to win or compel it by argumentative analysis. In my conception at least, the lines rejected as of no value do, with the exception of the two first, differ as much and as little from the language of common life, as those which he has printed in italics as possessing genuine excellence. Of the five lines thus honorably distinguished, two of them differ from prose even more widely than the lines which either precede or follow, in the position of the words:

> *A different object do these eyes require;*
> My lonely anguish melts no heart but mine;
> *And in my breast the imperfect joys expire.*

But were it otherwise, what would this prove but a truth of which no man ever doubted?—videlicet, that there are sentences, which would be equally in their place both in verse and prose. Assuredly it does not prove the point which alone requires proof; namely, that there are not passages, which would suit the one and not suit the other. The first line of this sonnet is distinguished from the ordinary language of men by the epithet to morning. (For we will set aside, at present, the consideration, that the particular word "smiling" is hackneyed, and—as it involves a sort of personification—not quite congruous with the common and material attribute of shining.) And, doubtless, this adjunction of epithets for the purpose of additional description, where no particular attention is demanded for the quality of the thing, would be noticed as giving a poetic cast to a man's conversation. Should the sportsman exclaim, "Come boys!

the rosy morning calls you up," he will be supposed to have some
song in his head. But no one suspects this when he says, "A wet
morning shall not confine us to our beds." This then is either a defect
in poetry, or it is not. Whoever should decide in the affirmative, I
would request him to re-peruse any one poem of any confessedly
great poet from Homer to Milton, or from Æschylus to Shakespeare;
and to strike out (in thought I mean) every instance of this kind.
If the number of these fancied erasures did not startle him, or if he
continued to deem the work improved by their total omission, he
must advance reasons of no ordinary strength and evidence, reasons
grounded in the essence of human nature. Otherwise I should not
hesitate to consider him as a man not so much proof against all authority as dead to it.

The second line,

And reddening Phœbus lifts his golden fire,

has indeed almost as many faults as words. But then it is a bad line,
not because the language is distinct from that of prose, but because
it conveys incongruous images, because it confounds the cause and
the effect, the real thing with the personified representative of the
thing; in short, because it differs from the language of good sense.
That the "Phœbus" is hackneyed, and a schoolboy image, is an accidental fault, dependent on the age in which the author wrote, and
not deduced from the nature of the thing. That it is part of an ex-
ploded mythology, is an objection more deeply grounded. Yet when
the torch of ancient learning was rekindled, so cheering were its
beams, that our eldest poets, cut off by Christianity from all accredited machinery, and deprived of all acknowledged guardians and
symbols of the great objects of nature, were naturally induced to
adopt, as a poetic language, those fabulous personages, those forms of
the supernatural in nature, which had given them such dear delight
in the poems of their great masters. Nay, even at this day what
scholar of genial taste will not so far sympathize with them, as to
read with pleasure in Petrarch, Chaucer, or Spenser, what he would
perhaps condemn as puerile in a modern poet?

I remember no poet, whose writings would safelier stand the test
of Mr. Wordsworth's theory, than Spenser. Yet will Mr. Wordsworth say, that the style of the following stanzas is either undistinguished from prose, and the language of ordinary life? Or that it is
vicious, and that the stanzas are blots in the *Faërie Queene*?

By this the northern waggoner had set
His sevenfold teme behind the stedfast starre,
That was in ocean waves yet never wet,
But firme is fixt and sendeth light from farre
To all that in the wild deep wandering arre.
And chearfull chanticleer with his note shrill
Had warned once that Phœbus' fiery carre
In hast was climbing up the easterne hill,
Full envious that night so long his roome did fill.

Book I, Canto 2, stanza 1.

At last the golden orientall gate
Of greatest heaven gan to open fayre,
And Phœbus fresh as brydegrome to his mate,
Came dauncing forth, shaking his deawie hayre,
And hurl'd his glist'ring beams through gloomy ayre;
Which when the wakeful elfe perceived, streightway
He started up, and did him selfe prepayre
In sun-bright armes, and battailous array;
For with that pagan proud he combat will that day.

Book I, Canto 5, stanza 2.

On the contrary, to how many passages, both in hymn books and in blank verse poems, could I (were it not invidious) direct the reader's attention, the style of which is most unpoetic, because, and only because, it is the style of prose? He will not suppose me capable of having in my mind such verses as

I put my hat upon my head
And walked into the Strand;
And there I met another man,
Whose hat was in his hand.

To such specimens it would indeed be a fair and full reply, that these lines are not bad because they are unpoetic, but because they are empty of all sense and feeling; and that it were an idle attempt to prove that "an ape is not a Newton, when it is evident that he is not a man." But the sense shall be good and weighty, the language correct and dignified, the subject interesting and treated with feeling; and yet the style shall, notwithstanding all these merits, be justly blameable as prosaic, and solely because the words and the order of the words would find their appropriate place in prose, but are not suitable to metrical composition. The *Civil Wars* of Daniel

is an instructive, and even interesting work: but take the following
stanzas (and from the hundred instances which abound I might
probably have selected others far more striking):

> And to the end we may with better ease
> Discern the true discourse, vouchsafe to show
> What were the times foregoing near to these,
> That these we may with better profit know.
> Tell how the world fell into this disease;
> And how so great distemperture did grow;
> So shall we see with what degrees it came;
> How things at full do soon wax out of frame.
>
> Ten kings had from the Norman conqu'ror reign'd
> With intermixt and variable fate,
> When England to her greatest height attain'd
> Of power, dominion, glory, wealth, and state;
> After it had with much ado sustain'd
> The violence of princes with debate
> For titles, and the often mutinies
> Of nobles for their ancient liberties.
>
> For first the Norman, conqu'ring all by might,
> By might was forced to keep what he had got;
> Mixing our customs and the form of right
> With foreign constitutions, he had brought;
> Mastering the mighty, humbling the poorer wight,
> By all severest means that could be wrought;
> And making the succession doubtful, rent
> His new-got state and left it turbulent.
>
> Book I, stanzas 7, 8, 9.

Will it be contended, on the one side, that these lines are mean
and senseless? Or on the other, that they are not prosaic, and for
that reason unpoetic? This poet's well-merited epithet is that of the
"well-languaged Daniel"; but likewise and by the consent of his
contemporaries no less than of all succeeding critics, the "prosaic
Daniel." Yet those, who thus designate this wise and amiable writer
from the frequent incorrespondency of his diction to his metre in
the majority of his compositions, not only deem them valuable and
interesting on other accounts, but willingly admit that there are to
be found throughout his poems, and especially in his *Epistles* and in
his *Hymen's Triumph*, many and exquisite specimens of that style
which, as the neutral ground of prose and verse, is common to both.

A fine and almost faultless extract, eminent as for other beauties so for its perfection in this species of diction, may be seen in Lamb's *Dramatic Specimens, etc.,* a work of various interest from the nature of the selections themselves (all from the plays of Shakespeare's contemporaries), and deriving a high additional value from the notes, which are full of just and original criticism, expressed with all the freshness of originality.

Among the possible effects of practical adherence to a theory that aims to identify the style of prose and verse (if it does not indeed claim for the latter a yet nearer resemblance to the average style of men in the *vivâ voce* intercourse of real life) we might anticipate the following as not the least likely to occur. It will happen, as I have indeed before observed, that the metre itself, the sole acknowledged difference, will occasionally become metre to the eye only. The existence of prosaisms, and that they detract from the merits of a poem, must at length be conceded, when a number of successive lines can be rendered, even to the most delicate ear, unrecognizable as verse, or as having even been intended for verse, by simply transcribing them as prose: when if the poem be in blank verse, this can be effected without any alteration, or at most by merely restoring one or two words to their proper places, from which they had been transplanted [1] for no assignable cause or reason but that of the au-

---

[1] As the ingenious gentleman under the influence of the Tragic Muse contrived to dislocate, "I wish you a good morning, Sir! Thank you, Sir, and I wish you the same," into two blank-verse heroics:

> To you a morning good, good Sir! I wish.
> You, Sir! I thank: to you the same wish I.

In those parts of Mr. Wordsworth's works which I have thoroughly studied, I find fewer instances in which this would be practicable than I have met in many poems, where an approximation of prose has been sedulously and on system guarded against. Indeed, excepting the stanzas already quoted from the *Sailor's Mother,* I can recollect but one instance: *viz.* a short passage of four or five lines in the *Brothers,* that model of English pastoral, which I never yet read with unclouded eye. "James, pointing to its summit, over which they had all purposed to return together, informed them that he would wait for them there. They parted, and his comrades passed that way some two hours after, but they did not find him at the appointed place, *a circumstance of which they took no heed*: but one of them going by chance into the house, which at this time was James's house, learnt there that nobody had seen him all that day." The only change which has been made is in the position of the little word "there" in two instances, the position in the original being clearly such as is not adopted in ordinary conversation. The other words printed in italics were so marked because, though good and genuine English, they are not the phraseology of common conversation either in the word put in apposition, or in the connection by the genitive pronoun. Men in general would have said, "but that was a circumstance they paid no attention to, or took no notice of," and the language is, on the theory of the preface, justified only by the narrator's being the Vicar. Yet if any ear could suspect that these sentences were ever printed as metre, on those very words alone could the suspicion have been grounded. (Coleridge.)

thor's convenience; but if it be in rhyme, by the mere exchange of the final word of each line for some other of the same meaning, equally appropriate, dignified and euphonic.

The answer or objection in the preface to the anticipated remark "that metre paves the way to other distinctions," is contained in the following words:—"The distinction of rhyme and metre is voluntary and uniform, and not like that produced by (what is called) poetic diction, arbitrary and subject to infinite caprices, upon which no calculation whatever can be made. In the one case the reader is utterly at the mercy of the poet respecting what imagery or diction he may choose to connect with the passion." But is this a poet, of whom a poet is speaking? No, surely—rather of a fool or madman, or at best of a vain or ignorant phantast! And might not brains so wild and so deficient make just the same havoc with rhymes and metres as they are supposed to effect with modes and figures of speech? How is the reader at the mercy of such men? If he continue to read their nonsense, is it not his own fault? The ultimate end of criticism is much more to establish the principles of writing than to furnish rules how to pass judgment on what has been written by others; if indeed it were possible that the two could be separated. But if it be asked, by what principles the poet is to regulate his own style, if he do not adhere closely to the sort and order of words which he hears in the market, wake, high-road, or plough-field? I reply, by principles, the ignorance or neglect of which would convict him of being no poet, but a silly or presumptuous usurper of the name! By the principles of grammar, logic, psychology! In one word, by such a knowledge of the facts, material and spiritual, that most appertain to his art, as, if it have been governed and applied by good sense, and rendered instinctive by habit, becomes the representative and reward of our past conscious reasonings, insights, and conclusions, and acquires the name of taste. By what rule that does not leave the reader at the poet's mercy, and the poet at his own, is the latter to distinguish between the language suitable to suppressed, and the language which is characteristic of indulged, anger? Or between that of rage and that of jealousy? Is it obtained by wandering about in search of angry or jealous people in uncultivated society, in order to copy their words? Or not far rather by the power of imagination proceeding upon the all in each of human nature? By meditation, rather than by observation? And by the latter in consequence only of the former? As eyes, for which the former has predetermined their field of vision, and to which, as to its organ, it communicates a microscopic power?

There is not, I firmly believe, a man now living, who has from his own inward experience a clearer intuition than Mr. Wordsworth himself, that the last mentioned are the true sources of genial discrimination. Through the same process and by the same creative agency will the poet distinguish the degree and kind of the excitement produced by the very act of poetic composition. As intuitively will he know, what differences of style it at once inspires and justifies; what intermixture of conscious volition is natural to that state; and in what instances such figures and colors of speech degenerate into mere creatures of an arbitrary purpose, cold technical artifices of ornament or connection. For even as truth is its own light and evidence, discovering at once itself and falsehood, so is it the prerogative of poetic genius to distinguish by parental instinct its proper offspring from the changelings, which the gnomes of vanity or the fairies of fashion may have laid in its cradle or called by its names. Could a rule be given from without, poetry would cease to be poetry, and sink into a mechanical art. It would be $\mu\acute{o}\rho\phi\omega\sigma\iota\varsigma$ not $\pi o\acute{\iota}\eta\sigma\iota\varsigma$.[1] The rules of the imagination are themselves the very powers of growth and production. The words, to which they are reducible, present only the outlines and external appearance of the fruit. A deceptive counterfeit of the superficial form and colors may be elaborated; but the marble peach feels cold and heavy, and children only put it to their mouths. We find no difficulty in admitting as excellent, and the legitimate language of poetic fervor self-impassioned, Donne's apostrophe to the Sun in the second stanza of his *Progress of the Soul:*

> Thee, eye of heaven! this great Soul envies not:
> By thy male force is all we have begot.
> In the first East thou now beginn'st to shine,
> Suck'st early balm and island spices there;
> And wilt anon in thy loose-rein'd career
> At Tagus, Po, Seine, Thames, and Danow dine,
> And see at night this western world of mine:
> Yet hast thou not more nations seen than she,
> Who before thee one day began to be,
> And thy frail light being quenched, shall long, long outlive thee.

Or the next stanza but one:

> Great Destiny, the commissary of God,
> That hast marked out a path and period
> For ev'ry thing! Who, where we offspring took,

---

[1] "Forming," not "creating."

Our ways and ends see'st at one instant: thou
Knot of all causes! Thou, whose changeless brow
Ne'er smiles or frowns! O! vouchsafe thou to look,
And show my story in thy eternal book, &c.

As little difficulty do we find in excluding from the honors of
unaffected warmth and elevation the madness prepense of pseudo-
poesy, or the startling hysteric of weakness over-exerting itself,
which bursts on the unprepared reader in sundry odes and apostro-
phes to abstract terms. Such are the Odes to Jealousy, to Hope, to
Oblivion, and the like, in Dodsley's *Collection* and the magazines of
that day, which seldom fail to remind me of an Oxford copy of
verses on the two Suttons,[1] commencing with:

Inoculation, heavenly maid! descend!

It is not to be denied that men of undoubted talents, and even
poets of true though not of first-rate genius, have, from a mistaken
theory, deluded both themselves and others in the opposite extreme.
I once read to a company of sensible and well-educated women the
introductory period of Cowley's preface to his Pindaric odes, written in imitation of the style and manner of the odes of Pindar. "If,"
says Cowley, "a man should undertake to translate Pindar, word for
word, it would be thought that one madman had translated another;
as may appear when he that understands not the original reads the
verbal traduction of him into Latin prose, than which nothing seems
more raving." I then proceeded with his own free version of the
second Olympic, composed for the charitable purpose of rationaliz-
ing the Theban Eagle:

Queen of all harmonious things,
Dancing words and speaking strings,
What God, what hero wilt thou sing?
What happy man to equal glories bring?
Begin, begin thy noble choice,
And let the hills around reflect the image of thy voice.
Pisa does to Jove belong,
Jove and Pisa claim thy song.
The fair first-fruits of war, th' Olympic games,

[1] Daniel and Robert Sutton, sons of a Suffolk surgeon, so improved the practice of inoculation (before 1765) that it was rendered acceptable and popular. In 1769 Daniel
Sutton called himself "Professor of Inoculation in the kingdom of Great Britain, and in
all the dominions of his Britannic Majesty." (George Sampson, citing R. H. Fox,
Dr. John Fothergill and his Friends.)

Alcides offer'd up to Jove;
Alcides too thy strings may move!
But oh! what man to join with these can worthy prove?
Join Theron boldly to their sacred names;
Theron the next honor claims;
Theron to no man gives place;
Is first in Pisa's and in Virtue's race;
Theron there, and he alone,
Ev'n his own swift forefathers has outgone.

One of the company exclaimed, with the full assent of the rest, that if the original were madder than this, it must be incurably mad. I then translated the ode from the Greek, and as nearly as possible word for word; and the impression was, that in the general movement of the periods, in the form of the connections and transitions, and in the sober majesty of lofty sense, it appeared to them to approach more nearly than any other poetry they had heard to the style of our Bible in the prophetic books. The first strophe will suffice as a specimen:

Ye harp-controlling hymns! (or) ye hymns the sovereigns of harps!
What God? what Hero?
What Man shall we celebrate?
Truly Pisa indeed is of Jove.
But the Olympiad (or the Olympic games) did Hercules establish,
The first-fruits of the spoils of war.
But Theron for the four-horsed car,
That bore victory to him,
It behooves us now to voice aloud:
The Just, the Hospitable,
The Bulwark of Agrigentum,
Of renowned fathers
The Flower, even him
Who preserves his native city erect and safe.

But are such rhetorical caprices condemnable only for their deviation from the language of real life? and are they by no other means to be precluded, but by the rejection of all distinctions between prose and verse, save that of metre? Surely, good sense and a moderate insight into the constitution of the human mind would be amply sufficient to prove that such language and such combinations are the native produce neither of the fancy nor of the imagination; that their operation consists in the excitement of surprise by the juxtaposition and apparent reconciliation of widely different or incompatible things. As when, for instance, the hills are made to reflect the image of a voice. Surely no unusual taste is requisite to see clearly that this compulsory juxtaposition is not produced by the presentation of impressive or delightful forms to the inward vision, nor by any sympathy with the modifying powers with which the genius of the poet had united and inspirited all the objects of his thought; that it is therefore a species of wit, a pure work of the will, and implies a leisure and self-possession both of thought and of feeling, incompatible with the steady fervor of a mind possessed and filled with the grandeur of its subject. To sum up the whole in one sentence: When a poem, or a part of a poem, shall be adduced, which is evidently vicious in the figures and contexture of its style, yet for the condemnation of which no reason can be assigned, except that it differs from the style in which men actually converse, then, and not till then, can I hold this theory to be either plausible or practicable, or capable of furnishing either rule, guidance, or precaution, that might not, more easily and more safely, as well as more naturally, have been deduced in the author's own mind from considerations of grammar, logic, and the truth and nature of things, confirmed by the authority of works whose fame is not of one country, nor of one age.

Chapter XXII

The characteristic defects of Wordsworth's poetry, with the principles from which the judgment, that they are defects, is deduced—Their proportion to the beauties—For the greatest part characteristic of his theory only.

If Mr. Wordsworth have set forth principles of poetry which his arguments are insufficient to support, let him and those who have adopted his sentiments be set right by the confutation of those arguments, and by the substitution of more philosophical principles. And still let the due credit be given to the portion and importance of the truths, which are blended with his theory; truths, the too exclusive attention to which had occasioned its errors, by tempting him to carry those truths beyond their proper limits. If his mistaken theory have at all influenced his poetic compositions, let the effects be pointed out, and the instances given. But let it likewise be shown, how far the influence has acted; whether diffusively, or only by starts; whether the number and importance of the poems and passages thus infected be great or trifling compared with the sound portion; and lastly, whether they are inwoven into the texture of his works, or are loose and separable. The result of such a trial would evince beyond a doubt, what it is high time to announce decisively and aloud, that the supposed characteristics of Mr. Wordsworth's poetry, whether admired or reprobated; whether they are simplicity or simpleness; faithful adherence to essential nature, or wilful selections from human nature of its meanest forms and under the least attractive associations; are as little the real characteristics of his poetry at large, as of his genius and the constitution of his mind.

In a comparatively small number of poems he chose to try an experiment; and this experiment we will suppose to have failed. Yet even in these poems it is impossible not to perceive that the natural tendency of the poet's mind is to great objects and elevated conceptions. The poem entitled *Fidelity* is for the greater part written in language, as unraised and naked as any perhaps in the two volumes. Yet take the following stanza and compare it with the preceding stanzas of the same poem.

> There sometimes doth a leaping fish
> Send through the tarn a lonely cheer;
> The crags repeat the raven's croak,
> In symphony austere;
> Thither the rainbow comes—the cloud—
> And mists that spread the flying shroud;
> And sun-beams; and the sounding blast,
> That, if it could, would hurry past;
> But that enormous barrier holds it fast.

Or compare the four last lines of the concluding stanza with the former half.

> Yes, proof was plain that, since the day
> On which the Traveller thus had died,
> The Dog had watched about the spot,
> Or by his Master's side:
> *How nourish'd here through such long time*
> *He knows, who gave that love sublime,—*
> *And gave that strength of feeling, great*
> *Above all human estimate!*

Can any candid and intelligent mind hesitate in determining, which of these best represents the tendency and native character of the poet's genius? Will he not decide that the one was written because the poet *would* so write, and the other because he could not so entirely repress the force and grandeur of his mind, but that he must in some part or other of every composition write otherwise? In short, that his only disease is the being out of his element; like the swan, that, having amused himself, for a while, with crushing the weeds on the river's bank, soon returns to his own majestic movements on its reflecting and sustaining surface. Let it be observed that I am here supposing the imagined judge, to whom I appeal, to have already decided against the poet's theory, as far as it is different from the principles of the art, generally acknowledged.

I cannot here enter into a detailed examination of Mr. Wordsworth's works; but I will attempt to give the main results of my own judgment, after an acquaintance of many years, and repeated perusals. And though, to appreciate the defects of a great mind it is necessary to understand previously its characteristic excellences, yet I have already expressed myself with sufficient fulness, to preclude most of the ill effects that might arise from my pursuing a contrary arrangement. I will therefore commence with what I deem the prominent *defects* of his poems hitherto published.

The first characteristic, though only occasional defect, which I appear to myself to find in these poems is the *inconstancy* of the style. Under this name I refer to the sudden and unprepared transitions from lines or sentences of peculiar felicity—(at all events striking and original)—to a style, not only unimpassioned but undistinguished. He sinks too often and too abruptly to that style, which I should place in the second division of language, dividing it into the three species; first, that which is peculiar to poetry; second, that which is only proper in prose; and third, the neutral or common to both. There have been works, such as Cowley's *Essay on Cromwell*, in which prose and verse are intermixed (not as in the *Consolation* of Boethius, or the *Argenis* of Barclay, by the insertion of poems supposed to have been spoken or composed on occasions previously related in prose, but) the poet passing from one to the other, as the nature of the thoughts or his own feelings dictated. Yet this mode of composition does not satisfy a cultivated taste. There is something unpleasant in the being thus obliged to alternate states of feeling so dissimilar, and this too in a species of writing, the pleasure from which is in part derived from the preparation and previous expectation of the reader. A portion of that awkwardness is felt which hangs upon the introduction of songs in our modern comic operas; and to prevent which the judicious Metastasio (as to whose exquisite taste there can be no hesitation, whatever doubts may be entertained as to his poetic genius) uniformly placed the *aria* at the end of the scene, at the same time that he almost always raises and impassions the style of the recitative immediately preceding. Even in real life, the difference is great and evident between words used as the arbitrary marks of thought, our smooth market-coin of intercourse, with the image and superscription worn out by currency; and those which convey pictures either borrowed from one outward object to enliven and particularize some other; or used allegorically to body forth the inward state of the person speaking; or such as are at least the exponents of his peculiar turn and unusual extent of faculty. So much so indeed, that in the social circles of private life we often find a striking use of the latter put a stop to the general flow of conversation, and by the excitement arising from concentred attention produce a sort of damp and interruption for some minutes after. But in the perusal of works of literary art, we prepare ourselves for such language; and the business of the writer, like that of a painter whose subject requires unusual splendor and prominence, is so to raise the lower and neutral tints, that what in a different style would be the commanding colors, are here used as the means of that gentle *degradation* requisite in order to produce the effect of a whole. Where this is not achieved in a poem, the metre merely reminds the reader of his claims in order to disappoint them; and where this defect occurs frequently, his feelings are alternately startled by anticlimax and hyperclimax.

* * * *

The second defect I can generalize with tolerable accuracy, if the reader will pardon an uncouth and new-coined word. There is, I should say, not seldom a *matter-of-factness* in certain poems. This may be divided into, first, a laborious minuteness and fidelity in the representation of objects, and their positions, as they appeared to the poet himself; secondly, the insertion of accidental circumstances, in order to the full explanation of his living characters, their dispositions and actions; which circumstances might be necessary to establish the probability of a statement in real life, where nothing is taken for granted by the hearer; but appear superfluous in poetry, where the reader is willing to believe for his own sake. To this *accidentality* I object, as contravening the essence of poetry, which Aristotle pronounces to be σπουδαιότατον καὶ φιλοσοφώτατον γένος, the most intense, weighty and philosophical product of human art; adding, as the reason, that it is the most catholic and abstract. The following passage from Davenant's prefatory letter to Hobbes well expresses this truth. "When I considered the actions which I meant to describe (those inferring the persons), I was again persuaded rather to choose those of a former age, than the present; and in a century so far removed, as might preserve me from their improper examinations, who know not the requisites of a poem, nor how much pleasure they lose (and even the pleasures of heroic poesy are not unprofitable), who take away the liberty of a poet, and fetter his feet in the shackles of an historian. For why should a poet doubt in story to mend the intrigues of fortune by more delightful conveyances of probable fictions, because austere historians have entered into bond to truth? An obligation, which were in poets as foolish and unnecessary, as is the bondage of false martyrs, who lie in chains for a mistaken opinion. *But by this I would imply, that truth, narrative and past, is the idol of historians (who worship a dead thing), and truth operative, and by effects continually alive, is the mistress of poets, who hath not her existence in matter, but in reason.*"

For this minute accuracy in the painting of local imagery, the lines in *The Excursion*, pp. 96, 97, and 98, may be taken, if not as a striking instance, yet as an illustration of my meaning. It must be some strong motive—(as, for instance, that the description was necessary to the intelligibility of the tale)—which could induce me to describe in a number of verses what a draughtsman could present to the eye with incomparably greater satisfaction by half a dozen strokes of his pencil, or the painter with as many touches of his brush. Such descriptions too often occasion in the mind of a reader, who is determined to understand his author, a feeling of labor, not very dissimilar to that, with which he would construct a diagram, line by line, for a long geometrical proposition. It seems to be like taking the pieces of a dissected map out of its box. We first look at one part, and then at another, then join and dove-tail them; and when the successive acts of attention have been completed, there is a retrogressive effort of mind to behold it as a whole. The poet should paint to the imagination, not to the fancy; and I know no happier case to exemplify the distinction between these two faculties. Masterpieces of the former mode of poetic painting abound in the writings of Milton, for example:

> The fig-tree; not that kind for fruit renown'd,
> But such as at this day, to Indians known,
> In Malabar or Decan spreads her arms
> Branching so broad and long, that in the ground

The bended twigs take root, *and daughters grow*
About the mother tree, a pillar'd shade
High over-arch'd and ECHOING WALKS BETWEEN:
There oft the Indian herdsman, shunning heat,
Shelters in cool, and tends his pasturing herds
At hoop-holes cut through thickest shade:

This is creation rather than painting, or if painting, yet such, and with such co-presence of the whole picture flashed at once upon the eye, as the sun paints in a camera obscura. But the poet must likewise understand and command what Bacon calls the *vestigia communia* [1] of the senses, the latency of all in each, and more especially as by a magical *penna duplex*,[2] the excitement of vision by sound and the exponents of sound. Thus, "The echoing walks between," may be almost said to reverse the fable in tradition of the head of Memnon,[3] in the Egyptian statue. Such may be deservedly entitled the *creative words* in the world of imagination.

The second division respects an apparent minute adherence to *matter-of-fact* in character and incidents; *a biographical* attention to probability, and an *anxiety* of explanation and retrospect. Under this head I shall deliver, with no feigned diffidence, the results of my best reflection on the great point of controversy between Mr. Wordsworth and his objectors; namely, on *the choice of his characters*. I have already declared, and, I trust justified, my utter dissent from the mode of argument which his critics have hitherto employed. To *their* question,—"Why did you choose such a character, or a character from such a rank of life?"—the poet might in my opinion fairly retort: why with the conception of my character did you make wilful choice of mean or ludicrous associations not furnished by me, but supplied from your own sickly and fastidious feelings? How was it, indeed, probable, that such arguments could have any weight with an author, whose plan, whose guiding principle, and main object it was to attack and subdue that state of association, which leads us to place the chief value on those things on which man differs from man, and to forget or disregard the high dignities, which belong to Human Nature, the sense and the feeling, which may be, and ought to be, found in all ranks? The feelings with which, as Christians, we contemplate a mixed congregation rising or kneeling before their common Maker, Mr. Wordsworth would have us entertain at all

[1] common remainders.
[2] double feather.
[3] Said to utter a sound when the rays of the rising sun first struck it.

times, as men, and as readers; and by the excitement of this lofty, yet prideless impartiality in poetry, he might hope to have encouraged its continuance in real life. The praise of good men be his! In real life, and, I trust, even in my imagination, I honor a virtuous and wise man, without reference to the presence or absence of artificial advantages. Whether in the person of an armed baron, a laurelled bard, or of an old Pedlar, or still older Leech-gatherer, the same qualities of head and heart must claim the same reverence. And even in poetry I am not conscious that I have ever suffered my feelings to be disturbed or offended by any thoughts or images, which the poet himself has not presented.

But yet I object, nevertheless, and for the following reasons. First, because the object in view, as an *immediate* object, belongs to the moral philosopher, and would be pursued, not only more appropriately, but in my opinion with far greater probability of success, in sermons or moral essays, than in an elevated poem. It seems, indeed, to destroy the main fundamental distinction, not only between a poem and prose, but even between philosophy and works of fiction, inasmuch as it proposes *truth* for its immediate object, instead of *pleasure*. Now till the blessed time shall come, when truth itself shall be pleasure, and both shall be so united, as to be distinguishable in words only, not in feeling, it will remain the poet's office to proceed upon that state of association, which actually exists as general; instead of attempting first to make it what it ought to be, and then to let the pleasure follow. But here is unfortunately a small *hysteron-proteron*. For the communication of pleasure is the introductory means by which alone the poet must expect to moralize his readers. Secondly: though I were to admit, for a moment, *this* argument to be groundless: yet how is the moral effect to be produced, by merely attaching the name of some low profession to powers which are *least* likely, and to qualities which are assuredly not *more* likely, to be found in it? The Poet, speaking in his own person, may at once delight and improve us by sentiments, which teach us the independence of goodness, of wisdom, and even of genius, on the favors of fortune. And having made a due reverence before the throne of Antonine, he may bow with equal awe before Epictetus among his fellow-slaves—

and rejoice
In the plain presence of his dignity.

Who is not at once delighted and improved, when the Poet Wordsworth himself exclaims,

> Oh! many are the Poets that are sown
> By Nature; men endowed with highest gifts
> The vision and the faculty divine,
> Yet wanting the accomplishment of verse,
> Nor having e'er, as life advanced, been led
> By circumstance to take unto the height
> The measure of themselves, these favored Beings,
> All but a scattered few, live out their time,
> Husbanding that which they possess within,
> And go to the grave, unthought of. Strongest minds
> Are often those of whom the noisy world
> Hears least.

To use a colloquial phrase, such sentiments, in such language, do one's
heart good; though I for my part, have not the fullest faith in the
truth of the observation. On the contrary I believe the instances to
be exceedingly rare; and should feel almost as strong an objection to
introduce such a character in a poetic fiction, as a pair of black swans
on a lake, in a fancy landscape. When I think how many, and how
much better books than Homer, or even than Herodotus, Pindar or
Æschylus, could have read, are in the power of almost every man, in
a country where almost every man is instructed to read and write;
and how restless, how difficultly hidden, the powers of genius are;
and yet find even in situations the most favorable, according to Mr.
Wordsworth, for the formation of a pure and poetic language; in
situations which ensure familiarity with the grandest objects of the
imagination; but one Burns, among the shepherds of Scotland, and
not a single poet of humble life among those of English lakes and
mountains; I conclude, that Poetic Genius is not only a very delicate
but a very rare plant.

But be this as it may, the feelings with which,

> I think of Chatterton, the marvellous Boy,
> The sleepless Soul, that perished in his pride;
> Of Burns, who walk'd in glory and in joy
> Behind his plough, upon the mountain-side—

are widely different from those with which I should read a *poem*,
where the author, having occasion for the character of a poet and a

philosopher in the fable of his narration, had chosen to make him a chimney-sweeper; and then, in order to remove all doubts on the subject, had *invented* an account of his birth, parentage and education, with all the strange and fortunate accidents which had concurred in making him at once poet, philosopher, and sweep! Nothing, but biography, can justify this. If it be admissible even in a novel, it must be one in the manner of Defoe's, that were meant to pass for histories, not in the manner of Fielding's: in *The Life of Moll Flanders,* or *Colonel Jack,* not in a *Tom Jones,* or even a *Joseph Andrews.* Much less then can it be legitimately introduced in a poem, the characters of which, amid the strongest individualization, must still remain representative. The precepts of Horace, on this point, are grounded on the nature both of poetry and of the human mind. They are not more peremptory, than wise and prudent. For in the first place a deviation from them perplexes the reader's feelings, and all the circumstances which are feigned in order to make such accidents less improbable, divide and disquiet his faith, rather than aid and support it. Spite of all attempts, the fiction will appear, and unfortunately not as fictitious but as false. The reader not only knows that the sentiments and language are the poet's own, and his own too in his artificial character, as poet; but by the fruitless endeavors to make him think the contrary, he is not even suffered to forget it. The effect is similar to that produced by an Epic Poet, when the fable and the characters are *derived* from Scripture history, as in *The Messiah* of Klopstock, or in Cumberland's *Calvary,* and not merely *suggested* by it as in the *Paradise Lost* of Milton. That illusion, contradistinguished from delusion, that negative faith, which simply permits the images presented to work by their own force, without either denial or affirmation of their real existence by the judgment, is rendered impossible by their immediate neighborhood to words and facts of known and absolute truth. A faith, which transcends even historic belief, must absolutely *put out* this mere poetic *analogon* [1] of faith, as the summer sun is said to extinguish our household fires, when it shines full upon them. What would otherwise have been yielded to as pleasing fiction, is repelled as revolting falsehood. The effect produced in this latter case by the solemn belief of the reader, is in a less degree brought about in the instances, to which I have been objecting, by the baffled attempts of the author to *make* him believe.

Add to all the foregoing the seeming uselessness both of the project

[1] Analogue; a thing that is similar.

and of the anecdotes from which it is to derive support. Is there one word, for instance, attributed to the pedlar in *The Excursion,* characteristic of a pedlar? One sentiment, that might not more plausibly, even without the aid of any previous explanation, have proceeded from any wise and beneficent old man, of a rank or profession in which the language of learning and refinement are natural and to be expected? Need the rank have been at all particularized, where nothing follows which the knowledge of that rank is to explain or illustrate? When on the contrary this information renders the man's language, feelings, sentiments, and information a riddle, which must itself be solved by episodes of anecdote? Finally when this, and this alone, could have induced a genuine Poet to inweave in a poem of the loftiest style, and on subjects the loftiest and of most universal interest, such minute matters of fact (not unlike those furnished for the obituary of a magazine by the friends of some obscure "ornament of society lately deceased" in some obscure town), as

> Among the hills of Athol he was born:
> There, on a small hereditary Farm,
> An unproductive slip of rugged ground,
> His Father dwelt; and died in poverty;
> While He, whose lowly fortune I retrace,
> The youngest of three sons, was yet a babe,
> A little One—unconscious of their loss.
> But ere he had outgrown his infant days
> His widowed Mother, for a second Mate,
> Espoused the teacher of the Village School;
> Who on her offspring zealously bestowed
> Needful instruction.
>
> From his sixth year, the Boy of whom I speak,
> In summer tended cattle on the Hills;
> But, through the inclement and the perilous days
> Of long-continuing winter, he repaired
> To his Step-father's School,—&c.

For all the admirable passages interposed in this narration, might, with trifling alterations, have been far more appropriately, and with far greater verisimilitude, told of a poet in the character of a poet; and without incurring another defect which I shall now mention, and a sufficient illustration of which will have been here anticipated.

Third; an undue predilection for the *dramatic* form in certain poems, from which one or other of two evils result. Either the thoughts and diction are different from that of the poet, and then there arises an incongruity of style; or they are the same and indistinguishable, and then it presents a species of ventriloquism, where two are represented as talking, while in truth one man only speaks.

The fourth class of defects is closely connected with the former; but yet are such as arise likewise from an intensity of feeling disproportionate to such knowledge and value of the objects described, as can be fairly anticipated of men in general, even of the most cultivated classes; and with which therefore few only, and those few particularly circumstanced, can be supposed to sympathize: In this class, I comprise occasional prolixity, repetition, and an eddying, instead of progression, of thought. As instances, see pages 27, 28, and 62 of the Poems, Vol. I, and the first eighty lines of the VIth Book of *The Excursion*.

Fifth and last; thoughts and images too great for the subject. This is an approximation to what might be called mental bombast, as distinguished from verbal: for, as in the latter there is a disproportion of the expressions to the thoughts so in this there is a disproportion of thought to the circumstance and occasion. This, by the bye, is a fault of which none but a man of genius is capable. It is the awkwardness and strength of Hercules with the distaff of Omphale.

It is a well-known fact, that bright colors in motion both make and leave the strongest impressions on the eye. Nothing is more likely too, than that a vivid image or visual *spectrum*, thus originated, may become the link of association in recalling the feelings and images that had accompanied the original impression. But if we describe this in such lines, as

> They flash upon that inward eye,
> Which is the bliss of solitude!

in what words shall we describe the joy of retrospection, when the images and virtuous actions of a whole well-spent life, pass before that conscience which is indeed the *inward* eye: which is indeed "*the bliss of solitude*"? Assuredly we seem to sink most abruptly, not to say burlesquely, and almost as in a medley, from this couplet to—

> And then my heart with pleasure fills,
> And dances with the *daffodils*.   Vol. I, p. 328.

The second instance is from Vol. II, page 12, where the poet having gone out for a day's tour of pleasure, meets early in the morning with a knot of Gipsies, who had pitched their blanket-tents and straw-beds, together with their children and asses, in some field by the road-side. At the close of the day on his return our tourist found them in the same place. "Twelve hours," says he,

> Twelve hours, twelve bounteous hours are gone, while I
> Have been a traveller under open sky,
> Much witnessing of change and cheer,
> Yet as I left I find them here!

Whereat the poet, without seeming to reflect that the poor tawny wanderers might probably have been tramping for weeks together through road and lane, over moor and mountain, and consequently must have been right glad to rest themselves, their children and cattle, for one whole day; and overlooking the obvious truth, that such repose might be quite as necessary for them, as a walk of the same continuance was pleasing or healthful for the more fortunate poet; expresses his indignation in a series of lines, the diction and imagery of which would have been rather above, than below the mark, had they been applied to the immense empire of China improgressive for thirty centuries:

> The weary Sun betook himself to rest:—
> —Then issued Vesper from the fulgent west,
> Outshining, like a visible God,
> The glorious path in which he trod.
> And now, ascending, after one dark hour,
> And one night's diminution of her power,
> Behold the mighty Moon! this way
> She looks, as if at them—but they
> Regard not her:—oh, better wrong and strife,
> Better vain deeds or evil than such life!
> The silent Heavens have goings on:
> The stars have tasks!—but *these* have none!

The last instance of this defect (for I know no other than these already cited) is from the ode, page 351, Vol. II., where, speaking of a child, "a six years' darling of a pigmy size," he thus addresses him:

> Thou best Philosopher, who yet dost keep
> Thy heritage, thou Eye among the blind,
> That, deaf and silent, read'st the eternal deep,
> Haunted for ever by the Eternal Mind,—

Mighty Prophet! Seer blest!
On whom those truths do rest,
Which we are toiling all our lives to find!
Thou, over whom thy Immortality
Broods like the Day, a Master o'er a Slave,
A Presence which is not to be put by!

*   *   *   *

To these defects which, as appears by the extracts, are only occasional, I may oppose, with far less fear of encountering the dissent of any candid and intelligent reader, the following (for the most part correspondent) excellencies. First, an austere purity of language both grammatically and logically; in short a perfect appropriateness of the words to the meaning. Of how high value I deem this, and how particularly estimable I hold the example at the present day, has been already stated: and in part too the reasons on which I ground both the moral and intellectual importance of habituating ourselves to a strict accuracy of expression. It is noticeable, how limited an acquaintance with the masterpieces of art will suffice to form a correct and even a sensitive taste, where none but masterpieces have been seen and admired: while on the other hand, the most correct notions, and the widest acquaintance with the works of excellence of all ages and countries, will not perfectly secure us against the contagious familiarity with the far more numerous offspring of tastelessness or of a perverted taste. If this be the case, as it notoriously is, with the arts of music and painting, much more difficult will it be to avoid the infection of multiplied and daily examples in the practice of an art, which uses words, and words only, as its instruments. In poetry, in which every line, every phrase, may pass the ordeal of deliberation and deliberate choice, it is possible, and barely possible, to attain that *ultimatum* which I have ventured to propose as the infallible test of a blameless style; namely: its *untranslatableness* in words of the same language without injury to the meaning. Be it observed, however, that I include in the *meaning* of a word not only its correspondent object, but likewise all the associations which it recalls. For language is framed to convey not the object alone, but likewise the character, mood and intentions of the person who is representing it. In poetry it *is* practicable to preserve the diction uncorrupted by the affectations and misappropriations, which promiscuous authorship, and reading not promiscuous only because it is disproportionally most conversant with the compositions of the day, have rendered general. Yet even to the poet, composing in his own province, it is an arduous work: and as the result and pledge of a watchful good sense, of fine and luminous distinction, and of complete self-possession, may justly claim all the honor which belongs to an attainment equally difficult and valuable, and the more valuable for being rare. It is at *all* times the proper food of the understanding; but in an age of corrupt eloquence it is both food and antidote.

In prose I doubt whether it be even possible to preserve our style wholly unalloyed by the vicious phraseology which meets us everywhere, from the sermon to the newspaper, from the harangue of the legislator to the speech from the convivial chair, announcing a *toast* or sentiment. Our chains rattle, even while we are complaining of them. The poems of Boethius rise high in our estimation when we compare them with those of his contemporaries, as Sidonius Apollinaris, and others. They might even be referred to a purer age, but that the prose, in which they are set, as jewels in a crown of lead or iron, betrays the true age of the writer. Much however may be effected by education. I believe not only from grounds of reason, but from having in great measure assured myself of the fact by actual though limited experience, that, to a youth led from his first boyhood to investigate the meaning of every word and the reason of its choice and position, logic presents itself as an old acquaintance under new names.

On some future occasion, more especially demanding such disquisition, I shall attempt to prove the close connection between veracity and habits of mental accuracy; the beneficial after-effects of verbal precision in the preclusion of fanaticism, which masters the feelings more especially by indistinct watch-words; and to display the advantages which language alone, at least which language with incomparably greater ease and certainty than any other means, presents to the instructor of impressing modes of intellectual energy so constantly, so imperceptibly, and as it were by such elements and atoms, as to secure in due time the formation of a second nature. When we reflect that the cultivation of the judgment is a positive command of the moral law, since the reason can give the *principle* alone, and the conscience bears witness only to the *motive*, while the application and effects must depend on the judgment: when we consider, that the greater part of our success and comfort in life depends on distinguishing the similar from the same, that which is peculiar in each thing from that which it has in common with others, so as still to select the most probable, instead of the merely possible or positively unfit, we shall learn to value earnestly and with a practical seriousness a mean, already prepared for us by nature and society, of teaching the young mind to think well and wisely by the same unremembered process and with the same never forgotten results, as those by which it is taught to speak and converse. Now how much warmer the interest is, how much more genial the feelings of reality and practicability, and thence how much stronger the impulses to imitation are, which a *contemporary* writer, and especially a contemporary *poet*, excites in youth and commencing manhood, has been treated of in the earlier pages of these sketches. I have only to add, that all the praise which is due to the exertion of such influence for a purpose so important, joined with that which must be claimed for the infrequency of the same excellence in the same perfection, belongs in full right to Mr. Wordsworth. I am far however from denying that we have poets whose *general* style possesses the same excellence, as Mr. Moore, Lord Byron, Mr. Bowles, and, in all his later and more important works, our laurel-honoring Laureate.[1] But there are none, in whose works I do not appear to myself to find *more* exceptions, than in those of Wordsworth. Quotations or specimens would here be wholly out of place, and must be left for the critic who doubts and would invalidate the justice of this eulogy so applied.

The second characteristic excellence of Mr. Wordsworth's work is: a correspondent weight and sanity of the Thoughts and Sentiments,—won, not from books; but—from the poet's own meditative observation. They are *fresh* and have the dew upon them. His muse, at least when in her strength of wing, and when she hovers aloft in her proper element,

> Makes audible a linked lay of truth,
> Of truth profound a sweet continuous lay,
> Not learnt, but native, her own natural notes!

Even throughout his smaller poems there is scarcely one, which is not rendered valuable by some just and original reflection.

*   *   *   *

Both in respect of this and of the former excellence, Mr. Wordsworth strikingly resembles Samuel Daniel, one of the golden writers

[1] Robert Southey.

of our golden Elizabethan age, now most causelessly neglected: Samuel Daniel, whose diction bears no mark of time, no distinction of age which has been, and as long as our language shall last, will be so far the language of the to-day and for ever, as that it is more intelligible to us, than the transitory fashions of our own particular age. A similar praise is due to his sentiments. No frequency of perusal can deprive them of their freshness. For though they are brought into the full daylight of every reader's comprehension, yet are they drawn up from depths which few in any age are privileged to visit, into which few in any age have courage or inclination to descend. If Mr. Wordsworth is not equally with Daniel alike intelligible to all readers of average understanding in all passages of his works, the comparative difficulty does not arise from the greater impurity of the ore, but from the nature and uses of the metal. A poem is not necessarily obscure, because it does not aim to be popular. It is enough, if a work be perspicuous to those for whom it is written, and

> Fit audience find, though few.

To the *Ode on the Intimations of Immortality from Recollections of Early Childhood* the poet might have prefixed the lines which Dante addresses to one of his own Canzoni—

> Canzone, i' credo, che saranno radi
> Color, che tua ragione intendan bene,
> Tanto lor sei faticoso ed alto.

> O lyric song, there will be few, I think,
> Who may thy import understand aright:
> Thou art for *them* so arduous and so high!

But the ode was intended for such readers only as had been accustomed to watch the flux and reflux of their inmost nature, to venture at times into the twilight realms of consciousness, and to feel a deep interest in modes of inmost being, to which they know that the attributes of time and space are inapplicable and alien, but which yet can not be conveyed, save in symbols of time and space. For such readers the sense is sufficiently plain, and they will be as little disposed to charge Mr. Wordsworth with believing the Platonic pre-existence in the ordinary interpretation of the words, as I am to believe, that Plato himself ever meant or taught it.

*   *   *   *

Third (and wherein he soars far above Daniel), the sinewy strength and originality of single lines and paragraphs: the frequent *curiosa felicitas* of his diction, of which I need not here give specimens, having anticipated them in a preceding page. This beauty, and as eminently characteristic of Wordsworth's poetry, his rudest assailants have felt themselves compelled to acknowledge and admire.

Fourth; the perfect truth of nature in his images and descriptions as taken immediately from nature, and proving a long and genial intimacy with the very spirit which gives the physiognomic expression to all the works of nature. Like a green field reflected in a calm and perfectly transparent lake, the image is distinguished from the reality only by its greater softness and lustre. Like the moisture or the polish on a pebble, genius neither distorts nor false-colors its objects; but on the contrary brings out many a vein and many a tint, which escape the eye of common observation, thus raising to the rank of gems what had been often kicked away by the hurrying foot of the traveller on the dusty high road of custom.

Let me refer to the whole description of skating, vol. I, pages 42 to 47, especially to the lines

> So through the darkness and the cold we flew,
> And not a voice was idle: with the din
> Meanwhile the precipices rang aloud;
> The leafless trees and every icy crag
> Tinkled like iron; while the distant hills
> Into the tumult sent an alien sound
> Of melancholy, not unnoticed, while the stars,
> Eastward, were sparkling clear, and in the west
> The orange sky of evening died away.

Or to the poem on *The Green Linnet,* vol. I, page 244. What can be more accurate yet more lovely than the two concluding stanzas?

> Upon yon tuft of hazel trees,
> That twinkle to the gusty breeze,
> Behold him perched in ecstasies,
>   Yet seeming still to hover;
> There! where the flutter of his wings
> Upon his back and body flings
> Shadows and sunny glimmerings,
>   That cover him all over.
>
> While thus before my eyes he gleams,
> A Brother of the Leaves he seems;

When in a moment forth he teems
His little song in gushes:
As if it pleased him to disdain
And mock the Form which he did feign
While he was dancing with the train
Of Leaves among the bushes.

Or the description of the blue-cap, and of the noontide silence, page 284; or the poem to the cuckoo, page 299; or, lastly, though I might multiply the references to ten times the number, to the poem, so completely Wordsworth's, commencing

"Three years she grew in sun and shower"—

Fifth: a meditative pathos, a union of deep and subtle thought with sensibility; a sympathy with man as man; the sympathy indeed of a contemplator, rather than a fellow-sufferer or co-mate (*spectator, haud particeps*) but of a contemplator, from whose view no difference of rank conceals the sameness of the nature; no injuries of wind or weather, or toil, or even of ignorance, wholly disguise the human face divine. The superscription and the image of the Creator still remain legible to *him* under the dark lines, with which guilt or calamity had cancelled or cross-barred it. Here the Man and the Poet lose and find themselves in each other, the one as glorified, the latter as substantiated. In this mild and philosophic pathos, Wordsworth appears to me without a compeer. Such as he *is:* so he *writes*. See vol. I, pages 134 to 136, or that most affecting composition, *The Affliction of Margaret —— of ——*, pages 165 to 168, which no mother, and, if I may judge by my own experience, no parent can read without a tear. Or turn to that genuine lyric, in the former edition, entitled, *The Mad Mother*, pages 174 to 178, of which I cannot refrain from quoting two of the stanzas, both of them for their pathos, and the former for the fine transition in the two concluding lines of the stanza, so expressive of that deranged state, in which, from the increased sensibility, the sufferer's attention is abruptly drawn off by every trifle, and in the same instant plucked back again by the one despotic thought, bringing home with it, by the blending, *fusing* power of Imagination and Passion, the alien object to which it had been so abruptly diverted, no longer an alien but an ally and an inmate.

Suck, little babe, oh suck again!
It cools my blood; it cools my brain;

Thy lips, I feel them, baby! they
Draw from my heart the pain away.
Oh! press me with thy little hand;
It loosens something at my chest:
About that tight and deadly band
I feel thy little fingers prest.
The breeze I see is in the tree!
It comes to cool my babe and me.

Thy father cares not for my breast,
'Tis thine, sweet baby, there to rest;
'Tis all thine own!—and if its hue
Be changed, that was so fair to view,
'Tis fair enough for thee, my dove!
My beauty, little child, is flown,
But thou wilt live with me in love;
And what if my poor cheek be brown?
'Tis well for me, thou canst not see
How pale and wan it else would be.

Last, and pre-eminently, I challenge for this poet the gift of
Imagination in the highest and strictest sense of the word. In the
play of fancy, Wordsworth, to my feelings, is not always graceful,
and sometimes recondite. The *likeness* is occasionally too strange, or
demands too peculiar a point of view, or is such as appears the creature of predetermined research, rather than spontaneous presentation.
Indeed his fancy seldom displays itself, as mere and unmodified
fancy. But in imaginative power, he stands nearest of all modern
writers to Shakespeare and Milton; and yet in a kind perfectly un-
borrowed and his own. To employ his own words, which are at once
an instance and an illustration, he does indeed to all thoughts and to
all objects—

> add the gleam,
> The light that never was, on sea or land,
> The consecration, and the Poet's dream.

* * * *

The preceding criticism will not, I am aware, avail to overcome
the prejudices of those, who have made it a business to attack and
ridicule Mr. Wordsworth's compositions.

Truth and prudence might be imaged as concentric circles. The
poet may perhaps have passed beyond the latter, but he has confined himself far within the bounds of the former, in designating

these critics, as "too petulant to be passive to a genuine poet, and too feeble to grapple with him;***men of palsied imaginations, in whose minds all healthy action is languid;***who, therefore, feed as the many direct them, or with the many are greedy after vicious provocatives."

So much for the detractors from Wordsworth's merits. On the other hand, much as I might wish for their fuller sympathy, I dare not flatter myself, that the freedom with which I have declared my opinions concerning both his theory and his defects, most of which are more or less connected with his theory, either as cause or effect, will be satisfactory or pleasing to *all* the poet's admirers and advocates. More indiscriminate than mine their admiration may be: deeper and more sincere it cannot be. But I have advanced no opinion either for praise or censure, other than as texts introductory to the reasons which compel me to form it. Above all, I was fully convinced that such a criticism was not only wanted; but that, if executed with adequate ability, it must conduce, in no mean degree, to Mr. Wordsworth's *reputation*. His *fame* belongs to another age, and can neither be accelerated nor retarded. How small the proportion of the defects are to the beauties, I have repeatedly declared; and that no one of them originates in deficiency of poetic genius. Had they been more and greater, I should still, as a friend to his literary character in the present age, consider an analytic display of them as *pure gain*; if only it removed, as surely to all reflecting minds even the foregoing analysis must have removed, the strange mistake, so slightly grounded, yet so widely and industriously propagated, of Mr. Wordsworth's turn for *simplicity!* I am not half as much irritated by hearing his enemies abuse him for vulgarity of style, subject, and conception, as I am disgusted with the gilded side of the same meaning, as displayed by some affected admirers, with whom he is, forsooth, a "sweet, simple poet!" and *so* natural, that little master Charles and his younger sister are *so* charmed with them, that they play at "Goody Blake," or at "Johnny and Betty Foy"!

* * * *

Hazlitt

William Hazlitt (1778–1830), the son of a Unitarian clergyman, was born at Maidstone, Kent, and educated at home until he went to a Unitarian college at Hackney, to prepare for the ministry. His interests were rather philosophical and political than theological, however, and he soon turned to literature. In 1798 he met Coleridge and later, on a visit to him, made the acquaintance of Wordsworth. He began the study of painting, but gave it up when he realized that he would not succeed, although he continued to feel a critic's interest in the medium and saw nature through an artist's eye. In 1805 he published his first book—a treatise which he called an *Essay on the Principles of Human Action*. In London he served as a dramatic critic, contributed to various periodicals, and gave lectures on literary subjects. He wrote *Table Talks* in 1819 for the *London Magazine*, and in 1825 and 1826 published collections of his essays. The final years of his life were darkened by marital troubles and ill-health—in 1822 a divorce ended an unhappy marriage of fifteen years, and an unfortunate love-affair is recorded in his unique *Liber Amoris*. He died in 1830, after a long illness.

In Hazlitt we find a new type of critic, the familiar essayist who is personal, independent, wandering through the fields of literature at ease but with keen discrimination, appreciating what he discovers and imparting later the joy that he found. These critics, like Hazlitt, Lamb, Leigh Hunt, De Quincey, and Stevenson, are romantic, to be sure, but their emotion is nicely tempered by good sense. They are, as it were, personal guides or interpreters, introducing or explaining with enthusiasm a piece of literature to a new reader. Their attitude is neatly expressed later by Anatole France in his statement that criticism should be the relating of "the adventures of a soul with a masterpiece."

ON POETRY IN GENERAL [1]

(1818)

The best general notion which I can give of poetry is, that it is the natural impression of any object or event, by its vividness exciting an involuntary movement of imagination and passion, and producing, by sympathy, a certain modulation of the voice, or sounds, expressing it.

In treating of poetry, I shall speak first of the subject-matter of it, next of the forms of expression to which it gives birth, and afterwards of its connection with harmony of sound.

Poetry is the language of the imagination and the passions. It relates to whatever gives immediate pleasure or pain to the human mind. It comes home to the bosoms and businesses of men; for nothing but what so comes home to them in the most general and intelligible shape, can be a subject for poetry. Poetry is the universal language which the heart holds with nature and itself. He who has a contempt for poetry, cannot have much respect for himself, or for any thing else. It is not a mere frivolous accomplishment (as some persons have been led to imagine), the trifling amusement of a few idle readers or leisure hours—it has been the study and delight of mankind in all ages. Many people suppose that poetry is something to be found only in books, contained in lines of ten syllables, with like endings: but wherever there is a sense of beauty, or power, or harmony, as in the motion of a wave of the sea, in the growth of a flower that "spreads its sweet leaves to the air, and dedicates its beauty to the sun,"—*there* is poetry, in its birth. If history is a grave study, poetry may be said to be a graver: its materials lie deeper, and are spread wider. History treats, for the most part, of the cumbrous and unwieldy masses of things, the empty cases in which the affairs of the world are packed, under the heads of intrigue or war, in different states, and from century to century: but there is no thought or feeling that can have entered into the mind of man,

[1] From *Lectures on the English Poets*, first published in 1818; and, revised and corrected, in 1819.

which he would be eager to communicate to others, or which they would listen to with delight, that is not a fit subject for poetry. It is not a branch of authorship: it is "the stuff of which our life is made." The rest is "mere oblivion," a dead letter: for all that is worth remembering in life, is the poetry of it. Fear is poetry, hope is poetry, love is poetry, hatred is poetry; contempt, jealousy, remorse, admiration, wonder, pity, despair, or madness, are all poetry. Poetry is that fine particle within us, that expands, rarefies, refines, raises our whole being: without it "man's life is poor as beast's." Man is a poetical animal: and those of us who do not study the principles of poetry, act upon them all our lives, like Molière's *Bourgeois Gentilhomme*, who had always spoken prose without knowing it. The child is a poet in fact, when he first plays at hide-and-seek, or repeats the story of Jack the Giant-killer; the shepherd-boy is a poet, when he first crowns his mistress with a garland of flowers; the countryman, when he stops to look at the rainbow; the city-apprentice, when he gazes after the Lord Mayor's Show; the miser, when he hugs his gold; the courtier, who builds his hopes upon a smile; the savage, who paints his idol with blood; the slave, who worships a tyrant, or the tyrant, who fancies himself a god;—the vain, the ambitious, the proud, the choleric man, the hero and the coward, the beggar and the king, the rich and the poor, the young and the old, all live in a world of their own making; and the poet does no more than describe what all the others think and act. If his art is folly and madness, it is folly and madness at second hand. "There is warrant for it." Poets alone have not "such seething brains, such shaping fantasies, that apprehend more than cooler reason" can.

> The lunatic, the lover, and the poet
> Are of imagination all compact.
> One sees more devils than vast hell can hold;
> The madman. While the lover, all as frantic,
> Sees Helen's beauty in a brow of Egypt.
> The poet's eye in a fine frenzy rolling,
> Doth glance from heav'n to earth, from earth to heav'n;
> And as imagination bodies forth
> The forms of things unknown, the poet's pen
> Turns them to shape, and gives to airy nothing
> A local habitation and a name.
> Such tricks hath strong imagination.

If poetry is a dream, the business of life is much the same. If it is a fiction, made up of what we wish things to be, and fancy that they are, because we wish them so, there is no other nor better reality. Ariosto has described the loves of Angelica and Medoro: but was not Medoro, who carved the name of his mistress on the barks of trees, as much enamored of her charms as he? Homer has celebrated the anger of Achilles: but was not the hero as mad as the poet? Plato banished the poets from his Commonwealth, lest their descriptions of the natural man should spoil his mathematical man, who was to be without passions and affections, who was neither to laugh nor weep, to feel sorrow nor anger, to be cast down nor elated by any thing. This was a chimæra, however, which never existed but in the brain of the inventor; and Homer's poetical world has outlived Plato's philosophical Republic.

Poetry then is an imitation of nature, but the imagination and the passions are a part of man's nature. We shape things according to our wishes and fancies, without poetry; but poetry is the most emphatical language that can be found for those creations of the mind "which ecstasy is very cunning in." Neither a mere description of natural objects, nor a mere delineation of natural feelings, however distinct or forcible, constitutes the ultimate end and aim of poetry, without the heightenings of the imagination. The light of poetry is not only a direct but also a reflected light, that while it shows us the object, throws a sparkling radiance on all around it: the flame of the passions, communicated to the imagination, reveals to us, as with a flash of lightning, the inmost recesses of thought, and penetrates our whole being. Poetry represents forms chiefly as they suggest other forms; feelings, as they suggest forms or other feelings. Poetry puts a spirit of life and motion into the universe. It describes the flowing, not the fixed. It does not define the limits of sense, or analyze the distinctions of the understanding, but signifies the excess of the imagination beyond the actual or ordinary impression of any object or feeling. The poetical impression of any object is that uneasy, exquisite sense of beauty or power that cannot be contained within itself; that is impatient of all limit; that (as flame bends to flame) strives to link itself to some other image of kindred beauty or grandeur; to enshrine itself, as it were, in the highest forms of fancy, and to relieve the aching sense of pleasure by expressing it in the boldest manner, and by the most striking examples of the same quality in other instances. Poetry, according to Lord Bacon, for this reason, "has something divine in it, because it raises the mind and hurries it into sublimity, by conforming the shows of things to the desires of the soul, instead of subjecting the soul to external things, as reason and history do." It is strictly the language of the imagination; and the imagination is that faculty which represents objects, not as they are in themselves, but as they are moulded by other thoughts and feelings, into an infinite variety of shapes and combinations of power. This language is not the less true to nature, because it is false in point of fact; but so much the more true and natural, if it conveys the impression which the object under the influence of passion makes on the mind. Let an object, for instance, be presented to the senses in a state of agitation or fear—and the imagination will distort or magnify the object, and convert it into the likeness of whatever is most proper to encourage the fear. "Our eyes are made the fools" of our other faculties. This is the universal law of the imagination,

> That if it would but apprehend some joy,
> It comprehends some bringer of that joy:
> Or in the night imagining some fear,
> How easy is each bush suppos'd a bear!

When Iachimo says of Imogen,

> The flame o' th' taper
> Bows toward her, and would under-peep her lids
> To see the enclosed lights—

this passionate interpretation of the motion of the flame to accord with the speaker's own feelings, is true poetry. The lover, equally with the poet, speaks of the auburn tresses of his mistress as locks of shining gold, because the least tinge of yellow in the hair has, from novelty and a sense of personal beauty, a more lustrous effect to the imagination than the purest gold. We compare a man of gigantic stature to a tower: not that he is any thing like so large, but because the excess of his size beyond what we are accustomed to expect, or the usual size of things of the same class, produces by contrast a greater feeling of magnitude and ponderous strength than another object of ten times the same dimensions. The intensity of the feeling makes up for the disproportion of the objects. Things are equal to the imagination, which have the power of affecting the mind with an equal degree of terror, admiration, delight, or love. When Lear calls upon the heavens to avenge his cause, "for they are old like him," there is nothing extravagant or impious in this sublime identification of his age with theirs; for there is no other image which could do justice to the agonizing sense of his wrongs and his despair!

Poetry is the high-wrought enthusiasm of fancy and feeling. As in describing natural objects, it impregnates sensible impressions with the forms of fancy, so it describes the feelings of pleasure or pain, by blending them with the strongest movements of passion, and the most striking forms of nature. Tragic poetry, which is the most impassioned species of it, strives to carry on the feeling to the utmost point of sublimity or pathos, by all the force of comparison or contrast; loses the sense of present suffering in the imaginary exaggeration of it; exhausts the terror or pity by an unlimited indulgence of it; grapples with impossibilities in its desperate impatience of restraint; throws us back upon the past, forward into the future; brings every moment of our being or object of nature in startling review before us; and in the rapid whirl of events, lifts us from the depths of woe to the highest contemplations on human life. When Lear says of Edgar, "Nothing but his unkind daughters could have brought him to this," what a bewildered amazement, what a wrench of the imagination, that cannot be brought to conceive of any other cause of misery than that which has bowed it down, and absorbs all other sorrow in its own! His sorrow, like a flood, supplies the sources of all other sorrow. Again, when he exclaims in the mad scene, "The little dogs and all, Tray, Blanche, and Sweetheart, see, they bark at me!" it is passion lending occasion to imagination to make every creature in league against him, conjuring up ingratitude and insult in their least looked-for and most galling shapes, searching every thread and fibre of his heart, and finding out the last remaining image of respect or attachment in the bottom of his breast, only to torture and kill it! In like manner, the "So I am" of Cordelia gushes from her heart like a torrent of tears, relieving it of a weight of love and of supposed ingratitude, which had pressed upon it for years. What a fine return of the passion upon itself is that in Othello—with what a mingled agony of regret and despair he clings to the last traces of departed happiness—when he exclaims,

> Oh now, for ever
> Farewell the tranquil mind. Farewell content;
> Farewell the plumed troops and the big war,
> That make ambition virtue! Oh farewell!
> Farewell the neighing steed, and the shrill trump,

The spirit-stirring drum, th' ear-piercing fife,
The royal banner, and all quality,
Pride, pomp, and circumstance of glorious war:
And O you mortal engines, whose rude throats
Th' immortal Jove's dread clamors counterfeit,
Farewell! Othello's occupation's gone!

How his passion lashes itself up and swells and rages like a tide in its sounding course, when in answer to the doubts expressed of his returning love, he says,

Never, Iago. Like to the Pontic sea,
Whose icy current and compulsive course
Ne'er feels retiring ebb, but keeps due on
To the Propontic and the Hellespont:
Even so my bloody thoughts, with violent pace,
Shall ne'er look back, ne'er ebb to humble love,
Till that a capable and wide revenge
Swallow them up.—

The climax of his expostulation afterwards with Desdemona is at that line,

But there where I had garner'd up my heart,
To be discarded thence!—

One mode in which the dramatic exhibition of passion excites our sympathy without raising our disgust is, that in proportion as it sharpens the edge of calamity and disappointment, it strengthens the desire of good. It enhances our consciousness of the blessing, by making us sensible of the magnitude of the loss. The storm of passion lays bare and shows us the rich depths of the human soul: the whole of our existence, the sum total of our passions and pursuits, of that which we desire and that which we dread, is brought before us by contrast; the action and re-action are equal; the keenness of immediate suffering only gives us a more intense aspiration after, and a more intimate participation with, the antagonist world of good; makes us drink deeper of the cup of human life; tugs at the heart-strings; loosens the pressure about them; and calls the springs of thought and feeling into play with tenfold force.

Impassioned poetry is an emanation of the moral and intellectual part of our nature, as well as of the sensitive—of the desire to know, the will to act, and the power to feel; and ought to appeal to these different parts of our constitution, in order to be perfect. The domestic or prose tragedy, which is thought to be the most natural, is in this sense the least so, because it appeals almost exclusively to one of these faculties, our sensibility. The tragedies of Moore and Lillo,[1] for this reason, however affecting at the time, oppress and lie like a dead weight upon the mind, a load of misery which it is unable to throw off: the tragedy of Shakespeare, which is true poetry, stirs our inmost affections; abstracts evil from itself by combining it with all the forms of imagination, and with the deepest workings of the heart, and rouses the whole man within us.

The pleasure, however, derived from tragic poetry, is not any thing peculiar to it as poetry, as a fictitious and fanciful thing. It is not an anomaly of the imagination. It has its source and groundwork in the common love of strong excitement. As Mr. Burke observes, people flock to see a tragedy; but if there were a public execution in the next street, the theatre would very soon be empty. It is not then the difference between fiction and reality that solves the difficulty. Children are satisfied with the stories of ghosts and witches in plain prose: nor do the hawkers in full, true, and particular accounts of murders and executions about the streets, find it necessary to have them turned into penny ballads, before they can dispose of these interesting and authentic documents. The grave politician drives a thriving trade of abuse and calumnies poured out against those whom he makes his enemies for no other end than that he may live by them. The popular preacher makes less frequent mention of heaven than of hell. Oaths and nicknames are only a more vulgar sort of poetry or rhetoric. We are as fond of indulging our violent passions as of reading a description of those of others. We are as prone to make a torment of our fears, as to luxuriate in our hopes of good. If it be asked, Why we do so? the best answer will be, Because we cannot help it. The sense of power is as strong a principle in the mind as the love of pleasure. Objects of terror and pity exercise the same despotic control over it as those of love or beauty. It is as natural to hate as to love, to despise as to admire, to express our hatred or contempt, as our love or admiration.

> Masterless passion sways us to the mood
> Of what it likes or loathes.

Not that we like what we loath; but we like to indulge our hatred and scorn of it; to dwell upon it, to exasperate our idea of it by every

[1] Edward Moore (1712–1757) and George Lillo (1693–1739), eighteenth-century dramatists, were popular in their day.

refinement of ingenuity and extravagance of illustration; to make it a bugbear to ourselves, to point it out to others in all the splendor of deformity, to embody it to the senses, to stigmatize it by name, to grapple with it in thought, in action, to sharpen our intellect, to arm our will against it, to know the worst we have to contend with, and to contend with it to the utmost. Poetry is only the highest eloquence of passion, the most vivid form of expression that can be given to our conception of any thing, whether pleasurable or painful, mean or dignified, delightful or distressing. It is the perfect coincidence of the image and the words with the feeling we have, and of which we cannot get rid in any other way, that gives an instant "satisfaction to the thought." This is equally the origin of wit and fancy, of comedy and tragedy, of the sublime and pathetic. When Pope says of the Lord Mayor's Show,—

> Now night descending, the proud scene is o'er,
> But lives in Settle's [1] numbers one day more!

—when Collins makes Danger, "with limbs of giant mould,"

> Throw him on the steep
> Of some loose hanging rock asleep:

when Lear calls out in extreme anguish,

> Ingratitude, thou marble-hearted fiend,
> How much more hideous show'st in a child
> Than the sea-monster!

—the passion of contempt in the one case, of terror in the other, and of indignation in the last, is perfectly satisfied. We see the thing ourselves, and show it to others as we feel it to exist, and as, in spite of ourselves, we are compelled to think of it. The imagination, by thus embodying and turning them to shape, gives an obvious relief to the indistinct and importunate cravings of the will.—We do not wish the thing to be so; but we wish it to appear such as it is. For knowledge is conscious power; and the mind is no longer, in this case, the dupe, though it may be the victim, of vice or folly.

Poetry is in all its shapes the language of the imagination and the passions, of fancy and will. Nothing, therefore, can be more absurd than the outcry which has been sometimes raised by frigid and pedantic critics, for reducing the language of poetry to the standard

[1] Elkanah Settle (1648–1724), poet and dramatist, wrote most of the Lord Mayor's Shows from 1691 to 1708.

of common sense and reason: for the end and use of poetry, "both at the first and now, was and is to hold the mirror up to nature," seen through the medium of passion and imagination, not divested of that medium by means of literal truth or abstract reason. The painter of history might as well be required to represent the face of a person who has just trod upon a serpent with the still-life expression of a common portrait, as the poet to describe the most striking and vivid impressions which things can be supposed to make upon the mind, in the language of common conversation. Let who will strip nature of the colors and the shapes of fancy, the poet is not bound to do so; the impressions of common sense and strong imagination, that is, of passion and indifference, cannot be the same, and they must have a separate language to do justice to either. Objects must strike differently upon the mind, independently of what they are in themselves, as long as we have a different interest in them, as we see them in a different point of view, nearer or at a greater distance (morally or physically speaking) from novelty, from old acquaintance, from our ignorance of them, from our fear of their consequences, from contrast, from unexpected likeness. We can no more take away the faculty of the imagination, than we can see all objects without light or shade. Some things must dazzle us by their preternatural light; others must hold us in suspense, and tempt our curiosity to explore their obscurity. Those who would dispel these various illusions, to give us their drab-colored creation in their stead, are not very wise. Let the naturalist, if he will, catch the glow-worm, carry it home with him in a box, and find it next morning nothing but a little grey worm; let the poet or the lover of poetry visit it at evening, when beneath the scented hawthorn and the crescent moon it has built itself a palace of emerald light. This is also one part of nature, one appearance which the glow-worm presents, and that not the least interesting; so poetry is one part of the history of the human mind, though it is neither science nor philosophy. It cannot be concealed, however, that the progress of knowledge and refinement has a tendency to circumscribe the limits of the imagination, and to clip the wings of poetry. The province of the imagination is principally visionary, the unknown and undefined: the understanding restores things to their natural boundaries, and strips them of their fanciful pretensions. Hence the history of religious and poetical enthusiasm is much the same; and both have received a sensible shock from the progress of experimental philosophy. It is the undefined and uncommon that gives birth and scope to the imagination; we can only fancy what we do not know. As in looking into the mazes of a tangled wood we fill them with what shapes we please, with ravenous beasts, with caverns vast, and drear enchantments, so in our ignorance of the world about us, we make gods or devils of the first object we see, and set no bounds to the wilful suggestions of our hopes and fears.

> And visions, as poetic eyes avow,
> Hang on each leaf and cling to every bough.

There can never be another Jacob's dream. Since that time, the heavens have gone farther off, and grown astronomical. They have become averse to the imagination, nor will they return to us on the squares of the distances, or on Doctor Chalmers's *Discourses*.[1] Rembrandt's picture brings the matter nearer to us.—It is not only the progress of mechanical knowledge, but the necessary advances of civilization that are unfavorable to the spirit of poetry. We not only stand in less awe of the preternatural world, but we can calculate more surely, and look with more indifference, upon the regular routine of this. The heroes of the fabulous ages rid the world of monsters and giants. At present we are less exposed to the vicissitudes of good or evil, to the incursions of wild beasts or "bandit fierce," or to the unmitigated fury of the elements. The time has been that "our fell of hair would at a dismal treatise rouse and stir as life were in it." But the police spoils all; and we now hardly so much as dream of a midnight murder. *Macbeth* is only tolerated in this country for the sake of the music; and in the United States of America, where the philosophical principles of government are carried still farther in theory and practice, we find that the *Beggar's Opera* is hooted from the stage. Society, by degrees, is constructed into a machine that carries us safely and insipidly from one end of life to the other, in a very comfortable prose style.

> Obscurity her curtain round them drew,
> And siren Sloth a dull quietus sung.

The remarks which have been here made, would, in some measure, lead to a solution of the question of the comparative merits of painting and poetry. I do not mean to give any preference, but it should seem that the argument which has been sometimes set up, that paint-

---

[1] Thomas Chalmers (1780–1847) wrote a series of *Discourses*, attempting to reconcile science with religion.

ing must affect the imagination more strongly, because it represents the image more distinctly, is not well founded. We may assume without much temerity, that poetry is more poetical than painting. When artists or connoisseurs talk on stilts about the poetry of painting, they show that they know little about poetry, and have little love for the art. Painting gives the object itself; poetry what it implies. Painting embodies what a thing contains in itself: poetry suggests what exists out of it, in any manner connected with it. But this last is the proper province of the imagination. Again, as it relates to passion, painting gives the event, poetry the progress of events: but it is during the progress, in the interval of expectation and suspense, while our hopes and fears are strained to the highest pitch of breathless agony, that the pinch of the interest lies.

> Between the acting of a dreadful thing
> And the first motion, all the interim is
> Like a phantasma or a hideous dream.
> The mortal instruments are then in council;
> And the state of man, like to a little kingdom,
> Suffers then the nature of an insurrection.

But by the time that the picture is painted, all is over. Faces are the best part of a picture; but even faces are not what we chiefly remember in what interests us most.—But it may be asked then, Is there anything better than Claude Lorraine's landscapes, than Titian's portraits, than Raphael's cartoons,[1] or the Greek statues? Of the two first I shall say nothing, as they are evidently picturesque, rather than imaginative. Raphael's cartoons are certainly the finest comments that ever were made on the Scriptures. Would their effect be the same if we were not acquainted with the text? But the New Testament existed before the cartoons. There is one subject of which there is no cartoon, Christ washing the feet of the disciples the night before His death. But that chapter does not need a commentary! It is for want of some such resting place for the imagination that the Greek statues are little else than specious forms. They are marble to the touch and to the heart. They have not an informing principle within them. In their faultless excellence they appear sufficient to themselves. By their beauty they are raised above the frailties of passion or suffering. By their beauty they are deified. But they are

---

[1] Here, a design, or study, drawn as a model for the completed picture—not, as now, a drawing with a satirical significance.

not objects of religious faith to us, and their forms are a reproach to common humanity. They seem to have no sympathy with us, and not to want our admiration.

Poetry in its matter and form is natural imagery or feeling, combined with passion and fancy. In its mode of conveyance, it combines the ordinary use of language with musical expression. There is a question of long standing, in what the essence of poetry consists; or what it is that determines why one set of ideas should be expressed in prose, another in verse. Milton has told us his idea of poetry in a single line—

> Thoughts that voluntary move
> Harmonious numbers.

As there are certain sounds that excite certain movements, and the song and dance go together, so there are, no doubt, certain thoughts that lead to certain tones of voice, or modulations of sound, and change "the words of Mercury into the songs of Apollo." There is a striking instance of this adaptation of the movement of sound and rhythm to the subject, in Spenser's description of the Satyrs accompanying Una to the cave of Sylvanus.

> So from the ground she fearless doth arise
> And walketh forth without suspect of crime.
> They, all as glad as birds of joyous prime,
> Thence lead her forth, about her dancing round,
> Shouting and singing all a shepherd's rhyme;
> And with green branches strewing all the ground,
> Do worship her as queen with olive garland crown'd.
>
> And all the way their merry pipes they sound,
> That all the woods with doubled echoes ring;
> And with their horned feet do wear the ground,
> Leaping like wanton kids in pleasant spring;
> So towards old Sylvanus they her bring,
> Who with the noise awaked, cometh out.
>
> *Faerie Queene*, b. i. c. vi.

On the contrary, there is nothing either musical or natural in the ordinary construction of language. It is a thing altogether arbitrary and conventional. Neither in the sounds themselves, which are the voluntary signs of certain ideas, nor in their grammatical arrangements in common speech, is there any principle of natural imitation, or correspondence to the individual ideas, or to the tone of feeling with which they are conveyed to others. The jerks, the breaks, the inequalities, and harshnesses of prose, are fatal to the flow of a poetical imagination, as a jolting road or a stumbling horse disturbs the reverie of an absent man. But poetry makes these odds all even. It is the music of language, answering to the music of the mind, untying as it were "the secret soul of harmony." Wherever any object takes such a hold of the mind as to make us dwell upon it, and brood over it, melting the heart in tenderness, or kindling it to a sentiment of enthusiasm;—wherever a movement of imagination or passion is impressed on the mind, by which it seeks to prolong and repeat the emotion, to bring all other objects into accord with it, and to give the same movement of harmony, sustained and continuous, or gradually varied according to the occasion, to the sounds that express it—this is poetry. The musical in sound is the sustained and continuous; the musical in thought is the sustained and continuous also. There is a near connection between music and deep-rooted passion. Mad people sing. As often as articulation passes naturally into intonation, there poetry begins. Where one idea gives a tone and color to others, where one feeling melts others into it, there can be no reason why the same principle should not be extended to the sounds by which the voice utters these emotions of the soul, and blends syllables and lines into each other. It is to supply the inherent defect of harmony in the customary mechanism of language, to make the sound an echo to the sense, when the sense becomes a sort of echo to itself—to mingle the tide of verse, "the golden cadences of poetry," with the tide of feeling, flowing and murmuring as it flows—in short, to take the language of the imagination from off the ground, and enable it to spread its wings where it may indulge its own impulses—

> Sailing with supreme dominion
> Through the azure deep of air—

without being stopped, or fretted, or diverted with the abruptnesses and petty obstacles, and discordant flats and sharps of prose, that poetry was invented. It is to common language, what springs are to a carriage, or wings to feet. In ordinary speech we arrive at a certain harmony by the modulations of the voice: in poetry the same thing is done systematically by a regular collocation of syllables. It has been well observed, that every one who declaims warmly, or grows intent upon a subject, rises into a sort of blank verse or measured prose. The merchant, as described in Chaucer, went on his way "sounding always the increase of his winning." Every prose-writer has more or less of rhythmical adaptation, except poets, who, when deprived of the regular mechanism of verse, seem to have no principle of modulation left in their writings.

An excuse might be made for rhyme in the same manner. It is but fair that the ear should linger on the sounds that delight it, or avail itself of the same brilliant coincidence and unexpected recurrence of syllables, that have been displayed in the invention and collocation of images. It is allowed that rhyme assists the memory; and a man of wit and shrewdness has been heard to say, that the only four good lines of poetry are the well-known ones which tell the number of days in the months of the year.

> Thirty days hath September, &c.

But if the jingle of names assists the memory, may it not also quicken the fancy? and there are other things worth having at our fingers' ends, besides the contents of the almanac.—Pope's versification is tiresome, from its excessive sweetness and uniformity. Shakespeare's blank verse is the perfection of dramatic dialogue.

All is not poetry that passes for such: nor does verse make the whole difference between poetry and prose. The *Iliad* does not cease to be poetry in a literal translation; and Addison's *Campaign* has been very properly denominated a Gazette[1] in rhyme. Common prose differs from poetry, as treating for the most part either of such trite, familiar, and irksome matters of fact, as convey no extraordinary impulse to the imagination, or else of such difficult and laborious processes of the understanding, as do not admit of the wayward or violent movements either of the imagination or the passions.

I will mention three works which come as near to poetry as possible without absolutely being so, namely, the *Pilgrim's Progress*, *Robinson Crusoe*, and the *Tales* of Boccaccio. Chaucer and Dryden have translated some of the last into English rhyme, but the essence and the power of poetry was there before. That which lifts the spirit above the earth, which draws the soul out of itself with indescribable longings, is poetry in kind, and generally fit to become so in name, by being "married to immortal verse." If it is of the essence of poetry to strike and fix the imagination, whether we will or no, to make the eye of childhood glisten with the starting tear, to be

[1] The *Gazette* was a periodical giving Court news, word of foreign campaigns, and honors bestowed by the King.

never thought of afterwards with indifference, John Bunyan and Daniel Defoe may be permitted to pass for poets in their way. The mixture of fancy and reality in the *Pilgrim's Progress* was never equalled in any allegory. His pilgrims walk above the earth, and yet are on it. What zeal, what beauty, what truth of fiction! What deep feeling in the description of Christian's swimming across the water at last, and in the picture of the Shining Ones within the gates, with wings at their backs and garlands on their heads, who are to wipe all tears from his eyes! The writer's genius, though not "dipped in dews of Castalie," [1] was baptized with the Holy Spirit and with fire. The prints in this book are no small part of it. If the confinement of Philoctetes in the island of Lemnos was a subject for the most beautiful of all the Greek tragedies, what shall we say to Robinson Crusoe in his? Take the speech of the Greek hero on leaving his cave, beautiful as it is, and compare it with the reflections of the English adventurer in his solitary place of confinement. The thoughts of home, and of all from which he is for ever cut off, swell and press against his bosom, as the heaving ocean rolls its ceaseless tide against the rocky shore, and the very beatings of his heart become audible in the eternal silence that surrounds him. Thus he says:

> As I walked about, either in my hunting, or for viewing the country, the anguish of my soul at my condition would break out upon me on a sudden, and my very heart would die within me to think of the woods, the mountains, the deserts I was in; and how I was a prisoner, locked up with the eternal bars and bolts of the ocean, in an uninhabited wilderness, without redemption. In the midst of the greatest composures of my mind, this would break out upon me like a storm, and make me wring my hands, and weep like a child. Sometimes it would take me in the middle of my work, and I would immediately sit down and sigh, and look upon the ground for an hour or two together, and this was still worse to me, for if I could burst into tears or vent myself in words, it would go off, and the grief having exhausted itself would abate.

The story of his adventures would not make a poem like the *Odyssey*, it is true; but the relator had the true genius of a poet. It has been made a question whether Richardson's romances are poetry; and the answer perhaps is, that they are not poetry, because they are not romance. The interest is worked up to an inconceivable height; but it is by an infinite number of little things, by incessant labor and calls upon the attention, by a repetition of blows that have no

[1] A spring sacred to the Muses, on Parnassus.

rebound in them. The sympathy excited is not a voluntary contribution, but a tax. Nothing is unforced and spontaneous. There is a want of elasticity and motion. The story does not "give an echo to the seat where love is throned." The heart does not answer of itself like a chord in music. The fancy does not run on before the writer with breathless expectation, but is dragged along with an infinite number of pins and wheels, like those with which the Lilliputians dragged Gulliver pinioned to the royal palace.—Sir Charles Grandison is a coxcomb. What sort of a figure would he cut, translated into an epic poem, by the side of Achilles? Clarissa, the divine Clarissa, is too interesting by half. She is interesting in her ruffles, in her gloves, her samplers, her aunts and uncles—she is interesting in all that is uninteresting. Such things, however intensely they may be brought home to us, are not conductors to the imagination. There is infinite truth and feeling in Richardson; but it is extracted from a *caput mortuum* [1] of circumstances: it does not evaporate of itself. His poetical genius is like Ariel confined in a pine-tree, and requires an artificial process to let it out. Shakespeare says—

> Our poesy is as a gum
> Which issues whence 'tis nourished, our gentle flame
> Provokes itself, and like the current flies
> Each bound it chafes. [2]

I shall conclude this general account with some remarks on four of the principal works of poetry in the world, at different periods of history—Homer, the Bible, Dante, and let me add, Ossian. In Homer, the principle of action or life is predominant; in the Bible, the principle of faith and the idea of Providence; Dante is a personification of blind will; and in Ossian we see the decay of life, and the lag end of the world. Homer's poetry is the heroic: it is full of life and action: it is bright as the day, strong as a river. In the vigor of his intellect, he grapples with all the objects of nature, and enters into

---

[1] death's head.

[2] Burke's writings are not poetry, notwithstanding the vividness of the fancy, because the subject matter is abstruse and dry, not natural, but artificial. The difference between poetry and eloquence is, that the one is the eloquence of the imagination, and the other of the understanding. Eloquence tries to persuade the will, and convince the reason: poetry produces its effect by instantaneous sympathy. Nothing is a subject for poetry that admits of a dispute. Poets are in general bad prose-writers, because their images, though fine in themselves, are not to the purpose, and do not carry on the argument. The French poetry wants the forms of the imagination. It is didactic more than dramatic. And some of our own poetry which has been most admired, is only poetry in the rhyme, and in the studied use of poetic diction. (Hazlitt.)

all the relations of social life. He saw many countries, and the manners of many men; and he has brought them all together in his poem. He describes his heroes going to battle with a prodigality of life, arising from an exuberance of animal spirits: we see them before us, their number, and their order of battle, poured out upon the plain "all plumed like estriches, like eagles newly bathed, wanton as goats, wild as young bulls, youthful as May, and gorgeous as the sun at midsummer," covered with glittering armor, with dust and blood; while the gods quaff their nectar in golden cups, or mingle in the fray; and the old men assembled on the walls of Troy rise up with reverence as Helen passes by them. The multitude of things in Homer is wonderful; their splendor, their truth, their force, and variety. His poetry is, like his religion, the poetry of number and form: he describes the bodies as well as the souls of men.

The poetry of the Bible is that of imagination and of faith: it is abstract and disembodied: it is not the poetry of form, but of power; not of multitude, but of immensity. It does not divide into many, but aggrandizes into one. Its ideas of nature are like its ideas of God. It is not the poetry of social life, but of solitude: each man seems alone in the world, with the original forms of nature, the rocks, the earth, and the sky. It is not the poetry of action or heroic enterprise, but of faith in a supreme Providence, and resignation to the power that governs the universe. As the idea of God was removed farther from humanity, and a scattered polytheism, it became more profound and intense, as it became more universal, for the Infinite is present to every thing: "If we fly into the uttermost parts of the earth, it is there also; if we turn to the east or the west, we cannot escape from it." Man is thus aggrandized in the image of his Maker. The history of the patriarchs is of this kind; they are founders of a chosen race of people, the inheritors of the earth; they exist in the generations which are to come after them. Their poetry, like their religious creed, is vast, unformed, obscure, and infinite; a vision is upon it—an invisible hand is suspended over it. The spirit of the Christian religion consists in the glory hereafter to be revealed; but in the Hebrew dispensation, Providence took an immediate share in the affairs of this life. Jacob's dream arose out of this intimate communion between heaven and earth: it was this that let down, in the sight of the youthful patriarch, a golden ladder from the sky to the earth, with angels ascending and descending upon it, and shed a light upon the lonely place, which can never pass away. The story of Ruth, again, is as if all the depth of natural affection in the human race was involved in her breast. There are descriptions in the book of Job more prodigal of imagery, more intense in passion, than anything in Homer, as that of the state of his prosperity, and of the vision that came upon him by night. The metaphors in the Old Testament are more boldly figurative. Things were collected more into masses, and gave a greater *momentum* to the imagination.

Dante was the father of modern poetry, and he may therefore claim a place in this connection. His poem is the first great step from Gothic darkness and barbarism; and the struggle of thought in it to burst the thraldom in which the human mind had been so long held, is felt in every page. He stood bewildered, not appalled, on that dark shore which separates the ancient and the modern world; and saw the glories of antiquity dawning through the abyss of time, while revelation opened its passage to the other world. He was lost in wonder at what had been done before him, and he dared to emulate it. Dante seems to have been indebted to the Bible for the gloomy tone of his mind, as well as for the prophetic fury which exalts and kindles his poetry; but he is utterly unlike Homer. His genius is not a sparkling flame, but the sullen heat of a furnace. He is power, passion, self-will personified. In all that relates to the descriptive or fanciful part of poetry, he bears no comparison to many who had gone before, or who have come after him; but there is a gloomy abstraction in his conceptions, which lies like a dead weight upon the mind; a benumbing stupor, a breathless awe, from the intensity of the impression; a terrible obscurity, like that which oppresses us in dreams; an identity of interest, which moulds every object to its own purposes, and clothes all things with the passions and imaginations of the human soul,—that makes amends for all other deficiencies. The immediate objects he presents to the mind are not much in themselves, they want grandeur, beauty, and order; but they become every thing by the force of the character he impresses upon them. His mind lends its own power to the objects which it contemplates, instead of borrowing it from them. He takes advantage even of the nakedness and dreary vacuity of his subject. His imagination peoples the shades of death, and broods over the silent air. He is the severest of all writers, the most hard and impenetrable, the most opposite to the flowery and glittering; who relies most on his own power, and the sense of it in others, and who leaves most room to the imagination of his readers. Dante's only endeavor is to interest; and he interests by exciting our sympathy with the emotion by which he is himself possessed. He does not place before us the objects by which that emotion has been created; but he seizes on the attention, by showing us the effect they produce on his feelings; and his poetry accordingly gives the same thrilling and overwhelming sensation, which is caught by gazing on the face of a person who has seen some object of horror. The improbability of the events, the abruptness and monotony in the *Inferno,* are excessive: but the interest never flags, from the continued earnestness of the author's mind. Dante's great power is in combining internal feelings with external objects. Thus the gate of hell, on which that withering inscription is written, seems to be endowed with speech and consciousness, and to utter its dread warning, not without a sense of mortal woes. This author habitually unites the absolutely local and individual with the greatest wildness and mysticism. In the midst of the obscure and shadowy regions of the lower world, a tomb suddenly rises up with the inscription, "I am the tomb of Pope Anastasius the Sixth": and half the personages whom he has crowded into the *Inferno* are his own acquaintance. All this, perhaps, tends to heighten the effect by the bold intermixture of realities, and by an appeal, as it were, to the individual knowledge and experience of the reader. He affords few subjects for picture. There is, indeed, one gigantic one, that of Count Ugolino, of which Michael Angelo made a bas-relief, and which Sir Joshua Reynolds ought not to have painted.

Another writer whom I shall mention last, and whom I cannot persuade myself to think a mere modern in the groundwork, is Ossian.[1] He is a feeling and a name that can never be destroyed in the minds of his readers. As Homer is the first vigor and lustihead, Ossian is the decay and old age of poetry. He lives only in the recollection and regret of the past. There is one impression which he conveys more entirely than all other poets, namely, the sense of privation, the loss of all things, of friends, of good name, of country—he is even without God in the world. He converses only with the spirits of the departed; with the motionless and silent clouds. The cold moonlight sheds its faint lustre on his head; the fox peeps out of the ruined tower; the thistle waves its beard to the wandering gale; and the strings of his harp seem, as the hand of age, as the tale of other times,

---

[1] James Macpherson (1736–1796) pretended to have translated some ancient Gaelic and Erse poems, and aroused much interest in the "Ossianic" remains. To this day the controversy regarding their authenticity persists: if the originals ever existed, Macpherson doubtless took great liberties with them. He discovered (or composed) a body of poetry unlike anything which preceded it, and contributed to break up the tyranny of the "classical school" of the earlier eighteenth century. Johnson did not accept the poems as genuine Gaelic; his letter to Macpherson is a classic.

passes over them, to sigh and rustle like the dry reeds in the winter's wind! The feeling of cheerless desolation, of the loss of the pith and sap of existence, of the annihilation of the substance, and the clinging to the shadow of all things as in a mock-embrace, is here perfect. In this way, the lamentation of Selma for the loss of Salgar is the finest of all. If it were indeed possible to show that this writer was nothing, it would only be another instance of mutability, another blank made, another void left in the heart, another confirmation of that feeling which makes him so often complain, "Roll on, ye dark brown years, ye bring no joy on your wing to Ossian!"

De Quincey

Thomas DE QUINCEY (1785–1859), the son of a merchant, was born in Manchester and educated at various schools. After a period of wandering through Wales and leading a Bohemian life in London, he entered Oxford University, from which he did not graduate. During his student days he began to take opium, and could never free himself from the habit. In 1807 he formed friendships with Wordsworth, Coleridge, and Southey, and soon afterward, with Lamb. He visited the Lake District, and in 1809 settled in Grasmere. In 1816 he married, and three years later began his literary career, acting as editor of the *Westmoreland Gazette*. In 1821 he contributed the "Confessions of an English Opium-Eater" to the *London Magazine*. From this time on, he wrote for different periodicals many articles, which in later years he collected in book form. In 1830 he took his family to Edinburgh, where, save for two years in Glasgow (1841–43), he lived until his death in 1859.

De Quincey was a romantic critic, but a critic in whom, as with Longinus, emotion and intellect were balanced, one often giving rise to the other. Emotion could result in a statement like his definition of language as the "incarnation" of the soul. His intellect could produce a psychological analysis of the Porter's Scene in *Macbeth*, and establish the difference between the literature of power and the literature of knowledge—a distinction in the drawing of which De Quincey, like Lessing and Coleridge, proceeded scientifically to a conclusion which has ever since been accepted.

CONCERNING LITERATURE [1]

(1823)

*   *   *   *

The word *literature* is a perpetual source of confusion, because it is used in two senses, and those senses liable to be confounded with each other. In a philosophical use of the word, literature is the direct and adequate antithesis of books of knowledge. But in a popular use, it is a mere term of convenience for expressing inclusively the total books in a language. In this latter sense, a dictionary, a grammar, a spelling-book, an almanac, a pharmacopœia, a Parliamentary report, a system of farriery, a treatise on billiards, the Court Calendar, &c., belong to the literature. But, in the philosophical sense, not only would it be ludicrous to reckon these as parts of the literature, but even books of much higher pretensions must be excluded—as, for instance, books of voyages and travels, and generally all books in which the matter to be communicated is paramount to the manner or form of its communication ("ornari res ipsa negat, contenta doceri").[2]

It is difficult to construct the idea of "literature" with severe accuracy; for it is a fine art—the supreme fine art, and liable to the difficulties which attend such a subtle notion; in fact, a severe construction of the idea must be the *result* of a philosophical investigation into this subject, and cannot precede it. But, for the sake of obtaining some expression for literature that may answer our present purpose, let us throw the question into another form. I have said that the antithesis of literature is books of knowledge. Now, what is that antithesis to *knowledge,* which is here implicitly latent in the word literature? The vulgar antithesis is *pleasure* ("aut prodesse volunt, aut delectare poetæ").[3] Books, we are told, propose to *instruct* or to *amuse.* Indeed! However, not to spend any words upon it, I suppose you will admit that this wretched antithesis will be of no service to us. And, by the way, let me remark to you, in this, as in other cases, how men by their own errors of understanding, by feeble thinking, and inadequate distinctions, forge chains of meanness and servility for themselves. For, this miserable alternative being

[1] From "Letters to a Young Man whose Education has been Neglected," *London Magazine,* March, 1823. (Cf. Masson, x, 46.)

[2] The thing itself denies ornament, content to teach.

[3] Poets wish either to instruct or to please. See Horace above, p. 62.

once admitted, observe what follows. In which class of books does the *Paradise Lost* stand? Among those which instruct, or those which *amuse*? Now, if a man answers among those which instruct, he lies; for there is no instruction in it, nor could be in any great poem, according to the meaning which the word must bear in this distinction, unless it is meant that it should involve its own antithesis. But if he says, "No; amongst those which amuse," then what a beast must he be to degrade, and in this way, what has done the most of any human work to raise and dignify human nature. But the truth is, you see that the idiot does not wish to degrade it; on the contrary, he would willingly tell a lie in its favor, if that would be admitted; but such is the miserable state of slavery to which he has reduced himself by his own puny distinction; for, as soon as he hops out of one of his little cells, he is under a necessity of hopping into the other. The true antithesis [1] to knowledge, in this case, is not *pleasure*, but *power*. All that is literature seeks to communicate power; all that is not literature, to communicate knowledge. Now, if it be asked what is meant by communicating power, I, in my turn, would ask by what name a man would designate the case in which I should be made to feel vividly, and with a vital consciousness, emotions which ordinary life rarely or never supplies occasions for exciting, and which had previously lain unwakened, and hardly within the dawn of consciousness —as myriads of modes of feeling are at this moment in every human mind for want of a poet to organize them? I say, when these inert and sleeping forms *are* organized, when these possibilities *are* actualized, is this conscious and living possession of mine *power*, or what is it?

When, in *King Lear,* the height, and depth, and breadth, of human passion is revealed to us, and, for the purposes of a sublime antagonism, is revealed in the weakness of an old man's nature, and in one

---

[1] For which distinction, as for most of the sound criticism on poetry, or any subject connected with it that I have ever met with, I must acknowledge my obligations to many years' conversation with Mr. Wordsworth. Upon this occasion it may be useful to notice that there is a rhetorical use of the word "power," very different from the analytic one here introduced, which, also, is due originally to Mr. Wordsworth, and will be found in no book before 1798; this is now become a regular slang term in London conversation. In reference to which, it is worth notice that a critic, speaking of the late Mr. Shelley, a year or two ago, in the most popular literary journal of the day, said, "It is alleged that there is power in Mr. Shelley's poetry; now, there can be no power shown in poetry, except by writing good poems" (or words to that effect). Waiving, however, the question of Mr. Shelley's merits, so far is this remark from being true, that the word was originally introduced expressly to provide for the case where, though the poem was *not* good from defect in the *composition*, or from other causes, the stamina and *matériel* of good poetry as fine thinking and passionate conceptions, could not be denied to exist. (De Quincey.)

night two worlds of storm are brought face to face—the human world, and the world of physical nature—mirrors of each other, semichoral antiphonies, strophe and antistrophe heaving with rival convulsions, and with the double darkness of night and madness,—when I am thus suddenly startled into a feeling of the infinity of the world within me, is this power, or what may I call it? Space, again —what is it in most men's minds? The lifeless form of the world without us, a postulate of the geometrician, with no more vitality or real existence to their feelings than the square root of two. But, if Milton has been able to *inform* this empty theatre, peopling it with Titanic shadows, forms that sat at the eldest counsels of the infant world, chaos and original night,—

> Ghostly shapes,
> To meet at noontide, Fear and trembling Hope,
> Death the Skeleton,
> And Time the Shadow,—

so that, from being a thing to inscribe with diagrams, it has become under his hands a vital agent on the human mind,—I presume that I may justly express the tendency of the *Paradise Lost*, by saying that it communicates power; a pretension far above all communication of knowledge. Henceforth, therefore, I shall use the antithesis power and knowledge as the most philosophical expression for literature (that is, *Literæ Humaniores*) and anti-literature (that is, *Literæ didacticæ—παιδεία*).

* * * *

ON THE KNOCKING AT THE GATE IN *MACBETH*[1]

From my boyish days I had always felt a great perplexity on one point in *Macbeth*. It was this:—the knocking at the gate which succeeds to the murder of Duncan produced to my feelings an effect for which I never could account. The effect was that it reflected back upon the murderer a peculiar awfulness and a depth of solemnity; yet, however obstinately I endeavored with my understanding to comprehend this, for many years I never could see *why* it should produce such an effect.

Here I pause for one moment to exhort the reader never to pay

---

[1] *London Magazine,* October, 1823. (Cf. Masson, x, 389.)

any attention to his understanding when it stands in opposition to any other faculty of his mind. The mere understanding, however useful and indispensable, is the meanest faculty in the human mind and the most to be distrusted; and yet the great majority of people trust to nothing else,—which may do for ordinary life, but not for philosophical purposes. Of this, out of ten thousand instances that I might produce, I will cite one. Ask of any person whatsoever who is not previously prepared for the demand by a knowledge of perspective, to draw in the rudest way the commonest appearance which depends upon the laws of that science—as, for instance, to represent the effect of two walls standing at right angles to each other, or the appearance of the houses on each side of a street, as seen by a person looking down the street from one extremity. Now, in all cases, unless the person has happened to observe in pictures how it is that artists produce these effects, he will be utterly unable to make the smallest approximation to it. Yet why? For he has actually seen the effect every day of his life. The reason is that he allows his understanding to overrule his eyes. His understanding, which includes no intuitive knowledge of the laws of vision, can furnish him with no reason why a line which is known and can be proved to be a horizontal line should not *appear* a horizontal line; a line that made any angle with the perpendicular less than a right angle would seem to him to indicate that his houses were all tumbling down together. Accordingly he makes the line of his houses a horizontal line, and fails of course to produce the effect demanded. Here then is one instance out of many, in which not only the understanding is allowed to overrule the eyes, but where the understanding is positively allowed to obliterate the eyes, as it were; for not only does the man believe the evidence of his understanding in opposition to that of his eyes, but (what is monstrous) the idiot is not aware that his eyes ever gave such evidence. He does not know that he has seen (and therefore *quoad* his consciousness has *not* seen) that which he *has* seen every day of his life.

But to return from this digression. My understanding could furnish no reason why the knocking at the gate in *Macbeth* should produce any effect, direct or reflected. In fact, my understanding said positively that it could *not* produce any effect. But I knew better; I felt that it did; and I waited and clung to the problem until further knowledge should enable me to solve it. At length, in 1812, Mr. Williams made his *début* on the stage of Ratcliffe Highway, and executed those unparalleled murders which have procured for him such a brilliant and undying reputation. On which murders, by the way, I must observe, that in one respect they have had an ill effect, by making the connoisseur in murder very fastidious in his taste, and dissatisfied with anything that has been since done in that line. All other murders look pale by the deep crimson of his; and, as an amateur once said to me in a querulous tone, "There has been absolutely nothing *doing* since his time, or nothing that's worth speaking of." But this is wrong, for it is unreasonable to expect all men to be great artists, and born with the genius of Mr. Williams. Now it will be remembered that in the first of these murders (that of the Marrs) the same incident (of a knocking at the door soon after the work of extermination was complete) did actually occur which the genius of Shakespeare has invented; and all good judges, and the most eminent dilettanti, acknowledged the felicity of Shakespeare's suggestion as soon as it was actually realized. Here, then, was a fresh proof that I had the right in relying on my own feeling in opposition to my understanding; and again I set myself to study the problem. At length I solved it to my own satisfaction; and my solution is this:—Murder, in ordinary cases, where the sympathy is wholly directed to the case of the murdered person, is an incident of coarse and vulgar horror; and for this reason,—that it flings the interest exclusively upon the natural but ignoble instinct by which we cleave to life; an instinct which, as being indispensable to the primal law of self-preservation, is the same in kind (though different in degree) amongst all living creatures. This instinct, therefore, because it annihilates all distinctions, and degrades the greatest of men to the level of "the poor beetle that we tread on," exhibits human nature in its most abject and humiliating attitude. Such an attitude would little suit the purposes of the poet. What then must he do? He must throw the interest on the murderer. Our sympathy must be with *him* (of course I mean a sympathy of comprehension, a sympathy by which we enter into his feelings, and are made to understand them—not a sympathy of pity or approbation).[1] In the murdered person all strife of thought, all flux and reflux of passion and of purpose, are crushed by one overwhelming panic; the fear of instant death smites him

---

[1] It seems almost ludicrous to guard and explain my use of a word in a situation where it would naturally explain itself. But it has become necessary to do so, in consequence of the unscholarlike use of the word sympathy, at present so general, by which, instead of taking it in its proper sense, as the act of reproducing in our minds the feelings of another, whether for hatred, indignation, love, pity, or approbation, it is made a mere synonym of the word *pity;* and hence, instead of saying, "sympathy *with* another," many writers adopt the monstrous barbarism of "sympathy *for* another." (De Quincey.)

"with its petrific mace." But in the murderer, such a murderer as a poet will condescend to, there must be raging some great storm of passion—jealousy, ambition, vengeance, hatred—which will create a hell within him; and into this hell we are to look.

In *Macbeth,* for the sake of gratifying his now enormous and teeming faculty of creation, Shakespeare has introduced two murderers; and, as usual in his hands, they are remarkably discriminated; but—though in Macbeth the strife of mind is greater than in his wife, the tiger spirit not so awake, and his feelings caught chiefly by contagion from her—yet, as both were finally involved in the guilt of murder, the murderous mind of necessity is finally to be presumed in both. This was to be expressed; and on its own account, as well as to make it a more proportionable antagonist to the unoffending nature of their victim, "the gracious Duncan," and adequately to expound "the deep damnation of his taking off," this was to be expressed with peculiar energy. We were to be made to feel that the human nature—i. e., the divine nature of love and mercy, spread through the hearts of all creatures, and seldom utterly withdrawn from man—was gone, vanished, extinct, and that the fiendish nature had taken its place. And, as this effect is marvellously accomplished in the *dialogues* and *soliloquies* themselves, so it is finally consummated by the expedient under consideration; and it is to this that I now solicit the reader's attention. If the reader has ever witnessed a wife, daughter, or sister, in a fainting fit, he may chance to have observed that the most affecting moment in such a spectacle is that in which a sigh and a stirring announce the recommencement of suspended life. Or, if the reader has ever been present in a vast metropolis on the day when some great national idol was carried in funeral pomp to his grave, and, chancing to walk near the course through which it passed, has felt powerfully, in the silence and desertion of the streets and in the stagnation of ordinary business, the deep interest which at that moment was possessing the heart of man,—if all at once he should hear the death-like stillness broken up by the sound of wheels rattling away from the scene, and making known that the transitory vision was dissolved, he will be aware that at no moment was his sense of the complete suspension and pause in ordinary human concerns so full and affecting as at that moment when the suspension ceases, and the goings-on of human life are suddenly resumed. All action in any direction is best expounded, measured, and made apprehensible, by reaction. Now apply this to the case in *Macbeth.* Here, as I have said, the retiring of the human heart and the entrance of the fiendish heart was to be expressed and made sensible. Another world has stepped in; and the murderers are taken out of the region of human things, human purposes, human desires. They are transfigured: Lady Macbeth is "unsexed"; Macbeth has forgot that he was born of woman; both are conformed to the image of devils; and the world of devils is suddenly revealed. But how shall this be conveyed and made palpable? In order that a new world may step in, this world must for a time disappear. The murderers, and the murder, must be insulated—cut off by an immeasurable gulf from the ordinary tide and succession of human affairs—locked up and sequestered in some deep recess; we must be made sensible that the world of ordinary life is suddenly arrested—laid asleep—tranced—racked into a dread armistice; time must be annihilated, relation to things without abolished; and all must pass self-withdrawn into a deep syncope and suspension of earthly passion. Hence it is that, when the deed is done, when the work of darkness is perfect, then the world of darkness passes away like a pageantry in the clouds: the knocking at the gate is heard, and it makes known audibly that the reaction has commenced; the human has made its reflux upon the fiendish; the pulses of life are beginning to beat again; and the re-establishment of the goings-on of the world in which we live first makes us profoundly sensible of the awful parenthesis that had suspended them.

O mighty poet! Thy works are not as those of other men, simply and merely great works of art, but are also like the phenomena of nature, like the sun and the sea, the stars and the flowers, like frost and snow, rain and dew, hail-storm and thunder, which are to be studied with entire submission of our own faculties, and in the perfect faith that in them there can be no too much or too little, nothing useless or inert, but that, the farther we press in our discoveries, the more we shall see proofs of design and self-supporting arrangement where the careless eye had seen nothing but accident!

THE LITERATURE OF KNOWLEDGE AND THE LITERATURE OF POWER [1]

What is it that we mean by *literature?* Popularly, and amongst the thoughtless, it is held to include everything that is printed in a

---

[1] From the review of "The Works of Alexander Pope, Esquire. By W. Roscoe, Esq." *North British Review*, August, 1848. (Cf. Masson, xi, 51.) It is not to be confused with the article on *Pope* which De Quincey wrote for the seventh edition of the *Encyclopædia Britannica*. (Cf. Masson, iv, 280.)

book. Little logic is required to disturb *that* definition; the most thoughtless person is easily made aware, that in the idea of *literature,* one essential element is,—some relation to a general and common interest of man, so that, what applies only to a local, or professional, or merely personal interest, even though presenting itself in the shape of a book, will not belong to literature. So far the definition is easily narrowed; and it is as easily expanded. For not only is much that takes a station in books not literature; but inversely, much that really *is* literature never reaches a station in books. The weekly sermons of Christendom, that vast pulpit literature which acts so extensively upon the popular mind—to warn, to uphold, to renew, to comfort, to alarm, does not attain the sanctuary of libraries in the ten-thousandth part of its extent. The drama again, as for instance, the finest of Shakespeare's plays in England, and all leading Athenian plays in the noontide of the Attic stage, operated as a literature on the public mind, and were (according to the strictest letter of that term) *published* through the audiences that witnessed [1] their representation some time before they were published as things to be read; and they were published in this scenical mode of publication with much more effect than they could have had as books, during ages of costly copying, or of costly printing.

Books, therefore, do not suggest an idea co-extensive and interchangeable with the idea of literature; since much literature, scenic, forensic, or didactic (as from lecturers and public orators), may never come into books; and much that *does* come into books, may connect itself with no literary interest.[2] But a far more important correction, applicable to the common vague idea of literature, is to be sought—not so much in a better definition of literature, as in a sharper distinction of the two functions which it fulfils. In that great social organ, which, collectively, we call literature, there may be distinguished two separate offices that may blend and often *do* so, but capable, severally, of a severe insulation, and naturally fitted for

---

[1] Charles I, for example, when Prince of Wales, and many others in his father's court, gained their known familiarity with Shakespeare—not through the original quartos, so slenderly diffused, nor through the first folio of 1623, but through the court representations of his chief dramas at Whitehall. (De Quincey.)

[2] What are called *The Blue Books*, by which title are understood the folio Reports issued every session of Parliament by committees of the two Houses, and stitched into blue covers,—though often sneered at by the ignorant as so much waste paper, will be acknowledged gratefully by those who have used them diligently, as the main well-heads of all accurate information as to the Great Britain of this day. As an immense depository of faithful (*and not superannuated*) statistics, they are indispensable to the honest student. But no man would therefore class the *Blue Books* as literature. (De Quincey.)

reciprocal repulsion. There is, first, the literature of *knowledge*; and, secondly, the literature of *power*. The function of the first is—to *teach*; the function of the second is—to *move*: the first is a rudder; the second, an oar or a sail. The first speaks to the *mere* discursive understanding; the second speaks ultimately, it may happen, to the higher understanding or reason, but always *through* affections of pleasure and sympathy. Remotely, it may travel towards an object seated in what Lord Bacon calls *dry* light; but, proximately, it does and must operate, else it ceases to be a literature of *power*, on and through that *humid* light which clothes itself in the mists and glittering *iris* of human passions, desires, and genial emotions. Men have so little reflected on the higher functions of literature, as to find it a paradox if one should describe it as a mean or subordinate purpose of books to give information. But this is a paradox only in the sense which makes it honorable to be paradoxical. Whenever we talk in ordinary language of seeking information or gaining knowledge, we understand the words as connected with something of absolute novelty. But it is the grandeur of all truth, which *can* occupy a very high place in human interests, that it is never absolutely novel to the meanest of minds: it exists eternally by way of germ or latent principle in the lowest as in the highest, needing to be developed, but never to be planted. To be capable of transplantation is the immediate criterion of a truth that ranges on a lower scale. Besides which, there is a rarer thing than truth, namely, *power*, or deep sympathy with truth. What is the effect, for instance, upon society, of children? By the pity, by the tenderness, and by the peculiar modes of admiration, which connect themselves with the helplessness, with the innocence, and with the simplicity of children, not only are the primal affections strengthened and continually renewed, but the qualities which are dearest in the sight of heaven—the frailty, for instance, which appeals to forbearance; the innocence which symbolizes the heavenly, and the simplicity which is most alien from the worldly, are kept up in perpetual remembrance, and their ideals are continually refreshed. A purpose of the same nature is answered by the higher literature, viz., the literature of power. What do you learn from *Paradise Lost*? Nothing at all. What do you learn from a cookery-book? Something new—something that you did not know before, in every paragraph. But would you therefore put the wretched cookery-book on a higher level of estimation than the divine poem? What you owe to Milton is not any knowledge, of which a million separate items are still but a million of advancing steps on the same earthly level; what you owe, is *power*, that is, exercise and expansion to your own latent capacity of sympathy with the infinite, where every pulse and each separate influx is a step upwards—a step ascending as upon a Jacob's ladder from earth to mysterious altitudes above the earth. *All* the steps of knowledge, from first to last, carry you further on the same plane, but could never raise you one foot above your ancient level of earth: whereas, the very *first* step in power is a flight—is an ascending movement into another element where earth is forgotten.

Were it not that human sensibilities are ventilated and continually called out into exercise by the great phenomena of infancy, or of real life as it moves through chance and change, or of literature as it recombines these elements in the mimicries of poetry, romance, &c., it is certain that, like any animal power or muscular energy falling into disuse, all such sensibilities would gradually droop and dwindle. It is in relation to these great *moral* capacities of man that the literature of power, as contradistinguished from that of knowledge, lives and has its field of action. It is concerned with what is highest in man; for the Scriptures themselves never condescended to deal by suggestion or co-operation, with the mere discursive understanding: when speaking of man in his intellectual capacity, the Scriptures speak not of the understanding, but of *"the understanding heart,"* —making the heart, i. e., the great *intuitive* (or non-discursive) organ, to be the interchangeable formula for man in his highest state of capacity for the infinite. Tragedy, romance, fairy tale, or epopee, all alike restore to man's mind the ideals of justice, of hope, of truth, of mercy, of retribution, which else (left to the support of daily life in its realities) would languish for want of sufficient illustration. What is meant, for instance, by *poetic justice?*—It does not mean a justice that differs by its object from the ordinary justice of human jurisprudence; for then it must be confessedly a very bad kind of justice; but it means a justice that differs from common forensic justice by the degree in which it *attains* its object, a justice that is more omnipotent over its own ends, as dealing—not with the refractory elements of earthly life—but with the elements of its own creation, and with materials flexible to its own purest preconceptions. It is certain that, were it not for the literature of power, these ideals would often remain amongst us as mere arid notional forms; whereas, by the creative forces of man put forth in literature, they gain a vernal life of restoration, and germinate into vital activities.

The commonest novel, by moving in alliance with human fears and hopes, with human instincts of wrong and right, sustains and quickens those affections. Calling them into action, it rescues them from torpor. And hence the pre-eminency over all authors that merely *teach*, of the meanest that *moves;* or that teaches, if at all, indirectly *by* moving. The very highest work that has ever existed in the literature of knowledge, is but a *provisional* work: a book upon trial and sufferance, and *quamdiu bene se gesserit.*[1] Let its teaching be even partially revised, let it be but expanded, nay, even let its teaching be but placed in a better order, and instantly it is superseded. Whereas the feeblest works in the literature of power, surviving at all, survive as finished and unalterable amongst men. For instance, the *Principia* of Sir Isaac Newton was a book *militant* on earth from the first. In all stages of its progress it would have to fight for its existence: first, as regards absolute truth; secondly, when that combat was over, as regards its form or mode of presenting the truth. And as soon as a La Place, or anybody else, builds higher upon the foundations laid by this book, effectually he throws it out of the sunshine into decay and darkness; by weapons won from this book he superannuates and destroys this book, so that soon the name of Newton remains, as a mere *nominis umbra,*[2] but his book, as a living power, has transmigrated into other forms. Now, on the contrary, the *Iliad*, the *Prometheus* of Æschylus,—the *Othello* or *King Lear*,—the *Hamlet* or *Macbeth*,—and the *Paradise Lost*, are not militant but triumphant for ever as long as the languages exist in which they speak or can be taught to speak. They never *can* transmigrate into new incarnations. To reproduce *these* in new forms, or variations, even if in some things they should be improved, would be to plagiarize. A good steam-engine is properly superseded by a better. But one lovely pastoral valley is not superseded by another, nor a statue of Praxiteles by a statue of Michael Angelo. These things are separated not by imparity, but by disparity. They are not thought of as unequal under the same standard, but as different in *kind*, and if otherwise equal, as equal under a different standard. Human works of immortal beauty and works of nature in one respect stand on the same footing; they never absolutely repeat each other; never approach so near as not to differ; and they differ not as better and worse, or simply by more and less: they differ by undecipherable and incommunicable differences, that cannot be caught by mimicries,

[1] As long as it behaves itself.
[2] Shadow of a name.

that cannot be reflected in the mirror or copies, that cannot become ponderable in the scales of vulgar comparison.

Applying these principles to Pope, as a representative of fine literature in general, we would wish to remark the claim which he has, or which an equal writer has, to the attention and jealous winnowing of those critics, in particular, who watch over public morals. Clergymen, and all the organs of public criticism put in motion by clergymen, are more especially concerned in the just appreciation of such writers, if the two canons are remembered, which we have endeavored to illustrate, viz., that all works in this class, as opposed to those in the literature of knowledge, first, work by far deeper agencies; and, secondly, are more permanent; in the strictest sense they are κτήματα ἐς ἀεί: [1] and what evil they do, or what good they do, is commensurate with the national language, sometimes long after the nation has departed. At this hour, five hundred years since their creation, the tales of Chaucer, never equalled on this earth for their tenderness, and for life of picturesqueness, are read familiarly by many in the charming language of their natal day, and by others in the modernizations of Dryden, of Pope, and Wordsworth. At this hour, one thousand eight hundred years since their creation, the Pagan tales of Ovid, never equalled on this earth for the gaiety of their movement and the capricious graces of their narrative, are read by all Christendom. This man's people and their monuments are dust; but *he* is alive: he has survived them, as he told us that he had it in his commission to do, by a thousand years; "and *shall* a thousand more."

All the literature of knowledge builds only ground-nests, that are swept away by floods, or confounded by the plough; but the literature of power builds nests in aërial altitudes of temples sacred from violation, or of forests inaccessible to fraud. *This* is a great prerogative of the *power* literature; and it is a greater which lies in the mode of its influence. The *knowledge* literature, like the fashion of this world, passeth away. An Encyclopædia is its abstract; and, in this respect, it may be taken for its speaking symbol—that, before one generation has passed, an Encyclopædia is superannuated; for it speaks through the dead memory and unimpassioned understanding, which have not the repose of higher faculties, but are continually enlarging and varying their phylacteries. But all literature, properly so called—literature κατ᾽ ἐξοχήν,[2] for the very reason that it

[1] perpetual possessions.
[2] *Par excellence.*

is so much more durable than the literature of knowledge, is (and by the very same proportion it is) more intense and electrically searching in its impressions. The directions in which the tragedy of this planet has trained our human feelings to play, and the combinations into which the poetry of this planet has thrown our human passions of love and hatred, of admiration and contempt, exercise a power bad or good over human life, that cannot be contemplated, when stretching through many generations, without a sentiment allied to awe.[1] And of this let every one be assured—that he owes to the impassioned books which he has read, many a thousand more of emotions than he can consciously trace back to them. Dim by their origination, these emotions yet arise in him, and mould him through life like forgotten incidents of his childhood.

* * * *

[1] The reason why the broad distinctions between the two literatures of power and knowledge so little fix the attention, lies in the fact, that a vast proportion of books— history, biography, travels, miscellaneous essays, &c., lying in a middle zone, confound these distinctions by interblending them. All that we call "amusement" or "entertainment," is a diluted form of the power belonging to passion, and also a mixed form; and where threads of direct *instruction* intermingle in the texture with these threads of *power*, this absorption of the duality into one representative *nuance* neutralizes the separate perception of either. Fused into a *tertium quid*, or neutral state, they disappear to the popular eye as the repelling forces, which, in fact, they are. (De Quincey.)

Shelley

Percy Bysshe SHELLEY (1792–1822) was born near Horsham, in Sussex, and was educated at Brentford, Eton, and Oxford University, from which he was expelled in 1811, after acknowledging the authorship of a pamphlet, *The Necessity of Atheism*. Well-grounded in the classics, he studied Plato, who aroused his enthusiasm and influenced his subsequent views, notably his Utopian speculations. In 1811 he offended his father, Sir Timothy, by marrying Harriet Westbrook, the young daughter of a retired innkeeper; and in 1814 he eloped with Mary Wollstonecraft, the daughter of William Godwin, whom he married after his wife's suicide in 1816. In 1818, the year in which his second wife wrote *Frankenstein*, Shelley took up his residence in Italy, staying with Byron in Venice, and later visiting Naples, Rome, Florence, and Leghorn, before he settled in Pisa. During these years he wrote *The Cenci, Prometheus Unbound, Epipsychidion, Adonais, Hellas,* and many lyrics, including the famous odes. In 1822 he was drowned while sailing in the Gulf of Spezzia; his ashes were buried in the Protestant Cemetery at Rome.

The *Defence of Poetry*, Shelley's only critical writing, was a general reply to an essay, *Four Ages of Poetry*, by his friend, and later his executor, Thomas Love Peacock, the novelist. It grew out of their correspondence, was written the year before Shelley's death, and was published twenty years later by his wife.

The student will readily perceive that Shelley is a disciple of Plato in his philosophy, but not in his aversion to poets as members of the State. Shelley believed that poets catch the visitations of the Divine to man, and also that they are the unacknowledged legislators of the world. The essay is both intellectual and emotional, and, like that of Sir Philip Sidney's, inspires the reader not only by its content, but also by the way the ideas are expressed.

From A DEFENCE OF POETRY[1]

(1821)

According to one mode of regarding those two classes of mental action which are called reason and imagination, the former may be considered as mind contemplating the relations borne by one thought to another, however produced, and the latter as mind acting upon those thoughts so as to color them with its own light, and composing from them, as from elements, other thoughts, each containing within itself the principle of its own integrity. The one is the τὸ ποιεῖν,[2] or the principle of synthesis, and has for its object those forms which are common to universal nature and existence itself; the other is the τὸ λογίζειν,[3] or principle of analysis, and its action regards the relations of things simply as relations; considering thoughts not in their integral unity, but as the algebraical representations which conduct to certain general results. Reason is the enumeration of quantities already known; imagination is the perception of the value of those quantities, both separately and as a whole. Reason respects the differences, and imagination the similitudes of things. Reason is to imagination as the instrument to the agent, as the body to the spirit, as the shadow to the substance.

Poetry, in a general sense, may be defined to be the expression of the imagination; and poetry is connate with the origin of man. Man is an instrument over which a series of external and internal impressions are driven, like the alternations of an ever-changing wind over an Æolian lyre, which move it by their motion to ever-changing melody. But there is a principle within the human being, and perhaps within all sentient beings, which acts otherwise than in a lyre, and produces not melody alone, but harmony, by an internal adjustment

[1] In 1821, Shelley wrote Thomas Love Peacock that he had composed part of an essay designed as an antidote to the latter's *Four Ages of Poetry*. The last two parts were never written, and the essay as he left it first appeared in the collection of Shelley's prose writings brought out by his wife in 1840.

[2] to make.

[3] to reason.

of the sounds and motions thus excited to the impressions which excite them. It is as if the lyre could accommodate its chords to the
motions of that which strikes them, in a determined proportion of
sound; even as the musician can accommodate his voice to the sound
of the lyre. A child at play by itself will express its delight by its
voice and motions; and every inflection of tone and every gesture
will bear exact relation to a corresponding antitype in the pleasurable impressions which awakened it; it will be the reflected image of
that impression; and as the lyre trembles and sounds after the wind
has died away, so the child seeks, by prolonging in its voice and motions the duration of the effect, to prolong also a consciousness of the
cause. In relation to the objects which delight a child, these expressions are what poetry is to higher objects. The savage (for the
savage is to ages what the child is to years) expresses the emotions
produced in him by surrounding objects in a similar manner; and
language and gesture, together with plastic or pictorial imitation,
become the image of the combined effect of those objects and his
apprehension of them. Man in society, with all his passions and his
pleasures, next becomes the object of the passions and pleasures of
man; an additional class of emotions produces an augmented treasure
of expression; and language, gesture, and the imitative arts, become
at once the representation and the medium, the pencil and the picture, the chisel and the statue, the chord and the harmony. The social
sympathies, or those laws from which, as from its elements, society
results, begin to develop themselves from the moment that two
human beings co-exist; the future is contained within the present as
the plant within the seed; and equality, diversity, unity, contrast,
mutual dependence, become the principles alone capable of affording
the motives according to which the will of a social being is determined to action, inasmuch as he is social; and constitute pleasure in
sensation, virtue in sentiment, beauty in art, truth in reasoning, and
love in the intercourse of kind. Hence men, even in the infancy of
society, observe a certain order in their words and actions, distinct
from that of the objects and the impressions represented by them, all
expression being subject to the laws of that from which it proceeds.
But let us dismiss those more general considerations which might involve an inquiry into the principles of society itself, and restrict our
view to the manner in which the imagination is expressed upon its
forms.

In the youth of the world, men dance and sing and imitate natural
objects, observing in these actions, as in all others, a certain rhythm

or order. And, although all men observe a similar, they observe not the same order in the motions of the dance, in the melody of the song, in the combinations of language, in the series of their imitations of natural objects. For there is a certain order or rhythm belonging to each of these classes of mimetic representation, from which the hearer and the spectator receive an intenser and purer pleasure than from any other; the sense of an approximation to this order has been called taste by modern writers. Every man, in the infancy of art, observes an order which approximates more or less closely to that from which this highest delight results; but the diversity is not sufficiently marked as that its gradations should be sensible, except in those instances where the predominance of this faculty of approximation to the beautiful (for so we may be permitted to name the relation between this highest pleasure and its cause) is very great. Those in whom it exists to excess are poets, in the most universal sense of the word; and the pleasure resulting from the manner in which they express the influence of society or nature upon their own minds, communicates itself to others, and gathers a sort of reduplication from the community. Their language is vitally metaphorical; that is, it marks the before unapprehended relations of things and perpetuates their apprehension, until words, which represent them, become, through time, signs for portions or classes of thought instead of pictures of integral thoughts; and then, if no new poets should arise to create afresh the associations which have been thus disorganized, language will be dead to all the nobler purposes of human intercourse. These similitudes or relations are finely said by Lord Bacon to be "the same footsteps of nature impressed upon the various subjects of the world" [1]—and he considers the faculty which perceives them as the storehouse of axioms common to all knowledge. In the infancy of society every author is necessarily a poet, because language itself is poetry; and to be a poet is to apprehend the true and the beautiful,—in a word, the good which exists in the relation subsisting, first between existence and perception, and secondly between perception and expression. Every original language near to its source is in itself the chaos of a cyclic poem; in the copiousness of lexicography and the distinctions of grammar are the works of a later age, and are merely the catalogue and the forms of the creations of poetry.

But poets, or those who imagine and express this indestructible order, are not only the authors of language and of music, of the

---

[1] *Advancement of Learning*, II, 5.

dance, and architecture, and statuary, and painting: they are the institutors of laws, and the founders of civil society, and the inventors of the arts of life, and the teachers who draw into a certain propinquity with the beautiful and the true that partial apprehension of the agencies of the invisible world which is called religion. Hence all original religions are allegorical, or susceptible of allegory, and, like Janus, have a double face of false and true. Poets, according to the circumstances of the age and nation in which they appeared, were called, in the earlier epochs of the world, legislators or prophets; a poet essentially comprises and unites both these characters. For he not only beholds intensely the present as it is, and discovers those laws according to which present things ought to be ordered, but he beholds the future in the present, and his thoughts are the germs of the flower and the fruit of latest time. Not that I assert poets to be prophets in the gross sense of the word, or that they can foretell the form as surely as they foreknow the spirit of events; such is the pretense of superstition, which would make poetry an attribute of prophecy, rather than prophecy an attribute of poetry. A poet participates in the eternal, the infinite, and the one; as far as relates to his conceptions, time and place and number are not. The grammatical forms which express the moods of time, and the difference of persons, and the distinction of place, are convertible with respect to the highest poetry without injuring it as poetry; and the choruses of Æschylus, and the Book of *Job*, and Dante's *Paradise*, would afford, more than any other writings, examples of this fact, if the limits of this essay did not forbid citation. The creations of music, sculpture, and painting are illustrations still more decisive.

Language, color, form, and religious and civil habits of action, are all the instruments and materials of poetry; they may be called poetry by that figure of speech which considers the effect as a synonym of the cause. But poetry in a more restricted sense expresses those arrangements of language, and especially metrical language, which are created by that imperial faculty whose throne is curtained within the invisible nature of man. And this springs from the nature itself of language, which is a more direct representation of the actions and passions of our internal being, and is susceptible of more various and delicate combinations, than color, form, or motion, and is more plastic and obedient to the control of that faculty of which it is the creation. For language is arbitrarily produced by the imagination, and has relation to thoughts alone; but all other materials, instruments, and conditions of art have relations among each other, which limit and interpose between conception and expression. The former is as a mirror which reflects, the latter as a cloud which enfeebles, the light of which both are mediums of communication. Hence the fame of sculptors, painters, and musicians, although the intrinsic powers of the great masters of these arts may yield in no degree to that of those who have employed language as the hieroglyphic of their thoughts, has never equalled that of poets in the restricted sense of the term; as two performers of equal skill will produce unequal effects from a guitar and a harp. The fame of legislators and founders of religions, so long as their institutions last, alone seems to exceed that of poets in the restricted sense; but it can scarcely be a question, whether, if we deduct the celebrity which their flattery of the gross opinions of the vulgar usually conciliates, together with that which belonged to them in their higher character of poets, any excess will remain.

We have thus circumscribed the word poetry within the limits of that art which is the most familiar and the most perfect expression of the faculty itself. It is necessary, however, to make the circle still narrower, and to determine the distinction between measured and unmeasured language; for the popular division into prose and verse is inadmissible in accurate philosophy.

Sounds as well as thoughts have relation both between each other and towards that which they represent, and a perception of the order of those relations has always been found connected with a perception of the order of the relations of thoughts. Hence the language of poets has ever affected a sort of uniform and harmonious recurrence of sound, without which it were not poetry, and which is scarcely less indispensable to the communication of its influence than the words themselves without reference to that peculiar order. Hence the vanity of translation; it were as wise to cast a violet into a crucible that you might discover the formal principles of its color and odor, as seek to transfuse from one language into another the creations of a poet. The plant must spring again from its seed, or it will bear no flower—and this is the burthen of the curse of Babel.

An observation of the regular mode of the recurrence of harmony in the language of poetical minds, together with its relation to music, produced metre, or a certain system of traditional forms of harmony and language. Yet it is by no means essential that a poet should accommodate his language to this traditional form, so that the harmony, which is its spirit, be observed. The practice is indeed convenient and popular, and to be preferred especially in such composition as includes much action; but every great poet must inevitably innovate upon the example of his predecessors in the exact structure of his peculiar versification. The distinction between poets and prose writers is a vulgar error. The distinction between philosophers and poets has been anticipated. Plato was essentially a poet—the truth and splendor of his imagery, and the melody of his language, are the most intense that it is possible to conceive. He rejected the harmony of the epic, dramatic, and lyrical forms, because he sought to kindle a harmony in thoughts divested of shape and action, and he forbore to invent any regular plan of rhythm which would include, under determinate forms, the varied pauses of his style. Cicero sought to imitate the cadence of his periods, but with little success. Lord Bacon was a poet. His language has a sweet and majestic rhythm which satisfies the sense, no less than the almost superhuman wisdom of his philosophy satisfies the intellect; it is a strain which distends and then bursts the circumference of the reader's mind, and pours itself forth together with it into the universal element with which it has perpetual sympathy. All the authors of revolutions in opinion are not only necessarily poets as they are inventors, nor even as their words unveil the permanent analogy of things by images which participate in the life of truth; but as their periods are harmonious and rhythmical, and contain in themselves the elements of verse; being the echo of the eternal music. Nor are those supreme poets, who have employed traditional forms of rhythm on account of the form and action of their subjects, less capable of perceiving and teaching the truth of things, than those who have omitted that form. Shakespeare, Dante, and Milton (to confine ourselves to modern writers) are philosophers of the very loftiest power.

A poem is the very image of life expressed in its eternal truth. There is this difference between a story and a poem, that a story is a catalogue of detached facts, which have no other connection than time, place, circumstance, cause and effect; the other is the creation of actions according to the unchangeable forms of human nature, as existing in the mind of the creator, which is itself the image of all other minds. The one is partial, and applies only to a definite period of time, and a certain combination of events which can never again recur; the other is universal, and contains within itself the germ of a relation to whatever motives or actions have place in the possible varieties of human nature. Time, which destroys the beauty and the use of the story of particular facts, stripped of the poetry which should invest them, augments that of poetry, and for ever develops new and wonderful applications of the eternal truth which it contains. Hence epitomes have been called the moths of just history; they eat out the poetry of it. A story of particular facts is as a mirror which obscures and distorts that which should be beautiful; poetry is a mirror which makes beautiful that which is distorted.

The parts of a composition may be poetical, without the composition as a whole being a poem. A single sentence may be considered as a whole, though it may be found in the midst of a series of unassimilated portions; a single word even may be a spark of inextinguishable thought. And thus all the great historians, Herodotus, Plutarch, Livy, were poets; and although the plan of these writers, especially that of Livy, restrained them from developing this faculty in its highest degree, they made copious and ample amends for their subjection, by filling all the interstices of their subjects with living images.

Having determined what is poetry, and who are poets, let us proceed to estimate its effects upon society.

Poetry is ever accompanied with pleasure: all spirits on which it falls open themselves to receive the wisdom which is mingled with its delight. In the infancy of the world, neither poets themselves, nor their auditors are fully aware of the excellency of poetry, for it acts in a divine and unapprehended manner, beyond and above consciousness; and it is reserved for future generations to contemplate and measure the mighty cause and effect in all the strength and splendor of their union. Even in modern times, no living poet ever arrived at the fulness of his fame; the jury which sits in judgment upon a poet, belonging as he does to all time, must be composed of his peers; it must be impanelled by Time from the selectest of the wise of many generations. A poet is a nightingale, who sits in darkness and sings to cheer its own solitude with sweet sounds; his auditors are as men entranced by the melody of an unseen musician, who feel that they are moved and softened, yet know not whence or why. The poems of Homer and his contemporaries were the delight of infant Greece; they were the elements of that social system which is the column upon which all succeeding civilization has reposed. Homer embodied the ideal perfection of his age in human character; nor can we doubt that those who read his verses were awakened to an ambition of becoming like to Achilles, Hector, and Ulysses; the truth and beauty of friendship, patriotism, and persevering devotion to an object, were unveiled to their depths in these immortal creations; the sentiments of the auditors must have been refined and enlarged by a sympathy with such great and lovely impersonations, until from admiring they imitated, and from imitation they identified themselves with the objects of their admiration. Nor let it be objected that these characters are remote from moral perfection, and that they are by no means to be considered as edifying patterns for general imitation. Every epoch, under names more or less specious, has deified its peculiar errors; Revenge is the naked idol of the worship of a semi-barbarous age; and Self-deceit is the veiled image of unknown evil, before which luxury and satiety lie prostrate. But a poet considers the vices of his contemporaries as the temporary dress in which his creations must be arrayed, and which cover without concealing the eternal proportions of their beauty. An epic or dramatic personage is understood to wear them around his soul, as he may the ancient armor or modern uniform around his body; whilst it is easy to conceive a dress more graceful than either. The beauty of the internal nature can not be so far concealed by its accidental vesture, but that the spirit of its form shall communicate itself to the very disguise, and indicate the shape it hides from the manner in which it is worn. A majestic form and graceful motions will express themselves through the most barbarous and tasteless costume. Few poets of the highest class have chosen to exhibit the beauty of their conceptions in its naked truth and splendor; and it is doubtful whether the alloy of costume, habit, etc., be not necessary to temper this planetary music for mortal ears.

The whole objection, however, of the immorality of poetry rests upon a misconception of the manner in which poetry acts to produce the moral improvement of man. Ethical science arranges the elements which poetry has created, and propounds schemes and proposes examples of civil and domestic life; nor is it for want of admirable doctrines that men hate, and despise, and censure, and deceive, and subjugate one another. But poetry acts in another and diviner manner. It awakens and enlarges the mind itself by rendering it the receptacle of a thousand unapprehended combinations of thought. Poetry lifts the veil from the hidden beauty of the world, and makes familiar objects be as if they were not familiar; it reproduces all that it represents, and the impersonations clothed in its Elysian light stand thenceforward in the minds of those who have once contemplated them, as memorials of that gentle and exalted content which extends itself over all thoughts and actions with which it co-exists. The great secret of morals is love; or a going out of our own nature, and an identification of ourselves with the beautiful which exists in thought, action, or person, not our own. A man, to be greatly good, must imagine intensely and comprehensively; he must put himself in the place of another and of many others; the pains and pleasures of his species must become his own. The great instrument of moral good is the imagination; and poetry administers to the effect by acting upon the cause. Poetry enlarges the circumference of the imagination by replenishing it with thoughts of ever new delight, which have the power of attracting and assimilating to their own nature all other thoughts, and which form new intervals and interstices whose void for ever craves fresh food. Poetry strengthens the faculty which is the organ of the moral nature of man, in the same manner as exercise strengthens a limb. A poet therefore would do ill to embody his own conceptions of right and wrong, which are usually those of his place and time, in his poetical creations, which participate in neither. By this assumption of the inferior office of interpreting the effect, in which perhaps after all he might acquit himself but imperfectly, he would resign a glory in the participation of the cause. There was little danger that Homer, or any of the eternal poets, should have so far misunderstood themselves as to have abdicated this throne of their widest dominion. Those in whom the poetical faculty, though great, is less intense, as Euripides, Lucan, Tasso, Spenser, have frequently affected a moral aim, and the effect of their poetry is diminished in exact proportion to the degree in which they compel us to advert to this purpose.

*   *   *   *

But let us not be betrayed from a defence into a critical history of poetry and its influence on society. Be it enough to have pointed out the effects of poets, in the large and true sense of the word, upon their own and all succeeding times.

But poets have been challenged to resign the civic crown to reasoners and mechanics, on another plea. It is admitted that the exercise of the imagination is most delightful, but it is alleged that that of reason is more useful. Let us examine, as the grounds of this distinction, what is here meant by utility. Pleasure or good, in a general sense, is that which the consciousness of a sensitive and intelligent being seeks, and in which, when found, it acquiesces. There are two kinds of pleasure, one durable, universal, and permanent; the other transitory and particular. Utility may either express the means of producing the former or the latter. In the former sense, whatever strengthens and purifies the affections, enlarges the imagination, and adds spirit to sense, is useful. But a narrower meaning may be assigned to the word utility, confining it to express that which banishes the importunity of the wants of our animal nature, the surrounding men with security of life, the dispersing the grosser delusions of superstition, and the conciliating such a degree of mutual forbearance among men as may consist with the motives of personal advantage.

Undoubtedly the promoters of utility, in this limited sense, have their appointed office in society. They follow the footsteps of poets, and copy the sketches of their creations into the book of common life. They make space and give time. Their exertions are of the highest value, so long as they confine their administration of the concerns of the inferior powers of our nature within the limits due to the superior ones. But whilst the skeptic destroys gross superstitions, let him spare to deface, as some of the French writers have defaced, the eternal truths charactered upon the imaginations of men. Whilst the mechanist abridges, and the political economist combines labor, let them beware that their speculations, for want of correspondence with those first principles which belong to the imagination, do not tend, as they have in modern England, to exasperate at once the extremes of luxury and of want. They have exemplified the saying, "To him that hath, more shall be given; and from him that hath not, the little that he hath shall be taken away." [1] The rich have become richer, and the poor have become poorer; and the vessel of the state is driven between the Scylla and Charybdis of anarchy and despotism. Such are the effects which must ever flow from an unmitigated exercise of the calculating faculty.

It is difficult to define pleasure in its highest sense, the definition involving a number of apparent paradoxes. For, from an inexplicable defect of harmony in the constitution of human nature, the pain of the inferior is frequently connected with the pleasures of the superior portions of our being. Sorrow, terror, anguish, despair itself, are often the chosen expressions of an approximation to the highest good. Our sympathy in tragic fiction depends on this principle; tragedy delights by affording a shadow of that pleasure which exists in pain. This is the source also of the melancholy which is inseparable from the sweetest melody. The pleasure that is in sorrow is sweeter than the pleasure of pleasure itself. And hence the saying, "It is better to go to the house of mourning than to the house of mirth." [2] Not that this highest species of pleasure is necessarily linked with

[1] Matthew, xxv: 29.
[2] Ecclesiastes, vii: 2 and 4.

pain. The delight of love and friendship, the ecstasy of the admiration of nature, the joy of the perception and still more of the creation of poetry, is often wholly unalloyed.

The production and assurance of pleasure in this highest sense is true utility. Those who produce and preserve this pleasure are poets or poetical philosophers.

The exertions of Locke, Hume, Gibbon, Voltaire, Rousseau,[1] and their disciples, in favor of oppressed and deluded humanity, are entitled to the gratitude of mankind. Yet it is easy to calculate the degree of moral and intellectual improvement which the world would have exhibited, had they never lived. A little more nonsense would have been talked for a century or two; and perhaps a few more men, women, and children burnt as heretics. We might not at this moment have been congratulating each other on the abolition of the Inquisition in Spain. But it exceeds all imagination to conceive what would have been the moral condition of the world if neither Dante, Petrarch, Boccaccio, Chaucer, Shakespeare, Calderón, Lord Bacon, nor Milton, had ever existed; if Raphael and Michael Angelo had never been born; if the Hebrew poetry had never been translated; if a revival of the study of Greek literature had never taken place; if no monuments of ancient sculpture had been handed down to us; and if the poetry of the religion of the ancient world had been extinguished together with its belief. The human mind could never, except by the intervention of these excitements, have been awakened to the invention of the grosser sciences, and that application of analytical reasoning to the aberrations of society which it is now attempted to exalt over the direct expression of the inventive and creative faculty itself.

We have more moral, political, and historical wisdom than we know how to reduce into practice; we have more scientific and economical knowledge than can be accommodated to the just distribution of the produce which it multiplies. The poetry in these systems of thought is concealed by the accumulation of facts and calculating processes. There is no want of knowledge respecting what is wisest and best in morals, government, and political economy, or at least what is wiser and better than what men now practice and endure. But we let "*I dare not* wait upon *I would*, like the poor cat in the adage." We want the creative faculty to imagine that which we know; we want the generous impulse to act that which we imagine;

[1] Although Rousseau has been thus classed, he was essentially a poet. The others, even Voltaire, were mere reasoners. (Shelley.)

we want the poetry of life: our calculations have outrun conception; we have eaten more than we can digest. The cultivation of those sciences which have enlarged the limits of the empire of man over the external world, has, for want of the poetical faculty, proportionally circumscribed those of the internal world; and man, having enslaved the elements, remains himself a slave. To what but a cultivation of the mechanical arts in a degree disproportioned to the presence of the creative faculty, which is the basis of all knowledge, is to be attributed the abuse of all invention for abridging and combining labor, to the exasperation of the inequality of mankind? From what other cause has it arisen that the discoveries which should have lightened have added a weight to the curse imposed on Adam? Poetry, and the principle of Self of which money is the visible incarnation, are the God and Mammon of the world.

The functions of the poetical faculty are two-fold: by one it creates new materials of knowledge, and power, and pleasure; by the other it engenders in the mind a desire to reproduce and arrange them according to a certain rhythm and order which may be called the beautiful and the good. The cultivation of poetry is never more to be desired than at periods when, from an excess of the selfish and calculating principle, the accumulation of the materials of external life exceed the quantity of the power of assimilating them to the internal laws of human nature. The body has then become too unwieldy for that which animates it.

Poetry is indeed something divine. It is at once the centre and circumference of knowledge; it is that which comprehends all science, and that to which all science must be referred. It is at the same time the root and blossom of all other systems of thought; it is that from which all spring, and that which adorns all; and that which, if blighted, denies the fruit and the seed, and withholds from the barren world the nourishment and the succession of the scions of the tree of life. It is the perfect and consummate surface and bloom of all things; it is as the odor and the color of the rose to the texture of the elements which compose it, as the form and splendor of unfaded beauty to the secrets of anatomy and corruption. What were virtue, love, patriotism, friendship; what were the scenery of this beautiful universe which we inhabit; what were our consolations on this side of the grave, and what were our aspirations beyond it,—if poetry did not ascend to bring light and fire from those eternal regions where the owl-winged faculty of calculation dare not ever soar? Poetry is not like reasoning, a power to be exerted according to the determination of the will. A man cannot say, "I will compose poetry." The greatest poet even cannot say it; for the mind in creation is as a fading coal, which some invisible influence, like an inconstant wind, awakens to transitory brightness; this power arises from within, like the color of a flower which fades and changes as it is developed, and the conscious portions of our nature are unprophetic either of its approach or its departure. Could this influence be durable in its original purity and force, it is impossible to predict the greatness of the results; but when composition begins, inspiration is already on the decline, and the most glorious poetry that has ever been communicated to the world is probably a feeble shadow of the original conceptions of the poet. I appeal to the greatest poets of the present day whether it is not an error to assert that the finest passages of poetry are produced by labor and study. The toil and the delay recommended by critics can be justly interpreted to mean no more than a careful observation of the inspired moments, and an artificial connection of the spaces between their suggestions by the intertexture of conventional expressions; a necessity only imposed by the limitedness of the poetical faculty itself; for Milton conceived the *Paradise Lost* as a whole before he executed it in portions. We have his own authority also for the muse having "dictated" to him the "unpremeditated song." And let this be an answer to those who would allege the fifty-six various readings of the first line of the *Orlando Furioso*. Compositions so produced are to poetry what mosaic is to painting. The instinct and intuition of the poetical faculty is still more observable in the plastic and pictorial arts: a great statue or picture grows under the power of the artist as a child in the mother's womb; and the very mind which directs the hands in formation is incapable of accounting to itself for the origin, the gradations, or the media of the process.

Poetry is the record of the best and happiest moments of the happiest and best minds. We are aware of evanescent visitations of thought and feeling, sometimes associated with place or person, sometimes regarding our own mind alone, and always arising unforeseen and departing unbidden, but elevating and delightful beyond all expression; so that even in the desire and the regret they leave, there cannot but be pleasure, participating as it does in the nature of its object. It is as it were the interpenetration of a diviner nature through our own; but its footsteps are like those of a wind over the sea, which the morning calm erases, and whose traces remain only, as on the wrinkled sand which paves it. These and corresponding conditions of being are experienced principally by those of the most delicate sensibility and the most enlarged imagination; and the state of mind produced by them is at war with every base desire. The enthusiasm of virtue, love, patriotism, and friendship is essentially linked with such emotions; and whilst they last, self appears as what it is, an atom to a universe. Poets are not only subject to these experiences as spirits of the most refined organization, but they can color all that they combine with the evanescent hues of this ethereal world; a word, a trait in the representation of a scene or a passion will touch the enchanted chord, and reanimate, in those who have ever experienced these emotions, the sleeping, the cold, the buried image of the past. Poetry thus makes immortal all that is best and most beautiful in the world; it arrests the vanishing apparitions which haunt the interlunations of life, and, veiling them or in language or in form, sends them forth among mankind, bearing sweet news of kindred joy to those with whom their sisters abide—abide, because there is no portal of expression from the caverns of the spirit which they inhabit into the universe of things. Poetry redeems from decay the visitations of the divinity in man.

Poetry turns all things to loveliness; it exalts the beauty of that which is most beautiful, and it adds beauty to that which is most deformed; it marries exultation and horror, grief and pleasure, eternity and change; it subdues to union under its light yoke all irreconcilable things. It transmutes all that it touches, and every form moving within the radiance of its presence is changed by wondrous sympathy to an incarnation of the spirit which it breathes; its secret alchemy turns to potable gold the poisonous waters which flow from death through life; it strips the veil of familiarity from the world, and lays bare the naked and sleeping beauty which is the spirit of its forms.

All things exist as they are perceived: at least in relation to the percipient.

> The mind is its own place, and in itself
> Can make a Heaven of Hell, a Hell of Heaven.[1]

But poetry defeats the curse which binds us to be subjected to the accident of surrounding impressions. And whether it spreads its own figured curtain, or withdraws life's dark veil from before the scene of things, it equally creates for us a being within our being. It

[1] *Paradise Lost*, I, 254–55.

makes us the inhabitant of a world to which the familiar world is a chaos. It reproduces the common universe of which we are portions and percipients, and it purges from our inward sight the film of familiarity which obscures from us the wonder of our being. It compels us to feel that which we perceive, and to imagine that which we know. It creates anew the universe, after it has been annihilated in our minds by the recurrence of impressions blunted by reiteration. It justifies the bold and true word of Tasso: *Non merita nome di creatore, se non Iddio ed il Poeta.*[1]

A poet, as he is the author to others of the highest wisdom, pleasure, virtue, and glory, so he ought personally to be the happiest, the best, the wisest, and the most illustrious of men. As to his glory, let time be challenged to declare whether the fame of any other institutor of human life be comparable to that of a poet. That he is the wisest, the happiest, and the best, inasmuch as he is a poet, is equally incontrovertible: the greatest poets have been men of the most spotless virtue, of the most consummate prudence, and, if we would look into the interior of their lives, the most fortunate of men; and the exceptions, as they regard those who possessed the poetic faculty in a high yet inferior degree, will be found on consideration to confirm rather than destroy the rule. Let us for a moment stoop to the arbitration of popular breath, and, usurping and uniting in our own persons the incompatible characters of accuser, witness, judge, and executioner, let us decide without trial, testimony, or form, that certain motives of those who are "there sitting where we dare not soar"[2] are reprehensible. Let us assume that Homer was a drunkard, that Virgil was a flatterer, that Horace was a coward, that Tasso was a madman, that Lord Bacon was a peculator, that Raphael was a libertine, that Spenser was a poet laureate. It is inconsistent with this division of our subject to cite living poets, but posterity has done ample justice to the great names now referred to. Their errors have been weighed and found to have been dust in the balance; if their sins were as scarlet, they are now white as snow; they have been washed in the blood of the mediator and redeemer, Time. Observe in what a ludicrous chaos the imputations of real or fictitious crime have been confused in the contemporary calumnies against poetry and poets; consider how little is as it appears—or appears as it is; look to your own motives, and judge not, lest ye be judged.

1 No one deserves the name of creator except God and the poet.
2 *Paradise Lost*, IV, 829.

Poetry, as has been said, differs in this respect from logic, that it is not subject to the control of the active powers of the mind, and that its birth and recurrence have no necessary connection with the consciousness or will. It is presumptuous to determine that these are the necessary conditions of all mental causation, when mental effects are experienced insusceptible of being referred to them. The frequent recurrence of the poetical power, it is obvious to suppose, may produce in the mind a habit of order and harmony correlative with its own nature and with its effects upon other minds. But in the intervals of inspiration—and they may be frequent without being durable—a poet becomes a man, and is abandoned to the sudden reflux of the influences under which others habitually live. But as he is more delicately organized than other men, and sensible to pain and pleasure, both his own and that of others, in a degree unknown to them, he will avoid the one and pursue the other with an ardor proportioned to this difference. And he renders himself obnoxious to calumny when he neglects to observe the circumstances under which these objects of universal pursuit and flight have disguised themselves in one another's garments.

But there is nothing necessarily evil in this error, and thus cruelty, envy, revenge, avarice, and the passions purely evil, have never formed any portion of the popular imputations on the lives of poets.

I have thought it most favorable to the cause of truth to set down these remarks according to the order in which they were suggested to my mind, by a consideration of the subject itself, instead of observing the formality of a polemical reply; but if the view which they contain be just, they will be found to involve a refutation of the arguers against poetry, so far at least as regards the first division of the subject. I can readily conjecture what should have moved the gall of some learned and intelligent writers who quarrel with certain versifiers; I, like them, confess myself unwilling to be stunned by the *Theseids* of the hoarse Codri [1] of the day. Bavius and Mævius [2] undoubtedly are, as they ever were, insufferable persons. But it belongs to a philosophical critic to distinguish rather than confound.

The first part of these remarks has related to poetry in its elements and principles; and it has been shown, as well as the narrow limits assigned them would permit, that what is called poetry in a restricted

---

[1] Codrus, an insignificant Latin poet, would read his play about Theseus, it is said, to anyone who would listen.

[2] As poets, in the same class as Codrus.

sense, has a common source with all other forms of order and of beauty according to which the materials of human life are suscepti-ble of being arranged, and which is poetry in a universal sense.

The second part will have for its object an application of these principles to the present state of the cultivation of poetry, and a defence of the attempt to idealize the modern forms of manners and opinions, and compel them into a subordination to the imaginative and creative faculty. For the literature of England, an energetic de-velopment of which has ever preceded or accompanied a great and free development of the national will, has arisen as it were from a new birth. In spite of the low-thoughted envy which would under-value contemporary merit, our own will be a memorable age in intel-lectual achievements, and we live among such philosophers and poets as surpass beyond comparison any who have appeared since the last national struggle for civil and religious liberty. The most unfailing herald, companion, and follower of the awakening of a great people to work a beneficial change in opinion or institution, is poetry. At such periods there is an accumulation of the power of communicat-ing and receiving intense and impassioned conceptions respecting man and nature. The persons in whom this power resides may often, as far as regards many portions of their nature, have little apparent correspondence with that spirit of good of which they are the min-isters. But even whilst they deny and abjure, they are yet compelled to serve the power which is seated on the throne of their own soul. It is impossible to read the compositions of the most celebrated writ-ers of the present day without being startled with the electric life which burns within their words. They measure the circumference and sound the depths of human nature with a comprehensive and all-penetrating spirit, and they are themselves perhaps the most sin-cerely astonished at its manifestations; for it is less their spirit than the spirit of the age. Poets are the hierophants of an unapprehended inspiration; the mirrors of the gigantic shadows which futurity casts upon the present; the words which express what they understand not; the trumpets which sing to battle and feel not what they in-spire; the influence which is moved not, but moves. Poets are the unacknowledged legislators of the world.

Sainte-Beuve

Charles Augustin SAINTE-BEUVE (1804–1869) was born at Boulogne-sur-Mer, where he had his first schooling, and went to Paris in 1818 for study at the Collège Charlemagne and the Collège Bourbon. He began a medical course, but gave it up for literature in 1824, with contributions to periodicals, which won him, for a time, the friendship of Victor Hugo. His novels, poems, and plays gained him an election, in 1844, to the Académie Française. In addition to his writing, he gave courses at the Collège de France, and at the University of Liège.

In 1849 he began his series of critical articles on literary subjects, under the title, *Causeries du Lundi*, which, in two series, ran for almost twenty years, and gave him a wide reputation both at home and abroad. In *Port Royal*, he wrote a history of Jansenism—the doctrines of a Catholic group opposed to the Jesuits—which took its name from the chief Jansenist centre, near Paris. He was appointed a Senator in 1865, and died at Paris four years later.

Sainte-Beuve, the greatest French critic of the nineteenth century, displayed enthusiasm and impeccable taste in his personal judgments. He strove, however, as in the essay below, to find a classical or a rational basis for criticism.

WHAT IS A CLASSIC? [1]

(1850)

This is a delicate question, and one of which a good many different solutions might have been given at different periods and seasons. A clever man has this day propounded it to me, and even if I cannot

[1] Translated by A. J. Butler in *Select Essays of Sainte-Beuve*, London, n.d.

solve it, I want at least to try to examine and discuss it before our readers, were it only to induce them to reply to it themselves, and if I can, to clear up their ideas and mine upon it. And why should not one occasionally venture to treat in criticism of some of those subjects which are not personal, in which not someone, but something, is spoken of, and which our neighbors the English have so successfully made into a complete branch, under the modest title of Essays? It is true that, in order to treat of such subjects, which are always in a measure abstract and moral, one must speak in a calm atmosphere, be sure of one's own attention and that of others, and seize one of those quarters of an hour of silence, moderation, and leisure, which are seldom granted to our beloved France, and which her brilliant genius bears with impatience, even when she is wishing to be good, and has given up making revolutions.

A classic, according to the usual definition, is an author of past times, already hallowed by general admiration, who is an authority in his own style. The word *classic,* taken in this sense, begins to appear among the Romans. With them the *classici,* properly so-called, were not all the citizens of the different classes, but only those of the highest class, who possessed, at least, an income of a certain fixed figure. All those who had a lower income were known by the appellation of *infra classem,* below *the* class properly so-called. For example, we find the word *classicus* used by Aulus Gellius and applied to writers: a writer of worth and mark is *classicus assiduusque scriptor,* a writer who counts, who has some possessions under the sun, and who is not confounded with the proletariat crowd. Such an expression presupposes an age sufficiently advanced for a criticism and classification, as it were, of literature to have come into existence.

For the moderns, the true and only classics were, in the first instance, naturally the ancients. The Greeks, who by rare good fortune had—a happy relief to their intellect—no other classics than themselves, were at first the sole classics of the Romans, who spent much trouble and ingenuity on imitating them. They in their turn, after the fine ages of their literature, after Cicero and Virgil, had their own classics, and they became almost exclusively the classics of the centuries which succeeded. The Middle Ages, which, though not as ignorant as might be thought of Latin antiquity, were wanting in the sense of proportion and taste, confused the ranks and orders. Ovid was put on a better footing than Homer, and Boethius appeared to be a classic at least equal to Plato. The "new birth" of literature in the fifteenth and sixteenth centuries came to clear up this long confusion, and then only was admiration graduated. The real classic authors of the twofold antiquity stood out for the future on a luminous background, and formed two harmonious groups on their two eminences.

Meanwhile, modern literature had been born, and some of the more precocious members of it, like the Italian, already had their own fashion of antiquity. Dante had appeared, and his posterity had lost no time in saluting him as a classic. Italian poetry may have retreated greatly since then, but when she has desired, she has already recovered and always retained some impulse, some reverberation, from this high origin. It is of no slight importance for a poetry thus to take its point of departure, its classic source in a lofty place—rather, for example, to descend from a Dante than to issue laboriously from a Malherbe.

Modern Italy had her classics, and Spain had every right to believe she was also in possession of hers, when France still had hers to seek. Indeed, a few writers of talent endowed with originality and exceptional raciness, a few brilliant efforts isolated and without successors, shattered immediately and needing always to be begun afresh, do not suffice to confer upon a nation the solid and imposing basis of literary wealth. That idea of a *classic* implies in itself something which has sequence and solidity, which forms a whole and makes a tradition, something which has "composition," is handed on to posterity and lasts. It was only after the brilliant years of Louis XIV that the nation felt with a thrill of pride that this happiness had come to it. All voices then told it to Louis XIV with flattery, exaggeration, and emphasis, and yet with a certain perception of truth. Then appeared a singular and quaint inconsistency: the men who were most in love with the wonders of that age of Louis the Great, and who went so far as to sacrifice all the ancients to the moderns, those men, of whom Perrault was the chief, tended to exalt and consecrate those very men in whom they found the most ardent and contradictory adversaries. Boileau defended and supported the ancients with anger against Perrault, who cried up the moderns, that is to say Corneille, Molière, Pascal, and the eminent men of his century, including Boileau as one of the first. The good La Fontaine, when he took Doctor Huet's part in the quarrel, did not perceive that he himself, in spite of his oversight, was in his turn on the eve of waking up to find himself a classic.

An instance is the best definition: France possessed her century of Louis XIV, and could consider it at a little distance; she knew what it was to be classic better than by any reasoning. The eighteenth century, till its upheaval, added to this idea by a few fine works due to its four great men. Read Voltaire's *Siècle de Louis XIV*, Montesquieu's *La Grandeur et la Décadence des Romains*, Buffon's *Époques de Nature*, the *Vicaire Savoyard*, and the fine pages of meditations and descriptions of nature by Jean-Jacques, and say whether the eighteenth century in its memorable past has not known how to reconcile tradition with independence and liberty of development. But at the beginning of this century and under the Empire, in presence of the first attempts of a decidedly novel and somewhat daring literature, the idea of a classic among some refractory minds, influenced more by vexation than by severity, contracted and shrank strangely. The first Dictionary of the Academy (1694) simply defined a classic author as "an ancient author, highly approved, who is an authority in the subject he treats of." The Dictionary of the Academy of 1835 urges this definition much more closely, and makes it exact and even narrow instead of, as it was, somewhat vague. It defines classic authors as "those who have become *models* in any language," and, in the articles which follow, these expressions—*models*, *rules* established for composition and style, *strict rules* of the art to which you must *conform*, are continually recurring. This definition of the *classic* has evidently been made by our respectable precursors of the Academy, in presence and in sight of what was then called the *romantic*, that is to say, in sight of the enemy. It seems to me that the time ought now to have come to renounce these restricting and timid definitions and to widen their spirit.

A true classic, as I should like to hear it defined, is an author who has enriched the human mind, who has really augmented its treasures, who has made it take one more step forward, who has discovered some unequivocal moral truth, or has once more seized hold of some eternal passion in that heart where all seemed known and explored; who has rendered his thought, his observation, or his discovery under no matter what form, but broad and large, refined, sensible, sane, and beautiful in itself; who has spoken to all in a style of his own which yet belongs to all the world, in a style which is new without neologisms, new and ancient, easily contemporaneous with every age.

Such a classic may have been revolutionary for a moment, or at least may have seemed to be, but he is not so; he has not, in the first instance, fallen upon everything around him; he has overthrown only what was in his way so as quickly to replace the balance in favor of order and beauty.

You can, if you will, set down some names under this definition, which I would purposely make grand and compendious, or in one word, generous. I should place there first the Corneille of *Polyeucte*, of *Cinna,* of *Les Horaces*. I should place there Molière, the most complete and the richest genius we have had in French.

"Molière is so great," said Goethe (that king of criticism), "that he surprises us afresh every time we read him. He is a man who stands alone; his plays verge on the tragic, and no one has had the courage to imitate them. His *Avare*, where the vice destroys all affection between father and son, is one of the most sublime of works, and dramatic in the highest degree. Every action in a play for the stage must be important in itself and tend towards a still greater event. *Tartuffe* is a model in this respect. What a setting out of the subject is the first scene! Everything is highly significant from the beginning, and makes you anticipate something still more important. The outset of any similar play of Lessing's which may be cited is very fine; but that of *Tartuffe* is unique. It is the greatest thing of the kind. . . . Every year I read a play of Molière's, just as from time to time I gaze at some engraving after the old Italian masters."

I do not pretend to say that this definition of a classic which I have just given does not go somewhat beyond the idea one generally forms for oneself under that name. It is especially made to comprise conditions of order, wisdom, moderation, and reasonableness, which prevail over and contain all others. Having occasion to praise M. Royer-Collard, M. de Rémusat said: "If he gets from our classics a pure taste, appropriate terms, variety of phrase, a careful attention in suiting expression to thought, to himself alone he owes the character which he gives to it all." One sees here that the part allotted to classic qualities seems rather to depend on selection and nicety of meaning, to an ornate and restrained style, and that, too, is the general opinion. In this sense the classics, properly so called, would be writers of the second rank—correct, sensible, elegant, always clear, expressing themselves with a passion not devoid of nobility, and a power kept slightly in reserve. Marie-Joseph Chénier has traced the poetic spirit of these temperate and accomplished writers in these lines, where he shows himself their apt disciple:

> C'est le bon sens, la raison qui fait tout,
> Vertu, génie, esprit, talent et goût.

Qu'est-ce vertu? raison mise en pratique;
Talent? raison produite avec éclat;
Esprit? raison qui finement s'exprime;
Le goût n'est rien qu'un bon sens delicat;
Et le génie est la raison sublime.[1]

In writing these lines he was evidently thinking of Pope, Despréaux [Boileau], and Horace, the master of them all. The real essence of this theory, which makes imagination and even feeling subordinate to reason, and of which Scaliger, perhaps, struck the first note among modern writers, is, strictly speaking, the *Latin* theory, and this has also for a long time been the French theory. It has some truth in it if it is only used in the right place, if that word *reason* is not misused; but it is evident that it is misused, and that if reason, for instance, can be confused with poetic genius and their union results in a moral epistle, it cannot be the same thing as that genius which we find so varied and so diversely creative in expressing the passions of the drama or the epic. Where will you find reason in the fourth book of the *Æneid*, and in the ecstasies of Dido? Where will you find it in the madness of Phædra? Be this as it may, the spirit which has prompted this theory tends to place in the first rank of the classics those writers who have governed their inspiration rather than those who have given themselves more up to it, to place Virgil there more certainly than Homer, Racine more than Corneille. The masterpiece which this theory loves to quote, and which does indeed unite every condition of prudence, strength, progressive daring, moral elevation and greatness, is *Athalie*. In Turenne, in his last two campaigns, and Racine in *Athalie*, we have the great examples of what wise and prudent men can do when they come into possession of the full maturity of their genius, and enter upon their crowning exploits.

Buffon, in his *Discourse on Style*, in which he insists on that oneness of plan, arrangement, and execution which is the stamp of really classic work, has said: "Every subject is one only; and *however spacious it may be it can be comprised in a single treatise*. Interruptions, pauses, and sections should only be used when different subjects are treated of, or when, having to speak of great, complicated, or incongruous matters, the march of genius finds itself impeded by the multiplicity of the obstacles in its way and constrained by the re-

---

[1] Good sense, reason, make everything—virtue, genius, wit, talent, and taste. What is virtue? reason in action; talent? reason produced with brilliance; spirit? reason finely expressed. Taste is only a delicate good sense, and genius is sublime reason.

quirements of the circumstances; otherwise a great number of divisions, far from making a work more solid, destroy its unity; the book seems clearer at first sight, but the author's intention remains obscure." And he continues his criticism, having in his mind Montesquieu's *l'Esprit des Lois,* a book excellent at bottom, but all cut up into segments, into which the illustrious author, worn out before the end, could not breathe all his spirit, nor even to some extent arrange all his matter. Yet I find it hard to believe that Buffon was not thinking in the same place by way of contrast of Bossuet's *Discours sur l'Histoire Universelle,* a subject, indeed, both vast and single, and which the great author has yet been able to comprise in one solitary treatise. Let anyone open the first edition of 1681, before the division into chapters which was introduced later, and which has passed from the margin into the text and cut it up; everything is there unfolded in one sequence and almost at one breath, and one would say that the orator has here done like the Nature of whom Buffon writes, that he *has worked on an eternal plan and has nowhere deviated from it,* so far does he seem to have penetrated into the intimacy of the counsels of Providence.

Athalie and the *Discours sur l'Histoire Universelle,* such are the highest masterpieces which the strict classic theory can offer alike to its friends and its enemies. Yet in spite of all the admirable simplicity and majesty with which these unique productions are executed, we should like for the practical purposes of art to extend this idea a little, and to show that there is room for enlarging it without going so far as to relax it. Goethe, whom I like to quote on such a subject, says:

"I call all *healthy* work classic, all *unhealthy* work romantic. The poem of the *Nibelungen* is for me as classic as Homer; both are healthy and vigorous. It is not because they are new that the works of the day are romantic, but because they are weak, sickly, or diseased. It is not because they are old that the works of past times are classic, but because they are energetic, fresh, and healthy. If we were to consider the romantic and the classic from these two points of view, we should soon all be agreed." [1]

And, indeed, I should like every free mind to travel round the world and give itself up to the contemplation of the different literatures in their primitive vigor and their infinite variety before marking down and fixing its ideas on this subject. What would such a mind see? First of all a Homer, the father of the classic world, but

[1] Cf. above, p. 336.

himself less certainly a single and very distinct individual than the vast and living expression of an active period and a semi-barbarous civilization. To make a classic properly so called of him, it has been necessary to attribute to him a design, a plan, literary intentions, qualities of criticism and urbanity as an afterthought, of which he would certainly never have dreamt in the overflowing development of his natural inspiration. And whom do we see beside him? imposing and venerable men of antiquity it is true, such as Æschylus or Sophocles, but all mutilated, and standing there only to represent to us the wreck of themselves, all that remains of many others doubtless as worthy as they to survive, who have perished for ever beneath the ill-treatment of the ages. This thought alone might teach a man of well-balanced mind not to look at literature as a whole, even classic literature, with too simple and too limited a view, and he may learn from it that that exact and well proportioned order which has had so much force since, has been introduced only artificially into our admiration of the past.

And how would it be when we enter the modern world? The greatest names we perceive at the outset of literature are those which most shock and disturb certain restricted ideas of the beautiful and the fitting which it has been thought desirable to convey in poetry. Is Shakespeare a classic, for instance? Yes, he is so to-day, for England and for the world; but in the time of Pope he was not. Pope and his friends were the only classics in the full sense; they seemed to become so indubitably the day after their death. To-day they are still classics and they deserve to be; but they are only in the second rank, and there they may be seen for ever, surpassed and kept in their place by him who has again his place on the topmost skyline.

I shall certainly not be the one to speak evil of Pope or of his excellent followers, especially when they are as sweet and natural as Goldsmith; next to the greatest, these, between writers and poets, are perhaps the best fitted for imparting charm to life. One day, when Lord Bolingbroke was writing to Dr. Swift, Pope put a postscript to the letter, in which he said: "I imagine that if we three were to spend even three years together, the result might be some advantage to our century." No, we must never speak lightly of those who have had the right to say such things of themselves without boasting, and it would be much better to envy the favored and fortunate ages when men of talent could suggest such unions, which were not then chimærical. These ages, whether we call them by the name of Louis XIV or of Queen Anne, are the only really classic ages, using the word in its limited sense, the only ones which offer a propitious climate and shelter to perfected talent. We here, in our disconnected period, are but too well aware of it, when talents possibly equal to theirs have got lost and dissipated through the uncertain ties and hardships of the times. Anyway, let us apportion to each kind of greatness its due influence and superiority. The true master genius triumphs over those difficulties which wreck others; Dante, Shakespeare, and Milton knew how to attain to their supremacy and to produce their imperishable works in spite of obstacles, persecutions, and storms. The opinions of Byron about Pope have been the subject of much discussion, and an attempt has been made to explain that kind of contradiction which has led the singer of *Don Juan* and of *Childe Harold* to extol the purely classic school, and declare it to be the only good one, while he himself took so different a course. Goethe has once more said the right word about this, when he remarks that Byron, so great in the outburst and spring of his poetry, yet feared Shakespeare, who is more capable than he of creating and putting life into his characters. He would have liked to deny him; he was irked by that unselfish superiority; he felt that he could never comfortably display himself beside him. He has never renounced Pope because he did not fear him; he well knew that Pope was a *wall* beside him.

If the school of Pope had kept the supremacy, and a kind of honorary empire over the past, as Byron wished, Byron would have been the first and only one of his kind; the erection of Pope as that wall hid Shakespeare's great form from sight, whereas, while Shakespeare reigns and dominates in all his height, Byron is only second.

We in France had no great classic before the era of Louis XIV; we lacked Dantes and Shakespeares, those original authorities to which one returns sooner or later in the days of emancipation. We have had only, as it were, the rough drafts of great poets, such as Mathurin Régnier and Rabelais, without any ideal, without the passion and the gravity which give consecration. Montaigne was a sort of classic before his time, of the Horatian breed, but one who, for want of worthy surroundings, abandoned himself like a strayed child to all the libertine fancies of his pen and his humor. The result is that we have earned less than any other nation the right to claim loudly one day, through our author-ancestors, our literary liberties and charters, and that it has been a still greater difficulty to us to work out our freedom and remain classic. Yet, with Molière and La Fontaine among our classics of the great era, there is sufficient cause for refusing no rights of legitimacy to any who will make the venture with knowledge.

The important thing now seems to me to be to preserve the notion and the cult, and at the same time to widen it. There is no recipe for making classics; this point must sooner or later be clearly recognized. To think that by imitating certain qualities of purity, of sobriety, of correctness and elegance, quite independently even of character and the divine spark, you will become a classic, is to think that after Racine the father there is room for Racine the son; an estimable and melancholy rôle which is the worst thing in poetry. Yet more: it is not a good thing to appear too quickly and right off, to one's contemporaries, as a pure classic; see how faint the color looks at a distance of twenty-five years! How many there are of these precocious classics who do not last and are only ephemeral! You turn round one morning and are surprised to find them no longer standing behind you. They have only been there, in the gay phrase of Madame de Sévigné, as a breakfast for the sun. With regard to classics the most spontaneous are still the best and the greatest: ask those virile geniuses who are really born immortal and who flourish perpetually, whether it is not so. Apparently the least classic of the four poets of Louis XIV was Molière; he was applauded then far more than he was esteemed; people enjoyed him without knowing his value. After him the least classic seemed to be La Fontaine; and see what came of it—for both of them—two centuries later. Far before Boileau, before even Racine, are they not to-day unanimously recognized as the most fruitful writers, the richest as regards the characteristics of universal morality?

After all, we need really sacrifice nothing—depreciate nothing. The temple of taste, I quite believe, needs rebuilding; but in rebuilding it, it is merely a question of making it greater, and of letting it become the Pantheon of all the nobility of mankind—of all those who have had a notable and lasting share in increasing the sum of the pleasures and possessions of the mind. As for me, who would in no sense pretend (as is evident) to be the architect or director of such a temple, I will confine myself to expressing some wishes—competing for the specification, as it were. Above all, I would exclude no one worthy to enter, and I would give everyone the place due to him, from Shakespeare, the most unfettered of creative geniuses and unconsciously the greatest of the classics, to Andrieux, the very last of the classics in miniature. "In my Father's house are many mansions." Let that be no less true of the kingdom of the beautiful here than of the kingdom of heaven above. Homer always and every-where would be the first in it, the most like a god; but behind him, like the attendant train of the three kings of the East, would follow those three grand poets, those three Homers long ignored by us, who also themselves have made grand and admirable epics, the Hindoo poets Valmiki and Vyasa, and the Persian Firdousi. In the realm of taste, it is a good thing to know, at least, that such men exist, and not to split up the human race. Having paid this homage to what it is sufficient to perceive and recognize, we would quit our own bound-aries no more, and we would divert our eyes with a thousand splendid or agreeable sights, and rejoice in a thousand various and surprising meetings; yet their apparent confusion would never be wanting in concord and harmony. The most ancient of sages and poets—those who have put human morality into maxims and have chanted it in plain-song—would converse with each other in rare suave speech, and would not be surprised to understand each other at the very first word. Solon, Hesiod, Theognis, Job, Solomon, and why not Confu-cius himself? would greet the most ingenious modern authors, La Rochefoucauld or La Bruyère, who would say to each other as they listened to them: "They knew all that we know, and we have found nothing new by bringing experience up to date." On the hill most in sight, with the most easy slopes, Virgil surrounded by Menander, Tibullus, Terence, Fénelon, would abandon himself with them to converse full of charm and a sacred enchantment; his gentle face would beam with radiance and the hue of modesty, as on that day when, entering the Roman theatre just as they had been reciting his verses, he saw the entire assembly rise in front of him by a simultane-ous movement and pay him the same homage as to Augustus himself. Not far from him, and regretting to be separated from so dear a friend, Horace would preside in his turn (so far as a poet and sage so keen of wit can be said to preside) over the group of the poets of civic life and of those who have known how to talk as well as sing— Pope and Despréaux, the one grown less irritable and the other less censorious. That true poet, Montaigne, would be there with them, and his presence would completely remove all appearance of a liter-ary academy from this charming corner. La Fontaine would forget himself there, and, henceforth less flighty, would be content to re-main. Voltaire would pass by, but he would not have the patience to stop, though at the same time delighting in it. On the same hill as Virgil, a little lower down, Xenophon would be seen with an unaf-fected look very little like a captain, but of a kind to make him rather resemble a priest of the Muses. He would gather around him the Attic minds of every language and of every country—Addison, Pellisson, Vauvenargues, all who feel the value of suave expression, exquisite simplicity, and a sweet, though not unadorned, carelessness. In the centre of the place three great men would often like to meet before the portico of the principal temple (for there would be several within the enclosure), and if those should be together, there would not be a fourth, however great, to whom it would occur to take part in their intercourse or their silence, so great would appear their beauty, their grand proportions, and that perfection of harmony which has only once been seen when first the world was young. Their three names have become the ideal of all art—Plato, Sophocles, and Demosthenes. And, moreover, having duly honored these demigods, do you not see yonder a numerous and familiar crowd of excellent spirits, who always prefer to follow Cervantes, Molière—the practical painters from the life—those indulgent friends who are still the first of benefactors, who seize the whole man with laughter, pour out experience for him in mirth, and are aware of the powerful influence of rational, hearty, lawful joy? I will not here go on any longer with this description, which would occupy a whole book if it were complete. Be sure that the Middle Ages and Dante would fill some of the sacred heights; Italy would wholly unfold herself like a garden at the feet of the singer of Paradise; Boccaccio and Aristotle would disport themselves there, and Tasso would find once more the orange groves of Sorrento. In short, the different nations would have each a special nook kept for it, but the authors would delight in coming out of it, and as they walk about they would recognize, where least they expect it, their brothers or their masters. Lucretius, for instance, would love to discuss with Milton the origin of the world and the disentanglement of chaos; but as they argue each after his manner, they will but agree about the divine representations of poetry and nature.

These are our classics; everybody's imagination can complete the sketch, and even choose his favorite group for himself. For there must be a choice, and the first condition of taste when all has been surveyed is not to roam ceaselessly, but once for all to stay with a settled opinion. Nothing palls on the mind so much and is so injurious to taste as ceaseless roamings; the poetic spirit is not the Wandering Jew. Notwithstanding all this, my concluding advice when I speak of choosing and of forming an opinion is not to imitate even those who please us the most among our masters in the past. Let us be satisfied with feeling them, with interpreting them, with admiring them, and for ourselves, late comers that we are, let us try at least to be ourselves. Let us make our choice with our own proper instincts. Let us have the sincerity and naturalness of our own thoughts, our own feelings—that always is possible. Let us add to it what is more difficult, a high aim, an impetus towards some lofty ideal; and while we speak our own language and submit to the conditions of the age in which we are placed, and from which we draw alike our strength and our failings, let us ask ourselves from time to time, while we lift our brow towards the hills and fasten our eyes on the group of reverend beings: *What would they say of us?*

But why do we speak continually of being an author, of writing? An age, perchance, is coming when there will be no more writing. Happy are those who read and read again, who can obey their free inclinations in their reading! There comes a period in life when, our wanderings all finished and our experiences all acquired, there is no keener pleasure than to study and deepen the things we know, to relish what we taste, just as when you behold again and again the people you love; purest delight of the mature mind and taste. It is then that this word *classic* assumes its true meaning, and is defined by the irresistible and discerning choice of every man of taste. Taste has now been created, it is formed and defined; the right meaning is now achieved if we are to have it at all. There is no longer any time to try about, nor any wish to make further discoveries. You stand by your friends, by those who have been proved by a long connection. Old wine, old books, old friends. You say to yourself like Voltaire in those delightful lines:

> Jouissons, écrivons, vivons, mon cher Horace!

> *   *   *   *

> J'ai vécu plus que toi: mes vers dureront moins:
> Mais, au bord du tombeau, je mettrai tous mes soins
> À suivre les leçons de ta philosophie,
> À mépriser la mort en savourant la vie,
> À lire tes écrits pleins de grâce et de sens,
> Comme on boit d'un vin vieux qui rajeunit les sens.[1]

---

[1] Let us play, let us write, let us live, my dear Horace! . . . I have lived longer than you; my verses will last less time: but, on the edge of the tomb, I will take every care to follow the lessons of your philosophy, to despise death in enjoying life, to read your writings full of grace and good sense, as one drinks an old wine which brings youth to the senses.

Finally, be it Horace or another, whoever the author is that we prefer, and that gives us back our own thoughts in full richness and maturity, we shall at any rate beg from one of these good and ancient spirits a perpetual entertainment, an unwavering friendship which will never fail us, and that habitual impression of serenity and sweetness, which reconciles us, who so often need it, to mankind and to ourselves.

Poe

Edgar Allan POE (1809–1849) was born in Boston, Massachusetts, where his actor-parents were playing. Both died when he was a young child, and he was adopted by his godfather, John Allan, of Richmond, Virginia, who, with his wife, treated him indulgently. In 1815 he was taken to England where he was put to school; on his return, six years later, his education was continued at Richmond and at the University of Virginia. Here he distinguished himself as a student; but his gambling debts led to his removal by his foster-parent. After a short, enforced stay in Mr. Allan's counting-house, he ran away to Boston, where an early volume of poems was published. Poor and friendless, he enlisted in the army, and for a while attended West Point; but he disliked the rigid discipline and got himself dismissed. When Mr. Allan died without making provision for him, he contributed to various periodicals poetry and prose tales which attracted attention and had considerable influence abroad, especially in France. He later took up editorial work, serving with the New York *Quarterly Review*, the *Gentleman's Magazine* (Philadelphia), and *Graham's Magazine*, in which some of his best work appeared. In 1836 he married his cousin, Virginia Clemm, who remained devotedly attached to him until her death in 1847, despite his indulgence in opium and intoxicants, and the poverty which resulted. In 1842 he resigned the editorship of *Graham's*, and for a brief time managed the *Broadway Journal* in New York; but when this enterprise failed, he gave up editorial work permanently. Grieved by the loss of his wife, he struggled against sickness and opium for two years, and died in Baltimore, where he was taken ill on a journey from Richmond to New York. He was buried there, near the grave of his grandfather, General David Poe.

Poe is the first American critic of distinction. In his creative writing he is like Coleridge, with his predilection for the supernatural and his skill in making it seem natural. He has the madness that Plato thought was inherent in a poet, but he practices what he expressed in his essays: this madness—or sublimity—should be accompanied by precise composition.

His criticism is like Coleridge's, too, in its impersonal analysis of what poetry is. Besides the essay below, the student should read his *Rationale of Verse*, and the *Philosophy of Composition*. The latter, Poe's account of how he wrote *The Raven*, is as thrilling as a detective story.

THE POETIC PRINCIPLE [1]

(1850)

In speaking of the Poetic Principle, I have no design to be either thorough or profound. While discussing, very much at random, the essentiality of what we call Poetry, my principal purpose will be to cite for consideration some few of those minor English or American poems which best suit my own taste, or which, upon my own fancy, have left the most definite impression. By "minor poems" I mean, of course, poems of little length. And here, in the beginning, permit me to say a few words in regard to a somewhat peculiar principle, which, whether rightfully or wrongfully, has always had its influence in my own critical estimate of the poem. I hold that a long poem does not exist. I maintain that the phrase, "a long poem," is simply a flat contradiction in terms.

I need scarcely observe that a poem deserves its title only inasmuch as it excites, by elevating the soul. The value of the poem is in the ratio of this elevating excitement. But all excitements are, through a psychal necessity, transient. That degree of excitement which would entitle a poem to be so called at all cannot be sustained throughout a

[1] First published in *Sartain's Union Magazine*, October, 1850. The text here printed has been collated with that edited by E. C. Stedman and G. E. Woodberry in their ten-volume edition of Poe's *Works*.

composition of any great length. After the lapse of half an hour, at the very utmost, it flags—fails—a revulsion ensues—and then the poem is, in effect, and in fact, no longer such.

There are, no doubt, many who have found difficulty in reconciling the critical dictum that the *Paradise Lost* is to be devoutly admired throughout, with the absolute impossibility of maintaining for it, during perusal, the amount of enthusiasm which that critical dictum would demand. This great work, in fact, is to be regarded as poetical, only when, losing sight of that vital requisite in all works of Art, Unity, we view it merely as a series of minor poems. If, to preserve its Unity—its totality of effect or impression—we read it (as would be necessary) at a single sitting, the result is but a constant alternation of excitement and depression. After a passage of what we feel to be true poetry, there follows, inevitably, a passage of platitude which no critical pre-judgment can force us to admire; but if, upon completing the work, we read it again omitting the first book—that is to say, commencing with the second—we shall be surprised at now finding that admirable which we before condemned—that damnable which we had previously so much admired. It follows from all this that the ultimate, aggregate, or absolute effect of even the best epic under the sun, is a nullity:—and this is precisely the fact.

In regard to the *Iliad*, we have, if not positive proof, at least very good reason, for believing it intended as a series of lyrics; but, granting the epic intention, I can say only that the work is based on an imperfect sense of Art. The modern epic is, of the supposititious ancient model, but an inconsiderate and blindfold imitation. But the day of these artistic anomalies is over. If, at any time, any very long poem *were* popular in reality, which I doubt, it is at least clear that no very long poem will ever be popular again.

That the extent of a poetical work is, *ceteris paribus*,[1] the measure of its merit, seems undoubtedly, when we thus state it, a proposition sufficiently absurd—yet we are indebted for it to the Quarterly Reviews. Surely there can be nothing in mere *size*, abstractly considered—there can be nothing in mere *bulk*, so far as a volume is concerned, which has so continuously elicited admiration from these saturnine pamphlets! A mountain, to be sure, by the mere sentiment of physical magnitude which it conveys, *does* impress us with a sense of the sublime—but no man is impressed after *this* fashion by the material grandeur of even *The Columbiad*.[2] Even

[1] Other things being equal.

[2] By Joel Barlow, American poet and patriot (1754–1812).

the Quarterlies have not instructed us to be so impressed by it. *As yet*, they have not *insisted* on our estimating Lamartine [1] by the cubic foot, or Pollok [2] by the pound—but what else are we to *infer* from their continued prating about "sustained effort"? If, by "sustained effort," any little gentleman has accomplished an epic, let us frankly commend him for the effort—if this indeed be a thing commendable—but let us forbear praising the epic on the effort's account. It is to be hoped that common sense, in the time to come, will prefer deciding upon a work of art, rather by the impression it makes, by the effect it produces, than by the time it took to impress the effect or by the amount of "sustained effort" which had been found necessary in effecting the impression. The fact is, that perseverence is one thing, and genius quite another—nor can all the Quarterlies in Christendom confound them. By-and-by, this proposition, with many which I have been just urging, will be received as self-evident. In the mean time, by being generally condemned as falsities, they will not be essentially damaged as truths.

On the other hand, it is clear that a poem may be improperly brief. Undue brevity degenerates into mere epigrammatism. A *very* short poem, while now and then producing a brilliant or vivid, never produces a profound or enduring effect. There must be the steady pressing down of the stamp upon the wax. De Béranger [3] has wrought innumerable things, pungent and spirit-stirring; but, in general, they have been too imponderous to stamp themselves deeply into the public attention; and thus, as so many feathers of fancy, have been blown aloft only to be whistled down the wind.

A remarkable instance of the effect of undue brevity in depressing a poem—in keeping it out of the popular view—is afforded by the following exquisite little serenade: [4]

> I arise from dreams of thee
> In the first sweet sleep of night,
> When the winds are breathing low,
> And the stars are shining bright;
> I arise from dreams of thee,
> And a spirit in my feet

1 Alphonse Marie Louis de Lamartine (1790–1869), famous French poet.
2 Robert Pollok (1789–1827), whose best-known poem, *The Course of Time*, has faint reminiscences of Milton and Young. Popular in its day, it is now rarely read.
3 Pierre Jean de Béranger (1780–1857), a French lyric poet.
4 *The Indian Serenade*, written in 1819 and published in 1822.

Hath led me—who knows how?—
To thy chamber-window, sweet!

The wandering airs, they faint
 On the dark, the silent stream;
The champak odors fail
 Like sweet thoughts in a dream;
The nightingale's complaint,
 It dies upon her heart,
As I must die on thine,
 Oh, beloved as thou art!

Oh, lift me from the grass!
I die! I faint! I fail!
Let thy love in kisses rain
 On my lips and eyelids pale.
My cheek is cold and white, alas!
 My heart beats loud and fast:
Oh! press it close to thine again,
 Where it will break at last!

Very few, perhaps, are familiar with these lines—yet no less a
poet than Shelley is their author. Their warm, yet delicate and
ethereal imagination will be appreciated by all—but by none so
thoroughly as by him who has himself arisen from sweet dreams of
one beloved to bathe in the aromatic air of a southern midsummer
night.

One of the finest poems by Willis [1]—the very best in my opinion, which he has ever written—has, no doubt, through this same
defect of undue brevity, been kept back from its proper position,
not less in the critical than in the popular view.

The shadows lay along Broadway,
 'Twas near the twilight tide,
And slowly there a lady fair
 Was walking in her pride.
Along walked she; but, viewlessly,
 Walked spirits at her side.

Peace charmed the street beneath her feet
 And Honor charmed the air;

[1] Nathaniel Parker Willis (1806–1867), American poet and journalist, was born at
Portland, educated at Yale; he travelled much abroad (for a time was attached to the American Embassy in Paris). He was very popular in his day, but is almost forgotten now.

And all astir looked kind on her,
    And called her good as fair,
For all God ever gave to her
    She kept with chary care.

She kept with care her beauties rare
    From lovers warm and true,
For her heart was cold to all but gold,
    And the rich came not to woo—
But honored well are charms to sell
    If priests the selling do.

Now walking there was one more fair—
    A slight girl, lily pale;
And she had unseen company
    To make the spirit quail:
'Twixt Want and Scorn she walked forlorn,
    And nothing could avail.

No mercy now can clear her brow
    For this world's peace to pray;
For, as love's wild prayer dissolved in air,
    Her woman's heart gave way!—
But the sin forgiven by Christ in heaven
    By man is cursed alway!

In this composition we find it difficult to recognize the Willis who has written so many mere "verses of society." The lines are not only richly ideal, but full of energy; while they breathe an earnestness—an evident sincerity of sentiment—for which we look in vain throughout all the other works of this author.

While the epic mania—while the idea that, to merit in poetry, prolixity is indispensable—has, for some years past, been gradually dying out of the public mind, by mere dint of its own absurdity—we find it succeeded by a heresy too palpably false to be long tolerated, but one which, in the brief period it has already endured, may be said to have accomplished more in the corruption of our Poetical Literature than all its other enemies combined. I allude to the heresy of *The Didactic*. It has been assumed, tacitly and avowedly, directly and indirectly, that the ultimate object of all Poetry is Truth. Every poem, it is said, should inculcate a moral; and by this moral is the poetical merit of the work to be adjudged. We Americans, especially, have patronized this happy idea; and we Bos-

tonians,[1] very especially, have developed it in full. We have taken
it into our heads that to write a poem simply for the poem's sake,
and to acknowledge such to have been our design, would be to confess ourselves radically wanting in the true Poetic dignity and
force:—but the simple fact is, that, would we but permit ourselves
to look into our own souls, we should immediately there discover
that under the sun there neither exists nor *can* exist any work more
thoroughly dignified—more supremely noble than this very poem
—this poem *per se*—this poem which is a poem and nothing more—
this poem written solely for the poem's sake.

With as deep a reverence for the True as ever inspired the bosom
of man, I would, nevertheless, limit, in some measure, its modes of
inculcation. I would limit to enforce them. I would not enfeeble
them by dissipation. The demands of Truth are severe. She has no
sympathy with the myrtles.[2] All *that* which is so indispensable in
Song, is precisely all *that* with which *she* has nothing whatever to
do. It is but making her a flaunting paradox, to wreathe her in gems
and flowers. In enforcing a truth, we need severity rather than
efflorescence of language. We must be simple, precise, terse. We
must be cool, calm, unimpassioned. In a word, we must be in that
mood which, as nearly as possible, is the exact converse of the
poetical. He must be blind, indeed, who does not perceive the radical and chasmal differences between the truthful and the poetical
modes of inculcation. He must be theory-mad beyond redemption
who, in spite of these differences, shall still persist in attempting to
reconcile the obstinate oils and waters of Poetry and Truth.

Dividing the world of mind into its three most obvious distinctions, we have the Pure Intellect, Taste, and the Moral Sense. I
place Taste in the middle, because it is just this position which in
the mind it occupies. It holds intimate relations with either extreme; but from the Moral Sense is separated by so faint a difference that Aristotle has not hesitated to place some of its operations
among the virtues themselves. Nevertheless, we find the *offices* of
the trio marked with a sufficient distinction. Just as the Intellect
concerns itself with Truth, so Taste informs us of the Beautiful,
while the Moral Sense is regardful of Duty. Of this latter, while
Conscience teaches the obligation, and Reason the expediency, Taste
contents herself with displaying the charms:—waging war upon

---

[1] Poe was born in Boston, and lived there for a while in later life.
[2] The ancients considered the myrtle sacred to Venus, goddess of love.

Vice solely on the ground of her deformity—her disproportion, her animosity to the fitting, to the appropriate, to the harmonious—in a word, to Beauty.

An immortal instinct, deep within the spirit of man, is thus, plainly, a sense of the Beautiful. This it is which administers to his delight in the manifold forms, and sounds, and odors, and sentiments amid which he exists. And just as the lily is repeated in the lake, or the eyes of Amaryllis in the mirror, so is the mere oral or written repetition of these forms, and sounds, and colors, and odors, and sentiments, a duplicate source of delight. But this mere repetition is not poetry. He who shall simply sing, with however glowing enthusiasm, or with however vivid a truth of description, of the sights, and sounds, and odors, and colors, and sentiments, which greet *him* in common with all mankind—he, I say, has yet failed to prove his divine title. There is still a something in the distance which he has been unable to attain. We have still a thirst unquenchable, to allay which he has not shown us the crystal springs. This thirst belongs to the immortality of Man. It is at once a consequence and an indication of his perennial existence. It is the desire of the moth for the star. It is no mere appreciation of the Beauty before us—but a wild effort to reach the Beauty above. Inspired by an ecstatic prescience of the glories beyond the grave, we struggle, by multiform combinations among the things and thoughts of Time, to attain a portion of that Loveliness whose very elements, perhaps, appertain to eternity alone. And thus when by Poetry—or when by Music, the most entrancing of the Poetic moods—we find ourselves melted into tears—we weep then—not as the Abbaté Gravina [1] supposes—through excess of pleasure, but through a certain, petulant, impatient sorrow at our inability to grasp *now,* wholly, here on earth, at once and forever, those divine and rapturous joys, of which *through* the poem, or *through* the music, we attain to but brief and indeterminate glimpses.

The struggle to apprehend the supernal Loveliness—this struggle, on the part of souls fittingly constituted—has given to the world all *that* which it (the world) has ever been enabled at once to understand and *to feel* as poetic.

The Poetic Sentiment, of course, may develop itself in various modes—in Painting, in Sculpture, in Architecture, in the Dance—very especially in Music—and very peculiarly, and with a wide field, in the composition of the Landscape Garden. Our present

---

[1] John Vincent Gravina (1664–1718), Italian legal authority and critic.

theme, however, has regard only to its manifestation in words. And here let me speak briefly on the topic of rhythm. Contenting myself with the certainty that Music, in its various modes of metre, rhythm, and rhyme, is of so vast a moment in Poetry as never to be wisely rejected—is so vitally important an adjunct, that he is simply silly who declines its assistance, I will not now pause to maintain its absolute essentiality. It is in Music, perhaps, that the soul most nearly attains the great end for which, when inspired by the Poetic Sentiment, it struggles—the creation of supernal Beauty. It *may* be, indeed, that here this sublime end is, now and then, attained *in fact*. We are often made to feel, with a shivering delight, that from an earthly harp are stricken notes which *cannot* have been unfamiliar to the angels. And thus there can be little doubt that in the union of Poetry with Music in its popular sense, we shall find the widest field for the Poetic development. The old Bards and Minnesingers [1] had advantages which we do not possess —and Thomas Moore,[2] singing his own songs, was, in the most legitimate manner, perfecting them as poems.

To recapitulate, then:—I would define, in brief, the Poetry of words as *The Rhythmical Creation of Beauty*. Its sole arbiter is Taste. With the Intellect or with the Conscience, it has only collateral relations. Unless incidentally, it has no concern whatever either with Duty or with Truth.

A few words, however, in explanation. *That* pleasure which is at once the most pure, the most elevating, and the most intense, is derived, I maintain, from the contemplation of the Beautiful. In the contemplation of Beauty we alone find it possible to attain that pleasurable elevation, or excitement, *of the soul*, which we recognize as the Poetic Sentiment, and which is so easily distinguished from Truth, which is the satisfaction of the Reason, or from Passion, which is the excitement of the heart. I make Beauty, therefore—using the word as inclusive of the sublime—I make Beauty the province of the poem, simply because it is an obvious rule of Art that effects should be made to spring as directly as possible from their causes:—no one as yet having been weak enough to deny that the peculiar elevation in question is at least *most readily* attainable in the poem. It by no means follows, however, that the incitements of Passion, or the precepts of Duty, or even the lessons of Truth, may not be introduced into a poem, and with advantage;

[1] Minnesingers were mediæval German love-poets.
[2] Thomas Moore (1779–1852), the still popular Irish poet.

for they may subserve, incidentally, in various ways, the general purposes of the work:—but the true artist will always contrive to tone them down in proper subjection to that *Beauty* which is the atmosphere and the real essence of the poem.

I cannot better introduce the few poems, which I shall present for your consideration, than by the citation of the Proem to Mr. Longfellow's *Waif:* [1]

> The day is done, and the darkness
>   Falls from the wings of Night,
> As a feather is wafted downward
>   From an eagle in his flight.
>
> I see the lights of the village
>   Gleam through the rain and the mist,
> And a feeling of sadness comes o'er me,
>   That my soul cannot resist:
>
> A feeling of sadness and longing,
>   That is not akin to pain,
> And resembles sorrow only
>   As the mist resembles the rain.
>
> Come, read to me some poem,
>   Some simple and heartfelt lay,
> That shall soothe this restless feeling,
>   And banish the thoughts of day.
>
> Not from the grand old masters,
>   Not from the bards sublime,
> Whose distant footsteps echo
>   Through the corridors of Time.
>
> For, like strains of martial music,
>   Their mighty thoughts suggest
> Life's endless toil and endeavor;
>   And to-night I long for rest.
>
> Read from some humbler poet,
>   Whose songs gushed from his heart,
> As showers from the clouds of summer,
>   Or tears from the eyelids start;
>
> Who, through long days of labor,
>   And nights devoid of ease,

---

[1] Now included in his collected works under *Songs,* with the title "The Day is Done."

Still heard in his soul the music
Of wonderful melodies.

Such songs have power to quiet
The restless pulse of care,
And come like the benediction
That follows after prayer.

Then read from the treasured volume
The poem of thy choice,
And lend to the rhyme of the poet
The beauty of thy voice.

And the night shall be filled with music,
And the cares that infest the day,
Shall fold their tents, like the Arabs,
And as silently steal away.

With no great range of imagination, these lines have been justly admired for their delicacy of expression. Some of the images are very effective. Nothing can be better than—

the bards sublime
Whose distant footsteps echo
Down the corridors of Time.

The idea of the last quatrain is also very effective. The poem, on the whole, however, is chiefly to be admired for the graceful *insouciance* [1] of its metre, so well in accordance with the character of the sentiments, and especially for the *ease* of the general manner. This "ease," or naturalness, in a literary style, it has long been the fashion to regard as ease in appearance alone—as a point of really difficult attainment. But not so:—a natural manner is difficult only to him who should never meddle with it—to the unnatural. It is but the result of writing with the understanding, or with the instinct, that *the tone*, in composition, should always be that which the mass of mankind would adopt—and must perpetually vary, of course, with the occasion. The author who, after the fashion of the *North American Review*, should be, upon *all* occasions, merely "quiet," must necessarily, upon *many* occasions, be simply silly, or stupid; and has no more right to be considered "easy," or "nat-

---

[1] Lack of rigidity—literally "carelessness," or "carefree" quality. Perhaps "ease" is an adequate translation.

ural," than a Cockney exquisite,[1] or than the sleeping Beauty in the wax-works.

Among the minor poems of Bryant, none has so much impressed me as the one which he entitles *June*. I quote only a portion of it:

> There, through the long, long summer hours,
>   The golden light should lie,
> And thick young herbs and groups of flowers
>   Stand in their beauty by.
> The oriole should build and tell
> His love-tale, close beside my cell;
>   The idle butterfly
> Should rest him there, and there be heard
> The housewife-bee and humming-bird.
>
> And what if cheerful shouts at noon
>   Come, from the village sent,
> Or songs of maids, beneath the moon,
>   With fairy laughter blent?
> And what if, in the evening light,
> Betrothèd lovers walk in sight
>   Of my low monument?
> I would the lovely scene around
> Might know no sadder sight nor sound.
>
> I know, I know I should not see [2]
>   The season's glorious show,
> Nor would its brightness shine for me,
>   Nor its wild music flow;
> But if, around my place of sleep,
> The friends I love should come to weep,
>   They might not haste to go.
> Soft airs, and song, and light, and bloom
> Should keep them lingering by my tomb.
>
> These to their softened hearts should bear
>   The thought of what has been,
> And speak of one who cannot share
>   The gladness of the scene;
> Whose part, in all the pomp that fills
> The circuit of the summer hills,
>   Is—that his grave is green;
> And deeply would their hearts rejoice
> To hear again his living voice.

[1] A lower-class Londoner putting on airs.
[2] In Bryant the line reads, "I know that I no more should see."

The rhythmical flow, here, is even voluptuous—nothing could be more melodious. The poem has always affected me in a remarkable manner. The intense melancholy which seems to well up, perforce, to the surface of all the poet's cheerful sayings about his grave, we find thrilling us to the soul—while there is the truest poetic elevation in the thrill. The impression left is one of a pleasurable sadness. And if, in the remaining compositions which I shall introduce to you, there be more or less of a similar tone always apparent, let me remind you that (how or why we know not) this certain taint of sadness is inseparably connected with all the higher manifestations of true Beauty. It is, nevertheless,

> A feeling of sadness and longing
> That is not akin to pain,
> And resembles sorrow only
> As the mist resembles the rain.

The taint of which I speak is clearly perceptible even in a poem so full of brilliancy and spirit as the *Health* of Edward Coate Pinkney: [1]

> I fill this cup to one made up
> Of loveliness alone,
> A woman, of her gentle sex
> The seeming paragon;
> To whom the better elements
> And kindly stars have given
> A form so fair, that, like the air,
> 'Tis less of earth than heaven.
>
> Her every tone is music's own,
> Like those of morning birds,
> And something more than melody
> Dwells ever in her words;
> The coinage of her heart are they,
> And from her lips each flows
> As one may see the burdened bee
> Forth issue from the rose.
>
> Affections are as thoughts to her,
> The measures of her hours;

[1] Pinkney was born in 1802 in London, where his father was United States Ambassador. He wrote light, graceful short poems. Falling a victim to ill-health and melancholy he died at the early age of twenty-six. In 1838, a new edition of his poems was published; in the edition of 1844 an introductory notice by Willis was included.

Her feelings have the fragrancy,
    The freshness of young flowers;
And lovely passions, changing oft,
    So fill her, she appears
The image of themselves by turns,—
    The idol of past years!

Of her bright face one glance will trace
    A picture on the brain,
And of her voice in echoing hearts
    A sound must long remain;
But memory, such as mine of her,
    So very much endears,
When death is nigh my latest sigh
    Will not be life's, but hers.

I fill this cup to one made up
    Of loveliness alone,
A woman, of her gentle sex
    The seeming paragon—
Her health! and would on earth there stood
    Some more of such a frame,
That life might be all poetry,
    And weariness a name.

It was the misfortune of Mr. Pinkney to have been born too far south. Had he been a New Englander, it is probable that he would have been ranked as the first of American lyrists, by that magnanimous cabal which has so long controlled the destinies of American Letters, in conducting the thing called the *North American Review*. The poem just cited is especially beautiful; but the poetic elevation which it induces, we must refer chiefly to our sympathy in the poet's enthusiasm. We pardon his hyperboles for the evident earnestness with which they are uttered.

It was by no means my design, however, to expatiate upon the *merits* of what I should read you. These will necessarily speak for themselves. Boccalini,[1] in his *Advertisements from Parnassus,* tells us that Zoilus once presented Apollo a very caustic criticism upon a very admirable book:—whereupon the god asked him for the beauties of the work. He replied that he only busied himself about the errors. On hearing this, Apollo, handing him a sack of unwinnowed wheat, bade him pick out *all the chaff* for his reward.

---

[1] Trajan Boccalini (1556–1613) was an Italian satirist, whose *Advertisements from Parnassus* (1612) dealt frankly with political and literary matters.

Now this fable answers very well as a hit at the critics—but I am by no means sure that the god was in the right. I am by no means certain that the true limits of the critical duty are not grossly misunderstood. Excellence, in a poem especially, may be considered in the light of an axiom, which need only be properly *put*, to become self-evident. It is *not* excellence if it require to be demonstrated as such:—and thus, to point out too particularly the merits of a work of Art is to admit that they are *not* merits altogether.

Among the *Melodies* of Thomas Moore, is one whose distinguished character as a poem proper seems to have been singularly left out of view. I allude to his lines beginning—"Come, rest in this bosom." The intense energy of their expression is not surpassed by anything in Byron. There are two of the lines in which a sentiment is conveyed that embodies the *all in all* of the divine passion of love —a sentiment which, perhaps, has found its echo in more, and in more passionate, human hearts than any other single sentiment ever embodied in words:

> Come, rest in this bosom, my own stricken deer,
> Though the herd have fled from thee, thy home is still here;
> Here still is the smile, that no cloud can o'ercast,
> And a heart and a hand all thy own to the last.
>
> Oh! what was love made for, if 'tis not the same
> Through joy and through torment, through glory and shame?
> I know not, I ask not, if guilt's in that heart,
> I but know that I love thee, whatever thou art.
>
> Thou hast called me thy Angel in moments of bliss,
> And thy Angel I'll be, 'mid the horrors of this,—
> Through the furnace, unshrinking, thy steps to pursue,
> And shield thee, and save thee,—or perish there too!

It has been the fashion, of late days, to deny Moore imagination, while granting him fancy—a distinction originating with Coleridge —than whom no man more fully comprehended the great powers of Moore. The fact is, that the fancy of this poet so far predominates over all his other faculties, and over the fancy of all other men, as to have induced, very naturally, the idea that he is fanciful *only*. But never was there a greater mistake. Never was a grosser wrong done the fame of a true poet. In the compass of the English language I can call to mind no poem more profoundly—more weirdly *imaginative*, in the best sense, than the lines commencing—"I would

I were by that dim lake"—which are the composition of Thomas Moore. I regret that I am unable to remember them.

One of the noblest—and, speaking of fancy, one of the most singularly fanciful of modern poets, was Thomas Hood.[1] His *Fair Ines* had always, for me, an inexpressible charm:

> O saw ye not fair Ines?
> She's gone into the West,
> To dazzle when the sun is down,
> And rob the world of rest:
> She took our daylight with her,
> The smiles that we love best,
> With morning blushes on her cheek,
> And pearls upon her breast.
>
> O turn again, fair Ines,
> Before the fall of night,
> For fear the Moon should shine alone,
> And stars unrivalled bright;
> And blessèd will the lover be
> That walks beneath their light,
> And breathes the love against thy cheek
> I dare not even write!
>
> Would I had been, fair Ines,
> That gallant cavalier,
> Who rode so gaily by thy side,
> And whispered thee so near!
> Were there no bonny dames at home,
> Or no true lovers here,
> That he should cross the seas to win
> The dearest of the dear?
>
> I saw thee, lovely Ines,
> Descend along the shore,
> With bands of noble gentlemen,
> And banners waved before;
> And gentle youth and maidens gay,
> And snowy plumes they wore;
> It would have been a beauteous dream,
> If it had been no more!

[1] Thomas Hood (1799–1845) was an illustrator, magazine editor, and writer, who, despite hardship and ill-health, produced some of the best comic verse in the language. He is remembered especially for his *Bridge of Sighs* and *The Song of the Shirt*, poems that reflect his compassion and restrained tenderness.

Alas, alas, fair Ines,
  She went away with song,
With Music waiting on her steps,
  And shoutings of the throng;
But some were sad, and felt no mirth,
  But only Music's wrong,
In sounds that sang Farewell, Farewell,
  To her you've loved so long.

Farewell, farewell, fair Ines,
  That vessel never bore
So fair a lady on its deck,
  Nor danced so light before,—
Alas for pleasure on the sea,
  And sorrow on the shore!
The smile that blest one lover's heart
  Has broken many more!

The Haunted House, by the same author, is one of the truest poems ever written—one of the *truest*—one of the most unexceptionable—one of the most thoroughly artistic, both in its theme and in its execution. It is, moreover, powerfully ideal—imaginative. I regret that its length renders it unsuitable for the purposes of this Lecture. In place of it, permit me to offer the universally appreciated *Bridge of Sighs*.

One more Unfortunate,
  Weary of breath,
Rashly importunate,
  Gone to her death!

Take her up tenderly,
  Lift her with care;—
Fashioned so slenderly,
  Young, and so fair!

Look at her garments
Clinging like cerements;
Whilst the wave constantly
Drips from her clothing;
Take her up instantly,
Loving, not loathing.

Touch her not scornfully;
Think of her mournfully,

Gently and humanly;
Not of the stains of her,
All that remains of her
Now is pure womanly.

Make no deep scrutiny
Into her mutiny
Rash and undutiful;
Past all dishonor,
Death has left on her
Only the beautiful.

Still, for all slips of hers,
One of Eve's family—
Wipe those poor lips of hers
Oozing so clammily.
Loop up her tresses
Escaped from the comb,
Her fair auburn tresses;
Whilst wonderment guesses
Where was her home?

Who was her father?
Who was her mother?
Had she a sister?
Had she a brother?
Or was there a dearer one
Still, and a nearer one
Yet, than all other?

Alas! for the rarity
Of Christian charity
Under the sun!
Oh! it was pitiful!
Near a whole city full,
Home she had none.

Sisterly, brotherly,
Fatherly, motherly
Feelings had changed:
Love, by harsh evidence,
Thrown from its eminence;
Even God's providence
Seeming estranged.

There is many a pang to pursue me:
　They may crush, but they shall not contemn—
They may torture, but shall not subdue me—
　'Tis of *thee* that I think—not of them.

Though human, thou didst not deceive me,
　Though woman, thou didst not forsake,
Though loved, thou forborest to grieve me,
　Though slandered, thou never couldst shake,—
Though trusted, thou didst not disclaim me,
　Though parted, it was not to fly,
Though watchful, 'twas not to defame me,
　Nor mute, that the world might belie.

Yet I blame not the world, nor despise it,
　Nor the war of the many with one—
If my soul was not fitted to prize it,
　'Twas folly not sooner to shun:
And if dearly that error hath cost me,
　And more than I once could foresee,
I have found that whatever it lost me,
　It could not deprive me of *thee*.

From the wreck of the past, which hath perished,
　Thus much I at least may recall,
It hath taught me that which I most cherished,
　Deserved to be dearest of all:
In the desert a fountain is springing,
　In the wide waste there still is a tree,
And a bird in the solitude singing,
　Which speaks to my spirit of *thee*.

Although the rhythm here is one of the most difficult, the versification could scarcely be improved. No nobler *theme* ever engaged the pen of poet. It is the soul-elevating idea, that no man can consider himself entitled to complain of Fate while, in his adversity, he still retains the unwavering love of woman.

From Alfred Tennyson—although in perfect sincerity I regard him as the noblest poet that ever lived—I have left myself time to cite only a very brief specimen. I call him, and *think* him, the noblest of poets—*not* because the impressions he produces are, at *all* times, the most profound—*not* because the poetical excitement which he induces is, at *all* times, the most intense—but because it *is*, at all times, the most ethereal—in other words, the most elevat-

ing and the most pure. No poet is so little of the earth, earthy.
What I am about to read is from his last long poem, *The Princess:*

> Tears, idle tears, I know not what they mean,
> Tears from the depth of some divine despair
> Rise in the heart, and gather to the eyes,
> In looking on the happy autumn fields,
> And thinking of the days that are no more.
>
> Fresh as the first beam glittering on a sail
> That brings our friends up from the underworld,
> Sad as the last which reddens over one
> That sinks with all we love below the verge;
> So sad, so fresh, the days that are no more.
>
> Ah, sad and strange as in dark summer dawns
> The earliest pipe of half-awaken'd birds
> To dying ears, when unto dying eyes
> The casement slowly grows a glimmering square;
> So sad, so strange, the days that are no more.
>
> Dear as remembered kisses after death,
> And sweet as those by hopeless fancy feigned
> On lips that are for others; deep as love,
> Deep as first love, and wild with all regret;
> O Death in Life, the days that are no more.

Thus, although in a very cursory and imperfect manner, I have
endeavored to convey to you my conception of the Poetic Principle. It has been my purpose to suggest that, while this Principle
itself is, strictly and simply, the Human Aspiration for Supernal
Beauty, the manifestation of the Principle is always found in *an
elevating excitement of the Soul*—quite independent of that passion
which is the intoxication of the Heart—or of that truth which is
the satisfaction of the Reason. For, in regard to Passion, alas! its
tendency is to degrade, rather than to elevate the Soul. Love, on the
contrary—Love—the true, the divine Eros—the Uranian, as distinguished from the Dionæan Venus [1]—is unquestionably the purest and truest of all poetical themes. And in regard to Truth—if,
to be sure, through the attainment of a truth, we are led to perceive a harmony where none was apparent before, we experience,
at once, the true poetical effect—but this effect is referable to the
harmony alone, and not in the least degree to the truth which
merely served to render the harmony manifest.

[1] Heavenly, as distinguished from earthly.

We shall reach, however, more immediately a distinct conception of what the true Poetry is, by mere reference to a few of the simple elements which induce in the Poet himself the true poetical effect. He recognizes the ambrosia which nourishes his soul, in the bright orbs that shine in Heaven—in the volutes of the flower—in the clustering of low shrubberies—in the waving of the grain-fields —in the slanting of tall, Eastern trees—in the blue distance of mountains—in the grouping of clouds—in the twinkling of half-hidden brooks—in the gleaming of silver rivers—in the repose of sequestered lakes—in the star-mirroring depths of lonely wells. He perceives it in the songs of birds—in the harp of Æolus—in the sighing of the night-wind—in the repining voice of the forest—in the surf that complains to the shore—in the fresh breath of the woods—in the scent of the violet—in the voluptuous perfume of the hyacinth—in the suggestive odor that comes to him, at eventide, from far-distant, undiscovered islands, over dim oceans, illimitable and unexplored. He owns it in all noble thoughts—in all unworldly motives—in all holy impulses—in all chivalrous, generous, and self-sacrificing deeds. He feels it in the beauty of woman—in the grace of her step—in the lustre of her eye—in the melody of her voice— in her soft laughter—in her sigh—in the harmony of the rustling of her robes. He deeply feels it in her winning endearments—in her burning enthusiasms—in her gentle charities—in her meek and devotional endurances—but above all—ah, far above all—he kneels to it—he worships it in the faith, in the purity, in the strength, in the altogether divine majesty—of her *love*.

Let me conclude—by the recitation of yet another brief poem— one very different in character from any that I have before quoted. It is by Motherwell,[1] and is called *The Song of the Cavalier*. With our modern and altogether rational ideas of the absurdity and impiety of warfare, we are not precisely in that frame of mind best adapted to sympathize with the sentiments, and thus to appreciate the real excellence of the poem. To do this fully, we must identify ourselves, in fancy, with the soul of the old cavalier.

> Then mounte! then mounte, brave gallants, all,
>   And don your helmes amaine:
> Death's couriers, Fame and Honor, call
>   Us to the field againe.

[1] William Motherwell (1797–1835) was a Scotch poet, antiquarian, and authority on ballad literature (which he collected).

No shrewish teares shall fill our eye
    When the sword-hilt's in our hand,—
Heart-whole we'll part, and no whit sighe
    For the fayrest of the land;
Let piping swaine, and craven wight,
    Thus weepe and puling crye,
Our business is like men to fight,
    And hero-like to die!

Hebbel

Christian Friedrich HEBBEL (1813–1863) was born in Wesselburen, Holstein, the only son of a poor bricklayer. The hardships of his youth developed a sharp directness of writing and an ability to face unvarnished facts. Interested friends made schooling possible for him, and he prepared himself at Hamburg for the University of Heidelberg, where he studied law, and Munich, where he followed courses in philosophy, history, and literature. His first play, *Judith,* was printed in 1841. Travel in Denmark and France inspired further composition, and in 1844 he wrote *Mary Magdalena,* a tragedy of common life, produced while Ibsen, who later felt his influence profoundly, was yet a boy. He settled in Vienna, where, in 1846, he married a beautiful and wealthy actress, who created many parts in his later plays, inspiring his best work. After a period of peace and serenity, he died in Vienna.

Hebbel was primarily a dramatist. He and Kleist and Grillparzer, worthy successors in the German theatre to Lessing, Goethe, and Schiller, stand at the head of European playwrights during the first half of the nineteenth century. In his criticism, Hebbel is not systematic, nor does he write essays. He enters in his *Tagebücher,* or diaries, highly compressed, often disconnected, statements, which give one the impression that they are either standards that he set down for his own guidance as an artist, or principles that he evolved from his creative writing. He gives only his conclusions, and valuable they are, omitting the steps or stages that led to them.

From his JOURNAL [1]

(1836)

Poetic and plastic art are alike in being both formative; that is to say, they are intended to bring to view a limited amount of matter in definite relations which are fixed by nature; and when the poet gives expression to an idea, the process is exactly the same as when a painter or sculptor represents the noble or beautiful outlines of a body.

It is a sign of mediocre intelligence to be able to fix one's attention upon details when contemplating a great work of art; on the other hand, it is a sign of the mediocrity of a work of art (poetic or plastic) if one cannot get beyond the details, if they, so to speak, impede the way to the whole.

*　　*　　*　　*

(1837)

Many simply introduce logic into their poetry and believe this is equivalent to motivation.

All reasoning (and here belongs what Schiller, under the trademark of the sentimental, would smuggle in as poetry) is onesided and allows the heart and mind no further activity than simply to deny or affirm. On the contrary, all that is actual and objective (and here belong the so-called natural sounds, which reveal the innermost essence of a state or a human personality) is infinite, and offers to those who are in sympathy and to those who are not the widest scope for the employment of all their powers.

Philosophy strives ever and always for the absolute, and yet that is properly speaking the task of poetry.

With every human being (let him be who he will) disappears from the world a mystery, that, owing to his peculiar construction, he alone could reveal, and that no one will reveal after him.

It is dangerous to think in images, but it cannot always be avoided; for often, especially in regard to the highest things, image and thought are identical.

*　　*　　*　　*

[1] *The German Classics*, edited by Kuno Francke; Albany, [1914], vol. ix. Hebbel's *Journal* is translated by Frances H. King.

(1838)

When the poet attempts to delineate characters by making them speak, he must be careful not to allow them to speak about their own inner life. All their utterances must relate to something external; only then does their inner nature come out vividly and expressively, for it fashions itself only in reflections of the world and of life.

To depict two kindred characters one by means of the other, to have them mutually reflect one another without their becoming aware of it, would surely be the triumph of delineation.

A double process must take place in the mind of the true poet before it can evolve anything. The crude matter must be resolved into an idea, and the idea must condense again into a form.

The first and last aim of art is to render intuitively perceptible the process of life itself, to show how the soul of man develops in the atmosphere surrounding him, let it be suited to him or not; how good engenders evil within him, and evil in turn produces something less evil, and how this eternal growth has a limit so far as our apprehension is concerned, but none at all in reality; this is symbolization. It is an error when men say that only the fully developed is matter for the poet; on the contrary, what is in process of development, what is first begotten in conflict with the elements of creation, that is matter for him. What is finished can be only a plaything of the waves, it can only be destroyed and devoured by them; can art have anything to do with that which is most common, in other words, most universal? But what is in process of development must pass from one form into another at the hands of the poet, it must never as formless soft clay dissolve before our eyes into chaos and confusion; it must always, in a certain sense, be at the same time a finished product, just as in the universe we never encounter naked raw material. Man exists only because of his future; an inexplicable mystery, but one that may not be denied. Man, therefore, cannot be brought before us as something complete in himself; for not how he affects the world but how the world affects him arouses our interest and is of importance to us; the great forces and powers outside of him find embodiment by exerting an influence over him, and thus lose their formidableness; the riddle of the universe is solved as soon as it finds utterance, and even though at the end a question remains, we can bear this much easier than an empty nothing.

Not only in art but in history as well life sometimes assumes a form, and art should not seek her subjects and her themes where this has occurred.

God was a mystery to Himself before the creation; He had to create in order to understand Himself.

The motives before a deed are usually transformed during the deed, and at least seem quite different after the deed: this is an important circumstance which most dramatists overlook.

Lyric poetry has something childlike about it, dramatic poetry something manly, epic poetry something senile.

(1840)

All life is a struggle of the individual with the universe.

Duality pervades all our intuitions and thoughts and every moment of our being, and is our supreme, our last idea. Beside it we have absolutely no fundamental idea. Life and death, health and sickness, time and eternity: we can imagine and picture to ourselves how one gradually shades off into the other, but not that which lies behind these divided dualities as a common solvent and reconciliation.

(1845)

A genuine drama may be compared to one of those great buildings which have almost as many passages and rooms below the earth as above it. Ordinary people only know the former; the architect knows the latter also.

(1847)

To present the necessary, but in the form of the accidental: that is the whole secret of dramatic style.

If the characters do not negate the moral idea, what does it matter that the piece affirms it? The negation of the individual factors must be so very decided, precisely in order to give emphasis to the affirmation of the whole.

Human institutions require a man to be a man like other men; but man, whoever and whatever he may be, wishes to be an individual, indeed is, as such, individualized. Hence the rupture.

Let the understanding question in a work of art, but do not let it answer.

(1848)

The understanding no more makes poetry than salt makes food, but it is necessary to poetry as salt is to food.

(1849)

One does not sit down to play on the piano in order to verify mathematical laws. Just as little does one write poetry in order to demonstrate something. Oh, if people would only learn to comprehend that! Indeed the beauty of all the higher activity of man is precisely the fact, that ends which the individual never even thinks of are attained thereby.

(1859)

Ideas are the same thing in the drama that counterpoint is in music; nothing in themselves but the primary condition for everything.

(1863)

I do not know the world, for although I myself represent a piece of it, this is such a minutely small part that no conclusion as to the true nature of the world can be deduced therefrom. Man, however, I know, for I am myself a man, and even though I do not know how he originates in the world, yet I know very well how, having once originated, he reacts upon it. I therefore conscientiously respect the laws of the human soul; in reference to everything else, however, I believe that imagination draws inspiration from the same depths out of which the world itself arose, that is to say, the multifarious series of phenomena which exists at present, but which at some future time, may perhaps be replaced by another.

. . . For systems are not dreamed, but neither are works of art made by minute calculations, nor, what amounts to the same thing, since thinking is only a higher kind of arithmetic, thought out. The artistic imagination is the organ which drains those depths of the world which are inaccessible to the other faculties, and in accordance herewith, my mode of viewing things puts, in place of the false realism which takes the part for the whole, only the true realism, which also comprises what does not lie on the surface. For the rest, this false realism is not curtailed thereby, for even though one can no more prepare oneself for writing poetry than for dreaming, yet dreams will always reflect daily and yearly impressions, and no less do poems reflect the sympathies and antipathies of the author. I believe all these propositions are simple and comprehensible.

Trollope

Anthony TROLLOPE (1815–1882) was born in London, the son of an unsuccessful barrister. After a youth shadowed by poverty—but with an education at Harrow—he obtained a position in the Post Office, a department in which he served with distinction for thirty-three years. In the odd moments of his active life, which involved much professional travel, he wrote the novels which rank him high as a satirist. He lived in Ireland, and later in various parts of England; he visited, at different times, the West Indies, the United States, and Australia. His official work involved considerable labor in the regulation of foreign mails and rural deliveries (among other improvements, he invented and introduced the postal pillar- or letter-box), and, like many other English authors, he was interested in international copyright laws. Toward the end of his life he became a familiar figure at London clubs; but he lived near enough to the country to be often out with the hounds and to keep up his favorite sport of riding.

Trollope is, of course, really not a critic. His essay is important, however, in calling attention to a new kind of criticism, "reviewing," which, in the nineteenth century, with the growth of magazines and newspapers, assumed a steadily increasing authority; and also in giving a creative artist's reaction to this type of criticism. The paper raises the question, too, whether literary criticism exists to help readers form judgments or to give artists advice and direction.

ON CRITICISM [1]

(1876)

Literary criticism in the present day has become a profession— but it has ceased to be an art. Its object is no longer that of proving that certain literary work is good, and other literary work is bad, in accordance with rules which the critic is able to define. English criticism at present rarely even pretends to go so far as this. It attempts, in the first place, to tell the public whether a book be or be not worth public attention; and, in the second place, so to describe the purport of the work as to enable those who have not time or inclination for reading it to feel that by a short-cut they can become acquainted with its contents. Both these objects, if fairly well carried out, are salutary. Though the critic may not be a profound judge himself, though not unfrequently he be a young man making his first literary attempts, with tastes and judgment still unfixed, yet he probably has a conscience in the matter, and would not have been selected for that work had he not shown some aptitude for it. Though he may not be the best possible guide to the undiscerning, he will be better than no guide at all. Real substantial criticism must, from its nature, be costly, and that which the public wants should, at any rate, be cheap. Advice is given to many thousands, which, though it may not be the best advice possible, is better than no advice at all. Then that description of the work criticized, that compressing of the much into very little—which is the work of many modern critics or reviewers—does enable many to know something of what is being said, who without it would know nothing.

I do not think it is incumbent on me at present to name periodicals in which this work is well done, and to make complaints of others by which it is scamped. I should give offence, and might probably be unjust. But I think I may certainly say that as some of these periodicals are certainly entitled to great praise for the manner in which the work is done generally, so are others open to very severe censure —and that the praise and that the censure are chiefly due on behalf of one virtue and its opposite vice. It is not critical ability that we have a right to demand, or its absence that we are bound to deplore. Critical ability for the price we pay is not attainable. It is a faculty not peculiar to Englishmen, and when displayed is very frequently not appreciated. But that critics should be honest we have a right to

[1] This essay is from Trollope's *Autobiography*, first edition, London, 1883, chapter xiv.

demand, and critical dishonesty we are bound to expose. If the writer will tell us what he thinks, though his thoughts be absolutely vague and useless, we can forgive him; but when he tells us what he does not think, actuated either by friendship or by animosity, then there should be no pardon for him. This is the sin in modern English criticism of which there is most reason to complain.

It is a lamentable fact that men and women lend themselves to this practice who are neither vindictive nor ordinarily dishonest. It has become "the custom of the trade," under the veil of which excuse so many tradesmen justify their malpractices. When a struggling author learns that so much has been done for A by the *Barsetshire Gazette*, so much for B by the *Dillsborough Herald*, and, again, so much for C by that powerful metropolitan organ the *Evening Pulpit*, and is told also that A and B and C have been favored through personal interest, he also goes to work among the editors, or the editors' wives—or, perhaps, if he cannot reach their wives, with their wives' first or second cousins. When once the feeling has come upon an editor or a critic that he may allow himself to be influenced by other considerations than the duty he owes to the public, all sense of critical or of editorial honesty falls from him at once. *Facilis descensus Averni.*[1] In a very short time that editorial honesty becomes ridiculous to himself. It is for other purpose that he wields the power; and when he is told what is his duty, and what should be his conduct, the preacher of such doctrine seems to him to be quixotic. "Where have you lived, my friend, for the last twenty years," he says in spirit, if not in word, "that you come out now with such stuff as old-fashioned as this?" And thus dishonesty begets dishonesty, till dishonesty seems to be beautiful. How nice to be good-natured! How glorious to assist struggling young authors, especially if the young author be also a pretty woman! How gracious to oblige a friend! Then the motive, though still pleasing, departs further from the border of what is good. In what way can the critic better repay the hospitality of his wealthy literary friend than by good-natured criticism, or more certainly ensure for himself a continuation of hospitable favors?

Some years since a critic of the day, a gentleman well known then in literary circles, showed me the manuscript of a book recently published, the work of a popular author. It was handsomely bound, and was a valuable and desirable possession. It had just been given to him by the author, as an acknowledgment for a laudatory review

[1] The descent to hell is easy.

in one of the leading journals of the day. As I was expressly asked whether I did not regard such a token as a sign of grace both in the giver and in the receiver, I said that I thought it should neither have been given nor have been taken. My theory was repudiated with scorn, and I was told that I was strait-laced, visionary, and impracticable! In all that the damage did not lie in the fact of that one present, but in the feeling on the part of the critic that his office was not debased by the acceptance of presents from those whom he criticized. This man was a professional critic, bound by his contract with certain employers to review such books as were sent to him. How could he, when he had received a valuable present for praising one book, censure another by the same author?

While I write this I well know that what I say, if it be ever noticed at all, will be taken as a straining at gnats, as a pretence of honesty, or, at any rate, as an exaggeration of scruples. I have said the same thing before, and have been ridiculed for saying it. But none the less am I sure that English literature generally is suffering much under this evil. All those who are struggling for success have forced upon them the idea that their strongest efforts should be made in touting for praise. Those who are not familiar with the lives of authors will hardly believe how low will be the forms which their struggles will take; how little presents will be sent to men who write little articles; how much flattery may be expended, even on the keeper of a circulating library; with what profuse and distant genuflexions approaches are made to the outside railing of the temple which contains within it the great thunderer of some metropolitan periodical publication! The evil here is not only that done to the public when interested counsel is given to them, but extends to the debasement of those who have, at any rate, considered themselves fit to provide literature for the public.

I am satisfied that the remedy for this evil must lie in the conscience and deportment of authors themselves. If once the feeling could be produced that it is disgraceful for an author to ask for praise—and demands for praise are, I think, disgraceful in every walk of life—the practice would gradually fall into the hands only of the lowest, and that which is done only by the lowest soon becomes despicable even to them. The sin, when perpetuated with unflagging labor, brings with it at best very poor reward. That work of running after critics, editors, publishers, the keepers of circulating libraries, and their clerks, is very hard, and must be very disagreeable. He who does it must feel himself to be dishonored—or she. It may, perhaps, help to sell an edition, but can never make an author successful.

I think it may be laid down as a golden rule in literature that there should be no intercourse at all between an author and his critic. The critic, as critic, should not know his author, nor the author, as author, his critic. As censure should beget no anger, so should praise beget no gratitude. The young author should feel that criticisms fall upon him as dew or hail from heaven—which, as coming from heaven, man accepts as fate. Praise let the author try to obtain by wholesome effort; censure let him avoid, if possible, by care and industry. But when they come, let him take them as coming from some source which he cannot influence, and with which he should not meddle.

I know no more disagreeable trouble into which an author may plunge himself than that of a quarrel with his critics, or any more useless labor than that of answering them. It is wise to presume, at any rate, that the reviewer has simply done his duty, and has spoken of the book according to the dictates of his conscience. Nothing can be gained by combating the reviewer's opinion. If the book which he has disparaged be good, his judgment will be condemned by the praise of others; if bad, his judgment will be confirmed by others. Or if, unfortunately, the criticism of the day be in so evil a condition generally that such ultimate truth cannot be expected, the author may be sure that his efforts made on behalf of his own book will not set matters right. If injustice be done him, let him bear it. To do so is consonant with the dignity of the position which he ought to assume. To shriek, and scream, and sputter, to threaten actions, and to swear about the town that he has been belied and defamed in that he has been accused of bad grammar or a false metaphor, of a dull chapter, or even of a borrowed heroine, will leave on the minds of the public nothing but a sense of irritated impotence.

If, indeed, there should spring from an author's work any assertion by a critic injurious to the author's honor, if the author be accused of falsehood or of personal motives which are discreditable to him, then, indeed, he may be bound to answer the charge. It is hoped, however, that he may be able to do so with clean hands, or he will so stir the mud in the pool as to come forth dirtier than he went into it.

I have lived much among men by whom the English criticism of the day has been vehemently abused. I have heard it said that to the public it is a false guide, and that to authors it is never a trustworthy mentor. I do not concur in this wholesale censure. There is, of course, criticism and criticism. There are at this moment one or two periodicals to which both public and authors may safely look for guidance, though there are many others from which no spark of literary advantage may be obtained. But it is well that both public and authors should know what is the advantage which they have a right to expect. There have been critics—and there probably will be again, though the circumstances of English literature do not tend to produce them—with power sufficient to entitle them to speak with authority. These great men have declared, *tanquam ex cathedrâ*,[1] that such a book has been so far good and so far bad, or that it has been altogether good or altogether bad; and the world has believed them. When making such assertions they have given their reasons, explained their causes, and have carried conviction. Very great reputations have been achieved by such critics, but not without infinite study and the labor of many years.

Such are not the critics of the day, of whom we are now speaking. In the literary world as it lives at present some writer is selected for the place of critic to a newspaper, generally some young writer, who for so many shillings a column shall review whatever book is sent to him and express an opinion—reading the book through for the purpose, if the amount of honorarium as measured with the amount of labor will enable him to do so. A laborer must measure his work by his pay or he cannot live. From criticism such as this must for the most part be, the general reader has no right to expect philosophical analysis, or literary judgment on which confidence may be placed. But he probably may believe that the books praised will be better than the books censured, and that those which are praised by periodicals which never censure are better worth his attention than those which are not noticed. And readers will also find that by devoting an hour or two on Saturday to the criticisms of the week, they will enable themselves to have an opinion about the books of the day. The knowledge so acquired will not be great, nor will that little be lasting; but it adds something to the pleasure of life to be able to talk on subjects of which others are speaking; and the man who has sedulously gone through the literary notices in the *Spectator* and the *Saturday* may perhaps be justified in thinking himself as well able to talk about the new book as his friend who has brought that new book on the *tapis*, and who, not improbably, obtained his information from the same source.

[1] As if from the chair (of authority).

As an author, I have paid careful attention to the reviews which have been written on my own work; and I think that now I well know where I may look for a little instruction, where I may expect only greasy adulation, where I shall be cut up into mince-meat for the delight of those who love sharp invective, and where I shall find an equal mixture of praise and censure so adjusted, without much judgment, as to exhibit the impartiality of the newspaper and its staff. Among it all there is much chaff, which I have learned how to throw to the winds, with equal disregard whether it praises or blames; but I have also found some corn, on which I have fed and nourished myself, and for which I have been thankful.

Ruskin

John RUSKIN (1819–1900) was born in London, the son of a wealthy merchant, who brought him up under intellectually and morally bracing Puritan influences. He went to Oxford University, where his studies were interrupted by a severe illness. In 1840 he made the acquaintance of the painter, Turner, who aroused his interest in art, which was further stimulated by a visit to Venice. In 1842 he took his degree at Oxford, and the next year published the first volume of *Modern Painters*. He married in 1848, but the union proved unhappy and was dissolved in 1855. In 1864 the death of his father left him rich; but he gradually disposed of his fortune in aiding the poor and making generous gifts to museums and schools. With his interest in art he combined a study of economics and sociology. From 1851 he expounded his theories, and continued to develop his views, not only in many books and lectures to all kinds of audiences, but in practical experiments relating to popular education. In 1870 he was appointed the first Slade Professor of the Fine Arts at Oxford, where he endowed a school of drawing. After the death of his mother, in 1871, he purchased a small property in the Lake District. This same year he was elected Lord Rector of St. Andrew's University. Cambridge University made him an LL. D. in 1867; in 1884 he resigned his Oxford professorship; and in 1893 Oxford conferred upon him the D. C. L. degree.

Better known, perhaps, as an art-critic and philanthropist, or as an economist interested in stressing the human element of the "dismal science," Ruskin was also concerned with matters of style and the psychology of literary criticism. He had, without doubt, taste and a sensitive appreciation of beauty, along with the gift of writing clear and rhythmical prose. His deeply felt humanitarianism, on the other hand, made him stress the moral obligation of the artist to create art with an ethical import for the forgotten man.

From MODERN PAINTERS [1]

(1856)

OF THE PATHETIC FALLACY

§ 1. German dullness, and English affectation, have of late much multiplied among us the use of two of the most objectionable words that were ever coined by the troublesomeness of metaphysicians,— namely, "Objective" and "Subjective."

No words can be more exquisitely, and in all points, useless; and I merely speak of them that I may, at once and for ever, get them out of my way, and out of my reader's. But to get that done, they must be explained.

The word *blue*, say certain philosophers, means the sensation of color which the human eye receives in looking at the open sky, or at a bell gentian.

Now, say they farther, as this sensation can only be felt when the eye is turned to the object, and as, therefore, no such sensation is produced by the object when nobody looks at it, therefore the thing, when it is not looked at, is not blue; and thus (say they) there are many qualities of things which depend as much on something else as on themselves. To be sweet, a thing must have a taster; it is only sweet while it is being tasted, and if the tongue had not the capacity of taste, then the sugar would not have the quality of sweetness.

And then they agree that the qualities of things which thus depend upon our perception of them, and upon our human nature as affected by them, shall be called Subjective; and the qualities of things which they always have, irrespective of any other nature, as roundness or squareness, shall be called Objective.

From these ingenious views the step is very easy to a farther opinion, that it does not much matter what things are in themselves, but only what they are to us; and that the only real truth of them is

[1] *Modern Painters* was published between 1843 and 1860. This selection is chapter xii of the Fourth Part, printed in 1856.

their appearance to, or effect upon, us. From which position, with a hearty desire for mystification, and much egotism, selfishness, shallowness, and impertinence, a philosopher may easily go so far as to believe, and say, that everything in the world depends upon his seeing or thinking of it, and that nothing, therefore, exists, but what he sees or thinks of.

§ 2. Now, to get rid of all these ambiguities and troublesome words at once, be it observed that the word "blue" does *not* mean the *sensation* caused by a gentian on the human eye; but it means the *power* of producing that sensation: and this power is always there, in the thing, whether we are there to experience it or not, and would remain there though there were not left a man on the face of the earth. Precisely in the same way gunpowder has a power of exploding. It will not explode if you put no match to it. But it has always the power of so exploding, and is therefore called an explosive compound, which it very positively and assuredly is, whatever philosophy may say to the contrary.

In like manner, a gentian does not produce the sensation of blueness if you don't look at it. But it has always the power of doing so; its particles being everlastingly so arranged by its Maker. And, therefore, the gentian and the sky are always verily blue, whatever philosophy may say to the contrary; and if you do not see them blue when you look at them, it is not their fault but yours.[1]

§ 3. Hence I would say to these philosophers: If, instead of using the sonorous phrase, "It is objectively so," you will use the plain old phrase, "It *is* so"; and if instead of the sonorous phrase, "It is subjectively so," you will say, in plain old English, "It *does* so," or "It seems so to me," you will, on the whole, be more intelligible to your fellow-creatures; and besides, if you find that a thing which generally "does so" to other people (as a gentian looks blue to most men), does *not* so to you, on any particular occasion, you will not fall into the impertinence of saying that the thing is not so, or did not so, but you will say simply (what you will be all the better for speedily finding out), that something is the matter with you. If you

---

[1] It is quite true, that in all qualities involving sensation, there may be a doubt whether different people receive the same sensation from the same thing (compare Part II, sect. i. ch. v. § 6); but, though this makes such facts not distinctly explicable, it does not alter the facts themselves. I derive a certain sensation, which I call sweetness, from sugar. That is a fact. Another person feels a sensation, which *he* also calls sweetness, from sugar. That is also a fact. The sugar's power to produce these two sensations, which we suppose to be, and which are, in all probability, very nearly the same in both of us, and, on the whole, in the human race, is its sweetness. (Ruskin.)

find that you cannot explode the gunpowder, you will not declare that all gunpowder is subjective, and all explosion imaginary, but you will simply suspect and declare yourself to be an ill-made match. Which, on the whole, though there may be a distant chance of a mistake about it, is, nevertheless, the wisest conclusion you can come to until further experiment.[1]

§ 4. Now, therefore, putting these tiresome and absurd words quite out of our way, we may go on at our ease to examine the point in question,—namely, the difference between the ordinary, proper, and true appearances of things to us; and the extraordinary, or false appearances, when we are under the influence of emotion, or contemplative fancy; [2] false appearances, I say, as being entirely unconnected with any real power or character in the object, and only imputed to it by us.

For instance—

> The spendthrift crocus, bursting through the mould
> Naked and shivering, with his cup of gold.[3]

This is very beautiful, and yet very untrue. The crocus is not a spendthrift, but a hardy plant; its yellow is not gold, but saffron. How is it that we enjoy so much the having it put into our heads that it is anything else than a plain crocus?

It is an important question. For, throughout our past reasonings about art, we have always found that nothing could be good or useful, or ultimately pleasurable, which was untrue. But here is some-

[1] In fact (for I may as well, for once, meet our German friends in their own style), all that has been objected to us on this subject seems subject to this great objection; that the subjection of all things (subject to no exceptions) to senses which are, in us, both subject and object, and objects of perpetual contempt, cannot but make it our ultimate object to subject *ourselves* to the senses, and to remove whatever objections existed to such subjection. So that, finally, that which is the subject of examination or object of attention, uniting thus in itself the characters of subness and obness (so that, that which has no obness in it should be called sub-subjective, or a sub-subject, and that which has no subness in it should be called upper or ober-objective, or an ob-object); and we also, who suppose ourselves the objects of every arrangement, and are certainly the subjects of every sensual impression, thus uniting in ourselves, in an obverse or adverse manner, the characters of obness and subness, must both become metaphysically dejected or rejected, nothing remaining in *us* objective, but subjectivity, and the very objectivity of the object being lost in the abyss of this subjectivity of the Human.

There is, however, some meaning in the above sentence, if the reader cares to make it out; but in a pure German sentence of the highest style there is often none whatever. See Appendix II. "German Philosophy." (Ruskin.)

[2] Contemplative, in the sense explained in Part III, Sec. ii. Chap. iv. (Ruskin.)

[3] Holmes (Oliver Wendell), quoted by Miss Mitford in her *Recollections of a Literary Life.* (Ruskin.) The lines are from *Astræa,* a poem delivered before the Phi Beta Kappa Society of Yale College. (1850.)

thing pleasurable in written poetry, which is nevertheless *un*true. And what is more, if we think over our favorite poetry, we shall find it full of this kind of fallacy, and that we like it all the more for being so.

§ 5. It will appear also, on consideration of the matter, that this fallacy is of two principal kinds. Either, as in this case of the crocus, it is the fallacy of wilful fancy, which involves no real expectation that it will be believed; or else it is a fallacy caused by an excited state of the feelings, making us, for the time, more or less irrational. Of the cheating of the fancy we shall have to speak presently; but, in this chapter, I want to examine the nature of the other error, that which the mind admits when affected strongly by emotion. Thus, for instance, in *Alton Locke,—*

> They rowed her in across the rolling foam—
> The cruel, crawling foam.[1]

The foam is not cruel, neither does it crawl. The state of mind which attributes to it these characters of a living creature is one in which the reason is unhinged by grief. All violent feelings have the same effect. They produce in us a falseness in all our impressions of external things, which I would generally characterize as the "pathetic fallacy."

§ 6. Now we are in the habit of considering this fallacy as eminently a character of poetical description, and the temper of mind in which we allow it, as one eminently poetical, because passionate. But, I believe, if we look well into the matter, that we shall find the greatest poets do not often admit this kind of falseness,— that it is only the second order of poets who much delight in it.[2]

Thus, when Dante describes the spirits falling from the bank of Acheron "as dead leaves flutter from a bough," he gives the most

[1] Kingsley's *Sands of Dee*, (1850).

[2] I admit two orders of poets, but no third; and by these two orders I mean the Creative (Shakespeare, Homer, Dante), and Reflective or Perceptive (Wordsworth, Keats, Tennyson). But both of these must be *first*-rate in their range, though their range is different; and with poetry second-rate in *quality* no one ought to be allowed to trouble mankind. There is quite enough of the best,—much more than we can ever read or enjoy in the length of a life; and it is a literal wrong or sin in any person to encumber us with inferior work. I have no patience with apologies made by young pseudo-poets, "that they believe there is *some* good in what they have written: that they hope to do better in time," etc. *Some* good! If there is not *all* good, there is no good. If they ever hope to do better, why do they trouble us now? Let them rather courageously burn all they have done, and wait for the better days. There are few men, ordinarily educated, who in moments of strong feeling could not strike out a poetical thought, and afterwards polish it so as to be presentable. But men of sense know better than so to waste their time; and those who sincerely love

perfect image possible of their utter lightness, feebleness, passiveness, and scattering agony of despair, without, however, for an instant losing his own clear perception that *these* are souls, and *those* are leaves: he makes no confusion of one with the other. But when Coleridge speaks of

> The one red leaf, the last of its clan,
> That dances as often as dance it can,[1]

he has a morbid, that is to say, a so far false, idea about the leaf: he fancies a life in it, and will, which there are not; confuses its powerlessness with choice, its fading death with merriment, and the wind that shakes it with music. Here, however, there is some beauty, even in the morbid passage; but take an instance in Homer and Pope. Without the knowledge of Ulysses, Elpenor, his youngest follower, has fallen from an upper chamber in the Circean palace, and has been left dead, unmissed by his leader or companions, in the haste of their departure. They cross the sea to the Cimmerian land; and Ulysses summons the shades from Tartarus. The first which appears is that of the lost Elpenor. Ulysses, amazed, and in exactly the spirit of bitter and terrified lightness which is seen in Hamlet,[2] addresses the spirit with the simple, startled words:—

"Elpenor! How camest thou under the shadowy darkness? Hast thou come faster on foot than I in my black ship?"[3]

Which Pope renders thus:—

> O, say, what angry power Elpenor led
> To glide in shades, and wander with the dead?
> How could thy soul, by realms and seas disjoined,
> Outfly the nimble sail, and leave the lagging wind?

I sincerely hope the reader finds no pleasure here, either in the nimbleness of the sail, or the laziness of the wind! And yet how is it

---

poetry, know the touch of the master's hand on the chords too well to fumble among them after him. Nay, more than this, all inferior poetry is an injury to the good, inasmuch as it takes away the freshness of rhymes, blunders upon and gives a wretched commonalty to good thoughts; and, in general, adds to the weight of human weariness in a most woful and culpable manner. There are few thoughts likely to come across ordinary men, which have not already been expressed by greater men in the best possible way; and it is a wiser, more generous, more noble thing to remember and point out the perfect words, than to invent poorer ones, wherewith to encumber temporarily the world. (Ruskin.)

[1] *Christabel*, i, 49–50.

[2] "Well said, old mole! can'st work i' the ground so fast?" (Ruskin.)

[3] *Odyssey*, xi, 56–7.

that these conceits are so painful now, when they have been pleasant to us in the other instances?

§ 7. For a very simple reason. They are not a *pathetic* fallacy at all, for they are put into the mouth of the wrong passion—a passion which never could possibly have spoken them—agonized curiosity. Ulysses wants to know the facts of the matter; and the very last thing his mind could do at the moment would be to pause, or suggest in any wise what was *not* a fact. The delay in the first three lines, and conceit in the last, jar upon us instantly, like the most frightful discord in music. No poet of true imaginative power could possibly have written the passage.[1]

Therefore, we see that the spirit of truth must guide us in some sort, even in our enjoyment of fallacy. Coleridge's fallacy has no discord in it, but Pope's has set our teeth on edge. Without farther questioning, I will endeavor to state the main bearings of this matter.

§ 8. The temperament which admits the pathetic fallacy, is, as I said above, that of a mind and body in some sort too weak to deal fully with what is before them or upon them; borne away, or over-clouded, or over-dazzled by emotion; and it is a more or less noble state, according to the force of the emotion which has induced it. For it is no credit to a man that he is not morbid or inaccurate in his perceptions, when he has no strength of feeling to warp them; and it is in general a sign of higher capacity and stand in the ranks of being, that the emotions should be strong enough to vanquish, partly, the intellect, and make it believe what they choose. But it is still a grander condition when the intellect also rises, till it is strong enough to assert its rule against, or together with, the utmost efforts of the passions; and the whole man stands in an iron glow, white hot, perhaps, but still strong, and in no wise evaporating; even if he melts, losing none of his weight.

So, then, we have the three ranks: the man who perceives rightly,

---

[1] It is worth while comparing the way a similar question is put by the exquisite sincerity of Keats:—

> He wept, and his bright tears
> Went trickling down the golden bow he held.
> Thus, with half-shut, suffused eyes, he stood;
> While from beneath some cumbrous boughs hard by,
> With solemn step an awful goddess came,
> And there was purport in her looks for him,
> Which he with eager guess began to read
> Perplexed, the while, melodiously he said,
> *"How camest thou over the unfooted sea?"* (Ruskin.)

because he does not feel, and to whom the primrose is very accurately the primrose, because he does not love it. Then, secondly, the man who perceives wrongly, because he feels, and to whom the primrose is anything else than a primrose: a star, or a sun, or a fairy's shield, or a forsaken maiden. And then, lastly, there is the man who perceives rightly in spite of his feelings, and to whom the primrose is for ever nothing else than itself—a little flower, apprehended in the very plain and leafy fact of it, whatever and how many soever the associations and passions may be, that crowd around it. And, in general, these three classes may be rated in comparative order, as the men who are not poets at all, and the poets of the second order, and the poets of the first; only however great a man may be, there are always some subjects which *ought* to throw him off his balance; some, by which his poor human capacity of thought should be conquered, and brought into the inaccurate and vague state of perception, so that the language of the highest inspiration becomes broken, obscure, and wild in metaphor, resembling that of the weaker man, overborne by weaker things.

§ 9. And thus, in full, there are four classes: the men who feel nothing, and therefore see truly; the men who feel strongly, think weakly, and see untruly (second order of poets); the men who feel strongly, think strongly, and see truly (first order of poets); and the men who, strong as human creatures can be, are yet submitted to influences stronger than they, and see in a sort untruly, because what they see is inconceivably above them. This last is the usual condition of prophetic inspiration.

§ 10. I separate these classes, in order that their character may be clearly understood; but of course they are united each to the other by imperceptible transitions, and the same mind, according to the influences to which it is subjected, passes at different times into the various states. Still, the difference between the great and less man is, on the whole, chiefly in this point of *alterability*. That is to say, the one knows too much, and perceives and feels too much of the past and future, and of all things beside and around that which immediately affects him, to be in any wise shaken by it. His mind is made up; his thoughts have an accustomed current; his ways are steadfast; it is not this or that new sight which will at once unbalance him. He is tender to impression at the surface, like a rock with deep moss upon it; but there is too much mass of him to be moved. The smaller man, with the same degree of sensibility, is at once carried off his feet; he wants to do something he did not want to do before; he views all the universe in a new light through his tears; he is gay or enthusiastic, melancholy or passionate, as things come and go to him. Therefore the high creative poet might even be thought, to a great extent, impassive (as shallow people think Dante stern), receiving indeed all feelings to the full, but having a great centre of reflection and knowledge in which he stands serene, and watches the feeling, as it were, from afar off.

Dante, in his most intense moods, has entire command of himself, and can look around calmly, at all moments, for the image or the word that will best tell what he sees to the upper or lower world. But Keats and Tennyson, and the poets of the second order, are generally themselves subdued by the feelings under which they write, or, at least, write as choosing to be so; and therefore admit certain expressions and modes of thought which are in some sort diseased or false.

§ 11. Now so long as we see that the *feeling* is true, we pardon, or are even pleased by, the confessed fallacy of sight which it induces: we are pleased, for instance, with those lines of Kingsley's, above quoted, not because they fallaciously describe foam, but because they faithfully describe sorrow. But the moment the mind of the speaker becomes cold, that moment every such expression becomes untrue, as being for ever untrue in the external facts. And there is no greater baseness in literature than the habit of using these metaphorical expressions in cold blood. An inspired writer, in full impetuosity of passion, may speak wisely and truly of "raging waves of the sea, foaming out their own shame"; but it is only the basest writer who cannot speak of the sea without talking of "raging waves," "remorseless floods," "ravenous billows," etc.; and it is one of the signs of the highest power in a writer to check all such habits of thought, and to keep his eyes fixed firmly on the *pure fact*, out of which if any feeling comes to him or his reader, he knows it must be a true one.

To keep to the waves, I forget who it is who represents a man in despair desiring that his body may be cast into the sea,

> *Whose changing mound, and foam that passed away,*
> Might mock the eyes that questioned where I lay.

Observe, there is not here a single false, or even overcharged, expression. "Mound" of the sea wave is perfectly simple and true; "changing" is as familiar as may be; "foam that passed away," strictly literal; and the whole line descriptive of the reality with a degree of accuracy which I know not any other verse, in the range of poetry, that altogether equals. For most people have not a distinct idea of the clumsiness and massiveness of a large wave. The word *wave* is used too generally of ripples and breakers, and bendings in light drapery or grass: it does not by itself convey a perfect image. But the word *mound* is heavy, large, dark, definite; there is no mistaking the kind of wave meant, nor missing the sight of it. Then the term *changing* has a peculiar force also. Most people think of waves as rising and falling. But if they look at the sea carefully, they will perceive that the waves do not rise and fall. They change. Change both place and form, but they do not fall; one wave goes on, and on, and still on; now lower, now higher, now tossing its mane like a horse, now building itself together like a wall, now shaking, now steady, but still the same wave, till at last it seems struck by something, and changes, one knows not how,—becomes another wave.

The close of the line insists on this image, and paints it still more perfectly,—"foam that passed away." Not merely melting, disappearing, but passing on, out of sight, on the career of the wave. Then, having put the absolute ocean fact so far as he may before our eyes, the poet leaves us to feel about it as we may, and to trace for ourselves the opposite fact,—the image of the green mounds that do not change, and the white and written stones that do not pass away; and thence to follow out also the associated images of the calm life with the quiet grave, and the despairing life with the fading foam:—

Let no man move his bones.[1]

As for Samaria, her king is cut off like the foam upon the water.[2]

But nothing of this is actually told or pointed out, and the expressions, as they stand, are perfectly severe and accurate, utterly uninfluenced by the firmly governed emotion of the writer. Even the word *mock* is hardly an exception, as it may stand merely for "deceive" or "defeat," without implying any impersonation of the waves.

§ 12. It may be well, perhaps, to give one or two more instances to show the peculiar dignity possessed by all passages which thus limit their expression to the pure fact, and leave the hearer to gather

[1] 2 Kings, xxiii: 18.
[2] Hosea, x: 7.

what he can from it. Here is a notable one from the *Iliad*. Helen, looking from the Scæan gate of Troy over the Grecian host, and telling Priam the names of its captains, says at last:—

"I see all the other dark-eyed Greeks; but two I cannot see,—Castor and Pollux,—whom one mother bore with me. Have they not followed from fair Lacedæmon, or have they indeed come in their sea-wandering ships, but now will not enter into the battle of men, fearing the shame and the scorn that is in me?"

Then Homer:—

So she spoke. But them, already, the life-giving earth possessed, there in Lacedæmon, in the dear fatherland.

Note, here, the high poetical truth carried to the extreme. The poet has to speak of the earth in sadness, but he will not let that sadness affect or change his thoughts of it. No; though Castor and Pollux be dead, yet the earth is our mother still, fruitful, life-giving. These are the facts of the thing. I see nothing else than these. Make what you will of them.

[Here Ruskin comments on "Casimir de la Vigne's terrible ballad," *La Toilette de Constance*.]

* * * *

§ 14. . . . A poet is great, first in proportion to the strength of his passion, and then, that strength being granted, in proportion to his government of it; there being, however, always a point beyond which it would be inhuman and monstrous if he pushed this government, and, therefore, a point at which all feverish and wild fancy becomes just and true. Thus the destruction of the kingdom of Assyria cannot be contemplated firmly by a prophet of Israel. The fact is too great, too wonderful. It overthrows him, dashes him into a confused element of dreams. All the world is, to his stunned thought, full of strange voices. "Yea, the fir-trees rejoice at thee, and the cedars of Lebanon, saying, 'Since thou art gone down to the grave, no feller is come up against us.' " [1] So, still more, the thought of the presence of Deity cannot be borne without this great astonishment. "The mountains and the hills shall break forth before you into singing, and all the trees of the field shall clap their hands." [2]

§ 15. But by how much this feeling is noble when it is justified by

[1] Isaiah, xiv: 8.
[2] *Ibid.*, lv: 12.

the strength of its cause, by so much it is ignoble when there is not cause enough for it; and beyond all other ignobleness is the mere affectation of it, in hardness of heart. Simply bad writing may almost always, as above noticed, be known by its adoption of these fanciful metaphorical expressions as a sort of current coin; yet there is even a worse, at least a more harmful condition of writing than this, in which such expressions are not ignorantly and feelinglessly caught up, but, by some master, skilful in handling, yet insincere, deliberately wrought out with chill and studied fancy; as if we should try to make an old lava-stream look red hot again, by covering it with dead leaves, or white-hot, with hoar-frost.

When Young is lost in veneration, as he dwells on the character of a truly good and holy man, he permits himself for a moment to be overborne by the feeling so far as to exclaim—

> Where shall I find him? angels, tell me where.
> You know him; he is near you; point him out.
> Shall I see glories beaming from his brow,
> Or trace his footsteps by the rising flowers? [1]

This emotion has a worthy cause, and is thus true and right. But now hear the cold-hearted Pope say to a shepherd girl—

> Where'er you walk, cool gales shall fan the glade;
> Trees, where you sit, shall crowd into a shade; . . .
> Your praise the birds shall chant in every grove,
> And winds shall waft it to the powers above.
> But would you sing, and rival Orpheus' strain,
> The wondering forests soon should dance again;
> The moving mountains hear the powerful call,
> And headlong streams hang, listening, in their fall. [2]

This is not, nor could it for a moment be mistaken for, the language of passion. It is simple falsehood, uttered by hypocrisy; definite absurdity, rooted in affectation, and coldly asserted in the teeth of nature and fact. Passion will indeed go far in deceiving itself; but it must be a strong passion, not the simple wish of a lover to tempt his mistress to sing. Compare a very closely parallel passage in Wordsworth, in which the lover has lost his mistress:

> Three years had Barbara in her grave been laid,
> When thus his moan he made:—

[1] *Night Thoughts,* ii, 325–8.
[2] *Pastorals,* ii, 73–84.

"Oh, move, thou cottage, from behind yon oak,
  Or let the ancient tree uprooted lie,
That in some other way yon smoke
  May mount into the sky.
If still behind yon pine-tree's ragged bough,
  Headlong, the waterfall must come,
Oh, let it, then, be dumb—
  Be anything, sweet stream, but that which thou art now." [1]

Here is a cottage to be moved, if not a mountain, and a water-fall to be silent, if it is not to hang listening: but with what different relation to the mind that contemplates them! Here, in the extremity of its agony, the soul cries out wildly for relief, which at the same moment it partly knows to be impossible, but partly believes possible, in a vague impression that a miracle *might* be wrought to give relief even to a less sore distress,—that nature is kind, and God is kind, and that grief is strong; it knows not well what *is* possible to such grief. To silence a stream, to move a cottage wall,—one might think it could do as much as that!

§ 16. I believe these instances are enough to illustrate the main point I insist upon respecting the pathetic fallacy,—that so far as it *is* a fallacy, it is always the sign of a morbid state of mind, and comparatively of a weak one. Even in the most inspired prophet it is a sign of the incapacity of his human sight or thought to bear what has been revealed to it. In ordinary poetry, if it is found in the thoughts of the poet himself, it is at once a sign of his belonging to the inferior school; if in the thoughts of the characters imagined by him, it is right or wrong according to the genuineness of the emotion from which it springs; always, however, implying necessarily *some* degree of weakness in the character.

Take two most exquisite instances from master hands. The Jessy of Shenstone, and the Ellen of Wordsworth, have both been betrayed and deserted. Jessy, in the course of her most touching complaint, says:

"If through the garden's flowery tribes I stray,
  Where bloom the jasmines that could once allure,
'Hope not to find delight in us,' they say,
  'For we are spotless, Jessy; we are pure.' "

Compare with this some of the words of Ellen:

1 Inaccurately quoted, with omissions, from *Tis Said That Some Have Died for Love.*

"Ah, why," said Ellen, sighing to herself,
"Why do not words, and kiss, and solemn pledge,
And nature, that is kind in woman's breast,
And reason, that in man is wise and good,
And fear of Him Who is a righteous Judge,—
Why do not these prevail for human life,
To keep two hearts together, that began
Their springtime with one love, and that have need
Of mutual pity and forgiveness, sweet
To grant, or be received; while that poor bird—
O, come and hear him! Thou who hast to me
Been faithless, hear him;—though a lowly creature,
One of God's simple children, that yet know not
The Universal Parent, *how* he sings!
As if he wished the firmament of heaven
Should listen, and give back to him the voice
Of his triumphant constancy and love;
The proclamation that he makes, how far
His darkness doth transcend our fickle light." [1]

The perfection of both these passages, as far as regards truth and tenderness of imagination in the two poets, is quite insuperable. But, of the two characters imagined, Jessy is weaker than Ellen, exactly in so far as something appears to her to be in nature which is not. The flowers do not really reproach her. God meant them to comfort her, not to taunt her; they would do so if she saw them rightly.

Ellen, on the other hand, is quite above the slightest erring emotion. There is not the barest film of fallacy in all her thoughts. She reasons as calmly as if she did not feel. And, although the singing of the bird suggests to her the idea of its desiring to be heard in heaven, she does not for an instant admit any veracity in the thought. "As if," she says,—"I know he means nothing of the kind; but it does verily seem as if." The reader will find, by examining the rest of the poem, that Ellen's character is throughout consistent in this clear though passionate strength. [2]

---

[1] *The Excursion*, vi, 869–87.

[2] I cannot quit this subject without giving two more instances, both exquisite, of the pathetic fallacy, which I have just come upon, in *Maud*:

> For a great speculation had fail'd;
> And ever he mutter'd and madden'd, and ever wann'd with despair;
> And out he walk'd, when the wind like a broken worldling wail'd,
> And the *flying gold of the ruin'd woodlands drove thro' the air.*

> There has fallen a splendid tear
> From the passion-flower at the gate.

It then being, I hope, now made clear to the reader in all respects that the pathetic fallacy is powerful only so far as it is pathetic, feeble so far as it is fallacious, and, therefore, that the dominion of Truth is entire, over this, as over every other natural and just state of the human mind, we may go on to the subject for the dealing with which this prefatory inquiry became necessary; and why necessary, we shall see forthwith.[1]

The red rose cries, "She is near, she is near!"
And the white rose weeps, "She is late."
The larkspur listens, "I hear, I hear!"
And the lily whispers, "I wait." (Ruskin.)

[1] "Of Classical Landscape" and "Of Modern Landscape" follow.

Arnold

Matthew ARNOLD (1822–1888), son of Dr. Thomas Arnold, the famous head of Rugby, was born at Laleham, Middlesex. Educated at Winchester, Rugby, and Oxford University (where, in 1843, he won the Newdigate Prize with a poem on *Cromwell*), he was elected in 1845 a Fellow of Oriel College. After a short career as classical master at Rugby and secretary to the Marquis of Lansdowne, he was appointed an inspector of schools (1851)—a post which he held until 1886, when Gladstone gave him a civil-list pension which enabled him to retire. He performed the routine duties of his office conscientiously, irksome as they were, and influenced English secondary education markedly. During these years he composed much of his verse, publishing *Empedocles on Etna* (1852), and two volumes of poetry in 1853 and 1855. In 1857 he was appointed to the Professorship of Poetry at Oxford, a chair which he held for ten years. During the next two decades and a half he wrote chiefly on critical and religious topics. The first of a long series of famous prose essays, *On Translating Homer* (1861), was followed by *Essays in Criticism* (1865), *On the Study of Celtic Literature* (1867), *Culture and Anarchy* (1869), and *Literature and Dogma* (1873), in which year he took up his residence at Cobham. In 1883, and again in 1886, he visited the United States, lecturing in the principal cities. He died suddenly of a heart attack in Liverpool in 1888.

Arnold was thoroughly equipped for criticism. To a deep knowledge of the classics, he added a wide but accurate understanding of Continental literatures, especially those of Germany and France. For him criticism was not merely an evaluation of literature or any other art, but the appraisal of life in all its phases. He had flawless taste, but he submitted it, like Lessing and Coleridge, to tests that might determine its validity. His ideal was culture. This he defined in a memorable paragraph in his essay, *Sweetness and Light*, (*Culture and Anarchy*, 1869):

> Culture . . . shows its single-minded love of perfection, its desire simply to make reason and the will of God prevail, its freedom from fanaticism, by its attitude towards all this machinery, even while it insists that it *is* machinery. Fanatics, seeing the mischief men do themselves by their blind belief in some machinery or other —whether it is wealth and industrialism, or whether it is the cultivation of bodily strength and activity, or whether it is a political organization—or whether it is a religious organization—oppose with might and main the tendency to this or that political and religious organization, or to games and athletic exercises, or to wealth and industrialism, and try violently to stop it. But the flexibility which sweetness and light give, and which is one of the rewards of culture pursued in good faith, enables a man to see that a tendency may be necessary, and even, as a preparation for something in the future, salutary, and yet that the generations or individuals who obey this tendency are sacrificed to it, that they fall short of the hope of perfection by following it; and that its mischiefs are to be criticized, lest it should take too firm a hold and last after it has served its purpose.

Arnold's criticism had a great influence in his day, and still has. Witness the general use of words and phrases to which he gave currency: "high seriousness," "Philistine," "culture," "sweetness and light" (a phrase which he borrowed from Swift), "to see life steadily and see it whole," "criticism of life"—and many others.

THE STUDY OF POETRY[1]

(1880)

"The future of poetry is immense, because in poetry, where it is worthy of its high destinies, our race, as time goes on, will find an ever surer and surer stay. There is not a creed which is not shaken, not an accredited dogma which is not shown to be questionable, not a received tradition which does not threaten to dissolve. Our religion has materialized itself in the fact, in the supposed fact; it has attached its emotion to the fact, and now the fact is failing it. But for poetry the idea is everything; the rest is a world of illusion, of divine illusion. Poetry attaches its emotion to the idea; the idea *is* the fact. The strongest part of our religion to-day is its unconscious poetry."

Let me be permitted to quote these words of my own, as uttering the thought which should, in my opinion, go with us and govern us in all our study of poetry. In the present work it is the course of one great contributory stream to the world-river of poetry that we are invited to follow. We are here invited to trace the stream of English poetry. But whether we set ourselves, as here, to follow only one of the several streams that make the mighty river of poetry, or whether we seek to know them all, our governing thought should be the same. We should conceive of poetry worthily, and more highly than it has been the custom to conceive of it. We should conceive of it as capable of higher uses, and called to higher destinies, than those which in general men have assigned to it hitherto. More and more mankind will discover that we have to turn to poetry to interpret life for us, to console us, to sustain us. Without poetry, our science will appear incomplete; and most of what now passes with us for religion and philosophy will be replaced by poetry. Science, I say, will appear incomplete without it. For finely and truly does Wordsworth call poetry "the impassioned expression which is in the countenance of all science"; and what is a countenance without its expression? Again, Wordsworth finely and truly calls poetry "the breath and finer spirit of all knowledge": our religion, parading evidences such as those on which the popular mind relies now; our philosophy, pluming itself on its reasonings about causation and finite and infinite being; what are they but the shadows and dreams

[1] This essay was first printed as the General Introduction to *The English Poets*, a four-volume anthology edited by Thomas Humphry Ward in 1880. Used by the kind permission of The Macmillan Company.

and false shows of knowledge? The day will come when we shall wonder at ourselves for having trusted to them, for having taken them seriously; and the more we perceive their hollowness, the more we shall prize "the breath and finer spirit of knowledge" offered to us by poetry.

But if we conceive thus highly of the destinies of poetry, we must also set our standard for poetry high, since poetry, to be capable of fulfilling such high destinies, must be poetry of a high order of excellence. We must accustom ourselves to a high standard and to a strict judgment. Sainte-Beuve relates that Napoleon one day said, when somebody was spoken of in his presence as a charlatan: "Charlatan as much as you please; but where is there *not* charlatanism?" —"Yes," answers Sainte-Beuve, "in politics, in the art of governing mankind, that is perhaps true. But in the order of thought, in art, the glory, the eternal honor is that charlatanism shall find no entrance; herein lies the inviolableness of that noble portion of man's being." It is admirably said, and let us hold fast to it. In poetry, which is thought and art in one, it is the glory, the eternal honor, that charlatanism shall find no entrance; that this noble sphere be kept inviolate and inviolable. Charlatanism is for confusing or obliterating the distinctions between excellent and inferior, sound and unsound or only half-sound, true and untrue or only half-true. It is charlatanism, conscious or unconscious, whenever we confuse or obliterate these. And in poetry, more than anywhere else, it is unpermissible to confuse or obliterate them. For in poetry the distinction between excellent and inferior, sound and unsound or only half-sound, true and untrue or only half-true, is of paramount importance. It is of paramount importance because of the high destinies of poetry. In poetry, as a criticism of life under the conditions fixed for such a criticism by the laws of poetic truth and poetic beauty, the spirit of our race will find, we have said, as time goes on and as other helps fail, its consolation and stay. But the consolation and stay will be of power in proportion to the power of the criticism of life. And the criticism of life will be of power in proportion as the poetry conveying it is excellent rather than inferior, sound rather than unsound or half-sound, true rather than untrue or half-true.

The best poetry is what we want; the best poetry will be found to have a power of forming, sustaining, and delighting us, as nothing else can. A clearer, deeper sense of the best in poetry, and of the strength and joy to be drawn from it, is the most precious benefit which we can gather from a poetical collection such as the present. And yet in the very nature and conduct of such a collection there is inevitably something which tends to obscure in us the consciousness of what our benefit should be, and to distract us from the pursuit of it. We should therefore steadily set it before our minds at the outset, and should compel ourselves to revert constantly to the thought of it as we proceed.

Yes; constantly in reading poetry, a sense for the best, the really excellent, and of the strength and joy to be drawn from it, should be present in our minds and should govern our estimate of what we read. But this real estimate, the only true one, is liable to be superseded, if we are not watchful, by two other kinds of estimate, the historic estimate and the personal estimate, both of which are fallacious. A poet or a poem may count to us historically, they may count to us on grounds personal to ourselves, and they may count to us really. They may count to us historically. The course of development of a nation's language, thought, and poetry, is profoundly interesting; and by regarding a poet's work as a stage in this course of development we may easily bring ourselves to make it of more importance as poetry than in itself it really is, we may come to use a language of quite exaggerated praise in criticizing it; in short, to over-rate it. So arises in our poetic judgments the fallacy caused by the estimate which we may call historic. Then, again, a poet or a poem may count to us on grounds personal to ourselves. Our personal affinities, likings, and circumstances, have great power to sway our estimate of this or that poet's work, and to make us attach more importance to it as poetry than in itself it really possesses, because to us it is, or has been, of high importance. Here also we over-rate the object of our interest, and apply to it a language of praise which is quite exaggerated. And thus we get the source of a second fallacy in our poetic judgments—the fallacy caused by an estimate which we may call personal.

Both fallacies are natural. It is evident how naturally the study of the history and development of a poetry may incline a man to pause over reputations and works once conspicuous but now obscure, and to quarrel with a careless public for skipping, in obedience to mere tradition and habit, from one famous name or work in its national poetry to another, ignorant of what it misses, and of the reason for keeping what it keeps, and of the whole process of growth in its poetry. The French have become diligent students of their own early poetry, which they long neglected; the study makes many of them dissatisfied with their so-called classical poetry, the court-tragedy of the seventeenth century, a poetry which Pellisson long ago reproached with its want of the true poetic stamp, with its *politesse stérile et rampante*,[1] but which nevertheless has reigned in France as absolutely as if it had been the perfection of classical poetry indeed. The dissatisfaction is natural; yet a lively and accomplished critic, M. Charles d'Héricault, the editor of Clément Marot, goes too far when he says that "the cloud of glory playing round a classic is a mist as dangerous to the future of a literature as it is intolerable for the purposes of history." "It hinders," he goes on, "it hinders us from seeing more than one single point, the culminating and exceptional point; the summary, fictitious and arbitrary, of a thought and of a work. It substitutes a halo for a physiognomy, it puts a statue where there was once a man, and hiding from us all trace of the labor, the attempts, the weaknesses, the failures, it claims not study but veneration; it does not show us how the thing is done, it imposes upon us a model. Above all, for the historian this creation of classic personages is inadmissible; for it withdraws the poet from his time, from his proper life, it breaks historical relationships, it blinds criticism by conventional admiration, and renders the investigation of literary origins unacceptable. It gives us a human personage no longer, but a God seated immovable amidst his perfect work, like Jupiter on Olympus; and hardly will it be possible for the young student, to whom such work is exhibited at such a distance from him, to believe that it did not issue ready made from that divine head."

All this is brilliantly and tellingly said, but we must plead for a distinction. Everything depends on the reality of a poet's classic character. If he is a dubious classic, let us sift him; if he is a false classic, let us explode him. But if he is a real classic, if his work belongs to the class of the very best (for this is the true and right meaning of the word *classic, classical*), then the great thing for us is to feel and enjoy his work as deeply as ever we can, and to appreciate the wide difference between it and all work which has not the same high character. This is what is salutary, this is what is formative; this is the great benefit to be got from the study of poetry. Everything which interferes with it, which hinders it, is injurious. True, we must read our classic with open eyes, and not with eyes blinded with superstition; we must perceive when his work comes short, when it drops out of the class of the very best, and we must rate it,

---

[1] Its cold and fierce conventionality.

in such cases, at its proper value. But the use of this negative criticism is not in itself, it is entirely in its enabling us to have a clearer sense and a deeper enjoyment of what is truly excellent. To trace the labor, the attempts, the weaknesses, the failures of a genuine classic, to acquaint oneself with his time and his life and his historical relationships, is mere literary dilettantism unless it has that clear sense and deeper enjoyment for its end. It may be said that the more we know about a classic the better we shall enjoy him; and, if we lived as long as Methuselah and had all of us heads of perfect clearness and wills of perfect steadfastness, this might be true in fact as it is plausible in theory. But the case here is much the same as the case with the Greek and Latin studies of our schoolboys. The elaborate philological groundwork which we require them to lay is in theory an admirable preparation for appreciating the Greek and Latin authors worthily. The more thoroughly we lay the groundwork, the better we shall be able, it may be said, to enjoy the authors. True, if time were not so short, and schoolboys' wits not so soon tired and their power of attention exhausted; only, as it is, the elaborate philological preparation goes on, but the authors are little known and less enjoyed. So with the investigator of "historic origins" in poetry. He ought to enjoy the true classic all the better for his investigations; he often is distracted from the enjoyment of the best, and with the less good he overbusies himself, and is prone to over-rate it in proportion to the trouble which it has cost him.

The idea of tracing historic origins and historical relationships cannot be absent from a compilation like the present. And naturally the poets to be exhibited in it will be assigned to those persons for exhibition who are known to prize them highly, rather than to those who have no special inclination towards them. Moreover the very occupation with an author, and the business of exhibiting him, disposes us to affirm and amplify his importance. In the present work, therefore, we are sure of frequent temptation to adopt the historic estimate, or the personal estimate, and to forget the real estimate; which latter, nevertheless, we must employ if we are to make poetry yield us its full benefit. So high is that benefit, the benefit of clearly feeling and of deeply enjoying the really excellent, the truly classic in poetry, that we do well, I say, to set it fixedly before our minds as our object in studying poets and poetry, and to make the desire of attaining it the one principle to which, as the *Imitation* [1] says,

---

[1] Thomas à Kempis (properly Thomas Hamerken or Hämmerlein), (1380–1471), a German ecclesiastic, was the author of *De Imitatione Christi.*

whatever we may read or come to know, we always return. *Cum multa legeris et cognoveris, ad unum semper oportet redire principium.*[1]

The historic estimate is likely in especial to affect our judgment and our language when we are dealing with ancient poets; the personal estimate when we are dealing with poets, our contemporaries, or at any rate modern. The exaggerations due to the historic estimate are not in themselves, perhaps, of very much gravity. Their report hardly enters the general ear; probably they do not always impose even on the literary men who adopt them. But they lead to a dangerous abuse of language. So we hear Cædmon, amongst our own poets, compared to Milton. I have already noticed the enthusiasm of one accomplished French critic for "historic origins." Another eminent French critic, M. Vitet, comments upon that famous document of the early poetry of his nation, the *Chanson de Roland*. It is indeed a most interesting document. The *joculator* or *jongleur* Taillefer, who was with William the Conqueror's army at Hastings, marched before the Norman troops, so said the tradition, singing "of Charlemagne and of Roland and of Oliver, and of the vassals who died at Roncevaux"; and it is suggested that in the *Chanson de Roland* by one Turoldus or Théroulde, a poem preserved in a manuscript of the twelfth century in the Bodleian Library at Oxford, we have certainly the matter, perhaps even some of the words, of the chant which Taillefer sang. The poem has vigor and freshness; it is not without pathos. But M. Vitet is not satisfied with seeing in it a document of some poetic value, and of very high historic and linguistic value; he sees in it a grand and beautiful work, a monument of epic genius. In its general design he finds the grandiose conception, in its details he finds the constant union of simplicity with greatness, which are the marks, he truly says, of the genuine epic, and distinguish it from the artificial epic of literary ages. One thinks of Homer; this is the sort of praise which is given to Homer, and justly given. Higher praise there cannot well be, and it is the praise due to epic poetry of the highest order only, and to no other. Let us try, then, the *Chanson de Roland* at its best. Roland, mortally wounded, lays himself down under a pine-tree, with his face turned towards Spain and the enemy—

> De plusurs choses à remembrer li prist,
> De tantes teres cume li bers cunquist,

---

[1] The Latin repeats the thought just expressed.

De dulce France, des humes de sun lign,
De Carlemagne sun seignor ki l'nurrit.[1]

That is primitive work, I repeat, with an undeniable poetic quality of
its own. It deserves such praise, and such praise is sufficient for it.
But now turn to Homer:—

Ὣς φάτο· τοὺς δ' ἤδη κατέχεν φυσίζοος αἶα
ἐν Λακεδαίμονι αὖθι, φίλῃ ἐν πατρίδι γαίῃ.[2]

We are here in another world, another order of poetry altogether;
here is rightly due such supreme praise as that which M. Vitet gives
to the *Chanson de Roland*. If our words are to have any meaning, if
our judgments are to have any solidity, we must not heap that supreme praise upon poetry of an order immeasurably inferior.

Indeed there can be no more useful help for discovering what
poetry belongs to the class of the truly excellent, and can therefore do us most good, than to have always in one's mind lines and
expressions of the great masters, and to apply them as a touchstone
to other poetry. Of course we are not to require this other poetry
to resemble them; it may be very dissimilar. But if we have any tact
we shall find them, when we have lodged them well in our minds,
an infallible touchstone for detecting the presence or absence of high
poetic quality, and also the degree of this quality, in all other poetry
which we may place beside them. Short passages, even single lines,
will serve our turn quite sufficiently. Take the two lines which I
have just quoted from Homer, the poet's comment on Helen's mention of her brothers;—or take his

Ἀ δειλώ, τί σφῶϊ δόμεν Πηλῆϊ ἄνακτι
θνητῷ; ὑμεῖς δ' ἐστὸν ἀγήρω τ' ἀθανάτω τε.
ἦ ἵνα δυστήνοισι μετ' ἀνδράσιν ἄλγε' ἔχητον;[3]

the address of Zeus to the horses of Peleus;—or take finally his

Καὶ σέ, γέρον, τὸ πρὶν μὲν ἀκούομεν ὄλβιον εἶναι·[4]

---

[1] "Then began he to call many things to remembrance,—all the lands which his valor
conquered, and pleasant France, and the men of his lineage, and Charlemagne his liege lord
who nourished him."—*Chanson de Roland*, iii, 939–42. (Arnold.)

[2] "So said she; they long since in Earth's soft arms were reposing,
There, in their own dear land, their father-land, Lacedæmon."
     Iliad, iii, 243–4 (translated by Dr. Hawtrey). (Arnold.) Cf. p. 532 above.

[3] "Ah, unhappy pair, why gave we you to King Peleus, to a mortal? but ye are without
old age, and immortal. Was it that with men born to misery ye might have sorrow?" *Iliad*,
xvii, 443–5. (Arnold.)

[4] "Nay, and thou too, old man, in former days wast, as we hear, happy."—*Iliad*, xxiv,
543. (Arnold.)

the words of Achilles to Priam, a suppliant before him. Take that incomparable line and a half of Dante, Ugolino's tremendous words—

> Io no piangeva; si dentro impietrai.
> Piangevan elli . . .[1]

take the lovely words of Beatrice to Virgil—

> Io son fatta da Dio, sua mercè, tale,
> Che la vostra miseria non mi tange,
> Nè fiamma d'esto incendio non m'assale . . .[2]

take the simple, but perfect, single line—

> In la sua volontade è nostra pace.[3]

Take of Shakespeare a line or two of Henry the Fourth's expostulation with sleep—

> Wilt thou upon the high and giddy mast
> Seal up the ship-boy's eyes, and rock his brains
> In cradle of the rude imperious surge . . .

and take, as well, Hamlet's dying request to Horatio—

> If thou didst ever hold me in thy heart,
> Absent thee from felicity awhile,
> And in this harsh world draw thy breath in pain
> To tell my story . . .

Take of Milton that Miltonic passage—

> Darken'd so, yet shone
> Above them all the arch-angel; but his face
> Deep scars of thunder had intrench'd, and care
> Sat on his faded cheek . . .

add two such lines as—

> And courage never to submit or yield
> And what is else not to be overcome . . .

and finish with the exquisite close to the loss of Proserpine, the loss

---

[1] "I wailed not, so of stone grew I within;—*they* wailed."—*Inferno*, xxxiii, 39, 40. (Arnold.)

[2] "Of such sort hath God, thanked be his mercy, made me, that your misery toucheth me not, neither doth the flame of this fire strike me."—*Inferno*, ii, 91-3. (Arnold.)

[3] "In His will is our peace."—*Paradiso*, iii, 85. (Arnold.)

. . . which cost Ceres all that pain
To seek her through the world.

These few lines, if we have tact and can use them, are enough even
of themselves to keep clear and sound our judgments about poetry,
to save us from fallacious estimates of it, to conduct us to a real
estimate.

The specimens I have quoted differ widely from one another, but
they have in common this: the possession of the very highest poetical quality. If we are thoroughly penetrated by their power, we shall
find that we have acquired a sense enabling us, whatever poetry may
be laid before us, to feel the degree in which a high poetical quality
is present or wanting there. Critics give themselves great labor to
draw out what in the abstract constitutes the characters of a high
quality of poetry. It is much better simply to have recourse to concrete examples;—to take specimens of poetry of the high, the very
highest quality, and to say: The characters of a high quality of
poetry are what is expressed *there*. They are far better recognized
by being felt in the verse of the master, than by being perused in the
prose of the critic. Nevertheless if we are urgently pressed to give
some critical account of them, we may safely, perhaps, venture on
laying down, not indeed how and why the characters arise, but
where and in what they arise. They are in the matter and substance
of the poetry, and they are in its manner and style. Both of these, the
substance and matter on the one hand, the style and manner on the
other, have a mark, an accent, of high beauty, worth, and power.
But if we are asked to define this mark and accent in the abstract,
our answer must be: No, for we should thereby be darkening the
question, not clearing it. The mark and accent are as given by the
substance and matter of that poetry, by the style and manner of
that poetry, and of all other poetry which is akin to it in quality.

Only one thing we may add as to the substance and matter
of poetry, guiding ourselves by Aristotle's profound observation
that the superiority of poetry over history consists in its possessing a higher truth and a higher seriousness (φιλοσοφώτερον καὶ
σπουδαιότερον).[1] Let us add, therefore, to what we have said, this:
that the substance and matter of the best poetry acquire their special
character from possessing, in an eminent degree, truth and seriousness. We may add yet further, what is in itself evident, that to the
style and manner of the best poetry their special character, their ac-

[1] More philosophical and more serious. Cf. above, page 401, where Coleridge wrongly
uses the superlative instead of the comparative.

cent, is given by their diction, and, even yet more, by their movement. And though we distinguish between the two characters, the two accents, of superiority, yet they are nevertheless vitally connected one with the other. The superior character of truth and seriousness, in the matter and substance of the best poetry, is inseparable from the superiority of diction and movement marking its style and manner. The two superiorities are closely related, and are in steadfast proportion one to the other. So far as high poetic truth and seriousness are wanting to a poet's matter and substance, so far also, we may be sure, will a high poetic stamp of diction and movement be wanting to his style and manner. In proportion as this high stamp of diction and movement, again, is absent from a poet's style and manner, we shall find, also, that high poetic truth and seriousness are absent from his substance and matter.

So stated, these are but dry generalities; their whole force lies in their application. And I could wish every student of poetry to make the application of them for himself. Made by himself, the application would impress itself upon his mind far more deeply than made by me. Neither will my limits allow me to make any full application of the generalities above propounded; but in the hope of bringing out, at any rate, some significance in them, and of establishing an important principle more firmly by their means, I will, in the space which remains to me, follow rapidly from the commencement the course of our English poetry with them in my view.

Once more I return to the early poetry of France, with which our own poetry, in its origins, is indissolubly connected. In the twelfth and thirteenth centuries, that seed-time of all modern language and literature, the poetry of France had a clear predominance in Europe. Of the two divisions of that poetry, its productions in the *langue d'oïl* and its productions in the *langue d'oc*,[1] the poetry of the *langue d'oc*, of southern France, of the troubadours, is of importance because of its effect on Italian literature;—the first literature of modern Europe to strike the true and grand note, and to bring forth, as in Dante and Petrarch it brought forth, classics. But the predominance of French poetry in Europe, during the twelfth and thirteenth centuries, is due to its poetry of the *langue d'oïl*, the poetry of northern France and of the tongue which is now the French language. In the twelfth century the bloom of this romance-poetry was earlier and stronger in England, at the court of our

---

[1] These were two mediæval dialects in France, distinguished by the words for "yes" (Provençal *oc* and Northern *oïl*).

Anglo-Norman kings, than in France itself. But it was a bloom of French poetry; and as our native poetry formed itself, it formed itself out of this. The romance-poems which took possession of the heart and imagination of Europe in the twelfth and thirteenth centuries are French; "they are," as Southey justly says, "the pride of French literature, nor have we anything which can be placed in competition with them." Themes were supplied from all quarters: but the romance-setting which was common to them all, and which gained the ear of Europe, was French. This constituted for the French poetry, literature, and language, at the height of the Middle Age, an unchallenged predominance. The Italian Brunetto Latini, the master of Dante, wrote his *Treasure* in French because, he says, "la parleure en est plus délitable et plus commune à toutes gens." [1] In the same century, the thirteenth, the French romance-writer, Christian of Troyes, formulates the claims, in chivalry and letters, of France, his native country, as follows:—

> Or vous ert par ce livre apris,
> Que Gresse ot de chevalerie
> Le premier los et de clergie;
> Puis vint chevalerie à Rome,
> Et de la clergie la some,
> Qui ore est en France venue.
> Diex doinst qu'ele i soit retenue
> Et que li lius li abelisse
> Tant que de France n'isse
> L'onor qui s'i est arestée!

"Now by this book you will learn that first Greece had the renown for chivalry and letters; then chivalry and the primacy in letters passed to Rome, and now it is come to France. God grant it may be kept there; and that the place may please it so well, that the honor which has come to make stay in France may never depart thence!" [2]

Yet it is now all gone, this French romance-poetry, of which the weight of substance and the power of style are not unfairly represented by this extract from Christian of Troyes. Only by means of the historic estimate can we persuade ourselves now to think that any of it is of poetical importance.

But in the fourteenth century there comes an Englishman nourished on this poetry; taught his trade by this poetry, getting words,

---

[1] The spoken language is more delightful and more common to everybody.
[2] From the opening passage of *Cligès*.

rhyme, metre from this poetry; for even of that stanza which the Italians used, and which Chaucer derived immediately from the Italians, the basis and suggestion was probably given in France. Chaucer (I have already named him) fascinated his contemporaries, but so too did Christian of Troyes and Wolfram of Eschenbach. Chaucer's power of fascination, however, is enduring; his poetical importance does not need the assistance of the historic estimate; it is real. He is a genuine source of joy and strength, which is flowing still for us and will flow always. He will be read, as time goes on, far more generally than he is read now. His language is a cause of difficulty for us; but so also, and I think in quite as great a degree, is the language of Burns. In Chaucer's case, as in that of Burns, it is a difficulty to be unhesitatingly accepted and overcome.

If we ask ourselves wherein consists the immense superiority of Chaucer's poetry over the romance-poetry, why it is that in passing from this to Chaucer we suddenly feel ourselves to be in another world, we shall find that his superiority is both in the substance of his poetry and in the style of his poetry. His superiority in substance is given by his large, free, simple, clear yet kindly view of human life,—so unlike the total want, in the romance-poets, of all intelligent command of it. Chaucer has not their helplessness; he has gained the power to survey the world from a central, a truly human point of view. We have only to call to mind the Prologue to *The Canterbury Tales*. The right comment upon it is Dryden's: "It is sufficient to say, according to the proverb, that *here is God's plenty*." And again: "He is a perpetual fountain of good sense." It is by a large, free, sound representation of things, that poetry, this high criticism of life, has truth of substance; and Chaucer's poetry has truth of substance.

Of his style and manner, if we think first of the romance-poetry and then of Chaucer's divine liquidness of diction, his divine fluidity of movement, it is difficult to speak temperately. They are irresistible, and justify all the rapture with which his successors speak of his "gold dew-drops of speech." Johnson misses the point entirely when he finds fault with Dryden for ascribing to Chaucer the first refinement of our numbers, and says that Gower also can show smooth numbers and easy rhymes. The refinement of our numbers means something far more than this. A nation may have versifiers with smooth numbers and easy rhymes, and yet may have no real poetry at all. Chaucer is the father of our splendid English poetry; he is our "well of English undefiled," because by the lovely charm of his diction, the lovely charm of his movement, he makes an epoch and founds a tradition. In Spenser, Shakespeare, Milton, Keats, we can follow the tradition of the liquid diction, the fluid movement, of Chaucer; at one time it is his liquid diction of which in these poets we feel the virtue, and at another time it is his fluid movement. And the virtue is irresistible.

Bounded as is my space, I must yet find room for an example of Chaucer's virtue, as I have given examples to show the virtue of the great classics. I feel disposed to say that a single line is enough to show the charm of Chaucer's verse; that merely one line like this—

> O martyr souded [1] in virginitee!

has a virtue of manner and movement such as we shall not find in all the verse of romance-poetry;—but this is saying nothing. The virtue is such as we shall not find, perhaps, in all English poetry, outside the poets whom I have named as the special inheritors of Chaucer's tradition. A single line, however, is too little if we have not the strain of Chaucer's verse well in our memory; let us take a stanza. It is from *The Prioress's Tale*, the story of the Christian child murdered in a Jewry:—

> My throte is cut unto my nekke-bone
> Saidè this child, and as by way of kinde
> I should have deyd, yea, longè time agone;
> But Jesu Christ, as ye in bookès finde,
> Will that his glory last and be in minde,
> And for the worship of his mother dere
> Yet may I sing O *Alma* loud and clere.

Wordsworth has modernized this Tale, and to feel how delicate and evanescent is the charm of verse, we have only to read Wordsworth's first three lines of this stanza after Chaucer's:—

> My throat is cut unto the bone, I trow,
> Said this young child, and by the law of kind
> I should have died, yea, many hours ago.

The charm is departed. It is often said that the power of liquidness and fluidity in Chaucer's verse was dependent upon a free, a licentious dealing with language, such as is now impossible; upon a liberty, such as Burns too enjoyed, of making words like *neck, bird,* into a dissyllable by adding to them, and words like *cause, rhyme,*

---

[1] The French *soudé*: soldered, fixed fast. (Arnold.)

into a dissyllable by sounding the *e* mute. It is true that Chaucer's fluidity is conjoined with this liberty, and is admirably served by it; but we ought not to say that it was dependent upon it. It was dependent upon his talent. Other poets with a like liberty do not attain to the fluidity of Chaucer; Burns himself does not attain to it. Poets again, who have a talent akin to Chaucer's, such as Shakespeare or Keats, have known how to attain to his fluidity without the like liberty.

And yet Chaucer is not one of the great classics. His poetry transcends and effaces, easily and without effort, all the romance-poetry of Catholic Christendom; it transcends and effaces all the English poetry contemporary with it, it transcends and effaces all the English poetry subsequent to it down to the age of Elizabeth. Of such avail is poetic truth of substance, in its natural and necessary union with poetic truth of style. And yet, I say, Chaucer is not one of the great classics. He has not their accent. What is wanting to him is suggested by the mere mention of the name of the first great classic of Christendom, the immortal poet who died eighty years before Chaucer,—Dante. The accent of such verse as

In la sua volontade è nostra pace . . .

is altogether beyond Chaucer's reach; we praise him, but we feel that this accent is out of the question for him. It may be said that it was necessarily out of the reach of any poet in the England of that stage of growth. Possibly; but we are to adopt a real, not an historic, estimate of poetry. However we may account for its absence, something is wanting, then, to the poetry of Chaucer, which poetry must have before it can be placed in the glorious class of the best. And there is no doubt what that something is. It is the σπουδαιότης, the high and excellent seriousness, which Aristotle assigns as one of the grand virtues of poetry. The substance of Chaucer's poetry, his view of things and his criticism of life, has largeness, freedom, shrewdness, benignity; but it has not this high seriousness. Homer's criticism of life has it, Dante's has it, Shakespeare's has it. It is this chiefly which gives to our spirits what they can rest upon; and with the increasing demands of our modern ages upon poetry, this virtue of giving us what we can rest upon will be more and more highly esteemed. A voice from the slums of Paris, fifty or sixty years after Chaucer, the voice of poor Villon out of his life of riot and crime, has at its happy moments (as, for instance, in the last stanza of *La*

Belle Heaulmière [1]) more of this important poetic virtue of seriousness than all the productions of Chaucer. But its apparition in Villon, and in men like Villon, is fitful; the greatness of the great poets, the power of their criticism of life, is that their virtue is sustained.

To our praise, therefore, of Chaucer as a poet there must be this limitation: he lacks the high seriousness of the great classics, and therewith an important part of their virtue. Still, the main fact for us to bear in mind about Chaucer is his sterling value according to that real estimate which we firmly adopt for all poets. He has poetic truth of substance, though he has not high poetic seriousness, and corresponding to his truth of substance he has an exquisite virtue of style and manner. With him is born our real poetry.

For my present purpose I need not dwell on our Elizabethan poetry, or on the continuation and close of this poetry in Milton. We all of us profess to be agreed in the estimate of this poetry; we all of us recognize it as great poetry, our greatest, and Shakespeare and Milton as our poetical classics. The real estimate, here, has universal currency. With the next age of our poetry divergency and difficulty begin. An historic estimate of that poetry has established itself; and the question is, whether it will be found to coincide with the real estimate.

The age of Dryden, together with our whole eighteenth century which followed it, sincerely believed itself to have produced poetical classics of its own, and even to have made advance, in poetry, beyond all its predecessors. Dryden regards as not seriously disputable the opinion "that the sweetness of English verse was never understood or practised by our fathers." Cowley could see nothing at all in Chaucer's poetry. Dryden heartily admired it, and, as we have

---

[1] The name *Heaulmière* is said to be derived from a head-dress (helm) worn as a mark by courtesans. In Villon's ballad, a poor old creature of this class laments her days of youth and beauty. The last stanza of the ballad runs thus:—

> Ainsi le bon temps regretons
> Entre nous, pauvres vieilles sottes,
> Assises bas, à croppetons,
> Tout en ung tas comme pelottes;
> A petit feu de chenevottes
> Tost allumées, tost estainctes.
> Et jadis fusmes si mignottes!
> Ainsi enprend à maintz et maintes.

"Thus amongst ourselves we regret the good time, poor silly old things, low-seated on our heels, all in a heap like so many balls; by a little fire of hemp-stalks, soon lighted, soon spent. And once we were such darlings! So fares it with many and many a one." (Arnold.)

seen, praised its matter admirably; but of its exquisite manner and movement all he can find to say is that "there is the rude sweetness of a Scotch tune in it, which is natural and pleasing, though not perfect." Addison, wishing to praise Chaucer's numbers, compares them with Dryden's own. And all through the eighteenth century, and down even into our own times, the stereotyped phrase of approbation for good verse found in our early poetry has been, that it even approached the verse of Dryden, Addison, Pope, and Johnson.

Are Dryden and Pope poetical classics? Is the historic estimate, which represents them as such, and which has been so long established that it cannot easily give way, the real estimate? Wordsworth and Coleridge, as is well known, denied it; but the authority of Wordsworth and Coleridge does not weigh much with the young generation, and there are many signs to show that the eighteenth century and its judgments are coming into favor again. Are the favorite poets of the eighteenth century classics?

It is impossible within my present limits to discuss the question fully. And what man of letters would not shrink from seeming to dispose dictatorially of the claims of two men who are, at any rate, such masters in letters as Dryden and Pope; two men of such admirable talent, both of them, and one of them, Dryden, a man, on all sides, of such energetic and genial power? And yet, if we are to gain the full benefit from poetry, we must have the real estimate of it. I cast about for some mode of arriving, in the present case, at such an estimate without offence. And perhaps the best way is to begin, as it is easy to begin, with cordial praise.

When we find Chapman, the Elizabethan translator of Homer, expressing himself in his preface thus: "Though truth in her very nakedness sits in so deep a pit, that from Gades [1] to Aurora and Ganges few eyes can sound her, I hope yet those few here will so discover and confirm that, the date being out of her darkness in this morning of our poet, he shall now gird his temples with the sun,"— we pronounce that such a prose is intolerable. When we find Milton writing: "And long it was not after, when I was confirmed in this opinion, that he, who would not be frustrate of his hope to write well hereafter in laudable things, ought himself to be a true poem,"—we pronounce that such a prose has its own grandeur, but that it is obsolete and inconvenient. But when we find Dryden telling us: "What Virgil wrote in the vigor of his age, in plenty and at ease, I have undertaken to translate in my declining years; struggling with

[1] *Gades*, the Latin form of Cádiz, in Spain.

wants, oppressed with sickness, curbed in my genius, liable to be misconstrued in all I write,"—then we exclaim that here at last we have the true English prose, a prose such as we would all gladly use if we only knew how. Yet Dryden was Milton's contemporary.

But after the Restoration the time had come when our nation felt the imperious need of a fit prose. So, too, the time had likewise come when our nation felt the imperious need of freeing itself from the absorbing preoccupation which religion in the Puritan age had exercised. It was impossible that this freedom should be brought about without some negative excess, without some neglect and impairment of the religious life of the soul; and the spiritual history of the eighteenth century shows us that the freedom was not achieved without them. Still, the freedom was achieved; the preoccupation, an undoubtedly baneful and retarding one if it had continued, was got rid of. And as with religion amongst us at that period, so it was also with letters. A fit prose was a necessity; but it was impossible that a fit prose should establish itself amongst us without some touch of frost to the imaginative life of the soul. The needful qualities for a fit prose are regularity, uniformity, precision, balance. The men of letters, whose destiny it may be to bring their nation to the attainment of a fit prose, must of necessity, whether they work in prose or in verse, give a predominating, an almost exclusive attention to the qualities of regularity, uniformity, precision, balance. But an almost exclusive attention to these qualities involves some repression and silencing of poetry.

We are to regard Dryden as the puissant and glorious founder, Pope as the splendid high-priest, of our age of prose and reason, of our excellent and indispensable eighteenth century. For the purposes of their mission and destiny their poetry, like their prose, is admirable. Do you ask me whether Dryden's verse, take it almost where you will, is not good?

> A milk-white Hind, immortal and unchanged,
> Fed on the lawns and in the forest ranged.[1]

I answer: Admirable for the purposes of the inaugurator of an age of prose and reason. Do you ask me whether Pope's verse, take it almost where you will, is not good?

> To Hounslow Heath I point, and Banstead Down;
> Thence comes your mutton, and these chicks my own.[2]

[1] Dryden, *The Hind and the Panther*, i, 1–2.
[2] Pope, *The Second Satire of the Second Book of Horace*, 143–4.

I answer: Admirable for the purposes of the high-priest of an age of prose and reason. But do you ask me whether such verse proceeds from men with an adequate poetic criticism of life, from men whose criticism of life has a high seriousness, or even, without that high seriousness, has poetic largeness, freedom, insight, benignity? Do you ask me whether the application of ideas to life in the verse of these men, often a powerful application, no doubt, is a powerful *poetic* application? Do you ask me whether the poetry of these men has either the matter or the inseparable manner of such an adequate poetic criticism; whether it has the accent of

> Absent thee from felicity awhile . . .

or of

> And what is else not to be overcome . . .

or of

> O martyr souded in virginitee!

I answer: It has not and cannot have them; it is the poetry of the builders of an age of prose and reason. Though they may write in verse, though they may in a certain sense be masters of the art of versification, Dryden and Pope are not classics of our poetry, they are classics of our prose.

Gray is our poetical classic of that literature and age; the position of Gray is singular, and demands a word of notice here. He has not the volume or the power of poets who, coming in times more favorable, have attained to an independent criticism of life. But he lived with the great poets, he lived, above all, with the Greeks, through perpetually studying and enjoying them; and he caught their poetic point of view for regarding life, caught their poetic manner. The point of view and the manner are not self-sprung in him, he caught them of others; and he had not the free and abundant use of them. But whereas Addison and Pope never had the use of them, Gray had the use of them at times. He is the scantiest and frailest of classics in our poetry, but he is a classic.

And now, after Gray, we are met, as we draw towards the end of the eighteenth century, we are met by the great name of Burns. We enter now on times where the personal estimate of poets begins to be rife, and where the real estimate of them is not reached without difficulty. But in spite of the disturbing pressures of personal partiality, of national partiality, let us try to reach a real estimate of the poetry of Burns.

By his English poetry Burns in general belongs to the eighteenth century, and has little importance for us.

> Mark ruffian Violence, distain'd with crimes,
> Rousing elate in these degenerate times;
> View unsuspecting Innocence a prey,
> As guileful Fraud points out the erring way;
> While subtle Litigation's pliant tongue
> The life-blood equal sucks of Right and Wrong! [1]

Evidently this is not the real Burns, or his name and fame would have disappeared long ago. Nor is Clarinda's love-poet, Sylvander, the real Burns either. But he tells us himself: "These English songs gravel me to death. I have not the command of the language that I have of my native tongue. In fact, I think that my ideas are more barren in English than in Scotch. I have been at *Duncan Gray* to dress it in English, but all I can do is desperately stupid." We English turn naturally, in Burns, to the poems in our own language, because we can read them easily; but in those poems we have not the real Burns.

The real Burns is of course in his Scotch poems. Let us boldly say that of much of this poetry, a poetry dealing perpetually with Scotch drink, Scotch religion, and Scotch manners, a Scotchman's estimate is apt to be personal. A Scotchman is used to this world of Scotch drink, Scotch religion, and Scotch manners; he has a tenderness for it; he meets its poet half way. In this tender mood he reads pieces like the *Holy Fair* or *Hallowe'en*. But this world of Scotch drink, Scotch religion, and Scotch manners is against a poet, not for him, when it is not a partial countryman who reads him; for in itself it is not a beautiful world, and no one can deny that it is of advantage to a poet to deal with a beautiful world. Burns's world of Scotch drink, Scotch religion, and Scotch manners, is often a harsh, a sordid, a repulsive world; even the world of his *Cotter's Saturday Night* is not a beautiful world. No doubt a poet's criticism of life may have such truth and power that it triumphs over its world and delights us. Burns may triumph over his world, often he does triumph over his world, but let us observe how and where. Burns is the first case we have had where the bias of the personal estimate tends to mislead; let us look at him closely, he can bear it.

Many of his admirers will tell us that we have Burns, convivial, genuine, delightful, here:—

[1] *On the Death of Robert Dundas, Esq.*, 25-30.

Leeze me on drink! it gies us mair
      Than either school or college;
   It kindles wit, it waukens lair,
      It pangs us fou o' knowledge.
   Be 't whisky gill or penny wheep
      Or ony stronger potion,
   It never fails, on drinking deep,
      To kittle up our notion
            By night or day.[1]

There is a great deal of that sort of thing in Burns, and it is unsatisfactory, not because it is bacchanalian poetry, but because it
has not that accent of sincerity which bacchanalian poetry, to do it
justice, very often has. There is something in it of bravado, something which makes us feel that we have not the man speaking to
us with his real voice; something, therefore, poetically unsound.

   With still more confidence will his admirers tell us that we have
the genuine Burns, the great poet, when his strain asserts the independence, equality, dignity, of men, as in the famous song *For a'*
that and a' that:—

   A prince can mak' a belted knight,
      A marquis, duke, and a' that;
   But an honest man 's aboon his might,
      Guid faith he manna fa' that!
         For a' that, and a' that,
            Their dignities, and a' that,
         The pith o' sense, and pride o' worth,
            Are higher rank than a' that.

Here they find his grand, genuine touches; and still more, when
this puissant genius, who so often set morality at defiance, falls
moralizing:—

   The sacred lowe o' weel-placed love
      Luxuriantly indulge it;
   But never tempt th' illicit rove,
      Tho' naething should divulge it.
   I waive the quantum o' the sin,
      The hazard o' concealing,
   But och! it hardens a' within,
      And petrifies the feeling.[2]

Or in a higher strain:—

[1] *The Holy Fair*, 163–71.
[2] *Epistle to a Young Friend*, 41–8.

Who made the heart, 't is He alone
Decidedly can try us;
He knows each chord, its various tone;
Each spring, its various bias.
Then at the balance let 's be mute,
We never can adjust it;
What's *done* we partly may compute,
But know not what 's resisted.[1]

Or in a better strain yet, a strain, his admirers will say, unsurpass-
able:—

To make a happy fire-side clime
To weans and wife,
That 's the true pathos and sublime
Of human life.[2]

There is criticism of life for you, the admirers of Burns will say to
us; there is the application of ideas to life! There is, undoubtedly.
The doctrine of the last-quoted lines coincides almost exactly with
what was the aim and end, Xenophon tells us, of all the teaching of
Socrates. And the application is a powerful one; made by a man of
vigorous understanding, and (need I say?) a master of language.

But for supreme poetical success more is required than the powerful application of ideas to life; it must be an application under the conditions fixed by the laws of poetic truth and poetic beauty.
Those laws fix as an essential condition, in the poet's treatment of
such matters as are here in question, high seriousness;—the high
seriousness which comes from absolute sincerity. The accent of high
seriousness, born of absolute sincerity, is what gives to such verse as

In la sua volontade è nostra pace . . .

to such criticism of life as Dante's, its power. Is this accent felt
in the passages which I have been quoting from Burns? Surely not;
surely, if our sense is quick, we must perceive that we have not in
those passages a voice from the very inmost soul of the genuine
Burns; he is not speaking to us from these depths, he is more or less
preaching. And the compensation for admiring such passages less,
for missing the perfect poetic accent in them, will be that we shall
admire more the poetry where that accent is found.

No; Burns, like Chaucer, comes short of the high seriousness of

[1] *Address to the Unco Guid*, 57–64.
[2] *To Dr. Blacklock*, 51–4.

the great classics, and the virtue of matter and manner which goes with that high seriousness is wanting to his work. At moments he touches it in a profound and passionate melancholy, as in those four immortal lines taken by Byron as a motto for *The Bride of Abydos*, but which have in them a depth of poetic quality such as resides in no verse of Byron's own:—

> Had we never loved sae kindly,
> Had we never loved sae blindly,
> Never met, or never parted,
> We had ne'er been broken-hearted.[1]

But a whole poem of that quality Burns cannot make; the rest, in the *Farewell to Nancy*, is verbiage.

We arrive best at the real estimate of Burns, I think, by conceiving his work as having truth of matter and truth of manner, but not the accent or the poetic virtue of the highest masters. His genuine criticism of life, when the sheer poet in him speaks, is ironic; it is not:—

> Thou Power Supreme, whose mighty scheme
> These woes of mine fulfil,
> Here firm I rest, they must be best
> Because they are Thy will![2]

It is far rather: *Whistle owre the lave o't!* Yet we may say of him as of Chaucer, that of life and the world, as they come before him, his view is large, free, shrewd, benignant,—truly poetic, therefore; and his manner of rendering what he sees is to match. But we must note, at the same time, his great difference from Chaucer. The freedom of Chaucer is heightened, in Burns, by a fiery, reckless energy; the benignity of Chaucer deepens, in Burns, into an overwhelming sense of the pathos of things;—of the pathos of human nature, the pathos, also, of non-human nature. Instead of the fluidity of Chaucer's manner, the manner of Burns has spring, bounding swiftness. Burns is by far the greater force, though he has perhaps less charm. The world of Chaucer is fairer, richer, more significant than that of Burns; but when the largeness and freedom of Burns gets full sweep, as in *Tam o' Shanter*, or still more in that puissant and splendid production, *The Jolly Beggars*, his world may be what it will, his poetic genius triumphs over it. In the world of *The Jolly*

---

[1] *Ae Fond Kiss*, 13–6. (*Farewell to Nancy* in *The English Poets*.)
[2] *Winter*, 17–20.

Beggars there is more than hideousness and squalor, there is bestiality; yet the piece is a superb poetic success. It has a breadth, truth, and power which make the famous scene in Auerbach's Cellar, of Goethe's *Faust,* seem artificial and tame beside it, and which are only matched by Shakespeare and Aristophanes.

Here, where his largeness and freedom serve him so admirably, and also in those poems and songs, where to shrewdness he adds infinite archness and wit, and to benignity infinite pathos, where his manner is flawless, and a perfect poetic whole is the result,—in things like the address to the Mouse whose home he had ruined, in things like *Duncan Gray, Tam Glen, Whistle and I'll come to you my Lad, Auld Lang Syne* (this list might be made much longer),— here we have the genuine Burns, of whom the real estimate must be high indeed. Not a classic, nor with the excellent σπουδαιότης of the great classics, nor with a verse rising to a criticism of life and a virtue like theirs; but a poet with thorough truth of substance and an answering truth of style, giving us a poetry sound to the core. We all of us have a leaning towards the pathetic, and may be inclined perhaps to prize Burns most for his touches of piercing, sometimes almost intolerable, pathos; for verse like—

> We twa hae paidl't i' the burn
> From mornin' sun till dine;
> But seas between us braid hae roar'd
> Sin auld lang syne . . .[1]

where he is as lovely as he is sound. But perhaps it is by the perfection of soundness of his lighter and archer masterpieces that he is poetically most wholesome for us. For the votary misled by a personal estimate of Shelley, as so many of us have been, are, and will be,—of that beautiful spirit building his many-colored haze of words and images

> Pinnacled dim in the intense inane—[2]

no contact can be wholesomer than the contact with Burns at his archest and soundest. Side by side with the

> On the brink of the night and the morning
> My coursers are wont to respire,
> But the Earth has just whispered a warning
> That their flight must be swifter than fire . . .

[1] *Auld Lang Syne,* 13–6.
[2] *Prometheus Unbound,* act iii, last line.

of *Prometheus Unbound,* how salutary, how very salutary, to place this from *Tam Glen:*—

> My minnie does constantly deave me
> And bids me beware o' young men;
> They flatter, she says, to deceive me;
> But wha can think sae o' Tam Glen?

But we enter on burning ground as we approach the poetry of times so near to us—poetry like that of Byron, Shelley, and Wordsworth—of which the estimates are so often not only personal, but personal with passion. For my purpose, it is enough to have taken the single case of Burns, the first poet we come to of whose work the estimate formed is evidently apt to be personal, and to have suggested how we may proceed, using the poetry of the great classics as a sort of touchstone, to correct this estimate, as we had previously corrected by the same means the historic estimate where we met with it. A collection like the present, with its succession of celebrated names and celebrated poems, offers a good opportunity to us for resolutely endeavoring to make our estimates of poetry real. I have sought to point out a method which will help us in making them so, and to exhibit it in use so far as to put any one who likes in a way of applying it for himself.

At any rate the end to which the method and the estimate are designed to lead, and from leading to which, if they do lead to it, they get their whole value,—the benefit of being able clearly to feel and deeply to enjoy the best, the truly classic, in poetry—is an end, let me say it once more at parting, of supreme importance. We are often told that an era is opening in which we are to see multitudes of a common sort of readers, and masses of a common sort of literature; that such readers do not want and could not relish anything better than such literature, and that to provide it is becoming a vast and profitable industry. Even if good literature entirely lost currency with the world, it would still be abundantly worth while to continue to enjoy it by oneself. But it never will lose currency with the world, in spite of momentary appearances; it never will lose supremacy. Currency and supremacy are insured to it, not indeed by the world's deliberate and conscious choice, but by something far deeper,—by the instinct of self-preservation in humanity.

Bagehot

Walter BAGEHOT (1826–1877) was born at Langport, Somersetshire, of a distinguished banking family. He went to school in Bristol and graduated from the University of London (B. A., 1846; M. A., 1848), with honors in mathematics and philosophy. He read widely in poetry, metaphysics, and history; he studied law and was called to the Bar in 1852, but never practiced. Although he became associated with his father in banking, his business career did not prevent him from contributing striking articles to various periodicals. He edited the *National Review* from 1855 to 1864 and, from 1860 until his sudden death, acted as the editor of the *Economist,* which had been founded by his father-in-law, James Wilson, during the anti-corn-law agitation, to represent free-trade principles.

In addition to his other duties, Bagehot found time to write much on banking, finance, and politics, and produced two volumes of literary studies. His papers were edited by R. H. Hutton (1878–80).

Bagehot enjoyed literature. He clearly derived much pleasure, too, from trying to find out why he liked things and then attempting, as an economist, to discover, if possible, the underlying laws or reasons for his appreciation. His analysis of the three major poets of his day is a stimulating, if oversimplified, study, even though, at times, his enthusiasm pushes aside logic and accuracy.

From PURE, ORNATE, AND GROTESQUE
ART IN ENGLISH POETRY[1]

(1864)

We couple these two books [2] together, not because of their likeness, for they are as dissimilar as books can be, nor on account of the eminence of their authors, for in general two great authors are too much for one essay, but because they are the best possible illustration of something we have to say upon poetical art—because they may give to it life and freshness. The accident of contemporaneous publication has here brought together two books, very characteristic of modern art, and we want to show how they are characteristic.

Neither English poetry nor English criticism have ever recovered the *eruption* which they both made at the beginning of this century into the fashionable world. The poems of Lord Byron were received with an avidity that resembles our present avidity for sensation novels, and were read by a class which at present reads little but such novels. Old men who remember those days may be heard to say, "We hear nothing of poetry now-a-days; it seems quite down." And "down" it certainly is, if for poetry it be a descent to be no longer the favorite excitement of the more frivolous part of the "upper" world. That stimulating poetry is now little read. A stray schoolboy may still be detected in a wild admiration for the *Giaour* or the *Corsair* (and it is suitable to his age, and he should not be reproached for it), but the *real* posterity—the quiet students of a past literature—never read them or think of them. A line or two linger in the memory; a few telling strokes of occasional and felicitous energy are quoted, but this is all. As wholes, these exaggerated stories were worthless; they taught nothing, and, therefore, they are forgotten. If now-a-days a dismal poet were, like Byron, to lament the fact of his birth, and to hint that he was too good for the world, the *Saturday Review* would say that "they doubted if he *was* too good; that a sulky poet was a questionable addition to a tolerable world; that he need not have been born, as far as they were concerned." Doubtless, there is much in Byron besides his dismal exaggeration, but it was that exaggeration which made "the sensation," which gave him a wild moment of dangerous

---

[1] This first appeared in the *National Review,* November, 1864.

[2] *Enoch Arden, &c.* By Alfred Tennyson, D.C.L., Poet Laureate. *Dramatis Personæ.* By Robert Browning.

name. As so often happens, the cause of his momentary fashion is the cause also of his lasting oblivion. Moore's former reputation was less excessive, yet it has not been more permanent. The prettiness of a few songs preserves the memory of his name, but as a poet to *read* he is forgotten. There is nothing to read in him; no exquisite thought, no sublime feeling, no consummate description of true character. Almost the sole result of the poetry of that time is the harm which it has done. It degraded for a time the whole character of the art. It said by practice, by a most efficient and successful practice, that it was the aim, the *duty* of poets, to catch the attention of the passing, the fashionable, the busy world. If a poem "fell dead," it was nothing; it was composed to please the "London" of the year, and if that London did not like it, why it had failed. It fixed upon the minds of a whole generation, it engraved in popular memory and tradition, a vague conviction that poetry is but one of the many *amusements* for the light classes, for the lighter hours of all classes. The mere notion, the bare idea, that poetry is a deep thing, a teaching thing, the most surely and wisely elevating of human things, is even now to the coarse public mind nearly unknown.

As was the fate of poetry, so inevitably was that of criticism. The science that expounds which poetry is good and which is bad is dependent for its popular reputation on the popular estimate of poetry itself. The critics of that day had *a* day, which is more than can be said for some since; they professed to tell the fashionable world in what books it would find new pleasure, and therefore they were read by the fashionable world. Byron counted the critic and poet equal. The *Edinburgh Review* penetrated among the young, and into places of female resort where it does not go now. As people ask, "Have you read *Henry Dunbar*? [1] and what do you think of it?" so they then asked, "Have you read the *Giaour*? and what do you think of it?" Lord Jeffrey, a shrewd judge of the world, employed himself in telling it what to think; not so much what it ought to think, as what at bottom it did think, and so by dexterous sympathy with current society he gained contemporary fame and power. Such fame no critic must hope for now. His articles will not penetrate where the poems themselves do not penetrate. When poetry was noisy, criticism was loud; now poetry is a still small voice, and criticism must be smaller and stiller. As the function of

---

[1] A novel by Mary Elizabeth Braddon (Mrs. John Maxwell), (1837-1915), which appeared in 1864, the year of this essay.

such criticism was limited so was its subject. For the great and (as time now proves) the *permanent* part of the poetry of his time —for Shelley and for Wordsworth—Lord Jeffrey had but one word. He said, "It won't do." And it will not do to amuse a drawing-room.

The doctrine that poetry is a light amusement for idle hours, a metrical species of sensational novel, has not indeed been without gainsayers wildly popular. Thirty years ago, Mr. Carlyle most rudely contradicted it. But perhaps this is about all that he has done. He has denied, but he has not disproved. He has contradicted the floating paganism, but he has not founded the deep religion. All about and around us a *faith* in poetry struggles to be extricated, but it is not extricated. Some day, at the touch of the true word, the whole confusion will by magic cease; the broken and shapeless notions cohere and crystallize into a bright and true theory. But this cannot be yet.

But though no complete theory of the poetic art as yet be possible for us, though perhaps only our children's children will be able to speak on this subject with the assured confidence which belongs to accepted truth, yet something of some certainty may be stated on the easier elements, and something that will throw light on these two new books. But it will be necessary to assign reasons, and the assigning of reasons is a dry task. Years ago, when criticism only tried to show how poetry could be made a good amusement, it was not impossible that criticism itself should be amusing. But now it must at least be serious, for we believe that poetry is a serious and a deep thing.

There should be a word in the language of literary art to express what the word "picturesque" expresses for the fine arts. *Picturesque* means fit to be put into a picture; we want a word *literatesque*, "fit to be put into a book." An artist goes through a hundred different country scenes, rich with beauties, charms, and merits, but he does not paint any of them. He leaves them alone; he idles on till he finds the hundred-and-first—a scene which many observers would not think much of, but which *he* knows by virtue of his art will look well on canvas, and this he paints and preserves. Susceptible observers, though not artists, feel this quality too; they say of a scene, "How picturesque!" meaning by this a quality distinct from that of beauty, or sublimity, or grandeur—meaning to speak not only of the scene as it is in itself, but also of its fitness for imitation by art; meaning not only that it is good, but that its goodness is such as ought to be transferred to paper; meaning not simply that it fascinates, but also that its fascination is such as ought to be copied by man. A fine and insensible instinct has put language to this subtle use; it expresses an idea without which fine art criticism could not go on, and it is very natural that the language of pictorial should be better supplied with words than that of literary criticism, for the eye was used before the mind, and language embodies primitive sensuous ideas, long ere it expresses, or need express, abstract and literary ones.

The reason why a landscape is "picturesque" is often said to be that such landscape represents an "idea." But this explanation, though in the minds of some who use it it is near akin to the truth, fails to explain that truth to those who did not know it before; the word *idea* is so often used in these subjects when people do not know anything else to say; it represents so often a kind of intellectual insolvency, when philosophers are at their wits' end, that shrewd people will never readily on any occasion give it credit for meaning anything. A wise explainer must, therefore, look out for other words to convey what he has to say. *Landscapes,* like everything else in nature, divide themselves as we look at them into a sort of rude classification. We go down a river, for example, and we see a hundred landscapes on both sides of it, resembling one another in much, yet differing in something; with trees here, and a farmhouse there, and shadows on one side, and a deep pool far on; a collection of circumstances most familiar in themselves, but making a perpetual novelty by the magic of their various combinations. We travel so for miles and hours, and then we come to a scene which also has these various circumstances and adjuncts, but which combines them best, which makes the best whole of them, which shows them in their best proportion at a single glance before the eye. Then we say, "This is the place to paint the river; this is the picturesque point!" Or, if not artists or critics of art, we feel without analysis or examination that somehow this bend or sweep of the river shall in future *be the river to us:* that it is the image of it which we will retain in our mind's eye, by which we will remember it, which we will call up when we want to describe or think of it. Some fine countries, some beautiful rivers, have not this picturesque quality; they give us elements of beauty, but they do not combine them together; we go on for a time delighted, but *after* a time somehow we get wearied; we feel that we are taking in nothing and learning nothing; we get no collected image before our mind; we see the accidents and circumstances of that sort of scenery, but the summary scene we do not see; we find *disjecta membra*,[1] but no form; various and many and faulty approximations are displayed in succession; but the absolute perfection in that country's or river's scenery—its *type*—is withheld. We go away from such places in part delighted, but in part baffled; we have been puzzled by pretty things; we have beheld a hundred different inconsistent specimens of the same sort of beauty; but the rememberable idea, the full development, the characteristic individuality of it, we have not seen.

We find the same sort of quality in all parts of painting. We see a portrait of a person we know, and we say, "It is like—yes, like, of course, but it is not *the man*"; we feel it could not be anyone else, but still, somehow it fails to bring home to us the individual as we know him to be. *He* is not there. An accumulation of features like his are painted, but his essence is not painted; an approximation more or less excellent is given, but the characteristic expression, the *typical* form, of the man is withheld.

Literature—the painting of words—has the same quality but wants the analogous word. The word *literatesque* would mean, if we possessed it, that perfect combination in the *subject-matter* of literature, which suits the *art* of literature. We often meet people, and say to them, sometimes meaning well and sometimes ill, "How well so-and-so would do in a book!" Such people are by no means the best people; but they are the most effective people—the most rememberable people. Frequently when we first know them, we like them because they explain to us so much of our experience; we have known many people "like that," in one way or another, but we did not seem to understand them; they were nothing to us, for their traits were indistinct; we forgot them, for they *hitched* on to nothing, and we could not classify them; but when we see the *type* of the genus, at once we seem to comprehend its character; the inferior specimens are explained by the perfect embodiment; the approximations are definable when we know the ideal to which they draw near. There are the infinite number of classes of human beings, but in each of these classes there is a distinctive type which, if we could expand it out in words, would define the class. We cannot expand it in formal terms any more than a landscape or a species of landscape; but we have an art, an art of words, which can draw it. Travellers and others often bring home, in addition to their long journals—which though so living to them, are so dead, so

[1] scattered limbs.

inanimate, so undescriptive to all else—a pen-and-ink sketch, rudely done very likely, but which, perhaps, even the more for the blots and strokes, gives a distinct notion, an emphatic image, to all who see it. They say at once, *now* we know the sort of thing. The sketch has *hit* the mind. True literature does the same. It describes sorts, varieties, and permutations, by delineating the type of each sort, the ideal of each variety, the central, the marking trait of each permutation.

On this account, the greatest artists of the world have ever shown an enthusiasm for reality. To care for notions, and abstractions; to philosophize; to reason out conclusions; to care for schemes of thought, are signs in the artistic mind of secondary excellence. A Schiller, an Euripides, a Ben Jonson, cares for *ideas*—for the parings of the intellect, and the distillation of the mind; a Shakespeare, a Homer, a Goethe, finds his mental occupation, the true home of his natural thoughts, in the real world—"which is the world of all of us"—where the face of nature, the moving masses of men and women, are ever changing, ever multiplying, ever mixing one with the other. The reason is plain—the business of the poet, of the artist, is with *types*; and those types are mirrored in reality. As a painter must not only have a hand to execute, but an eye to distinguish—as he must go here and there through the real world to catch the picturesque man, the picturesque scene, which is to live on his canvas—so the poet must find in that reality, the *literatesque* man, the *literatesque* scene which nature intends for him, and which will live in his page. Even in reality he will not find this type complete, or the characteristics perfect; but there, at least, he will find *something*, some hint, some intimation, some suggestion; whereas, in the stagnant home of his own thoughts he will find nothing pure, nothing *as it is*, nothing which does not bear his own mark, which is not somehow altered by a mixture with himself.

The first conversation of Goethe and Schiller illustrates this conception of the poet's art. Goethe was at that time prejudiced against Schiller, we must remember, partly from what he considered the *outrages* of *The Robbers*, partly because of the philosophy of Kant. Schiller's *Essay on Grace and Dignity*, he tells us, "was yet less of a kind to reconcile me. The philosophy of Kant, which exalts the dignity of mind so highly, while appearing to restrict it, Schiller had joyfully embraced: it unfolded the extraordinary qualities which Nature had implanted in him; and in the lively feeling of freedom and self-direction, he showed himself unthankful to the

Great Mother, who surely had not acted like a step-dame towards him. Instead of viewing her as self-subsisting, as producing with a living force, and according to appointed laws, alike the highest and the lowest of her works, he took her up under the aspect of some empirical native qualities of the human mind. Certain harsh passages I could even directly apply to myself: they exhibited my confession of faith in a false light; and I felt that if written without particular attention to me, they were still worse; for in that case, the vast chasm which lay between us, gaped but so much the more distinctly." After a casual meeting at a Society for Natural History, they walked home, and Goethe proceeds:

We reached his house; the talk induced me to go in. I then expounded to him, with as much vivacity as possible, the *Metamorphosis of Plants*,[1] drawing out on paper, with many characteristic strokes, a symbolic plant for him, as I proceeded. He heard and saw all this, with much interest and distinct comprehension; but when I had done, he shook his head and said: "This is no experiment, this is an idea." I stopped with some degree of irritation; for the point which separated us was most luminously marked by this expression. The opinions in *Dignity and Grace* again occurred to me; the old grudge was just awakening; but I smothered it, and merely said: "I was happy to find that I had got ideas without knowing it, nay that I saw them before my eyes."

Schiller had much more prudence and dexterity of management than I; he was also thinking of his periodical the *Horen*, about this time, and of course rather wished to attract than repel me. Accordingly he answered me like an accomplished Kantite; and as my stiff-necked Realism gave occasion to many contradictions, much battling took place between us, and at last a truce, in which neither party would consent to yield the victory, but each held himself invincible. Positions like the following grieved me to the very soul: *How can there ever be an experiment, that shall correspond with an idea? The specific quality of an idea is, that no experiment can reach it or agree with it.* Yet if he held as an idea, the same thing which I looked upon as an experiment, there must certainly, I thought, be some community between us, some ground whereon both of us might meet!

With Goethe's natural history, or with Kant's philosophy, we have here no concern, but we can combine the expressions of the two great poets into a nearly complete description of poetry. The "symbolic plant" is the *type* of which we speak, the ideal at which

---

[1] A curious physiologico-botanical theory by Goethe, which appears to be entirely unknown in this country: though several eminent continental botanists have noticed it with commendation. It is explained at considerable length, in this same *Morphologie*. (Bagehot.)

inferior specimens aim, the class-characteristic in which they all share, but which none shows forth fully. Goethe was right in searching for this in reality and nature; Schiller was right in saying that it was an "idea," a transcending notion to which approximations could be found in experience, but only approximations— which could not be found there itself. Goethe, as a poet, rightly felt the primary necessity of outward suggestion and experience; Schiller as a philosopher, rightly felt its imperfection.

But in these delicate matters, it is easy to misapprehend. There is, undoubtedly, a sort of poetry which is produced as it were out of the author's mind. The description of the poet's own moods and feelings is a common sort of poetry—perhaps the commonest sort. But the peculiarity of such cases is, that the poet does not describe himself *as* himself: autobiography is not his object; he takes himself as a specimen of human nature; he describes, not himself, but a distillation of himself: he takes such of his moods as are most characteristic, as most typify certain moods of certain men, or certain moods of all men; he chooses preponderant feelings of special sorts of men, or occasional feelings of men of all sorts; but with whatever other difference and diversity, the essence is that such self-describing poets describe what is *in* them, but not *peculiar* to them,—what is generic, not what is special and individual. Gray's *Elegy* describes a mood which Gray felt more than other men, but which most others, perhaps all others, feel too. It is more popular, perhaps, than any English poem, because that sort of feeling is the most diffused of high feelings, and because Gray added to a singular nicety of fancy an habitual proneness to a *contemplative*—a discerning but unbiassed—meditation on death and on life. Other poets cannot hope for such success: a subject so popular, so grave, so wise, and yet so suitable to the writer's nature is hardly to be found. But the same ideal, the same unautobiographical character is to be found in the writings of meaner men. Take sonnets of Hartley Coleridge,[1] for example:—

I

To a Friend

When we were idlers with the loitering rills,
The need of human love we little noted:
Our love was nature; and the peace that floated

[1] Hartley Coleridge (1796–1849) was the eldest son of Samuel Taylor Coleridge; he is chiefly remembered for his *Sonnets*.

On the white mist, and dwelt upon the hills,
To sweet accord subdued our wayward wills:
One soul was ours, one mind, one heart devoted,
That, wisely doating, ask'd not why it doated,
And ours the unknown joy, which knowing kills.
But now I find, how dear thou wert to me;
That man is more than half of nature's treasure,
Of that fair Beauty which no eye can see,
Of that sweet music which no ear can measure;
And now the streams may sing for others' pleasure,
The hills sleep on in their eternity.

II

To the Same

In the great city we are met again,
Where many souls there are, that breathe and die,
Scarce knowing more of nature's potency,
Than what they learn from heat, or cold, or rain,
The sad vicissitude of weary pain;—
For busy man is lord of ear and eye,
And what hath nature, but the vast, void sky,
And the thronged river toiling to the main?
Oh! say not so, for she shall have her part
In every smile, in every tear that falls,
And she shall hide her in the secret heart,
Where love persuades, and sterner duty calls:
But worse it were than death, or sorrow's smart,
To live without a friend within these walls.

III

To the Same

We parted on the mountains, as two streams
From one clear spring pursue their several ways;
And thy fleet course hath been through many a maze
In foreign lands, where silvery Padus gleams
To that delicious sky, whose glowing beams
Brightened the tresses that old Poets praise;
Where Petrarch's patient love, and artful lays,
And Ariosto's song of many themes,
Moved the soft air. But I, a lazy brook,
As close pent up within my native dell,
Have crept along from nook to shady nook,

Where flowrets blow, and whispering Naiads dwell
Yet now we meet, that parted were so wide,
O'er rough and smooth to travel side by side.

The contrast of instructive and enviable locomotion with refining but instructive meditation is not special and peculiar to these
two, but general and universal. It was set down by Hartley Coleridge because he was the most meditative and refining of men.

What sort of literatesque types are fit to be described in the sort
of literature called poetry, is a matter on which much might be
written. Mr. Arnold, some years since, put forth a theory that the
art of poetry could only delineate *great actions*. But though, rightly
interpreted and understood—using the word *action* so as to include
high and sound activity in contemplation—this definition may suit
the highest poetry, it certainly cannot be stretched to include many
inferior sorts and even many good sorts. Nobody in their senses
would describe Gray's *Elegy* as the delineation of a "great action";
some kinds of mental contemplation may be energetic enough to
deserve this name, but Gray would have been frightened at the
very word. He loved scholarlike calm and quiet inaction; his very
greatness depended on his *not* acting, on his "wise passiveness," on
his indulging the grave idleness which so well appreciates so much
of human life. But the best answer—the *reductio ad absurdum*—of
Mr. Arnold's doctrine, is the mutilation which it has caused him to
make of his own writings. It has forbidden him, he tells us, to re-
print *Empedocles*—a poem undoubtedly containing defects and
even excesses, but containing also these lines:—

And yet what days were those, Parmenides!
When we were young, when we could number friends
In all the Italian cities like ourselves,
When with elated hearts we join'd your train,
Ye Sun-born virgins! on the road of Truth.
Then we could still enjoy, then neither thought
Nor outward things were clos'd and dead to us,
But we receiv'd the shock of mighty thoughts
On simple minds with a pure natural joy;
And if the sacred load oppress'd our brain,
We had the power to feel the pressure eas'd,
The brow unbound, the thoughts flow free again,
In the delightful commerce of the world.
We had not lost our balance then, nor grown
Thought's slaves, and dead to every natural joy.

The smallest thing could give us pleasure then—
The sports of the country people;
A flute note from the woods;
Sunset over the sea:
Seed-time and harvest;
The reapers in the corn;
The vinedresser in his vineyard;
The village-girl at her wheel.
Fullness of life and power of feeling, ye
Are for the happy, for the souls at ease,
Who dwell on a firm basis of content.
But he who has outliv'd his prosperous days,
But he, whose youth fell on a different world
From that on which his exil'd age is thrown;
Whose mind was fed on other food, was train'd
By other rules than are in vogue to-day;
Whose habit of thought is fix'd, who will not change,
But in a world he loves not must subsist
In ceaseless opposition, be the guard
Of his own breast, fetter'd to what he guards,
That the world win no mastery over him;
Who has no friend, no fellow left, not one;
Who has no minute's breathing space allow'd
To nurse his dwindling faculty of joy:—
Joy and the outward world must die to him
As they are dead to me.

What freak of criticism can induce a man who has written such poetry as this, to discard it, and say it is not poetry? Mr. Arnold is privileged to speak of his own poems, but no other critic could speak so and not be laughed at.

We are disposed to believe that no very sharp definition can be given—at least in the present state of the critical art—of the boundary line between poetry and other sorts of imaginative delineation. Between the undoubted dominions of the two kinds there is a debatable land; everybody is agreed that the *Œdipus at Colonus, is* poetry: everyone is agreed that the wonderful appearance of Mrs. Veal is *not* poetry. But the exact line which separates grave novels in verse like *Aylmer's Field* or *Enoch Arden*, from grave novels not in verse like *Silas Marner* or *Adam Bede*, we own we cannot draw with any confidence. Nor, perhaps, is it very important; whether a narrative is thrown into verse or not certainly depends in part on the taste of the age, and in part on its mechanical helps. Verse is the only mechanical help to the memory in rude times, and there is little writing till a cheap something is found to write upon, and a cheap something to write with. Poetry—verse at least—is the literature of *all work* in early ages; it is only later ages which write in what *they* think a natural and simple prose. There are other casual influences in the matter too; but they are not material now. We need only say here that poetry, because it has a more marked rhythm than prose, must be more intense in meaning and more concise in style than prose. People expect a "marked rhythm" to imply something worth marking; if it fails to do so they are disappointed. They are displeased at the visible waste of a powerful instrument; they call it "doggerel," and rightly call it, for the metrical expression of full thought and eager feeling—the burst of metre—incident to high imagination, should not be wasted on petty matters which prose does as well,—which it does better— which it suits by its very limpness and weakness, whose small changes it follows more easily, and to whose lowest details it can fully and without effort degrade itself. Verse, too, should be *more concise*, for long continued rhythm tends to jade the mind, just as brief rhythm tends to attract the attention. Poetry should be memorable and emphatic, intense, and *soon over*.

The great divisions of poetry, and of all other literary art, arise from the different modes in which these *types*—these characteristic men, these characteristic feelings—may be variously described. There are three principal modes which we shall attempt to describe —the *pure*, which is sometimes, but not very wisely, called the classical; the *ornate*, which is also unwisely called romantic; and the *grotesque*, which might be called the mediæval. We will describe the nature of these a little. Criticism we know must be brief —not, like poetry, because its charm is too intense to be sustained —but on the contrary, because its interest is too weak to be prolonged; but elementary criticism, if an evil, is a necessary evil; a little while spent among the simple principles of art is the first condition, the absolute pre-requisite, for surely apprehending and wisely judging the complete embodiments and miscellaneous forms of actual literature.

The definition of *pure* literature is that it describes the type in its simplicity; we mean, with the exact amount of accessory circumstance which is necessary to bring it before the mind in finished perfection, and *no more* than that amount. The *type* needs some accessories from its nature—a picturesque landscape does not consist wholly of picturesque features. There is a setting of surroundings—as the Americans would say, of *fixings*—without which the reality is not itself. By a traditional mode of speech, as soon as we see a picture in which a complete effect is produced by detail so rare and so harmonized as to escape us, we say how "classical." The whole which is to be seen appears at once and through the detail, but the detail itself is not seen: we do not think of that which gives us the idea; we are absorbed in the idea itself. Just so in literature the pure art is that which works with the fewest strokes; the fewest, that is, for its purpose, for its aim is to call up and bring home to men an idea, a form, a character, and if that idea be twisted, that form be involved, that character perplexed, many strokes of literary art will be needful. Pure art does not mutilate its object; it represents it as fully as is possible with the slightest effort which is possible; it shrinks from no needful circumstances, as little as it inserts any which are needless. The precise peculiarity is not merely that no incidental circumstance is inserted which does not tell on the main design: no art is fit to be called *art* which permits a stroke to be put in without an object; but that only the minimum of such circumstance is inserted at all. The form is sometimes said to be bare, the accessories are sometimes said to be invisible, because the appendages are so choice that the shape only is perceived.

The English literature undoubtedly contains much impure literature; impure in its style if not in its meaning; but it also contains one great, one nearly perfect, model of the pure style in the literary expression of typical *sentiment;* and one not perfect, but gigantic and close approximation to perfection in the pure delineation of objective character. Wordsworth, perhaps, comes as near to choice purity of style in sentiment as is possible; Milton, with exceptions and conditions to be explained, approaches perfection by the strenuous purity with which he depicts character.

A wit once said, that *"pretty* women had more features than *beautiful* women," and though the expression may be criticized, the meaning is correct. Pretty women seem to have a great number of attractive points, each of which attracts your attention, and each one of which you remember afterwards; yet these points have not *grown together*, their features have not linked themselves into a single inseparable whole. But a beautiful woman is a whole as she is; you no more take her to pieces than a Greek statue; she is not an aggregate of divisible charms, she is a charm in herself. Such ever is the dividing test of pure art; if you catch yourself admiring its details, it is defective; you ought to think of it as a single whole which you must remember, which you must admire, which somehow subdues you while you admire it, which is a "possession" to you "for ever."

Of course no individual poem embodies this ideal perfectly; of course every human word and phrase has its imperfections, and if we choose an instance to illustrate that ideal, the instance has scarcely a fair chance. By contrasting it with the ideal we suggest its imperfections; by protruding it as an example, we turn on its defectiveness the microscope of criticism. Yet these two sonnets of Wordsworth may be fitly read in this place, not because they are quite without faults, or because they are the very best example of their kind of style; but because they are *luminous* examples; the compactness of the sonnet and the gravity of the sentiment, hedging in the thoughts, restraining the fancy, and helping to maintain a singleness of expression.

THE TROSACHS

There's not a nook within this solemn Pass,
But were an apt Confessional for one
Taught by his summer spent, his autumn gone,
That Life is but a tale of morning grass
Withered at eve. From scenes of art which chase
That thought away, turn, and with watchful eyes
Feed it 'mid Nature's old felicities,
Rocks, rivers, and smooth lakes more clear than glass
Untouched, unbreathed upon. Thrice happy guest,
If from a golden perch of aspen spray
(October's workmanship to rival May)
The pensive warbler of the ruddy breast
That moral sweeten by a heaven-taught lay,
Lulling the year, with all its cares, to rest!

COMPOSED UPON WESTMINSTER BRIDGE, SEPTEMBER 3, 1802

Earth has not anything to show more fair:
Dull would he be of soul who could pass by
A sight so touching in its majesty:
This city now doth, like a garment, wear
The beauty of the morning; silent, bare,
Ships, towers, domes, theatres, and temples lie
Open unto the fields and to the sky;
All bright and glittering in the smokeless air.

Never did sun more beautifully steep
In his first splendor, valley, rock, or hill;
Ne'er saw I, never felt, a calm so deep!
The river glideth at his own sweet will:
Dear God! The very houses seem asleep;
And all that mighty heart is lying still!

Instances of barer style than this may easily be found, instances of colder style—few better instances of purer style. Not a single expression (the invocation in the concluding couplet of the second sonnet perhaps excepted) can be spared, yet not a single expression rivets the attention. If, indeed, we take out the phrase—

The city now doth, like a garment, wear
The beauty of the morning,

and the description of the brilliant yellow of autumn—

October's workmanship to rival May,

they have independent value, but they are not noticed in the sonnet when we read it through; they fall into place there, and being in their place, are not seen. The great subjects of the two sonnets, the religious aspect of beautiful but grave nature—the religious aspect of a city about to awaken and be alive, are the only ideas left in our mind. To Wordsworth has been vouchsafed the last grace of the self-denying artist; you think neither of him nor his style, but you cannot help thinking of—you *must* recall—the exact phrase, the *very* sentiment he wished.

[Here Bagehot digresses to discuss Milton and Shelley.]

We are fortunate in not having to hunt out of past literature an illustrative specimen of the ornate style. Mr. Tennyson has just given one admirable in itself, and most characteristic of the defects and the merits of this style. The story of *Enoch Arden*, as he has enhanced and presented it, is a rich and splendid composite of imagery and illustration. Yet how simple that story is in itself. A sailor who sells fish, breaks his leg, gets dismal, gives up selling fish, goes to sea, is wrecked on a desert island, stays there some years, on his return finds his wife married to a miller, speaks to a landlady on the subject, and dies. Told in the pure and simple, the unadorned and classical style, this story would not have taken three pages, but Mr. Tennyson has been able to make it the principal—the largest tale in his new volume. He has done so only by giving to every event and incident in the volume an accompanying commentary. He tells a great deal about the torrid zone which a rough sailor like Enoch Arden certainly would not have perceived; and he gives to the fishing village, to which all the characters belong, a softness and a fascination which such villages scarcely possess in reality.

The description of the tropical island on which the sailor is thrown, is an absolute model of adorned art:—

> The mountain wooded to the peak, the lawns
> And winding glades high up like ways to Heaven,
> The slender coco's drooping crown of plumes,
> The lightning flash of insect and of bird,
> The lustre of the long convolvuluses
> That coil'd around the stately stems, and ran
> Ev'n to the limit of the land, the glows
> And glories of the broad belt of the world,
> All these he saw; but what he fain had seen
> He could not see, the kindly human face,
> Nor ever hear a kindly voice, but heard
> The myriad shriek of wheeling ocean-fowl,
> The league-long roller thundering on the reef,
> The moving whisper of huge trees that branch'd
> And blossom'd in the zenith, or the sweep
> Of some precipitous rivulet to the wave,
> As down the shore he ranged, or all day long
> Sat often in the seaward-gazing gorge,
> A shipwreck'd sailor, waiting for a sail:
> No sail from day to day, but every day
> The sunrise broken into scarlet shafts
> Among the palms and ferns and precipices;
> The blaze upon the waters to the east;
> The blaze upon his island overhead;
> The blaze upon the waters to the west;
> Then the great stars that globed themselves in Heaven,
> The hollower-bellowing ocean, and again
> The scarlet shafts of sunrise—but no sail.

No expressive circumstance can be added to this description, no enhancing detail suggested. A much less happy instance is the description of Enoch's life before he sailed:—

> While Enoch was abroad on wrathful seas,
> Or often journeying landward; for in truth

Enoch's white horse, and Enoch's ocean spoil
In ocean-smelling osier, and his face,
Rough-redden'd with a thousand winter gales,
Not only to the market-cross were known,
But in the leafy lanes behind the down,
Far as the portal-warding lion-whelp,
And peacock yew-tree of the lonely Hall,
Whose Friday fare was Enoch's ministering.

So much has not often been made of selling fish.

The essence of ornate art is in this manner to accumulate round the typical object, everything which can be said about it, every associated thought that can be connected with it without impairing the essence of the delineation.

The first defect which strikes a student of ornate art—the first which arrests the mere reader of it—is what is called a want of simplicity. Nothing is described as it is, everything has about it an atmosphere of *something else*. The combined and associated thoughts, though they set off and heighten particular ideas and aspects of the central and typical conception, yet complicate it: a simple thing—"a daisy by the river's brim"—is never left by itself, something else is put with it; something not more connected with it than "lion-whelp" and the "peacock yew-tree" are with the "fresh fish for sale" that Enoch carries past them. Even in the highest cases ornate art leaves upon a cultured and delicate taste, the conviction that it is not the highest art, that it is somehow excessive and over-rich, that it is not chaste in itself or chastening to the mind that sees it—that it is in an explained manner unsatisfactory, "a thing in which we feel there is some hidden want!"

That want is a want of "definition." We must all know landscapes, river landscapes especially, which are in the highest sense beautiful, which when we first see them give us a delicate pleasure; which in some—and these the best cases—give even a gentle sense of surprise that such things should be so beautiful, and yet when we come to live in them, to spend even a few hours in them, we seem stifled and oppressed. On the other hand there are people to whom the seashore is a companion, an exhilaration; and not so much for the brawl of the shore as for the *limited* vastness, the finite infinite of the ocean as they see it. Such people often come home braced and nerved, and if they spoke out the truth, would have only to say, "We have seen the horizon line;" if they were let alone indeed, they would gaze on it hour after hour, so great to them is the fascination, so full the sustaining calm, which they gain from that union of form and greatness. To a very inferior extent, but still, perhaps, to an extent which most people understand better, a common arch will have the same effect. A bridge completes a river landscape; if of the old and many-arched sort it regulates by a long series of defined forms the vague outline of wood and river which before had nothing to measure it; if of the new scientific sort it introduces still more strictly a geometrical element; it stiffens the scenery which was before too soft, too delicate, too vegetable. Just such is the effect of pure style in literary art. It calms by conciseness; while the ornate style leaves on the mind a mist of beauty, an excess of fascination, a complication of charm, the pure style leaves behind it the simple, defined, measured idea, as it is, and by itself. That which is chaste chastens; there is a poised energy—a state half thrill, and half tranquillity—which pure art gives, which no other can give; a pleasure justified as well as felt; an ennobled satisfaction at what ought to satisfy us, and must ennoble us.

Ornate art is to pure art what a painted statue is to an unpainted. It is impossible to deny that a touch of color *does* bring out certain parts, does convey certain expressions, does heighten certain features, but it leaves on the work as a whole, a want, as we say, "of something;" a want of that inseparable chasteness which clings to simple sculpture, an impairing predominance of alluring details which impairs our satisfaction with our own satisfaction; which makes us doubt whether a higher being than ourselves will be satisfied even though we are so. In the very same manner, though the *rouge* of ornate literature excites our eye, it also impairs our confidence.

Mr. Arnold has justly observed that this self-justifying, self-*proving* purity of style, is commoner in ancient literature than in modern literature, and also that Shakespeare is not a great or an unmixed example of it. No one can say that he is. His works are full of undergrowth, are full of complexity, are not models of style; except by a miracle nothing in the Elizabethan age could be a model of style; the restraining taste of that age was feebler and more mistaken than that of any other equally great age. Shakespeare's mind so teemed with creation that he required the most just, most forcible, most constant restraint from without. He most needed to be guided of poets, and he was the least and worst guided. As a whole no one can call his works finished models of the pure style, or of any style. But he has many passages of the most pure style, passages which could be easily cited if space served. And we must remember that the task which Shakespeare undertook was the most difficult which any poet has ever attempted, and that it is a task in which after a million efforts every other poet has failed. The Elizabethan drama— as Shakespeare has immortalized it—undertakes to delineate in five acts, under stage restrictions, and in mere dialogue, a whole list of *dramatis personæ*, a set of characters enough for a modern novel, and with the distinctness of a modern novel. Shakespeare is not content to give two or three great characters in solitude and in dignity, like the classical dramatists; he wishes to give a whole *party* of characters in the play of life, and according to the nature of each. He would "hold the mirror up to nature," not to catch a monarch in a tragic posture, but a whole group of characters engaged in many actions, intent on many purposes, thinking many thoughts. There is life enough, there is action enough, in single plays of Shakespeare to set up an ancient dramatist for a long career. And Shakespeare succeeded. His characters, taken *en masse*, and as a whole, are as well known as any novelist's characters; cultivated men know all about them, as young ladies know all about Mr. Trollope's novels. But no other dramatist has succeeded in such an aim. No one else's characters are staple people in English literature, hereditary people whom everyone knows all about in every generation. The contemporary dramatists, Beaumont and Fletcher, Ben Jonson, Marlowe, &c., had many merits; some of them were great men. But a critic must say of them the worst thing he has to say: "they were men who failed in their characteristic aim;" they attempted to describe numerous sets of complicated characters, and they failed. No one of such characters, or hardly one, lives in common memory; the Faustus of Marlowe, a really great idea, is not remembered. They undertook to write what they could not write, five acts full of real characters, and in consequence, the fine individual things they conceived are forgotten by the mixed multitude, and known only to a few of the few. Of the Spanish theatre we cannot speak; but there are no such characters in any French tragedy: the whole aim of that tragedy forbade it. Goethe has added to literature a few great characters; he may be said almost to have added to literature the idea of "intellectual creation,"—the idea of describing the great characters through the intellect; but he has not added to the common stock what Shakespeare added, a new *multitude* of men and women; and these not in simple attitudes, but amid the most complex parts of life, with all their various natures roused, mixed, and strained. The severest art must have allowed many details, much overflowing circumstance to a poet who undertook to describe what almost defies description. Pure art would have *commanded* him to use details lavishly, for only by a multiplicity of such could the required effect have been at all produced. Shakespeare could accomplish it, for his mind was a *spring*, an inexhaustible fountain of human nature, and it is no wonder that being compelled by the task of his time to let the fulness of his nature overflow, he sometimes let it overflow too much, and covered with erroneous conceits and superfluous images characters and conceptions which would have been far more justly, far more effectually, delineated with conciseness and simplicity. But there is an infinity of pure art *in* Shakespeare, although there is a great deal else also.

It will be said, if ornate art be as you say, an inferior species of art, why should it ever be used? If pure art be the best sort of art, why should it not always be used?

The reason is this: literary art, as we just now explained, is concerned with literatesque characters in literatesque situations; and the *best* art is concerned with the *most* literatesque characters in the *most* literatesque situations. Such are the subjects of pure art; it embodies with the fewest touches, and under the most select and choice circumstances, the highest conceptions; but it does not follow that only the best subjects are to be treated by art, and then only in the very best way. Human nature could not endure such a critical commandment as that, and it would be an erroneous criticism which gave it. *Any* literatesque character may be described in literature under *any* circumstances which exhibit its literatesqueness.

The essence of pure art consists in its describing what is as it is, and this is very well for what can bear it, but there are many inferior things which will not bear it, and which nevertheless ought to be described in books. A certain kind of literature deals with illusions, and this kind of literature has given a coloring to the name romantic. A man of rare genius, and even of poetical genius, has gone so far as to make these illusions the true subject of poetry—almost the sole subject. "Without," says Father Newman, of one of his characters, "being himself a poet, he was in the season of poetry, in the sweet springtime, when the year is most beautiful because it is new. Novelty was beauty to a heart so open and cheerful as his; not only because it was novelty, and had its proper charm as such, but because when we first see things, we see them in a gay confusion, which is a principal element of the poetical. As time goes on, and we number and sort and measure things,—as we gain views,—we advance towards philosophy and truth, but we recede from poetry.

"When we ourselves were young, we once on a time walked on a hot summer day from Oxford to Newington,—a dull road, as anyone who has gone it knows; yet it was new to us; and we protest to you, reader, believe it or not, laugh or not, as you will, to us it seemed on that occasion quite touchingly beautiful; and a soft melancholy came over us, of which the shadows fall even now, when we look back upon that dusty, weary journey. And why? because every object which met us was unknown and full of mystery. A tree or two in the distance seemed the beginning of a great wood, or park, stretching endlessly; a hill implied a vale beyond, with that vale's history; the bye-lanes, with their green hedges, wound on and vanished, yet were not lost to the imagination. Such was our first journey; but when we had gone it several times, the mind refused to act, the scene ceased to enchant, stern reality alone remained; and we thought it one of the most tiresome, odious roads we ever had occasion to traverse." That is to say, that the function of the poet is to introduce a "gay confusion," a rich medley which does not exist in the actual world—which perhaps could not exist in any world—but which would seem pretty if it did exist. Everyone who reads *Enoch Arden* will perceive that this notion of all poetry is exactly applicable to this one poem. Whatever be made of Enoch's "Ocean-spoil in ocean-smelling osier," of the "portal-warding lion-whelp, and the peacock yew-tree," everyone knows that in himself Enoch could not have been charming. People who sell fish about the country (and that is what he did, though Mr. Tennyson won't speak out, and wraps it up) never are beautiful. As Enoch was and must be coarse, in itself the poem must depend for a charm on a "gay confusion"—on a splendid accumulation of impossible accessories.

Mr. Tennyson knows this better than many of us—he knows the country world; he has proved it that no one living knows it better; he has painted with pure art—with art which describes what is a race perhaps more refined, more delicate, more conscientious, than the sailor—the *Northern Farmer,* and we all know what a splendid, what a living thing, he has made of it. He could, if he only would, have given us the ideal sailor in like manner—the ideal of the natural sailor we mean—the characteristic present man as he lives and is. But this he has not chosen. He has endeavored to de-

scribe an exceptional sailor, at an exceptionally refined port, performing a graceful act, an act of relinquishment. And with this task
before him, his profound taste taught him that ornate art was a
necessary medium—was the sole effectual instrument—for his purpose. It was necessary for him if possible to abstract the mind from
reality, to induce us *not* to conceive or think of sailors as they are
while we are reading of his sailors, but to think of what a person
who did not know might fancy sailors to be. A casual traveller on
the seashore, with the sensitive mood and the romantic imagination Mr. Newman has described, might fancy, would fancy, a
seafaring village to be like that. Accordingly, Mr. Tennyson has
made it his aim to call off the stress of fancy from real life, to occupy it otherwise, to bury it with pretty accessories; to engage it
on the "peacock yew-tree," and the "portal-warding lion-whelp."
Nothing, too, can be more splendid than the description of the tropics
as Mr. Tennyson delineates them, but a sailor would not have felt
the tropics in that manner. The beauties of nature would not have
so much occupied him. He would have known little of the scarlet
shafts of sunrise and nothing of the long convolvuluses. As in Robinson Crusoe, his own petty contrivances and his small ailments would
have been the principal subject to him. "For three years," he might
have said, "my back was bad, and then I put two pegs into a piece
of drift wood and so made a chair, and after that it pleased God to
send me a chill." In real life his piety would scarcely have gone
beyond that.

It will indeed be said, that though the sailor had no words for,
and even no explicit consciousness of the splendid details of the
torrid zone, yet that he had, notwithstanding, a dim latent inexpressible conception of them: though he could not speak of them
or describe them, yet they were much to him. And doubtless such
is the case. Rude people are impressed by what is beautiful—deeply
impressed—though they could not describe what they see, or what
they feel. But what is absurd in Mr. Tennyson's description—absurd
when we abstract it from the gorgeous additions and ornaments with
which Mr. Tennyson distracts us—is, that his hero feels nothing
else but these great splendors. We hear nothing of the physical
ailments, the rough devices, the low superstitions, which really would
have been the *first* things, the favorite and principal occupations
of his mind. Just so when he gets home he *may* have had such fine
sentiments, though it is odd, and he *may* have spoken of them to
his landlady, though that is odder still,—but it is incredible that

his whole mind should be made up of fine sentiments. Beside those sweet feelings, if he had them, there must have been many more obvious, more prosaic, and some perhaps more healthy. Mr. Tennyson has shown a profound judgment in distracting us as he does. He has given us a classic delineation of the *Northern Farmer* with no ornament at all—as bare a thing as can be—because he then wanted to describe a true type of real men: he has given us a sailor crowded all over with ornament and illustration, because he then wanted to describe an unreal type of fancied men,—not sailors as they are, but sailors as they might be wished.

Another prominent element in *Enoch Arden* is yet more suitable to, yet more requires the aid of, ornate art. Mr. Tennyson undertook to deal with *half belief*. The presentiments which Annie feels are exactly of that sort which everybody has felt, and which everyone has half believed—which hardly anyone has more than half believed. Almost everyone, it has been said, would be angry if anyone else reported that he believed in ghosts; yet hardly anyone, when thinking by himself, wholly disbelieves them. Just so such presentiments as Mr. Tennyson depicts, impress the inner mind so much that the outer mind—the rational understanding—hardly likes to consider them nicely or to discuss them sceptically. For these dubious themes an ornate or complex style is needful. Classical art speaks out what it has to say plainly and simply. Pure style cannot hesitate; it describes in concisest outline what is, as it is. If a poet really believes in presentiments he can speak out in pure style. One who could have been a poet [1]—one of the few in any age of whom one can say certainly that they could have been, and have not been—has spoken thus:—

> When Heaven sends sorrow,
>   Warnings go first,
>   Lest it should burst
>   With stunning might
>   On souls too bright
>   To fear the morrow.
>
> Can science bear us
>   To the hid springs
>   Of human things?
>   Why may not dream,
>   Or thought's day-gleam,
>   Startle, yet cheer us?

[1] Cardinal Newman.

> Are such thoughts fetters,
> While faith disowns
> Dread of earth's tones,
> Recks but Heaven's call,
> And on the wall,
> Reads but Heaven's letters? [1]

But if a poet is not sure whether presentiments are true or not true; if he wishes to leave his readers in doubt; if he wishes an atmosphere of indistinct illusion and of moving shadow, he must use the romantic style, the style of miscellaneous adjunct, the style "which shirks, not meets" your intellect, the style which as you are scrutinizing disappears.

Nor is this all, or even the principal lesson, which *Enoch Arden* may suggest to us, of the use of ornate art. That art is the appropriate art for an *unpleasing type*. Many of the characters of real life, if brought distinctly, prominently, and plainly before the mind, as they really are, if shown in their inner nature, their actual essence, are doubtless very unpleasant. They would be horrid to meet and horrid to think of. We fear it must be owned that Enoch Arden is this kind of person. A dirty sailor who did *not* go home to his wife is not an agreeable being: a varnish must be put on him to make him shine. It is true that he acts rightly; that he is very good. But such is human nature that it finds a little tameness in mere morality. Mere virtue belongs to a charity school-girl, and has a taint of the catechism. All of us feel this, though most of us are too timid, too scrupulous, too anxious about the virtue of others, to speak out. We are ashamed of our nature in this respect, but it is not the less our nature. And if we look deeper into the matter there are many reasons why we should not be ashamed of it. The soul of man, and as we necessarily believe of beings greater than man, has many parts beside its moral part. It has an intellectual part, an artistic part, even a religious part, in which mere morals have no share. In Shakespeare or Goethe, even in Newton or Archimedes, there is much which will not be cut down to the shape of the commandments. They have thoughts, feelings, hopes—immortal thoughts and hopes—which have influenced the life of men, and the souls of men, ever since their age, but which the "whole duty of man," the ethical compendium, does not recognize. Nothing is more unpleasant than a virtuous person with a mean mind. A highly

[1] *Warnings.*

developed moral nature joined to an undeveloped intellectual nature, an undeveloped artistic nature, and a very limited religious nature, is of necessity repulsive. It represents a bit of human nature—a good bit, of course—but a bit only, in disproportionate, unnatural, and revolting prominence; and therefore, unless an artist use delicate care, we are offended. The dismal act of a squalid man needed many condiments to make it pleasant, and therefore Mr. Tennyson was right to mix them subtly and to use them freely.

A mere act of self-denial can indeed scarcely be pleasant upon paper. An heroic struggle with an external adversary, even though it end in a defeat, may easily be made attractive. Human nature likes to see itself look grand, and it looks grand when it is making a brave struggle with foreign foes. But it does not look grand when it is divided against itself. An excellent person striving with temptation is a very admirable being in reality, but he is not a pleasant being in description. We hope he will win and overcome his temptation, but we feel that he would be a more interesting being, a higher being, if he had not felt that temptation so much. The poet must make the struggle great in order to make the self-denial virtuous, and if the struggle be too great, we are apt to feel some mixture of contempt. The internal metaphysics of a divided nature are but an inferior subject for art, and if they are to be made attractive, much else must be combined with them. If the excellence of Hamlet had depended on the ethical qualities of Hamlet, it would not have been the masterpiece of our literature. He acts virtuously of course, and kills the people he ought to kill, but Shakespeare knew that such goodness would not much interest the pit. He made him a handsome prince, and a puzzling meditative character; these secular qualities relieve his moral excellence, and so he becomes "nice." In proportion as an artist has to deal with types essentially imperfect, he must disguise their imperfections; he must accumulate around them as many first-rate accessories as may make his readers forget that they are themselves second-rate. The sudden *millionaires* of the present day hope to disguise their social defects by buying old places, and hiding among aristocratic furniture; just so a great artist who has to deal with characters artistically imperfect will use an ornate style, will fit them into a scene where there is much else to look at.

For these reasons ornate art is within the limits as legitimate as pure art. It does what pure art could not do. The very excellence of pure art confines its employment. Precisely because it gives the best things by themselves and exactly as they are, it fails when it is necessary to describe inferior things among other things, with a list of enhancements and a crowd of accompaniments that in reality do not belong to it. Illusion, half-belief, unpleasant types, imperfect types, are as much the proper sphere of ornate art, as an inferior landscape is the proper sphere for the true efficacy of moonlight. A really great landscape needs sunlight and bears sunlight; but moonlight is an equalizer of beauties; it gives a romantic unreality to what will not stand the bare truth. And just so does romantic art.

There is, however, a third kind of art which differs from these on the point in which they most resemble one another. Ornate art and pure art have this in common, that they paint the types of literature in as good perfection as they can. Ornate art, indeed, uses undue disguises and unreal enhancements; it does not confine itself to the best types; on the contrary it is its office to make the best of imperfect types and lame approximations; but ornate art, as much as pure art, catches its subject in the best light it can, takes the most developed aspect of it which it can find, and throws upon it the most congruous colors it can use. But grotesque art does just the contrary. It takes the type, so to say, *in difficulties*. It gives a representation of it in its minimum development, amid the circumstances least favorable to it, just while it is struggling with obstacles, just where it is encumbered with incongruities. It deals, to use the language of science, not with normal types but with abnormal specimens; to use the language of old philosophy, not with what nature is striving to be, but with what by some lapse she has happened to become.

This art works by contrast. It enables you to see, it makes you see, the perfect type by painting the opposite deviation. It shows you what ought to be by what ought not to be; when complete it reminds you of the perfect image, by showing you the distorted and imperfect image. Of this art we possess in the present generation one prolific master. Mr. Browning is an artist working by incongruity. Possibly hardly one of his most considerable efforts can be found which is not great because of its odd mixture. He puts together things which no one else would have put together, and produces on our minds a result which no one else would have produced, or tried to produce. His admirers may not like all we may have to say of him. But in our way we too are among his admirers. No one ever read him without seeing not only his great ability but his great *mind*. He not only possesses superficial useable talents, but the strong something, the inner secret something which uses them and controls them; he is great, not in mere accomplishments, but in himself. He has applied a hard strong intellect to real life; he has applied the same intellect to the problems of his age. He has striven to know what *is:* he has endeavored not to be cheated by counterfeits, not to be infatuated with illusions. His heart is in what he says. He has battered his brain against his creed till he believes it. He has accomplishments too, the more effective because they are mixed. He is at once a student of mysticism, and a citizen of the world. He brings to the club sofa distinct visions of old creeds, intense images of strange thoughts: he takes to the bookish student tidings of wild Bohemia, and little traces of the *demi-monde*. He puts down what is good for the naughty and what is naughty for the good. Over women his easier writings exercise that imperious power which belongs to the writings of a great man of the world upon such matters. He knows women, and therefore they wish to know him. If we blame many of Browning's efforts, it is in the interest of art, and not from a wish to hurt or degrade him.

If we wanted to illustrate the nature of grotesque art by an exaggerated instance we should have selected a poem which the chance of late publication brings us in this new volume. Mr. Browning has undertaken to describe what may be called *mind in difficulties*— mind set to make out the universe under the worst and hardest circumstances. He takes Caliban, not perhaps exactly Shakespeare's Caliban, but an analogous and worse creature; a strong thinking power, but a nasty creature—a gross animal, uncontrolled and unelevated by any feeling of religion or duty. The delineation of him will show that Mr. Browning does not wish to take undue advantage of his readers by a choice of nice subjects.

> Will sprawl, now that the heat of day is best,
> Flat on his belly in the pit's much mire,
> With elbows wide, fists clenched to prop his chin;
> And, while he kicks both feet in the cool slush,
> And feels about his spine small eft-things course,
> Run in and out each arm, and make him laugh;
> And while above his head a pompion-plant,
> Coating the cave-top as a brow its eye,
> Creeps down to touch and tickle hair and beard,
> And now a flower drops with a bee inside,
> And now a fruit to snap at, catch and crunch:

This pleasant creature proceeds to give his idea of the origin of the Universe, and it is as follows. Caliban speaks in the third person, and is of opinion that the maker of the Universe took to making it on account of his personal discomfort:—

> Setebos, Setebos, and Setebos!
> 'Thinketh, He dwelleth i' the cold o' the moon.
>
> 'Thinketh He made it, with the sun to match,
> But not the stars: the stars came otherwise;
> Only made clouds, winds, meteors, such as that:
> Also this isle, what lives and grows thereon,
> And snaky sea which rounds and ends the same.
>
> 'Thinketh, it came of being ill at ease:
> He hated that He cannot change His cold,
> Nor cure its ache. 'Hath spied an icy fish
> That longed to 'scape the rock-stream where she lived,
> And thaw herself within the lukewarm brine
> O' the lazy sea her stream thrusts far amid,
> A crystal spike 'twixt two warm walls of wave;
> Only she ever sickened, found repulse
> At the other kind of water, not her life
> (Green-dense and dim-delicious, bred o' the sun)
> Flounced back from bliss she was not born to breathe,
> And in her old bounds buried her despair,
> Hating and loving warmth alike: so He.
>
> 'Thinketh, He made thereat the sun, this isle,
> Trees and the fowls here, beast and creeping thing.
> Yon otter, sleek-wet, black, lithe as a leech;
> Yon auk, one fire-eye, in a ball of foam,
> That floats and feeds; a certain badger brown
> He hath watched hunt with that slant white-wedge eye
> By moonlight; and the pie with the long tongue
> That pricks deep into oakwarts for a worm,
> And says a plain word when she finds her prize,
> But will not eat the ants; the ants themselves
> That build a wall of seeds and settled stalks
> About their hole—He made all these and more,
> Made all we see, and us, in spite: how else?

It may seem perhaps to most readers that these lines are very difficult, and that they are unpleasant. And so they are. We quote them to illustrate, not the *success* of grotesque art, but the *nature* of grotesque art. It shows the end at which this species of art aims, and if it fails it is from over-boldness in the choice of a subject by the artist, or from the defects of its execution. A thinking faculty more in difficulties—a great type—an inquisitive, searching intellect under more disagreeable conditions, with worse helps, more likely to find falsehood, less likely to find truth, can scarcely be imagined. Nor is the mere description of the thought at all bad: on the contrary, if we closely examine it, it is very clever. Hardly anyone could have amassed so many ideas at once nasty and suitable. But scarcely any readers—any casual readers—who are not of the sect of Mr. Browning's admirers will be able to examine it enough to appreciate it. From a defect, partly of subject, and partly of style, many of Mr. Browning's works make a demand upon the reader's zeal and sense of duty to which the nature of most readers is unequal. They have on the turf the convenient expression "staying power": some horses can hold on and others cannot. But hardly any reader not of especial and peculiar nature can hold on through such composition. There is not enough of "staying power" in human nature. One of his greatest admirers once owned to us that he seldom or never began a new poem without looking on in advance, and foreseeing with caution what length of intellectual adventure he was about to commence. Whoever will work hard at such poems will find much mind in them: they are a sort of quarry of ideas, but who ever goes there will find these ideas in such a jagged, ugly, useless shape that he can hardly bear them.

We are not judging Mr. Browning simply from a hasty recent production. All poets are liable to misconceptions, and if such a piece as *Caliban upon Setebos* were an isolated error, a venial and particular exception we should have given it no prominence. We have put it forward because it just elucidates both our subject and the characteristics of Mr. Browning. But many other of his best known pieces do so almost equally; what several of his devotees think his best piece is quite enough illustrative for anything we want. It appears that on Holy Cross day at Rome the Jews were obliged to listen to a Christian sermon in the hope of their conversion, though this is, according to Mr. Browning, what they really said when they came away:—

> Fee, faw, fum! bubble and squeak!
> Blessedest Thursday's the fat of the week.
> Rumble and tumble, sleek and rough,

Stinking and savoury, smug and gruff,
Take the church-road, for the bell's due chime
Gives us the summons—'t is sermon-time.

Boh, here's Barnabas! Job, that's you?
Up stumps Solomon—bustling too?
Shame, man! greedy beyond your years
To handsel the bishop's shaving-shears?
Fair play's a jewel! leave friends in the lurch?
Stand on a line ere you start for the church.

Higgledy, piggledy, packed we lie,
Rats in a hamper, swine in a stye,
Wasps in a bottle, frogs in a sieve,
Worms in a carcase, fleas in a sleeve.
Hist! square shoulders, settle your thumbs
And buzz for the bishop—here he comes.[1]

[Here follow ten more stanzas from the poem.]

It is very natural that a poet whose wishes incline, or whose genius conducts him to a grotesque art, should be attracted towards mediæval subjects. There is no age whose legends are so full of grotesque subjects, and no age where real life was so fit to suggest them. Then, more than at any other time, good principles have been under great hardships. The vestiges of ancient civilization, the germs of modern civilization, the little remains of what had been, the small beginnings of what is, were buried under a cumbrous mass of barbarism and cruelty. Good elements hidden in horrid accompaniments are the special theme of grotesque art, and these mediæval life and legends afford more copiously than could have been furnished before Christianity gave its new elements of good, or since modern civilization has removed some few at least of the old elements of destruction. A *buried* life like the spiritual mediæval was Mr. Browning's natural element, and he was right to be attracted by it. His mistake has been, that he has not made it pleasant; that he has forced his art to topics on which no one could charm, or on which he, at any rate, could not; that on these occasions and in these poems he has failed in fascinating men and women of sane taste.

We say "sane" because there is a most formidable and estimable *insane* taste. The will has great though indirect power over the taste, just as it has over the belief. There are some horrid beliefs from

[1] *Holy-Cross Day.*

which human nature revolts, from which at first it shrinks, to which, at first, no effort can force it. But if we fix the mind upon them they have a power over us just because of their natural offensiveness. They are like the sight of human blood: experienced soldiers tell us that at first men are sickened by the smell and newness of blood almost to death and fainting, but that as soon as they harden their hearts and stiffen their minds, as soon as they *will* bear it, then comes an appetite for slaughter, a tendency to gloat on carnage, to love blood, at least for the moment, with a deep eager love. It is a principle that if we put down a healthy instinctive aversion, nature avenges herself by creating an unhealthy insane attraction. For this reason the most earnest truth-seeking men fall into the worst delusions; they will not let their mind alone; they force it towards some ugly thing, which a crotchet of argument, a conceit of intellect recommends, and nature punishes their disregard of her warning by subjection to the holy one, by belief in it. Just so the most industrious critics get the most admiration. They think it unjust to rest in their instinctive natural horror: they overcome it, and angry nature gives them over to ugly poems and marries them to detestable stanzas.

Mr. Browning possibly, and some of the worst of Mr. Browning's admirers certainly, will say that these grotesque objects exist in real life, and therefore they ought to be, at least may be, described in art. But though pleasure is not the end of poetry, pleasing is a condition of poetry. An exceptional monstrosity of horrid ugliness cannot be made pleasing, except it be made to suggest—to recall—the perfection, the beauty, from which it is a deviation. Perhaps in extreme cases no art is equal to this; but then such self-imposed problems should not be worked by the artist; these out-of-the-way and detestable subjects should be let alone by him. It is rather characteristic of Mr. Browning to neglect this rule. He is the most of a realist, and the least of an idealist of any poet we know. He evidently sympathizes with some part at least of Bishop Blougram's apology. Anyhow this world exists. "There *is* good wine—there *are* pretty women—there *are* comfortable benefices—there *is* money, and it is pleasant to spend it. Accept the creed of your age and you get these; reject that creed and you lose them. And for what do you lose them? For a fancy creed of your own, which no one else will accept, which hardly anyone will call a 'creed,' which most people will consider a sort of unbelief." Again, Mr. Browning evidently loves what we may call the realism, the grotesque realism, of orthodox Christianity. Many parts of it in which great divines have felt keen difficulties are quite pleasant to him. He must *see* his religion, he must have an "object-lesson" in believing. He must have a creed that will *take*, which wins and holds the miscellaneous world, which stout men will heed, which nice women will adore. The spare moments of solitary religion—the "obdurate questionings," the high "instincts," the "first affections," the "shadowy recollections,"

> Which, do they what they may,
> Are yet the fountain-light of all our day—
> Are yet a master-light of all our seeing;

the great but vague faith—the unutterable tenets—seem to him worthless, visionary; they are not enough immersed in matter; they move about "in worlds not realized." We wish he could be tried like the prophet once; he would have found God in the earthquake and the storm; he could have deciphered from them a bracing and a rough religion; he would have known that crude men and ignorant women felt them too, and he would accordingly have trusted them; but he would have distrusted and disregarded the "still small voice"; he would have said it was "fancy"—a thing you thought you heard to-day, but were not sure you had heard to-morrow: he would call it a nice illusion, an immaterial prettiness; he would ask triumphantly, "How are you to get the mass of men to heed this little thing?" he would have persevered and insisted, *"My wife does not hear it."*

But although a suspicion of beauty, and a taste for ugly reality, have led Mr. Browning to exaggerate the functions, and to caricature the nature of grotesque art, we own, or rather we maintain, that he has given many excellent specimens of that art within its proper boundaries and limits. Take an example, his picture of what we may call the *bourgeois* nature in *difficulties;* in the utmost difficulty, in contact with magic and the supernatural. He has made of it something homely, comic, true; reminding us of what *bourgeois* nature really is.

[Here Bagehot quotes several passages from *The Pied Piper of Hamelin.*]

Something more we had to say of Mr. Browning, but we must stop. It is singularly characteristic of this age that the poems which rise to the surface, should be examples of ornate art, and grotesque art, not of pure art. We live in the realm of the *half* educated. The number of readers grows daily, but the quality of readers does not improve rapidly. The middle class is scattered, headless; it is well-meaning but aimless; wishing to be wise, but ignorant how to be wise. The aristocracy of England never was a literary aristocracy, never even in the days of its full power—of its unquestioned predominance did it guide—did it even seriously try to guide—the taste of England. Without guidance young men, and tired men are thrown amongst a mass of books; they have to choose which they like; many of them would much like to improve their culture, to chasten their taste, if they knew how. But left to themselves they take, not pure art, but showy art; not that which permanently relieves the eye and makes it happy whenever it looks, and as long as it looks, but *glaring* art which catches and arrests the eyes for a moment, but which in the end fatigues it. But before the wholesome remedy of nature—the fatigue—arrives the hasty reader has passed on to some new excitement, which in its turn stimulates for an instant, and then is passed by for ever. These conditions are not favorable to the due appreciation of pure art—of that art which must be known before it is admired—which must have fastened irrevocably on the brain before you appreciate it—which you must love ere it will seem worthy of your love. Women too, whose voice in literature counts as well as that of men—and in a light literature counts for more than that of men—women, such as we know them, such as they are likely to be, ever prefer a delicate unreality to a true or firm art. A dressy literature, an exaggerated literature, seem to be fated to us. These are our curses, as other times had theirs.

*   *   *   *

Taine

Hippolyte Adolphe TAINE (1828–1893), critic and historian, was born at Vouziers, Ardennes. Graduating from the École Normale, in Paris, he became a teacher, but soon resigned his post to devote himself to literature. In 1864 he was appointed to a professorship in the École des Beaux-Arts, where his lectures on the history of art brought him fame. When the régime of Napoleon III came to an end, he turned his attention to the philosophy of history. His erudite studies of contemporary France alienated all parties, but his history of English literature gained attention abroad. In 1871 he received the degree of D. C. L. from Oxford University, and in 1878 was made a member of the Académie Française. He died in Paris fifteen years later.

Taine is one of a number of writers in the nineteenth century who tried to make of literary criticism a science. He evolved the well-known theory that literature is the product of race, epoch, and surroundings. This doctrine, which has the advantage of being both definite and flexible, has had a marked influence upon the study of history, social and political as well as literary. Taine applied it with happy results in his famous *History of English Literature*. He remains second only to Sainte-Beuve among French critics of his time.

INTRODUCTION TO THE "HISTORY OF ENGLISH LITERATURE" [1]

(1856)

The historian might place himself in the centre of the human soul for a given period, say a series of ages, and with some particular people; he might study, describe, relate, all the events, all the transformations, all the revolutions which had been accomplished in the internal man; and when he had finished his work, he would have a history of the civilization of the people and the period he had selected.—GUIZOT: *Civilization in Europe,* p. 25.

History has been transformed, within a hundred years in Germany, within sixty years in France, and that by the study of their literatures.

It was perceived that a literary work is not a mere individual play of imagination, the isolated caprice of an excited brain, but a transcript of contemporary manners, a manifestation of a certain kind of mind. It was concluded that we might recover, from the monuments of literature, a knowledge of the manner in which men thought and felt centuries ago. The attempt was made, and it succeeded.

Pondering on these modes of feeling and thought, men decided that they were facts of the highest kind. They saw that these facts bore reference to the most important occurrences, that they explained them, and were explained by them, that it was necessary thenceforth to give them a place, and one of the highest places, in history. This they have been given, and from that moment history has undergone a complete change in its subject-matter, its system, its machinery, its appreciation of laws and of causes. It is this change, such as it is and must be, that we shall here endeavor to explain.

I

On turning over the great, stiff leaves of a folio, the yellow sheets of a manuscript—a poem, a code of laws, a creed, what is your first remark? This, you say, did not come into existence all alone. It is but a mould, like a fossil shell, an imprint, like one of those shapes embossed in stone by an animal which has lived and perished. Under

---

[1] This translation by H. van Laun (1873) has been compared with the 1891 (ninth) French edition by John M. Smith.

the shell there was an animal, and, behind the document, there was a man. Why do you study the shell, except to bring before you the animal? So you study the document, only to know the man. The shell and the document are lifeless wrecks, valuable only as a clue to the entire and living existence. We must get hold of this existence, endeavor to reconstruct it. It is a mistake to study the document, as if it were isolated. This were to treat things like a simple scholar, to fall into the error of the bibliomaniac. Neither mythology nor languages exist in themselves; but only men, who arrange words and imagery according to the necessities of their physical being and the original bent of their minds. A dogma is nothing in itself; study the people who have made it,—a portrait, for instance, of the sixteenth century, say the stern, powerful face of an English archbishop or martyr. Nothing exists except through some individual man; it is this individual with whom we must become acquainted. When we have established the filiation of dogmas, or the classification of poems, or the progress of constitutions, or the transformation of idioms, we have only cleared the ground; genuine history is brought into existence only when the historian begins to unravel, across the lapse of time, the living man, toiling, impassioned, entrenched in his customs, with his voice and features, his gestures and his dress, distinct and complete as he from whom we have just parted in the street. Let us endeavor, then, to annihilate as far as possible this great interval of time, which prevents us from seeing man with our eyes, *with the eyes of our head*. What have we under the fair velvety pages of a modern poem?—a modern poet, who has studied and travelled, a man like Alfred de Musset, Victor Hugo, Lamartine, or Heine, in a black coat and gloves, looked upon with favor by the ladies, and making every evening his fifty bows and his score of bon-mots in society, reading the papers in the morning, lodging as a rule on a third floor; not over gay, because he has nerves, and especially because, in this dense democracy where we stifle one another, the discredit of the dignities of office has exaggerated his claims while increasing his importance, and because the keenness of his feelings in general disposes him somewhat to believe himself a deity. This is what we see behind modern *Meditations* or *Sonnets*. In the same way, behind a tragedy of the seventeenth century there is a poet, like Racine for instance, elegant, staid, a courtier, a fine talker, with a majestic wig and beribboned shoes, at heart a royalist and a Christian, who says, "God has been so gracious to me, that in whatever company I find myself I never have occasion to blush for the Gospel or the King"; [1] clever at entertaining the prince, and rendering for him into good French the "old-fashioned dialect of Amyot"; very respectful to the great, always "knowing his place"; as anxious to serve and as reserved at Marly as at Versailles,[2] amidst the regular pleasures of polished and ornate nature, amidst the salutations, graces, airs, and fopperies of the lords in their gold lace, who rose early in the morning to obtain the promise of a *survivance* [3] and amongst charming ladies who count their genealogies on their fingers in order to obtain a *tabouret*.[4] On that head, consult Saint-Simon and the engravings of Pérelle, as recently you have consulted Balzac and the water-colors of Eugène Lami. Similarly, when we read a Greek tragedy, our first care should be to picture to ourselves the Greeks, that is, the men who live half naked, in the gymnasia, or in the public squares, under a glowing sky, surrounded by the finest and the most noble landscapes, bent on making their bodies lithe and strong, on conversing, discussing, voting, carrying on patriotic piracies, yet idle and temperate, with three jugs in their house, two anchovies in a jar of oil for their food, waited on by slaves, so as to give them leisure to cultivate their understanding and exercise their limbs, with no desire beyond that of having the most beautiful town, the most beautiful processions, the most beautiful ideas, the most beautiful men. About these things, a statue such as the Meleager or the Theseus of the Parthenon, or still more, a glimpse of the Mediterranean, blue and lustrous as a silken tunic, from which protrude islands like marble bodies, plus twenty select phrases from Plato and Aristophanes, will teach you much more than a multitude of dissertations and commentaries. And so again, in order to understand an Indian Purāna, begin by imagining to yourself the father of a family, who, "having seen a son on his son's knees," retires, according to the law, into solitude, with an axe and a bowl under a banana tree, by the brook-side, ceases to speak, adds fast to fast, dwells naked between four fires, and under a fifth—that terrible sun, which devours and renews without end all things living; who, for weeks at a time, fixes his imagination first upon the feet of Brahma, next upon his knee, next upon his thigh, next upon his navel, and so on,

---

[1] Mary Wollstonecraft, in her *Historical and Moral View of the French Revolution*, p. 25, says in quoting this passage, "What could be expected from the courtier who could write in these terms to Madame de Maintenon?"—(van Laun.)

[2] Marly, a private residence of the King—Versailles, the Court.

[3] An appointment to some office in case of the death of the present holder.

[4] The right of sitting down in the presence of the King or Queen.

until, beneath the strain of this intense meditation, hallucinations begin to appear, until all the forms of existence, transformed and mingled the one with the other, quiver in his dazzled and giddy brain, until the motionless man, holding his breath, with fixed gaze, beholds the universe vanishing like a smoke in the universal void of Being into which he hopes to be absorbed. To this end, a voyage to India would be the best instructor; or failing that, the accounts of travellers, books of geography, botany, and ethnology, will take its place. In either case, the investigation should be the same. Language, legislation, creeds, are only abstract things: the complete thing is the man who acts, the man corporeal and visible, who eats, walks, fights, labors. Leave aside the theory and the mechanism of constitutions, religions and their systems, and try to see men in their workshops, in their offices, in their fields, with their sky and soil, their houses, their dress, their crops, their meals, as you do, when, landing in England or Italy, you look at faces and gestures, sidewalks and inns, a burgher taking his walk, a workman drinking. Our great care should be to supply as much as possible the lack of actual, personal, and direct observation which we cannot carry on at first hand; for it is our only means of knowing men. Let us make the past present: in order to judge of a thing, it must be before us; there is no experience of what is absent. Doubtless this reconstruction is always incomplete; it can produce only incomplete judgments; but that we cannot help. It is better to have an imperfect knowledge than none at all or a false one; and the only means of acquainting ourselves approximately with the events of olden times, is to *see,* even if faintly, the men of former days.

This is the first step in history; it was made in Europe at the revival of imagination, toward the close of the last century, by Lessing and Walter Scott; a little later in France, by Chateaubriand, Augustin Thierry, Michelet, and others. And now for the second step.

II

When you observe with your eyes the visible man, what do you look for? The invisible man. The words which enter your ears, the gestures, the way he carries his head, the clothes he wears, the visible acts and deeds of every kind, are, as far as you are concerned, merely expressions of what is revealed beneath them; that is, a soul. An inner man is concealed beneath the outer man; and the second but reveals the first. You look at his house, furniture, dress; and that in order to discover in them indications of his habits and tastes, the degree of his refinement or rusticity, his extravagance or his thrift, his stupidity or his acuteness. You listen to his conversation, and you note the inflections of his voice, the changes in his attitudes; in order to judge of his vivacity, his abandon and his gaiety, or his energy or his rigidity. You consider his writings, his artistic productions, his business transactions or political ventures; and that in order to measure the scope and limits of his intelligence, his inventiveness, his self-possession, to find out the order, the character, the general force of his ideas, the manner in which he thinks and resolves. All these externals are but avenues converging towards a centre; and you are concerned only with that centre. The real man is there.—I mean that mass of faculties and feelings which is the product of all these things. We have reached a new world, which is infinite, because every action which we see involves an infinite association of reasonings, emotions, sensations new and old, which has served to force it up to the light, and which, like great rocks deep-seated in the ground, crops out above the surface. The study of this subterranean world is the second phase, the historian's real field of research. If his critical education is sufficient, he can lay bare, under every detail of architecture, every stroke in a picture, every sentence in a writing, the special feeling whence detail, stroke, or sentence had issue; he is present at the drama which was enacted in the soul of artist or writer; the choice of a word, the brevity or length of a sentence, the nature of a metaphor, the accent of a verse, the development of an argument—everything is a symbol to him; while his eyes read the text, his soul and mind pursue the continuous development and the ever-changing succession of emotions and conceptions out of which the text has sprung: in short, he works out its *psychology*. If you would observe this operation, consider the originator and model of all our great contemporary culture, Goethe, who, before writing his *Iphigenia*, employed days in making drawings of the most finished statues, and who at last, his eyes filled with the noble forms of ancient landscape, his mind permeated by the harmonious loveliness of ancient life, succeeded in reproducing so exactly in himself the habits and tendencies of the Greek imagination, that he gives us almost the twin sister of the Antigone of Sophocles, and the goddesses of Phidias. This precise and accurate recapture of vanished sensations has given to history, in our days, a second birth; hardly anything of the sort was known to the preceding century. Men of every race and century were considered all but identical; the Greek, the barbarian, the Hindoo, the man of the Renaissance, and the man of the eighteenth century, as if they had been turned out of a common mould; and all in conformity with a certain abstract conception, which served for the whole human race. Man was known, but not men; one had not penetrated to the soul; one had not seen the infinite diversity and marvellous complexity of souls; one did not know that the moral structure of a people or an age is as particular and distinct as the physical structure of a family of plants or an order of animals. To-day, history, like zoölogy, has found its anatomy; and whatever the branch of history to which we devote ourselves, philology, linguistics, or mythology, it is by these means we must strive to produce new fruit. Among so many writers who, since the time of Herder, Ottfried Müller, and Goethe, have ceaselessly carried on and improved this great method, let the reader consider only two historians and two works: Carlyle's *Cromwell,* and Sainte-Beuve's *Port-Royal:* he will see with what accuracy, precision, exactness, depth of insight, a man may discover a soul beneath its actions and its works; how, behind the old general, in place of a vulgar hypocritical schemer, we recover a man troubled with the cloudy reveries of a melancholic imagination, but with practical instincts and faculties, English to the core, strange and incomprehensible to one who has not studied the climate and the race; how, with some hundred scattered letters and a score of mutilated speeches, we may follow him from his farm and teams, to the general's tent and to the Protector's throne, in his transmutation and development, in his pricks of conscience and his political sagacity, until the machinery of his mind and actions becomes visible, and the inner tragedy, ever changing and renewed, which tortured this great, darkling soul, passes, like one of Shakespeare's, into the soul of the onlooker. He will see (in the other case) how, behind the squabbles of the monastery, or the contumacies of nuns, he may find a great province of human psychology; how fifty personalities, that had been buried under the uniformity of a circumspect narrative, reappear in the light of day, each with its own relief and its countless diversities; how, beneath theological disquisitions and monotonous sermons, we can unearth the beatings of living hearts, the convulsions and apathies of monastic life, the unforeseen reassertions and surging turmoil of nature, the inroads of surrounding worldliness, the intermittent victories of grace, with such a variety of lights and shades, that the most exhaustive description and the most flexible style can hardly gather the inexhaustible harvest, which criticism has caused to spring up in this abandoned field. The same is true elsewhere. Germany, with its genius so pliant, so comprehensive, so prompt at transformation, so well fitted to reproduce the most remote and anomalous states of human thought; England, with its intellect so precise, so well calculated to grapple closely with moral questions, to render them exact with figures, weights and measures, geography, statistics, with Scripture texts and common sense; France, with her Parisian culture, with her drawing-room manners, with her untiring analysis of characters and actions, her irony so ready to point out a weakness, her finesse so practiced in the discrimination of shades of thought;—all have worked the same ground, and we begin to understand that there is no region of history where it is not imperative to till this deeper soil, if we would see a profitable harvest rise among the furrows.

This is the second step; we are in a fair way to its completion. It is the outstanding accomplishment of contemporary criticism. No one has worked so well, so splendidly as Sainte-Beuve: in this respect, we are all his pupils; his method is revolutionizing, to-day, in books, and even in newspapers, every kind of literary, of philosophical and religious criticism. From it we must set out in order to begin the further development. I have more than once endeavored to indicate this development; there is here, in my opinion, a new path open to history, and I will try to describe it more in detail.

III

When you have observed and noted in a man one, two, three, then a multitude of sentiments, does this suffice, and does your knowledge appear complete? Is psychology only a series of observations? No; here as elsewhere we must search out the causes after we have collected the facts. No matter whether the facts be physical or moral, they always have their causes; there is a cause for ambition, for courage, for veracity, as there is for digestion, for muscular movement, for animal heat. Vice and virtue are products, like vitriol and sugar; and every complex condition arises from other more simple conditions upon which it depends. Let us then seek the simple condition for moral qualities, as we seek them for physical qualities; and let us take the first fact that presents itself: for example, religious music, that of a Protestant Church. There is an inner cause which has turned the minds of the faithful toward these grave and monotonous melodies, a cause broader than its effect; I mean the general idea of the true, external worship which man owes to God. It is this which has modelled the architecture of Protestant places of worship, thrown down the statues, removed the pictures, destroyed the ornaments, curtailed the ceremonies, shut up the worshippers in high pews which prevent them from seeing anything, and regulated the thousand details of decoration, posture, and general externals. This again comes from another more general cause, the idea of human conduct in all its comprehensiveness, internal and external, prayers, demeanor, duties of every kind which man owes to God; it is this which has enthroned the doctrine of grace, lowered the status of the clergy, transformed the sacraments, suppressed various practices, and changed a disciplinary religion into a moral religion. This second idea, in its turn, depends upon a third still more general, that of moral perfection, such as is met with in the perfect God, the unerring judge, the stern watcher of souls, before whom every soul is sinful, worthy of punishment, incapable of righteousness or salvation, except through the sting of conscience which He inflicts, and the renewal of heart which He produces. That is the master idea, which consists in setting up duty as the absolute king of human life, and in prostrating all ideal models before a moral model. Here we touch the depth of man's being; for to explain this conception it is necessary to consider the race itself, the German and Northman, the structure of his character and mind, his general processes of thought and feeling, the sluggishness and coldness of sensation which prevent his falling easily and headlong under the sway of the pleasures of the senses, the coarseness of his taste, the unpredictable acrobatics in the formation of ideas, which arrest in him the birth of order and harmony of form, the disdain of appearances, the need of truth, the attachment to bare and abstract ideas, which develop in him conscience, at the expense of all else. There our search is at an end; we have come upon some primitive disposition, a trait characteristic of all the sensations, and all the conceptions of a century or a race, a special feature inseparable from all the working of its mind and heart. Here lie the great causes, for they are the universal and permanent causes, present at every moment and in every case, everywhere and always in action, indestructible, and in the end infallibly supreme, since the accidents with which they meet, being limited and partial, end by yielding to the dull and incessant repetition of their efforts; so that the general structure of things, and the chief features of events, are their work; and religions, philoso-

phies, poetries, industries, forms of society and of family, are in fact
only the imprints stamped by their seal.

IV

There is, then, a system in human sentiments and ideas: and this
system has for its motive power certain general traits, certain characteristics of the intellect and the heart common to men of one race,
age, or country. As in mineralogy the crystals, however diverse,
spring from certain simple physical forms, so in history, civilizations,
however diverse, are derived from certain simple spiritual forms. The
former are explained by a primitive geometrical element, as the
others are by a primitive psychological element. In order to master
the classification of mineralogical species, we must first consider a
regular and general solid, its sides and angles, and observe in this
the countless transformations of which it is capable. Likewise, if you
would understand the system of historical varieties, consider first a
human soul generally, with its two or three fundamental faculties,
and in this compendium you will perceive the principal forms which
it can present. After all, this kind of ideal picture, geometrical as
well as psychological, is not very complex, and we fairly speedily
see the limits of the frame in which civilizations, like crystals, are
constrained to exist.

What is really the mental structure of man? Images or *representations* of things, which float within him, exist for a time, are effaced,
and return again, after he has been looking upon a tree, an animal,
any visible object. This is the material of which the rest is made, the
development whereof is twofold, either speculative or practical, according as the representations resolve themselves into a *general conception* or an *active resolution*. Here we have an abridgment of the
whole of man; and in these narrow limits, human diversities meet,
sometimes in the bosom of the primordial matter, sometimes in the
twofold primordial development. However minute in their elements,
they are enormous in the aggregate, and the least alteration in the
factors produces vast alterations in the results. According as the
representation is clear and, as it were, punched out, or confused and
faintly defined, according as it embraces a great or small number of
the characteristics of the object, according as it is violent and accompanied by impulses, or quiet and surrounded by calm, all the
operations and processes of the human machine are transformed. So,
again, according as the subsequent development of the representation

varies, the whole human development varies. If the general conception in which it results is a mere dry notation (in the Chinese fashion), language becomes a sort of algebra, religion and poetry dwindle, philosophy is reduced to a kind of moral and practical common sense, science to a collection of utilitarian formulas, classifications, mnemonics, and the whole mind takes a positivist bent. If, on the contrary, the general conception in which the representation ends, is a poetical and figurative creation, a living symbol, as among the Aryan races, language becomes a sort of delicately-shaded and colored epic poem, in which every word is an actor, poetry and religion assume a magnificent and inexhaustible amplitude, metaphysics is widely and subtly developed, without regard to positive applications; the whole mind in spite of the inevitable deviations and shortcomings of its effort, is smitten with the beautiful and the sublime, and conceives an ideal capable by its nobleness and its harmony of rallying round it the devotion and enthusiasm of the human race. If, again, the general conception in which the representation results is poetical but not kept in hand; if man arrives at it not by an uninterrupted gradation, but by a quick intuition; if the original operation is not a regular development, but a violent explosion,—then, as with the Semitic races, metaphysics is absent, religion conceives God only as a king, solitary and devouring, science cannot grow, the mind is too rigid and unbending to reproduce the delicate operations of nature, poetry can give birth only to vehement and grandiose exclamations, language cannot unfold the web of argument and of eloquence, man is reduced to a lyric enthusiasm, an uncheckable passion, a fanatical and shallow action. In this interval between the particular representation and the universal conception are found the germs of the greatest human differences. Some races, such as the classical, pass from the first to the second by a graduated scale of ideas, regularly arranged, and progressively more general; others, such as the Germanic, traverse the same ground by leaps, without uniformity, after vague and prolonged groping. Some, like the Romans and English, stop on the first rungs; others, like the Hindoos and Germans, mount to the last. If, again, after considering the passage from the representation to the idea, we consider that from the representation to the resolution, we should find elementary differences of like importance and like order, according as the impression is sharp, as in southern climates, or dull, as in northern; according as it results in action instantly, as among barbarians, or slowly, as in civilized nations; according as it is capable or not of growth, inequality, persistence, and restraint. The whole network of human passions, the chances of peace and public security, the sources of labor and action, spring from thence. The same is true of other primordial differences, the results of which embrace an entire civilization; and we may compare them with those algebraical formulas which, within a narrow limit, contain in advance the whole curve of which they form the law. Not that this law is always active to the very end; occasionally there are perturbing forces; but when such is the case, it is not that the law was false, but that it was not the sole actor. New elements become mingled with the old; great forces from without counteract the primitive. A race emigrates, as did the Aryan, and the change of climate alters in its case the whole economy of its intelligence, and organization of its society. A people is conquered, as was the Saxon nation, and a new political structure imposes on it customs, capacities, and inclinations which it did not have. A nation installs itself in the midst of a conquered people, downtrodden and threatening, as did the ancient Spartans; and the necessity of living like troops in the field violently distorts in a single direction the whole moral and social composition. In each case, the mechanism of human history is the same. We continually find, as the original impulse, some very general disposition of mind and soul, either innate and appended by nature to the race, or acquired and produced by some circumstance acting upon the race. These impulses, once admitted, produce their effect gradually: I mean that after some centuries they bring the nation into a new religious, literary, social, economic condition; a new condition which, combined with their renewed effort, produces another condition, sometimes good, sometimes bad, sometimes slowly, sometimes quickly, and so forth; so that we may regard the whole progress of each distinct civilization as the effect of a permanent force which, at every stage, varies its product by modifying the circumstances of its action.

V

Three different sources contribute to produce this elementary moral state—RACE, SURROUNDINGS, and EPOCH. What we call *the race* are the innate and hereditary dispositions which man brings with him into the world, and which, as a rule, are united with marked differences in the temperament and structure of the body. They vary with various peoples. There are, naturally, different kinds

of men, as of bulls and horses, some brave and intelligent, some timid
and dependent, some capable of superior conceptions and creations,
some reduced to rudimentary ideas and inventions, some more specially fitted to special works, and gifted more richly with particular
instincts, as we meet with species of dogs better favored than others,
—these for racing, those for fighting, those for hunting, these again
for house dogs or shepherds' dogs. We have here a distinct force,—so
distinct, that amidst the vast deviations which the other two motive
forces impose upon it, one can recognize it still; and a race, like the
old Aryans, scattered from the Ganges as far as the Hebrides, settled in every clime, and found in every stage of civilization, transformed by thirty centuries of revolutions, nevertheless manifests in
its languages, religions, literatures, and philosophies, the community
of blood and of spirit which to this day binds its offshoots together.
Different as they are, their parentage is not obliterated; barbarism,
culture, and grafting, differences of sky and soil, fortunes good and
bad, have labored in vain: the main features of the original model
have persisted, and we find again the two or three principal linea-
ments of the primitive stamp underneath the secondary imprints
which time has laid upon them. There is nothing astonishing in this
extraordinary tenacity. Although the vastness of the distance lets
us but half perceive—and dimly lighted—the origin of species,[1] the
events of history sufficiently illumine the events anterior to history,
to explain the almost unshakable solidity of the primordial characteristics. When we meet with them, fifteen, twenty, thirty centuries before our era, in an Aryan, an Egyptian, a Chinese, they
represent the work of a great many ages, perhaps of several myriads
of centuries. For, as soon as an animal begins to exist, it has to
reconcile itself with its surroundings; it breathes and renews itself,
is differently affected according to the variations in air, food, temperature. Different climates and situations bring it different needs, and
consequently a different course of activity; and this, again, a different set of habits; and still again, a different set of aptitudes and
instincts. Man, forced to accommodate himself to circumstances,
acquires a temperament and a character corresponding to them;
both his character, and his temperament, are acquisitions the more
stable, in proportion as the external impression is made upon him
by more numerous repetitions, and is transmitted to his progeny
by a more ancient descent. So that at any moment we may consider

---

[1] Darwin, *The Origin of Species.*—Prosper Lucas, *On Heredity.* (Taine.)

the character of a people as an abridgment of all its preceding actions and sensations; that is, as a quantity and as a weight, not infinite,[1] since everything in nature is finite, but nearly so, and almost impossible to lift, since every moment of an almost infinite past has contributed to increase it, and since, in order to tip the balance, one must place in the opposite pan a still greater number of actions and sensations. Such is the first and richest source of these master-faculties from which historical events take their rise; and one sees at the outset, that if it be powerful, it is because this is no simple spring, but a kind of lake, a deep reservoir wherein other springs have for a multitude of centuries, discharged their several streams.

Having thus outlined the interior structure of a race, we must consider the surroundings in which it exists. For man is not alone in the world; nature surrounds him, and his fellow-men surround him; accidental and secondary tendencies grow over his primitive tendencies, and physical or social circumstances disturb or complete the character committed to their charge. Sometimes climate has had its effect. Though we can follow only obscurely the Aryan peoples from their common fatherland to their final places of settlement, we can yet assert that the profound differences which are manifest between the German races on the one hand, and the Greek and Latin on the other, arise for the most part from the difference between the countries in which they are settled. We find the former in cold moist lands, deep in rugged marshy forests or on the shores of a wild ocean, beset by melancholy or violent sensations, prone to drunkenness and gluttony, bent on a fighting, blood-spilling life; the latter, within the loveliest landscapes, on a bright and pleasant seacoast, enticed to navigation and commerce, exempt from gross cravings of the stomach, inclined from the beginning to social ways, to a settled organization of the state, to feelings and dispositions such as develop the art of oratory, the talent for enjoyment, the invention of science, letters, arts. Sometimes political circumstances have been at work, as in the two Italian civilizations; the first wholly turned to action, conquest, government, legislation, because of its original situation as a city of refuge, as a frontier emporium, as an armed aristocracy, which, by importing and enlisting the foreigner and the vanquished, created two hostile armies, having no escape from its internal discords and its greedy instincts save through systematic warfare; the other, denied unity and great political ambition because of the permanence of the power of its cities, the cosmopolitan position of its

[1] Spinoza, *Ethics*, part iv, axiom. (Taine.)

pope, and the military intervention of neighboring nations, directed by the whole bent of its magnificent and harmonious genius towards the worship of pleasure and beauty. Sometimes social conditions have left their mark, as did Christianity eighteen centuries ago, and Buddhism twenty-five centuries ago, when around the Mediterranean, and in Hindostan, Aryan conquest and organization brought in their wake intolerable oppression, the subjugation of the individual, utter despair, a world accursed, along with the development of metaphysics and myth, so that man in this dungeon of misery, feeling his heart softened, begot abnegation, charity, love, gentleness, humility, the brotherhood of men: in the east, in an idea of universal nothingness, in the west, under the Fatherhood of God. Study the governing instincts and faculties implanted in a race—in short, its frame of mind when it thinks and acts at the present time: you will discover most often the work of some one of these prolonged situations, these surrounding circumstances, persistent and gigantic pressures, brought to bear upon an aggregate of men who, singly and together, from generation to generation, have never ceased to be bent and fashioned by their action; in Spain, a crusade against the Mussulmans which lasted eight centuries and more, until the exhaustion of the nation was completed by the expulsion of the Moors, the spoliation of the Jews, the establishment of the Inquisition, the Catholic wars; in England, a political establishment eight centuries old, which keeps a man erect and respectful, in independence and obedience, and accustoms him to strive unitedly, under the authority of the law; in France, a Latin organization, which, imposed first upon docile barbarians, then shattered in the universal crash, was reformed from within by the latent trend of the national instinct, was developed under hereditary kings, ends in a sort of administrative, centralized, republic where all are equal under dynasties constantly at the mercy of revolution. These are the most efficacious of the observable causes which mould the primitive man; they are to nations what education, profession, class, abode, are to individuals; and they seem to include everything, since they include all external powers which mould human material, and by which the external acts upon the internal.

There is yet a third kind of causes; for, in addition to the forces within and without, there is the result which they have already produced together, and this result itself contributes to produce a new one. Beside the permanent impulse and the given surroundings, there is the acquired momentum. When the national character and surrounding circumstances operate, it is not upon a smooth surface, but upon one on which imprints have already been made. According as one takes this surface at one epoch or another, the imprint is different; and that suffices to make the total effect different. Consider, for instance, two epochs of a literature or art,—French tragedy under Corneille and under Voltaire, the Greek drama under Æschylus and under Euripides, Italian painting under da Vinci and under Guido. Naturally, at either of these two extreme points the general idea has not changed; it is always the same human type which is its subject of representation or painting; the mould of verse, the structure of the drama, the form of body has endured. But among several differences there is this: the one artist is the precursor, the other the successor; the first has no model, the second has; the first sees objects face to face, the second sees them through the first; many details are perfected; simplicity and grandeur of impression have diminished; pleasing and refined forms have increased,—in short, the first work has influenced the second. Thus it is with a people as with a plant; the same sap, under the same temperature, and in the same soil, produces, at different steps of its progressive development, different formations, buds, flowers, fruits, seed-vessels, in such a manner that the one which follows must always be preceded by the former, and must spring up from its death. And if now you consider no longer a brief period, as we have just done, but one which embraces one or more centuries, like the Middle Ages, or our last classic age, the conclusion will be similar. A certain dominant idea has held sway; men, for two, for five hundred years, have taken as their model a certain ideal type of man: in the Middle Ages, the knight and the monk; in our classic age, the courtier, the polished speaker. This creative and universal idea made itself manifest over the whole field of action and thought; and after covering the world with its involuntarily systematic product, it faded, it died away, and lo, a new idea springs up, destined to have a like domination, and to produce as many creations. And here remember that the second depends in part upon the first, and that it is the first which, uniting its effect with those of national genius and surrounding circumstances, is going to impose on each new creation its bent and direction. The great historical currents are formed according to this law, I mean by that the long periods of domination by one intellectual pattern, or a master idea, such as the period of spontaneous creations called the Renaissance, or the period of oratorical models called the Classical Age, or the series of mystical systems called the Alexandrian and Christian

eras, or the series of mythological efflorescences which we meet with
in the infancy of the German, the Indian, and the Greek peoples.
Here, as elsewhere, we have only a mechanical problem; the total effect is a result, depending entirely on the magnitude and direction
of the producing causes. The only difference which separates these
moral problems from physical ones is, that their magnitudes and
directions cannot be appraised or computed in the first as in the second. If a need or a faculty is a quantity, capable of degrees, as is a
pressure or a weight, this quantity is not measurable as is pressure or
weight. We cannot define it in an exact or approximative formula;
we cannot have more, or give more, than a literary impression of
it; we are limited to noting and citing the salient points by which
it is manifested, and which indicate approximately and roughly how
far up it reaches on the measuring-stick. But though the means of
notation are not the same in the moral and physical sciences, yet
as in both the material is the same, equally made up of forces, magnitudes, and directions, we may say that in both the final effect is
produced according to the same rule. It is great or small, as the fundamental forces are great or small and act more or less exactly in
the same direction, according as the distinct effects of race, circumstance, and epoch combine to add the one to the other, or to annul
one another. Thus are explained the long periods of impotence and
the brilliant triumphs which make their appearance irregularly and
without apparent reason in the life of a people; they are caused by
internal concordances or contrarieties. There was such a concordance when in the seventeenth century the sociable character and the
conversational aptitude, innate in France, encountered the drawing-
room manners and the epoch of oratorical analysis; when in the
nineteenth century the profound and pliant genius of Germany encountered the age of philosophical systems and of cosmopolitan criticism. There was such a contrariety when in the seventeenth century
the harsh and lonely English genius tried blunderingly to adopt a
new-born urbanity; when in the sixteenth century the lucid and
prosaic French spirit tried vainly to bring forth a living poetry. That
hidden concordance of creative forces produced the finished *politesse*
and the noble and regular literature of the age of Louis XIV and
Bossuet, the lofty metaphysics and the broad critical sympathy of
the time of Hegel and Goethe. That hidden contrariety of creative
forces produced the imperfect literature, the scandalous comedy, the
abortive drama under Dryden and Wycherley, the feeble Greek im-
portations, the groping elaborate efforts, the petty partial beauties

under Ronsard and the Pléiade. This much we can say with confidence: the unknown creations toward which the current of the centuries conducts us, will be produced and governed by the three primordial forces; that if these forces could be measured and computed, we might deduce from them as from a formula the characteristics of future civilization; and that if, in spite of the evident crudeness of our notations, and the fundamental inexactness of our measurements, we try now to form some idea of our general destiny, it is upon an examination of these forces that we must base our prophecy. For in enumerating them, we complete the circle of active forces; and when we have considered RACE, SURROUNDINGS, and EPOCH, that is to say, the internal force, the external pressure, and the acquired momentum, we have exhausted not only the whole of the actual causes, but also the whole of the possible causes of motion.

VI

It remains for us to examine how these causes, when applied to a nation or an age, produce their results. As a spring, rising in high ground and flowing downwards spreads its waters, according to the contour of the land, and flows from level to level, until it reaches the lowest, so the disposition of mind or soul impressed on a people by race, circumstance, or epoch, spreads in different proportions and by regular descents, down the diverse orders of facts which make up its civilization.[1] If we arrange the map of a country, starting from the watershed, we find that below this common point the slopes form five or six principal basins, then each of these is divided into several secondary basins, and so on, until the whole country with its thousand details is included in the ramifications of this network. So, if we arrange the psychological map of the events and sensations of a human civilization, we find first of all five or six well-defined provinces—religion, art, philosophy, the state, the family, the industries; then in each of these provinces natural sub-divisions, and in each of these, smaller territories, until we arrive at the countless details of life such as may be observed within and around us every day. If now we examine and compare these diverse groups of facts, we find first of all that they are made up of parts, and that all have parts in common. Let us take first the three chief products of human

---

[1] For this scale of coördinate effects, consult Renan, *Langues Sémitiques*, ch. i; Mommsen, *Comparison of the Greek and Roman Civilizations*, third edition, Vol. I, ch. ii; and Tocqueville, *Consequences of Democracy in America*, Vol. III. (Taine.)

intelligence—religion, art, philosophy. What is a philosophy but a conception of nature and its primordial causes, expressed in the form of abstractions and formulas? What is there at the bottom of a religion or of an art but a conception of this same nature and of these same causes in the form of symbols more or less clear, and characters more or less precise; with this difference, that in the first we believe that they exist, in the second we believe that they do not exist? Let the reader consider a few of the great creations of the intelligence in India, Scandinavia, Persia, Rome, Greece, and he will see that, throughout, art is a kind of philosophy made perceptible to the senses, religion a poem believed to be true, philosophy an art and a religion dried up, and reduced to simple ideas. There is, therefore, at the core of each of these three groups, a common element, the conception of the world and its principles; and if they differ among themselves, it is because each combines with the common element, another wholly distinct: now the power to abstract, again the ability to personify and to believe, and finally the talent to personify and not believe. Let us now take the two chief products of human association, the family and the state. What forms the state but a sense of obedience, by which the many unite under the authority of a chief? And what forms the family but a sense of obedience by which wife and children live under the direction of a father and husband? The family is a natural, primitive and restricted state, as the state is an artificial, developed and expanded family; and underneath the differences arising from the number, origin, and condition of its members, we discover in the small group as in the great, a like fundamental disposition of mind which draws them together and unites them. Now suppose that this element acquires from environment, race, or epoch certain special characteristics, it is clear that all the groups into which it enters will be modified proportionately. If the sense of obedience is merely the result of fear,[1] you will find, as in most Oriental states, the brutalities of despotism, prodigality of punishment, exploitation of the subject, servility of manners, insecurity of property, impoverishment of production, the slavery of women, and the customs of the harem. If the sense of obedience has its root in the instinct of order, sociability, and honor, you will find, as in France, a perfect military organization, a fine administrative hierarchy, a lack of public spirit linked with occasional bursts of patriotism, ready docility of the subject combined with revolutionary impatience, the bowing of the courtier along with the independ-

[1] Montesquieu, *Esprit des lois, Principes des trois gouvernements.* (Taine.)

ence of the man of honor, the refined pleasure of conversation and society on the one hand, and the bickering at the family fireside on the other, the equality of husband and wife, the imperfection of the married state under the necessary constraint of the law. If, again, the sense of obedience has its root in the instinct of subordination and the idea of duty, you will find, as among the Germans, security and happiness in the household, a solid basis of domestic life, a tardy and incomplete development of high society, an innate respect for established dignities, a superstitious reverence for the past, the maintenance of social inequalities, natural and habitual regard for the law. So in a race, according as the aptitude for general ideas varies, religion, art, and philosophy will vary. If man is naturally inclined to the broadest universal conceptions, and at the same time apt to disturb them by the nervous tension of his over-sensitive organiza-tion, you will find, as in India, an astonishing abundance of gigantic religious creations, a brilliant flowering of vast, transparent epic poems, a strange tangle of subtle and imaginative philosophies, all so interwoven, and so penetrated with a common essence, as to be instantly recognized, by their breadth, their coloring, and their lack of order, as the products of the same climate and the same intelli-gence. If, on the other hand, a man naturally staid and well bal-anced limits of his own accord the scope of his ideas, in order the better to define their form, you will find, as in Greece, a theology of artists and tale-tellers; distinctive gods, early considered distinct from things, and transformed, almost at the outset, into recognizable characters; the sense of universal unity all but effaced, and barely preserved in the vague notion of Destiny; a philosophy rather closely-woven and delicate than broad and systematic, with shortcomings in higher metaphysics,[1] but incomparable for logic, sophistry, and mor-als; poetry and arts superior for clarity, simplicity, measure, truth, and beauty, to all that have ever been known. If, once more, man, reduced to narrow conceptions, and deprived of all speculative *finesse*, is at once both absorbed and tethered by practical occupa-tions, you will find, as in Rome, rudimentary deities, mere hollow names, serving to designate the trivial details of agriculture, genera-tion, household concerns, marriage-customs, rural life, and therefore a mythology, a philosophy, a poetry, either non-existent or bor-

[1] The Alexandrian philosophy was born through contact with the Orient. The metaphysi-cal views of Aristotle are isolated; moreover, with him as with Plato, they are only an outline. By way of contrast, consider the systematic vigor of Plotinus, Proclus, Schelling, and Hegel, or the wonderful boldness of Brahminical and Buddhistic speculation. (Taine.)

rowed. Here, as everywhere, the law of mutual dependence [1] comes into play. A civilization is a body, and its parts are connected with each other like the parts of an organic body. As in an animal, instincts, teeth, limbs, osseous structure, muscular envelope, are mutually connected, so that a change in one produces a corresponding change in the rest, and just as a clever naturalist can by a process of reasoning reconstruct out of a few fragments almost the whole body, so in a civilization, religion, philosophy, the organization of the family, literature, the arts, make up a system in which every local change induces a general change, so that an experienced historian, studying some particular part of it, can see in advance and can half predict the character of the rest. There is nothing vague in this dependence. The thing in the living body that governs it is, first, its tendency to produce a certain primordial type; then its necessity for organs whereby to provide for its needs and for harmony with itself in order that it may live. The thing that governs it in a civilization, is the presence, in every great human creation, of a productive element, present also in other surrounding creations,—that is, some outstanding, efficient faculty, aptitude, or disposition, which, being possessed of its special character, introduces it with itself into all the operations in which it participates, and, according to its variations, causes the whole product in the making of which it has coöperated, to vary also.

VII

At this point we can obtain a glimpse of the principal features of human transformations, and begin to search for the general laws which regulate, not events only, but classes of events, not a particular religion or literature, but a group of literatures or religions. If, for instance, it were admitted that a religion is a metaphysical poem accompanied by belief; and if furthermore we found that there are certain epochs, races, and circumstances in which belief, the poetical and metaphysical faculty, show themselves with an unwonted vigor; if we noticed that Christianity and Buddhism were produced at periods of lofty philosophical conceptions, and amid such miseries as those which produced the fanatics of the Cévennes; if we recognized, on the other hand, that primitive religions are born at the awakening of human reason, during the richest blossoming of human imagination, during a period of absolute simplicity and credulity; if we con-

---

[1] I have endeavored on several occasions to give expression to this law, notably in the preface to *Essais de Critique et d'Histoire*. (Taine.)

sidered, also, that Mohammedanism appeared with the dawning of poetic prose, and the conception of national unity, amongst a people destitute of science, at a period of sudden intellectual development,— we might then conclude that a religion is born, declines, is reformed and transformed according as circumstances strengthen and combine, more or less closely and energetically, its three generative instincts; and we should understand why it is endemic in India, amidst imaginative, philosophic, eminently fanatic brains; why it blossomed forth so strangely and grandly in the Middle Ages, in a society given to oppression, amid new tongues and literatures; why it rose again with a new character and an heroic enthusiasm, in the sixteenth century amid universal renascence, and during the awakening of the German races; why it breaks out into eccentric sects in the crude American democracy, and under the bureaucratic Russian despotism; why, in short, it is spread, at the present day, over Europe differing in proportion and character, according to the differences of race and civilization. And so for every kind of human production—for literature, music, the fine arts, philosophy, science, the state, industries, and so on. Each of these has for its direct cause a moral disposition, or a combination of moral dispositions: the cause given, they appear; the cause withdrawn, they vanish: the weakness or intensity of the cause measures their weakness or intensity. They are bound up with their causes, as a physical phenomenon with its condition, as the dew with the fall of the surrounding temperature, as expansion with heat. There are couples in the moral as in the physical world, just as rigorously bound together, and as universally extended in the one as in the other. Whatever in the one couple produces, alters, or suppresses the first term, produces, alters, or suppresses the second as a necessary consequence. Whatever lowers the surrounding temperature, causes the dew to be deposited. Whatever develops credulity side by side with a poetical conception of the world, engenders religion. Thus phenomena have been produced; thus they will be produced. As soon as we know the sufficient and necessary condition of one of these vast occurrences, our understanding grasps the future as well as the past. We can say with confidence in what circumstances it will reappear, foretell without presumption many chapters of its future history, and sketch cautiously some aspects of its subsequent development.

VIII

History now attempts, or rather is very near attempting, this method of research. The question now proposed is this: Given a liter-

ature, a philosophy, a society, an art, a group of arts, what is the
moral condition which produced it? what are conditions of race,
epoch, circumstance, most fitted to produce this moral condition?
There is a distinct moral condition for each of these fields and for
each of their branches; one for art in general, one for each kind of
art—for architecture, painting, sculpture, music, poetry; each has
its special germ in the wide field of human psychology; each has its
law, and it is by virtue of this law that we see it rise, apparently by
chance, quite alone, amid the miscarriage of its neighbors, like painting in Flanders and Holland in the seventeenth century, poetry in
England in the sixteenth, music in Germany in the eighteenth. At
that time, and in those countries, the conditions were ripe for one art,
not for others, and only one branch budded amid the general barrenness. History must search nowadays for these rules of human growth;
it must busy itself with the special psychology of each special field;
it must now endeavor to compose the finished picture of these characteristic conditions. No task is more delicate or more difficult; Montesquieu tried it, but in his time history was too new to admit of his
success; no one had yet even a suspicion of the road to be travelled,
and even now we are just beginning to catch sight of it. Just as
basically astronomy is a mechanical problem and physiology a chemical problem, so history is fundamentally *a psychological problem*.
There is a particular system of inner impressions and operations
which makes an artist, a believer, a musician, a painter, a man in a
nomadic or social state; and of each the filiation, the intensity, the
dependence of ideas and emotions, are different: each has his moral
history and his special structure, with some governing disposition
and some dominant feature. To explain each, it would be necessary
to write a chapter of intimate analysis, and as yet such a method has
been but roughly sketched. One man alone, Stendhal, with a peculiar
kind of mind and education, has undertaken it, and to this day the
majority of readers find his books paradoxical and obscure: his talent and his ideas were premature; his admirable divinations were not
understood, any more than his profound words casually spoken, or
the astonishing precision of his observations and of his logic. It was
not perceived that, under the exterior of a *causeur* and a man of
the world, he explained the most complicated internal mechanisms;
that he laid his finger on the great natural forces; that he introduced
into the history of the heart scientific processes, the art of notation,
decomposition, deduction; that he first marked the fundamental
causes, that is nationality, climate, temperament; in short, that he

treated feelings and emotions as they should be treated,—in the manner of the naturalist, and of the physicist, by classifying and weighing forces. For this very reason he was considered dry and eccentric: he remained solitary, writing novels, travels, notes, for which he sought and obtained a score of readers. And yet it is in his books that one will find even now the best attempts to open the road which I have endeavored to describe. No one has better taught us how to open our eyes and to look at, first, the men about us and the life around us, and then, the ancient and authentic documents, to read beyond the black and white of the pages, to recognize beneath the old print, under the scribbling of texts, the precise sentiment, the movement of ideas, the state of mind of the author when they were written. In his writings, in Sainte-Beuve, in the German critics, the reader will see all the wealth that may be drawn from a literary work: when the work is rich, and we know how to interpret it, we find there the psychology of a soul, frequently of an age, now and then of a race. In this respect, a great poem, a fine novel, the confessions of a superior man, are more instructive than a heap of historians with their histories. I would give fifty volumes of charters and a hundred volumes of state papers for the memoirs of Cellini, the epistles of St. Paul, the table-talk of Luther, or the comedies of Aristophanes. The importance of literary works lies in the fact that they are instructive because they are beautiful; their utility grows with their perfection; and if they furnish documents it is because they are monuments. The more a book makes sentiments visible, the more it is a work of literature; for the proper office of literature is to record sentiments. The more a book records important sentiments, the higher is its place in literature; for it is by representing the way of life of a whole nation and a whole age, that a writer rallies round him the sympathies of an entire age and an entire nation. This is why, of all the documents which set before our eyes the sentiments of preceding generations, a literature, and notably a great literature, is incomparably the best. It resembles those admirable apparatus of extraordinary sensitivity, by which physicists disentangle and measure the most hidden and delicate changes of a body. Constitutions, religions, do not approach it in importance; the articles of a code and of a creed only show us the spirit roughly and without delicacy. If there are any documents in which politics and dogma live, they are the eloquent discourses from pulpit and rostrum, memoirs, intimate confessions; and all these belong to literature: so that, literature in addition to its work as such, possesses all the good of non-literary documents. It is then chiefly by the study of literatures that one may construct a moral history, and advance toward the knowledge of the psychological laws upon which events depend.

I intend to write the history of a literature, and to seek in it the psychology of a people: if I have chosen the English nation in particular, it was not without a motive. I had to find a people with a great and complete literature, and this is rare: there are few nations who have, during their whole existence, really thought and written. Among the ancients, Latin literature is insignificant at the outset, then it borrowed and became imitative. Among the moderns, German literature does not exist for nearly two centuries.[1] Italian literature and Spanish literature end at the middle of the seventeenth century. Only ancient Greece, modern France and England offer a complete series of great significant monuments. I have chosen England, because being still living, and subject to direct examination, it may be better studied than a destroyed civilization, of which we retain but the relics, and because, being different from France, it has in the eyes of a Frenchman a more distinct character. Furthermore, there is a peculiarity in this civilization, in that besides its spontaneous development, it presents a forced deviation, it suffered the last and most effective of all conquests, and the three conditions whence it sprung, race, climate, the Norman invasion, may be observed in its monuments with perfect exactness; so that we may examine in this history the two most powerful moving forces of human transformation, natural bent and constraining force, and we may examine them without uncertainty or gap, in a series of authentic and unmutilated monuments.

I have endeavored to define these primitive impulses, to show their gradual effects, to explain how they finally brought to light great political, religious, and literary works, and developed the interior mechanism whereby the Saxon barbarian has been transformed into the Englishman of to-day.

[1] From 1550 to 1750. (Taine.)

Tolstóy

Count Leo Nikolayevich Tolstóy (1828–1910), novelist and moralist, was born at Yasnaya Polyana, in the province of Tula. He studied languages and law at the University of Kazan, and served in the army, taking part in the defence of Sebastopol during the Crimean War. He began his literary work at this time, with vivid descriptions of the Crimean campaign. When peace came, he left the army, and went to St. Petersburg, where he made the acquaintance of many distinguished Russian writers. In 1857 he took his first foreign journey, returning to live a simple life on his estate, where he interested himself in the condition of the peasantry and continued to write. In 1862 he married the daughter of a Moscow physician, and in the following years produced his best-known works, among them *War and Peace* (1865–68), *Anna Karenina* (1877), and *Resurrection* (1900). His characteristic views of religion led to his excommunication, in 1901, by the Russian Church. Thereafter his writings express his social and religious ideas, which he put into practice by giving up wealth and privileges to live a life of labor and service.

Tolstóy, a consummate artist, represents in his later life and in his writings, the eternal struggle that existed for Plato, Boethius, the Church Fathers, the Puritans, as to whether art should produce beauty and give pleasure only, or strive to bring about a brotherhood among men. He believed that an artist should produce in his particular medium an experience that could be felt and understood by every one.

From WHAT IS ART? [1]

(1898)

CHAPTER IV

Definitions of art founded on beauty. Taste not definable. A clear definition needed to enable us to recognize works of art.

To what do these definitions of beauty amount? Not reckoning the thoroughly inaccurate definitions of beauty which fail to cover the conception of art, and suppose beauty to consist either in utility, or in adjustment to a purpose, or in symmetry, or in order, or in proportion, or in smoothness, or in harmony of the parts, or in unity amid variety, or in various combinations of these,—not reckoning these unsatisfactory attempts at objective definition, all the æsthetic definitions of beauty lead to two fundamental conceptions. The first is that beauty is something having an independent existence (existing in itself), that it is one of the manifestations of the absolutely Perfect, of the Idea, of the Spirit, of Will, or of Good; the other is that beauty is a kind of pleasure received by us not having personal advantage for its object.

The first of these definitions was accepted by Fichte, Schelling, Hegel, Schopenhauer, and the philosophizing Frenchmen: Cousin, Jouffroy, Ravaisson, and others, not to enumerate the second-rate æsthetic philosophers. And this same objective-mystical definition of beauty is held by a majority of educated people of our day. It is a conception very widely spread especially among the elder generation.

The second view, that beauty is a certain kind of pleasure received by us not having personal advantage for its aim, finds favor chiefly among the English æsthetic writers and is shared by the other part of our society, principally by the younger generation.

So there are (and it could not be otherwise) only two definitions of beauty: the one objective, mystical, merging this conception into that of the highest perfection, God—a fantastic definition, founded on nothing; the other on the contrary a very simple, and intelligible, subjective one, which considers beauty to be that which pleases (I do not add to the word *pleases* the words "without the aim of advantage," because "pleases" naturally presupposes the absence of the idea of profit).

[1] Translated by Aylmer Maude, with Tolstóy's co-operation, for the Tolstóy Society, (Oxford and London, 1929).

On the one hand beauty is viewed as something mystical and very elevated, but unfortunately at the same time very indefinite, and consequently embracing philosophy, religion, and life itself (as in the theories of Schelling and Hegel and their German and French followers); or on the other hand (as necessarily follows from the definition of Kant and his adherents), beauty is simply a certain kind of disinterested pleasure received by us. And this conception of beauty, although it seems very clear, is unfortunately again inexact; for it widens out on the other side, that is, it includes the pleasure derived from drink, from food, from touching a delicate skin, and so forth, as is acknowledged by Guyau, Kralik, and others.

It is true that, following the development of the æsthetic doctrines of beauty, we may notice that though at first (in the times when the foundations of the science of æsthetics were being laid) the metaphysical definition of beauty prevailed, yet the nearer we get to our own times the more does an experimental definition (recently assuming a physiological form) come to the front, so that at last we even meet with æstheticians such as Véron and Sully, who try to escape entirely from the conception of beauty. But such æstheticians have very little success, and with the majority of the public as well as of artists and the learned, a conception of beauty is firmly held which agrees with the definitions contained in most of the æsthetic treatises, that is, which regards beauty either as something mystical or metaphysical, or as a special kind of enjoyment.

What then is this conception of beauty, so stubbornly held to by people of our circle and day as furnishing a definition of art?

In its subjective aspect, we call beauty that which supplies us with a particular kind of pleasure.

In its objective aspect, we call beauty something absolutely perfect, and we acknowledge it to be so only because we receive from the manifestation of this absolute perfection a certain kind of pleasure: so that this objective definition is nothing but the subjective conception differently expressed. In reality both conceptions of beauty amount to one and the same thing, namely, the reception by us of a certain kind of pleasure; that is to say, we call "beauty" that which pleases us without evoking in us desire.

Such being the position of affairs it would seem only natural that the science of art should decline to content itself with a definition of art based on beauty (that is, on that which pleases), and should seek a general definition applicable to all artistic productions, by reference to which we might decide whether a certain article belonged to the realm of art or not. But no such definition is supplied, as the reader may see from those summaries of æsthetic theories which I have given, and as he may discover even more clearly from the original æsthetic works if he will be at the pains to read them. All attempts to define absolute beauty in itself—whether as an imitation of nature, or as suitability to its object, or as a correspondence of parts, or as symmetry, or as harmony, or as unity in variety, and so forth—either define nothing at all, or define only some traits of some artistic productions and are far from including all that everybody has always held and still holds to be art.

There is no objective definition of beauty. The existing definitions (both the metaphysical and the experimental) amount only to one and the same subjective definition, which is (strange as it seems to say so), that art is that which makes beauty manifest, and beauty is that which pleases (without exciting desire). Many æstheticians have felt the insufficiency and instability of such a definition, and in order to give it a firm basis have asked themselves why a thing pleases. And they have converted the discussion on beauty into a question of taste, as did Hutcheson, Voltaire, Diderot, and others. But all attempts to define what taste is must lead to nothing, as the reader may see both from the history of æsthetics and experimentally. There is and can be no explanation of why one thing pleases one man and displeases another, or vice versa; so that the whole existing science of æsthetics fails to do what we might expect from it as a mental activity calling itself a science, namely, it does not define the qualities and laws of art, or of the beautiful (if that be the content of art), or the nature of taste (if taste decides the question of art and its merit), and then on the basis of such definitions acknowledge as art those productions which correspond to these laws and reject those which do not come under them. But this science of æsthetics consists in first acknowledging a certain set of productions to be art (because they please us), and then framing such a theory of art as all these productions which please a certain circle of people can be fitted into. There exists an art-canon according to which certain productions favored by our circle are acknowledged as being art,—the works of Phidias, Sophocles, Homer, Titian, Raphael, Bach, Beethoven, Dante, Shakespeare, Goethe, and others,—and the æsthetic laws must be such as to embrace all these productions. In æsthetic literature you will constantly meet with opinions on the merit and importance of art, founded not on any certain laws by which this or that is held to be good or bad, but merely on consideration as to whether this art tallies with the art-canon we have drawn up.

The other day I was reading a far from ill-written book by Folgeldt. Discussing the demand for morality in works of art, the author plainly says that we must not demand morality in art. And in proof of this he advances the fact that, if we admit such a demand, Shakespeare's *Romeo and Juliet* and Goethe's *Wilhelm Meister* would not come within the definition of good art; but since both these books are included in our canon of art, he concludes that the demand is unjust. And therefore it is necessary to find a definition of art which shall fit the works; and instead of a demand for morality Folgeldt postulates as the basis of art a demand for the important (*Bedeutungsvolles*).

All the existing æsthetic standards are built on this plan. Instead of giving a definition of true art and then deciding what is and what is not good art by judging whether a work conforms or does not conform to this definition, a certain class of works which for some reason pleases a certain circle of people is accepted as being art, and a definition of art is then devised to cover all these productions. I recently came upon a remarkable instance of this method in a very good German work, *The History of Art in the Nineteenth Century,* by Muther. Describing the pre-Raphaelites, the Decadents, and the Symbolists (who are already included in the canon of art), he not only does not venture to blame their tendency, but earnestly endeavors to widen his standard so that it may include them all, since they appear to him to represent a legitimate reaction from the excesses of realism. No matter what insanities appear in art, when once they find acceptance among the upper classes of our society a theory is quickly invented to explain and sanction them; just as if there had never been periods in history when certain special circles of people recognized and approved false, deformed, and insensate art which subsequently left no trace and has been utterly forgotten. And to what lengths the insanity and deformity of art may go, especially when as in our days it knows that it is considered infallible, may be seen by what is being done in the art of our circle to-day.

So that the theory of art founded on beauty, expounded by æsthetics and in dim outline professed by the public, is nothing but the setting up as good of that which has pleased and pleases us, that is, pleases a certain class of people.

In order to define any human activity, it is necessary to understand its sense and importance; and in order to do this it is primarily necessary to examine that activity in itself, in its dependence on its causes and in connection with its effects, and not merely in relation to the pleasure we can get from it.

If we say that the aim of any activity is merely our pleasure and define it solely by that pleasure, our definition will evidently be a false one. But this is precisely what has occurred in the efforts to define art. Now if we consider the food question it will not occur to any one to affirm that the importance of food consists in the pleasure we receive when eating it. Everybody understands that the satisfaction of our taste cannot serve as a basis for our definition of the merits of food, and that we have therefore no right to pre-suppose that dinners with cayenne pepper, Limburg cheese, alcohol, and so on, to which we are accustomed and which please us, form the very best human food.

In the same way beauty, or that which pleases us, can in no sense serve as a basis for the definition of art; nor can a series of objects which afford us pleasure serve as the model of what art should be.

To see the aim and purpose of art in the pleasure we get from it, is like assuming (as is done by people of the lowest moral development, for instance by savages) that the purpose and aim of food is the pleasure derived when consuming it.

Just as people who conceive the aim and purpose of food to be pleasure cannot recognize the real meaning of eating, so people who consider the aim of art to be pleasure cannot realize its true meaning and purpose, because they attribute to an activity the meaning of which lies in its connection with the other phenomena of life, the false and exceptional aim of pleasure. People come to understand that the meaning of eating lies in the nourishment of the body, only when they cease to consider that the object of that activity is pleasure. And it is the same with regard to art. People will come to understand the meaning of art only when they cease to consider that the aim of that activity is beauty, that is to say, pleasure. The acknowledgement of beauty (that is, of a certain kind of pleasure received from art) as being the aim of art, not only fails to assist us in finding a definition of what art is, but on the contrary by transferring the question into a region quite foreign to art (into metaphysical, psychological, physiological, and even historical, discussions as to why such a production pleases one person and such another displeases or pleases some one else), it renders such definition impossible. And since discussions as to why one man likes pears and another prefers meat do not help towards finding a definition of what is essential in nourishment, so the solution of questions of taste in art (to which the discussions on art involuntarily come) not only does not help to make clear in what this particular human activity which we call art really consists, but renders such elucidation quite impossible until we rid ourselves of a conception which justifies every kind of art at the cost of confusing the whole matter.

To the question, What is this art to which is offered up the labor of millions, the very lives of men, and even morality itself? we have extracted replies from the existing æsthetics which all amount to this: that the aim of art is beauty, that beauty is recognized by the enjoyment it gives, and that artistic enjoyment is a good and important thing, because it *is* enjoyment. In a word, that enjoyment is good because it is enjoyment. Thus what is considered the definition of art is no definition at all, but only a shuffle to justify existing art. Therefore, however strange it may seem to say so, in spite of the mountains of books written about art, no exact definition of art has been constructed. And the reason of this is that the conception of art has been based on the conception of beauty.

CHAPTER V

Definitions of art not founded on beauty. Tolstóy's definition. The extent and necessity of art. How people in the past distinguished good from bad in art.

What is art if we put aside the conception of beauty, which confuses the whole matter? The latest and most comprehensible definitions of art, apart from the conception of beauty, are the following:—(1) *a,* Art is an activity arising even in the animal kingdom, and springing from sexual desire and the propensity to play (Schiller, Darwin, Spencer), and *b,* accompanied by a pleasurable excitement of the nervous system (Grant Allen). This is the physiological-evolutionary definition. (2) Art is the external manifestation, by means of lines, colors, movements, sounds, or words, of emotions felt by man (Véron). This is the experimental definition. According to the very latest definition (Sully), (3) Art is "the production of some permanent object or passing action which is fitted not only to supply an active enjoyment to the producer, but to convey a pleasurable impression to a number of spectators or listeners, quite apart from any personal advantage to be derived from it."

Notwithstanding the superiority of these definitions to the metaphysical definitions which depended on the conception of beauty, they are yet far from exact. The first, the physiological-evolutionary definition (1) *a*, is inexact, because instead of speaking about the artistic activity itself, which is the real matter in hand, it treats of the derivation of art. The modification of it, *b*, based on the physiological effects on the human organism, is inexact because within the limits of such definition many other human activities can be included, as has occurred in the neo-æsthetic theories which reckon as art the preparation of handsome clothes, pleasant scents, and even of victuals.

The experimental definition, (2), which makes art consist in the expression of emotions, is inexact because a man may express his emotions by means of lines, colors, sounds, or words and yet may not act on others by such expression—and then the manifestation of his emotions is not art.

The third definition (that of Sully) is inexact because in the production of objects or actions affording pleasure to the producer and a pleasant emotion to the spectators or hearers apart from personal advantage, may be included the showing of conjuring tricks or gymnastic exercises, and other activities which are not art. And further, many things the production of which does not afford pleasure to the producer and the sensation received from which is unpleasant, such as gloomy, heart-rending scenes in a poetic description or a play, may nevertheless be undoubted works of art.

The inaccuracy of all these definitions arises from the fact that in them all (as also in the metaphysical definitions) the object considered is the pleasure art may give, and not the purpose it may serve in the life of man and of humanity.

In order to define art correctly it is necessary first of all to cease to consider it as a means to pleasure, and to consider it as one of the conditions of human life. Viewing it in this way we cannot fail to observe that art is one of the means of intercourse between man and man.

Every work of art causes the receiver to enter into a certain kind of relationship both with him who produced or is producing the art, and with all those who, simultaneously, previously, or subsequently, receive the same artistic impression.

Speech transmitting the thoughts and experiences of men serves as a means of union among them, and art serves a similar purpose. The peculiarity of this latter means of intercourse, distinguishing it from intercourse by means of words, consists in this, that whereas by words a man transmits his thoughts to another, by art he transmits his feelings.

The activity of art is based on the fact that a man receiving through his sense of hearing or sight another man's expression of feeling, is capable of experiencing the emotion which moved the man who expressed it. To take the simplest example: one man laughs, and another who hears becomes merry, or a man weeps, and another who hears feels sorrow. A man is excited or irritated, and another man seeing him is brought to a similar state of mind. By his movements or by the sounds of his voice a man expresses courage and determination or sadness and calmness, and this state of mind passes on to others. A man suffers, manifesting his sufferings by groans and spasms, and this suffering transmits itself to other people; a man expresses his feelings of admiration, devotion, fear, respect, or love, to certain objects, persons, or phenomena, and others are infected by the same feelings of admiration, devotion, fear, respect, or love, to the same objects, persons, or phenomena.

And it is on this capacity of man to receive another man's expression of feeling and to experience those feelings himself, that the activity of art is based.

If a man infects another or others directly, immediately, by his appearance or by the sounds he gives vent to at the very time he experiences the feeling; if he causes another man to yawn when he himself cannot help yawning, or to laugh or cry when he himself is obliged to laugh or cry, or to suffer when he himself is suffering —that does not amount to art.

Art begins when one person with the object of joining another or others to himself in one and the same feeling, expresses that feeling by certain external indications. To take the simplest example: a boy having experienced, let us say, fear on encountering a wolf, relates that encounter, and in order to evoke in others the feeling he has experienced, describes himself, his condition before the encounter, the surroundings, the wood, his own lightheartedness, and then the wolf's appearance, its movements, the distance between himself and the wolf, and so forth. All this, if only the boy when telling the story again experiences the feelings he had lived through, and infects the hearers and compels them to feel what he had experienced—is art. Even if the boy had not seen a wolf but had frequently been afraid of one, and if wishing to evoke in others the fear he had felt, he invented an encounter with a wolf and recounted it so as to make his hearers share the feelings he experienced when he feared the wolf, that also would be art. And just in the same way it is art if a man, having experienced either the fear of suffering or the attraction of enjoyment (whether in reality or in imagination), expresses these feelings on canvas or in marble so that others are infected by them. And it is also art if a man feels, or imagines to himself, feelings of delight, gladness, sorrow, despair, courage, or despondency, and the transition from one to another of these feelings, and expresses them by sounds so that the hearers are infected by them and experience them as they were experienced by the composer.

The feelings with which the artist infects others may be most various—very strong or very weak, very important or very insignificant, very bad or very good: feelings of love of one's country, self-devotion and submission to fate or to God expressed in a drama, raptures of lovers described in a novel, feelings of voluptuousness expressed in a picture, courage expressed in a triumphal march, merriment evoked by a dance, humor evoked by a funny story, the feeling of quietness transmitted by an evening landscape or by a lullaby, or the feeling of admiration evoked by a beautiful arabesque—it is all art.

If only the spectators or auditors are infected by the feelings which the author has felt, it is art.

To evoke in oneself a feeling one has once experienced and having evoked it in oneself then by means of movements, lines, colors, sounds, or forms expressed in words, so to transmit that feeling that others experience the same feeling—this is the activity of art.

Art is a human activity consisting in this, that one man consciously by means of certain external signs, hands on to others feelings he has lived through, and that others are infected by these feelings and also experience them.

Art is not, as the metaphysicians say, the manifestation of some mysterious Idea of beauty or God; it is not, as the æsthetic physiologists say, a game in which man lets off his excess of stored-up energy; it is not the expression of man's emotions by external signs; it is not the production of pleasing objects; and, above all, it is not pleasure; but it is a means of union among men joining them together in the same feelings, and indispensable for the life and progress towards well-being of individuals and of humanity.

As every man, thanks to man's capacity to express thoughts by words, may know all that has been done for him in the realms of thought by all humanity before his day, and can in the present, thanks to this capacity to understand the thoughts of others, become a sharer in their activity and also himself hand on to his contemporaries and descendants the thoughts he has assimilated from others as well as those that have arisen in himself; so, thanks to man's capacity to be infected with the feelings of others by means of art, all that is being lived through by his contemporaries is accessible to him, as well as the feelings experienced by men thousands of years ago, and he has also the possibility of transmitting his own feelings to others.

If people lacked the capacity to receive the thoughts conceived by men who preceded them and to pass on to others their own thoughts, men would be like wild beasts, or like Kasper Hauser.[1]

And if men lacked this other capacity of being infected by art, people might be almost more savage still, and above all more separated from, and more hostile to, one another.

And therefore the activity of art is a most important one, as important as the activity of speech itself and as generally diffused.

As speech does not act on us only in sermons, orations, or books, but in all those remarks by which we interchange thoughts and experiences with one another, so also art in the wide sense of the word permeates our whole life, but it is only to some of its manifestations that we apply the term in the limited sense of the word.

We are accustomed to understand art to be only what we hear and see in theatres, concerts, and exhibitions; together with buildings, statues, poems, and novels. . . . But all this is but the smallest part of the art by which we communicate with one another in life. All human life is filled with works of art of every kind—from cradle-song, jest, mimicry, the ornamentation of houses, dress, and utensils, to church services, buildings, monuments, and triumphal processions. It is all artistic activity. So that by art, in the limited

[1] "The foundling of Nuremberg," found in the market-place of that town on 23rd May 1828, apparently some sixteen years old. He spoke little and was almost totally ignorant even of common objects. He subsequently explained that he had been brought up in confinement underground and visited by only one man, whom he saw but seldom. (Translator's note.)

sense of the word, we do not mean all human activity transmitting feelings but only that part which we for some reason select from it and to which we attach special importance.

This special importance has always been given by men to that part of this activity which transmits feelings flowing from their religious perception, and this small part they have specifically called art, attaching to it the full meaning of the word.

That was how men of old—Socrates, Plato, and Aristotle—looked on art. Thus did the Hebrew prophets and the ancient Christians regard art. Thus it was, and still is, understood by the Mohammedans, and thus it still is understood by religious folk among our own peasantry.

Some teachers of mankind—such as Plato in his *Republic,* and people like the primitive Christians, the strict Mohammedans, and the Buddhists—have gone so far as to repudiate all art.

People viewing art in this way (in contradiction to the prevalent view of to-day which regards any art as good if only it affords pleasure) held and hold that art (as contrasted with speech, which need not be listened to) is so highly dangerous in its power to infect people against their wills, that mankind will lose far less by banishing all art than by tolerating each and every art.

Evidently such people were wrong in repudiating all art, for they denied what cannot be denied—one of the indispensable means of communication without which mankind could not exist. But not less wrong are the people of civilized European society of our class and day in favoring any art if it but serves beauty, that is, gives people pleasure.

Formerly people feared lest among works of art there might chance to be some causing corruption, and they prohibited art altogether. Now they only fear lest they should be deprived of any enjoyment art can afford, and they patronize any art. And I think the last error is much grosser than the first and that its consequences are far more harmful.

CHAPTER XV

THE QUALITY OF ART (WHICH DEPENDS ON ITS FORM) CONSIDERED APART FROM ITS SUBJECT-MATTER—The sign of art: infectiousness. Art is incomprehensible to those whose taste is perverted. Conditions of infection: Individuality, Clearness, and Sincerity of the feeling conveyed.

Art in our society has become so perverted that not only has bad art come to be considered good, but even the very perception of what art really is has been lost. In order to be able to speak about the art of our society it is, therefore, first of all necessary to distinguish art from counterfeit art.

There is one indubitable sign distinguishing real art from its counterfeit—namely, the infectiousness of art. If a man without exercising effort and without altering his standpoint, on reading, hearing, or seeing another man's work experiences a mental condition which unites him with that man and with others who are also affected by that work, then the object evoking that condition is a work of art. And however poetic, realistic, striking, or interesting, a work may be, it is not a work of art if it does not evoke that feeling (quite distinct from all other feelings) of joy and of spiritual union with another (the author) and with others (those who are also infected by it).

It is true that this indication is an *internal* one and that there are people who, having forgotten what the action of real art is, expect something else from art (in our society the great majority are in this state), and that therefore such people may mistake for this æsthetic feeling the feeling of diversion and a certain excitement which they receive from counterfeits of art. But though it is impossible to undeceive these people just as it may be impossible to convince a man suffering from color-blindness that green is not red, yet for all that, this indication remains perfectly definite to those whose feeling for art is neither perverted nor atrophied, and it clearly distinguishes the feeling produced by art from all other feelings.

The chief peculiarity of this feeling is that the recipient of a truly artistic impression is so united to the artist that he feels as if the work were his own and not some one else's—as if what it expresses were just what he had long been wishing to express. A real work of art destroys in the consciousness of the recipient the separation between himself and the artist, and not that alone, but also between himself and all whose minds receive this work of art. In this freeing of our personality from its separation and isolation, in this uniting of it with others, lies the chief characteristic and the great attractive force of art.

If a man is infected by the author's condition of soul, if he feels this emotion and this union with others, then the object which has effected this is art; but if there be no such infection, if there be not this union with the author and with others who are moved by the same work—then it is not art. And not only is infection a sure sign of art, but the degree of infectiousness is also the sole measure of excellence in art.

The stronger the infection the better is the art, as art, speaking of it now apart from its subject-matter—that is, not considering the value of the feelings it transmits.

And the degree of the infectiousness of art depends on three conditions:—

(1) On the greater or lesser individuality of the feeling transmitted; (2) on the greater or lesser clearness with which the feeling is transmitted; (3) on the sincerity of the artist, that is, on the greater or lesser force with which the artist himself feels the emotion he transmits.

The more individual the feeling transmitted the more strongly does it act on the recipient; the more individual the state of soul into which he is transferred the more pleasure does the recipient obtain and therefore the more readily and strongly does he join in it.

Clearness of expression assists infection because the recipient who mingles in consciousness with the author is the better satisfied the more clearly that feeling is transmitted which, as it seems to him, he has long known and felt and for which he has only now found expression.

But most of all is the degree of infectiousness of art increased by the degree of sincerity in the artist. As soon as the spectator, hearer, or reader, feels that the artist is infected by his own production and writes, sings, or plays, for himself, and not merely to act on others, this mental condition of the artist infects the recipient; and, on the contrary, as soon as the spectator, reader, or hearer, feels that the author is not writing, singing, or playing, for his own satisfaction—does not himself feel what he wishes to express, but is doing it for him, the recipient—resistance immediately springs up, and the most individual and the newest feelings and the cleverest technique not only fail to produce any infection but actually repel.

I have mentioned three conditions of contagion in art, but they may all be summed up into one, the last, sincerity; that is, that the artist should be impelled by an inner need to express his feeling. That condition includes the first; for if the artist is sincere he will express the feeling as he experienced it. And as each man is different from every one else, his feeling will be individual for every one else; and the more individual it is—the more the artist has drawn it from the depths of his nature—the more sympathetic and sincere will it be. And this same sincerity will impel the artist to find clear expression for the feeling which he wishes to transmit.

Therefore this third condition—sincerity—is the most important of the three. It is always complied with in peasant art, and this explains why such art always acts so powerfully; but it is a condition almost entirely absent from our upper-class art, which is continually produced by artists actuated by personal aims of covetousness or vanity.

Such are the three conditions which divide art from its counterfeits, and which also decide the quality of every work of art considered apart from its subject-matter.

The absence of any one of these conditions excludes a work from the category of art and relegates it to that of art's counterfeits. If the work does not transmit the artist's peculiarity of feeling and is therefore not individual, if it is unintelligibly expressed, or if it has not proceeded from the author's inner need for expression—it is not a work of art. If all these conditions are present even in the smallest degree, then the work even if a weak one is yet a work of art.

The presence in various degrees of these three conditions: individuality, clearness, and sincerity, decides the merit of a work of art as art, apart from subject-matter. All works of art take order of merit according to the degree in which they fulfil the first, the second, and the third, of these conditions. In one the individuality of the feeling transmitted may predominate; in another, clearness of expression; in a third, sincerity; while a fourth may have sincerity and individuality but be deficient in clearness; a fifth, individuality and clearness, but less sincerity; and so forth, in all possible degrees and combinations.

Thus is art divided from what is not art, and thus is the quality of art, as art, decided, independently of its subject-matter, that is to say, apart from whether the feelings it transmits are good or bad.

But how are we to define good and bad art with reference to its content or subject-matter? [This Tolstóy does in the following two chapters.]

CHAPTER XVIII

The purpose of human life is the brotherly union of man. Art must be guided by this perception.

The cause of the lie into which the art of our society has fallen was that people of the upper classes, having ceased to believe in the Church teaching (called Christian), did not resolve to accept true Christian teaching in its real and fundamental principles of sonship to God and brotherhood to man, but continued to live on without any belief, endeavoring to make up for the absence of belief—some by hypocrisy, pretending still to believe in the nonsense of the Church creeds; others by boldly asserting their disbelief; others by refined agnosticism; and others again by returning to the Greek worship of beauty, proclaiming egotism to be right, and elevating it to the rank of a religious doctrine.

The cause of the malady was the non-acceptance of Christ's teaching in its real, that is, its full, meaning. And the only cure lies in acknowledging that teaching in its full meaning. Such acknowledgement in our time is not only possible but inevitable. Already to-day a man standing on the height of the knowledge of our age, whether he be nominally a Catholic or a Protestant, cannot say that he really believes in the dogmas of the Church: in God being a Trinity, in Christ being God, in the Scheme of Redemption, and so forth, nor can he satisfy himself by proclaiming his unbelief or scepticism, nor by relapsing into the worship of beauty and egotism. Above all he can no longer say that we do not know the real meaning of Christ's teaching. That meaning has not only become accessible to all men of our times, but the whole life of man to-day is permeated by the spirit of that teaching and is, consciously or unconsciously, guided by it.

However differently in form people belonging to our Christian world may define the destiny of man: whether they see it in human progress (in whatever sense of the words), in the union of all men in a socialistic realm, or in the establishment of a commune; whether they look forward to the union of mankind under the guidance of one universal Church, or to the federation of the world—however various in form their definitions of the destination of human life may be, all men in our times already admit that the highest well-being attainable by men is to be reached by their union with one another.

However people of our upper classes (feeling that their ascendency can only be maintained as long as they separate themselves—the rich and learned—from the laborers—the poor and unlearned) may seek to devise new conceptions of life by which their privileges may be perpetuated—now the ideal of returning to antiquity, now mysticism, now Hellenism, now the cult of the superior person (supermanism)—they have, willingly or unwillingly, to admit the truth which is becoming clear upon all sides, voluntarily and involuntarily, namely, that our welfare lies only in the union and brotherhood of man.

This truth is unconsciously confirmed by the construction of means of communication—telegraphs, telephones, the press, and the ever-increasing attainability of material well-being for every one—and it is consciously affirmed by the destruction of superstitions which divide men, by the diffusion of the truths of knowledge, and by the expression of the ideal of the brotherhood of man in the best works of art of our time.

Art is a spiritual organ of human life which cannot be destroyed, and therefore, notwithstanding all the efforts made by people of the upper classes to conceal the religious ideal by which humanity lives, that ideal is more and more clearly recognized by man, and even in our perverted society is more and more often partially expressed by science and by art. During the present century works of the higher kind of religious art, permeated by a truly Christian spirit, have appeared more and more frequently both in literature and in painting, as also works of the universal art of common life accessible to all. So that even art knows the true ideal of our times and tends towards it. On the one hand the best works of art of our time transmit religious feelings urging towards the union and brotherhood of man (such are the works of Dickens, Hugo, Dostoévski; and, in painting, of Millet, Bastien Lepage, Jules Breton, Lhermitte, and others); on the other hand they strive towards the transmission, not of feelings which are natural to people of the upper classes only, but of feelings that may unite every one without exception. There are as yet few such works, but the need of them is already acknowledged. In recent times we also meet more and more frequently with attempts at publications, pictures, concerts, and theatres, for the people. All this is still very far from accomplishing what should be done, but the direction in which good art instinctively presses forward to regain the path natural to it, can already be discerned.

The religious perception of our time—which consists in acknowledging that the aim of life (both collective and individual) is the union of mankind—is already so sufficiently distinct that people have now only to reject the false theory of beauty—according to which enjoyment is considered to be the purpose of art—and religious perception will naturally take its place as the guide of the art of our time.

And as soon as this religious perception, which already unconsciously directs the life of man, is consciously acknowledged, then immediately and naturally the division of art into art for the lower and art for the upper classes will disappear. There will be one common, brotherly, universal art; and then first, that art will naturally be rejected which transmits feelings incompatible with the religious perception of our time—feelings which do not unite, but divide men—and later, that insignificant, exclusive art to which an unmerited importance is now attributed will be rejected.

And as soon as this occurs art will immediately cease to be what it has been in recent times, a means of making people coarser and more vicious, and it will become what it always used to be and should be, a means by which humanity progresses towards union and blessedness.

Strange as the comparison may sound, what has happened to the art of our circle and time is what happens to a woman who sells her womanly attractiveness, intended for maternity, for the gratification of those who desire such pleasures.

The art of our time and of our circle has become a prostitute. And this comparison holds good even in minute details. Like her it is not limited to certain times, like her it is always adorned, like her it is always saleable, and like her it is enticing and ruinous.

A real work of art can only arise in the soul of an artist occasionally, as the fruit of the life he has lived, just as a child is conceived by its mother. But counterfeit art is produced by artisans and handicraftsmen continually, if only consumers can be found.

Real art, like the wife of an affectionate husband, needs no ornaments. But counterfeit art, like a prostitute, must always be decked out.

The cause of the production of real art is the artist's inner need to express a feeling that has accumulated, just as for a mother the cause of sexual conception was love. The cause of counterfeit art, as of prostitution, is gain.

The consequence of true art is the introduction of a new feeling into the intercourse of life, as the consequence of a wife's love is the birth of a new man into life.

The consequences of counterfeit art are the perversion of man, pleasure which never satisfies, and the weakening of man's spiritual strength.

And this is what people of our day and of our circle should understand, in order to avoid the filthy torrent of depraved and prostituted art with which we are deluged.

*   *   *   *

Pater

Walter Horatio PATER (1839–1894) was born at Shadwell, son of a physician. Educated at the King's School, Canterbury, and at Oxford University, he took his degree in 1862. After travelling on the Continent, he gave up plans to take orders—humanistic idealism having replaced a faith in Christianity. On his election as a Fellow of Brasenose College, he made Oxford his principal home. In 1885, when *Marius the Epicurean* appeared, establishing his literary reputation, he moved to London, where he continued his association with the Pre-Raphaelites, and wrote on classical and Renaissance subjects. Besides *Marius,* his best-known works are *Studies in the History of the Renaissance* (1873), *Imaginary Portraits* (1887), *Appreciations* (1889), *Plato and Platonism* (1893), and *The Child in the House* (1894). *Greek Studies* and his unfinished *Gaston de Latour* were published posthumously.

Pater is at a pole opposite to Tolstóy, believing that art exists only for its own sake. His position is at variance, too, with that of Ruskin and of Arnold. This theory of *l'art pour l'art* is usually assigned to the end of the nineteenth century, and associated with his name and Whistler's. The idea, however, appears often in the writings of lesser known critics after 1800.

From APPRECIATIONS
(1876)

ROMANTICISM [1]

The words, *classical* and *romantic*, although, like many other critical expressions, sometimes abused by those who have understood them too vaguely or too absolutely, yet define two real tendencies in the history of art and literature. Used in an exaggerated sense, to express a greater opposition between those tendencies than really exists, they have at times tended to divide people of taste into opposite camps. But in that *House Beautiful*, which the creative minds of all generations—the artists and those who have treated life in the spirit of art—are always building together, for the refreshment of the human spirit, these oppositions cease; and the *Interpreter* of the *House Beautiful*, the true æsthetic critic, uses these divisions, only so far as they enable him to enter into the peculiarities of the objects with which he has to do. The term *classical*, fixed, as it is, to a well-defined literature, and a well-defined group in art, is clear, indeed; but then it has often been used in a hard, and merely scholastic sense, by the praisers of what is old and accustomed, at the expense of what is new, by critics who would never have discovered for themselves the charm of any work, whether new or old, who value what is old, in art or literature, for its accessories, and chiefly for the conventional authority that has gathered about it—people who would never really have been made glad by any Venus fresh-risen from the sea, and who praise the Venus of old Greece and Rome, only because they fancy her grown now into something staid and tame.

And as the term, *classical*, has been used in a too absolute, and therefore in a misleading sense, so the term, *romantic*, has been used much too vaguely, in various accidental senses. The sense in which Scott is called a romantic writer is chiefly this; that, in opposition to the literary tradition of the last century, he loved strange adventure, and sought it in the Middle Age. Much later, in a Yorkshire village, the spirit of romanticism bore a more really characteristic fruit in the work of a young girl, Emily Brontë, the romance of *Wuthering Heights*; the figures of Hareton Earnshaw, of Catherine Linton, and of Heathcliffe—tearing open Catherine's

---

[1] Originally an article in *Macmillan's Magazine*, November 1876, this essay became, with the addition of a final paragraph, the "Postscript" to *Appreciations* (1889).

grave, removing one side of her coffin, that he may really lie beside her in death—figures so passionate, yet woven on a background of delicately beautiful, moorland scenery, being typical examples of that spirit. In Germany, again, that spirit is shown less in Tieck, its professional representative, than in Meinhold, the author of *Sidonia the Sorceress* and the *Amber-Witch*. In Germany and France, within the last hundred years, the term has been used to describe a particular school of writers; and, consequently, when Heine criticizes the *Romantic School* in Germany—that movement which culminated in Goethe's *Goetz von Berlichingen;* or when Théophile Gautier criticizes the romantic movement in France, where, indeed, it bore its most characteristic fruits, and its play is hardly yet over; where, by a certain audacity, or *bizarrerie* of motive, united with faultless literary execution, it still shows itself in imaginative literature, they use the word, with an exact sense of special artistic qualities, indeed; but use it, nevertheless, with a limited application to the manifestation of those qualities at a particular period. But the romantic spirit is, in reality, an ever-present, an enduring principle, in the artistic temperament; and the qualities of thought and style which that, and other similar uses of the word *romantic* really indicate, are indeed but symptoms of a very continuous and widely working influence.

Though the words *classical* and *romantic*, then, have acquired an almost technical meaning, in application to certain developments of German and French taste, yet this is but one variation of an old opposition, which may be traced from the very beginning of the formation of European art and literature. From the first formation of anything like a standard of taste in these things, the restless curiosity of their more eager lovers necessarily made itself felt, in the craving for new motives, new subjects of interest, new modifications of style. Hence, the opposition between the classicists and the romanticists—between the adherents, in the culture of beauty, of the principles of liberty, and authority, respectively—of strength, and order or what the Greeks called κοσμιότης.[1]

Sainte-Beuve, in the third volume of the *Causeries du Lundi,* has discussed the question, *What is meant by a classic?* It was a question he was well fitted to answer, having himself lived through many phases of taste, and having been in earlier life an enthusiastic member of the romantic school: he was also a great master of that sort of "philosophy of literature," which delights in tracing tradi-

[1] decorum.

tions in it, and the way in which various phases of thought and sentiment maintain themselves, through successive modifications, from epoch to epoch. His aim, then, is to give the word *classic* a wider and, as he says, a more generous sense than it commonly bears, to make it expressly *grandiose et flottant* [1]; and, in doing this, he develops, in a masterly manner, those qualities of measure, purity, temperance, of which it is the especial function of classical art and literature, whatever meaning, narrower or wider, we attach to the term, to take care.

The charm, therefore, of what is classical, in art or literature, is that of the well-known tale, to which we can, nevertheless, listen over and over again, because it is told so well. To the absolute beauty of its artistic form, is added the accidental, tranquil, charm of familiarity. There are times, indeed, at which these charms fail to work on our spirits at all, because they fail to excite us. "*Romanticism*," says Stendhal, "is the art of presenting to people the literary works which, in the actual state of their habits and beliefs, are capable of giving them the greatest possible pleasure; *classicism*, on the contrary, of presenting them with that which gave the greatest possible pleasure to their grandfathers." But then, beneath all changes of habits and beliefs, our love of that mere abstract proportion—of music—which what is classical in literature possesses, still maintains itself in the best of us, and what pleased our grandparents may at least tranquillize us. The "classic" comes to us out of the cool and quiet of other times, as the measure of what a long experience has shown will at least never displease us. And in the classical literature of Greece and Rome, as in the classics of the last century, the essentially classical element is that quality of order in beauty, which they possess, indeed, in a pre-eminent degree, and which impresses some minds to the exclusion of everything else in them.

It is the addition of strangeness to beauty, that constitutes the romantic character in art; and the desire of beauty being a fixed element in every artistic organization, it is the addition of curiosity to this desire of beauty, that constitutes the romantic temper. Curiosity and the desire of beauty, have each their place in art, as in all true criticism. When one's curiosity is deficient, when one is not eager enough for new impressions, and new pleasures, one is liable to value mere academical proprieties too highly, to be satisfied with worn-out or conventional types, with the insipid orna-

[1] grand and compendious.

ment of Racine, or the prettiness of that later Greek sculpture, which passed so long for true Hellenic work; to miss those places where the handiwork of nature, or of the artist, has been most cunning; to find the most stimulating products of art a mere irritation. And when one's curiosity is in excess, when it overbalances the desire of beauty, then one is liable to value in works of art what is inartistic in them; to be satisfied with what is exaggerated in art, with productions like some of those of the romantic school in Germany; not to distinguish, jealously enough, between what is admirably done, and what is done not quite so well, in the writings, for instance, of Jean Paul. And if I had to give instances of these defects, then I should say, that Pope, in common with the age of literature to which he belonged, had too little curiosity, so that there is always a certain insipidity in the effect of his work, exquisite as it is; and, coming down to our own time, that Balzac had an excess of curiosity—curiosity not duly tempered with the desire of beauty.

But, however falsely those two tendencies may be opposed by critics, or exaggerated by artists themselves, they are tendencies really at work at all times in art, moulding it, with the balance sometimes a little on one side, sometimes a little on the other, generating, respectively, as the balance inclines on this side or that, two principles, two traditions, in art, and in literature so far as it partakes of the spirit of art. If there is a great overbalance of curiosity, then, we have the grotesque in art: if the union of strangeness and beauty, under very difficult and complex conditions, be a successful one, if the union be entire, then the resultant beauty is very exquisite, very attractive. With a passionate care for beauty, the romantic spirit refuses to have it, unless the condition of strangeness be first fulfilled. Its desire is for a beauty born of unlikely elements, by a profound alchemy, by a difficult initiation, by the charm which wrings it even out of terrible things; and a trace of distortion, of the grotesque, may perhaps linger, as an additional element of expression, about its ultimate grace. Its eager, excited spirit will have strength, the grotesque, first of all—the trees shrieking as you tear off the leaves; for Jean Valjean, the long years of convict life; for Redgauntlet, the quicksands of Solway Moss; then, incorporate with this strangeness, and intensified by restraint, as much sweetness, as much beauty, as is compatible with that. *Énergique, frais, et dispos*—these, according to Sainte-Beuve, are the characteristics of a genuine classic—*les ouvrages anciens ne sont pas classiques parce qu'ils sont vieux, mais parce qu'ils sont énergiques, frais, et dispos.*[1] Energy, freshness, intelligent and masterly disposition:—these are characteristics of Victor Hugo when his alchemy is complete, in certain figures, like Marius and Cosette, in certain scenes, like that in the opening of *Les Travailleurs de la Mer,* where Déruchette writes the name of *Gilliatt* in the snow, on Christmas morning; but always there is a certain note of strangeness discernible there, as well.

The essential elements, then, of the romantic spirit are curiosity and the love of beauty; and it is only as an illustration of these qualities, that it seeks the Middle Age, because, in the overcharged atmosphere of the Middle Age, there are unworked sources of romantic effect, of a strange beauty, to be won, by strong imagination, out of things unlikely or remote.

Few, probably, now read Madame de Staël's *De l'Allemagne,* though it has its interest, the interest which never quite fades out of work really touched with the enthusiasm of the spiritual adventurer, the pioneer in culture. It was published in 1810, to introduce to French readers a new school of writers—the romantic school, from beyond the Rhine; and it was followed, twenty-three years later, by Heine's *Romantische Schule,* as at once a supplement and a correction. Both these books, then, connect romanticism with Germany, with the names especially of Goethe and Tieck; and, to many English readers, the idea of romanticism is still inseparably connected with Germany—that Germany which, in its quaint old towns, under the spire of Strasburg or the towers of Heidelberg, was always listening in rapt inaction to the melodious, fascinating voices of the Middle Age, and which, now that it has got Strasburg back again, has, I suppose, almost ceased to exist. But neither Germany, with its Goethe and Tieck, nor England, with its Byron and Scott, is nearly so representative of the romantic temper as France, with Murger, and Gautier, and Victor Hugo. It is in French literature that its most characteristic expression is to be found; and that, as most closely derivative, historically, from such peculiar conditions, as ever reinforce it to the utmost.

For, although temperament has much to do with the generation of the romantic spirit, and although this spirit, with its curiosity, its thirst for a curious beauty, may be always traceable in excellent art (traceable even in Sophocles) yet still, in a limited sense, it may

[1] The works of ancient writers are not classics because they are old, but because they are energetic, fresh, and healthy.

be said to be a product of special epochs. Outbreaks of this spirit, that is, come naturally with particular periods—times, when, in men's approaches towards art and poetry, curiosity may be noticed to take the lead, when men come to art and poetry, with a deep thirst for intellectual excitement, after a long *ennui*, or in reaction against the strain of outward, practical things: in the later Middle Age, for instance; so that mediæval poetry, centering in Dante, is often opposed to Greek and Roman poetry, as romantic poetry to the classical. What the romanticism of Dante is, may be estimated, if we compare the lines in which Virgil describes the hazelwood, from whose broken twigs flows the blood of Polydorus, not without the expression of a real shudder at the ghastly incident, with the whole canto of the *Inferno*, into which Dante has expanded them, beautifying and softening it, meanwhile, by a sentiment of profound pity. And it is especially in that period of intellectual disturbance, immediately preceding Dante, amid which the romance languages define themselves at last, that this temper is manifested. Here, in the literature of Provence, the very name of *romanticism* is stamped with its true signification: here we have indeed a romantic world, grotesque even, in the strength of its passions, almost insane in its curious expression of them, drawing all things into its sphere, making the birds, nay! lifeless things, its voices and messengers, yet so penetrated with the desire for beauty and sweetness, that it begets a wholly new species of poetry, in which the *Renaissance* may be said to begin. The last century was pre-eminently a classical age, an age in which, for art and literature, the element of a comely order was in the ascendant; which, passing away, left a hard battle to be fought between the classical and the romantic schools. Yet, it is in the heart of this century, of Goldsmith and Stothard, of Watteau and the *Siècle de Louis XIV* —in one of its central, if not most characteristic figures, in Rousseau—that the modern or French romanticism really originates. But, what in the eighteenth century is but an exceptional phenomenon, breaking through its fair reserve and discretion only at rare intervals, is the habitual guise of the nineteenth, breaking through it perpetually, with a feverishness, an incomprehensible straining and excitement, which all experience to some degree, but yearning also, in the genuine children of the romantic school, to be *énergique, frais, et dispos*—for those qualities of energy, freshness, comely order; and often, in Murger, in Gautier, in Victor Hugo, for instance, with singular felicity attaining them.

It is in the terrible tragedy of Rousseau, in fact, that French romanticism, with much else, begins: reading his *Confessions* we seem actually to assist at the birth of this new, strong spirit in the French mind. The wildness which has shocked so many, and the fascination which has influenced almost everyone, in the squalid, yet eloquent figure we see and hear so clearly in that book, wandering among the apple-blossoms and under the vines of Neuchâtel or Vevey actually give it the quality of a very successful romantic invention. His strangeness or distortion, his profound subjectivity, his passionateness—the *cor laceratum* [1]—Rousseau makes all men in love with these. *Je ne suis fait comme aucun de ceux que j'ai sus. Mais si je ne vaux pas mieux, au moins je suis autre.*—"I am not made like any one else I have ever known: yet, if I am not better, at least I am different." These words, from the first page of the *Confessions*, anticipate all the Werthers, Renés, Obermanns,[2] of the last hundred years. For Rousseau did but anticipate a trouble in the spirit of the whole world; and thirty years afterwards, what in him was a peculiarity, became part of the general consciousness. A storm was coming: Rousseau, with others, felt it in the air, and they helped to bring it down: they introduced a disturbing element into French literature, then so trim and formal, like our own literature of the age of Queen Anne.

In 1815 the storm had come and gone, but had left, in the spirit of "young France," the *ennui* of an immense disillusion. In the last chapter of Edgar Quinet's *Révolution Française,* a work itself full of irony, of disillusion, he distinguishes two books, Senancour's *Obermann* and Chateaubriand's *Génie du Christianisme,* as characteristic of the first decade of the present century. In those two books we detect already the disease and the cure—in *Obermann* the irony, refined into a plaintive philosophy of "indifference"—in Chateaubriand's *Génie du Christianisme,* the refuge from a tarnished actual present, a present of disillusion, into a world of strength and beauty in the Middle Age, as at an earlier period—in *René* and *Atala*—into the free play of them in savage life. It is to minds in this spiritual situation, weary of the present, but yearning for the spectacle of beauty and strength, that the works of French romanticism appeal. They set a positive value on the intense, the exceptional; and a certain distortion is sometimes noticeable in them, as in conceptions like Victor Hugo's Quasimodo, or Gwyn-

---

[1] lacerated heart.

[2] Typical melancholy heroes of romanticism.

plaine,[1] something of a terrible grotesque, of the *macabre,* as the
French themselves call it; though always combined with perfect literary execution, as in Gautier's *La Morte Amoureuse,* or the scene
of the "maimed" burial-rites of the player, dead of the frost, in his
Capitaine Fracasse—true "flowers of the yew." It becomes grim humor in Victor Hugo's combat of Gilliatt with the devil-fish, or the
incident, with all its ghastly comedy drawn out at length, of the great
gun detached from its fastenings on shipboard, in *Quatre-Vingt-
Treize* (perhaps the most terrible of all accidents that can happen
by sea) and in the entire episode, in that book, of the *Convention.*
Not less surely does it reach a genuine pathos; for the habit of
noting and distinguishing one's own most intimate passages of sentiment makes one sympathetic, begetting, as it must, the power of
entering, by all sorts of finer ways, into the intimate recesses of
other minds; so that pity is another quality of romanticism, both
Victor Hugo and Gautier being great lovers of animals, and charming writers about them, and Murger being unrivalled in the pathos
of his *Scènes de la Vie de Jeunesse.* Penetrating so finely into all
situations which appeal to pity, above all, into the special or exceptional phases of such feeling, the romantic humor is not afraid of
the quaintness or singularity of its circumstances or expression,
pity, indeed, being of the essence of humor; so that Victor Hugo
does but turn his romanticism into practice, in his hunger and
thirst after practical *Justice!*—a justice which shall no longer
wrong children, or animals, for instance, by ignoring in a stupid,
mere breadth of view, minute facts about them. Yet the romanticists are antinomian,[2] too, sometimes, because the love of energy
and beauty, of distinction in passion, tended naturally to become
a little *bizarre,* plunging into the Middle Age, into the secrets of
old Italian story. *Are we in the Inferno?*—we are tempted to ask,
wondering at something malign in so much beauty. For over all a
care for the refreshment of the human spirit by fine art manifests
itself, a predominant sense of literary charm, so that, in their search
for the secret of exquisite expression, the romantic school went
back to the forgotten world of early French poetry, and literature
itself became the most delicate of the arts—like "goldsmith's work,"
says Sainte-Beuve, of Bertrand's *Gaspard de la Nuit*—and that pe-

[1] Characters in Victor Hugo's *Le Jongleur de Notre Dame* and *L'Homme Qui Rit.*

[2] Here, "inconsistent, self-contradictory." The word goes back to a reformed sect of
the sixteenth century which maintained that the moral law was not binding on Christians
under the "law of grace."

culiarly French gift, the gift of exquisite speech, *argute loqui*,[1] attained in them a perfection which it had never seen before.

Stendhal, a writer whom I have already quoted, and of whom English readers might well know much more than they do, stands between the earlier and the later growths of the romantic spirit. His novels are rich in romantic quality; and his other writings—partly criticism, partly personal reminiscences—are a very curious and interesting illustration of the needs out of which romanticism arose. In his book on *Racine and Shakespeare*, Stendhal argues that all good art was romantic in its day; and this is perhaps true in Stendhal's sense. That little treatise, full of "dry light" and fertile ideas, was published in the year 1823, and its object is to defend an entire independence and liberty in the choice and treatment of subject, both in art and literature, against those who upheld the exclusive authority of precedent. In pleading the cause of romanticism, therefore, it is the novelty, both of form and of motive, in writings like the *Hernani* of Victor Hugo (which soon followed it, raising a storm of criticism) that he is chiefly concerned to justify. To be interesting and really stimulating, to keep us from yawning even, art and literature must follow the subtle movements of that nimbly-shifting *Time-Spirit*, or *Zeit-Geist*, understood by French not less than by German criticism, which is always modifying men's taste, as it modifies their manners and their pleasures. This, he contends, is what all great workmen had always understood. Dante, Shakespeare, Molière, had exercised an absolute independence in their choice of subject and treatment. To turn always with that ever-changing spirit, yet to retain the flavor of what was admirably done in past generations, in the classics, as we say—is the problem of true romanticism. "Dante," he observes, "was pre-eminently the romantic poet. He adored Virgil, yet he wrote the *Divine Comedy*, with the episode of Ugolino, which is as unlike the *Æneid* as can possibly be. And those who thus obey the fundamental principle of romanticism, one by one become classical, and are joined to that ever-increasing common league, formed by men of all countries, to approach nearer and nearer to perfection."

Romanticism, then, although it has its epochs, is in its essential characteristics rather a spirit which shows itself at all times, in various degrees, in individual workmen and their work, and the amount of which criticism has to estimate in them taken one by one, than the peculiarity of a time or a school. Depending on the

[1] To speak brilliantly.

varying proportion of curiosity and the desire of beauty, natural tendencies of the artistic spirit at all times, it must always be partly a matter of individual temperament. The eighteenth century in England has been regarded as almost exclusively a classical period; yet William Blake, a type of so much which breaks through what are conventionally thought the influences of that century, is still a noticeable phenomenon in it, and the reaction in favor of naturalism in poetry begins in that century, early. There are, thus, the born romanticists and the born classicists. There are the born classicists who start with *form*, to whose minds the comeliness of the old, immemorial, well-recognized types in art and literature, have revealed themselves impressively; who will entertain no matter which will not go easily and flexibly into them; whose work aspires only to be a variation upon, or study from, the older masters. " 'Tis art's decline, my son!" they are always saying, to the progressive element in their own generation; to those who care for that which in fifty years' time every one will be caring for. On the other hand, there are the born romanticists, who start with an original, untried *matter*, still in fusion; who conceive this vividly, and hold by it as the essence of their work; who, by the very vividness and heat of their conception, purge away, sooner or later, all that is not organically appropriate to it, till the whole effect adjusts itself in clear, orderly, appropriate form; which form, after a very little time, becomes classical in its turn.

The romantic or classical character of a picture, a poem, a literary work, depends, then, on the balance of certain qualities in it; and in this sense, a very real distinction may be drawn between good classical and good romantic work. But all critical terms are relative; and there is at least a valuable suggestion in that theory of Stendhal's, that all good art was romantic in its day. In the beauties of Homer and Phidias, quiet as they now seem, there must have been, for those who confronted them for the first time, excitement and surprise, the sudden, unforeseen satisfaction of the desire of beauty. Yet the *Odyssey*, with its marvellous adventure, is more romantic than the *Iliad*, which nevertheless contains, among many other romantic episodes, that of the immortal horses of Achilles, who weep at the death of Patroclus. Æschylus is more romantic than Sophocles, whose *Philoctetes*, were it written now, might figure, for the strangeness of its motive and the perfectness of its execution, as typically romantic; while, of Euripides, it may be said, that his method in writing his plays is to sacrifice readily almost everything else, so that he may attain the fullness of a single romantic effect. These two tendencies, indeed, might be applied as a measure or standard, all through Greek and Roman art and poetry, with very illuminating results; and for an analyst of the romantic principle in art, no exercise would be more profitable, than to walk through the collection of classical antiquities at the Louvre, or the British Museum, or to examine some representative collection of Greek coins, and note how the element of curiosity, of the love of strangeness, insinuates itself into classical design, and record the effects of the romantic spirit there, the traces of struggle, of the grotesque even, though overbalanced here by sweetness; as in the sculpture of Chartres and Rheims, the real sweetness of mind in the sculptor is often overbalanced by the grotesque, by the rudeness of his strength.

Classicism, then, means for Stendhal, for that younger enthusiastic band of French writers whose unconscious method he formulated into principles, the reign of what is pedantic, conventional, and narrowly academical in art; for him, all good art is romantic. To Sainte-Beuve, who understands the term in a more liberal sense, it is the characteristic of certain epochs, of certain spirits in every epoch, not given to the exercise of original imagination, but rather to the working out of refinements of manner on some authorized matter; and who bring to their perfection, in this way, the elements of sanity, of order and beauty in manner. In general criticism, again, it means the spirit of Greece and Rome, of some phases in literature and art that may seem of equal authority with Greece and Rome, the age of Louis the Fourteenth, the age of Johnson; though this is at best an uncritical use of the term, because in Greek and Roman work there are typical examples of the romantic spirit. But explain the terms as we may, in application to particular epochs, there are these two elements always recognizable; united in perfect art—in Sophocles, in Dante, in the highest work of Goethe, though not always absolutely balanced there; and these two elements may be not inappropriately termed the classical and romantic tendencies.

*   *   *   *

James

Henry JAMES (1843–1916) was born in New York, son of Henry James (1811–1882), theologian and philosopher, and brother of the philosopher William James (1842–1910). Educated abroad, and in law at Harvard University, he began to contribute to magazines in 1866. From 1869 he lived in Europe, residing chiefly in Italy and England, visiting occasionally his native country—where, however, he hardly felt at home. During these years he published his delicately but vividly written novels upon which his reputation rests. Among them may be listed *Roderick Hudson* (1876), *The American* (1877), *Daisy Miller* (1879), *Portrait of a Lady* (1881), *The Awkward Age* (1899), *The Ambassadors* (1903), *The Golden Bowl* (1904), and *The American Scene* (1906).

The essay below, phrased in James's characteristic style, is the personal reaction of a novelist toward his profession. It contains provocative ideas, but it does not attempt to establish any rigid rules or standards.

THE ART OF FICTION [1]
(1884)

I should not have fixed so comprehensive a title to these few remarks, necessarily wanting in any completeness upon a subject the full consideration of which would carry us far, did I not seem to discover a pretext for my temerity in the interesting pamphlet

---

[1] First published in *Longman's Magazine* (1884), this essay provoked an answer from Robert Louis Stevenson, entitled "A Humble Remonstrance," which, originally published in *Longman's Magazine*, has been reprinted in *Memories and Portraits*.

lately published under this name by Mr. Walter Besant.[1] Mr. Besant's lecture at the Royal Institution—the original form of his pamphlet—appears to indicate that many persons are interested in the art of fiction, and are not indifferent to such remarks as those who practice it may attempt to make about it. I am therefore anxious not to lose the benefit of this favorable association, and to edge in a few words under cover of the attention which Mr. Besant is sure to have excited. There is something very encouraging in his having put into form certain of his ideas on the mystery of storytelling.

It is a proof of life and curiosity—curiosity on the part of the brotherhood of novelists as well as on the part of their readers. Only a short time ago it might have been supposed that the English novel was not what the French call *discutable*.[2] It had no air of having a theory, a conviction, a consciousness of itself behind it—of being the expression of an artistic faith, the result of choice and comparison. I do not say it was necessarily the worse for that: it would take much more courage than I possess to intimate that the form of the novel as Dickens and Thackeray (for instance) saw it had any taint of incompleteness. It was, however, *naïf* (if I may help myself out with another French word); and evidently if it be destined to suffer in any way for having lost its *naïveté* it has now an idea of making sure of the corresponding advantages. During the period I have alluded to there was a comfortable good-humored feeling abroad that a novel is a novel, as a pudding is a pudding, and that our only business with it could be to swallow it. But within a year or two, for some reason or other, there have been signs of returning animation—the era of discussion would appear to have been to a certain extent opened. Art lives upon discussion, upon experiment, upon curiosity, upon variety of attempt, upon the exchange of views and the comparison of standpoints; and there is a presumption that those times when no one has anything particular to say about it, and has no reason to give for practice or preference, though they may be times of honor, are not times of development —are times, possibly, even a little of dullness. The successful application of any art is a delightful spectacle, but the theory too is interesting; and though there is a great deal of the latter without the former I suspect there has never been a genuine success that

---

[1] Sir Walter Besant (1836–1901), was a novelist as well as an historian. Like Ruskin, he was interested in the poor, and founded the People's Palace in the East End of London.

[2] A proper subject for discussion.

has not had a latent core of conviction. Discussion, suggestion, formulation, these things are fertilizing when they are frank and sincere. Mr. Besant has set an excellent example in saying what he thinks, for his part, about the way in which fiction should be written, as well as about the way in which it should be published; for his view of the "art," carried on into an appendix, covers that too. Other laborers in the same field will doubtless take up the argument, they will give it the light of their experience, and the effect will surely be to make our interest in the novel a little more what it had for some time threatened to fail to be—a serious, active, inquiring interest, under protection of which this delightful study may, in moments of confidence, venture to say a little more what it thinks of itself.

It must take itself seriously for the public to take it so. The old superstition about fiction being "wicked" has doubtless died out in England; but the spirit of it lingers in a certain oblique regard directed toward any story which does not more or less admit that it is only a joke. Even the most jocular novel feels in some degree the weight of the proscription that was formerly directed against literary levity: the jocularity does not always succeed in passing for orthodoxy. It is still expected, though perhaps people are ashamed to say it, that a production which is after all only a "make-believe" (for what else is a "story"?) shall be in some degree apologetic— shall renounce the pretension of attempting really to represent life. This, of course, any sensible, wide-awake story declines to do, for it quickly perceives that the tolerance granted to it on such a condition is only an attempt to stifle it disguised in the form of generosity. The old evangelical hostility to the novel, which was as explicit as it was narrow, and which regarded it as little less favorable to our immortal part than a stage-play, was in reality far less insulting. The only reason for the existence of a novel is that it does attempt to represent life. When it relinquishes this attempt, the same attempt that we see on the canvas of the painter, it will have arrived at a very strange pass. It is not expected of the picture that it will make itself humble in order to be forgiven; and the analogy between the art of the painter and the art of the novelist is, so far as I am able to see, complete. Their inspiration is the same, their process (allowing for the different quality of the vehicle) is the same, their success is the same. They may learn from each other, they may explain and sustain each other. Their cause is the same, and the honor of one is the honor of another. The Mahometans think a picture an unholy thing, but it is a long time since any Christian did, and it is therefore the more odd that in the Christian mind the traces (dissimulated though they may be) of a suspicion of the sister art should linger to this day. The only effectual way to lay it to rest is to emphasize the analogy to which I just alluded —to insist on the fact that as the picture is reality, so the novel is history. That is the only general description (which does it justice) that we may give of the novel. But history also is allowed to represent life; it is not, any more than painting, expected to apologize. The subject-matter of fiction is stored up likewise in documents and records, and if it will not give itself away, as they say in California, it must speak with assurance, with the tone of the historian. Certain accomplished novelists have a habit of giving themselves away which must often bring tears to the eyes of people who take their fiction seriously. I was lately struck, in reading over many pages of Anthony Trollope, with his want of discretion in this particular. In a digression, a parenthesis or an aside, he concedes to the reader that he and this trusting friend are only "making believe." He admits that the events he narrates have not really happened, and that he can give his narrative any turn the reader may like best. Such a betrayal of a sacred office seems to me, I confess, a terrible crime; it is what I mean by the attitude of apology, and it shocks me every whit as much in Trollope as it would have shocked me in Gibbon or Macaulay. It implies that the novelist is less occupied in looking for the truth (the truth, of course I mean, that he assumes, the premises that we must grant him, whatever they may be) than the historian, and in doing so it deprives him at a stroke of all his standing-room. To represent and illustrate the past, the actions of men, is the task of either writer, and the only difference that I can see is, in proportion as he succeeds, to the honor of the novelist, consisting as it does in his having more difficulty in collecting his evidence, which is so far from being purely literary. It seems to me to give him a great character, the fact that he has at once so much in common with the philosopher and the painter; this double analogy is a magnificent heritage.

It is of all this evidently that Mr. Besant is full when he insists upon the fact that fiction is one of the *fine* arts, deserving in its turn of all the honors and emoluments that have hitherto been reserved for the successful profession of music, poetry, painting, architecture. It is impossible to insist too much on so important a truth, and the place that Mr. Besant demands for the work of the novelist may be represented, a trifle less abstractly, by saying that he demands not only that it shall be reputed artistic, but that it shall be reputed very artistic indeed. It is excellent that he should have struck this note, for his doing so indicates that there was need of it, that his proposition may be to many people a novelty. One rubs one's eyes at the thought; but the rest of Mr. Besant's essay confirms the revelation. I suspect in truth that it would be possible to confirm it still further, and that one would not be far wrong in saying that in addition to the people to whom it has never occurred that a novel ought to be artistic, there are a great many others who, if this principle were urged upon them, would be filled with an indefinable mistrust. They would find it difficult to explain their repugnance, but it would operate strongly to put them on their guard. "Art," in our Protestant communities, where so many things have got so strangely twisted about, is supposed in certain circles to have some vague injurious effect upon those who make it an important consideration, who let it weigh in the balance. It is assumed to be opposed in some mysterious manner to morality, to amusement, to instruction. When it is embodied in the work of the painter (the sculptor is another affair!) you know what it is: it stands there before you, in the honesty of pink and green and a gilt frame; you can see the worst of it at a glance, and you can be on your guard. But when it is introduced into literature it becomes more insidious—there is danger of its hurting you before you know it. Literature should be either instructive or amusing, and there is in many minds an impression that these artistic preoccupations, the search for form, contribute to neither end, interfere indeed with both. They are too frivolous to be edifying, and too serious to be diverting; and they are moreover priggish and paradoxical and superfluous. That, I think, represents the manner in which the latent thought of many people who read novels as an exercise in skipping would explain itself if it were to become articulate. They would argue, of course, that a novel ought to be "good," but they would interpret this term in a fashion of their own, which indeed would vary considerably from one critic to another. One would say that being good means representing virtuous and aspiring characters placed in prominent positions; another would say that it depends on a "happy ending," on a distribution at the last of prizes, pensions, husbands, wives, babies, millions, appended paragraphs, and cheerful remarks. Another still would say that it means being full of incident and movement, so that we shall wish to jump ahead, to see who was the mysterious stranger, and if the stolen will was ever found, and shall not be distracted from this pleasure by any tiresome analysis or "description." But they would all agree that the "artistic" idea would spoil some of their fun. One would hold it accountable for all the description, another would see it revealed in the absence of sympathy. Its hostility to a happy ending would be evident, and it might even in some cases render any ending at all impossible. The "ending" of a novel is, for many persons, like that of a good dinner, a course of dessert and ices, and the artist in fiction is regarded as a sort of meddlesome doctor who forbids agreeable aftertastes. It is therefore true that this conception of Mr. Besant's of the novel as a superior form encounters not only a negative but a positive indifference. It matters little that as a work of art it should really be as little or as much of its essence to supply happy endings, sympathetic characters, and an objective tone, as if it were a work of mechanics: the association of ideas, however incongruous, might easily be too much for it if an eloquent voice were not sometimes raised to call attention to the fact that it is at once as free and as serious a branch of literature as any other.

Certainly this might sometimes be doubted in presence of the enormous number of works of fiction that appeal to the credulity of our generation, for it might easily seem that there could be no great character in a commodity so quickly and easily produced. It must be admitted that good novels are much compromised by bad ones, and that the field at large suffers discredit from overcrowding. I think, however, that this injury is only superficial, and that the superabundance of written fiction proves nothing against the principle itself. It has been vulgarized, like all other kinds of literature, like everything else to-day, and it has proved more than some kinds accessible to vulgarization. But there is as much difference as there ever was between a good novel and a bad one: the bad is swept with all the daubed canvases and spoiled marble into some unvisited limbo, or infinite rubbish-yard beneath the back-windows of the world, and the good subsists and emits its light and stimulates our desire for perfection. As I shall take the liberty of making but a single criticism of Mr. Besant, whose tone is so full of love of his art, I may as well have done with it at once. He seems to me to mistake, in attempting to say so definitely beforehand, what sort of an affair the good novel will be. To indicate the danger of such an error as that has been the purpose of these few pages; to suggest that certain traditions on the subject, applied *a priori*, have already had much to answer for, and that the good health of an art which undertakes so immediately to reproduce life must demand that it be perfectly free. It lives upon exercise, and the very meaning of exercise is freedom. The only obligation to which in advance we may hold a novel, without incurring the accusation of being arbitrary, is that it be interesting. That general responsibility rests upon it, but it is the only one I can think of. The ways in which it is at liberty to accomplish this result (of interesting us) strike me as innumerable, and such as can only suffer from being marked out or fenced in by prescription. They are as various as the temperament of man, and they are successful in proportion as they reveal a particular mind, different from others. A novel is in its broadest definition a personal, a direct impression of life: that, to begin with, constitutes its value, which is greater or less according to the intensity of the impression. But there will be no intensity at all, and therefore no value, unless there is freedom to feel and say. The tracing of a line to be followed, of a tone to be taken, of a form to be filled out, is a limitation of that freedom and a suppression of the very thing that we are most curious about. The form, it seems to me, is to be appreciated after the fact: then the author's choice has been made, his standard has been indicated; then we can follow lines and directions and compare tones and resemblances. Then in a word we can enjoy one of the most charming of pleasures, we can estimate quality, we can apply the test of execution. The execution belongs to the author alone; it is what is most personal to him, and we measure him by that. The advantage, the luxury, as well as the torment and responsibility of the novelist, is that there is no limit to what he may attempt as an executant—no limit to his possible experiments, efforts, discoveries, successes. Here it is especially that he works, step by step, like his brother of the brush, of whom we may always say that he has painted his picture in a manner best known to himself. His manner is his secret, not necessarily a jealous one. He cannot disclose it as a general thing if he would; he would be at a loss to teach it to others. I say this with a due recollection of having insisted on the community of method of the artist who paints a picture and the artist who writes a novel. The painter *is* able to teach the rudiments of his practice, and it is possible, from the study of good work (granted the aptitude), both to learn how to paint and to learn how to write. Yet it remains true, without injury to the *rapprochement,* that the literary artist would be obliged to say to his pupil much more than the other, "Ah, well, you must do it as you can!" It is a question of degree, a matter of delicacy. If there are exact sciences, there are also exact arts, and the grammar of painting is so much more definite that it makes the difference.

I ought to add, however, that if Mr. Besant says at the beginning of his essay that the "laws of fiction may be laid down and taught with as much precision and exactness as the laws of harmony, perspective, and proportion" he mitigates what might appear to be an extravagance by applying his remark to "general" laws, and by expressing most of these rules in a manner with which it would certainly be unaccommodating to disagree. That the novelist must write from his experience, that his "characters must be real and such as might be met with in actual life"; that "a young lady brought up in a quiet country village should avoid descriptions of garrison life," and "a writer whose friends and personal experiences belong to the lower middle-class should carefully avoid introducing his characters into society"; that one should enter one's notes in a common-place book; that one's figures should be clear in outline; that making them clear by some trick of speech or of carriage is a bad method, and "describing them at length" is a worse one; that English Fiction should have a "conscious moral purpose"; that "it is almost impossible to estimate too highly the value of careful workmanship—that is, of style"; that "the most important point of all is the story," that "the story is everything": these are principles with most of which it is surely impossible not to sympathize. That remark about the lower middle-class writer and his knowing his place is perhaps rather chilling; but for the rest I should find it difficult to dissent from any one of these recommendations. At the same time, I should find it difficult positively to assent to them, with the exception, perhaps, of the injunction as to entering one's notes in a common-place book. They scarcely seem to me to have the quality that Mr. Besant attributes to the rules of the novelist— the "precision and exactness" of "the laws of harmony, perspective, and proportion." They are suggestive, they are even inspiring, but they are not exact, though they are doubtless as much so as the case admits of: which is a proof of that liberty of interpretation for which I just contended. For the value of these different injunctions —so beautiful and so vague—is wholly in the meaning one attaches to them. The characters, the situation, which strike one as real will be those that touch and interest one most, but the measure of reality is very difficult to fix. The reality of Don Quixote or of Mr. Micawber is a very delicate shade; it is a reality so colored by the author's vision that, vivid as it may be, one would hesitate to propose it as a model: one would expose one's self to some very embarrassing questions on the part of a pupil. It goes without saying that you will not write a good novel unless you possess the sense of reality; but it will be difficult to give you a recipe for calling that sense into being. Humanity is immense, and reality has a myriad forms; the most one can affirm is that some of the flowers of fiction have the odor of it, and others have not; as for telling you in advance how your nosegay should be composed, that is another affair. It is equally excellent and inconclusive to say that one must write from experience; to our supposititious aspirant such a declaration might savor of mockery. What kind of experience is intended, and where does it begin and end? Experience is never limited, and it is never complete; it is an immense sensibility, a kind of huge spider-web of the finest silken threads suspended in the chamber of consciousness, and catching every air-borne particle in its tissue. It is the very atmosphere of the mind; and when the mind is imaginative—much more when it happens to be that of a man of genius—it takes to itself the faintest hints of life, it converts the very pulses of the air into revelations. The young lady living in a village has only to be a damsel upon whom nothing is lost to make it quite unfair (as it seems to me) to declare to her that she shall have nothing to say about the military. Greater miracles have been seen than that, imagination assisting, she should speak the truth about some of these gentlemen. I remember an English novelist, a woman of genius, telling me that she was much commended for the impression she had managed to give in one of her tales of the nature and way of life of the French Protestant youth. She had been asked where she learned so much about this recondite being, she had been congratulated on her peculiar opportunities. These opportunities consisted in her having once, in Paris, as she ascended a staircase, passed an open door where, in the household of a *pasteur*, some of the young Protestants were seated at table round a finished meal. The glimpse made a picture; it lasted only a moment, but that moment was experience. She had got her direct personal impression, and she turned out her type. She knew what youth was, and what Protestantism; she also had the advantage of having seen what it was to be French, so that she converted these ideas into a concrete image and produced a reality. Above all, however, she was blessed with the faculty which when you give it an inch takes an ell, and which for the artist is a much greater source of strength than any accident of residence or of place in the social scale. The power to guess the unseen from the seen, to trace the implication of things, to judge the whole piece by the pattern, the condition of feeling life in general so completely that you are well on your way to knowing any particular corner of it—this cluster of gifts may almost be said to constitute experience, and they occur in country and in town, and in the most differing stages of education. If experience consists of impressions, it may be said that impressions *are* experience, just as (have we not seen it?) they are the very air we breathe. Therefore, if I should certainly say to a novice, "Write from experience and from experience only," I should feel that this was rather a tantalizing monition if I were not careful immediately to add, "Try to be one of the people on whom nothing is lost!"

I am far from intending by this to minimize the importance of exactness—of truth of detail. One can speak best from one's own taste, and I may therefore venture to say that the air of reality (solidity of specification) seems to me to be the supreme virtue of a novel—the merit on which all its other merits (including that conscious moral purpose of which Mr. Besant speaks) helplessly and submissively depend. If it be not there they are all as nothing, and if these be there, they owe their effect to the success with which the author has produced the illusion of life. The cultivation of this success, the study of this exquisite process, form, to my taste, the beginning and the end of the art of the novelist. They are his inspiration, his despair, his reward, his torment, his delight. It is here in very truth that he competes with life; it is here that he competes with his brother the painter in *his* attempt to render the look of things, the look that conveys their meaning, to catch the color, the relief, the expression, the surface, the substance of the human spectacle. It is in regard to this that Mr. Besant is well inspired when he bids him take notes. He cannot possibly take too many, he cannot possibly take enough. All life solicits him, and to "render" the simplest surface, to produce the most momentary illusion, is a very complicated business. His case would be easier, and the rule would be more exact, if Mr. Besant had been able to tell him what notes to take. But this, I fear, he can never learn in any manual; it is the business of his life. He has to take a great many in order to select a few, he has to work them up as he can, and even the guides and philosophers who might have most to say to him must leave him alone when it comes to the application of precepts, as we leave the painter in communion with his palette. That his characters "must be clear in outline" as Mr. Besant says—he feels that down to his boots; but how he shall make them so is a secret between his good angel and himself. It would be absurdly simple if he could be taught that a great deal of "description" would make them so, or that on the contrary the absence of description and the cultivation of dialogue, or the absence of dialogue and the multiplication of "incident," would rescue him from his difficulties. Nothing, for instance, is more possible than that he be of a turn of mind for which this odd, literal opposition of description and dialogue, incident and description, has little meaning and light. People often talk of these things as if they had a kind of internecine distinctness, instead of melting into each other at every breath, and being intimately associated parts of one general effort of expression. I cannot imagine composition existing in a series of blocks, nor conceive, in any novel worth discussing at all, of a passage of description that is not in its intention narrative, a passage of dialogue that is not in its intention descriptive, a touch of truth of any sort that does not partake of the nature of incident, or an incident that derives its interest from any other source than the general and only source of the success of a work of art—that of being illustrative. A novel is a living thing, all one and continuous, like any other organism, and in proportion as it lives will it be found, I think, that in each of the parts there is something of each of the other parts. The critic who over the close texture of a finished work shall pretend to trace a geography of items will mark some frontiers as artificial, I fear, as any that have been known to history. There is an old-fashioned distinction between the novel of character and the novel of incident which must have cost many a smile to the intending fabulist who was keen about his work. It appears to me as little to the point as the equally celebrated distinction between the novel and the romance—to answer as little to any reality. There are bad novels and good novels, as there are bad pictures and good pictures; but that is the only distinction in which I see any meaning, and I can as little imagine speaking of a novel of character as I can imagine speaking of a picture of character. When one says picture one says of character, when one says novel one says of incident, and the terms may be transposed at will. What is character but the determination of incident? What is incident but the illustration of character? What is either a picture or a novel that is *not* of character? What else do we seek in it and find in it? It is an incident for a woman to stand up with her hand resting on a table and look at you in a certain way; or if it be not an incident I think it will be hard to say what it is. At the same time it is an expression of character. If you say you don't see it (character in *that—allons donc!*), this is exactly what the artist who has reasons of his own for thinking he *does* see it undertakes to show you. When a young man makes up his mind that he has not faith enough after all to enter the Church as he intended, that is an incident, though you may not hurry to the end of the chapter to see whether perhaps he doesn't change once more. I do not say that these are extraordinary or startling incidents. I do not pretend to estimate the degree of interest proceeding from them, for this will depend upon the skill of the painter. It sounds almost puerile to say that some incidents are intrinsically much more important than others, and I need not take this precaution after having professed my sympathy for the major ones in remarking that the only classification of the novel that I can understand is into that which has life and that which has it not.

The novel and the romance, the novel of incident and that of character—these clumsy separations appear to me to have been made by critics and readers for their own convenience, and to help them out of some of their occasional predicaments, but to have little reality or interest for the producer, from whose point of view it is of course that we are attempting to consider the art of fiction. The case is the same with another shadowy category which Mr. Besant apparently is disposed to set up—that of the "modern English novel"; unless indeed it be that in this matter he has fallen into an accidental confusion of standpoints. It is not quite clear whether he intends the remarks in which he alludes to it to be didactic or historical. It is as difficult to suppose a person intending to write a modern English as to suppose him writing an ancient English novel: that is a label which begs the question. One writes the novel, one paints the picture, of one's language and of one's time, and calling it modern English will not, alas! make the difficult task any easier. No more, unfortunately, will calling this or that work of one's fellow-artist a romance—unless it be, of course, simply for the pleasantness of the thing, as for instance when Hawthorne gave this heading to his story of *Blithedale*. The French, who have brought the theory of fiction to remarkable completeness, have but one name for the novel, and have not attempted smaller things in it, that I can see, for that. I can think of no obligation to which the "romancer" would not be held equally with the novelist; the standard of execution is equally high for each. Of course it is of execution that we are talking—that being the only point of a novel that is open to contention. This is perhaps too often lost sight of, only to produce interminable confusions and cross-purposes. We must grant the artist his subject, his idea, his *donnée* [1]: our criticism is applied only to what he makes of it. Naturally I do not mean that we are bound to like it or find it interesting: in case we do not our course is perfectly simple—to let it alone. We may believe that of a certain idea even the most sincere novelist can make nothing at all, and the event may perfectly justify our belief; but the failure will have been a failure to execute, and it is in the execution that the fatal weakness is recorded. If we pretend to respect the artist at all, we must allow him his freedom of choice, in the face, in particular cases, of innumerable presumptions that the choice will not fructify. Art derives a considerable part of its beneficial exercise from flying in the face of presumptions, and some of the most interesting experiments of which it is capable are hidden in the bosom of common things. Gustave Flaubert has written a story about the devotion of a servant-girl to a parrot, and the production, highly finished as it is, cannot on the whole be called a success. We are perfectly free to find it flat, but I think it might have been interesting; and I, for my part, am extremely glad he should have written it; it is a contribution to our knowledge of what can be done—or what cannot. Ivan Turgénieff has written a tale about a deaf and dumb serf and a lap-dog, and the thing is touching, loving, a little masterpiece. He struck the note of life where Gustave Flaubert missed it—he flew in the face of a presumption and achieved a victory.

Nothing, of course, will ever take the place of the good old fashion of "liking" a work of art or not liking it: the most improved criticism will not abolish that primitive, that ultimate test. I mention this to guard myself from the accusation of intimating that the idea, the subject, of a novel or a picture, does not matter. It matters, to my sense, in the highest degree, and if I might put up a prayer it would be that artists should select none but the richest. Some, as I have already hastened to admit, are much more remunerative than others, and it would be a world happily arranged in which persons intending to treat them should be exempt from

[1] His given point of departure.

confusions and mistakes. This fortunate condition will arrive only, I fear, on the same day that critics become purged from error. Meanwhile, I repeat, we do not judge the artist with fairness unless we say to him, "Oh, I grant you your starting-point, because if I did not I should seem to prescribe to you, and heaven forbid I should take that responsibility. If I pretend to tell you what you must not take, you will call upon me to tell you then what you must take; in which case I shall be prettily caught. Moreover, it isn't till I have accepted your data that I can begin to measure you. I have the standard, the pitch; I have no right to tamper with your flute and then criticize your music. Of course I may not care for your idea at all; I may think it silly, or stale, or unclean; in which case I wash my hands of you altogether. I may content myself with believing that you will not have succeeded in being interesting, but I shall, of course, not attempt to demonstrate it, and you will be as indifferent to me as I am to you. I needn't remind you that there are all sorts of tastes: who can know it better? Some people, for excellent reasons, don't like to read about carpenters; others, for reasons even better, don't like to read about courtesans. Many object to Americans. Others (I believe they are mainly editors and publishers) won't look at Italians. Some readers don't like quiet subjects; others don't like bustling ones. Some enjoy a complete illusion, others the consciousness of large concessions. They choose their novels accordingly, and if they don't care about your idea they won't, *a fortiori*, care about your treatment."

So that it comes back very quickly, as I have said, to the liking: in spite of M. Zola, who reasons less powerfully than he represents, and who will not reconcile himself to this absoluteness of taste, thinking that there are certain things that people ought to like, and that they can be made to like. I am quite at a loss to imagine anything (at any rate in this matter of fiction) that people *ought* to like or to dislike. Selection will be sure to take care of itself, for it has a constant motive behind it. That motive is simply experience. As people feel life, so they will feel the art that is most closely related to it. This closeness of relation is what we should never forget in talking of the effort of the novel. Many people speak of it as a factitious, artificial form, a product of ingenuity, the business of which it is to alter and arrange the things that surround us, to translate them into conventional, traditional moulds. This, however, is a view of the matter which carries us but a very short way, condemns the art to an eternal repetition of a few familiar *clichés,* cuts short its development, and leads us straight up to a dead wall. Catching the very note and trick, the strange irregular rhythm of life, that is the attempt whose strenuous force keeps Fiction upon her feet. In proportion as in what she offers us we see life *without* rearrangement do we feel that we are touching the truth; in proportion as we see it *with* rearrangement do we feel that we are being put off with a substitute, a compromise and convention. It is not uncommon to hear an extraordinary assurance of remark in regard to this matter of rearranging, which is often spoken of as if it were the last word of art. Mr. Besant seems to me in danger of falling into the great error with his rather unguarded talk about "selection." Art is essentially selection, but it is a selection whose main care is to be typical, to be inclusive. For many people art means rose-colored window-panes, and selection means picking a bouquet for Mrs. Grundy. They will tell you glibly that artistic considerations have nothing to do with the disagreeable, with the ugly; they will rattle off shallow commonplaces about the province of art and the limits of art till you are moved to some wonder in return as to the province and the limits of ignorance. It appears to me that no one can ever have made a seriously artistic attempt without becoming conscious of an immense increase—a kind of revelation—of freedom. One perceives in that case—by the light of a heavenly ray—that the province of art is all life, all feeling, all observation, all vision. As Mr. Besant so justly intimates, it is all experience. That is a sufficient answer to those who maintain that it must not touch the sad things of life, who stick into its divine unconscious bosom little prohibitory inscriptions on the end of sticks, such as we see in public gardens—"It is forbidden to walk on the grass; it is forbidden to touch the flowers; it is not allowed to introduce dogs or to remain after dark; it is requested to keep to the right." The young aspirant in the line of fiction whom we continue to imagine will do nothing without taste, for in that case his freedom would be of little use to him; but the first advantage of his taste will be to reveal to him the absurdity of the little sticks and tickets. If he have taste, I must add, of course he will have ingenuity, and my disrespectful reference to that quality just now was not meant to imply that it is useless in fiction. But it is only a secondary aid; the first is a capacity for receiving straight impressions.

Mr. Besant has some remarks on the question of "the story" which I shall not attempt to criticize, though they seem to me to contain a singular ambiguity, because I do not think I understand them. I cannot see what is meant by talking as if there were a part of a novel which is the story and part of it which for mystical reasons is not—unless indeed the distinction be made in a sense in which it is difficult to suppose that any one should attempt to convey anything. "The story," if it represents anything, represents the subject, the idea, the *donnée* of the novel; and there is surely no "school"—Mr. Besant speaks of a school—which urges that a novel should be all treatment and no subject. There must assuredly be something to treat; every school is intimately conscious of that. This sense of the story being the idea, the starting-point, of the novel, is the only one that I see in which it can be spoken of as something different from its organic whole; and since in proportion as the work is successful the idea permeates and penetrates it, informs and animates it, so that every word and every punctuation-point contribute directly to the expression, in that proportion do we lose our sense of the story being a blade which may be drawn more or less out of its sheath. The story and the novel, the idea and the form, are the needle and thread, and I never heard of a guild of tailors who recommended the use of the thread without the needle, or the needle without the thread. Mr. Besant is not the only critic who may be observed to have spoken as if there were certain things in life which constitute stories, and certain others which do not. I find the same odd implication in an entertaining article in the *Pall Mall Gazette,* devoted, as it happens, to Mr. Besant's lecture. "The story is the thing!" says this graceful writer, as if with a tone of opposition to some other idea. I should think it was, as every painter who, as the time for "sending in" his picture looms in the distance, finds himself still in quest of a subject—as every belated artist not fixed about his theme will heartily agree. There are some subjects which speak to us and others which do not, but he would be a clever man who should undertake to give a rule—an *index expurgatorius*—by which the story and the no-story should be known apart. It is impossible (to me at least) to imagine any such rule which shall not be altogether arbitrary. The writer in the *Pall Mall* opposes the delightful (as I suppose) novel of *Margot la Balafrée* to certain tales in which "Bostonian nymphs" appear to have "rejected English dukes for psychological reasons." I am not acquainted with the romance just designated, and can scarcely forgive the *Pall Mall* critic for not mentioning the name of the author, but the title appears to refer to a lady who may have received a scar in some heroic adventure. I am inconsolable at not being acquainted with this episode, but am utterly at a loss to see why it is a story when the rejection (or acceptance) of a duke is not, and why a reason, psychological or other, is not a subject when a cicatrix is. They are all particles of the multitudinous life with which the novel deals, and surely no dogma which pretends to make it lawful to touch the one and unlawful to touch the other will stand for a moment on its feet. It is the special picture that must stand or fall, according as it seems to possess truth or to lack it. Mr. Besant does not, to my sense, light up the subject by intimating that a story must, under penalty of not being a story, consist of "adventures." Why of adventures more than of green spectacles? He mentions a category of impossible things, and among them he places "fiction without adventure." Why without adventure, more than without matrimony, or celibacy, or parturition, or cholera, or hydropathy, or Jansenism? This seems to me to bring the novel back to the hapless little *rôle* of being an artificial, ingenious thing —bring it down from its large, free character of an immense and exquisite correspondence with life. And what *is* adventure when it comes to that, and by what sign is the listening pupil to recognize it? It is an adventure—an immense one—for me to write this little article; and for a Bostonian nymph to reject an English duke is an adventure only less stirring, I should say, than for an English duke to be rejected by a Bostonian nymph. I see dramas within dramas in that, and innumerable points of view. A psychological reason is, to my imagination, an object adorably pictorial; to catch the tint of its complexion—I feel as if that idea might inspire one to Titianesque efforts. There are few things more exciting to me, in short, than a psychological reason, and yet, I protest, the novel seems to me the most magnificent form of art. I have just been reading, at the same time, the delightful story of *Treasure Island*, by Mr. Robert Louis Stevenson, and, in a manner less consecutive, the last tale from M. Edmond de Goncourt, which is entitled *Chérie*. One of these works treats of murders, mysteries, islands of dreadful renown, hairbreadth escapes, miraculous coincidences, and buried doubloons. The other treats of a little French girl who lived in a fine house in Paris, and died of wounded sensibility because no one would marry her. I call *Treasure Island* delightful, because it appears to me to have succeeded wonderfully in what it attempts; and I venture to bestow no epithet upon *Chérie*, which strikes me as having failed deplorably in what it attempts—that is, in tracing

the development of the moral consciousness of a child. But one of
these productions strikes me as exactly as much of a novel as the
other, and as having a "story" quite as much. The moral consciousness of a child is as much a part of life as the islands of the Spanish
Main, and the one sort of geography seems to me to have those
"surprises" of which Mr. Besant speaks quite as much as the other.
For myself (since it comes back in the last resort, as I say, to the
preference of the individual), the picture of the child's experience
has the advantage that I can at successive steps (an immense luxury, near to the "sensual pleasure" of which Mr. Besant's critic in
the *Pall Mall* speaks) say Yes or No, as it may be, to what the artist
puts before me. I have been a child in fact, but I have been on a
quest for a buried treasure only in supposition, and it is a simple
accident that with M. de Goncourt I should have for the most part
to say No. With George Eliot, when she painted that country with
a far other intelligence, I always said Yes.

The most interesting part of Mr. Besant's lecture is unfortunately the briefest passage—his very cursory allusion to the "conscious moral purpose" of the novel. Here again it is not very clear
whether he be recording a fact or laying down a principle; it is a
great pity that in the latter case he should not have developed his
idea. This branch of the subject is of immense importance, and
Mr. Besant's few words point to considerations of the widest reach,
not to be lightly disposed of. He will have treated the art of fiction
but superficially who is not prepared to go every inch of the way
that these considerations will carry him. It is for this reason that
at the beginning of these remarks I was careful to notify the reader
that my reflections on so large a theme have no pretension to be
exhaustive. Like Mr. Besant, I have left the question of the morality
of the novel till the last, and at the last I find I have used up my
space. It is a question surrounded with difficulties, as witness the
very first that meets us, in the form of a definite question, on the
threshold. Vagueness, in such a discussion, is fatal, and what is the
meaning of your morality and your conscious moral purpose? Will
you not define your terms and explain how (a novel being a picture) a picture can be either moral or immoral? You wish to paint
a moral picture or carve a moral statue: will you not tell us how
you would set about it? We are discussing the Art of Fiction; questions of art are questions (in the widest sense) of execution; questions of morality are quite another affair, and will you not let us
see how it is that you find it so easy to mix them up? These things

are so clear to Mr. Besant that he has deduced from them a law which he sees embodied in English Fiction, and which is "a truly admirable thing and a great cause for congratulation." It is a great cause for congratulation indeed when such thorny problems become as smooth as silk. I may add that in so far as Mr. Besant perceives that in point of fact English Fiction has addressed itself preponderantly to these delicate questions he will appear to many people to have made a vain discovery. They will have been positively struck, on the contrary, with the moral timidity of the usual English novelist; with his (or with her) aversion to face the difficulties with which on every side the treatment of reality bristles. He is apt to be extremely shy (whereas the picture that Mr. Besant draws is a picture of boldness), and the sign of his work, for the most part, is a cautious silence on certain subjects. In the English novel (by which of course I mean the American as well), more than in any other, there is a traditional difference between that which people know and that which they agree to admit that they know, that which they see and that which they speak of, that which they feel to be a part of life and that which they allow to enter into literature. There is the great difference, in short, between what they talk of in conversation and what they talk of in print. The essence of moral energy is to survey the whole field, and I should directly reverse Mr. Besant's remark and say not that the English novel has a purpose, but that it has a diffidence. To what degree a purpose in a work of art is a source of corruption I shall not attempt to inquire; the one that seems to me least dangerous is the purpose of making a perfect work. As for our novel, I may say lastly on this score that as we find it in England to-day it strikes me as addressed in a large degree to "young people," and that this in itself constitutes a presumption that it will be rather shy. There are certain things which it is generally agreed not to discuss, not even to mention, before young people.[1] That is very well, but the absence of discussion is not a symptom of the moral passion. The purpose of the English novel—"a truly admirable thing, and a great cause for congratulation"—strikes me therefore as rather negative.

There is one point at which the moral sense and the artistic sense lie very near together; that is in the light of the very obvious truth that the deepest quality of a work of art will always be the quality of the mind of the producer. In proportion as that intelligence

---

[1] Cf. *Our Mutual Friend*, Bk. I, ch. xi: "The question about everything was, would it bring a blush into the cheek of the young person?"

is fine will the novel, the picture, the statue partake of the substance of beauty and truth. To be constituted of such elements is, to my vision, to have purpose enough. No good novel will ever proceed from a superficial mind; that seems to me an axiom which, for the artist in fiction, will cover all needful moral ground: if the youthful aspirant take it to heart it will illuminate for him many of the mysteries of "purpose." There are many other useful things that might be said to him, but I have come to the end of my article, and can only touch them as I pass. The critic in the *Pall Mall Gazette,* whom I have already quoted, draws attention to the danger, in speaking of the art of fiction, of generalizing. The danger that he has in mind is rather, I imagine, that of particularizing, for there are some comprehensive remarks which, in addition to those embodied in Mr. Besant's suggestive lecture, might without fear of misleading him be addressed to the ingenuous student. I should remind him first of the magnificence of the form that is open to him, which offers to sight so few restrictions and such innumerable opportunities. The other arts, in comparison, appear confined and hampered; the various conditions under which they are exercised are so rigid and definite. But the only condition that I can think of attaching to the composition of the novel is, as I have already said, that it be sincere. This freedom is a splendid privilege, and the first lesson of the young novelist is to learn to be worthy of it. "Enjoy it as it deserves," I should say to him; "take possession of it, explore it to its utmost extent, publish it, rejoice in it. All life belongs to you, and do not listen either to those who would shut you up into corners of it and tell you that it is only here and there that art inhabits, or to those who would persuade you that this heavenly messenger wings her way outside of life altogether, breathing a superfine air, and turning away her head from the truth of things. There is no impression of life, no manner of seeing it and feeling it, to which the plan of the novelist may not offer a place; you have only to remember that talents so dissimilar as those of Alexandre Dumas and Jane Austen, Charles Dickens and Gustave Flaubert have worked in this field with equal glory. Do not think too much about optimism and pessimism; try and catch the color of life itself. In France to-day we see a prodigious effort (that of Émile Zola, to whose solid and serious work no explorer of the capacity of the novel can allude without respect), we see an extraordinary effort, vitiated by a spirit of pessimism on a narrow basis. M. Zola is magnificent, but he strikes an

English reader as ignorant; he has an air of working in the dark; if he had as much light as energy, his results would be of the highest value. As for the aberrations of a shallow optimism, the ground (of English fiction especially) is strewn with their brittle particles as with broken glass. If you must indulge in conclusions, let them have the taste of a wide knowledge. Remember that your first duty is to be as complete as possible—to make as perfect a work. Be generous and delicate and pursue the prize."

Conrad

Joseph CONRAD (1857–1924), born Teodor Jozef Konrad Korzeniowski, at Cracow, Poland, the son of a Polish revolutionist, went to sea at thirteen, and rose to a captaincy in the merchant marine. After long experience as a sailor, he settled in England and wrote many novels based on his experiences. The first was *Almayer's Folly* (1895); the third, *The Nigger of the "Narcissus"* (1897), decided for Conrad that he was to be a novelist and no longer a sailor. There followed a series of stories that established his high reputation among critics: *Lord Jim* (1900), *Youth* (1902), *The Heart of Darkness* (1902), *Typhoon* (1903), *Nostromo* (1904). In what is called his "second period," he produced novels that brought him public acclaim: *Chance* (1914), *Within the Tides* (1915), *Victory* (1915), *The Arrow of Gold* (1919), *The Rescue* (1920), and *The Rover* (1923).

Conrad, in a foreword to the American edition of *The Nigger of the "Narcissus,"* writes:

In the revulsion of feeling before the accomplished task, I understood that I had done with the sea, and that henceforth I had to be a writer. And almost without laying down the pen I wrote a preface, trying to express the spirit in which I was entering on the task of my new life. That preface on advice (which I now think was wrong) was never published with the book. But the late W. E. Henley, who had the courage at that time (1897) to serialize my "Nigger" in the *New Review*, judged it worthy to be printed as an afterword at the end of the last instalment of the tale.

This "suppressed" preface (first published with the novel in the American edition), a vivid declaration of faith by a literary artist at the beginning of his career, is printed in full below. The final paragraph is a fitting close to this book.

PREFACE TO *THE NIGGER OF THE* "*NARCISSUS*" [1]

(1897)

A work that aspires, however humbly, to the condition of art should carry its justification in every line. And art itself may be defined as a single-minded attempt to render the highest kind of justice to the visible universe, by bringing to light the truth, manifold and one, underlying its every aspect. It is an attempt to find in its forms, in its colors, in its light, in its shadows, in the aspect of matter and in the facts of life what of each is fundamental, what is enduring and essential—their one illuminating and convincing quality—the very truth of their existence. The artist, then, like the thinker or the scientist, seeks the truth and makes his appeal. Impressed by the aspect of the world the thinker plunges into ideas, the scientist into facts—whence, presently, emerging they make their appeal to those qualities of our being that fit us best for the hazardous enterprise of living. They speak authoritatively to our common-sense, to our intelligence, to our desire of peace or to our desire of unrest; not seldom to our prejudices, sometimes to our fears, often to our egoism—but always to our credulity. And their words are heard with reverence, for their concern is with weighty matters: with the cultivation of our minds and the proper care of our bodies, with the attainment of our ambitions, with the perfection of the means and the glorification of our precious aims.

It is otherwise with the artist.

Confronted by the same enigmatical spectacle the artist descends within himself, and in that lonely region of stress and strife, if he be deserving and fortunate, he finds the terms of his appeal. His appeal is made to our less obvious capacities: to that part of our nature which, because of the warlike conditions of existence, is necessarily kept out of sight within the more resisting and hard qualities—like the vulnerable body within a steel armor. His appeal is less loud, more profound, less distinct, more stirring—and sooner forgotten. Yet its effect endures forever. The changing wisdom of successive generations discards ideas, questions facts, demolishes theories. But the artist appeals to that part of our being which is not dependent on wisdom; to that in us which is a gift and not an acquisition—and, therefore, more permanently enduring. He speaks to our capacity for delight and wonder, to the sense of mystery surrounding our lives; to our sense of pity, and beauty, and pain; to the latent feeling of fellowship with all creation—and to the subtle but invincible conviction of solidarity that knits together the loneliness of innumerable hearts, to the solidarity in dreams, in joy, in sorrow, in aspirations, in illusions, in hope, in fear, which binds men to each other, which binds together all humanity—the dead to the living and the living to the unborn.

It is only some such strain of thought, or rather of feeling, that can in a measure explain the aim of the attempt, made in the tale which follows, to present an unrestful episode in the obscure lives of a few individuals out of all the disregarded multitude of the bewildered, the simple and the voiceless. For, if any part of truth dwells in the belief confessed above, it becomes evident that there is not a place of splendor or a dark corner of the earth that does not deserve, if only a passing glance of wonder and pity. The motive then, may be held to justify the matter of the work; but this preface, which is simply an avowal of endeavor, cannot end here— for the avowal is not yet complete.

Fiction—if it at all aspires to be art—appeals to temperament. And in truth it must be, like painting, like music, like all art, the appeal of one temperament to all the other innumerable temperaments whose subtle and resistless power endows passing events with their true meaning, and creates the moral, the emotional atmosphere of the place and time. Such an appeal to be effective must be an impression conveyed through the senses; and, in fact, it cannot be made in any other way, because temperament, whether individual or collective, is not amenable to persuasion. All art, therefore, appeals primarily to the senses, and the artistic aim when expressing itself in written words must also make its appeal through the senses, if its high desire is to reach the secret spring of responsive emotions. It must strenuously aspire to the plasticity of sculpture, to the color of painting, and to the magic suggestiveness of music— which is the art of arts. And it is only through complete, unswerving devotion to the perfect blending of form and substance; it is only through an unremitting never-discouraged care for the shape and ring of sentences that an approach can be made to plasticity, to color, and that the light of magic suggestiveness may be brought to play for an evanescent instant over the commonplace surface of words: of the old, old words, worn thin, defaced by ages of careless usage.

The sincere endeavor to accomplish that creative task, to go as far on that road as his strength will carry him, to go undeterred by faltering, weariness or reproach, is the only valid justification for the worker in prose. And if his conscience is clear, his answer to those who in the fullness of a wisdom which looks for immediate profit, demand specifically to be edified, consoled, amused; who demand to be promptly improved, or encouraged, or frightened, or shocked, or charmed, must run thus:—My task which I am trying to achieve is, by the power of the written word to make you hear, to make you feel—it is, before all, to make you *see*. That—and no more, and it is everything. If I succeed, you shall find there according to your deserts: encouragement, consolation, fear, charm—all you demand—and, perhaps, also that glimpse of truth for which you have forgotten to ask.

To snatch in a moment of courage, from the remorseless rush of time, a passing phase of life, is only the beginning of the task. The task approached in tenderness and faith is to hold up unquestioningly, without choice and without fear, the rescued fragment before all eyes in the light of a sincere mood. It is to show its vibration, its color, its form; and through its movement, its form, and its color, reveal the substance of its truth—disclose its inspiring secret: the stress and passion within the core of each convincing moment. In a single-minded attempt of that kind, if one be deserving and fortunate, one may perchance attain to such clearness of sincerity that at last the presented vision of regret or pity, of terror or mirth, shall awaken in the hearts of the beholders that feeling of unavoidable solidarity; of the solidarity in mysterious origin, in toil, in joy, in hope, in uncertain fate, which binds men to each other and all mankind to the visible world.

It is evident that he who, rightly or wrongly, holds by the convictions expressed above cannot be faithful to any one of the temporary formulas of his craft. The enduring part of them—the truth which each only imperfectly veils—should abide with him as the most precious of his possessions, but they all: Realism, Romanticism, Naturalism, even the unofficial sentimentalism (which like the poor, is exceedingly difficult to get rid of), all these gods must, after a short period of fellowship, abandon him—even on the very threshold of the temple—to the stammerings of his conscience and to the outspoken consciousness of the difficulties of his work. In that uneasy solitude the supreme cry of Art for Art itself, loses the exciting ring of its apparent immorality. It sounds far off. It has ceased to be a cry, and is heard only as a whisper, often incomprehensible, but at times and faintly encouraging.

Sometimes, stretched at ease in the shade of a roadside tree, we watch the motions of a laborer in a distant field, and after a time, begin to wonder languidly as to what the fellow may be at. We watch the movements of his body, the waving of his arms, we see him bend down, stand up, hesitate, begin again. It may add to the charm of an idle hour to be told the purpose of his exertions. If we know he is trying to lift a stone, to dig a ditch, to uproot a stump, we look with a more real interest at his efforts; we are disposed to condone the jar of his agitation upon the restfulness of the landscape; and even, if in a brotherly frame of mind, we may bring ourselves to forgive his failure. We understood his object, and, after all, the fellow has tried, and perhaps he had not the strength—and perhaps he had not the knowledge. We forgive, go on our way—and forget.

And so it is with the workman of art. Art is long and life is short, and success is very far off. And thus, doubtful of strength to travel so far, we talk a little about the aim—the aim of art, which, like life itself, is inspiring, difficult—obscured by mists. It is not in the clear logic of a triumphant conclusion; it is not in the unveiling of one of those heartless secrets which are called the Laws of Nature. It is not less great, but only more difficult.

To arrest, for the space of a breath, the hands busy about the work of the earth, and compel men entranced by the sight of distant goals to glance for a moment at the surrounding vision of form and color, of sunshine and shadows; to make them pause for a look, for a sigh, for a smile—such is the aim, difficult and evanescent, and reserved only for a very few to achieve. But sometimes, by the deserving and the fortunate, even that task is accomplished. And when it is accomplished—behold!—all the truth of life is there: a moment of vision, a sigh, a smile—and the return to an eternal rest.

BIBLIOGRAPHY

This is a selected bibliography, arranged under heads, to guide the reader toward further explorations in the field of literary criticism. Although the cases collected in this volume stress what might be called working, rather than theoretical or metaphysical, criticism, a list of books on æsthetics is included for the student who cares to follow another approach to the subject.

GENERAL

Abercrombie, L., *The Theory of Poetry*, London, 1924.

Alden, R. M., *English Verse*, N. Y., 1903.

Arnold, M., *Essays in Criticism* (First Series), London, 1865.

Arnold, M., *Essays in Criticism* (Second Series), London, 1888.

Babbitt, I., *The New Laocoön*, Boston, 1910.

Bradley, A. C., *Oxford Lectures on Poetry*, London, 1909.

Bray, J. W., *A History of English Critical Terms*, Boston, 1898.

Bronowski, J., *The Poet's Defence*, Cambridge, 1939.

Brownell, W. C., *The Genius of Style*, N. Y., 1924.

Brunetière, F., *L'Évolution des Genres dans l'Histoire de la Littérature*, Paris, 1898.

Brunetière, F., *Nouvelles Questions de Critique*, Paris, 1900.

Brunetière, F., *Questions de Critique*, Paris, 1889.

Buck, P. M., Jr., *Literary Criticism*, N. Y., 1930.

Cooper, L., *Theories of Style*, N. Y., 1907.

Courthope, W. J., *Life in Poetry; Law in Taste*, 3 vols., London, 1901.

Courtney, W. L., *Idea of Tragedy in Ancient and Modern Drama*, London, 1900.

Cross, W. L., *The Development of the English Novel*, N. Y., 1899.

Dudley, L., *The Study of Literature*, Boston, 1928.

Eastman, M., *The Enjoyment of Poetry*, N. Y., 1916.

Eastman, M., *The Sense of Humor*, N. Y., 1921.

Egan, Rose F., "The Genesis of the Theory of 'Art for Art's Sake' in Germany and in England," *Smith College Studies in Modern Languages*; Part I, in vol. ii, no. 4 (1920–21); Part II, in vol. v, no. 3 (1923–24).

Erskine, J., *Kinds of Poetry*, N. Y., 1920.

Forster, E. M., *Aspects of the Novel*, N. Y., 1927.

Garrod, H. W., *Poetry and the Criticism of Life*, Cambridge, 1931.

Garrod, H. W., *The Profession of Poetry*, Oxford, 1924.

Gayley, C. M., and Kurtz, B., *Methods and Materials of Literary Criticism*, Boston, 1920.

Gayley, C. M., and Scott, F. N., *An Introduction to the Methods and Materials of Literary Criticism*, Boston, 1899.

Gummere, F. B., *A Handbook of Poetics*, Boston, 1886.

Howells, W. D., *Criticism and Fiction*, N. Y., 1893.

Lanier, S., *The Science of English Verse*, N. Y., 1880.

Lowes, J. L., *Convention and Revolt in Poetry*, Boston, 1919.

Lubbuck, P., *The Craft of Fiction*, London, 1921.

Lucas, F. L., *The Criticism of Poetry*, London, 1933.

More, P. E., *Shelburne Essays*, 11 vols., 1904 ff.

Morley, J., *Studies in Literature*, London, 1891.

Neihardt, J. G., *Poetic Values, Their Reality and Our Need of Them*, N. Y., 1925.

Neilson, W. A., *Essentials of Poetry*, Boston, 1912.

Nietzsche, F., *Birth of Tragedy*, translated by W. A. Haussmann, Edinburgh, 1909.

Patterson, W. M., *Rhythms of Prose*, N. Y., 1917.

Perry, B., *A Study of Prose Fiction*, Boston, 1902.

Perry, B., *The Study of Poetry*, Boston, 1920.

Prescott, F. C., *The Poetic Mind*, N. Y., 1922.

Read, H., *Phases of English Poetry*, London, 1928.

Read, H., *Poetry and Anarchism*, N. Y., 1939.

Reynolds, Sir Joshua, *Fifteen Discourses Delivered in the Royal Academy* (Everyman's Library), London, 1907.

Richards, I. A., *Practical Criticism*, N. Y., 1929.

Richards, I. A., *Principles of Literary Criticism*, N. Y., 1926.

Richards, I. A., *Science and Poetry*, N. Y., 1926.

Rickert, E., *New Methods for the Study of Literature*, Chicago, 1927.

Robertson, J. M., *Essays towards a Critical Method*, London, 1889.

Saintsbury, G., *A History of Criticism and Literary Taste in Europe from the Earliest Texts to the Present Day*, 3 vols., Edinburgh, 1900–04.

Schopenhauer, A., *The Art of Literature*, translated by T. B. Saunders, London, 1891.

Scott-James, R. A., *The Making of Literature*, N. Y., [1929].

Seth, A., and Haldane, R. B., *Essays in Philosophical Criticism*, London, 1883.

Spingarn, J. E., *Creative Criticism*, N. Y., 1917.

Tinker, C. B., *The Good Estate of Poetry*, Boston, 1929.

Trent, W. P., *The Authority of Criticism, and Other Essays*, N. Y., 1899.

Winchester, C. T., *Some Principles of Literary Criticism*, N. Y., 1899.

Woodberry, G. E., *The Appreciation of Literature*, N. Y., 1907.

Worsfold, W. B., *The Principles of Criticism*, London, 1914.

SPECIAL

Atkins, J. W. H., *Literary Criticism in Antiquity*, 2 vols., Cambridge, 1934.

Babbitt, I., *The Masters of Modern French Criticism*, Boston, 1912.

Baldwin, C. S., *Ancient Rhetoric and Poetic*, N. Y., 1924.

Barstow, M. L., *Wordsworth's Theory of Poetic Diction*, New Haven, 1917.

Beatty, Arthur, *William Wordsworth, His Doctrine and Art in Their Historical Relations*, Madison, 1922.

Belis, A., *La Critique Français à la Fin du XIXe Siècle*, Paris, 1926.

Brown, J. E., *The Critical Opinions of Samuel Johnson*, Princeton, 1926.

Butcher, S. H., tr., *Aristotle's Theory of Poetry and Fine Art*, London, 1895.

Bywater, I., tr., *On the Art of Poetry*, Oxford, 1920.

Carton, H., *Histoire de la Critique Littéraire en France*, Paris, 1886.

Charleton, H. B., *Castelvetro's Theory of Poetry*, Manchester, 1913.

Clark, A. F. B., *Boileau and the French Classical Critics in England*, Paris, 1925.

Clark, D. L., *Rhetoric and Poetic in the Renaissance*, N. Y., 1922.

Cline, T. L., *Critical Opinion in the Eighteenth Century*, Ann Arbor, 1926.

Cooper, L., *An Aristotelian Theory of Comedy*, N. Y., 1922.

Cooper, L., tr., *On the Art of Poetry*, Boston, 1913.

Cooper, L., *The Poetics of Aristotle*, Boston, 1923.

D'Alton, J. F., *Roman Literary Criticism*, London, 1931.

De Mille, G. E., *Literary Criticism in America*, N. Y., 1931.

Eliot, T. S., *John Dryden: The Poet, the Dramatist, the Critic*, N. Y., 1932.

Eliot, T. S., *The Sacred Wood*, London, 1928.

Erskine, J., *The Elizabethan Lyric*, N. Y., 1904.

Foerster, N., *American Criticism: a Study in Literary Theory from Poe to the Present*, Boston, 1928.

Haldane, J. B. S., *Possible Worlds*, N. Y., 1928.

Houston, P. H., *Doctor Johnson: a Study in Eighteenth-Century Humanism*, Cambridge, Massachusetts, 1923.

Klein, D., *Literary Criticism from the Elizabethan Dramatists*, N. Y., 1910.

Lowes, J. L., *The Road to Xanadu*, Boston, 1927.

Lucas, F. L., *Tragedy in Relation to Aristotle's "Poetics,"* N. Y., 1928.

MacClintock, L., *Sainte-Beuve's Critical Theory and Practice After 1849*, Chicago, 1920.

Miller, G. M., *The Historical Point of View in English Literary Criticism from 1570 to 1770*, Heidelberg, 1913.

Monk, S. H., *The Sublime: a Study of Critical Theories in XVIII-Century England*, N. Y., 1935.

Nethercote, A. H., *The Road to Tryermaine*, Chicago, 1940.

Osgood, C. G., tr., *Boccaccio on Poetry*, Princeton, 1930.

Patterson, W. F., *Three Centuries of French Poetic Theory*, Ann Arbor, 1935.

Richards, I. A., and Ogden, C. K., *The Meaning of Meaning*, N. Y., 1925.

Roberts, W. Rhys, *Dionysius of Halicarnassus on Literary Composition*, London, 1910.

Roberts, W. Rhys, *Greek Rhetoric and Literary Criticism*, N. Y., 1928.

Robertson, J. G., *Lessing's Dramatic Theory*, N. Y., 1939.

Schelling, F. E., *Ben Jonson and the Classical School*, Baltimore, 1898.

Sikes, E. E., *The Greek View of Poetry*, N. Y., 1931.

Smith, N. C., *Wordsworth's Literary Criticism*, London, 1905.

Solve, M. T., *Shelley: His Theory of Poetry*, Chicago, 1927.

Spingarn, J. E., *History of Literary Criticism in the Renaissance*, N. Y., 1899.

Struckmeyer, O. K., *Croce and Literary Criticism*, Cambridge, 1921.

Thompson, G. A., *Elizabethan Criticism of Poetry*, Menasha, Wisconsin, 1914.

Warren, A., *Alexander Pope as Critic and Humanist*, Princeton, 1929.

COLLECTIONS

Bowman, J. C., *Contemporary American Criticism*, N. Y., 1926.

Brewster, W. T., *Specimens of Modern English Literary Criticism*, N. Y., 1908.

Burgum, E. B., *The New Criticism*, N. Y., 1930.

Clark, B., *European Theories of the Drama*, N. Y., 1930.

Cook, A. S., *Addison: Criticism on "Paradise Lost,"* N. Y., 1926.

Cook, A. S., *The Art of Poetry*, Boston, 1892.

Denniston, J. D., *Greek Literary Criticism*, London, 1924.

Durham, W. H., *Critical Essays of the Eighteenth Century, 1700–1725*, New Haven, 1915.

Foerster, N., *American Critical Essays: XIXth and XXth Centuries*, London, 1930.

George, A. J., *Coleridge's Principles of Criticism*, Boston, 1897.

Gilbert, A. H., *Literary Criticism, Plato to Dryden*, N. Y., 1940.

Jones, E. D., *English Critical Essays of the XIX Century*, London, 1922.

Lewisohn, L., *A Modern Book of Criticism* (Modern Library), N. Y., 1919.

Rhys, E., *Literary Pamphlets, Chiefly Relating to Poetry, from Sidney to Byron*, London, 1897.

Saintsbury, G., *Loci Critici*, Boston, 1903.

Shawcross, J., *Shelley's Literary and Philosophical Criticism*, London, 1909.

Smith, G. G., *Elizabethan Critical Essays*, 2 vols., Oxford, 1904.

Smith, J. H., and Parks, E. W., *The Great Critics*, N. Y., 1939.

Spingarn, J. E., *Critical Essays of the Seventeenth Century*, 3 vols., Oxford, 1908–1909.

Vaughan, C. E., *English Literary Criticism*, London, 1903.

Wilkinson, M., *The Way of the Makers*, N. Y., 1925.

Zabel, M. D., *Literary Opinion in America*, N. Y., 1937.

ÆSTHETICS

Allen, G., *Physiological Æsthetics*, London, 1877.

Baudouin, C., *Psycho-Analysis and Æsthetics*, translated by E. and C. Paul, London, 1924.

Bell, C., *Art*, London, 1914.

Bosanquet, B., *A History of Æsthetic*, London, 1922.

Bosanquet, B., *Three Lectures on Æsthetic*, London, 1892.

Buermeyer, L., *The Æsthetic Experience*, Merion, 1929.

Carritt, E. F., *The Theory of Beauty*, London, 1923.

Croce, B., *Æsthetic*, translated by D. Ainslie, London, 1922.

Gilbert, K., and Kuhn, H., *A History of Æsthetics*, N. Y., 1939.

Gordon, K., *Æsthetics*, N. Y., 1909.

Langfeld, H. S., *The Æsthetic Attitude*, N. Y., 1920.

Ogden, C. K., and others, *The Foundation of Æsthetics*, London, 1925.

Parker, D., *The Principles of Æsthetics*, N. Y., 1920.

Puffer, E. D., *The Psychology of Beauty*, Boston, 1905.

Santayana, G., *Reason in Art*, N. Y., 1906.

Santayana, G., *The Sense of Beauty*, N. Y., 1897.

INDEX

Proper names have not been listed in the index, except where the author has been discussed at some length.

THE ART OF LITERARY CRITICISM